Black is Back!

I dedicate this book - BLACK is BACK! - to my wife Ilus (Ilona), who believes that I deserve her borderless love and unconditional help in many ways.

I think I'm just a lucky bastard to have had her by my side in the past 21 years. But I'm not so foolish to tell her, so, dear readers, please keep it secret...!

Andras Adorjan

To the Readers of BLACK is BACK!

Experience shows that readers especially enjoy finding mistakes in books. I like my readers and would like to please them, but I'm having a problem: whatever I do is perfect, and so am I. Many people hate me for this but I can't help it.

However, for this book I thought of something. I've put four errors (or maybe more – I've forgotten), a major one among them – at several places in BLACK is Back (OK?). So you cannot say you're not being served well!

In case you find something, it's not necessary to write or call – just be proud of yourself!

With my compliments,
Andras (aa_ok@interware.hu)

Andras Adorjan

Black is Back!

What's White's Advantage Anyway?

New In Chess 2016

© 2016 New In Chess

Published by New In Chess, Alkmaar, The Netherlands
www.newinchess.com

Cover design: Ron van Roon
Supervision and proofreading: Frank Erwich
Production: Rik Weidema, Anton Schermer

Have you found any errors in this book?
Please send your remarks to editors@newinchess.com. We will collect all relevant corrections on the Errata page of our website www.newinchess.com and implement them in a possible next edition.

ISBN: 978-90-5691-661-9

Contents

Animate L. BARCZAY – A. Schnieder for A. Preston pg 279
.   A. Vegh – G. Felier pg 283

Explanation of Symbols

The chessboard with its coordinates:

h g f e d c b a

±	White stands slightly better
∓	Black stands slightly better
±	White stands better
∓	Black stands better
+−	White has a decisive advantage
−+	Black has a decisive advantage
=	balanced position
∞	the position is unclear
⯈	with compensation for the material
!	good move
!!	excellent move
?	bad move
??	blunder
!?	interesting move
?!	dubious move
⇄	with counterplay
→	with attack
↑	with initiative
#	mate

❑ White to move
■ Black to move
♚ King
♛ Queen
♜ Rook
♝ Bishop
♞ Knight

1−10   Game excitiment Level

QGD   Queen's Gambit Declined

Acknowledgements

I often wonder: when does Peter Boel sleep? Probably in winter. Otherwise it is very hard to explain his enormous productivity, intensive working tempo, and moral. He targets perfection, and really reminds me of my first Mentor and Editor GM Gedeon Barcza – see my remembrance of him in the 'Connections' Chapter. I hardly ever met such an attitude of tactfulness respect towards the Author, and humility in the face of the common task. By the way, we never met him personally – the whole book was written in cooperation via email!

Apart from the professional and human qualities he has of course weaknesses as well. Take this book. He tries to belittle his role, stating he was 'only' the editor, and his activity was limited to technical matters. This is just not true. He was my partner in composing the essence of this book, and I can tell you we've been having quarrels. The BLACK is Brutal series, for example, was his selection. I wasn't even allowed to save such classic games as the one against Kortchnoi (Cannes 1986) or another great performance against Portisch (Tungsram 1975). He kept repeating we were not supposed to repeat any material that had been published earlier, and I could not convince him that a book which has 8-10% of such material – naturally, revised and updated – can still be regarded as a brand new work. Finally we compromised. That's what editors do when you give in... Beware of editors!

On the other hand, Peter Boel had excellent creative suggestions and there is no part of the book he has not triple-checked. The extraordinary chapter with the Nakamura-Gelfand article belongs entirely to him. We just drew his attention to the 'fantastica'.

When I say 'we', here my wife Ilus (Ilona Oros) steps in, without whose help I wouldn't have been able to edit a single chapter decently. I am only a consumer of computer services, and my technical ability stops beyond handling ChessBase and writing. I may be a Stone Age man in people's eyes, not having a smartphone, but I'm still smart enough myself. I have my homephone (36-1-318-6259) which is good enough to call and be called. If worse comes to worst, you can reach me through Ilona's mobile (36-20-922-9207), but please, I prefer that you don't. I like to hear and understand what the other person says, and to be heard as well. It's called 'conversation' instead of exchanging stupid messages.

This book was actually planned, written and edited by three persons: Peter Boel, Ilona Oros and myself, AA. This is the fair and true story of it.

All the games in the book have been analysed at least three times since they were played. I don't think there are any of them that haven't been checked by IM Endre Vegh some time before the final version was born. I thank him as well for that.

Andras Adorjan
Budapest, July 2016

Foreword – Swan Song

They say swans sing their most beautiful song just before they die.

Well, I'm not planning to leave this life any time soon, but in any case it doesn't hurt to draw up the balance. I hope this is not only going to be my last opus, but also my best. It is a pleasant duty to conclude my 30-year mission of BLACK is OK!. Yes, it was 1985 when I had my first doubts about the dogma that says 'White is better'. All of the 11 books, hundreds of articles and thousands of analyses I've written, have been dedicated to the theme of BLACK is OK!, except for the booklet titled *Quo Vadis Garry?* (German edition 1989, English title 'The Change of a Child'). It is indeed hard to believe that in all of chess history there has been practically nobody who studied this territory of science and philosophy deeply – except me. This may sound Tarzan-like, but it is in fact rather sad that people do not seem to think in depth.

Some great players, like Steinitz, Lasker, Portisch, have declared that the perfect chess game ends in a draw. But all the same, players have descended into prejudice, strengthened by statistics. And all players are crazy about learning new and more new opening variations, but they find it unimportant to occupy themselves with the most important field of theory.

Our royal game is beloved by us, but there are other board games too. In some of them, the right to make the first move is an advantage. But in other cases it's just the opposite! Finally, we also have games where it is just the same either way. I have a large amount of evidence to show that chess belongs in the third group. Just you wait and see!

Well, dear reader, you have a long way to go but it's worth the trip. It may sound dry, but during the process there will be pleasure too. It's a cure which will eliminate all your complexes concerning playing with BLACK.

Either that, or your money back!

Andras Adorjan
Budapest, March 2016

Preface

When Andras Adorjan asked me to work with him on his new book, I felt deeply honoured. At New In Chess, we had worked with the famous Hungarian grandmaster for many years, and, to be honest, we had had our ups and downs. But no true chess fan would let an opportunity pass by to work with one of the chess giants of the 1970s and 80s, the years in which I myself 'grew up' as a chess player – of modest stature. In my opinion, at the end of the line Andras Adorjan is a great master and a noble soul who has given the world much more than he has received.

After we'd been working on the book for a couple of months, the bad tiding of Andras's serious illness reached me by way of his wife Ilona. Of course this meant a big delay. At first it wasn't even clear if we would ever finish the book. As for me, I never really stopped believing in it. And yes, after a while Andras, with Ilona's unfailing support, picked himself up again and wrote the final texts in a furious frenzy. Despite the fact that he was still ailing and had to see a doctor several times a week.

All the chess material in this book was supplied by Andras Adorjan. We have largely avoided games that were published in either of Adorjan's earlier *Black Is OK!* books. A notable exception is his victory over Karpov in Chapter 5, a game of which any World Champion could be proud. The analysis has been updated. So this is not so much a collection of Adorjan's best games, but rather an overview of his long career, with many treasures that had remained hidden so far. Apart from the spectacular games and analyses, there's the stories about Andras's career and contemporaries, written in the grandmaster's inimitable style: sharp, humoristic, not rarely melancholy or even melodramatic, but entertaining in every word. It may look like a bit of a hodgepodge, but there is so much humanity and life in there – it's got to be infectious. The analyses are in the same vein: you will find more inspiration than instruction in them. But isn't inspiration the best form of instruction?

My job was to collect and arrange the material – which wasn't as easy as it may sound! Andras also supplied the ground material for the chapter I wrote on the many black wins by Nakamura and Gelfand in their mutual games. I interviewed Gelfand on this subject via Skype – many thanks, Boris! – and my New In Chess colleague Dirk Jan ten Geuzendam posed Hikaru Nakamura a number of questions on my behalf. Thank you too, Dirk Jan and Hikaru! I've checked the existing analysis on these games (mostly from ChessBase), as well as some of the old analyses in the chapter 'Connections'. Inevitably, today's engines (Houdini, in my case) came up with some new conclusions here and there. Also, I've added a number of verbal commentaries in the 'Black Magic' chapter and elsewhere. So you see, not much harm done!

More than 90% of the analyses in here were done by Adorjan himself. You might be tempted to call these analyses biased – there are so many ∓'s as opposed to ±'s. You'd think Black is more than OK in a chess game. Well, first of all: what else would you expect in a book where every game is won by Black (except one – try to find it!)? Secondly, and more importantly, this reflects Adorjan's way of looking at the game. He just keeps on searching for the *most dynamic* possibilities for Black in every position, and this has led to many fantastic discoveries. Playing through the games in this book, you will be enchanted by the inexhaustible possibilities of our game.

I would also like to thank our publisher Allard Hoogland, who has been very patient and supportive all through this project, always keeping in touch with the process but never pushing too hard when things got tough.

Andras calls *Black Is Back* his swan song – well, you never know with a creative spirit like him. In any case, making this book together with him has been a thrilling experience for me. And, dear reader, I am convinced that reading it will be just as thrilling for you.

Peter Boel
Arnhem, June 2016

Chapter 1
Wishful Thinking?

Almost every chess player has (major) problems with black. Yet, I am sure that, apart from other crazies such as Alexander Morozevich, nobody uses more than 30-40% of their total training time to study the black side of chess science in general. The late IM Tibor Florian once said: 'People very much like to exercise things they already know well.'

I never expected to see BLACK is OK! clubs all over the world, or an international science movement under that name, but I hoped that the question would be a subject of serious, many-sided debate by the strongest players, trainers and analysts around. After all, the key, and only, question in chess is: what would be the result of a perfect game? Is it a draw? Or does White win? Or – surprise: would BLACK win? In quite a lot of board and other mind games, the 'Nachziehende' (not the 'second player'!) is the one who leads in the statistics.

Do you know that this is a world of right-handers? Once I read a serious essay where it was argued, with many examples, that left-handed people are handicapped in the use of many everyday tools and devices. I saw a demo film about it too. Blasphemy! Society doesn't bother too much – left-handers are few, and in schools, for example, they are the subject of bad jokes. They also become victims of an education that forces them to use their 'nice' hand. King George was only one of many famous victims. See The King's Speech – a wonderful film.

A left-handed boxer has a clear advantage. Of his potential opponents, the overwhelming majority will be right-handed. They face the usual 'service' in almost all of their matches and are trained that way (right vs. right). But our guy is different. This works in the favour of the left-handed fighter (for whom, by the way, it would also be odd to train only left vs. left), which may be very important between fighters of balanced strength. Now take the Almighty Initiative. Some fighters make a point of being the first to occupy the centre of the ring after the sounding of the gong. This is stupid and has no purpose. It's just a show. Even the achievement of pushing the opponent into the corner is worth nothing, unless the partner is already dizzy. Otherwise, a double-fist defence will cover everything while the defender still has a fair chance to swing some blows himself. You can do the same in chess: with white, play quietly and hope to win, but be objective and don't overdo it. There will be another day, when you can try to win with black. Your opponent will feel obliged to play for a win, and this may give you a good chance to land a counterblow – you don't have to push over your force. If it's going to be a game, you will have your psychological and professional chances too.

Let me conclude with some thoughts about happiness. In Hungary we have a great writer called Zsigmond Moricz, in whose novel 'The Happy Man' somebody asks an old peasant: 'Has your life been happy?' The answer is: 'I never thought about this.' He was a healthy character, who handled his problems only when he was sure to face them. A happy man.

I have always considered that with my talent I had a duty to serve. This is normal, I think. Even so, I sometimes felt that this was too much of a burden on my shoulders. Mahatma Gandhi once said: 'Let everybody have salvation by his own faith.' The leaders of certain religions, who visited him, were not very happy with this. One of them – guess who – said: 'But I suppose you agree that Jesus was the greatest prophet of all?' The little man just smiled and answered: 'Your words, not mine' (which was JC's answer to Pontius Pilate's question: 'Are you the king of the Jews?') After my near-death experience in a Budapest hospital earlier this year, such reflections naturally went through my head – not for the first time in my life, of course. What will happen when we pass away?

Strangely enough, after this whole chain of intensive suffering, humility and half-death in the first few months of 2016, all of a sudden something else came up. The human race is represented in billions of bodies and minds, but still it is one entity, and I am a part of it. And after passing away physically, I will somehow still be present in this spiritual community, by the things I've done – good or bad – and hopefully by my peak performances. It's difficult to imagine that Lenin, Stalin or Hitler would get away with their track record, but even this cannot be excluded. Clearly I have no reason to pity myself, or appeal for anybody's pity – as they say, everyone has his cross to bear. I won't disappear unnoticed. I did something in return for using up all that oxygen. I got credit for it too. Not enough, I feel. But that happens in every corner.

I don't miss the high official recognitions, the swords of honour, the Order of the Garter. I got a few (international) titles, not given by any jury. World Championship Candidate for one; three-time Hungarian champion. Olympic gold medallist. But I had badly hoped to have a serious influence on chess theory and practice with my true conviction that BLACK IS OK!.

30 years were not enough – I won't see a chain of BLACK IS OK! education centres where pupils are taught that:

In chess the initial position is equal – or rather, chances are even. The right of the first move offers no advantage and the result of the game is likely a draw.

Wishful thinking? Daydreaming? Instead I have seen in print such things as 'the aim of the chess game is to avoid getting mated'. If you think I'm joking – consult Wikipedia!

Appetizers

| Peter Hardicsay | 2345 | Robert Hübner | 2600 |
| Andras Adorjan | 2560 | Andras Adorjan | 2550 |

Hungary tt 1986   Bad Lauterberg m 1980 (9)

17.f2-f3??   **65.♖g8xg5**

17...♘d5!!   0-1   **65...♖c5??**
65...♖xh3-+.
66.♔xh4! ♖xg5   ½-½

| Zoltan Ribli | | Vladimir Liberzon | 2550 |
| Andras Adorjan | | Andras Adorjan | |

Hungary tt 1983   Amsterdam 1977 (15)

27.♕e3-c3   **45.g3xh4**

27...♗f1!!   0-1   **45...♗e1!**   0-1

Darko Gliksman
Andras Adorjan
Birmingham 1973

25.♘f3-e1

25...♖c1! 26.f3 ♘e2+　　　　**0-1**
27.♔f2　♕h4+;　27.♔h1　♘g3+
28.hxg3 (28.♔g1 ♖xa1 29.fxg4 ♘xf1)
28...♕h5+.

Bela Balogh
Andras Jocha
Hungary 1968

31.♖e1-d1

31...♗d4!! 32.♕xd4 ♖e1+　　　**0-1**

Lajos Portisch　　　2630
Andras Adorjan　　　2465
Amsterdam 1971 (15)

58.f2xe3

58...♘xb3! 59.axb3 c4　　　　**0-1**

Roland Sallay
Andras Jocha
Budapest 1966

34.♕e2-e4??

34...♖xg3!　　　　**0-1**
35.hxg3 ♕h3+ 36.♔g1 ♗c5+.
This game was played in the last round
of the semi-final for the Hungarian
Championship. I qualified and gained
the title of National Master.

Chapter 2
The Way It All Started

The Continuing Story of 'BLACK IS OK!'

Earlier versions of this text were published first in the 'BLACK IS OK!' zero copy in 1992, and then in the book 'Black is Still OK!' (2004). It has evolved over the years and can be regarded as a kind of manifesto. It is also a confession of love and gratitude to my mother, who showed me the way by her life and death.

My mother died in 1985. When death gathers its crops on a large scale, but at a safe distance, it is – regretfully but true – not such a big deal for us. But the loss of someone close to us tends to shake us deeply. It's not only that we cry for the deceased, as we know from Hemingway that, 'hearing the bell toll, you should never ask for whom it tolls. It tolls for you. It's preceded by the statement that it's me who loses something with every death. That's why you should never ask for whom the bell tolls.' (Actually it was John Donne who wrote this.)

Can there be anything good in losing someone you loved? Isn't it a morbid thought? I managed to tell my mother on her deathbed: 'Don't you be afraid, you of all people. You've done a lot of good to others in your life, and you are doing good to us even at the moment of your death. You're reminding us to keep together, and to leave as little debt as possible.' She was still teaching in a primary school a couple of months before her death (at the age of 70), in rather bad health. But she was happy at the school, surrounded by children, more than anywhere else.

When, in that fateful year 1985, I experienced how ephemeral human life is, it prompted me to ponder the meaning of our being here. After a quite long search for an answer, I figured we should do something in return for the oxygen we breathe in and transform into carbon-dioxide during our presence on earth. We must leave something lasting, something that lives on when we die.

That was the time when I started to think of building up a 'life-work'. I was not quite satisfied with my career in tournament chess, although I had had some big successes in that field. Writing seemed to be the right course of action for me. I had done quite a lot of writing from my teens onwards: chess articles, analyses, reports, prose and poetry (17 poems in English too), lyrics, occasionally even music. I am extremely extroverted, as a psychologist would put it, and so it was natural for me to take pen in hand.

I wanted to create something original, something novel and daring, and what I created had to have a certain common denominator, some kind of 'meaningful harmony', as Vassily Smyslov would put it. After a long while I suddenly realized that many of my most creative games and writings more or less supported Black's case. Then I recalled that I liked playing with black (or at least I wasn't afraid of the 'dark') already at 20 or even earlier, and in many tournaments most of my victories had been with black (as was the case with 5 of my 7 wins in the Riga Interzonal). I didn't actually feel that I had found my mission – it was the other way round. I was probably predestined to do this; it was my calling, all I had to do was listen to the message.

So I got down to work. I started with a 'black' approach to the Keres (IM Endre Vegh was my co-author), which was first published in two articles in New In Chess in December 1985 and January 1986. It was titled 'A Blow to the Keres Attack'. Other magazines followed in quick succession, in almost all the chess countries in the world. As the reception was encouraging, I then decided to pursue the 'BLACK IS OK' mission, committing myself to something that was much larger than just a nice-sounding witticism. It was, and is, something I believe in, and my belief is getting deeper and deeper. In the beginning, however, even my best friends looked at this thesis with – how to describe it – condescending cheerfulness, and regarded it as a strange hobby-horse. Nobody said anything nasty – but it was in the air, and I could smell it. I kept 'building my sand-castle' with persistence and dedication. It is not by chance that the 'logo' of our struggle features Don Quixote, as in the early days our efforts – to make people rethink things day by day instead of following dogmas – seemed just as futile as fighting windmills.

However, as time went on, the army of sceptics lessened, and I saw my pieces published in various chess magazines in 59 countries. The mission was spread in my books *Black Is OK!*, *Black Is Still OK!* and *Black Is OK Forever!*, and these works were favourably received worldwide. But what really matters is not what pleases me. More important is that me and my 'brothers-in-arms' have done our bit to 'straighten out' a little part of the world that had 'gone aslant'.

However, nowadays there are probably very few people left who completely reject the idea that it is quite tolerable to play with black. I received two letters where the writers went even further. One of them wrote that there is a limited number of 'good moves' for each player in the starting position, and if either of them runs out of good moves, he will only make things worse with any further move, and the 'right' to move actually becomes a burden. Now, as White starts the game, he will have to make the first 'bad move'. Therefore, with both players making the best possible moves, Black is the one who must win. Well… it looks a bit far-fetched, but it has its logic too.

My other penfriend challenged the view that it is White who determines the character of the game. I think he is right in saying that Black can also choose from a great variety of answers to White's first move, influencing the position at least as strongly as White does. He also told me that in some board games, e.g. in Nine-Men's Morris, it is disadvantageous to be the one who starts.

What I am claiming, though, is not more than 'BLACK IS OK'. I will probably repeat it on my deathbed, unlike Goethe, who in fact didn't want more Black but more 'light'. I am more like that other 'fellow-heretic', Galileo Galilei, who claimed: 'And yet the earth does move'.

I don't think I could deny it even in a torture chamber. Unless… someone convinced me it isn't true! My 'mission' is actually a scientific experiment to find out how each idea works in practice. It is all very nice that in my own practice playing with black was a bliss rather than a burden, and that my results support my thesis. But it is still rather like someone vaccinating himself with black pox, then with the serum he has invented, and surviving. It doesn't prove that the vaccine can be used all over the world – only that this particular guy didn't die from it. In clinical practice it takes 5-10 years to legalize a drug, to prove it isn't toxic, to rule out all harmful side effects, etc. Similarly, we can collect thousands of games by organizing theme tournaments, and see how my ideas will stand the test of serious tournament practice. With various friends I have organized theme tournaments on certain openings with black, and also events featuring alternative forms of the chess game, like Rainbow Chess and SwitChess – see my game with against Giorgadze in the chapter 'Black Is Brutal IV'. The statistics for black and white are always interesting to look at, and 99% of (wo-)men treat them as evidence. However, plain statistics don't prove anything, they are just collected findings, supposed to lead to a correct diagnosis. (My wife since 1998, Ilona, is a statistician, by the way...)

The ultimate goal of the experiment is not to confirm my thesis, and definitely not 'by all means' to claim that I am the one who is right, folks. It is to *discover the truth*. If after 5-10 years, it should turn out that BLACK is not OK at all, or maybe only a little bit OK, well, that would be a disappointment for me personally – and it would be quite unexpected for me! But it would still do great service to chess science, as even a refuted hypothesis takes us closer to the truth. So the strongest motivation of this work is (childish) *curiosity*. Curiosity that keeps asking, somewhere inside: What's going to become of all this? Will this be a fresh spring in chess theory, or will White reign until the end of time? Will White score a devastating 8-1 like in the K vs K match for the World Championship in 1986? Or even 7-0, as in the next match? Well, just remember that several 'invincible' empires have also fallen in world history!

So, in the distant future there may come a teacher who tells his amused students about what nonsense people got into their heads a couple of millennia ago. But sometimes I have another bizarre daydream. Centuries from today, triangle-headed, intelligent creatures with plastic legs and green bodies from outer space appear on Earth. These creatures, who are a whole lot cleverer than our proud human race, study the history of our culture. They come across my 'BLACK IS OK' book, and, since they can play chess (it would be a funny part of the galaxy if there were intelligent beings who couldn't play chess, right?), they have a look at it. And after reading it, they conclude with a sigh: 'What a pity! This poor devil was the only one who knew what it was all about. It's a shame he wasn't important and noisy enough to be listened to!'

Well, dear reader, only time will tell. As for me, I will keep 'laying my eggs'. Do you know the anecdote where a lady goes to the psychiatrist for help because her husband thinks he is a hen? The doctor asks 'How long has this been going on?' 'Some three years.' 'And only now you come to me?' 'You know, doctor, we are not well off, and the money for the eggs came in handy.' If you don't mind, I will win quite a few more games as BLACK, whether based on firm scientific grounds or just on the power of faith. In return, I promise that I am not going to push anyone to take my side. I will use only concrete facts, data from experiments, statistics – that is, objective factors, to recruit new 'converts'.

Some say about artists that they are tolerated by the rest of mankind and saved from Hell for their works only. If my BLACK IS OK! mission is successful, perhaps I can also hope for a place in Purgatory...

Adorjan Andras

Chapter 3
Black is Brutal I (1962 – 1968)

I played my tournament games from 1962 until 2000. I fell in love with chess, although the early encounters versus my brother, who is six years my senior, brought me not much joy. But still I somehow realized this was a beautiful game, and justice would be served to those who deserved it. The first bunch of games given below are from my early years, reflecting a romantic approach – at that age everybody plays gambits and sacrifices like crazy. The original analyses that I kept in several notebooks had longish beautiful variations, but sometimes there were holes in there, as you might expect. Still it was touching: almost all of them finishing with mate, and '!!!' can be seen after various moves as signs of enthusiasm.

These early games I played mostly against opponents who could have been my (grand-)father. In those days my name was Jocha. In 1968 it became Adorjan – see the preface to Chapter 5, 'Black is Brutal II'.

Karoly Jocha
Andras Jocha
Budapest 1962

'I beat Karcsi, mom!', I said, running to my mother with tears in my eyes. 'And I did it with a plan!' Karcsi was my six years' elder brother.

1.e4 c6 2.d4 d5 3.e5 c5 4.dxc5 e6 5.♗e3

Developing with 5.♘c3 ♘d7 6.♗b5 ♗xc5 7.♕g4 was more to the point.

5...♘c6 6.f4 d4 7.♗f2 ♗xc5 8.♘f3 ♕b6 9.b3 ♘ge7 10.♘bd2 ♘f5 11.♘e4 ♕a5+ 12.♘ed2

12...♘e3 13.♕b1

13.♕c1 ♗a3 14.♕b1 ♕c3 is not exactly an improvement.

13...♗b4 14.♕c1 ♗c3 15.♖b1 ♘b4 0-1

Here is a game from the 2nd category Championship of Budapest, which I went on to win.

Karolyi Vasvari
Andras Jocha
Budapest 1962

1.e4 c6 2.d4 d5 3.♘c3 dxe4 4.♘xe4 ♘f6 5.♘xf6+ gxf6 6.f4?! ♖g8 7.h3 ♗f5 8.c4 ♘d7 9.♕h5 ♗g6 10.♕e2 ♕c7 11.♘f3 0-0-0 12.g4

12...f5

12...e6.

13.g5 e6 14.c5 ♗h5 15.♗e3 ♗g7

There was a more forceful way to exploit the d4-weakness: 15...♕a5+! 16.♗d2 (16.♔f2 is a lesser evil) 16...♕a4 17.b3 ♗xf3 18.bxa4 ♗xe2 19.♗xe2 ♗g7 20.♗a5 b6 21.cxb6 axb6 22.♗c3 ♘c5

23.a5 ♘e4 24.♖c1 ♔b7 25.axb6 ♘xc3 26.♖xc3 ♖xd4 and Black is clearly better.

16.♗g2 ♘f8 17.♕f2 ♗xf3 18.♗xf3 ♘g6 19.♗g2 ♖d7

Systematic pressure. But again, 19...♕a5+ was stronger; Black is already winning.

20.0-0 ♖gd8 21.♖fd1 ♘e7

21...f6.

22.a3 ♘d5 23.♗c1 b6 24.♔h2 ♘e7 25.♗e3?

Just losing two pawns. He had to take on b6 first.

25...bxc5 26.d5 ♘xd5 27.♗xc5

27...♘xf4–+ 28.♖xd7 ♖xd7 29.♔h1 ♘xg2 30.♕xg2 ♖d5 31.♖c1 ♕f4 32.♖f1 ♕c4 33.♗xa7 ♖d2! 34.♕f3 ♕d5 35.b4 ♕xf3+

35...♖d3–+.

36.♖xf3 ♗d4 37.♗xd4 ♖xd4 38.♖c3 ♔b7 39.♔g2 ♔b6 40.♔g3 e5 41.h4 e4 42.♔f4 ♖d3 43.♖xd3 exd3 44.♔e3 ♔b5 45.♔xd3 ♔a4

0-1

The First Swallow

The following game was my first one ever published in a newspaper.

Sandor Szabo
Andras Jocha

Budapest 1963

1.e4 e5 2.♘f3 ♘c6 3.♗b5 a6 4.♗a4 ♘f6 5.0-0 ♗e7 6.♖e1 b5 7.♗b3 0-0 8.c3 d5 9.exd5 ♘xd5 10.♘xe5

♘xe5 11.♖xe5 ♘f6 12.d4 ♗d6 13.♖e1 ♘g4 14.g3?

It has since become well-known that 14.h3! ♕h4 15.♕f3 h5 (15...♘xf2? 16.♗d2! ♗xh3 17.gxh3 ♘xh3+ 18.♔f1±) 16.♗e3 ♘xe3 17.♖xe3 ♕f4 18.♕xf4 ♗xf4 19.♖e1 leads to a slight advantage for White.

14...♘xh2!?

Brave, nice, and good. But probably better is 14...♕f6!, continuing the attack: 15.♕e2 ♘xh2∓ or 15.♗e3 ♖e8∓.

15.♗d5

15.♔xh2 loses by force: 15...♕h4+ 16.♔g1 ♗xg3 17.♕f3! (after 17.fxg3 ♕xg3+ 18.♔h1 ♗g4 Black wins easily) 17...♕h2+ (17...♗h2+ 18.♔g2 ♗g4 19.♕d3 ♖ae8! with the idea 20.♖e3 ♗f4!–+) 18.♔f1 ♗h3+ 19.♔e2 ♖ae8+ (19...♗g4?! 20.♕xg4 ♕xf2+ 21.♔d3 ♕xe1 22.♗h6! ♕f1+ 23.♔c2 ♕f6 24.♗e3± (24.♕xg3 ♕xh6)) 20.♗e3 (20.♔d1 ♖xe1+ 21.♔xe1 ♕g1+ 22.♔d2 ♗h4–+) 20...♗g4!! 21.♕xg4 ♗xf2 22.♔d1 ♗xe1 23.♗c1 c5.

On the other hand, 15.♕h5! was very strong: 15...♘g4 16.♗g5 ♕d7 17.♗c2 (17.♘d2 ♕f5) 17...h6 with an unclear position.

15...♗xg3! 16.fxg3

Two months later the same position was reached in a team championship game. There, my opponent, Denkinger, chose the 'quicker death'. The game continued: 16.♗xa8 ♗g4 17.fxg3 (17.f3 ♕xa8 18.fxg4 ♘f3+ 19.♔g2

19

♘xe1+ 20.♔xg3 ♕g2+−+) 17...♗xd1
18.♔xh2 ♕xa8 19.♖xd1 ♖e8 20.d5
♖e2+ 21.♔h3 ♕c8+ 22.g4 h5 and
White resigned a few moves later.

**16...♕xd5 17.♔xh2 ♗b7 18.♖g1
♖ae8 19.♗f4**

History repeats itself: the game Belenkij-Pirogov (1959) saw this position first. I did not know this game, and only noticed the diagram among a number of other combination exercises.

The rest of the game was the same. To my great surprise I found another (full) example on this theme: Feco-Pohranc, Slovakia tt B 2003/04. Only 40 years after my game...

After 19.♗d2 Black could have obtained a decisive attack by 19...♖e6 and 20...♖fe8. However, the text allows a powerful finish.

19...♖e1!! 20.c4

The only move that doesn't lose at once.

20...♖xg1!

20...bxc4?? would run into 21.♘c3+−.

**21.cxd5 ♖xd1 22.♗xc7 ♖c8
23.♗b6 f5 24.♗c5 ♖e8**

The d-pawn can wait – Black is going for mate.

25.g4 f4 26.g5 ♖e2+ 27.♔h3 ♗c8+

And White resigned.

**K. Velinszky
Andras Jocha**

Budapest 1963

1.e4 e5 2.♘f3 ♘c6 3.♗c4 f5?

Jocha? Morphy! My gambit was not quite so original for, as I later learned, Paul Morphy had already played it.

4.d4 fxe4

4...exd4 is no better, cf. 5.♘xd4 ♘xd4 6.♕xd4 fxe4 7.♗xg8 ♖xg8 8.♕d5 ♖h8 9.♕h5+ g6 10.♕e5+ ♔f7 11.♘c3 ♗g7 12.♕d5+ ♔f8 13.0-0, which is quite pleasant for White.

5.♘xe5 d5 6.♕h5+??

As they say: patzer sees a check, patzer gives a check. Instead there were several ways for White to get an advantage: 6.♘xc6 bxc6 7.♕h5+ ♔e7 8.♗g5+ ♘f6 9.♗b3= or 6.♗b5! ♕d6 7.c4±.

6...g6 7.♘xg6

7.♘xc6 loses a piece to 7...gxh5 8.♘xd8 dxc4 9.♗g5 ♗e7 and the knight is caught.

7...♘f6 8.♕h4

8...hxg6

More convincing was 8...♘xd4! 9.♗b3 ♘f5 10.♕h3 ♘e7 – an even more humoristic knight catch.

9.♕xh8 dxc4 10.♗g5?

Better was 10.c3 ♔f7 11.♕h4, keeping some play.

10...♘xd4! 11.♘a3 ♔f7 12.0-0-0

12.c3 ♘e6 achieves nothing.

12...♗g4 13.♔b1

White had to try 13.f3, after which 13... exf3 14.gxf3 ♗xa3 15.♕xd8 ♖xd8 16.fxg4 ♘e2+ 17.♔b1 ♖xd1+ 18.♖xd1 ♘e4 should win for Black.

13...♗xd1 14.♖xd1 ♗xa3 15.♕h4 ♕d6

Taking over the attack.

16.bxa3 ♕b6+ 17.♔c1 c3 18.♖xd4 ♕xd4 19.♗xf6 ♕d2+   0-1

Termes
Andras Jocha
Budapest 1963

1.e4 e5 2.♘f3 ♘c6 3.♗b5 a6 4.♗a4 ♘f6 5.0-0 ♗e7 6.♖e1 b5 7.♗b3 0-0 8.c3 d5

Happy Marshall days...

9.exd5 ♘xd5 10.♘xe5 ♘xe5 11.♖xe5 ♘f6 12.♖e2!?

A very careful move, but it has its drawbacks too.

12...♗d6 13.d4 ♘h5

A trifle too gung-ho. 13...♗b7!? gives good compensation.

14.♕d3 ♕h4 15.g3 ♕h3 16.♗d5!

On 16.♕e4 Black has 16...♗g4.

16...♗f5 17.♗e4?!

17.♕e3±.

17...♗xe4 18.♖xe4

Not consistent. More logical was 18.♕xe4 ♘f6 (18...f5!?) 19.♕f3 ♖ae8 20.♗e3 ♘g4 21.♕g2 ♕h5 22.♘d2 ♖e6 23.♖ae1 ♖fe8, though Black has compensation here.

18...♖ae8 19.♖xe8 ♖xe8

20.♕f1

Some thematic shots are 20.♗d2? ♘f4! and 20.♘d2 ♘f4 21.♕f1 ♖e1!.

20...♕g4 21.♘d2

21.♗d2 was safer.

21...f5

22.f3?

A bad mistake. 22.a4 ♘f4 23.axb5 ♘e2+ 24.♔h1 was better. After the text, the white king's position will be easy to breach.

22...♕g6–+ 23.♕f2

On 23.♕g2 ♖e1+ 24.♘f1 Black blasts through with 24...♗xg3 25.hxg3 ♘xg3 26.♗g5 ♘e2+ 27.♔f2 ♖xa1 28.♔xe2 h6.

23...♘f4

Or again 23...♗xg3 24.hxg3 ♘xg3, winning easily since after 25.♘f1 ♘e2+ 26.♔h1 ♘xc1 White cannot take back due to 27...♕h6+.

24.♔h1 ♖e2 25.♕f1 ♕h6 26.h4 ♘h5! 27.♘e4

27...♘xg3+! 28.♔g1 ♕xh4 29.♘f2 ♘xf1   0-1

Bela Juhasz
Andras Jocha
Budapest 1963

This was a romantic game, if not without mistakes.

1.e4 e5 2.♘f3 ♘c6 3.d4 exd4 4.♘xd4 ♘f6 5.♗g5?! ♗c5

The play sharpens. The safer option was 5...h6 6.♗xf6 ♕xf6 7.c3 (7.♘b5 ♗c5 8.f3 ♕xb2 9.♘xc7+ ♔d8 10.♘xa8 ♕xa1 clearly favours Black) 7...♗c5 8.♘f3 0-0∓.

6.c3

6.♘xc6 bxc6 7.e5 doesn't work in view of 7...♕e7 8.♕e2 ♗d4! 9.exf6 ♕xe2+ 10.♗xe2 ♗xb2.

6...0-0

Also here, safer was 6...h6! 7.♘xc6 bxc6 8.♗xf6 (8.♗h4 g5 just loses a pawn) 8...♕xf6 9.♕d2 0-0 10.♗d3 d5 with lovely play for Black. 6...♕e7 was another good alternative.

7.f3 d5 8.♘xc6 bxc6 9.♘d2

9.e5 ♕e8 10.♕e2 runs into 10...♗a6!.

9...dxe4

It was stronger to increase the pressure on e4 with 9...♖e8. There's no safe shelter for the white king.

10.♗xf6?

An amusing line is 10.♘xe4 ♘xe4 (10...♕xd1+ 11.♖xd1 ♘xe4 12.fxe4 ♗e6∓) 11.♕xd8 (11.♗xd8 loses to 11...♗f2+ 12.♔e2 ♗a6+ 13.♕d3 ♗xd3+ 14.♔xd3 ♖axd8+) 11...♖xd8 12.♗xd8 ♘f2 13.♖g1 (13.♗e7! ♗b6 14.♖g1 ♘h3 15.♖h1) 13...♗f5 14.♗g5 ♘h3 (14...♖e8+ 15.♔d2 h6) 15.gxh3 ♗xg1, which still gives Black something of an edge.

10...♕xf6 11.♘xe4 ♖e8 12.♕c2

Black's attack is also strong after the developing move 12.♗d3 ♕g5 13.♔f1 ♖xe4! 14.fxe4 (14.♗xe4 ♗a6+ – again! – 15.♗d3 ♕e3–+) 14...♗g4 15.♕c2 ♖d8–+.

12...♖xe4+!?

There was a simpler win by 12...♕h4+! 13.g3 ♕h6 14.♗e2 ♗f5.

13.fxe4

On 13.♕xe4 Black has two good possibilities:

A) 13...♗f5!? 14.♕c4 (14.♕e2 ♔f8–+) 14...♖e8+ 15.♗e2 ♕e7 16.♖d1 a5 and the king cannot get away;

B) But more convincing is 13...♗d7 14.♗e2 ♖e8 15.♕c4 (15.♕c2 ♗f5–+) 15...♕g5 16.g4 h5 17.♖d1 ♗e6–+.

13...♗g4 14.♗d3

On 14.♗c4 ♕f4 is strong; I should have played this after the text move as well.

14...♖d8 15.♖f1 ♕h6?

15...♕d6!–+.

16.♗e2??

16.♗c4 ♕xh2 17.♖xf7 ♕h4+ 18.♖f2+ ♔h8 19.b4 ♗e3 wins for Black, but 16.g3 was a better defence; Black should then play 16...♗e3!.

16...♕h4+!–+ 17.g3 ♕xh2 18.♗d3 ♕xg3+ 19.♖f2 ♖xd3   0-1

Mihaly Gombi
Andras Jocha
Hungary tt 1963

With the king still on e1, there can only be one move here:

14...e3! 15.dxe3

15.fxe3 ♖xe3–+.

15...♗xc3+ 16.♔d1 ♕xd5+ 17.♗d2 ♕xd2#

Janos Havasi
Andras Jocha
Budapest jr 1964 (7)

Today we even see categories like Under-8 in junior tournaments. In our time we all played in one under-20 group. I was only 14 in this Championship, probably the youngest ever to win the competition – ahead of Tompa (17) and Szel (18), among others. It's funny, but later on my best result would be second place.

1.d4 d5 2.♘f3 ♘f6 3.e3 e6 4.c4 c5 5.♘c3 ♘c6 6.♗e2 dxc4 7.0-0 cxd4 8.exd4 ♗e7 9.♗xc4 0-0 10.a3 ♘d5 11.h3 ♘xc3 12.bxc3 ♗f6 13.♗f4 b6 14.♕e2 ♘a5 15.♗d3 ♗b7 16.♘e5 ♖c8 17.♖ac1 ♘b3 18.♖c2 ♕d5 19.♘f3

19.♕g4.

19...♕a5 20.♗d6 ♖fd8 21.♗b4 ♕d5 22.a4 a5 23.♗a3

23...♗xd4??

Bad, but winning. That's what happens in must-win situations.

Nice and fine was 23...♖xc3!? and now:

A) 24.♗xh7+ ♔xh7 25.♖xc3 ♘xd4 26.♕d3+ ♕e4 27.♕xe4+ ♗xe4 28.♖c7 ♘e2+ (28...♔g6) 29.♔h1 ♖d3!

23

(threatening mate in a few) 30.♖e1 ♖xf3 (a less romantic soul would win with 30...♖xa3 31.♖xe2 ♖xa4) 31.♖xe2 ♖xh3+ 32.♔g1 ♖xa3 33.♖xe4 ♖a1+ 34.♔h2 ♖xa4!! 35.♖e3 (35.♖xa4 ♗e5+) 35...♗g5 36.♖h3+ ♔g6, winning in the endgame;

B) 24.♖xc3 ♘xd4 25.♗xh7+ ♔h8 (or 25...♔xh7 as in line a) 26.♕e3 ♘xf3+ 27.gxf3 ♔xh7 (why give up that nice bishop on f6?) 28.♖c7 ♕xf3 29.♕xf3 ♗xf3 and Black is much better in the endgame after either 30.♗e7 ♗xe7 31.♖xe7 ♔g6 or 30.♖xf7 ♔g6 31.♖f8 ♖d4!.

The prosaic 23...♕c6! 24.♗b2 ♕xa4 is highly unclear after 25.♗b5.

24.♖d1 e5 25.cxd4 e4?

The best chance was 25...♘xd4 26.♕e3 ♘xc2 27.♗xc2 ♕c6±.

26.♖xc8 ♖xc8 27.♖e1 f5 28.♗c2

28.♗a6! was winning.

28...exf3

29.♕e5??

Still winning was 29.♕e7! ♘xd4 30.♗b2 and Black can't take either way because of mate.

29...♘xd4 30.♕xd5+ ♗xd5 31.♗d3 fxg2   **0-1**

Bela Vigh
Andras Jocha
Budapest blindfold 1964

I still remember this game very well. We were part of the 'crowd and soldiers' for a movie they were making

called 'White resigns'. Chess played an important part in the story. But we were rather bored and tired after a while and then started playing a blindfold game, which is given below.

1.d4 d5 2.c4 e6 3.♘c3 ♘f6 4.cxd5 exd5 5.♗g5 ♗e7 6.e3 0-0 7.♗d3 b6??

7...c6.

8.♘ge2?

Both of us didn't 'see' 8.♗xf6 ♗xf6 9.♕h5+−.

8...♗b7 9.0-0 ♘bd7 10.♕c2 ♘e4! 11.♗xe7 ♕xe7 12.♖ae1 c5 13.f3 ♘ef6 14.♘g3 c4 15.♗f5 g6 16.♗h3 ♖ae8 17.♗xd7?

17.e4!.

17...♕xd7 18.♔h1 b5 19.♕f2 b4 20.♘ce2 ♖e7 21.♘c1 ♖fe8 22.♖e2 h5 23.♖fe1 ♗a6 24.e4 c3 25.e5 ♗xe2 26.exf6 cxb2

27.♘b3

27.♘cxe2 loses to 27...♖xe2 28.♘xe2 ♕e6 (or also 28...♕f5 29.♕f1 h4−+) 29.♕f1 ♕e3.

27...♖e3 28.♘d2 ♕e6 29.h3 ♖d3
30.♖xe2

This loses, as do the alternatives 30.♘b1
♖xf3 and 30.♘b3 ♖xb3 31.axb3 ♗d3
32.♖xe6 b1♕+.

30...♕xe2! 31.♘xe2 ♖xd2 32.♕f1
♖dxe2 33.♔h2 ♖e1   0-1

Comment by the winner: 'Nice game.
Both the refutation of White's e3-e4
break and the way Black takes advantage
of the back-rank weakness are pretty.'

Laszlo Antal
Andras Jocha
Hungary tt 1965

1.e4 e5 2.d4 exd4 3.♕xd4 ♘c6
4.♕e3

White plays the Centre Gambit the way
Bela Bacsi played it – like myself, Laszlo was
his pupil. I've never understood why it is
called a gambit. A decent gambit involves
some sacrifice, while here White regains
the pawn immediately, giving two tempi
to Black. In addition, e3 can hardly be the

final station for the queen. It becomes a
target again after my real gambit move.
   4...f5!?
I am sure that this brainchild of mine is
at least as playable as any other healthy
move, but strangely enough, 21 years
would pass until somebody repeated it.
With success.
   5.exf5+
5.♘c3 ♘f6 (5...fxe4 6.♕xe4+ ♕e7
7.♕xe7+ ♗xe7 8.♗f4 gives White
an edge) 6.♘f3 fxe4 7.♘xe4 ♘xe4
8.♕xe4+ ♕e7=.
   5...♗e7 6.♗d3 ♘f6 7.♘e2
7.♘f3 0-0 8.0-0 d5 looks like a good
reversed King's Gambit for Black.
   7...0-0 8.0-0 d5
Also possible is 8...♘b4 – see Havasi-
Füsthy, Hungary tt 1986 in the
'Connections' chapter at the end of this
book.
   9.♘f4 ♕d6
The immediate 9...♘g4 doesn't work
very well due to 10.♕h3 ♘ge5
(10...♘ce5 11.♘e6 ♗xe6 12.fxe6±)
11.g4 ♗h4 12.♘d2 and White
consolidates.
   10.♖e1 ♘g4

   11.♕f3??
Now Black's set-up is justified. White
could win by making use of the pin on
the h2-b8 diagonal with 11.♕g3! ♘ce5
12.♘c3 c6 (12...♘xd3 13.cxd3 ♗xf5
14.♘fxd5 ♖ae8 15.♗f4 ♕d7 16.h3 ♘f6
17.♖xe7 ♖xe7

18.♘xe7+ ♕xe7 19.♗xc7+–) and now, even stronger than 13.h3 is 13.♘fxd5! cxd5 14.♗f4 ♗f6 15.♕xg4+–.

The text move wins a second pawn on d5, but after that Black gets fantastic piece play even (or should we say 'precisely'?) without the queens.

11...♘ce5 12.♕xd5+ ♕xd5 13.♘xd5

13...♗c5?

Strong was 13...♗h4! 14.♗e3 ♗xf5 15.♗xf5 ♖xf5 and now:

A) 16.♗c5 ♖xf2!;

B) 16.♖e2 c6 17.h3 cxd5 18.hxg4 ♘xg4 19.♘c3 ♘xe3 20.fxe3 ♗f6 or 19.♗d4 ♗xf2+! followed by ...♖af8;

C) 16.♖f1 c6 17.h3 cxd5 18.hxg4 ♘xg4 and Black remains a little better.

14.♗e3 ♘xd3?

The wrong exchange. After 14...♘xe3 15.fxe3 c6 16.♘c7 ♖b8 17.♘e6 ♗xe6 18.fxe6 ♖bd8 19.♘c3 ♘xd3 20.cxd3 ♖xd3 21.♖ad1 ♖xe3 22.♔h1 ♖xe1+ 23.♖xe1 ♖d8 24.g3 ♔f8 Black has his pawns back, with an edge.

15.cxd3 ♗d6

15...♘xe3 16.fxe3 ♗xf5 17.d4 ♗d6 18.e4 ♗e6 19.♘bc3 doesn't give enough compensation for the pawn.

16.h3

Or first 16.♗f4 ♘c5 17.♗g3 ♗xf5 18.♘e7+ ♔h8 19.h3 and White is slightly better.

16...♘e5 17.d4?

17.♗f4±; 17.f6±.

17...♘d3 18.♖e2 ♗xf5

More accurate may have been 18...c6 19.♘dc3 ♗xf5 20.♘d2 ♖ae8 with pressure for the pawn.

19.b3

White could have freed himself with 19.♘a3! ♘xb2 20.♘b5 ♘c4 21.♘dxc7 ♗xc7 22.♘xc7 ♖ac8 (22...♖ad8) 23.♘d5=.

19...♖ae8 20.♘d2 c6 21.♘c4 ♗b8 22.♘c3 ♖e6 23.♖d1

Or 23.♗g5 ♖g6 with initiative.

23...♖g6 24.♔h1

24.g4 h5 25.f3=; 24.♔f1.

24...b5 25.♘b2?

White cannot really disentangle in this way. He might have done so with 25.♘e5 ♘xe5 26.dxe5 ♗xe5 27.♗d4=.

25...♘xb2 26.♖xb2

26...b4

With the nice 26...♗xh3 27.f3 (27.gxh3 ♖f3 is the point) 27...♖e8 28.♗c1 ♗f5 Black could have obtained an advantage with his two bishop versus not a minus pawn.

27.♘a4 ♗e4

Again, 27...♗xh3! was possible.

28.♖g1?

This allows an immediate decision. White would also be in trouble after 28.f4 ♖g3 29.♖e1 ♖xh3+ 30.♔g1 ♖h4, winning the f-pawn.

**28...♖f3   29.♖c1   ♖xh3+   30.♔g1
♗f3   0-1**

The victim in this game was a talented player, but he did not become a professional. Forty years later, he told me why (half a bottle of whiskey makes you sincere): 'You know, when I realized that chess can be played the way you played it, I saw no reason to hope for a shining future. I sold my chess books the next day to a second-hand shop' (Ervin Nagy became sad when he heard this story and added 'Unfortunately, mine too, which I had lent him'). Instead, Laszlo Antal became a well-known name in the circles of European economists. And that's not the end of the story. We have a saying in Hungary: 'Blood doesn't turn into water'. Today we have a grandmaster called Gergely Antal – his son. I wish we had more parents with such sane self-criticism and more talented children. But give up chess? No! Chess can be played for fun as an amateur, and many people play it with pleasure until a high age.

**Kakoczki
Andras Jocha**

Hungary tt 1965

**1.e4   e5   2.♘f3   ♘c6   3.♗b5   a6
4.♗a4   ♘f6   5.0-0   ♗e7   6.♖e1   b5
7.♗b3   0-0**

8.c3
8.d4 ♘xd4!? (8...d6=) 9.♗xf7+ ♖xf7 10.♘xe5 ♖f8 11.♕xd4 gives Black interesting play for the pawn after 11...♗b7 12.♘c3 c5 13.♕d1 ♕c7 14.♘g4 ♘xg4 15.♕xg4 ♗d6 16.♕h4 ♗e5, with compensation. Also nice is 9.♘xd4 exd4 10.e5 ♘e8 11.♕xd4 ♗b7 (11...d6 12.♗d5 dxe5 13.♕xe5 ♗f6 (13...♗d6!? 14.♗xf7+ ♔h8) 14.♕h5 ♗g4! 15.♗xf7+ ♖xf7 16.♕xg4 ♗d4 with compensation) 12.♕d3 d6 13.e6 d5 14.♘c3 fxe6 15.♖xe6 c6=.

8...d5 9.exd5 e4!?
At best dubious, like Frank Marshall's original idea 9...♘xd5 10.♘xe5 ♘xe5 11.♖xe5 ♘f6?!. It's funny, but 11...c6 has become drawish these days, although it's pretty sharp.

10.dxc6 exf3 11.♕xf3
11.d4 fxg2 12.♗g5=.

**11...♗g4   12.♕g3   ♗d6   13.♕h4
♖e8 14.f3 ♗f5 15.d4**

15...♗xh2+!?
A move with a shock effect. Since chess is played by human beings, the psychological

side to the game is always important. My weaker opponent sees ghosts and falls victim to his own timidity:

16.♔h1??
16.♔xh2! ♘g4+ 17.♔g3 (17.♕xg4 ♗xg4 18.♖xe8+ ♕xe8 19.fxg4 ♕e1 offers roughly equal chances) 17...♕xh4+ 18.♔xh4 ♖xe1 19.fxg4 ♖xc1 (19...♗xb1 20.♖xb1 ♖ae8 21.d5+−) 20.gxf5 ♖e8 21.d5 ♖f1 22.d6 cxd6 23.g4 was better for White as Black is tied to the c6-pawn.

16...♖xe1+ 17.♕xe1 ♕d6
Winning.

18.♗e3
18.♕h4 ♖e8 19.♗d2 ♗g3−+.

18...♖e8 19.♕d2 ♘h5! 20.g4

White cannot survive such a weakening of his position.

20...♗f4! 21.♗xf4 ♘xf4 22.♗d1 ♗xb1 23.♔g1 ♕h6   0-1

Istvan Somogyi
Andras Jocha
Hungary tt 1965

38.♔d3
38.g4 fxg4 39.fxg4 ♔e4 40.♔c4 ♔f3 41.♔d4 ♔xg4 42.e4 h5 leads to a queen ending with a plus pawn for Black.

38...f4!!
It's almost incredible that this move, which gives White a protected passed pawn, not only wins, but is also the only move that wins.

On the other hand, 38...h5? 39.e4+ fxe4+ 40.fxe4+ ♔c5 (40...♔e5? 41.♔e3) 41.♔e3 ♔c4 42.♔e2 ♔d4 43.♔f3 ♔c5 44.♔e3 ♔c4 45.♔e2 is only a draw.

39.e4+
39.exf4 loses to the simple 39...gxf4 40.♔c3 ♔c5 when Black has the opposition; and if 39.♔c3, ♔c5! wins.

39...♔c5
Good enough. But simpler and quicker was 39...♔e5! in view of 40.♔c4 h5 41.♔b5 (41.♔d3 g4 42.♔e2 g3 and the a4-pawn falls.

The white king is paralysed by the threat of ...h4-h3) and now the well-known breakthrough 41...g4 42.♔xa5 h4 43.♔b6 h3 44.gxh3 gxf3 or 44...g3.

40.♔c3 h5 41.♔d3 g4 42.fxg4
42.♔e2 g3 43.♔d3 h4 44.♔e2 ♔b4 is the same story. If 42.e5 gxf3 43.gxf3 h4 wins.

42...hxg4 43.e5 ♔d5 44.e6 ♔xe6 45.♔e4

45...f3! 46.gxf3
46.♔e3 fxg2 47.♔f2 ♔d5−+.

46...g3 47.♔e3 ♔f5 48.♔e2

On 48.f4 ♔g4 49.f5 ♔h3! decides the issue.

48...♔f4 49.♔e1

49.♔f1 ♔xf3–+.

49...♔e3!

Not 49...♔xf3?? 50.♔f1=. Now the g-pawn is under control, and if Black gives it up for the a-pawn, the white king still reaches the queenside in time.

50.f4

50.♔f1 ♔xf3–+.

50...g2

White resigned.
Here 50...♔xf4 51.♔e2 ♔g4 52.♔f1 ♔h3 would also have won.

Andor Lilienthal
Andras Jocha

Budapest simul 1966

Andor Lilienthal was born in Hungary, but he travelled a lot and lived in the Soviet Union for thirty years. However, he often visited his native country Hungary, giving lectures and simuls.
Nobody likes to lose, not even in a simul. The game given below is one which he lost and I won.
He knew he was playing against the Junior Team of Hungary, but maybe he still wasn't careful enough. However, instead of flying into a rage he said: 'But my dear boy, you are a very good player already. Congratulations!'.

1.d4 ♘f6 2.c4 g6 3.♘c3 d5 4.♘f3 ♗g7 5.♕b3 dxc4 6.♕xc4 0-0 7.e4 ♘a6 8.e5 ♘d7 9.e6?

Too optimistic. Uncle Lili should have continued his development instead.

9...fxe6 10.♕xe6+ ♔h8 11.♕b3

In the event of 11.♕e2 ♘b4 (11...c5 12.♗e3) 12.♗g5 (12.♗e3) 12...♘f6 13.a3 ♘bd5 Black already has an edge due to his better development.

11...e5 12.d5

12.dxe5 is dangerous after 12...♘ac5∓.

12...♘dc5

13.♕d1

13.♕a3 e4 14.♗xa6 exf3 15.♕xc5 fxg2 16.♖g1 b6! 17.♕c4 (17.♕c6 ♗xa6 18.♖xg2 ♕e8+ 19.♗e3 ♕xc6 20.dxc6 ♖f6–+) 17...♗xa6 18.♕xa6 ♗xc3+ 19.bxc3 ♕f6 gives Black a winning attack; After 13.♕c4 c6! the position is opened up, which will be disastrous for White's undeveloped position.

13...e4 14.♘g5 ♘b4 15.♘gxe4 ♘xe4 16.♘xe4 ♗f5 17.a3

17...♕e7 18.axb4 ♕xe4+ 19.♗e3 ♗xb2 20.♗e2 ♗h3 21.gxh3 ♕xh1+
21...♗c3+–+.

22.♗f1 ♖ae8 23.♔d2 ♕xh2 24.♗e2 ♕e5   **0-1**

Zoltan Ribli
Andras Jocha

Balatonszeplak 1967 (6)

1.e4 e5 2.♘f3 ♘c6 3.♗b5 a6 4.♗a4 ♘f6 5.0-0 b5 6.♗b3 ♗b7 7.d4 ♘xd4 8.♗xf7+ ♔xf7 9.♘xe5+ ♔g8 10.♕xd4 c5 11.♕e3 ♕c7 12.♘f3 ♖e8 13.e5 ♘g4 14.♕f4 ♘xe5

15.♘xe5 ♛xe5 16.♛xe5 ♖xe5
17.♗f4 ♖f5 18.♗g3 ♔f7 19.♘d2 ♗e7

Since Zoltan and I were already friends at the time, and worked together, we avoided the variations we had analysed in our mutual games. My choice was luckier: Black is not only OK, he is already better here.

20.a4 c4 21.axb5 axb5 22.♖fe1 ♖e8 23.♘e4 ♗xe4 24.♖xe4 ♗f6 25.♖xe8 ♔xe8 26.♖e1+ ♔f7 27.♖d1 d5 28.b3 d4 29.♔f1 ♖c5 30.♔e2 ♔e6!

It's still too early for 30...d3+ 31.♔d2 ♖d5 32.bxc4 bxc4 33.♔c1 ♗e7 (33...♗c3!?) 34.cxd3 cxd3 35.♔d2 and White can contain the passed pawn.

31.bxc4 bxc4 32.f3 ♖b5 33.♗f2

33...d3+! 34.cxd3

Now 34.♔d2 fails tactically to 34...♖b2 35.♖c1 ♗g5+ (35...♖a2!?−+) 36.♗e3 ♖xc2+ 37.♖xc2 ♗xe3+.

34...♖b2+

35.♔e3

35.♖d2 loses immediately to 35...c3. 35.♔f1 c3 36.♗e3 c2 (36...♔d5 37.♖a1 c2 38.♖a5+ ♔d6 39.♖c5 ♗e5 40.d4 ♗xd4 41.♗xd4 ♖b1+ 42.♔f2 c1♛ 43.♖xc1 ♖xc1 44.♗xg7=) 37.♖c1 ♗e7 38.♗f4 ♗a3 39.♖e1+ ♔d5 40.♗c1 ♔d4 41.♖e4+ (41.♔e2 ♖a2−+) 41...♔c3 42.♔e2 ♖a2 43.♗d2+ ♔b3 44.♔f1 c1♛+ and wins − the power of the passed pawn!

35...c3 36.♖c1 ♔d5 37.♗e1 ♗d4+ 38.♔f4

38...♖e2 39.♖xc3

39.♔g3 c2−+; 39.♗xc3 ♗e3+−+.

39...♗e5+! 40.♔g4 ♖xg2+ 41.♔h3 ♖xh2+ 42.♔g4 h5+ 43.♔g5 ♗xc3 44.♗xc3 h4 45.♔f4 h3 46.♗xg7 ♖e2   **0-1**

Now the other passed pawn decides − 47.♔g3 ♖g2+.

Jan Timman
Andras Jocha

Groningen Ech jr 1967

I first met Jan Timman twice. How? In Groningen we played in the semi-final and both qualified for the A-group. That's the explanation. Our business could not have started better for me – I scored plus 2 (but it ended quite differently: minus 5).

1.c4 ♘f6 2.♘c3 d5 3.cxd5 ♘xd5 4.g3 g6 5.♗g2 ♘xc3 6.bxc3 ♗g7 7.♘f3 0-0 8.0-0 c5 9.♖b1 ♘c6 10.♕a4 ♕a5 11.♕xa5 ♘xa5 12.d4 ♗f5 13.♖b5 b6

14.♘h4

On 14.dxc5 Black has time for 14...♗d7.

14...♗d7 15.♖xa5 bxa5 16.♗xa8 ♖xa8

Ruining Black's structure, but the bishop pair should be worth something!

17.♗a3 cxd4 18.cxd4 ♗b5

18...♗e6!?.

19.♗xe7 ♗xe2 20.♖e1 ♗c4 21.a3 ♖e8 22.♖c1 ♗d5 23.♗c5 ♖e4 24.♖d1

24.♔f1 sets a nice little trap: 24...♗xd4? 25.f3 ♖xh4 26.gxh4 ♗e5 27.♔g2±. Instead Black should play 24...♗b7 25.♘f3 or 24...a6 25.♘f3 ♗f6, both with even chances.

24...♖e2

25.♗xa7 is met by 25...♗f8 26.♗c5 ♖c2! and Black dominates, although with good defence White can probably hold.

25.♘g2 ♖a2

With 25...♗h6 Black could have restricted the knight.

26.♘e3 ♗f3 27.♖b1 h5 28.d5 ♔h7 29.d6 ♖d2

30.♖e1

It's a draw after 30.♘c4 ♖d5 31.♗xa7 ♗e2 32.♖c1 ♗h6 33.f4 ♗xc4 34.♖xc4 ♖xd6=.

30...♗c3 31.♖c1

31.♘f1 ♖d3 32.♖e3 ♖xe3 33.♘xe3 ♗c6 34.♘c2 ♗a4 35.♗d4 ♗d2 36.♗e3 ♗c3 37.♗xa7 ♗e5 and now White forces opposite-coloured bishops with the trick 38.♗b8 ♗xc2 39.d7 ♗f6 40.♗c7=.

31...♗f6 32.♘c4 ♖d5 33.♘xa5??

A dramatic error. 33.♗xa7 ♗e2 34.♗b6 a4 was still equal.

33...♗b2–+ 34.♖b1 ♖xc5 35.♘b3 ♖d5 36.g4 ♖xd6 37.gxh5 ♖d1+ 38.♖xd1 ♗xd1 39.hxg6+ ♔xg6 40.♘a5 ♗xa3   **0-1**

Sandor Bodnar
Andras Jocha

Budapest ch-HUN sf 1967

In the game below, my opponent and I composed a piece together. It's not a classic, but it's entertaining.

1.e4 c5 2.♘f3 ♘c6 3.c3 ♘f6 4.d3 g6 5.♗e2 ♗g7 6.0-0 0-0 7.♗e3 d6 8.h3 b6 9.♘bd2 e5 10.d4 cxd4 11.cxd4 exd4 12.♘xd4 ♗b7 13.♕a4 ♘e7 14.f3 ♘h5

15.♔h2?

Black's more active pieces already gave him an edge, which is why White should have exchanged one with 15.♗a6 ♗xa6 16.♕xa6, though after 16...d5 Black is still slightly better.

15...d5 16.g4 dxe4! 17.gxh5 ♘d5 18.♗g1

On 18.h6 comes simply 18...♗h8.

18...♗e5+ 19.♔h1 ♕h4 20.♖f2

20.♗h2 ♗xh2 21.fxe4 ♕xh3 also loses.

20...e3 21.♖g2 exd2 22.♕d7

22...♘f4!

Killing.

23.♕xb7 ♘xg2 24.♔xg2 ♕g3+ 25.♔f1 ♕xh3+   0-1

Bela Balogh
Andras Jocha
Hungary tt 1968

Bela Balogh was a solid player, and our game was quiet for a long time, but then somehow it ended with a bolt from the blue

1.d4 ♘f6 2.♘f3 g6 3.c4 ♗g7 4.♘c3 d5 5.e3 0-0 6.♕b3 e6 7.♗d2 b6 8.cxd5 exd5 9.♗e2 ♗b7 10.0-0 ♘bd7 11.♘a4 ♖e8 12.♗b4 a5 13.♗a3 c6 14.♘c5 ♘xc5 15.♗xc5 ♘d7 16.♗d6 ♖e6 17.♗g3 h6 18.♖ac1 ♕f8 19.♖c3 a4 20.♕c2 ♕b4 21.a3 ♕a5 22.♘h4 ♘f6 23.f3 ♖ae8 24.♗e1 ♕a8 25.♗f2 ♘h5 26.♖e1 c5

27.♗b5

Black is winning after either 27.♕d2 ♗a6 or 27.dxc5 d4!.

27...cxd4 28.♖c7 dxe3 29.♗xe8 exf2+ 30.♕xf2 ♕xe8 31.♖d1

31.♖xe6 ♕xe6 32.♖xb7 loses to the same point...

31...♗d4!!

... only here it's prettier!

32.♕xd4 ♖e1+   0-1

Chapter 4

The Dogma is Dead – BLACK is BACK!

It is not only that fresh material has come up ever since my previous book *Black is OK forever!* (2005). No, it is simply that I have finally found a convincing refutation of the dogma (or, as the dogmatists believed it to be, the 'axiom') of hundreds, maybe even thousands of years: that White has any advantage. It is not true. Not in the beginning position, and not in the further development of the game. I have worked on this subject for over 30 years. Already in the beginning, in 1985, I declared that starting the game with white in no way means taking the initiative. Stating that White is the one who chooses the direction of the opening and, consequently, the rest of the game, is false. Every single move on either side gives a player the opportunity to find his own way.

(See *Black is OK*, Batsford 1988)

Years ago, my wife Ilona discovered a nice discussion on Wikipedia about the following question: is there a first-move advantage in chess? One argument in this discussion was that the perfect chess game naturally ends in a draw. It is good that Steinitz, Lasker, Capablanca and many great players supported this opinion, but what we still need is concrete evidence.

Well, the first piece of evidence – which I have hardly seen mentioned anywhere in serious chess literature – is that ever since chess has been played, nobody has ever won a game without a mistake by the opponent. This mistake may be identified and corrected, and then everything is in order. It's so easy to understand, and nobody has ever refuted or even questioned this basic truth. It is not in accordance with the 'official' standpoint, so they keep schtumm about it.

The more I studied this key subject, the less I understood the nature of White's so-called advantage. Grandmaster Sveshnikov and another reader drew my attention to the fact that it is *much easier to create a repertoire for Black than for White*.

A simple example: if White plays 1.e4 he must be prepared – and very carefully too; after all 'White should be better' – for at least 9 return moves, followed by a lot of different defences! If Black wants to play the Sveshnikov, he only has to know the target opening plus the Sicilian sub-variations (2.f4, 2.b3, 2.g3, 2.c3 etc). Only the last of this list is considered to be (relatively) serious, the rest may even be better for Black already. And, I never realized this before, but in case of 1.d4 the balance turns out to be approximately the same!

So, surprisingly enough, it turns out that *White has to prepare at least twice as many lines as Black*, who can choose his direction without learning a hell of a lot of other variations.

A good combination, for example, is the Sveshnikov with the Caro-Kann. This allows you to play in quite different styles, depending on the opponent and your ranking in the tournament.

We will illustrate this further on in the book, in Chapter 9, with a complete over-view of *all* the possible opening lines after 1.e4 and 1.d4, assembled by Endre Vegh.

This is already quite enough to refute the age-old dogma of White's superiority – who knows, it may have been in existence since the invention of chess when White won the first few games ever... The average player doesn't even try to win with black (the 'wrong colour') and gets into a slightly worse position, trying to hold it. Only two results are possible, so it is very comfortable to play with white.

This discovery of White's 'burden of preparation' will have a powerful effect on the whole opening and middlegame theory. It is easy to understand. If only you think about it a little, using your own mind.

So far everybody thought that already the starting position was better for White, and Black had to defend carefully (somehow they seemed to forgot about counter-attack), and that if the 'second' player did well he might equalize and laugh all the way to his hotel room with his draw. Not a word of this is true. There is not even a mathematical guarantee that White has a draw! Or if there is – show it to me!

The initial position is equal – or, more accurately: it offers chances for both sides. And that is that.

Statistics

My wife is a statistician, and she helps me understand a lot of things.

It was not her, however, but one of my readers, who drew my attention to the fact that if the whole body of statistics changed all of a sudden, and Black had had the upper hand for 50 years on end, it still wouldn't prove anything. Very true!

The reason is that statistics should be used for orientation, and their results certainly do not convey the ultimate truth. Soon I will give you a concrete example – sadly I have to tell you that in this discussion I have found very few facts and a lot of foggy, if not ridiculous, 'reasoning'. To say for example that 1.e4 or 1.d4 wins when we don't even know which of these moves is the better one, and others like 1.g4 are not serious and only make you look like a monkey – pardon my French. If you want to prove your opinion, pick a great player who won a lot of games with black or with white. Silly. I can produce at least 1000 games I won with black – many of them in good style – and in fact I will give you a nice selection in this book. However, tomorrow somebody else may rush in with 2000 white wins.

But!

Take a look at the statistics of the top players (101 men, 50 women) given below. Here you can see their games separated by colour. Believe it or not, there is only one player among the 151 who has a minus score with black – Peter Leko. Whenever I try to have a reasonable discussion with somebody about BLACK IS OK! there always comes a moment when (s)he nervously says: 'And what about the statistics?' Now I put the same question to you, my dear fellow chess players!

I'm not the kind of man who likes to manipulate: most of these players have even (much) better statistics for White. But this has a lot to do with BLACK IS OK! as well, because with white they play soberly, with no fear for tomorrow's black game. They don't think that the necessary points are to be collected by winning with white and surviving with black. They know from experience that it is possible to win with black as well. What is more, they don't have to force things to create a sharp fight, for an overwhelming majority plays aggressively with white. And a counter-attack can be very effective.

In the tables below, the numbers 1-4 refer to games played with BLACK; the numbers 5-8 refer to games played with white. In both cases first the average rating of the opponents is given, then the total number of games, then the score, and finally the score without counting draws.

Top Players December 2015

Name	Fed	Rating	Bd	1*	2*	3*	4*	5*	6*	7*	8*
Carlsen, Magnus	NOR	2834	1990	2627	923	57,2%	62,8%	2616	967	67,4%	77,2%
Topalov, Veselin	BUL	2803	1975	2655	1061	50,9%	51,7%	2647	1122	65,2%	76,1%
Anand, Viswanathan	IND	2796	1969	2654	1531	57,9%	67,3%	2622	1657	69,5%	83,4%
Kramnik, Vladimir	RUS	2796	1975	2666	1316	54,3%	59,5%	2652	1398	68,1%	83,1%
Nakamura, Hikaru	USA	2793	1987	2575	1007	59,9%	65,2%	2583	1011	68,3%	76,8%
Aronian, Levon	ARM	2788	1982	2638	1053	53,8%	58,2%	2636	1065	67,5%	79,1%
Caruana, Fabiano	USA	2787	1992	2579	744	55,1%	58,7%	2576	762	65,9%	74,0%
Giri, Anish	NED	2784	1994	2590	562	54,4%	58,6%	2591	569	64,8%	75,9%
Ding, Liren	CHN	2776	1992	2589	331	57,6%	63,7%	2571	340	67,5%	77,7%
So, Wesley	USA	2775	1993	2520	427	61,0%	72,6%	2522	423	72,0%	85,8%
Vachier-Lagrave, Maxime	FRA	2773	1990	2557	851	59,8%	67,8%	2542	894	69,4%	83,0%
Karjakin, Sergey	RUS	2766	1990	2638	1033	54,8%	58,9%	2636	1082	64,8%	74,6%
Eljanov, Pavel	UKR	2763	1983	2576	756	54,8%	58,5%	2573	776	66,7%	78,1%
Svidler, Peter	RUS	2751	1976	2636	1387	53,6%	57,6%	2633	1412	66,3%	79,4%
Li Chao b	CHN	2750	1989	2514	408	62,3%	69,7%	2510	427	69,6%	77,9%
Mamedyarov, Shakhriyar	AZE	2748	1985	2618	960	57,0%	62,0%	2611	1040	65,8%	75,3%
Grischuk, Alexander	RUS	2747	1983	2646	1182	55,0%	59,9%	2634	1239	68,1%	79,9%
Tomashevsky, Evgeny	RUS	2744	1987	2585	535	54,9%	61,1%	2578	542	66,8%	84,7%
Harikrishna, Pentala	IND	2743	1986	2543	790	53,7%	57,3%	2528	811	68,2%	81,6%
Adams, Michael	ENG	2737	1971	2585	1458	55,5%	61,1%	2567	1515	68,4%	81,5%
Jakovenko, Dmitry	RUS	2737	1983	2600	776	55,0%	60,7%	2596	787	65,1%	76,2%
Yu Yangyi	CHN	2736	1994	2541	375	59,1%	66,5%	2544	383	70,2%	81,9%
Andreikin, Dmitry	RUS	2732	1990	2550	582	56,4%	63,1%	2547	596	66,7%	79,9%
Dominguez Perez, Leinier	CUB	2732	1983	2581	725	54,1%	58,4%	2589	721	64,5%	79,1%
Gelfand, Boris	ISR	2731	1968	2661	1441	51,9%	54,2%	2654	1469	60,4%	70,7%
Navara, David	CZE	2730	1985	2520	946	59,7%	66,2%	2517	961	69,4%	78,2%
Wei Yi	CHN	2730	1999	2520	255	58,8%	66,4%	2521	251	68,3%	80,7%
Radjabov, Teimour	AZE	2726	1987	2650	812	52,3%	54,8%	2648	803	61,5%	73,1%
Wang Yue	CHN	2724	1987	2602	614	54,4%	60,0%	2592	637	65,2%	78,4%
Vitiugov, Nikita	RUS	2724	1987	2553	607	57,9%	65,8%	2559	629	67,7%	79,7%
Wojtaszek, Radoslaw	POL	2723	1987	2509	801	59,7%	67,0%	2510	853	70,2%	82,6%
Le Quang Liem	VIE	2718	1991	2527	618	63,9%	71,2%	2533	642	69,3%	77,9%
Rapport, Richard	HUN	2715	1996	2458	426	61,2%	66,6%	2452	449	67,6%	75,4%
Korobov, Anton	UKR	2713	1985	2491	663	61,0%	66,8%	2496	660	69,8%	78,4%
Bu Xiangzhi	CHN	2712	1985	2549	694	57,2%	64,0%	2546	702	69,7%	84,8%
Kryvoruchko, Yuriy	UKR	2711	1986	2481	499	59,5%	68,2%	2491	486	70,5%	82,8%
Ivanchuk, Vassily	UKR	2710	1969	2645	1846	55,6%	61,4%	2627	1890	67,0%	79,9%

Name	Fed	Rating	Bd	1*	2*	3*	4*	5*	6*	7*	8*
Ponomariov, Ruslan	UKR	2710	1983	2636	876	52,2%	54,0%	2634	895	63,9%	75,8%
Fressinet, Laurent	FRA	2707	1981	2521	1012	58,1%	64,4%	2511	1066	67,2%	78,2%
Nepomniachtchi, Ian	RUS	2707	1990	2590	776	56,4%	60,7%	2584	799	65,0%	72,9%
Wang Hao	CHN	2707	1989	2602	563	53,6%	56,8%	2596	571	67,6%	77,4%
Leko, Peter	HUN	2705	1979	2650	1145	49,6%	49,0%	2641	1185	59,4%	70,9%
Sargissian, Gabriel	ARM	2702	1983	2536	665	56,2%	62,4%	2536	697	67,5%	81,6%
Kasimdzhanov, Rustam	UZB	2702	1979	2565	774	58,3%	65,2%	2565	761	63,8%	73,5%
Naiditsch, Arkadij	AZE	2698	1985	2535	1059	55,6%	58,7%	2529	1093	68,4%	76,3%
Hammer, Jon Ludvig	NOR	2695	1990	2422	541	56,7%	61,0%	2409	567	67,7%	75,8%
Malakhov, Vladimir	RUS	2694	1980	2549	822	59,1%	67,4%	2542	811	70,0%	82,0%
Ni Hua	CHN	2693	1983	2527	686	58,2%	66,0%	2513	715	68,5%	80,6%
Bacrot, Etienne	FRA	2692	1983	2570	1209	55,5%	60,4%	2564	1230	65,9%	76,3%
Morozevich, Alexander	RUS	2692	1977	2645	1008	54,0%	56,1%	2646	978	63,9%	70,6%
Rublevsky, Sergei	RUS	2692	1974	2575	798	54,9%	59,8%	2569	867	66,4%	78,9%
Almasi, Zoltan	HUN	2690	1976	2553	950	56,0%	62,4%	2544	980	68,0%	80,8%
Moiseenko, Alexander	UKR	2689	1980	2512	823	58,4%	64,7%	2519	870	68,4%	80,8%
Howell, David	ENG	2688	1990	2416	671	56,9%	60,0%	2423	683	66,2%	72,0%
Ragger, Markus	AUT	2687	1988	2457	676	55,9%	61,1%	2455	656	66,8%	80,6%
Granda Zuniga, Julio	PER	2685	1967	2470	913	61,7%	68,0%	2466	911	71,2%	79,9%
Short, Nigel	ENG	2684	1965	2553	1404	53,8%	56,8%	2546	1518	67,3%	77,4%
Matlakov, Maxim	RUS	2684	1991	2479	546	57,8%	64,6%	2468	551	70,0%	82,9%
Hou Yifan	CHN	2683	1994	2488	648	58,3%	63,0%	2489	656	67,1%	76,0%
Cheparinov, Ivan	BUL	2682	1986	2503	784	58,4%	64,2%	2497	806	69,4%	79,5%
Kovalenko, Igor	LAT	2680	1988	2426	491	61,4%	65,1%	2431	509	72,6%	78,8%
Rodshtein, Maxim	ISR	2678	1989	2481	561	56,4%	61,3%	2471	586	67,4%	76,7%
Areshchenko, Alexander	UKR	2677	1986	2505	638	60,7%	69,2%	2485	649	71,3%	81,5%
Vallejo Pons, Francisco	ESP	2676	1982	2541	989	54,8%	57,8%	2536	1001	64,9%	74,7%
Shirov, Alexei	LAT	2676	1972	2602	1648	55,7%	60,5%	2589	1768	68,3%	79,0%
Artemiev, Vladislav	RUS	2676	1998	2448	256	61,5%	68,3%	2455	258	69,6%	80,2%
Nisipeanu, Liviu-Dieter	GER	2675	1976	2515	874	59,3%	70,1%	2509	896	70,3%	85,9%
Bareev, Evgeny	CAN	2675	1966	2588	970	53,4%	56,1%	2581	1006	65,1%	74,1%
Naer, Evgeniy	RUS	2674	1977	2532	854	54,7%	58,6%	2522	871	68,7%	77,7%
Jobava, Baadur	GEO	2673	1983	2539	687	57,1%	61,4%	2536	729	69,1%	76,7%
Postny, Evgeny	ISR	2670	1981	2480	794	58,8%	65,3%	2472	781	68,8%	80,8%
Kamsky, Gata	USA	2669	1974	2612	999	53,1%	55,4%	2617	960	65,4%	74,8%
McShane, Luke	ENG	2669	1984	2454	657	56,8%	60,4%	2449	681	65,3%	72,1%
Adhiban, Baskaran	IND	2669	1992	2407	449	61,1%	67,6%	2404	458	69,3%	79,6%
Inarkiev, Ernesto	RUS	2668	1985	2568	643	54,4%	57,4%	2560	689	64,1%	72,0%
Bruzon Batista, Lazaro	CUB	2666	1982	2499	797	59,5%	68,2%	2492	800	71,8%	84,6%
Lysyj, Igor	RUS	2666	1987	2491	550	56,6%	63,4%	2496	550	65,7%	76,9%
Amin, Bassem	EGY	2665	1988	2416	396	59,2%	62,9%	2429	406	68,2%	74,2%
Fedoseev, Vladimir	RUS	2664	1995	2451	365	56,7%	59,9%	2446	366	67,8%	75,8%
Negi, Parimarjan	IND	2664	1993	2469	531	55,6%	59,9%	2473	565	66,9%	76,2%
Onischuk, Alexander	USA	2664	1975	2551	770	56,4%	63,2%	2545	776	66,2%	80,0%
Duda, Jan-Krzysztof	POL	2663	1998	2374	309	62,8%	70,1%	2346	325	67,8%	75,4%

Name	Fed	Rating	Bd	1*	2*	3*	4*	5*	6*	7*	8*
Sadler, Matthew	ENG	2662	1974	2484	452	60,6%	67,9%	2468	454	70,0%	80,0%
Zviagintsev, Vadim	RUS	2662	1976	2558	769	53,6%	59,8%	2551	811	66,8%	85,5%
Tkachiev, Vladislav	FRA	2660	1973	2545	819	56,3%	62,6%	2544	859	66,8%	79,3%
Meier, Georg	GER	2660	1987	2467	590	57,0%	62,8%	2471	593	66,8%	78,3%
Ivanisevic, Ivan	SRB	2660	1977	2474	859	60,3%	67,9%	2482	859	67,6%	77,3%
Movsesian, Sergei	ARM	2659	1978	2549	1152	58,5%	66,4%	2542	1236	68,9%	80,8%
Robson, Ray	USA	2659	1994	2477	315	56,7%	60,5%	2474	332	63,1%	69,0%
Smirin, Ilia	ISR	2658	1968	2530	1101	57,9%	64,4%	2526	1099	66,3%	78,8%
Bukavshin, Ivan	RUS	2657	1995	2410	385	57,0%	61,7%	2392	409	69,3%	77,8%
Laznicka, Viktor	CZE	2655	1988	2486	707	57,2%	61,7%	2557	699	66,3%	75,0%
Dubov, Daniil	RUS	2655	1996	2539	303	53,6%	56,4%	2527	323	63,8%	73,1%
Zhigalko, Sergei	BLR	2655	1989	2492	586	56,1%	61,7%	2484	609	69,0%	81,4%
Melkumyan, Hrant	ARM	2654	1989	2494	438	56,4%	60,4%	2487	458	65,4%	72,5%
Bologan, Viktor	MDA	2654	1971	2547	1240	53,4%	55,1%	2546	1297	65,8%	73,3%
Saric, Ivan	CRO	2654	1990	2438	583	58,7%	64,2%	2432	595	67,5%	75,5%
Gharamian, Tigran	FRA	2654	1984	2432	372	62,8%	73,6%	2430	393	70,2%	84,1%
Khismatullin, Denis	RUS	2654	1984	2498	672	59,0%	63,6%	2495	672	67,6%	74,7%
Safarli, Eltaj	AZE	2653	1992	2482	541	54,9%	59,3%	2471	546	67,2%	78,8%
Motylev, Alexander	RUS	2653	1979	2547	789	53,9%	58,4%	2536	806	65,9%	75,9%
Top 100 men					78245	56,4%	61,7%		80517	67,2%	78,0%

Name - Women	Fed	Rating	Bd	1*	2*	3*	4*	5*	6*	7*	8*
Hou Yifan	CHN	2683	1994	2488	648	58,3%	63,0%	2489	656	67,1%	76,0%
Koneru, Humpy	IND	2583	1987	2428	641	55,4%	58,5%	2433	666	68,1%	76,3%
Muzychuk, Mariya	UKR	2561	1992	2340	573	58,2%	62,3%	2336	594	66,5%	73,2%
Dzagnidze, Nana	GEO	2559	1987	2379	675	61,0%	66,1%	2380	681	67,1%	73,0%
Ju Wenjun	CHN	2543	1991	2406	481	58,0%	63,7%	2402	485	66,0%	75,9%
Kosteniuk, Alexandra	RUS	2542	1984	2445	828	54,0%	55,6%	2441	858	63,8%	68,1%
Muzychuk, Anna	UKR	2535	1990	2388	736	60,9%	67,9%	2376	770	71,5%	81,9%
Cmilyte, Viktorija	LTU	2534	1983	2386	671	56,7%	59,5%	2380	684	65,4%	72,0%
Lagno, Kateryna	RUS	2529	1989	2438	707	54,9%	57,7%	2445	707	60,9%	67,5%
Cramling, Pia	SWE	2523	1963	2412	1328	54,4%	57,4%	2413	1350	64,3%	74,4%
Stefanova, Antoaneta	BUL	2521	1979	2418	1083	56,6%	60,4%	2411	1116	63,9%	71,7%
Zhao Xue	CHN	2519	1985	2402	735	58,3%	61,6%	2404	723	66,6%	71,8%
Harika, Dronavalli	IND	2513	1991	2367	724	57,5%	63,3%	2377	728	62,7%	72,2%
Gunina, Valentina	RUS	2502	1989	2358	635	59,4%	61,7%	2361	647	68,8%	73,5%
Batsiashvili, Nino	GEO	2498	1987	2317	312	54,5%	56,9%	2311	316	62,7%	67,1%
Khotenashvili, Bela	GEO	2496	1988	2369	417	52,6%	53,8%	2369	419	62,3%	66,6%
Goryachkina, Aleksandra	RUS	2493	1998	2291	350	52,1%	53,1%	2266	366	63,0%	68,3%
Tan Zhongyi	CHN	2493	1991	2342	340	59,3%	64,8%	2344	340	67,4%	75,9%
Sebag, Marie	FRA	2490	1986	2398	582	51,3%	51,8%	2392	601	63,4%	69,0%
Zhukova, Natalia	UKR	2488	1979	2376	702	55,1%	58,2%	2380	732	61,3%	67,9%
Javakhishvili, Lela	GEO	2486	1984	2337	577	53,7%	56,2%	2330	575	67,1%	74,8%
Zatonskih, Anna	USA	2478	1978	2340	589	57,6%	61,4%	2331	585	65,9%	73,7%
Shen Yang	CHN	2477	1989	2367	383	54,3%	56,4%	2365	393	61,5%	67,6%

Name	Fed	Rating	Bd	1*	2*	3*	4*	5*	6*	7*	8*
Pähtz, Elisabeth	GER	2475	1985	2361	1018	54,3%	56,3%	2366	1015	62,7%	70,2%
Galliamova, Alisa	RUS	2475	1972	2405	524	54,5%	56,0%	2410	527	63,0%	67,9%
Kosintseva, Tatiana	RUS	2475	1986	2417	662	53,5%	55,2%	2420	667	65,0%	71,4%
Kosintseva, Nadezhda	RUS	2471	1985	2396	551	56,3%	59,9%	2396	540	64,4%	71,4%
Krush, Irina	USA	2468	1983	2393	749	51,4%	52,1%	2400	759	59,6%	63,8%
Hoang Thanh Trang	HUN	2464	1980	2377	853	51,2%	52,1%	2372	863	61,6%	70,4%
Kovalevskaya, Ekaterina	RUS	2459	1974	2370	692	54,1%	57,6%	2370	703	63,4%	72,7%
Bodnaruk, Anastasia	RUS	2456	1992	2305	496	56,6%	58,7%	2302	485	62,2%	66,5%
Girya, Olga	RUS	2456	1991	2321	466	53,2%	54,8%	2324	471	65,1%	71,9%
Pogonina, Natalija	RUS	2454	1985	2340	617	56,7%	60,6%	2344	641	62,9%	70,0%
Skripchenko, Almira	FRA	2453	1976	2356	766	52,5%	53,7%	2346	776	61,0%	67,1%
Melia, Salome	GEO	2452	1987	2322	438	55,5%	58,6%	2309	457	65,9%	73,8%
Ushenina, Anna	UKR	2450	1985	2376	604	54,8%	57,9%	2379	587	65,1%	72,8%
Kashlinskaya, Alina	RUS	2448	1993	2286	458	51,1%	51,4%	2306	480	59,2%	62,3%
Munguntuul, Batkhuyag	MGL	2448	1987	2331	397	56,0%	59,1%	2309	398	67,0%	74,4%
Danielian, Elina	ARM	2445	1978	2390	650	50,6%	50,9%	2378	668	62,7%	69,7%
Lei Tingjie	CHN	2444	1997	2287	138	54,7%	57,0%	2278	134	71,3%	78,2%
Hunt, Harriet	ENG	2444	1978	2313	352	54,5%	56,7%	2305	373	66,8%	73,8%
Moser, Eva	AUT	2442	1982	2297	605	56,9%	59,9%	2288	614	64,1%	70,5%
Huang Qian	CHN	2441	1986	2359	405	55,4%	59,6%	2366	419	63,6%	71,3%
Mkrtchian, Lilit	ARM	2440	1982	2350	500	53,7%	56,2%	2359	511	64,6%	75,1%
Guseva, Marina	RUS	2439	1986	2295	237	51,5%	52,1%	2278	233	62,0%	65,9%
Padmini, Rout	IND	2437	1994	2249	374	54,3%	55,9%	2227	369	65,0%	71,9%
Socko, Monika	POL	2437	1978	2334	964	56,4%	59,0%	2324	969	63,6%	69,8%
Zawadzka, Jolanta	POL	2433	1987	2284	640	56,9%	60,2%	2297	656	61,2%	66,5%
Khurtsidze, Nino	GEO	2432	1975	2339	632	56,9%	60,7%	2336	620	63,3%	69,6%
Nomin-Erdene, D.	MGL	2430	2000	2262	55	53,6%	56,7%	2251	57	60,5%	65,8%
Top 50 women					29560	55,3%	58,1%		29984	64,2%	71,1%

Let's take an example which I studied in the early days of my 'BLACK IS OK!' mission. The Keres Attack against the Sicilian Defence was very successful for a long time. Even Garry Kasparov wrote to me: 'It's better to avoid it.' But I liked to play against it! And after we analysed my lines in his secret training camp he was ready to play it in the very first game of his World Championship match against Anatoly Karpov (1984). Karpov deviated. Around the same time I threw in my variation two times in a grandmaster tournament in Dortmund. The result: two wins against Sznapik and Schmittdiel, awarded with the Best Novelty prize in *Informant*. Now you listen to me carefully! Before this, the balance or the variation was something like 20-1 in favour of White. With all my brilliancy it only improved to 20-3. So statistically it's still quite fine for White. But *statistics don't help — the line is refuted*. Such things happen all the time.

All these statistics are derived from human anxiety — the result of a tremendous manipulation scheme against the black side. From a very early childhood we are taught that White is better. Just like that. The lone king that gets mated in instructional examples is always black! On diagrams, demonstration boards, etc., by the millions, things are always viewed from White's side. Isn't this just permanent manipulation? Switch on any chess software on your computer and the initial position is always shown in the same way. (I know of only one exception in the whole world: my own program, made by Laszlo Lovass, by which you can play classical chess in four versions: Black and White, Switchess, Rainbow Chess and Colour Chess. In the starting position I have my black army standing before me and not the opposing army.) Some programs offer the possibility to turn the board around, but at the online broadcasts, for example, there is no way to do this. Studies and problems? It's always: White to play and win! Why?

Generally the information given in statistics is that white players score 54 to 56%. But such statistics are tricky. It may be true if you only take black and white wins. But if you add 10-15 draws (that's 50-50 %) the balance significantly changes. 56%? Why not 101%? And anyway, all these results, summaries and statistics are the result of a psychological disadvantage, *insufficiently good preparation with black*, and the superstitious fear of defeat, just because you are the second to move. Nonsense!

It is simply ridiculous that even among the best players the score with white is much better than with black. Of the many Kasparov-Karpov matches I recall two: 8-1 and 7-0 (a total of 15-1) for White! That is why in one of my books I asked: How should I interpret this? Are we supposed to say they played like geniuses with white? Or maybe (rather) they both played like patzers with BLACK?' I got no answer. It is nonsense that the best players in the world are so one-sided. Isn't it? But these things keep happening all the time. In the World Championship matches of the first one hundred years, White won 234 games, Black 124. I say this is horrible and shows a low-level culture of defence and counter-attack. But you may say those were the romantic times. Our age is not at all romantic, but if you take the World Championship tournament in Mexico City in 2007, won by Anand, Black was smashed 18-2. In the most recent Candidates Tournament in Moscow (2016) the black players didn't fare much better: 12-3. Of course this is primitive, and it casts a shadow over the players' education and attitude. But this is not all. How is it possible that the 'experts' simply accepted this as a fact and — at least to my knowledge — nobody analysed the psychology? Or will somebody someday come up with the 'solution' that both sides have to play White? Like John Lennon and Yoko Ono?

Sorry — but it's not me being funny, it's them being ridiculous.

When in Wijk aan Zee Vladimir Kramnik came only 4th (behind the triple winners), he gave as a reason that he had played one more game with black! The reporter asked: 'Then why didn't you play something sharper than the Petroff all the time?' Answer: 'My repertoire is made for matches.' Needless to say, our friend did not play a single match in that year. What is this — a bad joke? Surrounded by seconds and technical help, shouldn't he be able to learn something else, something more? Such is the attitude of one of the best players in the world. He's playing just one variation — isn't he bored to death? Not to speak of the spectators...

Epilogue
The 2013 Dortmund Super-tournament ended with Kramnik having lost two games. Both of them with the Petroff. Countless experiences show that passive defence is tiring and may backfire on you, while it encourages the opponent.

Chapter 5
Black Is Brutal II (1969 – 1978)

I played under the name Jocha early in my career. And although it's not very rare to change your name, many people asked me many times why I did this, and why I opted for the name Adorjan.

To start with, I could say that it's nobody's business. In Alushta 1994, I played against a post-Soviet grandmaster called Nenashev, who later resided in Germany and continued under the name of Graf. By the way, I also played the 'real' Graf, an IM in the Bundesliga, so it might be a rather ordinary name. I'm told that it means 'Count', which doesn't bring me any further. The thing with Nenashev/Graf, however, is that in ChessBase it is as if nobody with the name Nenashev ever existed. All of his games are given under the name of Graf, including the very first. This I don't understand. I don't know if he agreed to it, or even asked for it, but anyway this is illegal and misguiding.

You cannot find any of my games under the name of Jocha in the databases, although I have been never asked for a re-baptisement. On the other hand, you can find our Ivanka Budinszky Maria (or vica versa), for she married Andras Budinszky – after winning 9 Hungarian Championships under the name of Maria Ivanka.

But let's clear it up! I became a Master in 1966 under the name Andras Jocha. The first time I played as Adorján in a FIDE tournament was at the Hungarian Championship in 1968. My timing was lucky, as I achieved my biggest successes from then on. The name of Jocha was a constant problem. People never got it right, they asked me to spell it, and so on. So I wanted to change it. Adorján is my mother's maiden name, beginning with the same letter as my first name. Adorján is also a Christian name for men. I like to be AA, OK?

Beating the Champion is of course everybody's dream, especially in a match. I succeeded in doing this. True, at the time Karpov was 'only' the fresh World Junior Champion of 1969 (with a 3-point margin) and this was a two-game mini-match, part of the USSR-Hungary contest (for men, women, juniors).

Anatoly Karpov
Andras Adorjan
Budapest tt 1969
1.d4 g6 2.c4 ♗g7 3.♘c3 d6 4.♘f3 ♘f6 5.g3 0-0 6.♗g2 ♘bd7 7.0-0 a6!?
IM Laszlo Navarovszky's move. The intentions behind it will become clear soon. We called it 'the Navary' and the whole subject was analysed at length in Yearbook 111.

8.e4
A) If 8.a4 a5!. One of the finesses of this line is that by giving up one tempo Black gets a chance to build up a permanent post on c5 for his knight.

Also, it confirms Steinitz' opinion, who said: 'pawns are strongest on their starting squares'. Moves by any other piece can be regretted and mended if proved wrong, but a pawn may only go forward. Too bad that you can never promote without reaching the back rank. Nothing is perfect, as the fox would say to the Little Prince...

Black has sufficient counterplay in all the following lines:

A1) 9.e4 e5 10.♗e3 (10.d5 ♘c5 11.♕c2 ♘e8 12.♗g5 f6 13.♗e3 f5);

A2) 9.b3 e5 10.e3!? ♖e8 11.♗b2 (11.♗a3 exd4 12.exd4 ♘b6=) 11...c6;

A3) 9.♕c2 c6 10.♖d1 ♕c7=;

A4) 9.♗e3 ♘g4 (9...c6!?) 10.♗f4 e5 11.♗g5 ♗f6 12.♗xf6 ♘gxf6=;

Alternatives for White to 8.a4 are:

B) 8.d5!? e5 (8...♘g4!?)

B1) On 9.e4, 9...b5 gives Black good counterplay, e.g. 10.cxb5 axb5 11.b4 ♘b6 12.♕d3 ♕e8 13.♖d1 ♗d7 14.♘d2 ♘a4 15.♘b3 ♘xc3 16.♕xc3 c6;

B2) 9.dxe6 fxe6 10.♘g5 ♘e5 11.b3 ♖b8 (11...h6! 12.♘h3 ♕e8 13.♗b2 ♖b8 with initiative) 12.f4 ♘f7 13.♘xf7 ♖xf7 14.♕d3 ♗d7 15.♗e3 ♕e7?! (15...♕e8!∓) 16.♖ac1 b6 17.♖fd1 ♕e8 ½-½ Flesch-Adorjan, Budapest ch-HUN 1969 – after 18.b4 ♗c6 19.♗xc6 ♕xc6 20.♗d4 ♖bf8 Black still has the initiative.

C) 8.b3 ♖b8 (8...c5!? 9.♗b2 ♖b8) 9.a4 (9.♗b2?! b5) 9...a5 10.♕d2 e5 11.♗b2 exd4 (11...c6!?) 12.♘xd4 ♘c5 13.♘d5 ♖e8=.

8...c5 9.♖e1

On 9.e5

A) 9...♘e8? was my original intention, with the following variation in mind: 10.exd6?! ♘xd6 11.dxc5 ♘xc5 12.♗e3 ♗xc3! 13.bxc3 ♕c7= (13...b6=).

However, 10.♗f4! gives White the advantage after 10...cxd4 (10...dxe5 11.dxe5 ♘c7 12.♖e1 (12.♕e2!?) 12...♘e6 is less clear) 11.♕xd4

analysis diagram

11...dxe5 (11...♖b8 12.♖ad1 b5 13.cxb5 ♗b7 14.♕d2±) 12.♗xe5!±.

B) 9...dxe5! is the best move, which was first played by the Czech future GM Karel Mokry nine years later: 10.dxe5 ♘g4 11.e6 fxe6 12.♕e2 ♘de5 and now:

B1) 13.♘xe5 ♘xe5 14.♗f4 (14.♖d1 ♕b6; 14.♗e3 ♕d3 15.♗xc5 ♕xe2∓ ½-½ Tiller-Mokry, Graz Wch jr 1978) 14...♕d3∓;

B2) 13.♘e1 ♕d4 14.h3 ♘f6 15.♘c2 ♕d6 16.♗f4 ♘h5 17.♖ad1 ♕c7 18.♗xe5 ♗xe5 19.♕e3 ♘g7 20.♖fe1 ♗d6 21.♕e4 ♘f5 22.♖d2 ♖b8

analysis diagram

In this position White has some compensation for the pawn, but it's questionable whether it is enough – the e6-pawn is defending d5. And, as another great chess philosopher said, it's not necessary to immediately use your pair of bishops, but simply to have it.

A nice trip down memory lane. Later it was discovered that 12.♘a4! more or less puts this line on the shelf. But that doesn't mean the old lines aren't instructive.

41

Another thematic example is 9.d5?! b5 10.Nd2 Nb6! 11.cxb5 (11.Qb3 b4 12.Na4 a5 13.e5 Ng4∓) 11...axb5 12.Nxb5 Ba6 13.Nc3 (13.Qe2? Qd7−+) 13...Bxf1 14.Nxf1 Qd7 with a clear advantage for Black.

Exactly two decades later, Gyula Horvath beat Attila Schneider after 9.h3 cxd4 10.Nxd4 Nc5 11.Be3 Bd7 12.Rc1 Qa5 13.a3 Na4 14.b4 Nxc3 15.Rxc3 Qa4 16.Qc1!? Rfc8 17.Kh2 Rc7 18.Bf3 Be8 19.Rd1 a5 20.b5? Rac8 21.Nc6 Bxc6 22.Rd4 Nxe4 23.Bd1 Nxc3 24.Bxa4 Bxd4 25.bxc6 Bxe3 26.Qxc3 Bc5 27.cxb7 Rxb7−+ ... 0-1, A.Schneider-Gy.Horvath, Budapest ch-HUN 1989.

9...cxd4 10.Nxd4 Nc5

The structure reminds me of the Maroczy Bind variation in the Dragon Sicilian. Now, however, Black's queen's knight has reached c5 (instead of c6) and is ready to be exchanged for the knight on c3, White's 'strongest' piece, after ...Na4. After this exchange, the weakness of the d5-square would disappear, and both the doubling of the black rooks on the c-file, and later the powerful manoeuvre ...Nd7-e5 would be feasible. Of course, I have only roughly outlined Black's plan.

11.h3

Normal. The more aggressive alternative doesn't promise much:

A) 11.b4!? Ne6 and now:

A1) 12.Be3 Ng4 13.Qxg4 (13.Nxe6 Nxe3∓) 13...Nxd4 14.Qd1 Nc6 (14...Nb5 15.Nxb5 axb5 16.cxb5 Bxa1 17.Qxa1 gives White good compensation) 15.Qb3 a5 16.b5 Nd4 with mutual chances;

A2) 12.e5 dxe5! 13.Nxe6 Bxe6 14.Bxb7 Ra7 15.Bd5 Rd7 (15...Bxd5 16.cxd5 Rc7 17.Qb3 Qc8 18.Bb2 Qh3 19.f3 Rfc8∓) 16.Qa4 Bxd5 17.Nxd5 Nxd5 18.cxd5 Qc8∓; 11.Nd5 Re8 12.Bg5 Nfd7 13.b4 Bxd4 14.Qxd4 Ne6 15.Qd2 Nxg5 16.Qxg5 Rb8=.

B) Or 11.b3 Bd7 12.Bb2 Rc8 13.Qe2 (13.a4? Ng4! 14.h3 Ne5 15.Bf1 Nc6!∓) 13...b5! 14.cxb5 axb5 15.Ndxb5 (15.Ncxb5 is worse due to 15...e5! 16.Nc2 Ncxe4! 17.a4 Re8! 18.Nca3 d5∓) 15...Nfxe4! 16.Nxe4 Bxb5 17.Qxb5 Bxb2 is roughly equal.

11...Bd7 12.Be3

12.e5 dxe5 13.Nxe5 Rc8 14.Re2 b6=; 12.b4 Ne6 13.Nxe6 Bxe6 14.e5 dxe5 15.Bxb7 Ra7 (or also 15...Bxh3 16.Bxa8 Qxa8 17.Nd5 Rd8) 16.Bg2 Bxc4 clearly favours Black.

12...Rc8

13.Rc1

13.b4?! Ne6 14.Qd3 Qc7 15.Nd5 Nxd5 16.cxd5 (less good is 16.exd5 Nxd4 17.Bxd4 Bf5 18.Qd2 Bxd4 19.Qxd4 Qxc4 20.Qxc4 Rxc4 21.Bxe7 (21.g4 Bc8 22.Rxe7 or 21...Bc2 22.Rxe7 Rxb4∓) 21...Rxb4 22.Rc1 h5) 16...Nxd4 17.Bxd4 Qc4 gives Black a slight edge.

13.Qd2!? leads to a sharp and close fight: 13...Qa5 14.Nd5 Qxd2 15.Nxe7+ Kh8 16.Bxd2 Rce8 17.Bf4 Nfxe4 18.Bxe4

Rxe7 19.Bxd6 Rxe4 20.Bxc5 Rfe8 21.Rxe4 Rxe4 22.Rd1 Bxh3 23.f3 Re8∓.

13...Qa5!

Not 13...b5? 14.cxb5 axb5 15.b4! Na6 16.a3±.

14.a3

A) 14.Qd2 Rfe8! 15.a3 Ne6 16.Nxe6 Bxe6 17.Nd5 Qxd2 18.Bxd2 Nxd5 19.cxd5 Bd7∓; not better is 19.exd5 Bf5 20.g4 Bd3 (20...Bd7 21.b4 f5 22.g5 Bb2 23.Rc2 Bd4=) 21.Re3 Bxb2 22.Rxd3 Bxc1 23.Bxc1 Rxc4∓;

B) A 'direct try' (though some might consider it a tempo loss) is 14.Rb1!? Na4 15.Nxa4 Qxa4 (15...Bxa4? 16.b4±) 16.Qxa4 Bxa4 17.b3 Bd7 18.f4 Nh5 19.Kh2 e5 20.Ne2 exf4 21.Nxf4 Nxf4 22.gxf4 (22.Bxf4 Be5= 23.Rbd1 Bc6 24.Rxd6!? Bxd6 25.Bxd6 Rfe8 26.e5 Bxg2 27.Kxg2 b6∓) 22...b5 23.Rbd1 bxc4 24.Rxd6 Be6=.

14...Na4!

15.b4!?

A consistent move, but it weakens the pawn on c4 and promotes Black's play on the queenside, although it will hang by a single hair that White's intended push c4-c5 fails.

On the other hand, after the modest 15.Nxa4 Bxa4 16.b3 (16.Qe2 Rfd8 17.b4 Qc7∓) 16...Be8! 17.Qd3 (17.a4 Nd7) 17...Nd7 Black would have fine counterplay (17...Qxa3? 18.Ra1 Qc5 19.Ne6).

If 15.Nb3 Qc7 16.Nxa4 Bxa4 17.c5 dxc5 18.Rxc5 Qd7 Black is also for choice.

15...Nxc3 16.Rxc3 Qa4!

17.Qb1

A) 17.Qd3 Rc7 18.Rec1 Rfc8 19.c5 e5! 20.Ne2 Bb5 21.Qc2 Qxc2 22.R1xc2 dxc5 23.bxc5 Bf8∓;

B) 17.Qc1!? was a very energetic try: 17...Rc7 18.e5!? dxe5 19.Nb3 e4 (only move!) 20.Nc5 Qc6 21.Bf4 Rcc8 22.Nxe4 Bxh3! (remember: God created the counterblow too – not only the defence!) 23.Nxf6+ Qxf6 24.Be5 Qxe5 25.Rxe5 Bxg2 26.Rxe7 Bxc3 27.Qxc3 (27.Kxg2 may give better winning chances, but Black maintains chances of building a fortress) 27...d5 28.c5 Rfe8. According to the engines, White is winning. Yes, sometimes, but not in this game! There is no way here for Black to go down unless by a blunder.

17...Rc7 18.Rec1 Rfc8 19.Qd3

19...Be8!!

Probably the best move of the game, and one that arose from a difficult decision. It took me ten minutes to give up my romantic dreams of somehow combining certain pawn advances. The bishop retreat heralds the manoeuvre ...♘f6-d7-e5, which White has no good way to prevent.

20.♗f3?

Better was 20.c5 dxc5 21.♖xc5 ♖xc5 22.♖xc5 ♖xc5 23.bxc5 ♘d7 24.♘c2 e6∓; or 20.f4 ♘h5 21.g4 (21.♔h2 e5 22.fxe5 ♗xe5) 21...♘xf4! 22.♗xf4 e5 23.♗e3 exd4 24.♗xd4 ♗e5 with mutual chances.

20...♘d7! 21.♖d1?

21.♕f1 might have been better, although after 21...♘e5 22.♗e2 ♕d7 23.c5 (23.♖3c2 b5! 24.cxb5 ♖xc2 25.♖xc2 ♖xc2 26.♘xc2 axb5 27.♘d4 ♕b7! 28.♗xb5 ♘f3+! 29.♘xf3 ♗xb5 30.♕b1 ♕a8! 31.♗c1 d5! 32.♘d2 dxe4 33.♘xe4 ♕d5!−+; 23.f4 ♘c6 24.♖d1 ♘xd4 25.♗xd4 ♕e6 26.♗xg7 ♔xg7 27.♗g4 f5 28.exf5 gxf5 29.♗e2 b5!) 23...♘c6 24.♖d1 ♘xd4 25.♗xd4 ♕a4 Black's prospects are slightly preferable.

21...♘e5 22.♕f1

22.♗xa4 ♘xd3 23.♖xd3 ♗xa4 24.♖dc3 (24.c5 b6) 24...f5! (24...♗b5!? 25.c5 ♗d7 26.♔h2 f5 27.f3 ♔f7∓; 24...♗d7 25.♔h2 f5! 26.exf5 gxf5−+) 25.exf5 (25.f3 fxe4 26.fxe4 ♗c6; 25.♘e6 ♗xc3 26.♘xc7 ♖xc7 27.♖xc3 fxe4∓) 25...gxf5 26.♘e6 ♗xc3 27.♘xc7 ♖xc7 28.♖xc3 d5 29.♗b6 ♖c8 30.c5 e5 31.♖d3 ♗c6 32.a4 d4 33.f4 ♗e4 34.♖d2 exf4 35.gxf4 d3 36.♔f2 ♔f7∓.

22...♕d7 23.c5?

More circumspect was 23.♗e2 b5! (23...♘c6 24.♖d1 ♘xd4 25.♗xd4 ♕a4 26.♗xg7 ♔xg7 27.♗g4 ♗d7=) 24.c5 dxc5 25.♖xc5 (25.bxc5 ♘c6∓) 25...♖xc5 26.bxc5 (26.♖xc5 ♖xc5 27.bxc5 ♘c4 28.c6 ♕c8 29.♗xc4 bxc4 30.♕xc4 e5 31.♘c2 ♕xc6) 26...♘c4 27.♗xc4 ♗xd4∓.

23...b5!

There will be trouble for White − both on the board and on the clock.

24.♗b3 **dxc5** **25.♖xc5** **♖xc5** **26.bxc5**

In the event of 26.♖xc5 ♖xc5 27.bxc5 ♕c8 28.f4, now 28...♘d7 is even stronger than 28...♘c4 29.♗xc4 ♕xc5 30.♗xf7+ ♗xf7 31.♕d3 ♕c8 32.♔h2 e5 33.fxe5 ♗c4.

26...♘c4!

All this is forced and leads to an ending that is clearly advantageous for Black. Also possible was 26...♘g4!? 27.c6 ♕d6 28.♘xb5 axb5 29.hxg4 ♖xc6 (19...♗b2? 30.♖c2 ♗xa3 31.♕xb5 ♗xc6 32.♕a6+−) 30.♖d1 ♕b8∓.

27.♗xc4 ♗xd4 28.♖d1 e5 29.♗xd4 exd4 30.♗d5 ♖xc5 31.♖xd4 ♕c8! 32.h4

Better was 32.♔h2.

32...♖c2?

Not the best move, but winning after White's reply.

32...♖c1! 33.♖d1 ♖c3 34.♖d3 ♕c5 was the way to go.

33.e5??

An awful blunder in time-trouble, immediately following Black's mistake. Objectively speaking, White could probably have saved his skin by 33.♔g2 ♕c5 34.♖d3 ♖c3 35.♖xc3 ♕xc3 36.a4.

33...♕c3!

Due to the constant threat of ...♖c1 White now has to surrender his e-pawn.

34.♖d3 ♕xe5 35.♕g2

35.♖e3 ♕xd5 36.♖xe8+ ♔g7 37.♕a1+ ♔h6−+.

35...♔g7

Less clear was 35...b4?! 36.♕e4! (on 36.axb4?, 36...♕e1+ 37.♕f1 ♕xf1+ 38.♔xf1 ♗b5 wins) 36...♕xe4 37.♗xe4

bxa3 38.♖xa3 ♖c1+ 39.♔g2 ♗c6
40.♗f3 ♗xf3+ 41.♔xf3 ♖c6∓.

36.♕f3?

The worst of all possible moves. But there was no salvation in 36.♕e4 ♕xe4 37.♗xe4 ♗c6 38.♗xc6 ♖xc6 or 36.♖e3 ♕xe3.

36...♕e1+ 37.♔g2 ♖c1 38.g4

38.♔h2 ♕g1+ 39.♔h3 ♗d7+ 40.g4 ♗xg4+! 41.♕xg4 ♕f1+–+; 38.♔h3 ♕f1+ 39.♔g4 ♖c2 40.♖d1 ♕xf2–+.

38...♕h1+ 39.♔g3 ♖g1+ 40.♔f4 ♕h2+ 41.♔e4 ♕xh4

And White resigned. 41...♖xg4+! 42.♔e3 ♖xh4 would also have won.

In the next game I drew 'from above', making the result 1½-½ in favour of me and Black. Regretfully I was never strong enough to have any kind of chance against Karpov later on...

We are all tempted to follow the top players by using their weapons. But as the game below shows, copying them is not the right way. Top players are feeble people too, and not all the variations they use are necessarily sound.

Juan Bellon Lopez
Andras Adorjan
Groningen Ech jr 1969 (5)

1.e4 c5 2.♘f3 ♘c6 3.d4 cxd4 4.♘xd4 g6 5.♘c3 ♗g7 6.♗e3 ♘f6 7.♗c4 0-0 8.f3 d6 9.♕e2?!

Maybe not worse than the casual 9.♕d2, but with a dubious intention.

9...♗d7 10.0-0-0 ♘a5!

11.♗d3?!

An idea of the great Paul Keres, which he first played against Lombardy, with full success (17/1/1969, Wijk aan Zee). But in that game Black was slow with his counterplay on the queenside. The present game convincingly shows the dark side of Keres' novelty.

11...♖c8 12.♔b1 a6 13.♘b3

I was expecting one of the moves h2-h4, g2-g4 or f3-f4. In all these cases my plan was 13...♖xc3! 14.bxc3 ♕c7 followed by ...e7-e5 and ...♗e6 or ...b7-b5 with fine compensation.

If 13.♕f2 ♘c4.

13...b5 14.♘xa5?

Bad. Better was 14.♘d5! ♘c4 (14...♘xd5∓) 15.♗d4 (on 15.♗xc4? bxc4 16.♗b6 cxb3! wins) 15...e5 16.♘xf6+ ♕xf6 17.♗e3 (17.♗c3 d5 18.exd5 ♘a3+ 19.♔c1 ♖xc3 20.bxc3 e4!–+) 17...♗e6 with mutual chances.

14...♕xa5

15.♕f2?

Very naive. Here is another example of the dangers which were threatening White: 15.♘d5 ♘xd5 16.exd5 b4! 17.♗c4 (17.♗xa6 b3!!) 17...♖xc4 18.♕xc4 ♖c8 19.♕e2 (19.♕b3 ♗a4; 19.♕d3 ♗f5) 19...♗f5 20.♖c1 ♗xb2 21.♔xb2 ♕a3+ 22.♔a1 ♕c3+ 23.♔b1 b3 and Black is winning.

15...♖xc3! 16.bxc3

16.♗b6 ♕b4 17.a3 ♖xa3 or 16.♗d2 b4 are both winning for Black.

16...♕xc3?!

16...♘g4!! (Peter Dely) was beautiful, and quicker too: 17.fxg4 ♗xc3−+.

17.♔c1

Three nice shots for Black are: 17.♕d2 ♘xe4; 17.♗d4 ♕b4+ 18.♔c1 ♘g4!; 17.♗d2 ♘xe4 18.♗xc3 ♘xf2.

17...♖c8 18.♗d4 ♕b4!

18...♘g4 was only second-best now, winning in the ending.

19.♕g1

19.a3 ♕xa3+ 20.♔d2 e5 21.♗a1 d5−+.

19...♗e6! 20.♖d2 ♗xa2 21.♔d1 e5 22.♗a1

If 22.♗e3 there comes 22...d5 with crushing effect: 23.exd5 ♗xd5 24.♔e2 e4−+.

22...♗h6 23.♕e1

23.♖f2 ♕b1+ 24.♔e2 ♖xc2+−+.

23...♗c4 24.♗xc4 ♖xc4 25.♔e2 ♘xe4!   **0-1**

Gambling was never my style. I tried to win fine games, not only points, even against relatively weaker opponents. I was wrong from the practical point of view. But this approach, targeting perfection, brought me eight brilliancy prizes and many brilliant games, to the delight of many chess lovers.

Aladar Kovacs
Andras Adorjan
Budapest ch-HUN sf 1969 (6)
1.e4 g6 2.d4 ♗g7 3.♘c3 d6 4.♗e3 a6 5.♗c4 b5 6.♗b3

6...♘f6?!

Pretty bad – setting up a primitive trap which proves to be tempting enough to the opponent.

6...e6 is better here.

7.e5! dxe5 8.♕f3?

White could have obtained a favourable queenless middlegame by 8.dxe5 ♕xd1+ 9.♖xd1 ♘g4 10.♘d5 ♗xe5 11.♗d4 0-0 12.♘xe7+ ♔g7 13.♗d5.

8...exd4! 9.♕xa8 dxe3 10.fxe3 ♘bd7 11.0-0-0 c5 12.♗d5

After 12.a3 c4 13.♗a2 ♕c7 14.♕f3 0-0 Black already clearly dominates.

12...0-0 13.♗b7 b4!? 14.♘d5

White doesn't solve his problems by 14.♕xc8 ♕a5 15.♕c6 bxc3 16.♕xa6 cxb2+ 17.♔b1 ♕xa6 18.♗xa6 ♘b6, but 14.♘a4 might have held..

14...♘xd5 15.♕xc8

15...♕a5! 16.♕xf8+

16.♕xd7 causes White to go down in flames: 16...♘xe3! 17.♔b1 (17.♖d3 b3!; 17.♘e2 ♕xa2 18.♔d2 ♗h6 19.♔e1 ♕xb2) 17...♗xb2 18.♔xb2 ♕a3+ 19.♔b1 ♘c4.

16...♗xf8 17.♗xd5 ♘b6 18.♔b1 ♘xd5 19.♖xd5 b3! 20.cxb3 ♕e1+ 21.♔c2 ♕f1 22.♖d2 ♗h6 23.♖d1 ♕xg2+ 24.♘e2 ♕xe2+ 25.♖d2 ♕xe3   **0-1**

Rovert Veress
Andras Adorjan
Budapest sf 1969
1.e4 g6 2.d4 ♗g7 3.c3 d6 4.f4

Very much in fashion in those days.

4...e5?!

4...♘f6 is normal and good, provoking 5.e5 (5.♗d3 0-0 6.♘f3 c5) 5...dxe5 6.fxe5 ♘d5 7.♘f3 0-0 8.♗c4 c5 9.dxc5 (9.0-0 ♘c6 10.dxc5 ♗e6∓) 9...♗e6 when Black is fine and active, cf.:

A) 10.♕d4 ♘c6 11.♕e4 ♘a5 12.♗b5 ♕c7 13.b4 ♘c6 14.♗xc6 ♕xc6 15.♕h4 (15.♘d4 ♕c7) 15...f6;

B) 10.♕b3 ♘c6 11.♕xb7 ♘a5 12.♕a6 ♘xc3 13.♗e2 and now the nice 13...♗c4 wins: 14.♗xc4 ♕d1+ 15.♔f2 ♘e4+ 16.♔e3 ♕xh1 17.♘a3 ♘xc4+ 18.♕xc4 ♘xc5 19.♕xc5 ♕xg2 and White's king is dead meat.

5.dxe5 ♕h4+ 6.g3 ♕e7

7.♘f3?!

A) Critical was 7.exd6 ♕xe4+ 8.♕e2 ♕xe2+ 9.♘xe2 cxd6 10.♘a3 ♘c6 (10...♗e6 11.♘b5 ♔d7 12.f5 gxf5?! 13.♗f4±) 11.♘b5 ♔e7 12.♗e3 (12.♗g2 ♘f6 13.0-0 ♖d8=) 12...♘f6 13.0-0-0 ♖d8 14.♘c7 ♖b8 15.♗g2 ♗f5 16.♖he1 ♔f8 17.♘d4 ♗g4 18.♖d2 and White is better thanks to his superior structure;

B) Less convincing is 7.♕a4+ ♗d7 8.♕b4 and now:

B1) 8...♘c6 9.♕xb7 ♖b8 10.♕xc7 dxe5 11.♗h3 f5! with strong counterplay, for instance: 12.♘d2 ♘f6 13.♘gf3 ♖c8 (13...exf4) 14.♕b7 exf4 15.0-0 fxg3 16.exf5 gxh2+ 17.♔xh2 0-0 18.fxg6 ♕d6+ 19.♔g2 ♗xh3+ 20.♔xh3 ♘h5−+.

Much better for White in this line is 8.exd6 cxd6 9.♗b5 ♘f6 10.♘d2 0-0 11.♘gf3 ♘xe4! 12.♕xe4 ♕xe4+

13.♘xe4 ♗xb5 14.♘xd6 ♗c6 15.0-0 ♖d8 16.♘c4 ♗b5 17.♘fd2 ♘c6 18.♖e1 ♖ac8 19.♘e5 (this just holds) 19...♘xe5 20.fxe5 ♖c5 21.♘f3 ♗c6 22.♔f2 ♗xf3 23.♔xf3 ♖d3+ 24.♗e3 ♗h6 25.♖ad1=.

7...dxe5 8.♘xe5 ♘d7!

Less clear, and a pity about the bishop too, was 8...♗xe5 9.fxe5 ♘c6 10.♗f4 ♗d7 11.♘a3 0-0-0.

But an interesting try is 8...♘c6!? 9.♗b5 ♗xe5 10.♗xc6+ bxc6 11.fxe5 ♕xe5 12.♕d4 (12.♗f4 ♕xe4+ 13.♔f2 ♕f5 14.♖e1+ ♗e6) 12...♕xd4 13.cxd4 f5 14.♗f4 ♘e7 15.exf5 ♘xf5 16.♘c3 ♘xd4 17.0-0-0 ♘e6 18.♖he1 0-0 19.♗e3 when Black's extra pawn isn't worth a lot.

9.♘xd7

9.♕a4 ♘f6 10.♗g2 0-0 11.♘d3 ♘e4 12.♕xe4 ♕xe4+ 13.♗xe4 ♖e8 would give Black what he wants.

9...♕xe4+ 10.♕e2 ♕xe2+ 11.♗xe2 ♗xd7 12.♗e3 ♘h6 13.♘d2 ♘g4

13...0-0-0!?.

14.♗xg4

14.♗c5 0-0-0∓.

14...♗xg4 15.♔f2 0-0-0 16.♘f3 ♖d5 17.♖ad1 ♖hd8 18.♖xd5 ♖xd5

BLACK is clearly BETTER.

19.h3

19.♖e1 ♖h5 20.h4 (20.♗xa7? b6 21.♖e7 ♗e6−+) 20...♖a5 21.a3 ♖d5∓.

19...♗d7 20.♗d4?!

20.♖e1 was much more stubborn.

20...♗xd4+ 21.♘xd4 c5 22.♘f3 ♖d3 23.♖h2

Horribly passive, but 23.♖e1 ♗xh3 24.♘g5 ♗g4 25.♖e7 f5 26.♖xh7 ♖d2+ 27.♔e3 ♖xb2 leaves White struggling to draw.

23...f6 24.g4 ♗c6 25.♘e1 ♖d1 26.♘f3 ♔c7 27.g5?

27.♔e3 ♖f1 was the lesser evil.

27...♖d3!

Simplifying into a winning ending.

28.♘e1 ♖d2+ 29.♔g3 ♖xh2 30.♔xh2 fxg5 31.fxg5 ♗e4

The point of the simplification. The knight is paralysed.

32.♔g3

The pawn ending is losing after 32.♘g2 ♗xg2 33.♔xg2 ♔d6 34.♔f3 ♔e5 35.b3 b6 36.h4 b5 37.a3 ♔f5 38.c4 bxc4 39.bxc4 ♔e5 40.♔e3 a6 41.a4 a5–+.

32...♔d6 33.♔f4 ♔d5 34.h4 b5 35.♔e3

Again, 35.♘f3 just loses to 35...♗xf3 36.♔xf3 ♔e5 37.♔e3 ♔f5 38.♔f3 a6 39.b3 a5 40.c4 (40.a3 b4) 40...b4 41.♔e3 ♔e5 42.♔f3 ♔d4 43.♔f4 ♔c3.

35...♔e5 36.b4 c4 37.♘f3+ ♗xf3 38.♔xf3 ♔f5 39.a3 a6 40.♔g3 ♔e4

White resigned.

A good technical performance!

Jacek Bielczyk
Andras Adorjan

Varna jr 1969

1.e4 c5 2.♘f3 ♘c6 3.d4 cxd4 4.♘xd4 g6

The Dragon Variation is one of the sharpest in the Sicilian. It was in fashion at that time, and I had analysed it together with Ribli.

5.♘c3 ♗g7 6.♗e3 ♘f6 7.♗c4 d6 8.f3 ♕a5 9.♕d2 ♗d7 10.0-0-0 0-0 11.♔b1 ♖fc8 12.♗b3 ♘e5

13.♗g5!?

Much more common is h2-h4.

13...♕d8

Inconsistent. 13...♘c4 led to a well-known ending where chances are roughly even: 14.♗xc4 ♖xc4 15.♗xf6 ♗xf6 16.♘d5 ♕xd2 17.♘xf6+ ♔g7 18.♘h5+ (a desperado to ruin Black's structure) 18...♔h6 (18...gxh5 19.♖xd2 h4 is also quite possible) 19.♖xd2 ♔xh5 20.♖e1 ♗e6=.

14.♖he1 ♘c4?

This error could have been fatal.

15.♕e2?

15.♗xc4 ♖xc4 and now 16.e5! (if White can make this push in the Dragon, it usually means bad news for Black) 16...dxe5 17.♘b3 ♖c7 18.♘b5 gave a decisive advantage to White: 18...♖cc8 (18...♖ac8 19.♘xc7 ♖xc7 20.♖xe5) 19.♗xf6 ♗xb5 20.♗xg7 ♕xd2 21.♖xd2 ♔xg7 22.♖xe5, winning a crucial pawn.

15...♘xb2!

A typical blow in this line.

16.♔xb2

16.♗xf6 ♘xd1.

16...♖xc3 17.♔xc3

17.♗xf6 ♖xb3+ 18.axb3 ♗xf6 19.f4 e5 20.fxe5 ♗xe5 gives Black more than enough play.

17...♕a5+ 18.♔b2 ♕xg5 19.c3?!

19.e5! would have led to a similar position as the game: 19...dxe5 20.♕xe5 ♕xe5 21.♖xe5 e6 22.♖c5 ♘e8 and Black has typical compensation for the exchange.

19...♖c8

19...♕e5!? 20.g3 ♖c8. But as it turns out, the push of the e-pawn is not to be feared now.

20.e5   dxe5   21.♕xe5   ♕xe5 22.♖xe5

22...♔f8! 23.♖e3 h5! 24.♖ed3 e6 25.♖e1 ♖c5 26.f4 ♔e7 27.♖ed1 b5 28.a3 a5 29.g3 ♗c8

29...h4!?.

30.a4

Searching for counterplay.

30...bxa4

30...b4! 31.cxb4 axb4 32.♖c1 ♘e4 looked good too.

31.♗xa4 ♘d5 32.♖c1 ♗a6 33.♖d2 h4!

Well done!

34.♔b3 ♗c4+ 35.♔b2 ♖c7?

35...♘b6! was strong.

36.♗b3 ♘b6! 37.♖a1

A time-trouble move.

37...♗xb3 38.♔xb3 a4+ 39.♔c2 ♘d5

40.♖xa4?

The decisive mistake. 40.♖a3 was a must: after 40...♘e3+ 41.♔d3 ♘c4 42.♖xa4 a draw is the logical outcome.

40...hxg3 41.hxg3 ♖xc3+ 42.♔d1 ♖xg3 43.♘e2 ♖f3 44.♖da2 ♗h6 45.♖a7+ ♔f8 46.♖b7 ♗xf4 47.♖aa7 ♗e5   0-1

The following game was the last of a six-game match with Ribli that had to decide who would represent Hungary in the Junior World Championship Stockholm, 1969. In those times these championships were played in a single field of U-20 players, and only for boys, in every second year. I was born in 1950, and this was my first and last opportunity, while Ribli would also have the option to play in the next championship. I had missed the U-20 championship in Haifa, 1967, because of the boycott of Israel by the so-called 'socialist' countries. On top of everything, my results were much better than Ribli's in those days, so the entire match was an injustice. But the Hungarian Chess Federation decided to favour it. I wonder how they would have acted if the match had ended in a draw? I won the first three games, but lost the next two. So...!

**Zoltan Ribli
Andras Adorjan**

Pecs m 1969 (6)

1.e4 g6 2.d4 ♗g7 3.♘c3 d6 4.♗e3 a6 5.a4 b6 6.♘ge2 ♗b7 7.♘g3 ♘d7 8.♗e2 ♘gf6 9.♕d2 h5! 10.h4

10...c5!

Sharp play for the needed draw! This is the right attitude – chickening will only backfire on you.

11.f4

11.d5 ♘e5=.

11...cxd4 12.♗xd4 ♖c8

12...e5!? is always an interesting possibility. In return for the weakness on d6 Black gets a strong square on e5.

13.e5 dxe5 14.fxe5 ♕c7?

An awful mistake! 14...♘g4 was right, without fearing 15.e6 ♗xd4 16.♗xg4 hxg4 17.♕xd4 ♘f6 18.exf7+ ♔xf7 as Black is for choice in this position.

15.exf6

15.♕f4 ♘g4 16.0-0 ♘gxe5 would be more than alright for Black.

15...♕xg3+ 16.♗f2 ♕xg2 17.fxg7

17.♖g1 ♗h6∓.

17...♕xh1+ 18.♗f1 ♖g8 19.0-0-0 ♕c6 20.♗g2 ♕c7 21.♗g3 e5

22.♗h3?

This looks winning. However, 22.♗xb7 ♕xb7 23.♘e4 ♕c6 (23...♖c6? 24.♗xe5+−)

24.♕xd7+ (stronger than 24.c3) 24...♕xd7 25.♘f6+ ♔e7 26.♘xd7 ♖cd8 27.♘xe5 ♖xd1+ 28.♔xd1 ♖xg7 29.♘c4± would probably have done the job.

22...f5?!

Better was 22...♖d8.

23.♕g5 ♔f7 24.♗xf5 gxf5 25.♕xf5+ ♔e7 26.♕g5+?

26.♖e1±.

26...♔e6 27.♖f1 ♕c4 28.♕f5+ ♔e7 29.♗xe5?

29.♕g5+ would have drawn.

29...♕xf1+! 30.♕xf1 ♘xe5 31.♕f4 ♘d7 32.♕g5+ ♘f6

32...♔f7 was also possible.

33.♕e3+ ♔f7 34.♕xb6 ♗f3 35.♕xa6

35...♖xc3?!

I was sure Black could not lose after this move, but today I have my doubts. 35...♖c7 may have been better.

36.bxc3 ♖xg7 37.a5 ♖g2 38.♕a7+ ♔g6 39.a6

39.♔b2.

39...♗e4 40.♕d4

Again, 40.♔b2.

40...♖xc2+ 41.♔d1

The sealed move.

41...♖a2 42.a7 ♔f5 43.c4?

43.♕c5+! ♔g6 44.c4 would still have given White some chances.

43...♘g4 44.♕c5+ ♔f4 45.♕g5+

45.♔e1 ♔f3! 46.♕e7 ♔e3= leads to a perpetual.

Worse is 45...♘e5 46.♕f8+ ♔g4 47.♕g7+ ♔f5 48.♕h7+ ♔f4 49.♕h6+

♔g3 50.♕g7+ ♘g4 51.c5 ♗f3 52.♕f7
♖e2+ 53.♔d1 ♘f2+ 54.♔c1 ♘d3+
55.♔b1 ♗e4 56.♔a1!±.

45...♔g3 46.♕g7

46.♕e7=.

46...♔f3 47.♕f8+

47.♔c1.

47...♔e3 48.♔c1??

In despair, and in the time scramble,
White makes his last mistake. He had
to play 48.♕c5+ ♔d3 49.♕d6+, when
Black can still hope for a win after
49...♔c3 50.♕g3+ ♗d3 51.♕e1+ ♔d4
52.♕e6 ♘e3+ 53.♔c1 ♖c2+ 54.♔b1
♖e2+ 55.♔c1 ♖e1+ 56.♔b2 ♘d1+
57.♔c1 ♖xe6 58.a8♕ ♘e3.

48...♖c2+   **0-1**

White has to give the queen to prevent
mate.

With this 4-2 result I could go for
the silver medal in the World Junior
Championship. Two years later, Ribli too
came second – behind Hug but ahead of
Vaganian (who was then already a GM)
and others. Happy endings!

As I wrote before my game against
Kovacs, gambling was never dominant
in my style. But sometimes I couldn't
resist!

**Gyorgy Biro
Andras Adorjan**

Hungary tt 1969

**1.e4 g6 2.d4 ♗g7 3.♘c3 d6 4.f4 a6
5.a4**

Not bad, but not necessary either.

5...b6

Normal is 5...♘f6.

6.♘f3 ♗b7

On 6...♘f6 7.♗c4 0-0 White has 8.e5.

7.♗c4 ♘f6

After 7...♘d7 Black would also be
in trouble, e.g., 8.♘g5 e6 (8...♘h6
9.♗xf7+ ♘xf7 10.♘e6) 9.f5+–.

8.e5 dxe5 9.fxe5 ♘d5 10.♘g5!

10.0-0±.

10...0-0 11.♕f3

11.e6 ♘xc3 12.bxc3 f5 13.0-0
♗d5 14.♘f7 ♖xf7 15.exf7+ ♔xf7
16.♕e2 e6 17.♗f4 ♕d7 18.♖ae1 was
overwhelming.

And so was 11.0-0! e6 12.♕g4 ♘xc3
(12...h5 13.♕h3 ♘xc3 14.bxc3) 13.♘xf7
♖xf7 14.♖xf7 ♘e2+ 15.♔f1 ♘xd4
16.♗g5 ♕e8 17.♖e7 ♕c6 18.♕xd4
♕xg2+ 19.♔e1+–.

11...e6 12.♕h3?

This looks winning, but...

12...h6 13.♘xe6?

White should have sobered up and
played 13.♘xf7!? ♖xf7 14.♕xe6 ♕h4+
(14...c6 15.♖f1 ♕e7 16.♕xg6 ♘d7
17.♖xf7 ♕xf7 18.♕xf7+ ♔xf7 19.♘e4)
15.g3 ♕xd4 16.♖f1 ♕xe5+ 17.♕xe5
♗xe5 18.♘xd5 ♖xf1+ 19.♔xf1 ♔h7,
which is about equal.

13...fxe6 14.♕xe6+ ♔h7 15.♘xd5

15.♗xd5 loses to the surprise strike
15...♗c8! 16.♕xc8 ♕xc8 17.♗xa8 c6 18.d5
♗xe5 19.♗d2 ♕g4 20.♗xc6 ♘xc6 21.dxc6
♗xc3 22.♗xc3 ♕e4+ 23.♔d1 ♖f2.

15...♕h4+ 16.♔d1

16...♘c6??

16...♗c8! 17.♕e7 ♕xd4+ was winning.
17.♗d3 ♕h5+ 18.g4 ♘xd4
19.♘f6+??

19.gxh5 ♘xe6 20.hxg6+ ♔h8 21.c4 was still highly unclear. Black has to keep the momentum with moves like ...♖ad8 and ...♘c5 to maintain compensation for the pawns.

19...♖xf6 20.exf6

20...♗f3+! 21.♗e2 ♗xe2+ 22.♕xe2 ♕d5

With a decisive attack:
23.♕f1 ♘f5+ 24.♔e1 ♖e8+ 25.♔f2 ♕d4+ 26.♔f3 ♖e3+ **0-1**

Bela Török
Andras Adorjan
Hungary tt 1969
1.e4 e5 2.♘f3 ♘c6 3.♗b5 a6 4.♗a4 ♘f6 5.d3 b5 6.♗b3 g6?
Normal is 6...♗e7 or 6...♗c5.

7.♘g5 d5 8.exd5?

Better is 8.♘c3 ♗b4 9.0-0 ♗xc3 10.bxc3 ♘a5 11.f4±.
8...♘d4

The only move. After 8...♘xd5?, 9.♕f3 ♗e6 10.♘xe6 fxe6 11.♗e3 is not bad for White, but 9.♘xf7 is classical. For example: 9...♔xf7 10.♕f3+ ♔e6 11.♘c3 ♘b4 12.♗g5! ♕xg5 (12...♕d6 13.♕f6+; 12...♗e7 13.♗xe7 ♔xe7 14.♘xd5+ ♘xd5 15.♗xd5; 12...♘xc2+ 13.♔d1) 13.♘xd5 ♘xc2+ 14.♗xc2 ♖a7 15.♗b3 and White should win.

9.c4

The old Master keeps the pawn. Alternatives were 9.d6!? ♘xb3 10.dxc7 ♕d5! (10...♕xc7 11.axb3 ♗g7 also gives Black good play for the pawn) 11.axb3 ♕xg2 12.♕f3 ♕xf3 13.♘xf3 ♗d6 14.♗h6 ♖g8∓ or 9.♘c3!?.
9...h6
9...♗c5.
10.♘e4

This move is not bad. A more defensive tactic was 10.♘f3 ♗g4 11.♘bd2 ♗b4 12.0-0 ♗xd2 13.♗xd2 ♗xf3 14.gxf3 ♘h5, unclear.
10...♘xe4 11.dxe4 ♗c5! 12.0-0 ♕h4 13.♔h1!

Another good defence was 13.♘c3!? ♗g4 14.♕d3 (14.♕e1?? ♘f3+−+) 14...b4 (14...0-0 15.♗d1) 15.♗d1!±.
13...0-0
13...f5? 14.f4+−.
14.♘d2 f5 15.f3

15...f4!?
The whole thing resembles a King's Indian. 15...♗d7 was more flexible.
16.♕e1
Stronger was 16.cxb5 axb5 17.d6+.
16...♕h5 17.♗d1 ♗d7!
Still, 17...♗e7 also came into consideration.
18.♖g1?
18.♘b3 was necessary. After the exchange of one of Black's attacking pieces, White will breathe more freely.
18...b4! 19.g4 ♕g5 20.b3
20.h4 ♕d8 21.♖g2 may have been better, with the idea 21...♗e7 22.♖h2.
20...♔f7
20...♕d8!?.
21.a4?
21.h4 ♕e7∓.
21...♕d8! 22.♖a2

22...h5!
We shall overcome!
23.g5 h4! 24.♘f1
Taking the pawn was tantamount to suicide: 24.♕xh4 ♖h8 25.♕e1 (25.♕f2

♘xb3) 25...♖xh2+! 26.♔xh2 ♕h8+ 27.♔g2 ♗h3+ 28.♔f2 ♕h4+ 29.♔g3 ♕xg3#.
24...h3 25.a5 ♖h8 26.♘g3
Desperation; similarly bad is 26.♘e3 fxe3 27.♗xe3 ♕e7–+.
26...♕xg5! 27.♘f5

27...♕xg1+
27...♘xf3 was simpler: 28.♗xf3 ♗xg1 29.♕xg1 ♕xg1+ 30.♔xg1 gxf5, winning. But the text is more pleasing to the eye.
28.♕xg1 gxf5 29.♖f2 ♖ag8 30.♕e1 fxe4?!
30...♖g2!–+.
31.fxe4 ♖g2! 32.♖f1
32.♗e3 ♖hg8∓; 32.♖xg2 hxg2+ 33.♔xg2 f3+ 34.♔h1 (34.♗xf3 ♖xh2+) 34...♗h3 35.♗e3 ♗g2+ 36.♔g1 ♘e2+ 37.♔f2 ♗e7 and White can resign.
32...♖hg8 33.♗e3

33...♗g4! 34.♗f2 ♘f3 35.♗g1 ♗xg1 36.♕g3 ♖xg3 37.hxg3 fxg3 38.♗xf3 ♗f2   0-1
A pet game of mine.

A game against the father of the future well-known GM Jeroen. Joop was not a bad player himself at the time.

Joop Piket
Andras Adorjan
Amsterdam 1970 (4)

1.e4 c5 2.d4 cxd4 3.c3

The Smith-Morra Gambit, which is refutable in many ways.

3...♘f6

Transposing into the 2.c3 variation, which is a very nice line for Black too. There follows some strategic entertainment.

4.e5 ♘d5 5.♗c4?!

5.♘f3 ♘c6 6.cxd4 d6 is the main line, for instance: 7.♗c4 ♘b6 8.♗b5 dxe5 9.♘xe5 ♗d7 10.♗xc6 (10.♘xd7 ♕xd7) 10...♗xc6 11.0-0 g6 12.♘xc6 bxc6 13.♖e1 ♗g7 14.♗g5 0-0! with a comfortable game for Black.

5...♕c7 6.♕e2

A) 6.♕xd4 ♘b6 7.♗b5 a6 (7...♘c6 8.♗xc6 dxc6 9.♘f3 ♗f5 10.0-0 e6∓) 8.♗e3 axb5 9.♕xb6 ♕xb6 10.♗xb6 ♘c6 11.♘a3 ♖a6 12.♗e3 ♘xe5 13.♘xb5 ♔d8.

analysis diagram

An original picture!

B) 6.♕b3 ♕xe5+ 7.♘e2 d3 8.♗xd3 ♘a6∓/∓;

C) 6.♗xd5 ♕xe5+.

6...♘b6 7.♗b3

7.♗d3 ♘c6 8.♘f3 d5 9.exd6 (9.cxd4?? ♘xd4) 9...♕xd6 10.♘xd4 ♘xd4 11.cxd4 g6 12.0-0 ♗g7 13.♗e3 0-0∓.

7...d3!

Putting White on the wrong foot.

8.♕e4

8.♕e3 d5 9.♘f3 ♗f5; 8.♕xd3 ♕xe5+ 9.♗e3 e6 10.♘f3 ♕c7 11.0-0 ♘a6∓.

8...♘a6 9.♗f4 ♕c6!

'This is the beginning of the end' (Churchill).

10.♘d2 ♘c5 11.♕f3 ♕xf3

11...e6 12.♕g3 h5! 13.h4 ♘d5∓.

12.♘gxf3

12...f6!

Undermining the proud centre. I could also have gone for the bishop pair by 12...e6 13.0-0-0 f6 14.♗e3 ♘xb3+ 15.axb3 ♘d5 16.♘e4 ♘xe3 17.fxe3 fxe5 18.♘xe5 b6 19.♖xd3 d5 with a different type of advantage.

13.0-0

On 13.0-0-0 d6 14.exd6 e5 Black builds a mighty centre, as in the game.

13...d6 14.exd6

14.♗e3 ♘xb3 15.axb3 ♘d5 16.exf6 gxf6 (16...♘xe3 17.f7+ ♔xf7 18.fxe3 ♔e8 19.♘c4=) 17.♗xa7 doesn't solve White's problems after 17...♗h6.

14...e5 15.♗e3 ♗xd6 16.♖fe1?!

16.♖fd1 was a better defence.

16...♘xb3 17.axb3 ♗c7 18.♗xb6 ♗xb6 19.♘c4 ♗c7 20.♖ad1 ♗d7 21.♖xd3 0-0-0 22.♘d6+ ♗xd6 23.♖xd6

Black has given up the pair of bishops for a winning endgame.

23...♗g4 24.♖xd8+

24.♖ed1 ♗xf3 25.gxf3 ♖xd6 26.♖xd6 ♖d8 27.♖xd8+ ♔xd8 28.♔g2 g5 29.♔g3 h5 and Black wins easily – à la Rubinstein!

24...♖xd8 25.♖a1 a6 26.h3 ♗h5

Also here, 26...♗xf3 27.gxf3 ♖d2 28.♖b1 ♔d7 29.♔g2 ♔e6 was an easy win.

27.g4?! ♗f7 28.b4 ♖d3 29.♘h4 ♖xh3 30.♘f5 ♗e6 31.♘e3

31...♖h6

31...h5! could have saved a lot of time. A whole session!

32.♔g2 ♖g6 33.♔f3 ♖g5 34.♖h1 ♖xg4! 35.♖xh7 ♖g5 36.♖h8+ ♔c7 37.♖e8 ♗d7 38.♖f8 ♗c6+ 39.♔e2 ♔d6 40.♖f7 ♔e6 41.♖c7 ♖g1 42.♔d2 g5 43.c4 f5 44.b5 axb5 45.cxb5 ♗f3 46.♘c4 f4 47.♘a5 ♖d1+ 48.♔c2 ♖d7 49.♖c8 g4 50.♘c4 ♗d5 51.♘b6 ♗e4+ 52.♔c3 ♖g7   **0-1**

● **Alexander Beliavsky**
Andras Adorjan
Groningen Ech jr 1970 (6)

This game is of historical value. Not for its level... Sasha was leading by 5/5, ahead of me (4½) and the field. So my task was simple. And (very) surprisingly easy thanks to his 'Absolute Zero Day' on this occasion. And so I became the European U-20 Champ.

1.e4 c5 2.d3 ♘c6 3.g3 g6 4.♗g2 ♗g7 5.f4 d6 6.♘f3 e6 7.♘bd2 ♘ge7 8.0-0 0-0 9.♘c4?

But on 9.♖b1 Black has 9...♘b4! with the idea 10.a3 (10.♖a1=) 10...♘a2∓.

9...b5 10.♘e3 ♖b8 11.♕e1 f5 12.♘h4?!

Even worse than 12.exf5.

12...d5 13.e5

13...g5!

The Total Blockade is being built.

14.♘f3

14.fxg5 ♘xe5 is structurally winning for Black.

14...g4 15.♘d2??

Already a blunder. Necessary was 15.♘h4 but also here White is in trouble: 15...♘g6 (after 15...♗b7 Black is also clearly better) 16.♘hxf5 (16.♘xg6 hxg6 17.h3 gxh3 18.♗xh3 d4 19.♘d1 ♘b4 20.♖f2 ♗b7) 16...♖xf5 17.♘xf5 exf5 18.♕f2.

15...d4 16.♘d1 ♘b4 17.♕e2 *SAves fork!*

A pawn just drops.

17...♘xc2 18.♖b1 ♘b4 19.a3 ♘bd5 20.♖f2 a5 21.a4 bxa4 22.♖a1

On 22.♘c4 I had planned 22...♘b6.

22...♗d7 23.♗f1 h5! 24.♘c4 h4 25.♗d2

25...h3!

⌐Simply cramping White.⌐ His lack of space will seal his fate.

26.♗xa5 ♕c8 27.♕e1 ♕a6 28.♖c2 ♘c6 29.♗d2 ♘db4 30.♖cc1 ♘a5

White could have resigned here.

31.♘xa5 ♕xa5 32.♖c4 ♖fc8 33.♘f2 ♕b6 34.♗e2 ♕b7 35.♗f1 ♗b5 36.♖ac1?♖ ♗xc4 37.♖xc4 ♖a8 38.♕c1 ♘d5 39.♖c2 ♗f8 40.♕d1 ♕g7 41.♕c1 ♖a6 42.♗e2 ♕b7 43.♕f1 **0-1**

The winner of this competition automatically received two further invitations: both to the IBM tournament in Amsterdam (1970) and the Hoogoven (1971) Master Tournament. At that time there were very few quality tournaments like these. And I went on to win the right to take part in both the IBM and the Wijk aan Zee GM group in the next year!

Tamas Hradeczky
Andras Adorjan
Budapest ch-HUN 1970

My opponent was (of course) another pupil of (Papp) Bela Bacsi, who was also called 'Uncle'.

1.d4 ♘f6 2.♘f3 g6 3.g3 ♗g7 4.♗g2 0-0 5.0-0 d6

Naturally, playing for a win with black too. 5...d5 is equal.

6.♘c3

6.c4 a6 7.♘c3 ♘bd7 leads to the Navary.

6...♘a6

A good alternative is the dynamic provocation 6...♘c6!? when after 7.d5 Black has a choice:

A) 7...♘e5 8.♘d4 e6 (8...c5 9.dxc6 ♘xc6 10.♘xc6 (10.♗xc6 bxc6 11.♘xc6 ♕d7 12.♘d4 ♗b7 (12...♕h3 13.f3 ♗b7)) 10...bxc6 11.♗xc6 ♗h3 12.♖e1 ♖b8) 9.dxe6 fxe6 10.f4 ♘f7;

B) 7...♘b4 8.a3 ♘a6 9.e4 e6 10.♘d4 exd5 11.exd5 ♗g4.

BLACK IS OK! in both cases.

7.d5

More ambitious is 7.e4 c5 and now:

A) 8.d5 b5! (8...♗g4 9.h3 ♗xf3 10.♕xf3 ♘d7 11.♕e2 ♘c7=) 9.♘xb5 (9.e5 ♘e8 10.♘xb5 dxe5 11.♖e1 ♘d6 12.a4 f6 leads to an unbalanced position where Black has his chances) 9...♘xe4 10.♖e1 ♘f6 11.c4 ♘c7 12.♘c3 ♖b8 13.♕e2 e6 14.dxe6 ♘xe6 15.h3 ♗b7 with a better structure for White, but several open lines in Black's possession;

B) 8.e5 ♘g4

B1) 9.exd6 ♕xd6 10.h3 cxd4 (10...♘f6 11.♗e3) 11.♘e4 ♕c6 12.♘xd4 ♕b6 13.c3 ♘e5 (less good is 13...♘f6 14.♘xf6+ ♗xf6 15.♕e2=) 14.♕e2 ♘c7 with chances for both sides;

B2) 9.dxc5 dxe5 10.h3 ♘f6 11.♘xe5 ♘xc5 12.♕e2 ♕b6 13.♘c4 ♕a6 14.♗e3 ♗e6 again with mutual chances.

7...e6

7...♘c5!? 8.♘d4 a5= to establish the knight.

8.dxe6 fxe6

8...♗xe6!? 9.♘d4 ♗c8 might be interesting psychologically.

9.♗g5 h6 10.♗e3 ♕e8 11.h3 ♗d7 12.♕d2 ♔h7 13.♘h2

13.♖ad1 ♗c6=.

13...♗c6

BLACK is already (a little) BETTER.

14.♘g4 ♘g8!

14...♘xg4 15.hxg4 ♗xg2 16.♔xg2 is only equal.

15.♗d4 e5 16.♗e3 ♗xg2 17.♔xg2 ♖d8 18.♕c1

The flight forward by 18.♕d5 is effectively countered by 18...c6 (18...b6 19.♕c4 ♘c5 20.♗xc5 bxc5=) 19.♕b3 (19.♕d2 d5!?) 19...♕e7∓. But now the black centre gets rolling.

18...d5

Winning just like that!

19.♗d2 ♘c5 20.b4 ♘e6 21.e4? dxe4 22.b5

If 22.♘xe4 White gets crushed on the diagonal: 22...♕c6 23.f3 ♘d4−+.

22...♘d4 23.♘xe4 ♕xb5　　　**0-1**

Do not forget: in every second game of your life you play with black! And it's up to you whether you handle these games as fearsome duties or as an opportunity for pleasure!

Gabor Kadas
Andras Adorjan
Budapest ch-HUN sf 1970

1.d4 ♘f6 2.c4 g6 3.♘c3 d5 4.♗f4 ♗g7 5.e3 0-0 6.h4?!

Adhering to the catastrophic conception that White can play anything during his first moves. 6.♘f3 should be played.

6...c5!

A flank *Angriff* is met by a central blow!

7.♗e5

After 7.dxc5 there can follow:

A) 7...♘e4 8.♖c1 ♘xc3 9.bxc3 e5 (9...♕a5 10.cxd5 ♗xc3+ 11.♔e2 ♘a6 12.♕c2 ♗g7 13.♔f3 e5 14.dxe6 ♗xe6∓) 10.♗g3 d4;

B) 7...♕a5 8.♖c1 (8.♕a4 ♕xc5 9.♘f3 ♘c6 10.♕b5 ♕xb5 11.♘xb5 ♘h5 12.cxd5 ♘b4 13.♖d1 ♘xf4 14.exf4 ♗f5 15.♘bd4 ♗g4∓) 8...♘e4 9.♘e2 e5 10.♗h2 d4 and BLACK is almost winning, for instance: 11.exd4 exd4 12.♘xd4 ♖d8 13.♗d6 ♘xc5 14.♘b3 ♘xb3 15.axb3 ♘a6 16.♕d2 ♗g4 17.f3 ♗e6 18.♖d1 ♘c5 19.♘b5 ♕xd2+ 20.♖xd2 ♘xb3 21.♖d1 ♖d7 22.c5 ♖ad8−+.

7...cxd4 8.exd4 ♘c6 9.h5?

More monkeying around. But the normal 9.cxd5 ♘xd5 10.♗xg7 ♔xg7 already favours Black strongly.

analysis diagram

After 11.h5 ♗f5 12.♕d2 ♘db4 13.0-0-0 ♖c8 Black takes over the attack: 14.♕e3 ♘xa2+ 15.♘xa2 ♘xd4+ 16.♔d2 ♘c2+ 17.♔e2 ♕xd1+ 18.♖xd1 ♘xe3+ 19.fxe3 ♖fd8+ 20.♔e1 ♖c2 and wins.

9...♘xe5 10.dxe5 ♘e4?!

Two better knight moves were 10...♘xh5 and 10...♘g4 11.hxg6 hxg6 12.♕xd5 ♕b6 13.♕d2 ♗e6 14.♘d5 ♗xd5 15.cxd5 ♖fd8−+.

11.hxg6   hxg6   12.♕d4   ♘xc3
13.bxc3   dxc4   14.♕h4   ♖e8∓
15.♗xc4   ♕a5   16.♘e2   ♕xe5
17.♕h7+   ♔f8 18.♔f1   ♗f5 19.♖d1
♖ad8 20.♖d4   ♕c5

21.g4

If 21.♖hh4, 21...♕xc4!! finishes beautifully.

21...♖xd4 22.cxd4   ♕xc4 23.gxf5
♕xa2 24.fxg6   ♕b1+   25.♔g2
♕xg6+ 26.♕xg6 fxg6 27.♔f3

White should have resigned here... modestly.

27...♖c8 28.♖b1   b6 29.♔e4   ♖c6
30.d5 ♖c4+ 31.♔d3 ♖a4 32.♖c1 ♗e5

33.♖c6 ♔f7 34.♖e6 ♗f6 35.f4 b5 36.♖c6 b4 37.♔c4 a5 38.♖b6 b3+ 39.♔xb3 ♖e4 40.♘c1 ♖xf4 41.d6 a4+ 42.♔c2 ♖c4+ 43.♔b1 exd6 44.♖xd6 g5 45.♖d3 g4 46.♘e2 ♗e5 47.♖e3 ♔f6 48.♔a2 ♔f5   **0-1**

Janos Rigo
Andras Adorjan
Budapest ch-HUN sf 1970

1.e4 c5 2.♘c3 ♘c6 3.f4

Dangerous − for White.

3...e6 4.♗c4 ♘f6!?

4...♘ge7 5.♘f3 d5 6.♗b5 d4 7.♘e2 a6 8.♗xc6+ ♘xc6∓ is the patented way to develop.

5.e5

If 5.♘f3 d5 6.exd5 exd5 7.♗b5 ♗e7 Black is already leading the dance. The white f4-pawn is just in the way of its bishop.

5...d5 6.♗b5 ♘d7 7.♘f3 ♗e7 8.0-0
0-0 9.♕e1?

At least consistent, but a bit silly. 9.♗xc6 was a must. If 9.d3 ♕c7.

9...♘b4! 10.♗a4 b5! 11.a3

11.♘xb5 opens the b-file favourably for Black: 11...♗a6 12.♕d1 ♖b8 13.c3 (13.c4   ♘b6) 13...♗xb5 14.♗xb5 ♖xb5 15.cxb4 ♖xb4 16.d4 cxd4 17.a3 (17.♘xd4 ♖xd4) 17...♖b6 18.♘xd4 a5 19.♗e3 ♖xb2 20.♘c6 ♕e8.

11...♘d3!

Killing. The c1-bishop is buried alive.

12.cxd3 bxa4 13.♕d1 ♗a6 14.♘e1
f6 15.♕g4 ♕b6−+ 16.♘xd5 exd5
17.♕xd7 ♖ad8 18.♕g4

58

On 18.♕xe7 ♖fe8 traps the queen.

**18...fxe5 19.f5 ♗c8 20.d4 c4
21.♘c2 g6 22.♕g3 ♗xf5 23.♘e3
♕xd4 24.h3 ♗h4 25.♕h2 ♗d3
26.♖xf8+ ♖xf8 27.♔h1 ♗f2 28.g4
♗xe3 29.dxe3 ♗e4+**

Oh my Goodness, oh my Goodness!
White resigned.

Gabor Kadas
Andras Adorjan
Hungary tt 1970

1.d4 ♘f6 2.c4 g6 3.♘c3 d5 4.h4?!
In my opinion, the whole idea of an
early h2-h4 against the Grünfeld is
cynical and groundless. Master Kadas,
however, regularly played 1.h4 too.
With a good score! Beating strong
players as well, sometimes.

4...c5!?
4...c6 is possible too; or 4...dxc4 5.e4
c5 6.♘f3 (6.d5 b5 7.e5 b4 8.exf6 bxc3
9.♗xc4 ♕a5 10.♔f1 ♗a6 11.♗xa6
♕xa6+ 12.♘e2 ♘d7 13.fxe7 ♗xe7
14.bxc3 0-0 15.h5 ♖ad8 16.♔g1 ♘b6)
6...♕a5 7.dxc5 ♘c6 8.♗xc4 ♗g7 9.0-0
♕xc5 10.♗b3 ♗g4 – now look at h4.

5.cxd5 ♘xd5

6.e4?!
Asking for punishment. He had to try
6.dxc5 ♘xc3 7.♕xd8+ ♔xd8 8.bxc3
♗g7 when Black has some plus in the
queenless middlegame after both bishop
moves: 9.♗d2 ♘a6 (9...♘d7 10.c6 bxc6
11.♘f3 ♗a6) 10.c6 bxc6 or 9.♗b2 ♘d7
10.♖d1 (or 10.0-0-0) 10...♔c7.

6...♘xc3 7.bxc3 ♗g7 8.e5
He could play 8.♗e3 but Black has an
extra tempo in the fight against d4,
whereas the pawn on h4 is still useless:
8...♘c6 9.♘e2 (9.♗b5 0-0 10.♗xc6
bxc6 11.h5 ♕a5∓) 9...♕a5 10.♕d2
cxd4 11.cxd4 (11.♘xd4 0-0 12.h5 ♖d8)
11...♕xd2+ 12.♔xd2 0-0 13.♖d1 ♖d8
14.♔c2 f5 and the white king is starting
to feel the draught.

8...♘c6 9.♗e3 ♕a5 10.♗d2
10.♕d2 is already unplayable due to
White's lag in development: 10...0-0
11.♖d1 ♖d8 12.f4 cxd4 13.cxd4
♘b4!–+.

10...0-0 11.♗c4 ♗f5

12.g4?
Suicide. There is no shelter for White's
king now. 12.♘e2 ♖ad8∓.

**12...♗e6 13.♗xe6 fxe6 14.♕b3
cxd4 15.cxd4 ♕d8 16.♕xe6+ ♔h8
17.♗e3 ♘xd4 18.♕c4 ♘c6 19.f4
♕a5+ 20.♔e2**
On 20.♗d2, 20...♘xe5 is quite aesthetic.

20...♘xe5! 21.fxe5 ♖ac8 22.♕d3
♖c3 23.♕xc3 ♕xc3 24.♖c1 ♕b2+
25.♗d2 ♕b5+ 26.♔e3 ♕xe5+
27.♔d3 ♕d4+ **0-1**

The counterattack was again devastating.

Andrey Makarov
Andras Adorjan

Hungary tt 1970

**1.e4 c5 2.♘f3 ♘c6 3.d4 cxd4
4.♘xd4 g6**

The sharp Dragon against an attacking
player!

**5.♘c3 ♗g7 6.♗e3 ♘f6 7.♗c4 0-0
8.♗b3 d6 9.f3 ♗d7 10.♕d2 ♕a5
11.0-0-0 ♖fc8 12.♔b1 ♘e5**

13.g4

13.h4 ♘c4 14.♗xc4 ♖xc4 15.♘b3 ♕a6
16.e5 dxe5 17.♘c5 ♕d6 18.♕e2 ♖d4
gives Black good compensation for the
exchange.

13...b5! 14.g5

14.♘cxb5 gets tricked by 14...♕xd2
15.♖xd2 ♘xf3!.

14...b4! 15.♘ce2

15.♘d5 ♘xd5 16.♗xd5 ♘c4 yields
Black the bishop pair and the initiative.

15...♘e8 16.h4 ♕c7 17.h5

More to the point was 17.♘f4 a5
18.♗d5, keeping the initiative on his
side.

17...♘c4 18.♗xc4 ♕xc4 19.hxg6

19.b3!? ♕c7 20.♘f4 e6 21.♕xb4 a5
22.♕d2 a4.

19...hxg6 20.♘g3

A little more solid was, also here,
20.b3 ♕c7 21.♘f4 e6 22.♕xb4 a5,
when Black will have to prove his
compensation for the pawn.

20...a5

The counterattack is often quicker!

21.f4 a4 22.f5 e5?!

The direct 22...a3!? 23.b3 ♕c3
24.♕xc3 ♖xc3 25.♖d3 ♖ac8 26.♘ge2
♖3c5! 27.fxg6 fxg6 would have given
Black an edge.

23.♘de2?!

Missing a chance to muddy the waters
by 23.f6! exd4 24.fxg7 ♘xg7 25.♕h2
♕xc2+ 26.♕xc2 ♖xc2 27.♔xc2 dxe3
28.♖xd6 ♗e6.

23...gxf5

And here Black could have struck
with 23...b3! 24.♘c3 bxc2+ 25.♔xc2
a3, although it was hard to foresee
that after 26.♕h2 axb2 27.f6 ♘xf6
28.gxf6 ♗xf6 is possible: 29.♖xd6
♕xc3 30.♕h7+ ♔f8 31.♗h6+
♔e7 32.♖xd7+ ♔xd7 33.♕xf7+
♔c6 34.♕xf6+ ♔b7 35.♕f7+ ♖c7
36.♕b3+ ♕xb3 37.axb3 ♖c3 38.♘e2
♖a1+ 39.♔xb2 ♖xh1−+.

24.exf5

Again, he should have played 24.b3.

24...b3 25.cxb3

After 25.♘c3 bxa2+ 26.♘xa2 a3 27.b3
♖ab8 White would have done best to
enter a double-edged ending by 28.♕d3.

25...axb3 26.♘c3 ♕g4! 27.♕f2?

27.a3 ♕xg3 28.f6 was his best chance,
when Black keeps the upper hand with

28...♕g4 29.fxg7?! ♗f5+ 30.♔a1 ♕b4 31.♘b5 ♕xd2.

27...♖xc3! 28.bxc3 ♖xa2 29.♖d2 ♗c6

29...♖a3−+.

30.♖xa2 bxa2+ 31.♔xa2 ♗xh1 32.♘xh1 ♘c7 33.♘g3 ♘d5 34.f6? ♕c4+ 0-1

That wasn't so dull, was it?

**Bela Török
Andras Adorjan**

Hungary tt 1970

1.e4 g6 2.d4 ♗g7 3.c3 d6 4.♗e3 ♘f6 5.f3 ♘bd7 6.♗c4?! d5!?

A fine reaction!

7.♗d3

A) 7.♗xd5 ♘xd5 8.exd5 0-0 and now:

A1) 9.c4 b5! 10.b3 (10.cxb5 ♘b6 (10...a6 11.bxa6 ♘b6 12.♘c3 ♗xa6 gives Black plenty of play for the material deficit) 11.♘c3 ♘xd5) 10...♘b6 11.♘a3 bxc4 12.bxc4 e6 13.dxe6 ♗xe6 14.♕d3 ♖e8 15.♘e2 ♘xc4 (15...♕e7−+)

16.♘xc4 ♗xc4 17.♕xc4 ♖xe3 18.0-0 c5 19.♖ad1 ♕h4 20.♕f2 ♖ae8∓;

A2) 9.♘a3 ♘b6 10.c4 e6 11.dxe6 ♗xe6 12.d5 ♗xd5 13.cxd5 ♗xb2 14.♘c2 ♗xa1 15.♕xa1 ♘xd5−+.

The timid 7.exd5 ♘b6 8.♗b5+ ♗d7 9.♗xd7+ ♕xd7 leads to a very OK position for BLACK.

7...e5 8.♘d2 0-0 9.♘e2

A picturesque position! Rather than further plumbing the d- and e-file, Black now opens it up:

9...dxe4 10.♘xe4 ♘xe4

10...♘d5!? also looks promising: 11.♗g5 f6 12.♗c1 f5 with initiative.

11.fxe4?!

For better or worse, he had to go for 11.♗xe4 ♘f6 12.0-0 (12.♗c2 ♘d5∓) 12...exd4 13.cxd4 c6∓; or 13.♗xd4 ♘xe4 14.fxe4 ♗g4 15.♗xg7 ♕xd1 16.♖axd1 ♔xg7 17.♖f2 ♖ad8∓.

11...exd4 12.cxd4 c5! 13.♗c4?!

There is hardly time for 13.0-0 cxd4 14.♘xd4 ♘c5 when Black has the upper hand also.

13...♘f6

13...♘b6! 14.♗b3 ♕h4+ was winning on the spot.

14.dxc5 ♕a5+ 15.♕d2 ♕xd2+ 16.♗xd2 ♘xe4 17.♗b4 ♗xb2 18.♖b1 a5

18...♗f6!?.

19.♖xb2 axb4 20.♖xb4 ♘xc5 21.♖b5?

21.0-0∓.

21...♘e4 22.♖b6

22...♗e6!

Keeping the white king in the centre.

23.♗xe6 fxe6 24.♘c1 ♖ac8 25.♘d3 ♖c3 26.♖xe6 ♘c5!

Over and out!

27.♘xc5 ♖c1+ 28.♔e2 ♖xh1 29.♘d7 ♖f7 30.♘f6+ ♔g7 31.♘g4 ♖a1 32.♘e3 ♖xa2+ 33.♔d3 ♖d7+ 34.♔e4 ♔f7 35.♖e5 ♖e7   **0-1**

Istvan Polgar
Andras Adorjan

Budapest 1970

1.e4 c5 2.♘f3 ♘c6 3.d4 cxd4 4.♘xd4 g6 5.♘c3 ♗g7 6.♗e3 ♘f6 7.♗c4 0-0 8.♗b3 d6 9.f3 ♕a5 10.♕d2 ♗d7 11.0-0-0 ♖fc8 12.h4 ♘e5 13.h5

Nobody wants to take prisoners!

13...♘xh5 14.♗h6 ♗xh6 15.♕xh6

15...♖xc3 16.bxc3 ♘f6

Grandmaster Bilek said many times that the exchange sac is the smallest sacrifice to make, especially if it ruins the opponent's pawn structure and

gains an extra pawn. I think he was dead right.

17.♔b1

17.♘e2 ♕a3+ 18.♔d2 (18.♔b1 a5 and Black attacks) 18...♗b5∓.

17...♖c8 18.♘e2 ♗e6?!

Good intention – poor execution.

A) 18...♗a4? was wrong due to 19.♘f4= when 19...♕xc3?? loses to 20.♘d5;

B) 18...♘c4!? is already luckier: 19.♖d5 ♕b6 with equal chances;

C) But 18...♗b5 is very serious indeed. Please take a look:

C1) 19.♘d4 ♗c4 (19...♗d7) 20.♖h3! (20.g4 ♕xc3 21.g5 ♗xb3 22.cxb3 (22. axb3 ♘h5 23.♖xh5 gxh5 24.♕xh5 ♖c5 25.♖h1 ♔f8 26.♕xh7 ♘g6–+) 22...♘h5 23.♘f5 ♘d3–+) 20...♖c5 21.♕h4 ♗a6 22.♕h6= (sobering up; 22.f4 ♘c4 23.♗xc4 ♖xc4 still favours Black slightly);

C2) 19.♘f4 ♗c4 (19...♕xc3?? 20.♘d5) 20.g4 ♕xc3 21.g5 ♗xb3 22.cxb3 ♕c2+ 23.♔a1 ♕c3+ 24.♔b1 ♕c2+ with a draw.

19.♗xe6

19.♘f4 ♗c4 20.g4 (not 20.♘d5 ♗xd5 21.♖xd5 ♕xc3–+) 20...♕xc3 21.g5 ♗xb3 22.cxb3 ♕c2+ 23.♔a1 ♕c3+ with a draw.

19...fxe6 20.♕h3

20...♕b5+

A) 20...♔f7 – remembrances of the Wild West! – 21.♘d4 ♕xc3!? 22.♕xe6+ ♔f8 23.f4 ♘c4 is a bold but irresponsible try: (23...♕b4+! 24.♕b3 (24.♔a1 ♕c3±) 24...♕xb3+ 25.cxb3 ♘eg4) 24.♕xc8+ ♔f7 25.♕xb7 ♘a3+ 26.♔c1

♕a1+ 27.♔d2 ♕xd4+ 28.♔e2 ♕c4+ 29.♔f3 d5! 30.♖xh7+ ♘xh7 31.♕xd5+ ♕xd5 32.♖xd5 ♘xc2 33.♖a5 ♘f6 34.♖xa7 ♘e1+ (34...♘d4+ 35.♔e3 ♘b5 36.♖a8+–; 34...g5 35.fxg5 ♘h7 36.♔g4+–) 35.♔f2 ♘c2 36.e5 ♘d5 37.g3 ♔e6 38.a4 g5 39.fxg5 ♔xe5 40.a5+–;

B) 20...♖c6! is just fantastic: 21.♕xe6+ ♔f8 22.♔a1 ♘c4 23.♖d5 ♕b6 24.♖b1

analysis diagram

24...♘a3!! 25.♖b3 ♕f2∓; or 25.♖xb6 ♖xb6 26.♖b5 ♖xb5 27.♕b3 ♖xb3 28.cxb3 ♘c2+ 29.♔b2 ♘e1 and Black wins.

21.♔a1 ♔f7 22.♕xe6+ ♔xe6 23.♘d4+ ♔f7 24.♘xb5 a6 25.♘a3?!

Sidetracking the knight. 25.♘d4 ♖xc3 26.♔b2 ♖c4 27.g4 was still equal.

25...♖xc3 26.♔b2 ♖c5 27.♖d4 b5

Black has fine compensation here.

28.♖e1 g5 29.♔b3

29.♖e3 h5 30.g3 h4 31.gxh4 gxh4 32.f4 ♘eg4 33.♖f3∓.

29...h5 30.♘b1 h4

Like an avalanche.

31.♘d2

31.♖e2 was preferable.

31...♘h5 32.♖d5 ♖c7 33.♘f1 ♘f4 34.♖d2

34...h3!

The best timing.

35.♘e3 hxg2 36.♖f2 g1♕ 37.♖xg1 ♘h3 38.♖gg2 ♘xf2 39.♖xf2 ♖c8 40.♖h2 ♖f8 41.♘f5 e6?!

41...♘xf3 was winning.

42.♘d4

42.♘xd6+ ♔e7.

42...♔g6 43.♖h3 ♖f4 44.c3 ♖h4 45.♖g3 ♔f6 46.a4 bxa4+ 47.♔xa4 ♘d3 48.♔a5 ♘c5 49.♔b6 ♘a4+ 50.♔xa6 ♘xc3 51.♔b7

Better was 51.♘c2 ♖f4 52.♘e1 g4 with good chances to win.

51...d5

The final blow.

52.♘xe6 ♔xe6 53.exd5+ ♔f5 54.d6 ♖d4 55.♔c6 ♘d5 56.♔d7 ♘f6+ 57.♔e7 ♖h4

Handshake!

This was my very first game for the Hungarian team. In total I made 2½/4, playing all my games with black!!

Petar Arnaudov
Andras Adorjan
Kapfenberg, Ech tt 1970 (1)

1.c4 c5 2.♘c3 g6 3.g3 ♗g7 4.♗g2 ♘c6 5.♘f3 e6

A very fine set-up!

6.b3 b6?!

The common continuation is 6...♘ge7 7.♗b2 0-0 and now:

A) 8.♘a4?! is no good: 8...e5 (8...♗xb2 9.♘xb2 d5∓) 9.♘xc5? e4 10.♗xg7 exf3 11.♗xf8 fxg2 12.♖g1 ♕xf8 13.♖xg2 d5−+ – a line by Bobby Fischer;

B) 8.0-0 d5 9.cxd5 exd5 (9...♘xd5 10.♕c1) 10.♘a4 ♗xb2 11.♘xb2 ♘f5=.

7.♗b2

Here White could have tried 7.d4!? ♘ge7 8.♗b2 d5 9.dxc5 bxc5 10.0-0 0-0 11.♘a4 ♗xb2 12.♘xb2 d4 13.e3 ♖b8.

7...♗b7 8.♕c1 d6 9.0-0

9.♘e4 shouldn't be a problem for Black after 9...♘f6 (9...e5 10.0-0 ♘ge7) 10.0-0 0-0=.

9...♘ge7 10.♘d5 e5 11.♘c3 0-0

And BLACK is BETTER!

12.e3 ♕d7 13.♘e1 ♘b4 14.a3 ♗xg2 15.♔xg2 ♘bc6 16.d3 f5 17.f4 exf4 18.gxf4 d5 19.♘e2 d4

20.exd4 ♘xd4 21.♘xd4 ♗xd4 22.♘f3 ♘c6 23.♕d2 ♕b7 24.♔g3 ♗xb2 25.♕xb2 ♖ad8

The fruit of Black's maintenance job of the d4-square: the blockaded pawn on d3 is chronically weak.

26.♖ad1 ♖fe8 27.♖fe1 ♘d4 28.♘xd4 ♖xe1 29.♖xe1 ♖xd4 30.♖e8+ ♔f7 31.♖e3 ♕c7 32.♕f2 g5−+ 33.♖f3 ♔f6 34.h4

If 34.♕f1 ♕d6 establishes a nasty zugzwang.

34...g4!

34...gxf4+ 35.♔h3 ♕d6 was also strong.

35.♖e3 ♕d6 36.♕f1 a5 37.h5 h6

38.b4

38.a4 ♔f7 and again – White to move!

38...axb4 39.axb4 cxb4 40.♕f2 b3 41.♕f1 b2   **0-1**

A nice strategic performance.

Jan Adamski
Andras Adorjan
Polanica Zdroj 1970 (11)

1.c4 g6 2.♘f3 ♗g7 3.e4 e5 4.d4 exd4 5.♘xd4 ♘f6!?

A novelty found over the board. I may have been inspired by my Polish girlfriend Alexandra's gentle kisses just minutes earlier. *Polak Wegier dwa bratanky i do swabry j do sklanky*, as the phrase says... (meaning: Polaks and Hungarians are two good brothers, fighting and drinking together). This move is surely better than 5...♘c6 6.♗e3 (6.♘c2!?)

6...♘ge7 7.♘c3 0-0 8.♗e2 d6 9.0-0 f5
10.♘xc6 (10.exf5 ♗xd4! 11.♗xd4 ♘xf5).

6.♘c3

6.e5 is met by 6...♘e4.

6...0-0 7.♗e2

A) 7.♗d3 d5! 8.cxd5 c6 9.0-0 cxd5
10.exd5 ♘xd5 11.♗e4 ♘xc3 12.bxc3
♕a5= Petrosian-Adorjan, Sochi 1977;

B) 7.♗e3 ♖e8 8.f3 c6! 9.♕d2 d5!
Or:

C) 7.♗g5 ♖e8 8.♕c2 h6 9.♗h4 ♘c6
10.♘xc6 bxc6 (10...dxc6 11.♖d1 ♕e7
12.♗d3 g5 13.♗g3 ♘h5) 11.♗d3 g5
12.♗g3 ♘h5 with good counterplay.

7...♖e8 8.f3

8...c6!

One of the key moves. In the 'regular'
King's Indian Black plays the move ...d6-
d5 after ...d7-d6. Here Black intends to
gain a tempo even at the cost of a pawn
sacrifice.

9.♘c2

A) 9.♗g5 h6 (9...♕b6 10.♘b3 ♘a6
11.♕d2 d5 12.♗e3 ♕b4 is unclear,
Vaganian-Jansa, Tallinn 1983) 10.♗h4 d5!.

analysis diagram

Here it is! Now:

A1) 11.cxd5 cxd5 12.♘xd5 g5 13.♗f2
(13.♘xf6+ ♗xf6 14.♗f2 ♕a5+ 15.♔f1
♖d8 (15...♘c6) 16.♕c1! ♘c6 17.♘xc6
bxc6 18.♕xc6 ♗e6 19.♗e1 ♕b6
20.♕xb6 axb6 21.♗c3 ♗xc3 22.bxc3
♖d2) 13...♘xd5 14.exd5 ♕xd5 and
Black is better, for example: 15.0-0
(15.♖c1 ♕xa2) 15...♗xd4 16.♗xd4 and
now 16...♖xe2! finishes White off;

A2) 11.exd5 cxd5 12.0-0 ♘c6 13.cxd5
(13.♘xc6 bxc6 14.♗f2 ♗e6 15.♘a4
♘h5∓ Bobotsov-Adorjan, Vrnjacka
Banja 1972, was another stem game (0-1))
13...♘xd4 14.♕xd4 ♘xd5!∓ (O.Smirin-A.
Khasin, Podolsk 1990) 15.♕xg7+
(15.♕xd5 ♕xh4) 15...♔xg7 16.♗xd8
♘xc3 17.bxc3 ♖xd8 18.♗c4 ♗f5.

B) 9.♘b3?! is an interesting try to
prevent ...d7-d5. But 9...a5 is an adequate
counter, for example: 10.a4 (10.c5? a4
11.♘d4 b6 12.cxb6 (12.♘xa4 bxc5−+)
12...♕xb6 13.♘xa4 ♕b4+ 14.♘c3
♘xe4!) 10...♘a6! 11.0-0 ♘b4! 12.c5
(for 12.♗g5 h6 13.♗h4 see 13...d5!)
12...b6 13.♗e3 bxc5 14.♘xc5 (14.♗xc5
d5!) 14...d6! 15.♘b3 d5 16.♘c5 ♘h5!
and Black is better.

9...d5! 10.cxd5 cxd5 11.♘xd5

A) 11.exd5 ♕b6 12.♔f1 (12.♕d4
♘bd7!) 12...♘a6 13.♗d2 ♗f5 14.♘a4
♕d6∓;

B) 11.♗g5 h6! 12.♗xf6 ♕xf6 13.♕xd5
(13.♘xd5 ♕xb2 14.0-0 ♘c6 15.♖b1 ♕e5
16.f4 ♕xe4 17.♗f3 ♕c4 18.♘c7 ♗f5!−+;

65

13.exd5 ♕b6!) 13...♗e6 14.♕b5 ♘c6 15.0-0 ♘d4 with good compensation, as in Gross-Stohl, Rimavska Sobota 1991.

11...♘xd5 12.♕xd5

12...♕h4+

This is probably worse than the two alternatives.

A) 12...♕c7!? is probably best, e.g. 13.♘d4 a6! with a strong initiative;

B) I will analyse the position after the queen swap 12...♕xd5 in length: 13.exd5 ♘a6 14.♔f2 (14.♘e3 ♗d4 15.♗xa6 bxa6 16.♔e2 ♗f5 17.g4 ♗c2 18.♖e1 ♖ad8 19.♔d2 ♗a4 20.♔d3 ♗f6∓) and now:

B1) 14...♗d7 15.♗xa6 (15.♘e3 ♗d4 16.♖d1 ♗b6 with compensation) 15...bxa6 and now:

B11) 16.♘e3 ♖ab8 17.♖d1 ♗a4! 18.♖d2 ♖b4 19.a3 ♖d4;

B12) 16.♘e3 ♖ab8 17.b3 ♖bc8 18.♘a3 ♗xa1 19.♖xa1 leads to another crossroads:

B121) 19...♖c7? was a rather bad mistake in a good position: 20.♘c4 ♗b5 21.♗f4 ♖c5 22.♘e3 ♖c3 23.d6 ♖d3 (23...f6!? was surely better) 24.♘g4 ♖c8 25.♖e1 h5 26.♘f6+ ♔g7 27.♘e4? (27.♗e5 ♔h6 28.a4 ♖c2+ 29.♔g3 ♗c6 30.♘g8+ ♔h7 31.♘f6±) 27...♖c2+ 28.♔g3 h4+ 29.♔xh4 ♖xg2 (29...f6!∓) 30.♘g5 ♗d7 31.♖e7 ♖d4 32.♘e4 ♖d5 33.♗e5+ ♔h6 34.♘f6?? (34.♗f4+ ♔g7 35.♗e5+ ♔h6 36.♗f4±) 34...g5# 0-1 Wirthensohn-Ree, Caorle 1972;

B122) 19...♖c3 is better, cf. 20.♗f4 a5 21.♖d1 a4 22.♖d4 axb3 23.♗d2 ♖c5 24.axb3 ♖e5 25.d6 ♖cd5 26.♖xd5 ♖xd5 27.♘c4 (27.♗f4 g5-+ 28.♗e3 ♖xd6 29.♘c4 ♖d3 30.♘e5 ♖d5-+) 27...♖d3 28.♗e3 a6 and Black wins.

B2) 14...♗f5 15.♘e3 ♗d4 16.♖d1 ♗b6 17.♗b5 (17.♗xa6 bxa6 18.g4 ♗c2 19.♖e1 ♖ad8 20.♔g2 ♗d3 21.♗d2 ♗xe3 22.♗xe3 ♖xd5 23.♗xa7 ♖e2+ 24.♖xe2 ♗xe2 25.♔f2 ♖d1=) 17...♘b4 (17...♖ed8 18.♔e2 ♗d7 19.♖xd7 ♖xd7 20.♘g4±; 17...♖e5 18.f4 ♗e7 19.d6 ♖e4 20.♔f3 ♘b4 21.♘xf5 ♖xb5 22.♘e7+ ♔f8 23.f5+−) 18.♗xe8 ♖xe8 19.g4 (19.♔g3! ♖xe3! (19...♗xe3 20.♗xe3 ♖xe3 21.♖ac1± (21.♖ac1 ♖e7 22.♖d4 ♘c2 23.♖d2 ♖d7=)) 20.♗xe3 ♗xe3 21.d6 ♘c2 22.♖ac1 ♗xc1 23.♖xc1 ♔f8=) 19...♗c2!∓.

13.g3 ♕f6 14.♖b1

Due to his weak pawn protection, 14.0-0!? doesn't mean that White is safe. Black has good compensation in all lines, for example:

A) 14...♕b6+ (14...♘c6 15.♖d1 ♖d8 16.♕b5 ♖xd1+ 17.♗xd1) 15.♔g2 ♗e6;

B) 14.♗g5 ♕xb2∓;

C) 14.♕g5!? ♕b6 15.♕b5 ♕xb5 16.♗xb5 ♗d7 17.♗xd7 ♘xd7 18.♔f2 ♖ac8.

14...♘c6 15.♗g5

White offered a draw here.

15.0-0 ♗e6 16.♕g5 ♗xa2 and 15.a3 ♗e6 16.♕b5 ♕e7 (16...♗a2!? 17.♖a1 ♕e6) were still slightly better for Black.

15...♕e6

16.♔f2?

This turns the tables.

A) 16.♗c4 ♘e5! 17.♘d4 (17.♕xe6 ♗xe6 18.♗xe6 ♘xf3+−+) 17...♕xd5 18.♗xd5 ♘d3+ 19.♔d2 ♘f2 20.♘b5 ♘xh1 21.♘c7;

B) 16.♘e3? h6! 17.♗f4 g5 18.♗d6 ♖d8 19.♕xe6 ♗xe6∓;

C) He might have had better chances in the endgame: 16.♕xe6 ♗xe6 17.b3 (17.a3 ♗b3 18.♗d1 (18.♘e3 ♘d4) 18...f5∓) 17...♖ac8! (17...f5 18.0-0 ♖ac8 19.♖bd1 fxe4 20.fxe4 ♘e5 21.♖d2 ♗h3 22.♖f2 ♘f7 with counterchances) 18.♗e3 (18.0-0 ♘d4!) 18...f5 19.0-0 ♗f7;

D) 16.b3 ♕xd5 17.exd5 ♗f5 looks fine for Black, but 18.dxc6 ♗xc2 19.cxb7 ♖ab8 20.♖c1 ♗d3 21.♖c8! wins for White!

16...♕xd5 17.exd5 ♘d4 18.♘xd4

18.♗d3?? runs into mate after 18...♘xc2 19.♗xc2 ♗d4+ 20.♔f1 (20.♔g2 ♖e2+) 20...♗h3#; whereas 18.♘e3? loses material due to White's clumsily placed pieces: 18...h6 19.♗f4 g5 20.♗c7 ♘xe2 21.♔xe2 ♗d4.

18...♗xd4+ 19.♔e1 ♗d7 20.♔d2

20.♖d1 ♗xb2 21.♔f2 ♖ac8 is dangerous – White has to play 22.♗d3 and hope for the best.

20...♖e5 21.♗f4 ♖xd5

The massage is in progress...

22.♗c4 ♖c5 23.♖bc1 ♖ac8 24.b3 b5?!

A) 24...♗b2!? 25.♖c2 ♗a3 26.♗e3 ♖5c6 27.♗d3 ♗b4+ 28.♔d1 ♖xc2 29.♗xc2 ♗c6 30.♖f1 a6∓;

B) 24...♗c6 looks good;

C) But most forceful was 24...g5! 25.♗e3 (25.♗d6 ♖5c6 26.♗a3 b5! 27.♗d3 ♗c3+ 28.♔e2 b4) 25...♗xe3+ 26.♔xe3 ♗e6 27.♖b1 ♗xc4 28.bxc4 b6 29.♖b5 ♖xb5 30.cxb5 ♖c3+ 31.♔e4 ♖a3.

The computer doesn't think this is very dramatic, but in practice it is hardly playable for White.

25.♗d3 ♗c3+

25...♗b2 doesn't promise Black much, see 26.♖xc5 ♖xc5 27.♔e2 ♖c8 28.♖b1=.

26.♔e2 b4 27.♖hd1 ♗e6

27...♖e8+ 28.♔f2 ♗d4+ 29.♔g2 ♖xc1 30.♖xc1 ♗c3 31.♖d1=.

28.♗e3 ♖e5 29.♔f2= a5 30.♗a6 ♖e8 31.♗f4 ♖f5 32.♗b7 h5 33.♗c6 ♖c8 34.♗b7 ♖e8 35.♗c6 ♖c8 36.♗b7 ♖f8

Only move!

37.♗e4 ♖b5 38.♗c6 ♖c5 39.♗b7 ♖e8

40.♗d6?

This is typical: the guy has survived the hard times but makes a mistake in the time scramble. And from then on he is walking on a tightrope...

40.♖d6!? or 40.♗e3 were still OK for White.

40...♗d4+! 41.♔g2 ♖xc1 42.♖xc1 ♗c3

The sealed move. White has to be very careful here.

43.♗c6

43.♖d1? ♖d8 44.f4 ♗f6−+; 43.♗f4 a4! 44.♗c6 axb3 45.axb3 ♖d8 46.♗a4 ♖d5!.

43...♖c8

43...♖d8 44.♗f4 (44.♗c7 ♖d2+ 45.♔g1 ♖xa2 46.♗a4 ♗h3−+) 44...f6 45.h4∓.

44.♗b5?!

44.♗b7 ♖d8 45.♗f4 still defends.

44...g5! 45.♗c2?

Less bad was 45.♖d1; 45.♗e7 f6; or 45.♖d1!.

45...♗d5 46.♗d3?

The wrong square. Still, it was difficult for White: 46.♖e2 g4 47.♖e8+ ♖xe8 48.♗xe8 ♗xf3+∓; 46.h3 g4 47.hxg4 hxg4 48.♗e2 ♖e8∓ (48...♖e8 49.♔f2 ♗d4+ 50.♔f1 gxf3∓); 46.♗e2 g4 47.♗f4 ♖e8 48.♔f2∓.

46...♖d8 47.♗c7 ♗xf3+ 48.♔xf3 ♖xd3+

From here on we were fiddling about a bit, but the outcome remains clear.

49.♔e4 ♖d4+ 50.♔e3 ♖d5 51.h3

51.♔e4 ♖c5 52.♗b6 ♖b5 53.♗c7 was more tenacious, but in the long run Black should win.

51...f5 52.h4?!

52.♖e2.

52...♖c5 53.♗d6

53.♗d8 loses to 53...♖d4+! 54.♔d3 ♖xc2 55.♔xc2 f4! 56.gxf4 g4 and the pawn promotes.

53...♖c6! 54.♗b8

54...♖d4+ 55.♔d3 ♖xc2 56.♔xc2 gxh4 57.gxh4 ♗f2−+ 58.♗c7 ♗xh4 59.♗xa5 ♗e7 60.♔d3 h4 61.♗c7 ♔f7 62.♔e3 ♔e6 63.♔f3 ♗d6 64.♗d8 h3 65.♗h4 ♔d5

65...f4! would have won a little more quickly.

66.♗f2 h2 67.♔g2 ♔e4 68.♗h4 ♔e3

68...♔d3 69.♗f2 ♔c2−+.

69.♗e1 ♔e2 70.♗h4 f4! 71.♔xh2 f3+ 72.♔h3 ♗c5!

This is 'cleaner' than 72...f2 73.♗xf2 ♔xf2 74.♔g4 ♔e2 75.♔f5 ♔d3 76.♔e6 ♗f8 77.♔d5 ♔c2 78.♔c4 ♔b2 79.♔d3 ♔xa2 80.♔c2 ♔a3−+.

73.♔g4 ♗f2 74.♗e7 ♗e1 75.♗c5 ♗d2 76.♔f5 ♗e3

And White finally gave up. You have just seen a game of great theoretical importance.

How to beat a 'patzer'?

Müller
Andras Adorjan
Hungary tt 1970

1.c4 g6 2.♘c3 ♗g7 3.b3?! d5!

A good start!

4.cxd5?

More solid was 4.e3 ♘f6 5.♗b2 0-0 6.♘f3 c5 7.♘xd5 ♘xd5 8.♗xg7 ♔xg7 (8...♘xe3 9.fxe3) 9.cxd5 ♕xd5 10.♗c4 ♕h5 11.0-0.

4...♘f6 5.♗b2 ♘xd5 6.♕b1 e5

Very serious. 6...0-0!? 7.♘xd5 ♕xd5 8.♘f3 ♗g4 9.♗xg7 ♔xg7 10.♕b2+ f6 gave a slight edge too.

7.♕d3

He's dying to exchange the queens.

7...♗e6 8.e4

8.♘f3 ♘c6.

8...♘b4 9.♕xd8+ ♔xd8 10.♖c1 ♘d7 11.a3

A must, since 11.♗a3 a5 would be problematic.

11...♘c6 12.b4

On 12.♘d5 I had planned 12...♘b6. 12...♗xd5 13.exd5 ♘d4 looks good as well, since any exchange makes White's pawns weaker.

12...a5 13.b5 ♘d4 14.♘a4?

Losing. He had to try 14.♘f3 ♘xf3+ 15.gxf3 f5∓.

14...♗b3 15.♗xd4

15.♘c3 ♘c2+ 16.♔e2 ♖e8 cannot be holdable.

15...exd4 16.♘b2 ♖e8 17.f3 f5 18.d3 ♖e5 19.a4 ♖c5

19...♗f8 was even stronger.

20.♘e2 c6 21.g4?

21.bxc6 bxc6 22.exf5 gxf5 23.g3 ♖b8 would mean disaster along the b-file. The text is worse.

21...fxg4 22.f4 cxb5 23.axb5 a4 24.♘c4 ♗xc4 25.dxc4 d3 26.♘g3 a3 27.e5 a2 28.♖a1

28...♘xe5   **0-1**

Jesus Christ on the cross!

Lajos Portisch	2630
Andras Adorjan	2465

Amsterdam 1971

A typical last-round game. Smyslov, who was leading Portisch by half a point, made his quick draw and happily went shopping. Soon there were no more players left in the hall but us, two Hungarians. The world-class player LP and me, a tiny 21-year-old IM.

1.d4 ♘f6 2.c4 g6 3.♘c3 d5 4.♘f3 ♗g7 5.♕b3 dxc4 6.♕xc4 0-0 7.e4 a6

The legendary Hungarian Variation!

8.♕b3 b5 9.e5 ♘fd7 10.e6 fxe6

11.♕xe6+?!

Neither does the assault 11.♘g5 yield much:

11...♘b6 12.♘xe6 ♗xe6 13.♕xe6+ ♔h8 14.♗e3 ♖f6 15.♕h3 (15.♕e4 ♖d6 16.0-0-0 ♘c6 17.d5 ♗xc3 18.bxc3 ♘xd5∓) 15...♘c6 and now: 16.♘e4 (16.♗d3 ♘xd4 17.♖d1) 16...♘xd4 17.♗d3 (worse is 17.♘xf6 ♘c2+ 18.♔e2 ♗xf6 19.♖d1 ♕g8 20.♗xb6 cxb6 21.b3 ♕b8∓) 17...♖c6 18.♘g5 ♕g8 19.0-0. These days 11.♗e3 is almost exclusively played.

11...♔h8 12.♕e4

On 12.♘g5 Black has a promising exchange sacrifice with 12...♘f6 13.♘f7+ ♖xf7 14.♕xf7 ♘c6 15.♗e3 ♘xd4 16.♗xd4 (16.♖d1 ♗e6 17.♕xe6 ♘xe6 18.♖xd8+ ♖xd8∓) 16...♘xd4 17.♗e2 ♕e5 18.♖d1 (18.f4 ♕c5∓) 18...♗g4∓.

Also playable is 12...♘e5 13.♕d5 ♕xd5 14.♘xd5 ♘ec6 15.♘xc7 ♘xd4 16.♘xa8 ♘c2+ 17.♔e2 ♘xa1 18.♘c7 ♗e5 19.♘ce6 ♗xe6 20.♘xe6 ♖c8=.

12...♘b6 13.♗e2 ♗f5 14.♕h4 ♘c6

The ...e7-e5 break is in the air.

15.♗h6

15.♗e3 e5 16.♗g5 (16.♕xd8 ♖axd8 17.dxe5 ♘xe5 18.♘xe5 ♗xe5∓) 16...♕e8 17.dxe5 b4∓.

15...e5 16.♘g5

16.♕xd8 ♖axd8 17.♗xg7+ ♔xg7 18.dxe5 ♖fe8, controlling the central files.

16...♗xh6! 17.♕xh6 ♕e7 18.dxe5 ♘d4!

BLACK has been somewhat BETTER for some time already.

19.♖d1

19.0-0-0 c5 (a nice trap was 19...♖ad8?? 20.♖xd4 ♖xd4 21.♘xh7+−) 20.♗f3 (stronger than 20.♖he1 b4 21.♘ce4 ♗xe4 22.♘xe4 ♖f5 23.♔b1 ♖xe5 24.f3 ♖e8 and Black has pressure) 20...♖ae8 21.♘ce4 ♗xe4 22.♗xe4 ♕g7 23.♕xg7+ ♔xg7 24.♘f3 ♘xf3 25.♗xf3=.

19...c5

Also here 19...♖ad8? runs into 20.♖xd4 ♖xd4 21.♘xh7+−.

20.♖d2 b4

Now 20...♖ad8!? was possible and natural.

21.♘d1

Not 21.♘ce4? ♗xe4 22.♘xe4 ♕xe5 23.f3 ♘d5 24.0-0 ♘f4 and Black wins.

21...♘d5 22.♗c4 ♘f4

23.♘f7+

There were various nasty forks in the position here:

A) 23.0-0 ♕xg5!! 24.♕xg5 ♘h3+ 25.gxh3 ♘f3+ 26.♔h1 ♘xg5∓;

B) 23.♘e3 ♘xg2+!! 24.♘xg2 ♕xg5! 25.♕xg5 ♘f3+ 26.♔e2 ♘xg5 27.f4 ♘e6 28.♖c1 ♘d4+ 29.♔e3 ♖a7=.

23...♖xf7 24.♕xf4 ♗e6 25.♕e4 ♖af8 26.♘e3

26.♗xe6 ♕xe6 27.0-0 ♖f4 would be tremendous for Black.

26...♖f4 27.♕d3

27.♕b1 ♗xc4 28.♘xc4 ♕g5 29.♔f1 (29.f3 ♘xf3+ 30.gxf3 ♖xc4−+) 29...♘f5−+.

27...♗xc4

A pretty 'reculer pour mieux sauter' was 27...♗c8! 28.0-0 ♕xe5.

28.♞xc4 ♕g5

29.♕g3

Black's attack has become irresistible, as see:

A) 29.♔f1 ♖xf2+!!–+;

B) 29.♞e3 ♕xe5 30.0-0 ♖h4 31.h3 ♖xh3!–+;

C) 29.f3 ♞xf3+ 30.gxf3 ♕h4+ 31.♔d1 ♖xc4 32.e6 ♖d4 33.♕e2 ♕f6∓.

29...♖g4 30.♕e3 ♖xg2

30...♕f5! would have finished off at once: 31.♕d3 (31.♔f1 ♞c2 32.♕d3 ♖xc4) 31...♕xd3 32.♖xd3 ♞c2+.

31.♕xg5 ♖xg5 32.♔d1 ♖g2 33.♖e1 ♔g7

I could have just gone for 33...♞f3 34.e6 ♞xd2 35.e7 ♖e8 36.♞d6 ♖xe7 37.♖xe7 ♞f3 with a winning endgame.

34.♞d6?

A mistake under pressure and in time-trouble. He could have put up more resistance here with 34.e6 ♖e8 35.e7 ♞f5 36.♞e3 ♞xe3+ 37.♖xe3 ♖xh2∓.

34...♞f3–+ 35.e6 ♞xe1 36.e7 ♞f3 37.exf8♕+ ♔xf8 38.♖d3 ♖g1+ 39.♔e2 ♞d4+ 40.♔d2 ♖b1 41.♞c4 ♖f1 42.♔e3 ♔e7 43.♞d2 ♖e1+ 44.♔f4 ♖e2! 45.♞g3 ♔d6

A slow kill.

46.♔g2 ♔d5 47.♔f1 ♖e7 48.b3 ♔c6 49.♞c4 ♖e6 50.h3 ♔d5 51.♖d2 h6 52.♞e3+ ♔c6 53.♞c4 ♔b5 54.♞b2 a5 55.♞a4 ♖e5 56.♖d3 ♖e4 57.♖e3

57.♞b2 ♖e2–+.

57...♖xe3! 58.fxe3

58...♞xb3!! 59.axb3 c4 0-1

Simple but pretty. This was my first victory over Lajos Portisch the Great.

Krzysztof Pytel	2320
Andras Adorjan	2465

Polanica Zdroj 1971 (7)

1.d4 ♞f6 2.c4 g6 3.♞c3 d5 4.♞f3 ♗g7 5.♗g5 ♞e4 6.cxd5 ♞xg5 7.♞xg5 e6 8.♕d2 h6 9.♞h3 exd5

10.♞f4

Timid. In this position, 10.♕e3+ is the only move that is connected with an idea of its own. Not a very sound one though... 10...♔f8 11.♞f4 and now:

A) 11...♞c6!? 12.♖d1 ♞e7 13.♕d2 c6 14.e3 ♔g8 15.♗d3 ♗f5=;

B) 11...c6!? 12.♕f3 ♗f6 13.e3 ♔g7=;

C) 11...c5 12.♕f3 (12.dxc5 d4 13.♕d2 ♞c6 14.0-0-0 (14.♞e4 b6)) 12...cxd4 13.♞xg6+? (two pieces are not enough to build up an attack with. Best here is 13.♞cxd5 ♔g8 14.g3 ♞c6 15.♗g2 ♕a5+

16.b4 ♘xb4 17.0-0 with compensation) 13...♔g8 14.♕xd5 (14.♘xh8 dxc3−+) 14...♕f6 15.♘b5 ♕xg6 16.♘c7 ♕c2 17.♘xa8 ♕xb2 18.♖d1 ♗e6 19.♕e4 d3 20.f3 ♕c3+ 21.♔f2 ♗d4+ 22.♔g3 ♗e5+ 23.♔f2 ♕c5+ 24.e3 ♕c2+ 25.♔g1 ♕xd1 26.♕xe5 d2−+.

10...0-0 11.e3

11.g3 ♖e8 12.e3 (12.♗g2 ♘c6∓) 12...c6=/∓. 11.♘fxd5 loses precious time after 11...c6 12.♘f4 ♕xd4∓.

11...c5

11...♖e8 12.♗e2 c6 with equality was the solid alternative – not for a Grünfeld player!

12.dxc5 d4 13.exd4

13.0-0-0 and the pseudo-queen sac 13...dxc3 has been played a few times since: 14.♕xd8 cxb2+ 15.♔b1 ♗f5+ 16.♕d3 ♖d8 17.♗e2 ♗xd3+ 18.♗xd3 (18.♖xd3 ♖xd3 19.♘xd3 ♘a6 20.♗f3 ♖d8=) 18...♘a6 19.♗f3 ♖ab8=/∓.

13...♕xd4

13...♘c6 allows White to consolidate with 14.d5 ♖e8+ 15.♗e2 ♘d4 16.0-0 ♕a5 17.♖fe1 ♕xc5 18.♗d3±.

14.♕xd4 ♗xd4

15.♗b5?!

Both 15.♘fd5 ♘c6 16.0-0-0 ♗xf2 17.♘e4 ♗d4= and 15.0-0-0 were better: 15...♗xf2 (15...♗xc5 16.♘e4 ♗b6 17.♘d5 ♘c6 18.♘xb6 axb6 19.a3 ♖a4 20.♘c3 ♖f4 21.f3 ♗e6 22.♗d3=) 16.♘fd5 ♘c6 17.♘e4 ♗d4 18.♗b5 ♗e5=.

15...♘a6

15...♗xc5!?= was a viable option.

16.♘fe2

16.c6 backfires as it opens the b-file for the black rook: 16...bxc6 (16...♘b4!? 17.cxb7 ♗xb7 18.0-0 ♖fd8 with compensation) 17.♗xc6 ♖b8 18.♘fe2 ♗e5 19.0-0-0 ♘b4 20.♗e4 ♗e6∓; 16.♗xa6 bxa6 17.c6 (17.0-0 ♗xc5∓) 17...♖e8+ 18.♔d2 ♖b8 19.♘d3 ♖b6 20.c7 ♗b7∓.

16...♗xc5 17.0-0 ♘c7 18.♗a4 ♗f5 19.♖fd1 ♖fd8 20.♗b3

20.♖xd8+ ♖xd8 21.♖d1 ♖xd1+ 22.♗xd1 b5∓.

20...♔g7 21.♘a4

21.♖ac1 ♖ac8∓. 21...♗e7 22.♘d4 ♗g4 23.f3 ♗d7 24.♖ac1 ♘a6!

Craftier than 24...♖ac8!?.

25.♘e2

25.♘c3 ♖ac8∓.

25...♗g5

26.♖c3?

A blunder, of course, but in a quite bad position already: 26.♖c2 ♗xa4!−+; 26.f4 ♗f6∓.

26...b5

BINGÓ!

Peter Szilagyi
Andras Adorjan

Hungary tt 1971

1.e4 g6 2.d4 ♗g7 3.♘c3 d6 4.f4 a6 5.♘f3 b5

They call this Tiger's Modern these days.

6.a4 b4 7.♘b1

Better was 7.♘a2.

7...♗b7 8.♘bd2 ♘f6 9.♗c4 0-0 10.e5 ♘d5 11.♘f1?!

What does he want? 11.♘b3 was the move.

11...♕c8

11...c5 12.dxc5 dxc5∓.

12.♘e3

Or 12.♗xd5 ♗xd5 13.♘e3 ♗b7 14.0-0 ♘d7 and, typically, White's centre will crumble.

12...♘xf4 13.0-0 c5 14.♘g5 d5 15.♗b3 h6

15...cxd4 16.♖xf4 (16.♘g4 ♘e6−+) 16...dxe3 17.♗xe3 ♘c6 is very nice for Black.

16.♖xf4 hxg5 17.♖f2

17...cxd4

Every healthy move is winning; also 17...c4, for instance.

18.♘g4

18.♘xd5 ♕c5 19.♕f3 g4 20.♘f6+ exf6 21.♕xb7 ♖a7∓ 22.♗xf7+ ♖xf7 23.♕xb8+ ♖f8 24.♕d6 ♕xd6 25.exd6 ♖d7 and the endgame should win for Black.

18...♘c6 19.♗xg5

19...♘xe5?!

Silly! 19...♕e6 was good.

20.♘xe5 ♗xe5 21.♗xe7 ♗xh2+! 22.♔xh2 ♕c7+ 23.♔g1 ♕xe7 24.♕xd4

White has some play for the pawn.

24...♖ac8 25.♖af1?!

25.a5 might have been roughly equal.

25...a5!

25...♕c5∓.

26.♗xd5 ♗xd5 27.♕xd5 ♖c5 28.♕d4 ♕c7 29.♕d3 ♖h5 30.♖f4 ♕c5+ 31.♕d4

31...♖d5!

It's not a shame to score in the ending.

32.♕xc5 ♖xc5 33.♖1f2 f5 34.♖d2

He should have played 34.g4 here or later, keeping chances of a draw.

34...♔g7 35.♔f1 ♖fc8 36.♖ff2 ♔h6 37.♔e1 ♔g5 38.♔d1 ♔g4 39.♖d6 g5 40.♖fd2 f4 41.♖d7 ♖e5 42.♖2d5 ♖ce8 43.♖xe5 ♖xe5 44.♖d3 ♔h5 45.♖h3+ ♔g6 46.♔d2 g4 47.♖h8 ♔g5 48.♖f8 ♖e3 49.♖a8

49...♖g3 50.♖xa5+ ♔h4 51.♖f5 ♖xg2+ 52.♔d3 f3 53.a5 ♖g1 54.c3 b3 55.c4 ♔g3 56.a6 ♖a1 57.♖f6 f2 0-1

How many chances does it take to win a won game?

Peter Szilagyi
Andras Adorjan

Hungary tt 1972

1.e4 g6 2.♘f3 c5 3.d4 cxd4 4.♘xd4 ♘c6 5.♘c3 ♗g7 6.♗e3 ♘f6 7.♗c4 0-0 8.f3

8.♗b3.

8...e6!?

An experiment. The usual move was 8...♕b6 9.♗b3 and now:

A) 9...♘g4 10.fxg4 (10.♘d5 ♘xe3 11.♘xb6 ♘xd1 12.♘xa8 ♘xb2 13.c3 ♘xd4∓) 10...♗xd4 (10...♘xd4 11.♘d5 ♕a5+ 12.c3 ♘c6 13.0-0=) 11.♗xd4 ♕xd4 12.♕xd4 ♘xd4 13.♘d5 ♘c6 14.g5=;

B) 9...♘xe4 10.♘d5 ♕a5+ 11.c3 ♘f6 12.♘xc6 dxc6 13.♘xe7+ ♔h8 14.♘xc8 ♖axc8=.

9.♗b3

There are of course several alternatives here:

A) 9.♘xc6 bxc6 10.♗c5 and now:

A1) Possible is 10...♖e8 with the point 11.♗d6 ♘d5! 12.♕d2 (for 12.♕d3 ♕b6 see next game) 12...♘xc3 13.bxc3 ♕a5 and after 14.♗b4 the road is cleared for ...d7-d5 – Black is better;

A2) 10...d5!? is therefore not necessary, but it is spectacular: 11.♗xf8 ♕xf8 12.♗d3 (12.♗b3 ♗a6) 12...♖b8 (it is also feasible to keep White's king in the centre by 12...dxe4 13.fxe4 ♕c5 14.♕f3 ♘d7 15.♘d1 ♘e5) and now:

A21) 13.♖b1 ♕c5 14.♘a4 (14.♕d2 ♘xe4 15.♘xe4 dxe4 16.♗xe4 ♗c3-+) 14...♕e3+ 15.♕e2 ♕d4 16.c4 (16.b3 ♕xa4) 16...♘h5 with good compensation;

A22) 13.0-0 ♖xb2 14.♘a4 ♖b7 15.e5 and now:

A221) 15...♘d7 16.f4 ♕a3 17.c3 ♘b6 18.♘xb6 axb6 19.♕b3 (19.c4 ♗f8∓) 19...♕c5+ 20.♔h1 f6 21.♖ae1 ♖f7 and Black is not worse here;

A222) But more promising looks 15...♘h5!? 16.♖e1 (16.f4 ♖b4 17.c3 ♖xf4 18.g4 ♕a3-+) 16...♕b4∓.

B) The knight sortie 9.♘db5 runs into the strong pawn sacrifice 9...d5, opening lines to the white king: 10.exd5 exd5 11.♘xd5 ♗e6 12.♘xf6+ ♕xf6 13.♗xe6 ♕xe6 14.♔f2 ♖ad8 15.♕c1 ♕f5 16.♘c3 ♖fe8∓;

C) 9.♘b3 d5 with the same idea and 9.0-0 d5 10.♗b3 ♖e8 gives Black all the play in the centre.

9...d5 10.0-0

10.exd5 ♘xd5 11.♘xd5 exd5 12.0-0 ♖e8 13.♘xc6 (13.♗f2 ♕g5∓) 13...bxc6 14.♗d4 ♗a6 15.♖f2 ♗xd4 16.♕xd4 ♕b6 17.c3 ♖e3 and Black is more active.

10...♖e8

10...dxe4?! doesn't quite work due to 11.♘xc6 (11.fxe4 ♘e5 12.h3 b6=) 11...bxc6 12.fxe4 ♗a6 13.♕xd8 ♖fxd8 14.♖fd1 ♘d7 15.♖d6 ♘e5=.
Or 10...♘a5 11.e5?! (11.exd5 ♘xd5 12.♘xd5 exd5=) 11...♘d7 12.f4 ♘b6∓.

11.♘xc6?

Strengthening Black's centre. The right order was 11.exd5 ♘xd5 12.♘xc6 (12.♘xd5 exd5 13.♗f2 ♗e5∓) 12...bxc6 13.♗d4, though Black has the upper hand here too: 13...♗a6 14.♗xg7 ♔xg7 (14...♗xf1 15.♕d4 c5 16.♕e5 f6 17.♗xf6 ♕xf6 18.♕xf6 ♘xf6 19.♖xf1 ♔f8) 15.♖f2 ♘xc3 16.bxc3 ♕b6 17.♕d4+ ♔g8 18.♖d2 (18.♖d1?? ♖ad8) 18...c5 19.♕f2 c4 20.♗a4 ♖ed8 21.♕xb6 (21.♖ad1?? ♖xd2) 21...axb6 22.♖xd8+ ♖xd8 23.♖b1 ♖d6.

11...bxc6 12.♕e1 ♗a6 13.♖f2 d4 14.♖d2

14.♖d1? dxe3−+.

14...c5

White is dead. The funeral services still take some time.

15.♗f2 ♕a5 16.♘e2 e5

Or 16...c4 when on 17.♘xd4 ♗h6 forces a winning endgame. The wedge on d4

will now keep White thumbscrewed until the end of the game.

17.c4 ♗h6 18.♖dd1 ♕xe1+ 19.♗xe1 ♘d7 20.♗a4

20.♗d2 ♗xd2 21.♖xd2 ♘b6∓.

20...♗xc4 21.♗xd7 ♖ed8 22.♘xd4 cxd4 23.♗h3

23.♗c6 ♖ac8 24.♗a5 ♗e2−+.

23...♗e2 24.♗d2

Resigning would have been more polite; if 24.♖db1 ♗d3−+.

24...♗xd1 25.♗xh6 ♗c2 26.♖c1 d3 27.♗d2 ♖ab8 28.b3 ♖b6 29.♔f2 ♖a6 30.a4 ♗xb3 31.♖c5 ♗e6 32.g4 ♖xa4 33.♖xe5 h5 34.♗f1 hxg4 35.f4 ♖a1 36.f5 gxf5 37.exf5 ♖d1 38.♗g5 ♖d5 0-1

Jozsef Pogats
Andras Adorjan
Budapest ch-HUN 1972

1.e4 g6

As you may have noticed, this is one of my pet openings, targeting activity with black as well.

2.d4 ♗g7 3.♘f3 d6 4.♗c4 ♘f6 5.♘bd2 0-0 6.♕e2 ♘c6 7.c3

7.e5 dxe5 8.dxe5 ♘g4 9.e6 f5∓.

7...e5 8.dxe5 ♘h5!?

An experiment: 8...♘xe5 9.♘xe5 dxe5 10.0-0 is equal.

9.0-0

9.exd6 ♘f4 10.♕f1 ♕xd6 11.h4 (11.g3 ♗h3 12.♕g1 ♘d3+ is not exactly attractive for White) 11...♘a5 with compensation.

9...dxe5

Better was 9...♘f4!? 10.♕e3 dxe5.

10.♖e1

10.♘b3!? ♘f4 11.♗xf4 exf4 12.h3 would have more or less solved White's kingside problems.

10...♘a5 11.♗b5?!

Losing his head – he wants to keep the bishop at any price. If 11.g3!? ♗g4.

11...a6 12.♗a4 ♘f4 13.♕f1 ♕d3

13...♕f6!?∓.

14.♖e3?!

BLACK was already BETTER, but this only makes things worse.

He should have essayed 14.♘b3 ♕xf1+ 15.♔xf1 ♘c4 16.♘c5 ♖d8∓.

14...♕xf1+ 15.♔xf1 ♖d8 16.♗c2 ♗d7 17.b3 ♗b5+! 18.c4 ♗e8 19.g3 ♘c6

Here we see the point of the check on the 17th move.

20.♗b2 ♘d4 21.♗d1 ♘fe6 22.♘xd4 exd4 23.♖e1 a5 24.♗g4 ♘c5 25.♗a3 ♘d3 26.♖ed1 ♘b4 27.♗b2 a4 28.♘f3 ♗c6–+ 29.♗xd4

29...♘c2?!

29...h5! would have won at once!

30.♗xg7

White played on for 20 more moves.

30...♘xa1 31.♖xd8+ ♖xd8 32.♗f6 ♖d1+

32...♖d6 33.♗e5 axb3 34.axb3 ♘xb3 35.♗xd6 cxd6 36.♔e2 h5 37.♗h3 ♗xe4∓.

33.♔e2 ♖b1?!

33...♖h1!.

34.♘d2 ♖c1 35.♗b2 ♖g1 36.b4

36.♔d3 was better.

36...b5 37.c5 ♘c2 38.a3

38...♘a1??

38...♔f8!.

39.e5??

He could have won back the exchange by 39.♗h3 ♘b3 40.♘f1 ♗xe4 41.f3 ♗f5 42.g4 ♗d7 43.♔f2 ♖xf1+ 44.♗xf1 ♘d2 45.♗e2.

39...♘b3 40.e6 ♘xd2 41.♔xd2 f5 42.♗e2 ♔f8 43.♗f6 ♖g2 44.h4 ♖xf2 45.♔e3 ♖g2 46.♗e5 ♔e7 47.♗xc7 ♔xe6 48.♗f4 ♖g1 0-1

It's not so easy to win a dead won game – you always have to watch out!

Sarkis Bohosjan
Andras Adorjan

Varna 1972

Here comes a picturesque move, although it's not the only way to win:

31...罝e3! 32.罝f1 豐xa3 33.奧d6 罝xf3 34.罝xf3 豐c1+ 35.含g2

35.罝f1 豐e3+−+.

35...罝xc2+ 36.罝f2 罝xf2+ 37.含xf2 豐d2+ 38.含f1 豐d1+ 39.含g2 豐e2+ 40.含h3

40.含g1 豐e3+ 41.豐xe3 dxe3 42.罝a2 奧c3.

40...豐h5+ 41.含g2 豐e2+ 42.含h3 豐f1+!

43.含h4

On 43.罝g2, the decisive diagonal is opened by 43...f4 44.奧xf4 豐h1+ 45.豐h2 奧e6+ 46.含g3 豐d1−+.

43...豐d1 44.含h3 f4

Again the key move, allowing the bishop to join the attack.

45.奧xf4 奧e6+ 46.含g2 奧f5 47.奧e3

Trying to get a few checks in, but...

47...豐e2+ 48.奧f2 奧e5   0-1

It is over after 49.豐h4 奧xd3 50.罝h1 奧e4+ 51.含g1 豐d1+ 52.奧e1 d3−+.

Zdenek Hlousek   2355
Andras Adorjan   2475

Graz Wch tt U26 1972 (2)

1.e4 c5 2.◎f3 ◎c6 3.d4 cxd4 4.◎xd4 g6 5.◎c3 奧g7 6.奧e3 ◎f6 7.奧c4 0-0 8.奧b3 d6 9.f3 奧d7 10.豐d2 ◎xd4! 11.奧xd4 b5

Tactical players don't like this 'back talk' variation. I think this concrete one is OK. Therefore it is advisable for White to avoid it by playing 10.h4 first, in which case 10...◎xd4?! 11.奧xd4 b5 12.◎d5 just gives him an extra tempo compared to the text. After 12...◎xd5 13.奧xd5 罝c8 14.h5 g5 15.h6 White is doing well.

12.a4 b4 13.◎e2 e5!?

My gambit. Solid, instead, is 13...a5.

14.奧e3

14...奧e6 15.奧xe6

15.0-0-0 奧xb3 16.cxb3 豐c8+ (16...d5 17.exd5 豐d6 18.奧g5 罝fd8 19.奧xf6 豐xf6 20.◎g3 豐b6 21.含b1 f5 is unclear) 17.含b1 豐e6 18.含a2 罝fd8 19.奧g5 罝ac8 20.豐xb4 d5 with good compensation for the pawn.

15...fxe6 16.♖d1

To take or not to take? And if yes, when? 16.♕xb4 ♖b8 17.♕a3 d5 18.♗c5 ♖f7 (18...dxe4!? 19.♗xf8 ♗xf8 20.♕a2 ♕b6 with compensation) 19.0-0 ♗f8 20.♗xf8 ♕xf8 21.♕xf8+ ♖fxf8 22.b3 dxe4 (22...♖fc8) 23.♘g3 e3 is very complicated, as is 23...exf3 24.♖xf3 e4 25.♖f2 e3 26.♖e2 ♘d5, with chances for both sides.

16...d5   17.♕xb4   ♖b8   18.♕a3 ♕a5+

18...♕c7!? 19.♕c5 ♕xc5 20.♗xc5 ♖fc8 21.b4 a5 22.c3 dxe4 23.♗d6 ♖b7 24.bxa5 exf3 25.gxf3 ♘d5 with a double-edged ending.

19.c3

19.b4?! ♕xb4+ 20.♕xb4 ♖xb4 21.exd5 exd5 22.♗c5 ♖xa4 23.♗xf8 ♗xf8∓; the a-pawn is rather strong.

19...dxe4 20.0-0 exf3 21.gxf3

If 21.♖xf3 ♕a6 22.♘g3 ♘d5 23.♗c5 (23.♖df1?? ♘xe3 24.♖xe3 ♕b6 25.c4 ♗h6) 23...♖f4 24.b4 ♗f8 25.b5 ♕xa4∓.

21...e4

Consistent, but not necessarily best. 21...♖f7!?∓; 21...♕a6 22.♘g3 ♘d5∓.

22.♗c5?

Better was 22.fxe4, but after 22...♕h5 23.♘f4 ♕g4+ 24.♘g2 ♘xe4 25.♗xa7 ♖xf1+ 26.♖xf1 ♖f8 27.♖xf8+ ♗xf8 28.♕a1 ♗d6 29.♕e1 ♘g5 30.♔h1 ♗xh2 31.♕h4 ♕d1+ 32.♘e1 ♗d6 Black will soon win.

22...exf3 23.♖xf3 ♖fd8

24.♖fd3?

The last mistake. 24.♖xd8+ offered better saving chances.

24...♖xd3 25.♖xd3 ♕a6!−+

Winning, and stronger than 25...♘e4!?∓.

26.♘f4 ♘d5 27.♖f3 ♕c4 28.♗d6 ♖f8!−+ 29.♗xf8 ♗xf8 30.♕a1 ♗c5+ 31.♔h1 ♕e4 32.♕f1 ♘xf4 33.b4 ♗d6 34.♔g1 g5 35.♕f2 g4 36.♕h4 ♘e2+ 37.♔f2 ♕xf3+ 38.♔e1 ♘xc3 39.♕g5+ ♔f7   0-1

My pleasure!

Laszlo Hazai 2200
Andras Adorjan 2515

Budapest ch-HUN 1973

1.e4 c5 2.d3 g6 3.g3 ♗g7 4.♗g2 ♘c6 5.♘c3 d6 6.f4 e6 7.♘f3 ♘ge7 8.0-0 0-0

The Closed Sicilian is a blunder of taste.

9.♖b1 b6 10.♖e1 ♗b7 11.♗d2 ♕d7 12.♘e2

12...d5

Or 12...f5 13.♗c3 e5 − see?

13.e5 d4 14.g4

If 14.a3 ♘f5 Black also gets an edge.

14...f6 15.exf6 ♖xf6 16.♘g3 ♘d5 17.♘g5 ♘xf4!?

17...h6 18.♘h3 ♖af8∓.

18.♗xf4   ♖xf4   19.♘xe6   ♖f7 20.♘xg7 ♔xg7 21.♕e2 ♘b4

21...♖af8 22.♖f1 ♔g8 was solid.

22.♗xb7

22.♘e4 ♖e8 23.♖f1 ♗xe4 24.♗xe4 ♘xa2∓.

22...♕xb7

23.♕e5+

A stauncher defence was 23.♖f1 ♖af8 24.♖xf7+.

23...♔g8 24.♘e4 ♞xc2 25.♖f1 ♞e3

25...♕e7! 26.♘f6+ ♔h8 would have finished off.

26.♖xf7 ♕xf7 27.♘f6+ ♔f8 28.♖e1 ♕e7

A slow and ghostlike killer. Speedier was 28...♖d8!? 29.♖e2 ♕e7 30.♕g5 ♔g7 31.♘h5+ ♔f7 32.♖f2+ ♔e6 and Black wins.

29.♕xe7+ ♔xe7 30.♘d5+ ♔d6 31.♘xe3 dxe3 32.♖xe3 ♖f8 33.♔g2 ♖f4 34.h3 a5

35.a3

White cannot keep out the black king in the pawn ending after 35.♖f3 ♖xf3 36.♔xf3 ♔e5 37.g5 ♔f5 38.h4 ♔e5 39.♔e3 a4 40.♔f3 (40.b3 a3–+; 40.a3 b5 41.♔f3 ♔d4 42.♔e2 b4 43.♔d2 ♔d5 44.♔e2 ♔e6 45.♔e3 ♔e5 46.♔f3 ♔d4 47.♔e2 bxa3 48.bxa3 ♔c3–+) 40...♔d4 41.♔e2 a3 42.bxa3 ♔c3 43.♔e3 ♔b2 44.d4 c4.

35...a4 36.♖e2

In the event of 36.♖e8 ♖d4 37.♔f2 ♔d7 38.♖e3 b5 Black slowly makes progress.

36...b5 37.♔g3?

A time-trouble mistake. More tenacious was 37.♖e8 ♖d4 38.♖d8+ ♔e5 39.♖c8 ♖d5 40.♖b8, but Black wins anyway after 40...♖xd3 41.♖xb5 ♔d4 42.♖b7 ♖b3.

37...♖f1

Penetration.

38.h4 ♖d1 39.♔f4 ♖xd3 40.♔g5 ♖h3 41.♖d2+

41.h5 gxh5 42.gxh5 b4–+.

41...♔c6 42.♖f2 b4 43.♖f7 h6+! 44.♔xg6

Or 44.♔xh6 ♖xh4+ 45.♔g5 ♖h2–+.

44...♖xh4 45.axb4 cxb4

And White resigned in view of 46.♖f4 ♔c5.

Dr. Bodo
Andras Adorjan
Hungary tt 1973

1.e4 g6 2.d4 ♗g7 3.♘e2?! c5 4.c3 cxd4 5.cxd4 d5 6.e5

6.exd5 ♘f6 7.♘bc3 ♘xd5 8.♕b3 ♘b6=/∓.

6...♘c6 7.b3 f6

8.f4?

Only weakening his king. He should have played 8.exf6.

8...♘h6 9.♘ec3 0-0 10.♗b5

White could have won a pawn by 10.♘xd5 but after 10...♗g4 11.♕d2 fxe5 12.dxe5 e6 13.♘dc3 ♘d4 the compensation is overwhelming.

10...♘f5 11.♗xc6 bxc6 12.g4 ♘h6

Interesting, and perhaps even stronger than the text, was the piece sacrifice 12...fxe5 13.gxf5 exd4 14.♘e2 d3 15.♘ec3 ♗xf5.

13.h3 fxe5 14.fxe5 e6 15.♗e3 c5 16.♕e2 ♕a5

Here, another promising exchange sac was possible: 16...♕h4+ 17.♗f2 ♖xf2 18.♕xf2 ♕xf2+ 19.♔xf2 cxd4 20.♘b5 ♗xe5 21.♖e1 ♗f6∓.

17.♕b5 ♕d8

Or also 17...♕xb5 18.♘xb5 ♘f7 and Black wins.

18.♘a3

The white centre is fatally weak: 18.♕e2 cxd4 19.♗xd4 ♕h4+ 20.♗f2 ♕g5 21.♗d4 ♘f7−+; or 18.♕xc5 ♕h4+ 19.♔e2 ♘xg4.

18...cxd4 19.♗xd4 ♕h4+ 20.♔e2

20...♘f5! 21.♕d3

21.♗f2 ♘g3+ also wins for Black. He can take on f2 next.

21...♗a6 22.♘ab5 ♘xd4+ 23.♕xd4 ♖ac8 24.a4 ♕g3   **0-1**

This must have been a painful lesson for the First Mover.

Ludwig Rellstab
Andras Adorjan

Hastings 1973 (7)

Uncle Rellstab had won the previous Hastings Challengers – that's how he got his invitation.

1.e4 c5 2.♘f3 ♘c6 3.d4 cxd4 4.♘xd4 g6 5.♘c3 ♗g7 6.♗e3 ♘f6

7.♗e2 0-0 8.♘b3 d6 9.0-0 ♗e6 10.f4 ♘a5

11.♘xa5

The normal continuation is 11.f5!? ♗c4 12.♗d3 when 12...d5 13.e5 ♘xb3 14.exf6 ♗xf6 15.axb3 ♗xd3 16.♕xd3 d4 is a liquidation that leads to approximate equality: 17.♘e4 (17. fxg6 dxe3 18.gxh7+ ♔h8 19.♕e4 ♕d4 20.♕xb7 e2+ 21.♖f2 ♕b6 22.♕f3 ♗d4 is not so clear, but should be OK for Black) 17...dxe3 18.♘xf6+ exf6 19.♕xe3 ♖e8 20.♕f2 ♔g7.

11...♕xa5 12.♗d4 ♖fd8

Better is 12...♖ac8!? with the idea 13.f5 ♗c4.

13.♕d3

Now he could and should have played 13.f5 ♗d7 (certainly not 13...gxf5 14.exf5 ♗xf5? 15.b4+−) 14.♕d3.

13...♖ac8 14.♕e3

In case of 14.♖ab1 ♗c4 15.♕e3 Black could give the pawn: 15...e5!? (or otherwise simply 15...♗xe2!? 16.♕xe2 a6) 16.fxe5 dxe5 17.♗xa7 ♗xe2 18.♗b6 ♘g4 19.♗xa5 ♘xe3 20.♖fe1 ♖d2 21.♘xe2 ♖dxc2 22.♗c3 f5∓.

14...♕b4 15.a3

15.♖fd1 ♕xb2 16.♖ab1 ♕a3 (Black could even try 16...♕xc2!? 17.♖dc1, now bailing out with 17...♖xc3 18.♖xc2 ♖xe3 19.♗xe3 b6 20.♗f3) 17.♖xb7 ♖d7 with pressure on White's pawns.

15...♕xb2

Poisoned?

16.♖fb1

The other way to try and punish Black was 16.f5 ♗d7 (or 16...♗xf5 17.exf5? ♘d5!–+, and 17.♖ab1 allows the same trick) 17.♖ab1 ♘g4 18.♗xg4 (18.♖xb2 ♘xe3 19.♗xe3 ♖xc3) 18...♗xd4 19.♕xd4 ♕xc3 20.♕xc3 ♖xc3 21.♖xb7 ♖xc2 or 21...♖xa3, and Black keeps an edge.

16...♘g4

Even better was 16...♕xc2 17.♖xb7 (17.♖c1 ♖xc3! 18.♖xc2 ♖xe3 19.♗xe3 ♘xe4 20.♖b1 b6 21.♖c7 ♘c3 22.♖e1 ♘d5) 17...♘xe4 18.♗xg7 ♘xc3 – Black is winning in all these lines.

17.♗xg4

17...♖xc3!

Black has to take drastic measures as 17...♗xd4 18.♕xd4 ♕xc3 19.♕xc3 ♖xc3 20.♗xe6 fxe6 21.♖xb7 ♔f7 22.♖xa7 ♖xc2 23.♖b1 is just equal.

18.♗xc3

18.♖xb2 ♖xe3 19.♗xe3 (19.♗xg7 ♗xg4 20.♗d4 ♖xe4 21.♗xa7 ♗c8∓) 19...♗xb2 20.♖b1 ♗xg4 21.♖xb2 b6∓; 18.♕f2 ♗xd4 19.♕xd4 ♕xc2.

18...♕xc3 19.♕xc3 ♗xc3 20.♗xe6 ♗xa1 21.♗b3 ♗d4+ 22.♔f1

And White played on for twenty more masochist moves:

22...♖c8 23.♖d1 ♗e3 24.g3 b5 25.♔e2 ♗c5 26.a4 bxa4 27.♗xa4 ♖b8 28.♗b3 ♖b4 29.♔f3 ♗d4 30.♖b1 a5 31.g4 ♔g7 32.h4 h5 33.g5 a4 34.♗a2 ♖xb1 35.♗xb1 ♗c3 36.♔g2 f6 37.♗a2 e5 38.fxe5 ♗xe5 39.♔f3 ♗b2 40.gxf6+ ♗xf6 41.♔g3 ♗c3   **0-1**

Milan Ilijc
Andras Adorjan
Novi Sad 1973

16.♔g2

It was tough for White anyway. Material doesn't count when there is somebody fiddling around with your king. You can have even three rooks, but if you have to face just two cruel bishops exactly on the right diagonals – forget it! Again: if you feel the spirit of the position you will surely find the right way, and the concrete moves. Let's see!

A) 16.g4 ♖xd5 17.cxd5 ♕xd5 18.♖h3 ♗e6 19.♖e3 ♖d8 (19...♗d4!?∓) 20.♕a4 ♗d4 21.♖e4 ♕a2 (21...c4!? 22.♘f3 b5) 22.♖ee1 ♗xg4 23.♕xa5 ♕d5, winning;

B) 16.♘f3 ♖xd5 17.cxd5 ♕xd5 18.♔g2 ♗xd3 19.♖e1 ♕f5 and Black holds all the trumps;

C) 16.♕f3 ♖xd5 (16...♕d7!?∓) 17.cxd5 c4 18.♖d1 ♗xd3+ 19.♖xd3 cxd3 20.♕xd3 ♗xb2 21.♕b3 ♗c1!? might have been the best defence.

16...♖xd5 17.cxd5 ♕xd5+ 18.♘f3

He could have gone for a queen exchange, but in the endgame the bishops are still dominant, for example: 18.♕f3 ♕xd3!? (18...♖d8 19.♕xd5 ♖xd5∓) 19.♕xd3 ♗xd3 20.♖d1 c4 21.♖d2 ♖a6 22.♘e2 ♖b6 23.♘c3 ♗xc3 24.bxc3 ♗b3∓.

18...♗xd3 19.♕d2 ♕f5 20.♖be1 ♗e4 21.♕f4 ♕xf4 22.gxf4 ♗c6

Also good was 22...f5 23.♖e2 ♖d8 24.b3 b5 25.♖c1 ♖d3 26.♖e3 ♖xe3 27.fxe3 c4 28.bxc4 ♗b2 29.♖d1 bxc4.

23.♖e2 ♖d8 24.♖c1

24...♗xb2!?

I couldn't resist this move. And it's not bad at all. Still, better and simpler may have been 24...♖d3 25.♖e3 ♖xe3 26.fxe3 ♗xb2 27.♖xc5 a4.

25.♖xc5

25.♖xb2 ♖d3 26.♖xc5 ♗xf3+∓.

25...♗xa3 26.♖xa5 ♗c1! 27.♖c5 ♗xf4 28.♖c3 h6 29.♔h3 ♖d6 30.♘e1 ♗b5

31.♖e4?

A blunder, of course, but it was made after a long and tiring defence, and still White was in trouble.

For instance: 31.♖e7 ♗d7+ 32.♔g2 ♗c6+ 33.♘f3 ♖d1–+.

31...♗d7+ 32.♔g2 ♗d2–+ 33.♖c2

33.♖d3 ♖xd3 34.♘xd3 ♗c6.

33...♗c6 34.♖xc6 bxc6 35.♖e8+ ♔g7 36.♘f3 ♗c3 37.♖c8 ♗f6 38.♖c7 ♗c3 39.♔g3 ♖f6 40.♖c8 ♗b4 41.♔g2 ♗c5   0-1

Jorge Cuadras Avellana
Andras Adorjan   2515

Olot 1974 (7)

1.e4 c5 2.♘f3 ♘c6 3.d4 cxd4 4.♘xd4 g6 5.♘c3 ♗g7 6.♗e3 ♘f6 7.♗c4 0-0 8.f3 e6!?

For 8...♕b6 9.♗b3 ♘g4 and 9...♘xe4 see the analyses in Szilagyi-Adorjan above.

9.♘xc6

9.♗b3 d5; 9.0-0 d5 10.exd5 ♘xd5.

9...bxc6 10.♗c5 ♖e8

For the exchange sacrifice 10...d5!? see the analysis in the game mentioned after move 8.

11.♗d6 ♘d5!

That's the idea!

12.♕d3

12.exd5 exd5+! (even stronger than 12...♕h4+) 13.♗e2 ♗xc3+ 14.bxc3 ♗a6 and it's finished!

12...♕b6!?N

12...♘xc3 13.bxc3 ♕b6 (or 13...♕a5, see again Szilagyi-Adorjan) 14.♖d1 ♗f8∓.

13.0-0-0

13.♘d1 ♘b4 14.♕d2 c5 15.e5 and now Black has a very annoying way to collect the ♗d6: 15...♘c6 16.♕f4 (16.♕c3 ♘a5 17.♗e2 ♘b7–+) 16...♘a5 17.♗d3 ♘b7 and Black is better, since on 18.♗e4 he simply sacrifices the exchange on a8 and collects the e5-pawn afterwards.

13...♘xc3 14.bxc3 ♕a5

White is facing his execution.

15.♔b2 ♗f8! 16.h4

16.e5 ♗xd6 17.♕xd6 ♗a6 18.♗b3 c5 19.c4 ♖ab8 20.♕d2 ♕xd2 leads to a sad endgame for White: 21.♖xd2 ♗xc4 22.♔c3 (22.♖xd7 ♗b5 23.♖xa7 c4 24.a4 cxb3 25.axb5 ♖xb5 26.f4 bxc2+ 27.♔xc2 ♖c8+ 28.♔d3 ♖b2 29.g3 ♖cc2∓) 22...♗b5 23.a4 ♗c6 24.♖d6 f6 25.exf6 ♔f7∓.

16...♗a6!! 17.♗xf8
The idea is 17.♗xa6 ♗xd6 18.♗c4 (he should play 18.♕xd6) 18...♕a3+ 19.♔a1 ♗e5 20.♗b3 a5 and now the other white bishop is trapped.
17...♗xc4 18.♕xc4 ♖xf8 19.h5
19.♖xd7 ♖ab8+ 20.♔c1 ♖fd8 spells trouble for the white king, e.g., 21.♖xd8+ ♖xd8 22.♔b1 ♕b6+ 23.♔a1 ♕f2∓.
19...♖ab8+ 20.♔a1 d5 21.♕d4 c5 22.♕d2
If 22.♕e5 d4−+.
22...dxe4 23.hxg6 hxg6

24.♕e3?
He should have taken on e4: 24.fxe4 ♖fd8 (24...♖b6) 25.♕e3 ♖xd1+

26.♖xd1 ♕b5 27.♕c1∓. Now he won't get any time for that.
24...♖b6 25.♖b1 ♖fb8 26.c4
Only move, as now 26.fxe4?? runs into 26...♕xa2+! 27.♔xa2 ♖a6#.
26...♖xb1+ 27.♖xb1 ♖xb1+ 28.♔xb1 ♕b4+ 29.♔c1 exf3 30.♕xf3 ♕e1+
Or 30...♕xc4 31.♕a8+ ♔g7 32.♕xa7 ♕d4−+.
31.♔b2
The young Spaniard knows no etiquette. Being short of time and also of a few pawns, he could have said 'Abandonado' in his mother tongue.
31...♕b4+ 32.♔c1 ♔g7 33.♕e3 a5 34.a3 ♕xc4 35.♕e5+ ♔h6 36.♕h8+ ♔g5 37.♕d8+ ♔g4 38.♕xa5 ♕d4 39.♕a8 ♕a1+ 40.♔d2 ♕d4+ 41.♔c1 f5 42.a4 c4 43.♕f3+ ♔g5 44.c3 ♕c5 45.♕g3+ ♔f6 46.♕h4+ ♔e5 47.♕g3+ ♔d5 48.♔c2 e5 49.♕h4 ♕c6 50.♕d8+ ♔e4 51.a5 ♕a4+ 52.♔d2 ♕a2+ 53.♔e1 ♕a1+ 54.♔f2 ♕b2+ 55.♔g1 ♕xc3 56.♕a8+ ♔f4 57.a6 ♔g3
The guy resigned by phone after first adjourning the game!

Arturo Pomar Salamanca 2435
Andras Adorjan 2515
Olot 1974 (9)

My opponent in this game passed away earlier this year at the age of 84. When he was 13, he defeated Alekhine in a regular game!
1.d4
White to play but Black to win! Okay?
1...g6 2.♘f3 ♗g7 3.c4 c5 4.♘c3 cxd4 5.♘xd4 ♘c6 6.e3 ♘f6 7.♗e2 0-0 8.0-0 d6
8...d5!? 9.cxd5 ♘xd5 10.♘xd5 ♕xd5 11.♗f3 ♕c4 12.♘xc6 bxc6 13.♕b3 ♗a6 14.♖d1 ♖fd8 is a piquant line.
9.b3

9...d5!?

A tricky switch!

10.♗f3

10.♗a3 ♕a5 11.♕c1 ♖e8 is unclear;
10.♘xc6 bxc6 11.♗b2 ♗f5=.

10...♘xd4

After 10...dxc4!? 11.♘xc6?! bxc6 12.bxc4
♗e6 13.♕c2 ♕c7 14.♖d1 ♘g4 15.♗xg4
♗xg4 16.f3 ♗f5 17.e4 ♗e6 Black has
good pressure.

11.exd4 dxc4 12.bxc4 ♗e6 13.d5

With 13.c5 ♘d5 14.♘xd5 ♗xd5
15.♗e3= he could have more or less
maintained the centre. If 13.♗xb7?
♖b8 14.♗f3 (14.♗a6 ♕a5; 14.♗d5
♗xd5 15.cxd5 ♘xd5 16.♘xd5 ♕xd5
17.♗e3 ♖fd8 18.♕a4 ♗xd4 19.♖ad1
e5) 14...♗xc4 15.♖e1 ♕d6∓.

13...♗f5 14.♗e3

14.♗b2 ♖c8 15.♕b3 (15.♕e2 ♕c7)
15...♘d7!?∓.

**14...♖c8 15.♕e2 ♘d7 16.♖ac1
♘e5 17.♗e4**

17.♘e4 ♕a5∓.

**17...♖xc4! 18.♗xf5 gxf5 19.f4 ♘g4
20.♗d2**

20.♕xc4 ♘xe3 21.♕b5 ♘xf1 22.♔xf1
♕b8 gives Black a good attack for his
plus pawn.

20...♕b6+ 21.♔h1 ♖fc8 22.h3

White is about to collapse; 22.♘a4 ♕a6.

22...♗xc3 23.♖xc3 ♖xc3 24.hxg4

24.♗xc3 would have allowed me to
finish with a flourish: 24...♘e3 25.♖c1

analysis diagram

25...♖xc3!! 26.♖xc3 ♕b1+ 27.♔h2 ♘f1+
28.♔g1 ♘g3+.

**24...♖c2 25.gxf5 ♕d4 26.♖d1
♕xf4 27.♕d3 ♕h4+ 28.♔g1 ♖8c4
29.♗e1 ♕g4 30.♗f2 ♕xd1+ 0-1**

All through the game a black storm was
raging!

**Richard Meulders
Andras Adorjan**

Teesside tt 1974

**1.e4 g6 2.d4 ♗g7 3.♘c3 d6 4.♗e3
c6 5.♕d2 b5 6.a4 b4 7.♘d1 a5 8.f3
♘f6 9.g4**

Bayonett auf!

**9...h5! 10.g5 ♘fd7 11.h4 0-0
12.c4 bxc3**

12...c5!? 13.d5 ♘b6 may have been preferable; Black is already better.

13.♘xc3 ♗a6 14.♘ge2

14.♗xa6 ♘xa6 15.♘ge2 ♖b8∓.

14...♘b6 15.b3 ♘8d7 16.♘g3 d5 17.♖c1

Leaving the doors open. The lesser evil was 17.♗xa6 ♖xa6 18.0-0 ♕b8∓.

17...e5 18.♗xa6 ♖xa6 19.exd5 ♘xd5 20.♘xd5 cxd5 21.♔f2 ♕b8 22.♖c3?

More solid though still insufficient, was 22.♖b1 ♖e8 23.♖hd1 when Black keeps the upper hand by 23...♖c6 or any other healthy move, like 23...♖b6.

22...f6?

Already decisive was 22...♖b6! 23.♖b1 (23.♘e2 ♖xb3) 23...♖b4.

23.♖hc1?

23.dxe5 ♕xe5 24.♗d4 would have put up some kind of defence.

23...fxg5 24.♖c7

24.hxg5 h4 25.♘f1 e4.

24...e4! 25.♗xg5 ♖a7! 26.♗f4 ♖xc7 27.♖xc7

27...♖xf4!

Beautiful!

28.♕xf4 ♗xd4+ 29.♔g2 ♗e5 30.♕h6 exf3+ 31.♔h3 ♕xc7 32.♕xg6+ ♔f8 33.♕xh5 ♕d6 0-1

| **Michael Basman** | 2395 |
| **Andras Adorjan** | 2515 |

London 1975

1.e4 g6 2.♘c3 ♗g7 3.f4?!

3.d4=.

3...c5 4.♘f3 ♘c6 5.♗b5 ♘d4 6.♗d3

6...d6

Black already has the upper hand, and he had another good choice here too: 6...♘f6 and now:

A) 7.♘xd4 cxd4 8.♘e2 0-0 (tactics!) 9.e5 (9.♘xd4 ♘xe4 10.♗xe4 ♗xd4 11.c3 d5! 12.♗c2 ♗f6 13.d4 ♗h4+! 14.g3 ♗f6 15.0-0 ♗h3 16.♖e1 ♕d7∓) 9...♘d5 10.♗e4 ♕a5 11.0-0 ♕c5 and Black is the side that is playing;

B) 7.e5 ♘h5 8.♘xd4 cxd4 9.♘e2 d6 10.exd6 (10.♗b5+ ♗d7 11.♗xd7+ ♕xd7∓) 10...♕xd6 11.0-0 0-0;

C) 7.0-0 0-0 8.e5 ♘e8 9.♘xd4 cxd4 10.♘e4 d6 – as you (will) see the d4-pawn is quite annoying for White.

7.♘xd4 cxd4 8.♘e2 ♘f6 9.0-0 0-0 10.c3 e5! 11.cxd4 exd4 12.b3 ♖e8

This happens when the 'first player' takes things too easy.

13.♘g3 h5! 14.f5

The Englishman prefers not to defend passively by 14.♖e1 ♗g4 15.♕c2 ♖c8 16.♕b1 h4 17.♘h1 ♘h5 (17...♗f5!? 18.♗b2 (18.♘f2? ♘xe4!−+) 18...♗d7∓) 18.♗b5 ♗d7 19.♗xd7 ♕xd7 20.d3 ♗h6 21.♖f1 d5 22.e5 ♕f5−+.

14...h4!

Come on sugar!

Even sharper, but also good, was 14...♘g4!? 15.fxg6 fxg6 16.h3 ♕h4 17.♘e2 (17.♘h1 ♗e5−+; 17.hxg4 ♗e5 18.♕f3 ♗e6∓) 17...♘e5 18.♗b5 ♗xh3! with a very strong attack.

15.♘e2 ♘xe4 16.♗xe4?

A more accurate defence was 16.fxg6 fxg6 17.♗xe4 ♖xe4 18.d3 ♖e8 19.♘f4 ♗f5∓.

16...♖xe4 17.d3 ♖e5 18.fxg6

18...♗g4 19.gxf7+ ♔h7 20.♖f4

20.♖f2 ♕e7 21.♔f1 ♖xe2! 22.♖xe2 ♕xf7+ 23.♔g1 ♖e8−+.

20...♗xe2

The rest is needless agony.

21.♕e1 ♗h5 22.♕xh4 ♕xh4 23.♖xh4 ♗f6 24.♖f4 ♔g7 25.♗a3 ♖e6 26.♖af1 ♖f8 27.♗b2 ♖xf7 28.g4 ♗e5 29.♗xd4 ♖xf4 30.♖xf4 ♗g6 31.♗xe5+ dxe5 32.♖a4 a6 33.♖b4 b5 34.d4 e4 35.♔f2 e3+ 36.♔e1 ♗d3   0-1

It was Crime and Punishment for the proud white player.

Craig Pritchett	2390
Andras Adorjan	2515

London 1975 (5)

1.e4 c5 2.♘f3 ♘c6 3.d4 cxd4 4.♘xd4 g6 5.♘c3 ♗g7 6.♗e3 ♘f6 7.♗c4 0-0 8.♗b3 d6 9.h3 ♘a5! 10.0-0 a6

10...b6!? is a wonderful option: 11.♕d3 ♗b7 12.♖fd1 ♖c8 13.♘d5 ♘d7 and now there is no punishment by 14.♗g5 ♖e8 15.c3 h6 16.♗h4 g5 17.♗g3 e6 − on the contrary, White loses a healthy e-pawn.

11.♖e1 b5 12.♘d5 ♗b7 13.♗g5

Here too − aggressive but groundless.

13...♖c8?!

13...♘xb3! was more accurate, cf. 14.♘xb3 (14.♗xf6 exf6 15.♘xb3 f5 16.exf5 ♗xb2 17.♖b1 ♗g7∓; 14.axb3 ♖e8 15.♗xf6 exf6 16.♘f3 f5 17.exf5 ♖xe1+ 18.♘xe1 ♗xb2 with two powerful bishops) 14...♖e8 15.♗xf6 exf6 16.♕d3 (16.♕d2 a5 17.c3 a4 18.♘d4 f5 19.♘xb5 ♖xe4 20.♖xe4 fxe4 21.♖e1 ♕d7 22.c4 ♖e8 is very unclear)

16...f5 17.exf5 ♗xb2 18.♖xe8+ ♕xe8 19.♖d1 ♖c8∓.

14.♗xf6 exf6 15.c3 ♖e8 16.a4 f5!

Just in time!

17.axb5 fxe4

17...♗xd4 is playable: 18.cxd4 fxe4 19.bxa6 ♗xa6 20.♗c2 ♗b7 21.♖xe4 ♗xd5 22.♖xe8+ ♕xe8 23.♖xa5 ♖xc2! 24.♖xd5 (24.♕xc2 ♕e1+–+) 24...♕e4=.

18.bxa6 ♗xa6 19.♗a4?!

The bishop goes astray, whereas Black's rook doesn't. Safer was 19.♗c2 ♗b7 20.♖xe4 ♘c4 (20...♖e5 21.♖xa5 ♕xa5 22.♘e7+ ♖xe7 23.♖xe7 ♗xg2? 24.♕g4+–) 21.♖xe8+ ♕xe8 22.♕f3 ♗xd4 23.cxd4 ♗xd5 24.♕xd5 ♘e3 25.fxe3 ♕xe3+ 26.♔h1 ♖xc2 when either of the sides will probably have to force the draw.

19...♖e5 20.♘e3 ♕b6 21.b4?!

21...♘c4

21...♖xc3?! would have produced a splendid torso, for example: 22.bxa5 ♖xa5 23.♘c6 ♖xc6 24.♖b1 ♗b5 25.♘d5 ♗xa4 26.♖xb6 ♖xb6 27.♕d2 ♖ba6 28.♖xe4 ♖xd5! 29.♕xd5 ♗c6

30.♕c4 ♖a1+ 31.♔h2 ♗xe4 32.♕xe4 ♗f6 with a difficult ending.

22.♘xc4?! ♖xc4 23.b5?

Downright bad. He should have gone 23.♕d2 ♗b7∓.

23...♗b7 24.♘c6

24...e3!

YES!

25.fxe3 ♖xe3 26.♔h1 ♗xc3 27.♖xe3 ♕xe3 28.♖a3 ♕g3 29.♕f3

On 29.♗c2, 29...♖xc6 30.bxc6 ♗xc6 finishes off neatly.

29...♕e1+ 30.♔h2 ♗e5+ 31.♘xe5 ♗xf3 32.♘xc4 ♗d5

32...♗xg2–+.

33.♖e3 ♕b4 34.♖e8+ ♔g7 35.♘b6 ♕f4+ 36.♔g1 ♕d4+ 37.♔h2 0-1

... and it's over and done with...

Laszlo Barczay   2465
Andras Adorjan   2515
Budapest 1978
1.e4 c5 2.♘f3 ♘c6 3.♘c3 g6 4.d4 cxd4 5.♘xd4 ♗g7 6.♗e3 ♘f6 7.♗e2 0-0

8.♕d2?!

A mistake which allows Black to play the centre blow ...d7-d5 in one move. White should play 8.♘b3 here, or 8.0-0 and now:

A) 8...d5 is still possible, though with a little less impact than in the game: 9.exd5 ♘xd5 (9...♘b4!? 10.d6 ♕xd6 11.♘cb5 ♕b8 12.c4 a6 13.♘c3 e5 14.♘c2 ♘c6 unclear) 10.♘xd5 ♕xd5 (keeping more play in the position than after 10...♘xd4 11.♗xd4 ♕xd5 12.♗xg7 ♕xd1 13.♖axd1 ♔xg7 14.♗f3 ♗e6 15.b3 ♖ac8 16.c4 b6=) 11.♗f3 ♕a5 with chances for both sides;

B) 8...d6 9.♕d2 ♘g4 10.♗xg4 ♗xg4 11.h3 ♗d7=.

8...d5! 9.exd5

9.♘xc6 bxc6 10.0-0-0 (10.e5 ♘d7 11.f4 e6∓) 10...♗e6 and Black's attack just may come first.

9...♘xd5 10.♘xc6

10.♘xd5 is met by 10...♘xd4! 11.♗c4 (11.♗xd4 ♕xd5 12.♗xg7 ♕xg2 13.0-0-0 ♔xg7∓) 11...♘f5 12.0-0-0 ♘xe3 13.♘xe3 ♕c7 14.♗b3 e6 15.♕d6 ♕xd6 16.♖xd6 b6 when the bishop pair will have its say.

10...bxc6 11.♖d1

11.♘xd5 cxd5 (Black is also more active in the endgame following 11...♕xd5 12.♕xd5 cxd5 13.c3 ♖d8 14.0-0-0 e5) 12.c3 ♕a5 13.0-0 ♖d8 14.♗f3 ♗f5 15.♖fe1 ♖ab8.

11.0-0-0? loses to 11...♗xc3 12.bxc3 ♕a5.

11...♗e6 12.♗d4

12.♘xd5 ♕xd5 13.♕xd5 loses a pawn for nothing after 13...♗xd5 14.0-0 (14.♗f3 ♗xf3 15.gxf3 ♗xb2 16.♖d7 ♗f6 17.♖xa7 ♖fd8 18.♖xd8+ ♖xd8 19.♗e3 ♖a8∓) 14...♗xb2 15.c4 ♗e6∓.

12...♗xd4 13.♕xd4 ♕a5

14.♕a4

White is in big trouble here – maybe already lost. For example: 14.♕e5 ♕b4 15.♕d4 ♕xd4 16.♖xd4 ♘xc3 17.bxc3 ♗xa2 18.♗f3 (18.c4 ♖fd8) 18...e5 19.♖a4 ♗d5 20.♔e2 e4!? (20...♖fd8 21.♖ha1 ♖d7 22.♗xd5 cxd5 23.c4 dxc4 24.♖xc4 ♖b8 25.♖c5 f6) 21.♗xe4 ♖fe8 22.♔d3 ♖xe4 23.♖xe4 ♗xe4+ 24.♔xe4 a5 25.♖a1 a4 26.♖a3 ♖a5 27.♔d4.

14...♕b6! 15.♕a3

15.♘xd5 ♗xd5 16.0-0 ♕xb2∓.

15...♖fb8 16.♘a4 ♕a5+

17.♖d2

17.c3 runs into a sudden crushing attack by 17...♘f4! 18.♗f3 ♕e5+ 19.♔d2 ♘xg2 20.♗xc6 ♕f4+ 21.♔c2 ♗f5+.

17...♖b4 18.♘c3

18.b3 ♘f4 19.♕c1 ♖d4−+.

18...♕xa3 19.bxa3 ♖b2

Can you see the ruins, Ladies and Gentlemen?

20.♘e4

20.♘xd5 ♗xd5 21.c4 ♖b1+ 22.♖d1 ♖xd1+−+.

20...♖xa2   21.c4   ♖a1+   22.♖d1 ♖xd1+ 23.♗xd1 ♘f4 24.g3 ♘d3+ 25.♔d2 ♖d8   0-1

Black wins a second pawn after 26.♔c3 f5 (or also 26...♗f5 27.♗f3 ♗xe4 28.♗xe4 ♘xf2) 27.♘g5 ♘xf2 28.♘xe6 ♘xd1+ 29.♔c2 ♘e3+.

Ivan Farago
Andras Adorjan
Budapest 1978

Four GMs played a double round robin playoff for one place to represent Hungary in the 1978 zonal: Csom, Farago, Adorjan and Vadasz. After beating the latter I led the field after the first full round, half a point ahead of Farago. So this next game would decide practically everything. I threw in the Nimzo for the first time in my life instead of my beloved (and expected) Grünfeld.

1.d4 ♘f6 2.c4 e6 3.♘c3 ♗b4 4.e3 b6 5.♗d3 ♗b7 6.♘f3 0-0 7.0-0 c5 8.♘a4 cxd4 9.a3 ♗e7 10.exd4 d6 11.♖e1 ♘bd7 12.♘c3

12...h6!?

This looks foggy, but it saves the h7-pawn in any case.

A) 12...♖e8 13.d5 exd5 14.cxd5 a6 (14...♘xd5? 15.♘xd5 ♗xd5 16.♗xh7+ ♔xh7 17.♕xd5±) 15.♗e3 g6=;

B) 12...a6!? 13.b4 (13.d5 exd5 14.cxd5 ♖e8; for 13.h3 see Pinter-Adorjan below) 13...♖c8 14.♗b2 is unclear;

C) 12...d5 might easily hold, but I played for a win so as to get my draw! There could follow:

C1) 13.b3 ♖c8 14.♗f4 ♘h5 15.♗e3 a6 16.♘e5 ♘hf6 17.♗f4 ♘xe5 18.♗xe5 (18.dxe5 dxc4) 18...♗d6 (18...♘d7 19.♗f4) 19.♕c2 h6 20.♕e2 (20.♖ad1 ♗xa3) 20...dxc4 21.bxc4 ♗xe5 22.♕xe5 b5 23.c5 ♕c7 with slightly better prospects, thanks to the long diagonal (d5!) and the d-file (d5!);

C2) 13.cxd5 ♘xd5 14.♘xd5 ♗xd5 15.♗f4 ♘f6 16.♖c1 ♖c8=.

13.b4

Gaining a spatial plus, which was considered advantageous for White at the time. 13.d5 exd5 14.cxd5 ♘xd5 15.♘xd5 ♗xd5 16.♗f4 gives White interesting compensation for the pawn.

13...♖e8 14.♗b2 a6 15.♘d2 ♗f8 16.♘b3 ♖c8 17.a4?!

Let's do something, the white player thought. The trouble in these Hedgehog-type positions is that if Black can get in ...d6-d5 or ...b6-b5, usually this doesn't just equalize!

17.♗f1!?; 17.♖c1!?.

17...d5! 18.c5

18.cxd5?? ♗xb4 19.dxe6 ♗xc3 20.♗xc3 ♖xc3–+.

18...a5!

The tables are turning as the white pawn squad falls apart.

19.♗b5

A) 19.bxa5!? bxc5 20.a6 ♗a8 21.dxc5 ♘xc5 22.♘xc5 ♗xc5 23.♘b5 ♘e4∓;

B) 19.♘a2 axb4 20.♗b5 bxc5 21.dxc5 ♗c6 (21...♘xc5!? is also tempting, for example: 22.♗xe8 ♘xe8 23.♘xb4 ♘e4 24.♘d3 ♘8d6 with compensation, for example: 25.f3? ♘c3) 22.♘xb4 (22.♗xc6 ♖xc6 23.♘xb4 ♖c8∓) 22...♗xb5 23.axb5 ♘xc5 24.♘c6 ♕b6 25.♗xf6 ♘xb3 (25...gxf6 26.♕g4+ ♗g7 27.♘xc5 ♕xc5 28.♖ac1 ♕xb5 29.♘e7+ ♖xe7 30.♖xc8+ ♔h7 31.♕g3 f5∓) 26.♕xb3 ♖xc6 27.♖a6 gxf6 28.♕a4 ♖d6 is similar to the game – BLACK is OK!

19...axb4 20.♘a2 bxc5

If 20...♗c6:

A) 21.♗a6?! ♗xa4 22.♗xc8 ♕xc8 23.♘xb4 ♗xb3 24.♕xb3 bxc5 25.dxc5 ♘xc5 26.♕e3 ♘fe4∓;

B) 21.♗xc6 ♖xc6 22.♘xb4 ♖c8∓;

C) 21.♘xb4 ♗xb5 22.axb5 bxc5 23.dxc5 ♘xc5 24.♘c6 ♕b6 – again

a complex liquidation similar to the game.

21.dxc5

21.♘xc5 ♘xc5 (21...♗xc5 22.dxc5 ♗c6 23.♘xb4 ♗xb5 24.axb5 ♖xc5 25.♘c6 ♕b6 26.♗d4 ♕xb5 27.♗xc5 ♕xc6 28.♗e3 e5 29.f4 ♘e4 30.fxe5 ♘xe5∓) 22.♗xe8 ♘xe8 23.dxc5 ♗xc5∓.

21...♗c6 22.♘xb4 ♗xb5 23.axb5 ♘xc5

23...♗xc5 comes down to an exchange sacrifice which may be playable, cf. 24.♘c6 ♕b6 25.♘xc5 ♕xc5 26.♗a3 (26.♖c1 ♕xb5 27.♘e7+ ♖xe7 28.♖xc8+ ♖e8 (only move) 29.♖xe8+ ♘xe8 is another playable exchange sac) 26...♕xb5 27.♘a7 ♕b6 28.♘xc8 ♖xc8, unclear.

24.♘c6 ♕b6 25.♗xf6 ♘xb3

25...gxf6 would probably result in a draw after 26.♕g4+ ♔h8 27.♘xc5 ♗xc5 28.♕h4 ♔g7 29.♕g3+.

26.♕xb3

26...♖xc6

Now definitely not 26...gxf6 27.♖a6 ♕b7? (27...♕c5 may still be tenable) 28.♖a7 ♕b6 29.♕g3+ ♗g7 30.♕d6 with a winning attack. We now enter an endgame where (as we saw before) Black's strong centre gives him compensation for his slight material deficit.

27.♖a6 gxf6 28.♕a4 ♖d6 29.♖xb6 ♖xb6 30.♖e3

30.♖b1 ♖eb8 31.g3=.

30...♗d6 31.♖h3

31.♕g4+ ♔f8 32.♖b3 ♖c8 33.g3=;
31.♖b3!? ♖c8 32.♖b1=.

31...♖c8 32.g3?

32.♔f1!?.

32...♗f8 33.♕g4+

White was in time-trouble and offered
a draw here.

**33...♗g7 34.♖xh6? ♖c4 35.♕h3
♖xb5?**

I was in time-trouble too! Winning
was 35...♗xh6! 36.♕xh6 e5 37.h4 d4
38.♕h5 d3.

36.♖h4 ♖bb4

36...♖bc5!?; 36...f5!?.

37.♖xc4 dxc4

Now it is Black who has a strong passed
pawn, which will be well supported by
the bishop.

38.♕g4 f5 39.♕g5

39.♕h4!?.

39...c3 40.♕d8+ ♔h7 41.♕c7 ♔g8

Stronger was 41...♔g6 42.h4 ♗d4
43.h5+ ♔g7 44.h6+ ♔g6 45.h7 ♗g7∓.

42.♕c8+ ♔h7 43.♔g2 ♗f6

43...♖b2 44.h4 ♗e5∓.

44.h4 ♔g7 45.h5

45.♕c5 ♖e4 46.♕c7 ♖e2 47.♕f4 ♔h7
48.♕c7 ♔g7 49.♕f4 ♖a2 and the
c-pawn should prevail.

45...♖e4

45...♖b2!? looks winning, but White has
a problematic save: 46.♕c4 c2 47.♔h3
♗g5 (47...♗e5 48.♕c5 ♔h7 doesn't
win as long as White keeps the queen
on the c-file) 48.♕c3+ ♔h7 49.♕c7!
(49.f4 ♗xf4! 50.gxf4 ♖b3! 51.♕xb3 c1♕

52.♕f3 ♕g1–+) 49...♔g7 50.♕c3+
♔f6 51.♕c5! and Black cannot make
any progress.

**46.♕e8 c2 47.h6+ ♔xh6 48.♕xf7
♗g7 49.♕c7 ♖e2 50.♕c4 ♔h7
51.♔f3**

**51...♗h6 52.♔xe2 c1♕ 53.♕xe6
♕c2+ 54.♔f3 ♕d3+?**

54...♕d1+ 55.♔g2 (55.♕e2 ♕h1#)
55...♕g4 56.f3 ♕g6 and if White trades
queens and plays f3-f4, Black is in time
to prevent g3-g4 with ...♔h5.

55.♔g2 ♕e4+

With the black pawn on the f-file it's a
win if Black's king is active enough, but
with the pawn on the e-file it isn't!
For example: 55...♔g7 56.g4 ♕e4+
57.♕xe4 fxe4 58.f3 e3 59.f4 ♗d4
60.♔f3 ♔g6 61.♔e2 ♔f6 62.♔d3 ♔e6
63.♔e2 ♗c5 64.♔f3 ♗a7 65.♔e2 ♔d5
66.♔d3 ♗d4 67.g5 ♔e6 68.g6 ♔f6
69.f5 with a draw.

56.♕xe4 fxe4 57.f3 e3

... and White resigned!

However, Black cannot win after 58.f4 ♗g7 59.♔f3 ♗d4 60.♔e2 ♔g6 61.g4 ♔f6 62.♔d3 ♔e6 63.♔e2 ♔d5 64.♔d3 ♗b6 65.g5 (but not 65.f5?? ♔e5 66.♔e2 ♗d4 67.♔f3 ♗c5 68.♔e2 ♔f4−+) 65...♔e6 66.g6 ♔f6 67.f5 ♗d4 68.♔e2 ♔xf5 69.g7.

Chess history has seen many upsets like this. Tseshkovsky resigned against Sax in a dead drawn rook ending, etc. Prolonged defence can lead to despair and hallucinations.

Anyhow, I qualified and thus became a World Championship Candidate (vs Robert Hübner) later in this period. Much later!

Jozsef Pinter
Andras Adorjan

Hungary tt 1977

1.d4 ♘f6 2.c4 e6 3.♘c3 ♗b4 4.e3 b6 5.♗d3 ♗b7 6.♘f3 0-0 7.0-0 c5 8.♘a4 cxd4 9.a3 ♗e7 10.exd4 d6 11.♖e1 ♘bd7 12.♘c3

12...a6

12...h6!? (very fine prevention! Compare this with the game Farago-Adorjan above) 13.d5 (13.b4 a6; for 13...♖e8 14.♗b2 a6 see Farago-Adorjan) 13... exd5 14.cxd5 ♘xd5 15.♘xd5 ♗xd5 16.♗h7+ (without taking!) 16...♔xh7 17.♕xd5 ♗f6 18.♗f4 ♗xb2 (18...♘e5 19.♘xe5 dxe5 20.♕e4+ ♔g8 21.♗xe5 ♖e8=) 19.♖ad1 ♖e8 (19...♘e5!?) 20.♕xf7 ♗xa3.

Here White can try something with 21.♗xh6! ♔xh6 22.♖e6+ ♖xe6 23.♕xe6+ g6 24.♕e3+ ♔g7 25.♕xa3 with good chances.

12...d5!? may be a sounder way to equalize, for example: 13.cxd5 ♘xd5 14.♘xd5 (14.♗d2 ♘xc3 15.bxc3 ♕c7=) 14...♗xd5 15.♗f4 ♘f6 16.♖c1 ♖c8=.

13.h3

It was possible to grab some space by 13.d5!? exd5 14.cxd5 b5 15.♗c2 ♘b6 16.♗b3 (16.♗g5 ♘bxd5 17.♕d3 g6 18.♖xe7 ♕xe7 19.♘xd5 ♗xd5 20.♕d4 ♔g7 21.♗xf6+ ♕xf6 22.♕xd5 ♕xb2 23.♕d1 ♖ac8 is materially OK for White, but Black's pieces are more active) 16...♖c8 17.♕d3 ♘c4, unclear.

13...♖e8 14.♗f4

Pinter and Farago were working together at the time. However, this variation did not bring either of them much luck against me.

14...♖c8

14...d5 15.cxd5 ♘xd5 16.♘xd5 ♗xd5 17.♖c1 b5 18.♗c7 ♕c8=.

15.♖c1

15.b4 g6 16.♖c1 ♗f8 and White is pushing against a 'Froschstellung'.

15...♕c7 16.♗h2?! ♕b8

17.♘e4?!

Against all principles. It was better to play 17.b4 ♕a8 18.♖e3. Now the indicated regrouping for Black is 18...♗f8 with the idea 19.♕e1 g6.

17...♘xe4 18.♗xe4 ♗xe4 19.♖xe4 b5!

Now that White is on the wrong foot. 19...♕b7!? 20.♖e2 d5 21.cxd5 ♕xd5 22.♖ec2 would have given White the somewhat freer play.

20.d5?

20.c5 ♕b7 was no good either, but 20.b3 ♕b6 (20...♞b6!? 21.♕d3 ♕b7 22.♖e2 a5 23.♖ec2 bxc4 24.bxc4 ♕a6) 21.♖e3 bxc4!? 22.bxc4 ♕a5 is still OK – the hanging pawns and the one on a3 are easily defensible and White has more space.

20...e5

Now the h2-bishop is out of play and Black is practically playing with a pawn up.

21.b3 ♞c5 22.♖e2

22.♖e3 was a bit better, after which Black keeps the upper hand by either 22...♕b7! or 22...e4 23.♞d4 (23.♞d2 ♗g5∓) 23...♞d3 (23...♗g5 24.♞f5).

22...bxc4 23.bxc4

23...♕b3! 24.♕xb3 ♞xb3 25.♖c3 ♞c5 26.♞e1 f5

And the game is practically over. You know why. By the way, Black could have grabbed a pawn by 26...♞a4! 27.♖c1 ♞b6 28.c5 (28.♖ec2 ♗g5) 28...♞xd5 29.c6 ♞c7∓.

27.g4 f4 28.♔g2 ♗f6

28...♖c7!?∓.

29.♖cc2 ♞b3 30.♖e4 ♞c5 31.♖ee2 ♖e7!

Oh YES!

32.f3 ♗h4! 33.♗g1 ♗xe1 34.♖xe1 ♖b7 35.♖ec1 ♔f7

Enjoying the position. Again there was a correct pawn grab: 35...♞d3 36.♖d1

♖b2 37.♖xb2 (37.♖dd2? ♞e1+–+) 37...♞xb2 38.♖b1 ♞xc4∓.

36.♖c3

The four-rook ending is pure torture: 36.♗xc5 ♖xc5 37.♖c3 ♔f6 38.h4 g6 39.g5+ ♔f5 40.♔f2 a5 41.♖1c2 a4∓/–+.

36...♔f6 37.h4 g6 38.♗f2 h5!

It's running like clockwork.

39.♔h3?

Again, after 39.♗xc5 ♖xc5 40.gxh5 gxh5 41.♔f2 ♔f5 penetration cannot be prevented.

39...♖b2 40.♖3c2 ♖b3 41.♖c3 ♖b2 42.♖3c2 hxg4+ 43.♔xg4

Forced, as 43.fxg4 runs into 43...♖b3+ 44.♖c3 ♖xc3+ 45.♖xc3 ♞e4.

43...♞d3 44.♗a7

44.♖xb2 ♞xb2 45.♖b1 ♞d3.

44...♖c7 45.♗g1 ♖cb7 46.♖xb2 ♖xb2 47.♖c3 ♖g2+ 48.♔h3 ♖g3+ 49.♔h2 ♖xf3

The win would have been achieved even more quickly by the following elegant knight dance: 49...♞e1 50.♗f2 ♞xf3+ 51.♔h1 ♖h3+ 52.♔g2 ♖h2+! 53.♔f1 ♞d2+ 54.♔e1 ♖xf2.

50.c5 dxc5 51.♗xc5 e4 52.♗d4+ ♔f5 53.♖c6 ♞e5

More crude was 53...e3 54.♖e6 ♖g3 55.♗c3 (55.♖e8 ♞e1) 55...♞f2 56.♗d4 ♞g4+ 57.♔h1 ♖f3 or 57...f3 58.♗xe3 ♞xe3 59.♖xe3 f2–+.

54.♗xe5 ♔xe5 55.♖xa6 ♔d5 56.♖xg6 e3 57.♔g2 e2 58.♖g5+ ♔e4 59.♖g8 ♖g3+ 0-1

Nice even movement by both!

Lots of back + forth moves till R93+, Rxf3!

Laszlo Kovacs
Andras Adorjan

Hungary tt 1978

1.e4 c5 2.♘f3 ♘c6 3.♘c3 ♘f6 4.d4 cxd4 5.♘xd4 e5 6.♘db5 d6 7.a4

Avoiding the extra-sharp Sveshnikov lines. But such defensive tactics are not often successful.

7...a6 8.♘a3 ♗e6 9.♘c4

9.♗c4 loses a pawn to the tactic 9...♘xe4! 10.♘xe4 (10.♗xe6 ♘xc3 11.♗xf7+ ♔xf7 12.bxc3 d5∓) 10...d5 11.♘g5 ♗xa3 12.♖xa3 (12.♘xe6 ♗b4+) 12...dxc4 13.♘xe6 ♕xd1+ 14.♔xd1 fxe6 with nice compensation for the extra doubled pawn.

9...♗e7 10.♗e3 0-0 11.f3

11.♗e2 ♘b4 12.♘b6 ♖b8 13.0-0 d5 14.exd5 ♘fxd5 15.♘bxd5 ♘xd5 16.♘xd5 ♗xd5=/∓.

11...b5!?

Grabbing the initiative at once! 11...♘b4 was also promising.

12.♘b6

Chickening out again. The proof of the pudding was in taking a bite:
12.axb5 axb5 13.♖xa8 ♕xa8 14.♘xb5 and now:

A) 14...♕b8 15.♘b6 ♗d8 16.♘d5 ♗xd5 17.exd5 ♘e7 18.c4 and now the question is: does Black have enough dark-square compensation for the pawn? It looks that way after 18...♗b6 18...♗a5+ (or 18...♗b6 19.♕d3) 19.♗d2 (19.♔f2 ♘f5) 19...♗xd2+ 20.♕xd2 ♕b6 21.♔f2 ♕a5+ 22.♕d2=.

B) Or also 14...♖b8 15.♘c7 ♕b7 16.♘xe6 fxe6 and ...d6-d5 is next (for if 17.♘b6 ♘d4!).

12...♖b8 13.♘bd5

Probably better was 13.axb5!? axb5 14.♘bd5.

13...♗xd5 14.exd5

14.♘xd5 bxa4 15.♖xa4 ♖xb2.

14...♘d4!

The position opens up anyway!

15.axb5 axb5 16.♗xd4 exd4 17.♕xd4

A must. Or else...
17.♘xb5?

A) 17...♕e8 starts a king hunt after 18.♕xd4 ♗d8+ 19.♔d1 ♖xb5 20.♗xb5 ♕xb5 21.♔c1 (21.c4 ♕b3+ 22.♔d2 ♘d7–+) 21...♗b6 22.c4 ♕b4 23.♕c3 ♕c5 24.♖e1 ♖c8 25.♔b1 ♕f2–+;

B) Even 17...♘xd5!? works, see 18.♕xd4 ♗h4+ 19.g3 ♘e3!' 20.♕d3 ♖e8 21.♔f2 ♕b6 22.♕d4 ♕xd4 23.♘xd4 ♗f6–+.

17...b4 18.♘d1?!

Better resistance could have been offered by 18.♘b5 ♖a8 19.♖xa8 ♕xa8 20.♗c4 ♕a1+ 21.♕d1 ♕xb2 22.0-0∓.

18...♘d7! 19.♗d3

On 19.♗e2, 19...♗f6 20.♕d3 ♖e8 keeps the initiative going.

19...♗f6

20.♕a7?

A fatal error – White was already short of time. Whichever way, Black's attack would have been very hard to parry:

A) 20.♕e3 ♖e8 21.♗e4 ♗g5–+;

B) 20.♕f4 ♖e8+ 21.♗e4 ♗d4;

C) 20.♕f2 ♖e8+ 21.♗e4 ♘c5 22.0-0 ♘xe4 23.fxe4 ♖xe4 24.c3 ♕e7∓.

20...♖e8+ 21.♔f2 ♘c5 22.♔f1 ♖b7 23.♕a5 ♕e7 24.♔f2 ♗h4+! 25.g3 ♘xd3+ 26.cxd3 ♕e2+ 27.♔g1

27...♗d8   **0-1**

A spectacular and brave attacking game. Wasn't it?

Chapter 6

It Doesn't Matter... Or Does It?

Nakamura vs Gelfand / Gelfand vs Nakamura

by Peter Boel

Even in this book we have to admit that it doesn't happen very often that statistics between two players are clearly in favour of Black. Certainly not at the top level. However, there is one quite notable exception. Between Boris Gelfand and Hikaru Nakamura the statistics favour the black side very strongly. Especially in the period until the end of 2013 the numbers were striking: 12 wins for Black versus 1 for White! How could this be? Do the 'chess laws' not apply to these two players?

With Nakamura we might perhaps expect the statistics to go topsy-turvy. Especially in his early years as an upcoming grandmaster, he liked to experiment in the openings – not necessarily gaining an advantage with white (playing openings like 1.e4 e5 2.♕h5), and displaying enormous resilience and fighting spirit with black (the King's Indian!).

'I don't really distinguish between Black and White', was Nakamura's initial reaction when asked during an interview with Dirk Jan ten Geuzendam at the World Cup in Baku, September 2015. 'I think it's equal. It depends on your style and the openings you use, but in general there is no advantage for White.' However, the American ace player immediately went on to mention some of the mechanisms we all recognize too well: 'With white you try to press; with black you try to play solidly and hold the draw.' Mind you, he said this in 2015, when he might have mellowed down a bit compared to earlier years. As Anish Giri wrote in his 2015 book After Magnus: 'Lately, Hikaru has become a lot more solid', and Jan Timman agreed in New In Chess 2016/2: 'With quiet positional play he maintains the tension, striking when his opponent loses the thread.' Still, for a fighter like Nakamura it remains interesting to play with black: 'Opponents try harder with white, which is more interesting for me because it becomes more dynamic.'

Nakamura's reply reflects the general philosophy that white players feel obliged to put pressure on their opponents because they have the first move. Which is not necessarily an advantage. This is what Anish Giri wrote in New In Chess 2015/7 in his report about the World Cup in Baku: 'I would have talked a lot about the importance of the white game in a two-game match, had I not lost in the semi-finals against Peter Svidler precisely due to my refusal to abandon the idea of the advantage of the white pieces, when I should have contented myself with a draw in my white game...' It is not unlike the pressure a stronger player may feel when he is paired against a weaker opponent: he is expected to win, and this subjects him to psychological pressure. The weaker player has nothing to lose, and this may lead to upsets now and then.

About pressuring and putting the squeeze on your opponent, Boris Gelfand wrote a fantastic book with Jacob Aagaard last year. In Positional Decision Making in Chess he elaborated on various ways to apply such pressure, in the style of his idol Rubinstein – in his white games. As Gelfand claims on page 71: often '...Black needs to find a way to solve his problems though White does not have an obvious advantage.' That does imply that White should have some edge from the start, doesn't it?

'Well, not an advantage', Gelfand replied during a Skype conversation with the author of this chapter. 'But in general White has more possibilities to determine the course of the game. Yes, if White plays 1.e4 Black can also determine what happens with his choice of move. But after, say, 1...c5, if White does not want too much theory he can play 2.c3, or 2.♘f3 and 3.♗b5. Generally White can strive for positions where Black can get no initiative, or has to create dubious complications to do this. With black you have a problem especially if you play someone who is dreaming of making a draw with you. If White wants a game, then there will be a game, and both players will have their chances.'

Of course Gelfand has also played many dynamic games in his career, as a top player's arsenal cannot be too one-sided. After all, White does not determine what happens entirely on his own. Gelfand himself writes, on page 61 of his book: 'These days, it is quite common for Black players to use dynamics as a way to counter the slight pressure White gets from the start.' 'In the next volumes after Positional Decision Making we will write more about the dynamic aspect of chess', the Israeli grandmaster announced on Skype.

A lot depends on who is sitting at the opposite side of the board. 'Against some players it doesn't matter much', Gelfand says. 'But in chess history, it was never nice to play Black against Polugaevsky or Portisch. Against Kortchnoi it didn't matter so much. There would always be a fight anyway. But for instance against Kramnik it is definitely better to have White. It started with Fischer, Polugaevsky and Portisch, I think. They tried to play classical chess with white, and with black they would play openings like the Najdorf and the King's Indian. With white they relied on their technique. If you gave them a tiny advantage, you would lose. This attitude has become common at the top level, and I would attribute that to these three players. For many years this worked for me too. It was my attitude even in my World Championship match with Anand (in 2012): with white, play classical chess, with black: play the Grünfeld or the Najdorf and try to put pressure on your opponent. Today things have become more flexible, as there are so many data available – even compared with, say, 10 years ago. Every player has a fully-fledged repertoire with white today.'

This reflects an approach that will not be alien to the majority of top grandmasters. All the more so, Gelfand's extreme plus score with black against Nakamura (and vice versa!) is a striking phenomenon. Until late 2013, Gelfand often was Black. And he won 9 times, against Nakamura 3 times.

'With Nakamura, if both sides go for an open game, then Black has chances', Gelfand says. 'I only look at games with a classical tempo, because with rapid or blitz strange things can happen. One time he flagged me when I was winning.'

That was the following game. By the way, for every game in this chapter we will add the ratings both players had at the time, for comparison.

7

Boris Gelfand	2741
Hikaru Nakamura	2741

Moscow Wch blitz 2010 (13)

34...♖xb2?

A little trap, as White cannot take on a4 due to 35...♕d1+. However, White has a nasty intermediate move. Black should have played 34...♕d2 or 34...♕d1+.

35.♖d4! ♕e8 36.♕xa5

Winning a piece due to the threat of 37.♖d8.

36...♗d7 37.♕c7 ♕a8 38.♖xd7 ♕a1+ 39.♗f1 ♕e1 40.♕c5 ♖b1 41.♕c4 ♖b2 42.♕d4 ♖b1 43.♕d3 ♖b2 44.♕f3 f6 45.♕e3 ♕a1 46.♔g2 ♖b1 47.♕d3 ♖b2 48.♕c4 ♔h7 49.♕xe6 **0-1**

Here Gelfand's flag fell.

Two days later in Moscow, he took his revenge – with black, when Nakamura, with white, overpressed. In those days, the young American's over-confidence could still play tricks on him.

Hikaru Nakamura	2741
Boris Gelfand	2741

Moscow Wch blitz 2010 (32)

Nakamura goes on the attack:

16.0-0 fxe5 17.dxe5?

But this looks like insufficient compensation. White is better after 17.♗xg6 ♖xf1+ 18.♖xf1 hxg6 19.♕xg6 exd4 20.exd4 and although Black can now quickly develop with 20...♘f8 21.♕c2 ♗e6, there is still some pressure after 22.♕b3.

17...♖xf1+ 18.♖xf1 ♘dxe5 19.♗xe5 ♕xe5 20.♕f3 ♗e6 21.♗xg6 hxg6

Black is just a healthy pawn up on the queenside now.

22.♘e2 ♖e8 23.b4 ♗f5 24.g4 ♗e4 25.♕f7+

This doesn't help much.

25...♔h7 26.♘d4

Of course not 26.♕xb7? ♗d3.

26...♕e7 27.♕xe7 ♖xe7 28.g5 ♔g8 29.h4 ♗d3

And since now White is the one with the weak pawns, Black won without much trouble.

'In another rapid game, in Odessa in 2007, I was losing, but he overpressed and even lost', Gelfand recalled. Again. Here is that game.

Hikaru Nakamura	2651
Boris Gelfand	2733

Odessa rapid 2007 (1)

34...♖h8!?

Gelfand doesn't want to wait passively. After the cool-headed 34...♔f7, or also 34...g5!?, clearing a square for the king, there is no win in sight for White. The text loses a pawn.

35.♖xa7+ ♔f6 36.♖b7

If 36.♔g1, Black wins by 36...♖d8 or 36...e3.

36...♖xh2 37.♖xb5 e3

Again, there is still this little peasant to annoy White.

38.a4 ♖f2+ 39.♔e1 ♖g2 40.a5 ♖xg3 41.a6 ♖g1+ 42.♔e2

42...♖a1?

After 42...g3! 43.a7 ♖a1 White would have had to give his a-pawn, as otherwise Black's kingside pawns will be first!

43.♖b6+ ♔g7 44.♔xe3

Now White is winning, even after Black creates two connected passed pawns:

44...g5 45.fxg5

The white king is too close, and he now threatens to push his c-pawn.

45...g3 46.♔f3 f4

47.a7?

He shouldn't have given up this pawn so easily. After 47.♖b7+ ♔g6 48.a7 ♔xg5 now White would have time for 49.c4, as 49...♖f1+ 50.♔g2 ♖f2+ 51.♔g1 f3, which would save Black after the immediate 47.c4, is too slow here: White has time to queen his a-pawn.

47...♖xa7 48.♖b4 ♖f7 49.♖d4 ♖f5 50.b4 ♖xg5!

Oops – no time to take on f4.

51.♖d2 ♔f6 52.c4 ♔e7 53.c5 ♖g6 54.♖g2 ♖f6 55.♖d2 ♖g6 56.♖e2+ ♔d8 57.♖g2 ♖f6 58.♖d2+ ♔c8 59.♖a2 ♖g6 60.♖d2 ♖g5 61.♖g2 ♖d5 62.♔e4 ♖d1 63.b5

63.♔xf4 ♖d4+ is also a draw, of course.

63...♖e1+

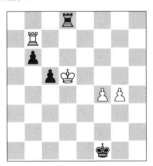

64.♔d5??

Nakamura wants too much and miscalculates. 64.♔xf4 was an easy draw.

64...f3 65.♖xg3 f2 66.♖g8+ ♔b7 67.♖g7+ ♔c8 68.♖g8+ ♔b7

After one more rook check Gelfand would probably have played the winning 70...♔d7 71.c6+ (71.♖g7+ ♔e8) 71...♔e7 72.c7 f1♕ 73.c8♕ ♖d1+ and Black wins in the attack.

69.c6+?? ♔b6

Now White runs out of checks.

70.♖b8+ ♔c7   0-1

Great fun for the spectators, but too many mistakes for a top player's taste. Classical chess is what really counts, Gelfand argues. 'In that discipline I beat him six times. Some of these wins were in the years when I was still clearly stronger than him.'

In Biel, 2005, a sharp theoretical Najdorf Sicilian set the scene for the first encounter between these two great fighters.

| Hikaru Nakamura | 2660 |
| Boris Gelfand | 2724 |

Biel 2005 (10)

1.e4 c5 2.♘f3 d6 3.d4 cxd4 4.♘xd4 ♘f6 5.♘c3 a6 6.♗g5 e6 7.f4 ♘bd7 8.♕f3 ♕c7 9.0-0-0 b5 10.♗d3 ♗b7 11.♖he1 ♕b6 12.♘d5

This sacrifice has been known since the famous game Chiburdanidze-Dvoirys, Tallinn 1980, which went 12...exd5 13.♘c6! and White won a beautiful game – the 'Tallinn Pearl'. But since then, a remedy for Black has been found:

12...♕xd4 13.♗xf6 gxf6 14.♗xb5 ♕c5 15.♘xf6+ ♔d8 16.♘xd7 ♕xb5 17.♘xf8 ♖xf8 18.♕a3 ♖c8 19.♕xd6+ ♔e8

20.c3

In a game with Krum Georgiev, in Saint Affrique later that year, Tony Kosten introduced the move 20.♖e3!. At first a few games were drawn after 20...♕c6 21.♕d2 ♔e7 22.♕b4+ ♔f6, but then, two years later, Fabiano Caruana tried 23.c3 ♕c5 (23...♕c7 24.e5+ ♔g7 25.f5 exf5 26.♕f4, and White's two pawns plus initiative still more than weigh up for the piece) 24.e5+ ♔f5 25.g4+ ♔g6 26.f5+ ♔g7 27.♕f4 ♔h8 28.♕h6 ♗g2 29.♖d2 (29.♖d7! ♕c4 30.b3 ♕f1+ 31.♔b2 ♕f2+ 32.♔a3 ♕g1 33.♖ed3 ♕c5+ 34.♔b2 ♕xe5 35.f6 ♕e2+ 36.♖d2 ♕xg4 37.♕g7+, or 37.♖7d3! and White is winning) 29...♕b5 (29...♕c4 30.♕f6+ ♔g8 31.♕g5+ ♔h8 32.b3 ♕f1+ 33.♔b2 a5! with sufficient counterplay) 30.b3 (30.♖f2!+−) 30...♖g8? (30...♕f1+ 31.♔b2 a5 32.a4! and White has a plus) 31.♔b2 ♕f1 32.♕f6+ ♖g7 33.♖ed3! ♗d5 34.fxe6 and Black resigned in Caruana-Dworakowska, Gibraltar 2007.

20...♕c6 21.♕b4 a5!

With this move Black gradually takes over. All the tactics work for him.

22.♕xa5 ♖a8 23.♕g5

23.♕b4 ♖xa2 24.♖d6 ♖a4! 25.♖xc6 ♖xb4 26.♖c7 ♖xe4 gives Black a clear advantage;

23.♕d5? ♕xc3+ – Gelfand.

23...f6

24.♕d5?

Elegant, but not best. Gelfand demonstrated that Black still has to fight for a draw after 24.♕h5+ ♖f7 25.a3 ♖xa3 26.bxa3 ♕xc3+=; or 24.♕g7 ♖xa2 25.♖d4 ♕b5 26.b3 (26.♖b4? ♕d3) 26...♖a1+ 27.♔d2 ♖a2+ 28.♔c1= (28.♔e3 e5).

24...♕xc3+! 25.bxc3 exd5 26.exd5+ ♔d7 27.♔b1 ♖a4 28.g3 ♖fa8!

With this accurate move, Black goes on to win.

29.♖d2 ♖8a5

Winning the d-pawn. After White's reply the bishop comes into action.

30.d6? ♗e4+ 31.♔a1 h5–+ 32.h3 ♗d5 33.g4 ♖xa2+ 34.♖xa2 ♖xa2+ 35.♔b1 ♖h2 36.♖e3 h4 37.♔c1 ♔xd6 38.f5 ♖f2 39.♔d1 ♖f3 0-1

And here is the first 'white sheep' from this chapter.

Boris Gelfand 2733
Hikaru Nakamura 2651
Odessa 2007 (1)

A good example of the 'Rubinstein squeeze'. Nakamura has been under pressure all along but has defended well. The endgame is nearly equal... nearly.

58.♗e3 ♗e1?!

He should have gone 58...♔f5!, when after 59.♗d7 Black has the tempo move 59...♗e1. There is no way to make progress for White now, for example: 60.♔c4 ♔e4 61.♗b6 ♘xf4.

59.♗d3 ♗g3 60.♔e4 ♗e1 61.f5

61...♘f8

More tenacious seems 61...♘g5+, but it's also depressing for Black after 62.♔d5 ♗c3 (62...♗b4 63.♗d4+ ♔e7 64.f6+ leaves Black without space) 63.♗b6 ♘f3 64.♗d8+ ♔g7 65.f6+! ♗xf6 66.♗xa5 and the a-pawn decides.

62.♗xh6 ♘d7 63.♗e3

Threatening to drive the king back again.

63...♗c3 64.h6 ♘e5 65.♗e2 ♘d7

66.♗d4+! ♗xd4 67.♔xd4 ♘f8 68.♔c5 ♔g5

On 68...♔xf5 69.h7 ♘xh7 70.♗d3+ is just one of several ways to win; White can also start with 69.♗d3+ and walk to the queenside.

69.♔b5 ♔xh6 70.♔xa5 ♔g5 71.♗d3 ♔f6 72.♔b5 ♔e5 73.♔c6   **1-0**

Another black win for Gelfand came two years later, in the Austrian team championship.

Hikaru Nakamura	2699
Boris Gelfand	2733

Austria Bundesliga 2008/09 (4)

Black's superiority here is mainly due to his better pawn structure, and the fact that he has more targets than White.

26.♘e4

Now the computer prefers withdrawing the queen to c7 or e7, but Gelfand confidently goes for the endgame. Perhaps he trusted Nakamura to make a desperate attempt when pushed far enough. If so, he was proved right.

26...♕b4 27.♕xb4 ♘xb4 28.f4!?

Yes, going wild already!

28...gxf4 29.g5 ♔f8

It looks dangerous for Black on the kingside, but he is always one step ahead as on 30.♘xf4, d4 is hanging.

30.♖gf1 ♘d5

Now threatening with a fork on e3, compelling White to give up the d-pawn.

31.♘xf4 ♘xf4 32.♖xf4 ♖xd4! 33.♖xd4 ♗xd4

34.♖f3

Black's point is 34.g6 (or 34.gxh6) 34...♖c1+! 35.♔xc1 ♗e3+ 36.♔c2 ♗xf4, in both cases with good winning chances in the ending. A nice 'echo line' is 34.♖xf7+ ♔xf7 35.♘d6+, but this is not serious as Black wins easily after 35...♔g8!.

34...♔e7! 35.gxh6 ♖h8 36.♖a3 b5 37.♖a5 f5 38.♘g3 ♗f2 39.♘h1 ♗b6 40.♖xb5 ♖xh6 41.a4 ♖xh5 42.♘g3 ♖g5 43.♘e2 ♖g2   **0-1**

The e- and f-pawns are a formidable force.

In those times, Nakamura gave the impression in many of his games that it didn't matter whether he was White or Black. His approach with black was not so dissimilar to Gelfand's: play a sharp opening and try to put pressure on the guy – more or less what he was doing with white! But his White approach has changed over the years.

'When Gelfand is White I tend to play the King's Indian', Nakamura says. 'Then he tries to punish me because I play the King's Indian and, you know, it's not "correct chess".' It's certainly an approach one would expect to see from Nakamura against an opponent who invariably plays 1.d4. As a matter of fact, however, the King's Indian came on the board only once in a decided game between these two rivals in this initial period. And it was a real show-stopper.

Excellent

Attack of the pawn people!

Boris Gelfand	2761
Hikaru Nakamura	2708

Bursa Wch tt 2010 (5)

1.d4 ♘f6 2.c4 g6 3.♘c3 ♗g7 4.e4 d6 5.♘f3 0-0 6.♗e2 e5 7.0-0 ♘c6 8.d5 ♘e7 9.♘d2 ♘e8 10.b4 f5 11.c5 ♘f6 12.f3 f4 13.♘c4 g5 14.a4 ♘g6 15.♗a3 ♖f7 16.b5 dxc5 17.♗xc5 h5 18.a5 g4 19.b6 g3 20.♔h1 ♗f8 21.d6 axb6 22.♗g1

22...♘h4!?

Vintage Nakamura – he goes all out on the kingside, never looking back at the ruins on his queenside.

23.♖e1

On 23.♘xe5, 23...♗h3! 24.♗d4 ♗xg2+ wins for Black, as Lubomir Ftacnik wrote in his analysis in ChessBase MegaBase at the time. But the Czech GM indicated as stronger 23.hxg3! fxg3 24.♗e3 and apparently the threats to g2 can be defended, for example: 24...♗h3 25.♖g1 ♗xg2+ 26.♖xg2 ♖g7 27.♘d5 ♗xd6. Now 28.♘dxb6 (Houdini) appears stronger than Ftacnik's 28.♘xd6 ♕xd6 29.axb6 (with only a small advantage for White), for example:

A) 28...cxb6 29.♘xd6 followed by a check on the a2-g8 diagonal: 29...bxa5 (29...♖xa5 30.♕b3+ ♔h7 31.♖d1!) 30.♗c4+ ♔h7 31.♖d2 ♕c7 32.♖c1 and White takes over – his king can go to g1;

B) 28...♖b8 29.♘xd6 cxd6 30.♕d2 or 30.♕b3 and White is clearly better.

23...♘xg2! 24.dxc7?

24.♔xg2 ♖g7 25.dxc7 gxh2+ 26.♔h1! hxg1♕+ 27.♖xg1 ♕xc7 28.axb6 ♖xa1 29.bxc7 ♖xd1 30.♗xd1 (Ftacnik) leads to an equal endgame.

24...♘xe1! 25.♕xe1 g2+! 26.♔xg2 ♖g7+ 27.♔h1 ♗h3 28.♗f1

28.♕f2 ♕xc7! 29.♘b5 (29.axb6 ♕b8 30.♖xa8 ♕xa8 31.♗f1 ♗c5!−+) 29...♕d8! followed by the lethal 30...♗c5.

28...♕d3!

Nice one, centurion!

29.♘xe5 ♗xf1 30.♕xf1

Obviously the queen still cannot be taken on account of mate on g2.

30...♕xc3 31.♖c1 ♕xe5 32.c8♕ ♖xc8 33.♖xc8 ♕e6   **0-1**

Later that year, Gelfand struck back again in the Youth versus Experience tournament in Amsterdam, 2010. For both players, this tournament was a great success. Gelfand became the overall winner with 7/10 (although

Both players push the maximum of risky moves. 24.dxc7!

Youth beat Experience in this last edition of the series) and Nakamura shared second place with Anish Giri on 6. Gelfand opines that Nakamura still had some way to go at the time. 'Probably he was deceived by his high rating, and he thought he could win. But I outplayed him.'

Still, this too was a real fight. 'He wasn't thinking of a draw, he was playing chess.'

Hikaru Nakamura	2729
Boris Gelfand	2739

Amsterdam 2010 (5)

1.c4 c6 2.e4 d5 3.exd5 cxd5 4.d4 ♘f6 5.♘c3 ♘c6 6.♗g5 e6 7.♘f3 ♗e7 8.♗d3? dxc4 9.♗xc4 0-0 10.0-0

Now a well-known position has come on the board, only with Black to move, because of White's tempo loss with 8.♗d3. Gelfand took a lot of time to decide whether he would fight for an advantage, instead of just maintaining equality. For the moment he carries on playing 'normal moves' – which is often the best way to get an advantage.

10...a6 11.♗d3 b5 12.♕e2!?

12...♘xd4!?

Gelfand goes for it! 'I felt that Black does not risk much with this exchange sacrifice', he wrote in his analysis of the game in ChessBase MegaBase. In the tournament Gelfand had already sacrificed the exchange against Caruana and Giri, 'but in those games I had no choice.' Here the sacrifice clearly is a bid to spice up the game.

The 'normal' way to play was 12...♗b7 13.♖ad1 ♖c8, with a typical isolani position which would be OK for Black, but obviously less adventurous. Gelfand is playing from a position of strength here: he considers himself to be the better player, and wants to give Nakamura a taste of his own medicine, as if to say: 'I can also beat you on your own turf'.

13.♘xd4 ♕xd4 14.♗e4 ♖b8 15.♗f4 ♘xe4 16.♗xb8 ♗b7

17.♗g3?!

17.♘xe4 ♖xb8 18.♖fe1 (18.♘c3 is also roughly balanced, according to Gelfand, but Black may still have something after 18...♕f4 or 18...b4 19.♖ad1 ♕f4 20.♘a4 ♗c6 21.♕xa6 ♕e4 22.f3 ♕e3+ 23.♖f2 ♗xa4 24.♕xa4 ♗c5) and now 18...♗d5 looks more solid than Gelfand's 18...♗xe4 19.♖ad1 ♕f6 20.♕xe4 ♕xb2, after which Black has to fight for the draw.

Gelfand feared the sharp 17.♖fd1!? but managed to calculate that Black is in no danger after 17...♘xc3 18.bxc3 ♕xc3 19.♗e5 ♕b4! 20.♖ab1 ♕e4.

17...♘xc3 18.bxc3 ♕d5 19.f3 ♕c5+ 20.♗f2 ♕xc3

Another squeeze! White has to wait and see what Black comes up with to win. It is really torturous for any player – especially a young one – to have to defend such a position. Sometimes you may be worse, and then you try to create some chaos to try and confuse the 'old guy'. There's no chance of that here. Black doesn't force anything, but keeps the tension, playing largely on intuition. Don't calculate too much, as then you might make mistakes.

21.a4! ♗d5

The queen swap 21...♛c4 might also still give winning chances, followed by slowly pushing his majority on the kingside.

22.♖fc1	**♛b3**	**23.axb5 axb5**
24.♗c5!	**♗xc5+**	**25.♖xc5 ♛b4**
26.♛e3	**♛b2**	**27.♖cc1 ♗c4**
28.♛c3		

Losing patience. With queens on the board White might have kept more counterchances.

28...♛xc3 29.♖xc3 g5! 30.♖ca3 ♗d5 31.♖b1 ♖b8 32.♖b4 ♗c4 33.h4?

Gelfand indicated 33.♖c3 ♖d8 34.♖bxc4 bxc4 35.♖xc4, sacrificing the exchange for a theoretical draw in the rook ending. He makes a very interesting addition here, citing Jacob Aagaard's trainer Henrik Mortensen, who said that 'you don't have a winning position unless you also know that you're going to win it'. Logically, this should also be

valid for drawn positions. These rook endings may be theoretically drawn, but even a world-class player can never be sure that he will draw it. We have seen many examples of the stronger side winning this ending, even at the highest level.

Gelfand wrote: 'In many of his interviews, my opponent did not assign much importance to endgame knowledge, and it's possible that he had to pay for that in this game.' Be that as it may, Nakamura's persistence has made up for this in many more recent cases.

33...gxh4 34.♔h2 ♖d8 35.♖e3 f5 36.♖e5 ♔f7 37.♔h3 ♔f6 38.♖c5 ♔g5 39.♖cxc4? bxc4 40.♖xc4 ♖d1! 41.♔h2 e5 42.♖a4 ♖d6 43.♔g1 ♖d4 44.♖a7 h6 45.♖h7 h3! 46.g3 ♖d3

Here and in the following there may have been quicker ways to win, but the squeeze has done its job.

47.♖g7+ ♔f6 48.♖h7 ♖xf3 49.♔h2 ♔g6 50.♖e7 ♖e3 51.♖e8 e4 52.♖f8 ♖f3 53.♔xh3 ♖f2 54.♖e8 ♔f7 55.♖a8 e3 56.♖a3 e2 57.♖e3 f4 58.gxf4 ♖f3+! 59.♖xf3 e1♛ 60.♔g2 ♛e2+ 61.♖f2 ♛g4+ 62.♔h2 h5 63.f5 ♔f6 64.♖g2 ♛h4+ 65.♔g1 ♛e1+ 66.♔h2 ♔xf5 67.♖g8 ♛e5+ 68.♔h3 ♛e6 69.♖g1 ♔f4+ 70.♔h2 ♛e4 71.♖g3 ♛e2+ 72.♖g2 ♛e1 73.♖g8 ♔f3 74.♖g2 ♛h4+ 75.♔g1 ♛g4

White resigned.

The return game in Amsterdam ended in a draw after a tense King's Indian fight. In that same year there followed two more draws: at the Olympiad in Khanty-Mansiysk, and at the Tal Memorial in Moscow. In early 2011 their blindfold game in Monaco also ended peacefully. But in the rapid game Black again came out on top.

Hikaru Nakamura 2774
Boris Gelfand 2733

Monte Carlo rapid 2011 (6)

14.dxc5?!

Nakamura wants to play against the hanging pawns, but it turns out that Black comes first, especially since he can put pressure on the pawn on b2.
With the standard 14.♘f4 cxd4 15.exd4 ♘xd4 16.♕d3 and taking back on d5, White could have maintained equality.

14...bxc5 15.♖fd1 c4! 16.♘f4 ♘e5 17.♕h3

17.♕g3 ♗d6 18.♕h3! might actually have been quite clever as the d6-bishop is in the queen's way and d5 is hanging.

17...♖b8

18.♖c2?

18.b3! ♖b7 (18...cxb3 19.axb3 ♖xb3 20.♗e1 ♗a3 21.♖c2 ♕c8 22.♕xc8 ♖xc8 23.♖a2=) 19.♗e1 ♖d7∓ is given as the best defence by Ftacnik in ChessBase MegaBase.

18...♘d3! 19.♕f3 d4! 20.exd4 ♖xb2 21.♖xb2 ♘xb2 22.♖c1 ♕xd4

Now Black is a pawn up while he keeps the initiative.

23.♗e3 ♕e5 24.g3 ♘d3 25.♘xd3 cxd3 26.♗d2 ♕d4 27.♖b1 ♕c4 28.♖b3 ♗b4 29.♔g2 a5 30.♘b1 ♖d8! 31.♗xb4 axb4 32.♘d2 ♕c2 33.♕f4 ♘d5 34.♕h4 f6

35.♕c4? ♕xd2   **0-1**

After the capture on d3 there is a knight check on f4.

At Tata Steel in the following year – the edition won by Aronian – it was again time for Nakamura to strike. He did well in the Dutch coastal town with 7½, while Gelfand had a bad tournament with 5 out of 13.

Excellent 10

Boris Gelfand 2739
Hikaru Nakamura 2759

Wijk aan Zee 2012 (6)

1.d4 f5

Not the King's Indian this time, but an even more provocative choice. Nakamura is still confident – even against his Nemesis!

2.g3 ♘f6 3.♗g2 g6 4.c4 ♗g7 5.♘c3 0-0 6.♘f3 d6 7.0-0 c6 8.d5

Kramnik had crushed Nakamura with 8.♖b1 two years earlier in the same tournament.

8...e5 9.dxe6 ♗xe6 10.b3

En Passant !

Best of Book

106

10...♖e8

Nakamura had also dabbled with 10...♘e4 11.♘xe4 fxe4 (11...♗xa1 12.♘xd6±) 12.♘d4 ♗f7 in 2010.

11.♗b2　♘a6　12.♘g5　♕e7
13.♘xe6　♕xe6　14.♕c2　♘c5
15.♖ad1　♖ad8　16.e3　♘ce4
17.♘xe4 fxe4 18.♖d2

This was a novelty. In an earlier game, Gelfand's second, Alexander Khuzman, had attacked the d-pawn by tripling on the d-file: 18.♖d4 d5 19.cxd5 cxd5 20.♕d2 ♖d7 21.♖d1 ♘h5 22.♖a4 ♗xb2 23.♕xb2 a6 24.♖ad4 ♘f6= Khuzman-Neiksans, Batumi 1999.

18...d5 19.cxd5 cxd5 20.♕c5 b6
21.♕b5 ♘h5 22.♗a3 ♗f8 23.♗b2
♗g7 24.♗a3

24...♗e5!?

Nakamura spurns the draw. He could also have tried 24...d4!? 25.exd4 ♗xd4 but the bishop can't escape its counterpart after 26.♗b2= (a line given by Mihail Marin in ChessBase MegaBase).

25.♖c1 ♘f6 26.♖dc2 d4 27.♖c6 ♕f5
28.exd4 ♗xd4 29.♕xf5 gxf5 30.♗h3
e3 31.♗xf5 exf2+ 32.♔f1 ♗e3

The f-pawn looks more dangerous than it actually is, but White does need to be careful.

33.♖b1 ♘e4 34.♗xe4 ♖xe4

35.♖c2?

As several more times in this book, this rook move is the decisive mistake!
Now the doubling on the d-file is immediately fatal. Necessary was 35.♖d6! ♖xd6 36.♗xd6 ♔g7 37.♖d1 ♔g6 38.♗b8 a5 39.♖d6+ ♔f5 40.♖d5+=; or 35...♖c8 36.♖bd1 ♖c2 37.♖d8+ and the black king cannot escape the checks either.

35...♖ed4 36.♔e2　♖d1 37.♖xd1
♖xd1　　　　　　　　　　　　0-1

And later that year Black was victorious once more, when Gelfand quite sneakily stepped away from his beloved Najdorf and tried the Sveshnikov. In this tournament, the roles were reversed again: Gelfand performed very well, ending shared first with Topalov and Mamedyarov, while Nakamura had probably his worst tournament ever, sharing last place with 4 out of 11 (and again, Giri had the same score).

Hikaru Nakamura　　　　　2783
Boris Gelfand　　　　　　2738
London 2012 (1)
1.e4 c5 2.♘f3 ♘c6 3.d4 cxd4 4.♘xd4
♘f6 5.♘c3 e5 6.♘db5 d6 7.♘d5

Avoiding the main line 7.♗g5.

7...♘xd5 8.exd5 ♘b8 9.a4 ♗e7 10.♗e2 0-0 11.0-0 ♘d7 12.♔h1 f5 13.f4 a6 14.♘a3 exf4

Quite straightforward. The more circumspect approach 14...♗f6 15.♘c4 ♘b6 had been tried several times earlier.

15.♗xf4 ♘e5 16.♕d2 ♗d7 17.♕b4

17...♖b8! 18.c4 a5! 19.♕b3 ♘g6 20.♗e3 b6

'Sealing off' the queenside.

21.♘b5 ♗xb5 22.axb5 ♗g5 23.♗g1 ♘e5 24.♕a3 ♗d2! 25.♖ad1 ♗b4 26.♕h3 ♕g5 27.♗e3 ♕f6 28.♗d4

28.g4! ♘xg4 (28...g6?? 29.gxf5 gxf5 30.♗d3!+−) 29.♗xg4 fxg4 30.♖xf6 gxh3 31.♖xf8+ ♔xf8 32.♖f1+ is equal (Sergey Erenburg, ChessBase MegaBase).

28...♗c5 29.♗c3 ♕g5

Gelfand was short of time here, so Nakamura changes the direction of the game. But it doesn't really work out.

30.♗xe5?! dxe5 31.g4 fxg4?!

31...f4 gave some winning chances. White can put up a blockade on the light squares, but Black can carefully prepare ...h7-h5.

32.♕xg4 ♕xg4 33.♗xg4 ♗d6 34.♗e6+ ♔h8 35.♔g2 g6 36.b3 ♔g7 37.h3?!

37.♖de1 would have prevented the following surprising and very dangerous push:

37...e4! 38.♗g4?!

It was not yet too late for 38.♖de1!. Then, 38...♖xf1 (38...♗c5 39.♖xe4 ♖xf1 40.♔xf1 ♖f8+ 41.♔e1 ♖f3 42.♔d2 with the idea 42...♖xb3 43.d6) 39.♖xf1 (39.♔xf1 ♖f8+ 40.♔g2 ♖f3) 39...♖f8 40.♖xf8 ♗xf8 leads to an opposite-coloured bishops ending where White has to suffer, but Sergey Erenburg analysed this to a draw: White controls the g- and h-pawns with ♗g8!, ♗f7! and ♗e8, and can then protect the b3-pawn with his king.

As Gelfand often stresses in *Positional Decision Making in Chess*, it doesn't matter whether such positions are objectively winning or not: 'It is simply easier to play positions where you are applying pressure than to play positions where everything you do will lead to an inferior position' (page 82).

38...h5

39.♗e2?

Now White cannot attack the e-pawn, and Black will double his rooks and get an attack. White could still go for the opposite-coloured bishops ending with 39.♗e6 ♗b4 40.♖xf8 ♖xf8 41.♖f1 ♖xf1 42.♔xf1, but in this version it's easier for the black king to penetrate to b3: 42...♔f6 43.♔e2 g5 and now the black kingside pawns are harder to control.

39...♖f6!? 40.♖de1

Again, the bishop ending after 40.♖xf6 ♔xf6 41.♖f1+ ♔e5 42.♖f7 ♖f8 is hard to defend for White, since his bishop is passive.

40...♖f5! 41.♗d1 ♖bf8 42.♖xf5

42.♗c2 ♖g5+ 43.♔h1 ♖f3! (Erenburg) with a big attack.

42...gxf5 43.♗xh5 ♔f6

The two centre pawns are an awesome force.

44.♖h1 ♔g5 45.♗d1 ♔h4 46.♖f1 ♖g8+ 47.♔h1 ♖g5 48.♗c2 ♔xh3 49.♖f2 ♔g3 50.♖h2 ♖g4 51.♖g2+ ♔f4 52.♖f2+ ♔g5 53.♖d2 ♖g3 54.♖e2 ♖h3+ 55.♔g1 ♔f4 56.♔g2 ♖h2+! 57.♔f1 ♖xe2 58.♔xe2 ♔e5

White resigned.

Nakamura's comment on this loss in New In Chess 2012/8 is interesting: 'Once I failed to draw that game, and then I didn't win the games in the middle, it all really just spiralled out of control.' The same can actually be said about the game itself. All the experts agreed that White missed the draw around move 37, but as Gelfand's comments make clear, that wasn't at all easy. In fact, it was more logical for Black to win the game even if it was objectively drawn. If you have managed to equalize with black, after that you often get a slight edge, and you are on your way to winning the game.

At the Tal Memorial in 2013, one of his greatest tournament successes, Gelfand beat Nakamura again with black. We will present that game in Chapter 8, which has that quite special tournament as its subject.

Later that year Gelfand won again – this time in a brilliant attacking game in his beloved Najdorf.

Hikaru Nakamura   2772
Boris Gelfand   2764

Elancourt 2013 (10)

21...♖fc8!

It's do or die in this position. For instance: 21...♘c4?! 22.♘d5! (22.♗xc4 ♗xc4 23.♗xg7 ♔xg7 24.f5 ♕e5+=) 22...♗xd5 23.exd5 ♘xb2 (otherwise Black simply loses material) 24.♔xb2 ♖c3 25.♗xg7! ♕xa3+ 26.♔b1 ♕b4+ 27.♔c1 and White wins.

22.♕g3?

On 22.fxe5 Black crashes through with 22...dxe5 23.♗a7 ♖xc3 24.bxc3 (24.♗d3 is more tenacious, but it does admit that Black was right) 24...♕xa3+ 25.♔d2 ♕xc3+, and Black is winning, for example: 26.♔c1 g3! 27.♕e2 ♗g4!. But better was the move Danny Gormally gave in ChessBase MegaBase: 22.f5!, in order to try and get a black piece on c4 prematurely, blocking its own attack: 22...♗c4 23.♗xc4 ♘xc4 (23...♖xc4? 24.♗b6) 24.♗xg7 ♔xg7 25.f6+ and after he puts his knight on d5, White's attack looks promising, though he had to reckon with Black's counter-stroke ...♘xa3!.

22...♘d7! 23.♗xg7 ♚xg7 24.f5

24...♖xc3!?

Playing in style. Objectively better was 24...♘e5!' for example: 25.♖d3!? (25. fxe6 ♖xc3 26.bxc3 ♖xc3 27.♕f2 ♖xa3 wins for Black – Gormally) 25...♗c4! 26.♖e3 h5 or, maybe even stronger, 26...♚h7.

25.bxc3 ♕xa3+

Again, 25...♘e5!, to involve one more piece in the attack.

26.♚d2 ♘f6 27.♕d3

27...♗c4

Black might as well have gone the whole hog with 27...♘xe4+! (the standard 27...♖xc3?? doesn't work as 28.♕xc3 pins the knight...) 28.♕xe4 ♕xc3+ 29.♚c1 ♕a3+ 30.♚d2 ♕a5+ 31.♚e2 (Gormally; 31.♚c1? ♗xf5) and now 31...♖c4! 32.♕d3 ♕e5+ 33.♚f2 ♖f4+ 34.♚g1 ♗xf5 35.♕d2 ♕c5+ 36.♚h2 g3+ 37.♚xg3 ♖g4+ 38.♚f3 e5 does not look very survivable.

28.♕d4 d5 29.exd5 ♗xd5 30.♖g1 ♗e4 31.♗d3 ♕a5!

White must have been dazzled by all those pins and forks.

32.♕b4! ♕c7 33.♗xe4?

33.♚c1 a5 34.♕d4 (Gormally) 34...♖d8 35.♕c4 ♕xc4 36.♗xc4 ♖xd1+ 37.♚xd1 ♗xf5 with an exciting endgame, probably slightly better for Black.

33...a5

33...♕f4+! 34.♚e2 ♘xe4 was winning.

34.♕xb7 ♕f4+

34...♕xc3+ 35.♚e2 ♖c4! 36.♗d3 ♕e5+ 37.♚d2 ♘d5! introduces some pretty mating motifs: 38.♖a7 (38.♖ge1 ♕f4+ 39.♚e2 ♘c3#) 38...♕f4+ 39.♚e1 ♖d4 40.g3 ♕e3+ 41.♚f1 ♖xd3 etc.

35.♚e2 ♖c7 36.♕b6 ♘xe4 37.♕d4+ ♚h7 38.c4?

38.♖gf1 ♘xc3+ 39.♕xc3 ♕xf1+ leads to a good, probably winning, rook ending for Black.

38...♖d7! 39.♕e3

Loses the queen. Also hopeless is 39.♕xd7 ♕f2+ 40.♚d3 ♘c5+.

39...♘g3+ 40.♔xg3 ♕xg3 41.♖xd7 ♕e5+ 0-1

After 42.♔d2 ♕xf5 White will also lose a rook.

Since the end of 2013, things have changed. White won four games, Black (Nakamura, in Zurich) only once. Was this a turnaround? Did something change or shift in the players' styles or attitudes in late 2013?

'Maybe we're a bit more cautious now', ventures Nakamura, 'so we tend to play more stable openings, trying to play for two results instead of three. Or maybe since that time I've just played better, that's also possible.' Has the American become 'old and wise'? Let's hope not, for the 'old and wise' tend to lose their ability to do the impossible – something which Nakamura has done several times. Gelfand thinks the numbers are relative. Most of their games since late 2013 were rapid or blitz games. 'We only played one classical game, in Tashkent, which Nakamura won due to a blunder from my side.'

First those rapid and blitz games.

Hikaru Nakamura	2786
Boris Gelfand	2777

London rapid 2013 (3)

1.d4 ♘f6 2.c4 g6 3.♘c3 d5 4.♘f3 ♗g7 5.♕b3 dxc4 6.♕xc4 0-0 7.e4 a6 8.e5 b5 9.♕b3 ♘fd7 10.♘g5 ♘c6

11.♘xf7

A little experiment. Before and since, white players have opted for 11.♗e3, with pretty disastrous results after either 11...♘b6 or 11...♘a5.

There seems little point in first playing 10.♘g5 and not following it up with some violence on f7. With that in mind, there is also another quite surprising move here: 11.♘e6!? ♘a5 (obviously best) 12.♘xd8 ♘xb3 13.axb3 ♖xd8 14.♘xb5. Thus White wins a pawn, but Black gets plenty of compensation by blowing up White's centre with 14...c6 15.♘c3 c5 16.♗g5 cxd4 17.♘d5 ♗b7 18.♘c7 ♖ac8 19.♗xe7 ♗xe5 20.♗xd8 ♖xd8 21.♘xa6 d3. The resulting positions are quite interesting.

11...♖xf7 12.e6 ♘xd4 13.exf7+ ♔f8 14.♕d1 ♘c5

Here also, Black has dangerous compensation for the material.

15.♗e3 ♗f5 16.♖c1 ♕d6 17.b4 ♘e4?

17...♕e6! 18.bxc5 ♖d8 19.♗e2 ♘c2+ 20.♕xc2 ♗xc2 21.♖xc2 b4 is good for Black, for example: 22.♘d1 ♕e4 23.♖c4 ♕xg2 and White cannot escape the grip.

18.♘xe4 ♗xe4 19.f3 ♗f5 20.♕d2 ♖d8 21.♔f2 ♔xf7 22.♗e2

Now White manages to consolidate.

22...♕f6?! 23.♖xc7 ♘e6 24.♖d7

Missed by Gelfand?!

24...♖c8 25.♗d3 ♖c3 26.♗xf5 gxf5 27.f4 ♖c4 28.♖c1 ♖e4 29.g3 h5 30.h4 ♕g6

31.♗c5 ♘f6 32.♖e1 ♛g4 33.♖xe4 fxe4 34.♕d1 ♕f5 35.♖d5 ♕h3 36.♕f1 **1-0**

Boris Gelfand 2777
Hikaru Nakamura 2789
Zurich blitz 2014 (1)

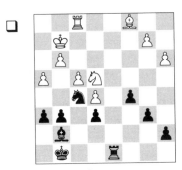

35.g4! ♘xh4+?!
After 35...♘e7 and 36...♖d4 Black would have been OK.

36.♔h3 g5
36...♖d4 37.♘f6+ ♗xf6 38.exf6 ♘f5 39.gxf5 exf5 followed by 40...♔f7 gave good chances to hold.

37.fxg5 ♘g6 38.♘f6+!
Active play is required.

38...♗xf6 39.♖xf6 ♖d3+
Or 39...♘xe5 40.gxh6 ♘d3 41.♗g5 and the black king gets encircled.

40.♔g2 ♘h4+ 41.♔f2 hxg5 42.♗xg5 ♖h3 43.♖h6 ♖f3+ 44.♔e2 ♖b3 45.♗xh4
And White won.

Boris Gelfand 2777
Hikaru Nakamura 2789
Zurich rapid 2014 (5)

Nakamura has provoked his opponent by playing Michael Basman's 2...h6 and 3...g5. Gelfand's treatment is thematic: he exploits the weakened light squares on Black's kingside by trading off all the minor pieces that control them.

21.♘g4 ♕d7 22.♘exf6+ ♗xf6 23.♘h6+ ♔g7 24.♘xf5+ ♕xf5 25.♔g2 ♖h8 26.♖h1 ♕g6 27.♗e4 ♕f7 28.♕g4 ♗e7 29.f3 ♖af8 30.♖xh8 ♖xh8 31.♖h1 ♖xh1 32.♔xh1

Another Rubinstein squeeze. Black has less space, his bishop is chronically passive, as opposed to White's, and he has several weak pawns. Against Gelfand, as we know by now, this is pure torture.

32...♕f8 33.♔g2 ♕d8 34.♕h5 ♗f6 35.♕h7+ ♔f8 36.♕f5 a5 37.♔f1 ♔g7 38.♔e2 ♕e7 39.♔d3 ♕d8 40.♔c2 ♔f8 41.♔b2 ♔f7 42.♕h7+ ♔f8 43.♕h6+ ♔e7 44.♕h3 ♔f8 45.♕e6 ♔g7 46.g4

There's still no clear winning path for White, but now Nakamura loses patience. It would have been a perfect example for the book *Positional Decision Making in Chess*: apply continuous pressure, and your opponent is bound to make a mistake sometime – however strong he is.

46...a4?! 47.bxa4 ♕b8+ 48.♔c2 ♕b4 49.♕d7+ ♔f8 50.♕b5 ♕e1

This looks active, but White's a-pawn will bring him the win. There are only a few checks to overcome.

51.a5 ♕a1 52.♔b3 ♕d1+ 53.♔c2 ♕xf3+ 54.♔a4 ♕c3 55.♔b3

Now the a-pawn has free passage. Nakamura played

55...c6

and resigned at the same time.

Boris Gelfand	2761
Hikaru Nakamura	2776

Zurich rapid 2014 (5)

30.♘e3?!

Missing something. Retreating with 30.♖d2 or 30.♖d1 (which is where it came from) was equal.

30...♘b6 31.♖d8 ♗e7 32.♖e8 ♔f7! 33.♖b8 ♘xa4 34.♘d5 ♗f6 35.♖b7+ ♔g6 36.f4 exf4 37.♘xf4+ ♔h7 38.♘e6 ♖c6

38...♗xb2! or, more simple, 38...♖c1+ 39.♔h2 ♗xb2, wins. Now there is an escape hatch for White.

39.e5! ♗g5

After 39...♖xe6 40.exf6 ♖xf6 41.♗e5 ♖g6 42.♗d4

analysis diagram

Black has no winning plan. A quite curious position!

40.♘xg7 ♘c5 41.♖a7 ♔g6 42.♘e8

With 42.h4! ♗c1 43.h5+ ♔g5 44.e6 ♘xe6 45.♘xe6+ ♖xe6 46.♖xa5+ ♔g4 47.♗e5 White could probably have saved himself, but this was difficult to find in a rapid game.

42...a4 43.h4 ♗e3+ 44.♔h2 a3 45.bxa3

45...b3!

How to stop the b-pawn now?

46.h5+?

Actually, after 46.♖g7+ ♔f5 47.e6 it's still quite complicated, as the white pieces cooperate surprisingly nicely:

A) 47...♔xe6 48.♘c7+ ♔f6 49.♘e8+ ♔e6 50.♘c7+ ♔f5 51.♘d5 b2 52.♘xe3+ ♔f6 53.♘d5+ (53.♖h7!?) 53...♔xg7 54.♗e5+ and Black will be hard put to win;

B) 47...♖xe6 48.♘d6+ ♔f6 (48...♖xd6 49.♗xd6 b2 50.♗xc5 ♗f4+ 51.g3 ♗xg3+ 52.♖xg3 b1♕ doesn't look like a win) 49.♖g8 ♘d7 50.♖g4 b2 51.♖b4 ♗c5 52.♖xb2 ♗xd6 and this is also still quite a job.

46...♔xh5 47.e6 ♘xe6 48.♖b7 ♖b6 49.♖xb6

And White resigned at the same time. After 49...♗xb6 50.♗e5 ♗d4 51.♘f6+ ♔g6 52.♗xd4 ♘xd4 53.♘e4 b2 54.♘c3 ♔f5 Black wins, as 55.♔g3 is not possible in view of 55...♘e2+.

And here is the second 'real' white sheep.

| Hikaru Nakamura | 2764 |
| Boris Gelfand | 2748 |

Tashkent 2014 (5)

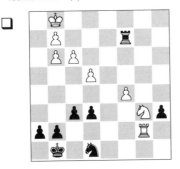

The black king and knight are terribly passive, and this will cost him the e-pawn.

There is some similarity between this position and the following one from a game between Giri and Leko, played one year later:

Anish Giri
Peter Leko

Baku 2015 (3)

Here the e-pawn is still protected by the f-pawn, but that one will inevitably fall while the black knight still cannot get out. Crowning an impressive performance, Giri hauled in the loot here, as follows:

42.♖e7 f5+ 43.♔h5 ♔h7 44.♖xe8 ♖b2 45.h3 ♖h2 46.♔h4   1-0

In the Nakamura-Gelfand game, there followed:

41.♖e7 ♔f8 42.♖xe6

Of course now Black cannot take on c5 due to the knight fork. But at least his own knight comes into play now.

42...♘c7 43.♖c6 ♘b5 44.♘d5 ♘d4 45.♖xa6 ♖xc5

A gruesome position. Can White ever win this? Nakamura gives it a good try.

46.♖a8+ ♔f7 47.♖a7+ ♔f8 48.♘f4 ♖c6 49.♖a8+ ♔f7 50.♖h8!

Creating a hole. A very annoying move for the defender. You never know when this will come in handy for your opponent, but you do know that it will one day.

50...h6 51.♖b8 ♖c7

Gormally has suggested a more active defence with 51...f5!? 52.♖b7+ ♔f6 53.exf5 ♘xf5 54.g4 ♘g3 55.♔f2 ♘h1+ 56.♔e3 ♘g3. Black has more space now, but it looks as if White can make progress with 57.♘d5+ ♔e6 58.♘b4

♖c4 59.♔d3 ♖f4 60.♘a6! and now 60...
h5 (60...♔f6 61.♘c7 ♘e5 62.♔e3 ♖a4
63.f4+! ♔d6 64.♘e8+) 61.♔e3 g5 (or
61...♖c4 62.♖xg7 hxg4 63.♖xg4 may
also still be a draw – or it may not)
62.gxh5 ♖h4 (62...♘xh5 63.♘c5+ ♔d5
64.♘e4) 63.♔f2 ♘h1+ 64.♔e1 ♖xh5
65.♘c5+ and after the coming ♘e4
Black seems to be in real trouble.

In the following phase Nakamura shows
that he has learned something from his
opponent!

**52.♖b6 ♖a7 53.♖d6 ♘b5 54.♖d5
♖b7 55.♔h2 ♘a7 56.♖d6 ♘c8
57.♖c6 ♘e7 58.♖a6 ♘g6 59.♘h5
♘e7 60.♘f4 ♘g6 61.♖d5 ♘e7
62.♘e3 ♖c7 63.g4 ♖c3 64.♘f1 ♖c7
65.♖a3 ♖b7 66.♘e3 ♖d7 67.♔g3
♖c7 68.♖a5 ♖c3 69.♔f2 ♖c7
70.♖b5 ♘g6 71.♘d5 ♖a7 72.♖c5
♖a2+ 73.♔g3 ♔g8 74.♖c7 ♖a3
75.♖b7 ♖a2 76.♖c7 ♖a3 77.♖d7
♖a2**

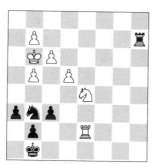

**78.♘e3! ♘e5 79.♖b7 ♖a3 80.♘f5
♘f7 81.♔h2 ♖a2 82.♖e7 ♖a8 83.f4!**
Finally, something is moving.
    **83...♔f8 84.♖c7 g6 85.♘h4 g5
86.♘f5 gxf4 87.♖c6**

87...♘g5?
Again, the weaker side cracks under the
pressure – only this time it is Gelfand!
More tenacious was 87...♔g8! 88.♖xf6
♖a4! 89.♖g6+ ♔f8 90.♖e6 ♖a5! as
Black needs to keep control of e5
(Gormally): 91.♖f6 ♔g8 92.♘h4 ♖a2
93.♖xf4 ♘e5. But here 94.♘f3!? looks
winning, and if not then White can also
try a slower way.
    88.♖xf6+ ♔g8 89.e5 ♖a2?
Hastens the end (if we can put it like
this after an excruciating 89 moves).
The black counterattack isn't sufficient.
    **90.e6! ♘f3+ 91.♔h3 ♘g1+ 92.♔h4
♖xg2 93.♔h5 ♘f3 94.♘xh6+ ♔h7
95.♖f7+ ♔h8 96.e7 ♖e2 97.♖xf4**
Black resigned.

Well, if all this proves anything, it is
that a game between two fighters always
gives both of them winning chances –
whether they are Black or White, in a
blitz game, a rapid game or a classical
game. Which is some proof for the
Black Is OK! theory. And if these two
gentlemen think otherwise, let them
prove it on the board! We will be glad
to watch.

Chapter 7
Black Is Brutal III (1979 – 1990)

It was in the seventies and eighties that I had my biggest successes. I became an international master in 1970, and a grandmaster in 1973. In the same year I came shared first in the Hungarian Championship with Ribli and Csom (playoff: 1.Ribli, 2.Adorjan, 3.Csom). The Hungarian team broke the Soviet hegemony by winning the Olympiad in Buenos Aires 1978. I was a member of the team.

In 1979-80 I became a World Champion Candidate following an incredibly long march, and nearly qualified for the semifinal, but blundered tragically against Hübner. I won the Hungarian Super Champion title in 1984 and came 2nd behind Dzindzichashvili in a 7-way tie together with Larsen, Portisch and other top players in the New York Open. Three years later I won the same event in a tie with Seirawan with 8/11, ahead of a field composed of 45 grandmasters! Between 1979 and 1986 I was Garry Kasparov's fellow worker and a second during his four matches.

A Bolt from the Blue
Two thin draws is what I started with in the Riga Interzonal, but in the end I miraculously qualified. On the players' list I occupied 11th/12th place, while beforehand I hadn't hoped for more than just a positive result.

TOO LONG

| Ljubomir Ljubojevic | 2590 |
| Andras Adorjan | 2525 |

Riga izt 1979 (3)

1.e4 c5 2.♘f3 ♘c6 3.d4 cxd4 4.♘xd4 ♘f6 5.♘c3 e6 6.♘db5 d6 7.♗f4 e5

When you play against a great fighter, be aggressive yourself. Chicken play will seal your fate. The Sveshnikov was quite a good weapon to fire back with. I was one of the world's leading specialists in it at that time. And – a romantic soul.

8.♗g5 a6 9.♘a3 b5 10.♘d5 ♗e7 11.♘xe7

11.♗xf6 ♗xf6 12.c3 is a quieter way to handle this line. Ljubo however was never known for being timid.

11...♘xe7 12.♗xf6

12.♗d3!? ♗b7 13.♕e2.

12...gxf6

13.c4

Taking it a little easy. This is not a mistake yet, but it is in connection with the next move.

13.♕f3 f5 14.exf5 ♗xf5 15.♗d3 ♗xd3 16.♕xd3 d5 17.c3=/∓.

13...♗b7!

Forced, but also good.

14.cxb5?!

It was not yet too late to wake up and get out of the troubled water. He who raises a sword sometimes falls by the sword, according to the Lord Jesus (a famous thinker): 14.♗d3! bxc4 15.♘xc4 d5 16.exd5 ♕xd5 17.♘d6+ ♔f8 18.♗e4 ♕a5+ 19.♕d2 ♕xd2+ 20.♔xd2 ♖d8 21.♗xb7 ♖xd6+=.

14...♗xe4 15.♕a4 d5 16.bxa6+ ♔f8 17.♕b4

17...♖g8!

The then known move 17...♔g7 was good enough (when 18.♗b5 is unclear), but the text is even more brutal.

18.f3 ♗f5 19.g4 ♗c8 20.0-0-0 ♗xa6 21.♔b1 ♔g7 22.♘b5?

White must have left his sense of danger at the hotel. He had big headaches already here, as can be seen in the line 22.♗xa6 ♖xa6 23.♖he1 ♘g6.

22...♘c6

22...d4 23.♕d6 ♘d5 was deadly too.

23.♕c5?!

Could it be that Ljubo, a great attacker himself, had said farewell to this game already?

23.♕d6 looks more stubborn here, but after 23...♕a5 24.a4 ♕xa4 25.♘c3 Black strikes with 25...♗d3+! with a winning attack.

23...♕a5!

The rest is silence.

24.a4

24.♕xc6 ♗xb5−+; 24.♕xd5 ♖gd8 25.♘d6 ♖xd6 26.♕xd6 ♗xf1 27.♕xc6 ♕xa2+ 28.♔c1 ♖b8 29.♕c2 ♗a6! 30.♖d6 ♖c8 31.♖c6 ♕a1+ 32.♔d2 ♖d8+−+.

24...♘d4! 25.b3

25.♖xd4 doesn't ward off the attack, as see 25...exd4 26.♕xd4 (26.♕c2 ♖gc8 27.♕d1 ♖e8 28.♗d3 ♖e3−+) 26...♕e1+ 27.♔c2 ♗xb5 28.axb5 ♖gc8+ 29.♔b3 ♕a1 and Black wins.

25...♘xb3 26.♕xd5 ♕b4

And the towel was thrown in...

Sensation! The guy (me) won with black! Yes, and so it was with four more (5 wins in total) of my seven full points. A good presentation of my thesis in an Interzonal.

| Edmar Mednis | 2510 |
| Andras Adorjan | 2525 |

Riga izt 1979 (7)

The game had been adjourned, and 41... a3 was the sealed move.

42.♘e2

Knight or bishop? It's one of the evergreen questions. These two pieces represent roughly even values, but they are of a quite different character. In closed or half-closed positions the knight – which can jump – may be stronger. Open structures or, especially, endings with passed pawns on both sides favour the bishop, which has a far range. In this ending Black stands to win. It only takes time. And patience.

A) 42.♔b3 a2! 43.♘xa2 ♗e1-+;

B) 42.♘d5 ♗e1 43.g4 hxg4 44.hxg5 fxg5 45.♔b3 g3 46.♘e3 ♗f2 47.♘g2 ♗xd4 48.♔xa3 ♔e5-+;

C) 42.d5+ ♔e5 43.♔b3 a2! 44.♘xa2 ♗e1-+.

42...♗d6

With the bishop covering both sides of the board, 42...f5! was very strong.

43.♔b3

43.hxg5 fxg5 44.♔b3 h4 45.gxh4 gxh4 46.♘g1 ♗e7 47.♔a2 (47.♘f3 h3 48.d5+ ♔f6 49.e5+ ♔f5 50.d6 ♗f8! 51.♔xa3 ♔f4-+). Now the black king needs to find a way in. Any move by White's centre pawns will just facilitate this: 47...♔f6 48.♘h3 ♔g6 49.♔b3 ♔h5 50.♘f2 ♔g5-+; 43.e5 fxe5 44.hxg5 ♔f5 and again the king cannot be kept out.

43...g4!

This may look odd. But even great discoveries are easy to understand afterwards. Here I must give credit to my second, IM Tompa, for his masterly analysing skills. The reader should not

be scared by the following sea of moves. The variations are long but their logic is very easy to follow:

44.♔a2 ♗e7! 45.♔b3 ♔d7 46.♔a2 ♔c7 47.♘c3

47.e5 fxe5 48.dxe5 ♗xe5 49.♔xa3 ♔d6 50.♔b4 ♔d5-+.

47...♗xg3

47...♔b6! 48.♘d5+ ♔xb5 49.♘xf6 ♗xg3 50.♘xh5 ♗xh4 51.♔xa3 ♔c4 52.d5 ♔d4 would have been quicker than the game; or 48.e5 fxe5 49.♘e4 ♗c7 50.d5 ♗d8!-+.

48.♘d5+ ♔b7 49.♘xf6 ♗xh4 50.♘xh5 ♔b6 51.♔xa3 ♔xb5 52.♔b3

52...g3 53.♘f4 ♗g5! 54.♘g2 a5 55.e5 ♗e7 56.d5 a4+ 57.♔a2

57.♔c3 ♗b4+ 58.♔d3 ♔c5 59.♘e3 a3 60.♔c2 a2 (forcing an entrance) 61.♔b2 ♗d2 62.♘g2 ♔xd5 63.♔xa2 ♔xe5 64.♔b3 ♔e4 65.♔c2 ♗g5 66.♘e1 ♔e3 67.♔d1 ♔f2 68.♘d3+ ♔f1-+.

57...♗c5 58.d6 ♔c6 59.♘e1 ♔d7 60.♔b2 ♗b4 61.♘f3 g2 62.♔c2 ♔e6 63.♔d3

Almost symmetrical opening!

63...♔d5! 64.d7 ♗e7 65.♔c3 ♔e4 66.♘g1 ♔xe5 67.♘e2 ♔e4 68.♔c4 ♔e3 69.♘g1 ♔d2 70.♘f3+ ♔c1

70...♔c2 71.♘e1+ ♔b2 72.♘xg2 a3 also wins.

71.♔c3 ♔b1 72.♘d2+ ♔a2 73.♘f3 ♗f6+ 74.♔c2 ♔a3 75.♘g1 ♔b4 76.♘f3 a3 77.♔b1

77...g1♕+! 0-1

I hope you agree it was worth the trouble to study all these lines. Even if this only means you will win or save one extra game, then your time hasn't been wasted.

Here is another eventful game from Riga. In the Interzonals there were always a few exotic players from weak zones. Bouaziz from Tunesia was one of them. Even these participants could be dangerous, and their rhapsodic doings may heavily influence the final score of the upper house. Dropping half a point against them (as I did against Bouaziz, Rodriguez and Greenfeld) could be a heavy blow.

My next opponent from Brazil, Francisco Trois, belonged to this group. Except I succeeded in beating him in a very critical tournament situation. I had started off well, but had then fallen behind and seemed to be losing my dreamed-of third place. I gave him a lot to think about, which he did. Got himself in big time-trouble and finally overstepped the time limit. The game itself is rich in beauty and fog. Enjoy it!

Francisco Trois 2415
Andras Adorjan 2525

Riga izt 1979 (13)

1.♘f3 ♘f6 2.c4 c5 3.♘c3 e6 4.e3 b6 5.♗e2 ♗b7 6.0-0 ♗e7 7.b3 0-0 8.♗b2 a6 9.♖c1 d6 10.d4 ♘bd7 11.a3

11.d5 exd5 12.♘xd5 (12.cxd5 b5 13.a3 ♖c8∓) 12...♘xd5 13.cxd5 ♗f6 14.♗c3 ♗xc3 15.♖xc3 ♖e8 favours Black; White's d5-pawn is a liability and Black's queenside pawn mass is strong.

11...♖e8 12.b4 cxd4

After the immediate 12...♖c8 the position may remain closed: 13.d5 exd5 14.cxd5 ♗f8 (14...b5 15.e4 ♘g4∓) 15.b5 axb5 16.♗xb5 g6 17.♕b3 ♗g7 18.♖fd1 ♕c7, unclear.

13.exd4 ♖c8 14.♘d2

White has a spatial advantage, which is formally considered very important. However, in the past 30-40 years it has become clear that as long as you can manoeuvre freely behind your pawn chain it's not a big deal. Especially in so-called Hedgehog-type positions.

14...♖c7 15.♖e1 ♕a8 16.♗f1 ♗f8 17.♕e2 ♖ec8

17...d5 18.cxd5 (18.c5 e5!∓) 18...exd5= was possible here, but not necessary.

18.♕e3 ♖e8?!

18...g6.

19.♘b3 g6

Don't worry about the following longish variations. They are not at all difficult to calculate: 19...h6 20.a4 d5 21.c5 a5 22.♘b5 ♖cc8 23.bxa5 bxc5 24.dxc5 ♘e4

(24...e5!?) 25.c6! (less strong is 25.♗a3 e5 26.♘d6 d4 27.♕h3 ♗xd6 28.cxd6=) 25...♗xc6 26.♘a7 ♖c7 27.♘xc6 ♖xc6 28.♗b5±.

20.a4 ♖ec8 21.a5

21.f3!? ♕b8 22.♗a3.

21...♖xc4!?

Actually sacrificing not one but two exchanges – it is quite correct, and handy in a must-win situation.

22.♗xc4 ♖xc4 23.♘d2 ♖xb4! 24.♗a3 bxa5 25.f3

25.♗xb4 axb4 26.♘a2 a5∓.

25...♖b5!?

Overdoing it a bit. 25...♕a7!∓ was better. Meanwhile the game rages on.

26.♘c4

26.♘xb5? axb5 27.♗b2 b4 28.♘e4 a4−+.

26...♘d5 27.♕d2 ♘xc3 28.♕xc3 ♖g5

28...♕b8∓.

29.♖f1

29.♗xd6 ♗xf3 30.g3 ♕d5 with good compensation.

29...♖d5 30.♘xa5

30...♘f6!

That's it! White would take over the initiative after either 30...♗h6 31.♖b1 ♖b5 32.♖xb5 axb5 33.♕c7 or 30...♗g7 31.♕c7 ♗xd4+ 32.♔h1 ♖xa5 33.♕xa5 ♗b6 (33...♘c5 34.♕c7 ♗d5 35.♖b1 ♕c6 36.♕d8+ ♔g7 37.♖b8+−) 34.♕a4 ♘c5 35.♕f4+±.

31.♕c7 ♖b5 32.♘xb7

32.♗xd6?? ♘e8−+.

32...♖xb7 33.♕c6 ♕a7 34.♗xd6 ♕xd4+ 35.♔h1 ♗xd6!!

35...♖b6 36.♗e5 ♕e3 37.♕c3 ♕xc3 38.♖xc3 ♘d5 39.♖c8 f6 40.♗d4 ♖b5 41.♖a1 would have given White an edge in the ending.

36.♕xb7?

In deep time-trouble, White finally takes the second rook. Things would have been less clear after 36.♖fd1 ♕b4 37.♕xd6 ♕xd6 38.♖xd6 ♘d5 39.♖xa6 h5.

36...♕h4

37.f4!?

Unexpected and cunning. But it does give up another pawn, after which the material balance becomes fairly strange.

A) 37.g3 ♗xg3 38.♖c2 ♗f4 39.♕xa6 ♘h5 40.♕c8+ ♔g7 41.♕c3+ ♔h6 and the black king weathers the storm, e.g., 42.♕e1 (42.♔g1 ♕g5+ 43.♔h1 ♕h4 44.♖b1 ♘g3+ 45.♔g1 ♘f5 46.♖e2 ♕g5+ 47.♖g2 ♕h4) 42...♕h3 43.♔g1 e5 44.♕e2 ♘g7 45.♖c3 ♘f5 and the forces roughly balance each other out;

B) 37.h3 ♕f4 38.♔g1 ♕h2+ 39.♔f2 ♗g3+ wins for Black.

37...♗xf4 38.g3

38.♖c8+ ♔g7 39.h3 ♕g3 40.♖xf4 ♕xf4 41.♕xa6 ♘e4 42.♕a1+ e5

Queen pin saves the day

43.♕e1 h5 with good chances for Black.

38...♗xg3   **0-1**

Here White overstepped the time-limit. It's funny, but after all these crazy complications the most likely outcome might have been a draw.

There might have followed: 39.♖c2 ♗e5 (39...♔g7 40.♕xa6 ♕e4+ 41.♖g2 ♗e5 42.♕e2 ♗d4∓) 40.♕xa6 ♕e4+ (40...♘e4 41.♖g2 ♘g3+? 42.♖xg3 ♗xg3 43.♕c8+ ♔g7 44.♕c3++−; 40...♘h5 41.♖g2 ♕e4 42.♕e2 is unclear) 41.♖g2 ♘g4 42.♕b5 ♔g7 43.h3 ♘e3 (43...♘h6 44.♕e2; 43...♘f6 44.♕e2) 44.♖xf7+! ♔xf7 45.♕d7+ ♔f8 46.♕d8+ ♔g7 47.♕e7+ ♔h6 48.♕g5+ with a draw.

A game that has remained memorable to me all my life. By winning it, I was able to continue my chase of the leaders.

Anthony Miles	2560
Andras Adorjan	2525

Riga izt 1979 (17)

An unforgettable last-round victory. With it I caught Ribli, who got busted by Romanishin's original attack. I could easily win back my sacrificed pawn twice, but decided to finish under the spell of beauty. This game qualified for a special prize among the wonderful games of this round, and I'm very proud of it. Chess is an art too! At least for me.

20...♕a7!?

I was playing this game in a kind of trance. I felt as if the pieces were heading for the right squares by themselves, and I was just helping them physically. Get the pawn back, with an endgame advantage? Yes, it was possible, but it didn't even cross my mind. Let's see what a cool-headed analysis and Fritz 38.5 had to say about it a little while later (24 years to be precise)!

A) Maybe 20...♘d5!, recommended by 'him' and analysed in a joint effort, would have been the 'right thing': 21.♕xb8 (21.♔h3 ♘e3 22.♕xb8 ♖cxb8∓) 21...♘e3+ 22.♔h3 ♖axb8 23.a3 f5! (23...♘xd1 24.♖xd1 f5∓) 24.♖e1 ♘5g4! 25.♘d1 ♘xd1 26.♖exd1 ♘f2+ 27.♔g2 ♘xd1 28.♖xd1 ♖c2−+;

B) 20...♕xb5 21.♘xb5 ♖cb8 22.♗xe5 dxe5 23.♘c3 ♗xb4 24.♘db1 ♗c5 25.♘e4 ♘xe4 26.fxe4 ♗d4 27.♖c2 g6∓.

Being only a feeble human player, I think I don't have to be ashamed that I missed this.

21.e4

21.♕a5 ♕e3 22.♘f1 ♕g5 23.♘b1 ♖e8!∓.

21...♕e3!!?

I thought it was over. The vicinity of his king is blackened by storm clouds, and I felt that my next move, planned long before, would be decisive. It was only during the final check of this game, which had been analysed frequently by lots of different people, that Fritz 38.5 'spat out' a move which holds the position for White. Had I known this, I would certainly have collected the b4-pawn and taken my time to collect the point as well.

Still, I am satisfied with the result, and let me quote the late Misha Tal, a lovable man as well as a genius: 'My sacrifices are sometimes refuted. Perhaps in two years, or in two months, sometimes even in two days. But I win the game!'

21...♖cb8! was too dry for me: 22.♕e2 ♖xb4 23.♖c2 ♖ab8 (23...♘c6 24.♘d5 ♘xd5 25.exd5 exd5 26.♗xg7 ♔xg7

27.♖xc6 ♖b2 28.a3 ♕d7∓) 24.♗a1 ♕a8! (or 24...♘c6 25.♕f2 ♕a6)∓.

22.♕f1

22.♖c2 ♕d3 (22...g5!?) 23.♕xd3 ♘xd3 24.♘db1 ♘xb4 25.♖cd2 ♘d7∓.

22...g5!

23.♖c2?

This rook move is not the most fortunate one in this book!

A) 23.♘e2 is the saving move of the Teutonic machine! Quite strange, but fully logical. In certain types of positions, computers are better than mortals, mainly because they have no emotions. In other cases, however, this rigidly exact way of 'thinking' does not only result in boredom on the board, it also brings victory to a sensitive, talented, resourceful man.

A1) 23...♖xc1 24.♘xc1 g4 25.♗xe5 dxe5 26.b5 and now:

analysis diagram

A11) 26...♖d8 27.♘cb3 ♕a7 28.♖a1 ♗b4 29.fxg4 ♘xg4 30.♕e2 ♘e3+ 31.♔h1 ♗xd2 32.♘xd2 ♕d4 33.♖e1 ♕xd2 34.♕xe3 ♕xe3 35.♖xe3 ♖d1+

36.♔g2 ♖d2+ 37.♔f3 ♖xa2 38.♖b3 ♖a7 (38...f5 39.b6 ♖a8 40.b7 ♖b8 41.exf5 exf5 42.g4+−) 39.b6 ♖b7 40.♔e3+−;

A12) 26...♗b4! 27.♘c4 ♕c3 (27...♕c5!?) 28.fxg4 (28.♕d3!) 28...♕c2+ 29.♔e2 ♖xa2! 30.♔f1 (30.♔f3 ♕c3+ 31.♕d3 ♖c2 32.♕xc3 ♖xc3+ 33.♘e3 ♗c5 34.♘d3 ♗xe3 35.♔xe3 ♘xg4+ 36.♔d2 ♖b3 37.h3 ♘f6 38.♔e3 ♖xb5∓) 30...♕xe2+ 31.♘xe2 ♘xg4 32.b6 ♘xh2+ 33.♔f2 ♗c5+ 34.♔e1 ♘f3+ 35.♔f1 ♘h2+=.

Coffee break!

A2) 23...g4 24.♗xe5 dxe5 and now:

A21) 25.♘c4 allows Black a choice between two attractive alternatives:

A211) 25...gxf3+ 26.♕xf3 ♕xe4 27.♕xe4 ♘xe4 28.a3 ♗g5 29.♖c2 ♘d2!! (29...f5 30.♖d7 ♘f6 31.♖d6 ♘g4 32.♔h1 ♖a7 33.♖xe6! ♖ac7 34.h3 ♘f2+ 35.♔g2 ♘e4 36.♖xe5 ♖xc4 37.♖xc4 ♖xc4 38.♖xf5=) 30.♖cxd2 ♖xc4 31.♖a2 ♖xb4 or 31.♖d3 ♖c2 32.♔f2 ♖a2∓;

A212) 25...♖xc4! 26.♖xc4 ♖xa2 27.♖e1 ♕d3!−+.

A22) 25.b5 ♖cb8 26.♘c3 ♗b4 27.♘db1 ♗xc3 28.♘xc3 ♖c8 29.♖d3 gxf3+ 30.♔h1 ♕h6 31.♖c2 ♘xe4 32.♕xf3 f5 33.♕e2 ♖xc3 (33...♖c4 34.♘xe4 ♖xe4 35.♕d1) 34.♖cxc3 ♘xc3 35.♖xc3 ♕g7 36.a3 ♕b7+ 37.♔g1 ♕d5 38.♕e3 ♔f7 39.b6 ♕d1+ 40.♔f2 ♖d8 41.♕e1 ♕d4+ 42.♔g2 ♕xb6 43.♕xe5 ♕b2+ 44.♔h3 ♕d2 45.♖e3 ♕d6=.

Time for tea!

B) 23.h3 h5! 24.♘e2 g4 25.♗xe5 dxe5 26.♘c4 and now:

B1) 26...gxf3+ 27.♕xf3 ♕xe4 28.♕xe4 ♘xe4 29.a3 ♗g5 30.♖c2 ♘d2! (30...♖c7 31.♘e3 ♖ca7 32.♘c4 ♖c7=) 31.♖cxd2 ♖xc4 32.♖d3 ♖c2 33.♔f2 e4 34.♖b3 ♖a2∓;

B2) 26...♖xc4! 27.♖xc4 ♖xa2 28.♖e1 ♕d3!−+.

23...♖xa2!

I decided to fall right into this trap!

24.♘d5

24...♖xc2! 25.♘xe3 ♖cxb2 26.♕e2 g4! 27.f4

27.♘xg4 ♘fxg4 28.fxg4 ♗g5–+.

27...♘xe4 28.♘ef1

28...♘xd2!?

28...♘c3! would have won the whole white army, but the text checkmates in a few moves.

29.♖xd2 ♖xd2 30.♘xd2 ♘f3 31.♕c4 ♖xd2+ 32.♔f1 ♗f6

And White surrendered, congratulating me standing up from his chair! Yes, it is possible to lose a game in such a dignified way. We remember you Tony! Rest in Peace.

Mark V (computer)
Andras Adorjan

Budapest blindfold simul 1980

These were the Spring days of computer chess. This engine was not very strong. But it had a fantastic skill: if it got a draw offer, it always accepted – in worse positions. In this game however there was not a word about peace. I had another memory of a year in Budapest where this exhibition of machines took place. After discovering their greediness I killed one of the primitive ones as follows:

1.e4 d5 2.♕h5!? dxe4 3.♘f3!! exf3 4.♗c4 fxg2 5.♗xf7+ ♔d7 6.♕d5 mate. Whenever I was blue I would do it three times to this fellow, and it really cheered me up.

1.d4 ♘f6 2.c4 c5 3.d5 g6 4.♘c3 ♗g7 5.e4 0-0!?

5...d6.

6.e5?!

6.♘f3.

6...♘e8

7.f4?!

Better was 7.♘f3 d6 8.exd6 ♘xd6 9.♗e2 ♗g4. Black has taken the initiative early on.

7...d6 8.♘f3 ♗g4 9.♕d3?

9.♗e2 ♗xf3 10.♗xf3 dxe5 11.fxe5 ♘d7 12.e6 ♘e5 13.exf7+ ♖xf7 14.0-0 ♘d6 clearly favours Black too.

9...♘d7 10.exd6

White's position, built of fragile panels, falls apart.

10.♗e2 ♗xf3 11.♕xf3 dxe5 12.0-0 ♘d6∓.

10...♘xd6 11.♗d2

11.♗e2 ♗f5 12.♕e3 e6 13.0-0 ♖e8∓.

11...b5!

The winning motif.

GAME BREAKING MOVE→

123

12.cxb5 c4 13.♕e2 ♘c5 14.0-0-0?
14.♕e3 ♗xf3 15.gxf3 (15.♕xc5 ♘e4)
15...♖c8 16.0-0-0 – escaping by suicide.
14...♘d3+ 15.♔c2
15.♔b1 ♖b8 16.a4 ♗f5 17.♕e3 ♘b4+
18.♔c1 ♕a5 19.♗e1 ♗xc3 20.♗xc3
♕xa4 is also game over.
15...♗f5 16.a4
Or 16.♕e3 ♘b4+ 17.♔c1 ♘xb5 18.♘e5
♘xc3 19.♗xc3 ♘xa2+ 20.♔d2 ♘xc3
21.bxc3 ♕xd5+–+.
16...♘c5+ 17.♘e4
Or 17.♔c1 ♘b3#.
White resigned.
Times are tougher for mankind since
we met the human-made programs.
But this whole game was still a bloody
massacre.

Tamas Kulcsar
Andras Adorjan
Budapest clock simul 1981

This game was played in a clock
simul against my first-league team on
the condition that we annotate the
whole harvest. Preferably verbally. The
original copy by this lyrical candidate
master was more than that – it had
poetry as well, and witty observations
made during the game. I still have it in
Hungarian together with the others. It
was a good method to get to know each
other's way of thinking.
With the overall result – I don't
remember exactly but it was something
like 7½-4½ – they cried all the (long)
way home. Just like two years earlier,
when I had scored 9½-2½.
**1.d4 ♘f6 2.c4 c5 3.d5 g6 4.♘c3
♗g7 5.e4 d6 6.f4 0-0 7.♘f3 b5
8.e5**
8.cxb5 a6 9.a4 was good, and much
safer.
**8...dxe5 9.fxe5 ♘g4 10.♘xb5
♘d7**

10...♘xe5 11.♗e2 a6 12.♘c3 ♘bd7∓.

Complicating matters deliberately.
My customer was known as a record-
breaking hesitater. Let's give him a
choice to suffer.
11.e6?!
Why not 11.♗e2 ?
11...fxe6 12.♗e2
12.dxe6 ♘b6 13.♕xd8 ♖xd8 14.♗e2
a6 15.♘c7 ♖a7 16.♘d5 ♘xd5
17.cxd5 ♖xd5 gives Black the upper
hand.
12...♘de5 13.0-0 ♖b8?!
Foggy business.
13...a6 14.♘c3 ♘xf3+ 15.♗xf3 ♘e5
16.♗e2 ♖xf1+ 17.♗xf1 ♖b8 gave Black
an edge, too.
14.d6?
14.♘xa7 was the move to play, when
after 14...♗b7 things are not clear. The
same goes for 14.♘xe5 ♖xf1+ 15.♗xf1
♘xe5 16.♘xa7 ♗b7.

14...♖xb5?!

PAWN SACRIFICE b5 is much more powerful than it seems !

But this is irresponsible. I'm mixing up originality and art pour l'art.

14...exd6!∓.

15.dxe7?

Cooperating till the bitter end out of excessive respect. Just because you are weaker you should not believe the Black Magician in everything...

15.cxb5 ♘xf3+ 16.♗xf3 ♗d4+ 17.♔h1 ♘f2+ 18.♖xf2 ♗xf2 19.♗h6 was a little better for White.

15...♘xf3+ 16.♗xf3 ♗d4+ 17.♔h1 ♕xe7 18.cxb5

18...♘xh2!　　　　　　**0-1**

But this is wonderful indeed. The viewers were thrilled. Paul Morphy would surely have liked this finish. Let's dedicate it to him.

Another last-round game from the Elekes Memorial, which I organized for the club's 50-year anniversary in GM and IM groups, with only the help of Tamas Kulcsar and my own enthusiasm. My participation was also a gesture, as at that time I did not play category 8 events. And the double role of playing and organizing is a constant headache. Try to avoid it! How much did it pay? Well... everything was done in a spirit of charity.

My partner was a reasonable IM and I had to win at all cost to become the tournament victor. Playing Black helped me to sharpen the game.

Gyorgy Rajna	2390
Andras Adorjan	2515

Budapest 1982

1.e4 c5 2.♘f3 e6 3.d4 cxd4 4.♘xd4 ♘f6 5.♘c3 d6 6.♗g5 ♗e7 7.♕d2 a6 8.f3

8.0-0-0 b5 and Black takes the initiative.

The key move for the so-called English Attack. This is practically a minus-tempo Keres Variation in which Black already stands very well. But the mass psychosis worked: British and other employees scored heavily with this global misunderstanding.

8...b5 9.♗e3

9.a4!? b4 10.♘a2 is unclear.

9...♗b7 10.g4 ♘c6

10...0-0 11.0-0-0 ♘fd7!?.

11.0-0-0 ♖c8 12.h4 ♘d7 13.g5

That's what I was talking about: White plays a 'soft Keres' where f2-f3 is a clear loss of tempo.

13...♘c5 14.♖g1

14.♘xc6!? ♗xc6 15.♔b1 is safer.

14...♘e5 15.♔b1

A) 15.h5? is too slow: 15...b4 16.♘b1 b3! 17.axb3 ♘xf3−+ or 17.♘xb3 ♘xb3+ 18.axb3 ♘xf3−+;

B) 15.f4 (in two moves!) 15...b4 (15...♘ed7 16.f5 b4 17.fxe6 fxe6 18.♘a4 ♗xe4) 16.♘b1 (16.fxe5 dxe5 (16... bxc3 17.♕xc3 0-0 18.exd6 ♗xd6∓) 17.♘de2 ♕c7 18.♗xc5 (18.♘b1 b3−+) 18...♗xc5 19.♖g3 0-0∓ or 19.♘a4 ♗e3−+) 16...b3 17.♘xb3 (17.axb3 ♘f3−+) 17...♘xb3+ 18.axb3 ♘f3 19.♕b4 ♕c7 20.♖g2 ♘xh4∓;

C) 15.a3 0-0 16.♔b1 ♕c7, preparing ...♖f8-d8-d5. There might be other things hanging in the air, such as ...♘xf3!? followed by ...♘xe4. No joke!

15...b4 16.♘ce2 ♘c4 17.♕c1

17...e5?

Totally unnecessary in a situation where Black is positionally winning. But I couldn't ignore my natural inclination to fish for pearls... did I tell you I got eight brilliancy prizes during my career by being faithful to Caissa's beauty? Sometimes I paid a heavy price for this attitude. Not in this book though!

A) 17...♘xe3 18.♕xe3 0-0 19.♗h3 ♕c7 20.h5 g6∓;

B) 17...♘a4!? 18.b3 ♘xe3 19.♕xe3 ♘c3+ 20.♘xc3 ♖xc3 21.♖d3 ♖xd3 22.♗xd3 ♕b6 23.♖d1 0-0 24.♘f5 ♕xe3 25.♘xe3 g6∓.

18.♘f5 ♘a4

The fellow almost fell from his chair. Bravo! said the public and the press afterwards.

19.g6?

An incredible upset. White is trying to surprise me back.

19.♘xg7+ ♔f8 20.♘d4 (20.g6 hxg6 21.♗h6 ♔g8−+) 20...♔xg7 21.♘f5+ ♔g8 22.♗xc4 ♖xc4 23.h5 is not clear, but 19.♘ed4! was the outright refutation of the ...e6-e5/...♘a4 cheapo. He didn't have 31 years to find this out, as I did: in 2013. Remember what Misha Tal said on this subject?

19...fxg6 20.♘xg7+

20.♘xe7 ♕xe7 21.♗h3 ♘axb2−+.

20...♔f7 21.♗h6 ♖g8 22.♘g3 ♘cxb2 23.♗h3 ♖xg7 24.♗xg7

24...♘c3+ 25.♔a1

On 25.♔xb2 ♕a5 Black mates in a fantastic way.

25...♘bxd1 26.♗xe5 dxe5 27.♕h6 ♕g8 28.♘f5 ♖c5 29.♘d4 exd4 30.♕f4+ ♔g7 **0-1**

Rejoice! Justice has been served to BLACK for so much suffering throughout history.

Laszlo Kovacs
Andras Adorjan
Budapest 1982
1.d4 ♘f6 2.c4 e6 3.♘f3 b6 4.a3 ♗b7 5.♗g5 ♗e7 6.♘c3 c5!

Black plays for a win. I hope you will realize that dynamism and flexibility give birth to a kind of activity where colours are of no importance. BLACK IS OK!

7.e3

A) 7.d5? ♘xd5! 8.cxd5 ♗xg5 9.dxe6 fxe6 10.♘b5 0-0 11.♘xg5 ♕xg5 12.♘c7 ♕f4 13.♘xa8 ♕xf2+ 14.♔d2 ♖f4!–+;

B) 7.♗xf6 ♗xf6 8.d5 0-0 9.e4 d6 10.♗e2 ♕e7 11.0-0 ♘d7=.

7...0-0

Stronger – more dynamic! – was 7...cxd4! 8.exd4 (8.♘xd4 a6∓) 8...♗xf3 9.♕xf3 ♘c6 and now:

A) 10.♕e3 ♘g4∓;

B) 10.d5 exd5 11.♗xf6 ♗xf6 12.♘xd5 (12.cxd5 ♕e7+∓) 12...♗e5 13.0-0-0=;

C) 10.♖d1 0-0 11.♗e2 ♖c8 with the idea ...♘a5.

8.♗e2 cxd4!

There shall be no symmetry!

9.exd4 d5 10.0-0 ♘c6 11.♖c1

... but 11.♗xf6 ♗xf6 12.cxd5 exd5 13.b4 ♘e7 was still equalish.

11...dxc4 12.♗xc4

12...♘d5!? 13.♗d2
13.♗xe7 ♘cxe7∓; and on either capture on d5, taking on g5 gives Black an edge.

13...♘f6
13...♘xc3!? leads after 14.♗xc3 ♗f6 15.d5 (only move) 15...♘a5! 16.♗xa5 (16.♗xf6 ♕xf6 17.dxe6 ♘xc4 18.♖xc4 ♗a6∓) 16...exd5 17.♗b4 dxc4 18.♗xf8 ♕xf8 to a position with more than abundant compensation for Black.

14.♗g5 h6! 15.♗f4
15.♗h4 ♘h5! 16.♗xe7 ♘xe7 is a dream position for Black in such lines.

15...♗d6 16.♘e5 ♖c8 17.♘b5?
Still more or less playable was 17.♗a2 ♘e7 18.♗b1 ♗b8 (18...♘f5 19.g4!? is not so clear) 19.♕d3 ♘f5 20.♖fd1 ♘d5 21.♗g3 even though Black has all the fun after 21...h5.

17...♗b8 18.♘xc6 ♖xc6 19.♗xb8

19...♕xb8
Soberly torturing the opponent till the end. However, an incredible switch was possible here: 19...♖xc4!? 20.♖xc4 (20.♗d6 ♖xc1 21.♕xc1 ♗a6! 22.♗xf8

♗xb5∓) 20...♕d5 21.♕f3! (21.f3?
♕xc4 22.♘d6 ♕c6 23.♘xb7 ♖xb8−+)
21...♕xc4 22.♕xb7 ♕xb5 23.♗d6
(23.♗xa7 ♘d5∓) 23...♖e8!? 24.♕xa7
♕xb2 25.♗e5 (25.♗b4? ♕xd4)
25...♘d5 when Black's knight dominates
and the d4-pawn becomes weak.

20.♗e2 ♖d8 21.♕a4

21.♕d2 loses material after 21...e5
22.♕e3 a6! 23.dxe5 ♘d5.

21...♖xc1 22.♖xc1 ♕f4! 23.♖c7

Time-trouble.

23...♘e4! 24.♗f3 ♕d2

24...♘c5 was available for gourmands...
25.♕c2 (25.♕d1 ♗xf3 26.gxf3 a6−+)
25...♗xf3 26.gxf3 ♕xf3, winning.

**25.♕d1   ♕xf2+   26.♔h1   ♕xb2
27.♔g1 ♕xb5**

27...♕f2+ 28.♔h1 ♕e3 would have
been quicker.

**28.♖xb7   ♘c3   29.♕f1   ♖xd4
30.♖xa7 ♕c5 31.♔h1 ♕f5 32.h3?**

32...♖d1!   **0-1**
A mercy killing.

'Beware of the Keres Attack', Garry
Kasparov wrote to me more than
once when we were working together
between 1979 and 1986. But I really
loved to play against it − and with a very
fine score thanks to my faith in Black's
opportunities. I discovered powerful
novelties against White's aggression, with
which he burns all the bridges behind
him. This game was followed by two
more in 1984, and when I sent them to
Kasparov and showed my ideas to him in
person, he gave in. What's more, he went
for it in the very first World Championship
match with Karpov in game one!

Amador Rodriguez Cespedes 2480
Andras Adorjan   2510

Toluca izt 1982 (2)

**1.e4 c5 2.♘f3 d6 3.d4 cxd4 4.♘xd4
♘f6 5.♘c3 e6 6.g4 h6 7.h4 ♘c6
8.♖g1 h5 9.g5**

9.gxh5 is better.

9...♘g4 10.♗e2

10...♕b6

10...d5!−see Sznapik-Adorjan, Dortmund
1984, awarded the best novelty by the
Chess Informant jury, accompanied by
another heavily commented game vs
Schmittdiel. Black adheres to the old
wisdom: if your opponent attacks on the
flank, break open the centre. If you are
educated by the right principles it is so
much easier to find concrete (counter-)
weapons to fight with!

11.♗xg4 hxg4 12.♘xc6 bxc6 13.♕xg4

Since White has committed himself to an early kingside attack, it seems logical to follow the classical advice and look for counterplay in the centre. This principle helped me to discover the move which keeps White busy here:

13...d5!

As you can see, number 13 doesn't always mean bad luck.

14.g6

If 14.b3 ♗b4 15.♗d2 ♕d4 and now:

A) 16.♖g3 e5 17.♕f3 ♖xh4 18.0-0-0 (18.exd5? ♗g4 19.♕g2 0-0-0 20.♖d3 ♖dh8 21.♖xd4 ♖h1+ 22.♕f1 exd4−+) 18...dxe4 19.♕e2 a5 with initiative;

B) 16.♕g3 ♗a6 (16...dxe4? 17.0-0-0) 17.0-0-0 ♗e2 18.♖de1 ♗h5 19.♕d3 ♕xd3 20.cxd3=/∓.

14...f6 15.h5 ♗c5 16.♕f3

16.♖g2 ♗d6∓ was played later between Nunn and Andersson as an improvement. But my next novelty again came earlier...

16...♗a6 17.h6

As on move 14, trying to develop the c1-bishop by 17.b3 invites tactical repercussions:

A) 17...♖xh5 18.♘a4 (18.♕xh5? ♗xf2+ 19.♔d1 0-0-0 20.♖g2 dxe4+ 21.♗d2 e3 22.♕g4 f5 23.♕a4 e2+ 24.♘xe2 ♖xd2+−+) 18...♕a5+ 19.♗d2 dxe4 20.♕g3 ♗b4 21.0-0-0 ♗xd2+ 22.♖xd2 ♖g5=;

B) Or also 17...♗b4! 18.♗d2 (18.a3 dxe4!) 18...d4 19.♘e2 d3! 20.cxd3 0-0-0∓.

17...0-0-0 18.♗d2?

Very naive or desperately tired? Whatever the reason, the text is a major blunder.

18.h7!?, targeting the promotion square, was no joke. For example, after 18...d4 19.♘d1 or 18...♗d4 19.exd5 exd5 20.♗e3! ♕xb2 21.♕g4+ f5 22.♕xd4 ♕xa1+ 23.♘d1 ♕xa2 24.♕xg7 it would still have been a game.

18...♕xb2 19.♖b1 ♕xc2 20.♕d1

White may have overlooked that 20.♖c1 fails to the nice 20...♕xd2+!.

20...♕d3

White resigned.

Imagine I started with 2½ out of 3 in this Interzonal after another splendid game against Hulak – who sadly passed away in early 2016. Unfortunately I finished only on 50%, winning and losing some more games like this.

**Enver Bukic
Andras Adorjan**
Banja Luka 1983

Another last-round game. I had to win against the very solid Yugoslav GM to be first. With BLACK, as usual.

1.d4 ♘f6 2.c4 g6 3.♘f3 ♗g7 4.♘c3 d5 5.cxd5 ♘xd5 6.e4 ♘xc3 7.bxc3 c5 8.♖b1

8...♕a5?

An original idea, but false, instead of the usual 8...cxd4 9.cxd4 ♕a5+ 10.♗d2 ♕xa2 11.♗e2 0-0 12.0-0 with hundreds of games, with a strong initiative for White. But I have always liked initiative over material.

9.♗d2?

Returning the favour in a big way.
The refutation was 9.♖b5, for instance:

A) 9...♕xc3+ 10.♗d2 ♕a3 11.♕c2! c4 (the only move; if 11...b6 12.♖b3 ♕a4 13.♗b5+) 12.♖b4 ♕a6 13.♗xc4 ♘c6 14.♗c3 ♕a3 15.♖b3± with a dream position for White – ergo, a nightmare for Black;

B) 9...♕xa2 10.♖xc5 ♘d7 11.♖b5 a6 12.♖b4±.

9...♕xa2 10.d5

10.♗b5+!? ♗d7 11.♗d3 with some compensation.

10...♕a5 11.♕c1 0-0 12.c4

12...♕a2

Moves like this are always risky. 12...♕c7 13.♗e2 ♗g4 14.h4 h5 was safer.

13.♗d3

13.e5?! ♗f5 14.♖b2 ♕a4 – unclear.

13...♗g4

13...♘a6!? 14.0-0 ♕a4.

14.♗c3 ♗xc3+ 15.♕xc3 ♕a6 16.♘d2 b6 17.f3 ♗d7 18.h4

18.e5 would have given White an attack.

18...♕c8

Trying to make up for my positional sin.

19.h5 ♘a6= 20.hxg6 fxg6 21.♔f2 ♘b4 22.♗e2 ♖f7 23.♘f1 a5 24.♘e3 ♕f8

BLACK is OK – better again!

25.♖b3 ♕g7 26.e5 ♖f4 27.g3 ♖d4 28.e6 ♗e8 29.♘g4 h5 30.♘e3 ♕f6 31.g4 h4 32.♖bb1 g5

Pleasant as a dream. Enjoy it!
32...a4 was also winning.

33.♘f5 ♗g6 34.♖bg1 ♖f8 35.♕e3

35.♘xd4 also fails on account of 35...cxd4 36.♕d2 d3.

35...♔h7

35...b5 was pretty brutal.

36.d6?

If 36.♖h2, again 36...b5!.

36...exd6! 37.♖d1 ♘c2 38.♕c1 ♖xd1 39.♖xd1 ♘d4 40.♘xd4 cxd4 41.♕b2 ♕xe6 42.♕xd4 ♕e5 43.♕xd6 ♕xd6 44.♖xd6 a4 45.♖xb6 ♖a8 46.♖b2 a3 47.♖a2 ♗b1 48.♖a1 a2 49.f4 gxf4 50.♔f3 ♖e8 51.♗f1 ♔h6 52.c5 ♔g5 53.♗c4 ♖e3+ 54.♔f2 ♖c3 0-1

If White were a masochist, he would have had a really good time here.

Fernand Gobet
Andras Adorjan

Biel 1983

1.e4 c5 2.♘f3 e6 3.d4 cxd4 4.♘xd4 ♘f6 5.♘c3 d6 6.g3

A pretty harmless set-up against the Scheveningen. I have played it with both colours, so I know.

6...♘c6 7.♗g2 ♗d7 8.0-0 ♗e7 9.♘ce2 a6 10.c4 ♖c8 11.b3 0-0 12.♗b2 ♕a5!

Even better than 12...b5 13.cxb5 ♘xd4 14.♘xd4 axb5 15.a3 ♕b6.

13.a3

13.♗c3 ♕h5 14.♘xc6 ♗xc6 15.♖e1 and now 15...e5!?, restricting the knight, equalizes (15...b5!? 16.♘d4); 13.♕e1 ♕h5 (13...♕c7!?) 14.♘f4 ♕c5 with mutual chances (14...♕h6!?).

13...♖fd8 14.♖e1

What else?

14.b4 mainly weakens c4: 14...♕h5 (14...♕b6!? 15.♘xc6 (15.♘b3 a5!) 15...

bxc6 16.♘f4 e5) 15.♖c1 ♘g4 16.h3 ♘ge5 17.♕b3 ♘xd4 (17...b5 18.♘f4 ♕h6 19.cxb5 ♘xd4 20.♗xd4 axb5 is a little less convenient) 18.♘xd4 b5 19.cxb5 axb5∓.

14...b5 15.cxb5 axb5 16.♘xc6 ♗xc6 17.♘d4 ♗a8

17...♗e8!?; 17...♗d7!? 18.♕d3 g6 19.♖ac1 e5.

18.♕e2 ♖b8 19.♖ec1 ♕b6

19...b4? fails tactically to 20.axb4 ♕xb4 and now 21.♖xa8 ♖xa8 22.♘c6 ♕b7 23.e5, while 21.♖a4! is also very annoying.

People are always surprised to hear me say, 'And BLACK is already BETTER'. Some even stay away from me.

20.♖c2 e5! 21.♘f5 ♗f8 22.♕d3

Better was 22.♖ac1. After 22...g6 White has to give up the e4-pawn with 23.♘e3 (23.♘h4 ♗h6∓). But Black should react with 23...♗h6, keeping the initiative – not 23...♘xe4? 24.♘g4 f5 25.♗xe4 fxe4 26.♘f6+ ♔g7 27.♖c7+ ♔xf6 28.♕g4 and White wins in the attack.

22...♕b7 23.♖ac1?

A big mistake.

A better defence was 23.♖e1 g6 24.♘h4 ♕b6 (24...♖bc8 25.♖ce2 ♗e7∓) 25.♘f3 ♖bc8 though Black has the initiative.

23...♘xe4! 24.♘e3

24.♕e3 ♕b6 25.♕xb6 (25.♕e2 ♘c5∓) 25...♖xb6 26.♖c8 ♖b8∓; 24.♖c7? ♘xf2!–+ is what Gobet may have overlooked.

24...♘c5!

The ending wins.

25.♖xc5 dxc5 26.♕xd8 ♕xg2+ 27.♘xg2 ♖xd8 28.♗xe5 ♖d3 29.♖b1 ♗e4?!

The start of a series of returned favours and second-best moves. Fortunately my advantage was bigger than my stupidity. 29...♗d5 was a winner, for example: 30.b4 ♗e4 (30...f6−+) 31.bxc5 ♖d5 32.♖e1 ♖xe5 33.f3 ♗xc5+ 34.♔h1 f5.

30.♘f4 ♖d2?!

30...♖xg3+! 31.hxg3 ♗xb1 32.a4 c4 was still good for the full point.

31.♖e1 ♗c6 32.♔f1 f6 33.♗c3 ♖c2 34.♖e3 ♖c1+?

Time-trouble... 34...♖a2−+.

35.♔e2 ♖b1 36.♗a5 ♖b2+ 37.♔e1 c4!

37...♗d7!?.

38.bxc4 ♗c5 39.♖e2?

39.♖e6 ♗d7! 40.♖e2 ♖b1+ 41.♔d2 bxc4∓.

39...♖b1+ 40.♔d2 bxc4 41.♗b4

41.♖e6 ♗d7∓.

41...♗xb4+ 42.axb4

42...g5!

42...♖xb4 43.♔c3 ♖a4 44.♖e7 would have allowed White to draw.

43.♖e6 ♗f3 44.♖e3 ♗g4 45.♘e6 ♖b2+ 46.♔c1

46.♔e1 c3−+.

46...♖xb4

I could have gone for the kingside pawns as well, as the b-pawn can be stopped, for example: 46...♖xf2 47.b5 ♖xh2 48.b6?! ♖h1+ 49.♔b2 ♗f5 50.♘d4 ♖b1+ 51.♔c3 ♗d3−+. But 48.♘d4! may hold the draw.

47.f3 ♗f5 48.g4 ♗g6 49.f4 ♖b1+ 50.♔d2 ♖b2+ 51.♔c3 ♖b3+

52.♔d2

It's not clear if there is a win for Black after 52.♔d4 ♗f7 53.♖e1 ♖h3 54.f5 (54.fxg5 ♖d3+! 55.♔c5 fxg5 56.♘d4 ♖h3 ∓/−+) 54...c3 55.♖e2 h5 56.♖a2 (56.gxh5 ♗xh5 57.♖c2 ♗g4 58.♖xc3 ♖xc3 59.♔xc3 ♗xf5∓) 56...♗xe6 57.fxe6 ♔f8 58.gxh5 ♔e7 59.♔d5 ♖d3+ 60.♔e4 (60.♔c4 loses to 60...♖d2−+) 60...♖d2 61.♖a6 ♖xh2 62.♖c6∓.

52...♗f7!

Now it is really over.

53.♖e4 gxf4 54.♘xf4 ♖b2+ 55.♔c3 ♖xh2 56.♘e6 ♖h4 57.♘d8 ♖h3+ 58.♔b4 c3 59.♘xf7 ♔xf7 60.♖c4 ♔g6 61.♔c5 ♖d3 62.♔b4 ♔g5 63.♔b3 h6 64.♔c2 ♖g3 **0-1**

What can I say? This game was not an evergreen, but it was 'green' in every part...

Krunoslav Hulak 2530
Andras Adorjan 2535

Indonesia 1983 (15)

1.e4 c5 2.♘f3 e6 3.d4 cxd4 4.♘xd4 ♘f6 5.♘c3 d6 6.f4 a6 7.♗d3

7.♕f3!?.

7...♘bd7 8.g4 h6 9.♕f3

Just bad.

9...e5! 10.♘f5

10.♘b3.

10...g6 11.♘e3

11.♘g3 loses the g4-pawn after 11...exf4 and now:

A) 12.♕xf4 g5 13.♕f1 ♘xg4 14.♗e2 ♘df6 (14...♘de5? 15.♘h5) 15.h3 ♘e5 16.♗e3 ♗e6 17.0-0-0 ♗e7 18.♘f5 ♗xf5 19.♕xf5 ♕d7 20.♕f2 0-0-0∓;

B) 12.♗xf4 g5 13.♗d2 ♘e5 14.♕g2 ♗xg4 15.♗e2 ♕c8∓.

11...exf4 12.♕xf4 ♘e5 13.h3 ♗e6

Believe it or not: Black has the upper hand after 13 moves.

14.♗d2 ♖c8 15.♗e2

If 15.0-0-0 ♘xd3+ (15...♗xa2!? 16.♗e2 ♗e6) 16.cxd3 ♗xa2 17.e5 ♘d7 18.exd6 ♗g7 and Black's king is safer than White's.

15...♗g7 16.♘cd5

If here 16.0-0-0 ♕b6 Black will come first as well.

16...♗xd5!

Less clear is 16...g5?! 17.♘xf6+ ♗xf6 18.♕f2 ♘g6 19.c3 ♘f4 20.♘f5 ♗e5 21.♗xf4 gxf4 22.♖d1 ♕c7 (22...♗xa2 23.♘xd6+ ♗xd6 24.e5) 23.a3 when White also has his trumps – chances are probably equal.

17.exd5 0-0 18.0-0-0 ♖e8 19.♖he1 ♖e7

19...♘ed7!? 20.♗f1 (20.♕xd6 ♘e4∓; 20.♗f3 ♕c7∓) 20...♖e4 21.♕xd6?! ♖a4, winning.

20.♔b1 ♕e8 21.♗f1

White could have created counter-chances here with 21.h4!? ♘ed7 22.h5.

21...♘fd7 22.♖e2 ♘b6 23.♕b4

23.b3 only walks into a decisive attack after 23...♘ec4! 24.bxc4 ♘xc4.

23...♘a4

24.♖f2

24.b3 ♘f3 25.♕xa4 ♘xd2+ 26.♖dxd2 ♖xe3 27.♕xe8+ ♖cxe8 28.c4 ♔f8∓.

24.♗c1 ♘f3 25.♖d3 doesn't work due to 25...♖e4!.

24...b5

24...♘xb2! 25.♖c1 (25.♕xb2 ♘d3) 25...b5 was crushing.

25.c3 ♘d7

25...♘c4! 26.♘xc4 (26.♗xc4 bxc4 27.♘xc4 ♖e4 28.b3 ♖exc4 29.bxc4 ♖b8) 26...bxc4 would have left White defenceless.

26.♘c2 ♘dc5 27.♖f3 ♖e5 28.♗f4 ♖e4 29.♕a5 ♘xb2

With 29...♗f6 Black could have gone for the white queen, but after 30.♖e3, 30...♘xb2 is again the winning move. 30...♗d8?! 31.♕b4 is much less clear. Some pretty motifs though!

30.♔xb2

30...♘a4+

In time-trouble there were too many ways to win here. It's a headless orgy of attack.

The most convincing was 30...♖a4 31.♕b6 ♕e4 (or also 31...♖xf4 32.♖xf4 ♕e5−+) 32.♖f2 ♗xc3+.

31.♔c1 ♘xc3 32.♕xa6 ♖a8?

32...♘e2+ 33.♗xe2 ♖xe2 34.♗d2 ♖xc2+ 35.♔xc2 ♕e4+ was winning.

33.♕c6 ♘xa2+ 34.♔d2

Now the king is an easy prey. It would still have been quite difficult after 34.♔b1 ♕d8 35.♕xd6 ♕a5 36.♖a3 ♘c3+ 37.♔c1 ♖a4∓.

34...♕d8 35.♕xb5?

A tougher defence was 35.♖e1 ♗c3+ 36.♖xc3 ♘xc3 37.♕xc3 ♖xf4 38.♗xb5 ♕g5.

35...♖b8 36.♕a6 ♕c7??

Just blundering the knight, while 36...♖b2 37.♖b1 ♘b4 would have won.

37.♕xa2 ♖xf4 38.♖xf4 ♕c3+ 39.♔c1 ♖b2

40.♕a4??

40.♖c4 would even have won for White – a bizarre position!

40...♖b1+!

With mate: White resigned.

Bojan Kurajica	2510
Andras Adorjan	2530

Sarajevo 1983 (8)

1.♘f3 c5 2.c4 ♘f6 3.g3 b6 4.♗g2 ♗b7 5.0-0 g6 6.b3 ♗g7 7.♗b2 0-0 8.♘c3

8...d6

8...d5 9.♘xd5 ♘xd5 10.♗xg7 ♔xg7 11.cxd5 ♕xd5 12.d4 ♘a6! is only equal. Black plays for a win, of course.

9.d3

Passive.

The alternative was 9.d4!? cxd4 10.♘xd4 (10.♕xd4 ♘bd7 11.♘d5?! b5!) 10...♗xg2 11.♔xg2 ♕c7 (11... d5 12.cxd5 ♘xd5 13.♘db5 is a draw) 12.e4 ♕b7 13.♖e1 a6 with a typical Hedgehog where BLACK IS OK!

9...a6 10.e4 e6 11.♖e1 ♘c6 12.♕d2 ♖b8 13.h3

What for?

13...♗a8

An interesting option was 13...♘d7!? 14.♘e2 ♗xb2 15.♕xb2 ♘de5 16.♘xe5 dxe5∓.

14.♘e2 b5 15.♖ab1

15...♖b6! 16.♗c3 ♕b8 17.♘h2

Black is for choice after both 17.♕b2 e5∓ and 17.♖bc1 bxc4 18.bxc4 ♘d7.

17...bxc4! 18.dxc4 e5 19.♘c1 ♘d4 20.♘d3 ♗c6 21.♗a5 ♖b7 22.g4

Wrong – this only creates more weaknesses.

22...h6 23.♗c3 ♕a8 24.f4

Oh my goodness! A harakiri attempt. 24.♘f1!? was the lesser evil.

24...♖d7 25.♘f2 exf4

25...♘e6!?.

26.♗xd4 cxd4 27.♕xf4 ♖e8 28.♘f1 ♖de7 29.♘d2

After 29.♕xd6 ♘d7 Black has all the play.

29...d5! 30.e5 ♘h7!

The other two knight moves were also promising for Black: 30...♘e4 31.♘fxe4 dxe4 32.♗xe4 ♖xe5 33.♗xc6 ♕xc6∓; 30...♘d7 31.♘d3 ♘xe5 32.♘b4 dxc4 33.♘xc6 ♘xc6 34.♖xe7 ♖xe7 35.♘xc4 ♕b8∓.

31.♕xd4

31.♘d3 ♘g5∓.

31...♗xe5 32.♕d3 ♘f6 33.♘f3 dxc4 34.bxc4 ♗f4 35.♖xe7 ♖xe7 36.♕d4 ♘e4 37.♖e1 ♖d7 38.♕b6 ♗g3 39.♘xe4 ♗xe4 40.♖f1 ♖d3 41.♕f6

The sealed move.

41...♕a7+ 42.♔h1 ♗b8

43.c5

You can see what White's actions on move 13 and 22 have done to his dark squares.

There was no more hope, for example:

A) 43.♖b1 ♖d6, winning the exchange;

B) 43.g5 ♗xf3 44.♖xf3 ♕c7, winning more;

C) 43.♕b2 ♕c7 44.♖b1 ♖d8 45.♖f1 ♕g3 46.♕f2 ♕xf2 47.♖xf2 ♖d1+ 48.♗f1 ♗a7, winning probably just as much;

D) 43.♖e1 ♕f2 44.♖f1 ♗xf3 45.♖xf2 ♖d1+ 46.♖f1 ♖xf1#.

43...♕c7 44.♕b2 ♕f4 45.♔g1

45.♖b1 ♗c7.

45...♗xf3 46.♖xf3

46.♗xf3 ♖d2−+.

46...♕h2+ 47.♔f2 ♗g3+   0-1

It was a BLACK day for poor Bojan K.

Ole Jakobsen	2445
Andras Adorjan	2530

Plovdiv Ech tt 1983 (3)

During this event, our stupid team captain (a founding member of the Hungarian Communist Party) was sitting opposite me at dinner. He tried to encourage me in the usual blackmail way of threatening to throw me out of the team for always playing for a draw. Just because I started off with two draws against the super-solid Keene and Kurajica.

I didn't sleep till dawn, and then started a four-game winning streak, of which the one given below was fought out in an awful mutual time scramble. Thus I became the best scorer of Hungary (5½/7) on our way to winning the bronze medal. From the Enemy of the State I became the Saver of the Nation. The monster was convinced that his friendly push had paprika'd me up. I've learned what suffering is in many ways, friends.

1.d4 ♘f6 2.c4 e6 3.♘c3 ♗b4 4.♘f3 c5 5.e3

5.g3!?.

5...♘c6 6.♗d2

A rare move, avoiding the so-called Hübner Variation and all the theory that goes with it. Not so bad either.

6.♗d3.

6...cxd4 7.exd4 0-0 8.a3 ♗xc3 9.♗xc3 b6

9...d5!?.

10.♗d3

10.d5? is *Selbstmord* due to 10...exd5 11.cxd5 ♖e8+ 12.♗e2 ♗a6 13.♘g1 ♘a5.

10...d5 11.b3 a5 12.a4?!

12.0-0!? ♗a6 13.♕e2 looks more natural.

12...♗a6 13.0-0 ♖c8 14.♖c1 ♕e7 15.♖e1 ♖fd8 16.♗b2

16.cxd5!? ♗xd3 17.dxc6 ♗a6 18.♗d2 ♘d5 19.♕c2 ♖d6 20.♘g5 g6 21.♕e4 ♕f6 22.♕h4 h5 would have kept me trying to serve the country.

16...♕b7 17.♗b1

17.♕e2.

17...♘e7

I couldn't find any forced wins as a loyal Hungarian citizen was expected to. The shadow-boxing continues.

17...h6!?.

18.♘e5 dxc4 19.bxc4 ♘g6 20.♗d3 ♕e7 21.d5

It was better to maintain the knight on e5 by 21.♗xg6 hxg6 22.♕f3.

21...♘xe5 22.♖xe5 ♕b4 23.♗c3

He might have given up his centre pawns, obtaining an initiative against my king: 23.♖e2!? ♗xc4 24.♖ec2 exd5 25.♗xf6 gxf6 26.♗f5.

23...♕d6 24.♖g5

In time-trouble, Ole Jacobsen gets over-ambitious. Bravo and Olé but not OK.

24...exd5 25.♗e5 ♕e7 26.♕f3 ♖c6 27.♖e1

27.♗xf6 ♖xf6.

27...h6 28.♖g3 ♖e6 29.♕f5?

He loses, drowning in his romantic dreams. 29.♕f4 ♔f8 30.♖ge3 dxc4 31.♗f5 ♘d5 32.♕g3 ♕g5 was already favouring Black.

29...dxc4

30.♖xg7+ ♔f8

Of course, I was also in time-trouble by now. 30...♔xg7 31.♕h7+ ♔f8 32.♕xh6+ ♔e8 33.♗f5 ♕b4 34.♕e3 ♘d5 35.♕e4 c3 was another devilish road to Hell.

31.♗c2 ♖d5 32.f4 ♖dxe5 33.fxe5 ♔xg7 34.exf6+ ♕xf6 35.♕h7+ ♔f8 36.♖f1 ♕d4+ 37.♔h1

37...♕f2!

A safe mercy killing.

38.♕xh6+ ♖xh6 39.♖xf2 ♖e6 40.h4 ♖d6 41.g4 ♖d4 42.♗g6 ♗b7+ 43.♔h2 ♗d5 44.♔g3 c3 45.♗c2 b5 46.axb5 a4 47.h5 a3 48.h6 a2 49.h7 ♔g7 50.♗f5 ♖xg4+ 0-1

Completely crazy. And so am I. Please pardon me for taking you with me.

Ivan Nemet	2395
Andras Adorjan	2535

Biel 1983

1.d4 ♘f6 2.c4 e6 3.♘c3 ♗b4 4.♕c2 0-0 5.a3 ♗xc3+ 6.♕xc3 b5!?

This is the counter-gambit with my idea of ...c7-c6. Alvis Vitolinsh played this move with the intention 7.cxb5 a6.

7.cxb5 c6!

Black tries to take advantage of the white queen's delicate situation on the c-file, combined with the exploitation of the light-square weaknesses by his advantage in development. A bright idea in general. But it needs co-operation and the benefit of the surprise effect. The great Geza Maroczy used to say: 'If you have a material advantage, look for a way to return it for something else.'

8.bxc6?! ♘xc6 9.♗g5

This would have been better one move earlier: 8.♗g5 cxb5 9.e3 with a normal position.

9.♘f3 ♗b7 (9...♗a6!? 10.♗g5 ♖c8) 10.♗g5 leads to the game continuation.

9...♗b7

9...♗a6!? would have been fine, also against 9.b4.

10.♘f3 ♖c8 11.♘d2?

There is a thing I call not colour blindness but white-colour drunkenness. You will see what this looks like.

11.♕d3.

11...h6 12.h4?

Another sign of 'white chauvinism'. With piece sacrifices you cannot always mate. Instead, an extra careful defence would have been advisable. A sense of danger is something white players often leave at home.

A) 12.♗xf6 ♕xf6 13.e3 e5 14.dxe5 ♘xe5 15.♕d4 (15.♕b3 ♘g4 16.f3 ♗d5!–+)

15...♖c2 16.♗e2 (16.♕xa7 ♘g4 17.f3 ♖xd2–+) 16...♗xg2 17.♖g1 ♗f3 18.♘xf3 ♕xf3 19.♕d1 ♕e4∓;

B) 12.♗h4 ♗a6!? (12...g5 13.♗g3 ♘d5 14.♕c5 ♘cb4 15.axb4 ♖xc5 16.bxc5 ♕a8∓) 13.b4 ♘e7 and now:

B1) 14.♕h3 ♘f5 15.e4 doesn't work in view of 15...♗xf1 16.exf5 ♗a6 17.♘e4 ♖c2! 18.♘c5 exf5 19.♘xa6 ♖e8+ 20.♔f1 (20.♔d1 ♖ee2–+) 20...♖c8 21.♘c5 d6 22.♕d3 ♖ee2 23.♕xe2 ♖xe2 24.♔xe2 g5 25.♗g3 dxc5–+;

B2) But 14.♕f3 ♘f5 15.♗xf6 ♕xf6 16.e3 ♗xf1 17.♘xf1, ♕g6 18.♘g3 ♘xg3 19.hxg3 ♕d3 does not give Black more than just enough compensation.

12...hxg5 13.hxg5 ♘g4 14.♘e4

Other moves are worse: 14.♕h3 f5 15.g6 ♘h6–+; 14.f3 ♘ce5 15.♕b4 ♕c7! 16.fxg4 ♘xg4–+; 14.♕d3 f5 15.f3 ♗a6 16.♕xa6 ♘xd4–+.

14...f5

Only moves are not at all difficult to find. The alternative is to resign. The problems begin when there are several tempting, seemingly equally strong candidate moves.

The choice is difficult, and this needs self-discipline, which was never my strongest point when chess beauty was at stake.

A) 14...♕c7 was strong, for example:

A1) 15.♕h3 f5 16.gxf6 ♘xf6 17.♘xf6+ ♖xf6–+;

A2) 15.♘f6+ ♘xf6 16.♕h3 (16.gxf6 ♕a5 17.b4 ♕f5 18.fxg7 ♔xg7–+) 16...♘h5 17.♕xh5 f6 18.♕h7+ (18.g6 ♕a5+ 19.♕xa5 ♘xa5–+) 18...♗f7 19.gxf6 ♖g8–+;

A3) But 15.d5 starts a crazy line in which White can put up a good fight: 15...♕f4 16.♕h3 f5 17.gxf6 ♘xf6 18.dxe6 dxe6 19.♕xe6+ ♖f7 20.♘d6 ♘d8 21.e3 ♕xf2+ 22.♔xf2 ♖c2+ 23.♔g1 ♘xe6 24.♘xf7 ♔xf7∓.

B) Strongest was 14...♕a5! 15.♘c5 (15.b4 ♘xb4 16.♕xb4 ♕xb4+ 17.axb4 ♗xe4 18.♖h4 f5 19.gxf6 ♘xf6–+) 15...♕xc3+ 16.bxc3 ♖c7 17.e4 ♗c8! 18.♗e2 d6 19.♘a4 e5 20.♖h4 ♘e7! 21.♖xg4 (21.♗xg4 ♘g6 22.♗xc8 ♘xh4–+) 21...♗xg4 22.♗xg4 exd4 23.cxd4 ♖c4∓/–+.

15.gxf6

15.♘d6 just loses to 15...♕xg5 16.♕h3 (16.♘xc8 ♖xc8 17.e3 f4 18.♖h3 fxe3 19.fxe3 ♘e7 20.♕d3 ♘f5–+) 16...♘h6 17.♘xc8 ♖xc8 18.♕h4 ♕xh4 19.♖xh4 ♘a5.

15...♘xf6

15...♘b4! would have fulfilled a double duty – winning, and also in style: 16.♘c5 ♕xf6 17.f3 ♘a6 18.♕d3 (18.fxg4 ♕f2+ 19.♔d1 ♘xc5–+) 18...♘xc5 19.♕h7+ ♔f7 20.♕h5+ ♔e7–+; or 16.♕xb4 ♗xe4 17.♕e7 ♕xe7 18.fxe7 ♖xf2–+.

16.♘d6   ♕c7   17.♘xc8   ♖xc8 18.♖h4

Black is better because his pieces can spring to life in a matter of seconds: 18.e3 ♘e4 19.♕c4 ♕a5+ 20.b4 ♕f5 21.♕a2 (21.f4 ♘e5 22.♕b5 ♕g4 23.♖h3 ♕xh3 24.gxh3 ♘f3+ 25.♔e2 ♘c3+–+) 21...♘e5! 22.dxe5 ♕xe5–+.

18...♕b6 19.f3

19.e3 runs into the pretty 19...♘e4!! 20.♖xe4 ♘a5 21.♕d3 ♘b3 and Black wins.

19...♘a5

Nothing is wrong yet, only the beauty has faded somewhat. Winning should still be a routine task, but instead something like a *kashmar* begins (this is a Russian word I learned from Garry which means 'nightmare'). You can lose any winning position even without taking it easy, and here I almost did just that.

19.g5! 20.d5 ♔f7–+.

20.♕b4 ♘b3 21.♖d1 ♕xb4+ 22.axb4 ♖c4 23.e3 ♖xb4 24.♗d3 a5??

24...♘c5!? 25.♗c2 ♖xb2.

25.♔f2 ♘c5 26.♗g6 ♖xb2+ 27.♔g3 ♘b3 28.e4

28...♔f8?

Incredible! 28...d6!? 29.e5 dxe5 30.dxe5 ♘d5 31.♖dh1 ♔f8 32.♖g4 ♔g8 33.♖gh4 ♔f8 34.♖g4 was still a draw.

29.e5 ♔e7 30.exf6+ ♔xf6 31.♗e4

31.♖b1!?±.

31...♗xe4 32.fxe4 a4 33.e5+ ♔f7 34.d5 a3 35.♖f4+ ♔g6 36.dxe6 dxe6 37.♖df1 ♔h7

Now it's a draw. 37...a2=.

38.♖g4

38.♖a4 a2 39.♖f8 a1♕ 40.♖h4+ ♔g6 41.♖g4+ would have secured the least likely result of a game like this: draw.

38...♔g8 39.♖a4 a2 40.♖a8+ ♔h7 41.♖a7

41...♔h6

And this stupid move... made White give up! Quite an upset in the stem game for this line.

41...♖b1 was winning. Instead, after 41...♔h6, 42.♔f4 ♖xg2 (42...♖b1 43.♖f3 a1♕ 44.♖h3+ ♔g6 45.♖g3+=) 43.♖a6 a1♕ 44.♖axa1 ♘xa1 45.♖xa1 ♖e2 46.♖h1+ ♔g6 47.♖g1+ ♔f7 48.♖b1 still gives White hopes of a draw.

Attila Groszpeter   2490
Andras Adorjan   2570
Budapest ch-HUN 1984

The young 'Groszpeti' seemed to be stealing the show in the Hungarian Super Championship of 1984. I was half a point behind him, and I had to beat him. Which is what I did, because I believed this is possible 'even with Black', as they say. I went on to win this event – it was the first of my three national titles. Rejoicing, I donated half of my prize to the Fund for Rebuilding Hungarian National Theatre. Yes! It was finally erected in 2002. I never got invited to visit it. Still, doing good feels great. Don't hesitate if you can do it!

1.d4 ♘f6 2.♘f3 e6 3.e3 c5 4.♗d3 b6 5.0-0 ♗b7 6.b3 ♘c6 7.♗b2 ♗e7 8.♘bd2

8...0-0

Attila Groszpeter deserves credit. Instead of playing for a draw, like an idiot he gave me a chance for a fight, mistakenly believing in White's chances. As almost everybody else does.

8...cxd4 9.exd4 ♘b4 10.♗e2 ♘bd5 and now:

A) 11.♘e1 ♗b4!? (11...♗a3? 12.♗xa3 ♘c3 13.♘c4 is fantastic for White!) 12.♘b1 ♘f4 13.♗f3 d5∓;

B) 11.♖e1 ♗b4∓;

C) 11.♘e5 0-0 12.♗f3 ♕c7 13.c4 ♘f4=.

9.a3 cxd4 10.exd4 ♖e8 11.♖e1 ♖c8 12.♖c1 d6 13.c4

13...♘b8!

The Moor has done his duty on c6, and now he is being regrouped to a different basis, challenging more activities of the opponent, who believes in White.

14.♘f1

14.♘b1!? d5 15.♘bd2=.

14...♘bd7 15.♘e3 ♗f8 16.d5

16.♗b1 a6 17.d5 exd5 (17...e5!?=) 18.♗f5 ♗e7=.

16...exd5 17.cxd5

17.♗f5 was better here.

17...♖xc1 18.♗xc1 ♕a8 19.♗b5

19.♗c4 a6 20.a4 g6 21.♗b2 ♗h6=.

19...♖d8 20.♗c4 a6 21.a4

With hindsight, 21.b4 was wiser, for example: 21...b5 (21...g6!? 22.♗b2 ♗h6=) 22.♗b3 and now:

A) Not 22...♘b6 23.♗b2 ♘bd7 (23...♘fxd5 runs into 24.♘g5 h6 25.♘xf7 ♔xf7 26.♕h5+ ♔g8 27.♘f5+−) 24.♘g5 h6 25.♘e6!+−;

B) But 22...♖e8 23.♗b2 ♘e5 is quite equal.

21...♘e5! 22.♗b2 b5

Blow!

23.axb5 axb5 24.♗xb5 ♘xd5

25.♘h4

Now White's position falls apart, but other roads would have led him astray in similar ways:

A) 25.♘xd5 ♘xf3+ 26.♕xf3 ♗xd5 27.♕f5 (27.♕g3? ♕a5−+) 27...♕a5 28.♖d1 ♗e6 29.♕d3 ♕a2∓/∓;

B) 25.♘xe5 dxe5 (25...♘xe3!? 26.♖xe3 dxe5 27.♖d3∓) and now:

B1) 26.♕e2 ♘f4 27.♕f1 ♗c5 28.♗xe5 ♗xg2 29.♘xg2 ♘h3+ 30.♔h1 ♘xf2+ 31.♔g1 ♖d1−+;

B2) 26.♘xd5 ♗xd5 27.f3 (27.♕g4 ♕a5 28.♕e2 f6∓) 27...♕a5 28.♕e2 ♗xb3∓/−+;

B3) 26.♕c1 ♘xe3 27.♕xe3 ♗xg2 28.♗xe5∓;

B4) 26.♕a1 ♕xa1 27.♗xa1 ♘xe3 28.fxe3 ♖d2 29.♗f1 f6∓.

25...♘f4! 26.♗f1 ♗e7 27.♘hf5 ♗f6

27...♘h3+? 28.gxh3 ♘f3+ allows White to 'get away with a black eye' by the queen sac 29.♕xf3 ♗xf3 30.♘xe7+ ♔f8 31.♘7f5=.

28.♗xe5

Both 28.♕a1? ♘h3+! and 28.♘d4 ♗e4 29.♕d2 ♗d3 would leave Black with a clear edge.

28...dxe5

29.♕g4?

Collapsing in time-trouble. With 29.♕c1!? he could have hung on longer, but the situation remains just as hopeless.

29...h5!−+ 30.♕g3 ♕a5 31.♖b1 ♕a2 32.♖e1 ♕d2!

32...♕xb3 33.♘g4 ♕xg3 34.♘xf6+ gxf6 35.hxg3 was nice, but not as good as the text.

33.♖a1

33.f3 g6−+; 33.♖d1 is met by the winning queen sac 33...♕xd1 34.♘xd1 ♖xd1 35.♕e3 ♗xg2 36.♘g3 h4−+.

33...♗e4 34.h4

Now after 34.♖d1, 34...♕xd1 35.♘xd1 ♖xd1 36.♕e3 ♗xf5 is even simpler.

34...♔h7 35.♔h2 ♕d7 36.♖d1 ♕c7 37.♖xd8 ♕xd8 38.f3 ♗d3 39.♗xd3 ♕xd3

White overstepped the time-limit in a lost position. Still I got not two points but just one for this double victory. A special prize was awarded to me nevertheless... the finish might have been 40.♕f2 g6 41.♘g3 ♗xh4.

Mershad Sharif	2220
Andras Adorjan	2580

New York 1984 (1)

I wonder if you have noticed the universal idiocy of calling openings like Sicilian, Benoni and alike 'defence'. All of these are attempts to take the initiative from the very first moment. The Najdorf, the Dragon, just to mention two of the many Sicilian variations. The Benoni is sharp as a razor. It's a kind of one-way thinking (White is better), otherwise there is no reasonable explanation. Why don't they call the Sicilian just Sicilian? Or Sicilian Variation? Think about it!

1.e4 c5 2.♘f3 e6 3.♘c3 d6 4.d4 cxd4 5.♘xd4 ♘f6 6.f4 a6 7.♕f3 ♘bd7 8.♗e3 e5

This switch is amazingly effective in these kinds of Sicilians. See Hulak-AA above. Action-reaction does not necessarily mean attack-defence. Counterplay-attack is an apter way of putting it. In tennis, you see aces but also winning returns. Again: use your own brain, don't blindly follow patterns drawn up by others! And God will bless you.

9.♘f5

Now belt up and be brave. You will find the many coming variations enriching; improving or refuting something here and there. In the meantime you gradually develop as a chess player. If you're talented, good. If you think you can sit on your laurels, you're a pitiful, simple-minded creature. Work and devotion cannot be replaced by anything.

A) 9.♘de2 and now:

A1) 9...b5 10.0-0-0 b4 (10...♗b7!? 11.g4 (11.♔b1 ♖c8) 11...b4 12.♘d5 ♘xd5 13.exd5 ♗e7=) 11.♘d5 ♘xd5 12.exd5 ♗e7=;

A2) 9...exf4 10.♕xf4 ♘e5 11.0-0-0 ♗e7; A21) 12.h3 ♗e6 13.♘d4 ♖c8 14.♘f5 ♘h5 15.♕f2 ♖xc3 (15...♗xf5!? 16.♗b6 ♗h4 17.♕xf5 ♕g5+ 18.♔b1 ♕xf5 19.exf5 ♖c6=) 16.bxc3 ♕a5 with compensation;

A22) 12.♔b1 ♘fg4 13.♗c1 ♘g6 14.♕f3 ♘6e5=.

B) 9.♘b3 ♗e7 10.0-0-0 0-0 11.♔b1 b5=.

9...g6 10.♘g3 exf4

This seems artificial, but in reality it is quite clever. Look for motifs like this in your games. Try to find your own self!

10...♗h6!? 11.0-0-0 exf4 12.♗xf4 ♘e5 13.♕e3 ♗xf4 14.♕xf4 ♗e6 15.♗e2 0-0=.

11.♕xf4

11.♗xf4 ♘e5=.

11...♘e5 12.♗e2 ♗g7 13.0-0 0-0 14.h3 ♗e6 15.♖ad1 ♖c8 16.♗d4

Do you realize that BLACK is already BETTER as early as here? Check it! If 16.♕h4 ♘c4 17.♗xc4 ♖xc4 18.♗g5? ♕b6+ and the strike on b2 decides.

16...♘fd7 17.♖d2 ♖e8 18.♖fd1

18...♕f6!

Black's attack continues after the exchange of queens. Am I in my right mind? But don't you know you can attack in the endgame too? That is what happens here.

19.♗e3

19.♕xf6 ♘xf6 (19...♗xf6!?) 20.♗e3 ♗c4 21.♗f4 (21.♖xd6? ♗xe2 22.♘gxe2 ♘c4−+; 21.♗d4 ♗h6∓) 21...b5 22.♖xd6 (22.b3 ♗xe2 23.♘cxe2 h5∓) 22...♗xe2 23.♘cxe2 ♘c4 24.♖xa6 ♘xe4 25.b3.

analysis diagram

And here it comes: 25...♘e3! 26.♗xe3 ♘xg3 27.♘xg3 ♖xe3∓.

19...♕xf4 20.♗xf4 ♘b6 21.♖b1
♘ec4 22.♖d3

22.♖dd1 ♖c6∓.

22...♘xb2

The crowning of Black's strategy – an
orgy of fine tactical motifs.

23.♖xb2 ♖xc3 24.♖xd6

24.♖xb6 ♖xd3 and 25...♗d4+.

**24...♘c8 25.♖xe6 fxe6 26.e5 b5
27.♘e4 ♖a3**

27...♖c6–+.

Some people try to get on your nerves
instead of behaving like gentlemen. Walter
Browne had a special method for such
cases: 'If you don't resign here (patzer),
you'll get a half an hour free lesson from a
six-time US Champion.' That was Browne,
of course, but I don't know many people
who could educate in that way.

28.c4 ♘b6 29.cxb5 ♘d5 30.♗h2

30.g3 ♘xf4 31.gxf4 ♖a4∓.

**30...axb5 31.♗xb5 ♖b8 32.♘f6+
♘xf6 33.exf6 ♗xf6 34.♗xb8 ♗xb2
35.♗c4 ♔f7 36.♗b3 ♖a5 37.♗d6
♗a3 38.♗c7 ♖c5 39.♗f4 ♖f5
40.♗d2 ♗c5+ 41.♔h2 ♖f1   0-1**

In the New York tournament of 1984,
my opponent in the following game had
played a 2.c3 Sicilian vs Kavalek some
rounds earlier, and he very easily drew
against the variation with 2...d5. When I
saw Zuckerman's third move I had a hunch
that he was again aiming at a half point, so
I decided to put aside my favourite move
and seek a less well trodden path – taking
a risk to gain the full point.

Bernard Zuckerman	2490
Andras Adorjan	2570

New York 1984 (7)

**1.e4 c5 2.♘f3 e6 3.c3 b6 4.d4 ♗b7
5.♗d3 ♘f6 6.♘bd2**

White should have sought an opening
advantage with 6.♕e2!? cxd4 7.cxd4
♘c6 (7...♗e7 8.♘c3 0-0 9.0-0 d6
10.♗f4) 8.a3! ♖c8 9.0-0 ♗e7=.

**6...cxd4 7.cxd4 ♗e7 8.0-0 0-0
9.♖e1 d6 10.a3 ♘bd7**

So we have the well-known Hedgehog
formation again! The little thorny thing
is lying in wait for the careless beast of
prey that tries to assault him.

11.e5?!

White is too impatient.

11.b4 ♖c8 12.♗b2 ♖c7 13.♕e2 ♕a8=;
11.♘f1 ♖c8 12.♘g3 ♖c7=; 11.♕e2!?
♖c8 12.b4=/±.

11...dxe5 12.dxe5 ♘g4

13.♕c2?!

White has already strayed from the right
path and now inflicts further damage
on himself.

A) 13.♗e4 was a better move, for example:

A1) 13...♕c7 14.♗xb7 ♕xb7 15.h3 ♘h6 16.♘e4 ♘f5 17.g4;

A2) 13...♗xe4 14.♖xe4 f5!? (14...♘h6) 15.exf6 ♘dxf6 16.♖d4 ♕e8=/∓ with the idea 17.h3 ♘xf2 18.♔xf2 ♗c5.

B) 13.h3 ♘dxe5 14.♖xe5 ♘xe5 15.♘xe5 f6 16.♘df3 ♗xe5 17.♘xe5 ♕d5 18.♕f3 ♖ad8 (18...♕xe5 19.♕xb7 ♕e1+ 20.♔h2 ♖ad8 21.♕e4 ♕xe4 22.♗xe4 ♖d1 23.♖b1 ♖fd8 24.♗e3=) 19.♕xd5 ♖xd5 20.♗f4 g5 21.♗g3 f6 22.♗e4 fxe5 23.♗xd5 ♗xd5 24.♗xe5 ♖c8 25.♗c3=.

13...♖c8

Black is on his way to a win!

14.♕b1

14.♗xh7+ ♔h8 15.♕a4 (15.♕d3 ♗c5−+) 15...♗xf2! leads to very fine prospects for Black: 16.♔xf2 ♘c5 17.♕c2 g6 18.♗xg6 ♘h4+ 19.g3 fxg6 20.♕xg6 ♖c7−+.

14...♗c5 15.♖e2

15...♗xf2+

15...♘xf2 was more forcing. For example: 16.♖xf2 (16.♗xh7+ ♔h8 17.b4 ♘d1+ 18.bxc5 ♘c3−+) 16...♘xe5 17.♘xe5 ♗xf2+ 18.♔xf2 (18.♔h1 ♖c5−+) 18...♕d4+ 19.♔f1 ♕xe5 and owing to White's undeveloped and unharmonious position, Black's victory cannot be in doubt.

16.♖xf2 ♘xf2 17.♔xf2 ♘xe5 18.♗e2

Forced.

18...♘g4+

19.♔g1

19.♔e1 ♘e3−+; 19.♔g3 f5−+.

19...b5?

A hasty move.

19...♕c7 was the proper continuation, when White would not have even the slightest chance. Let's see why: 20.b4 b5 21.h3 (21.♕d3 ♖fd8 22.♕xb5 ♖d5−+) 21...♕b6+ 22.♔h1 ♕f2 23.hxg4 ♕xe2−+ and White cannot escape from Black's grip.

20.♕d3 ♕c7

20.e5!?∓/−+.

21.h3 ♖fd8 22.♕xb5 ♘e3 23.♕g5

23.♘b3 ♘c2 24.♖b1 ♗d5 and 23.♘f1 ♘c2 24.♖b1 ♗e4 both lose.

23...♘c2 24.♖b1 ♕b6+ 25.♔h2 ♕f2 26.♗d1

How can you dance in fetters? My opponent had no answer to this question.

26.♘g1 ♘d4−+.

26...♘e3 27.♗b3

27...♖d7!

The destiny of the c1-bishop is sealed, as is that of the game. The following moves are motivated only by time pressure.

28.♕g3 ♕xg3+ 29.♔xg3 ♖dc7 30.♔f2 ♘f5 31.♘c4 ♖xc4 32.♗xc4 ♖xc4 33.♘d2 ♖c2 34.g4 ♘d4 35.b4 e5 36.b5 h6 37.a4 ♗e4 38.♔e3 ♗g6 39.♖a1 ♖c3+ 40.♔f2 ♖xh3 41.♔g2 ♖c3

White resigned. OK!

Mohamed Sharif
Andras Adorjan 2515

Thessaloniki ol 1984 (1)

1.d4 ♘f6 2.c4 e6 3.♘c3 ♗b4 4.e3 c5 5.♘e2 cxd4 6.exd4 0-0 7.a3 ♗e7 8.d5 exd5 9.cxd5 ♖e8 10.g3 ♗c5 11.b4

11...♗b6

Targeting f2. With the circumventive manoeuvre 11...♗d6!? 12.♗g2 ♗e5 (12...a5!? 13.♖b1 axb4 14.axb4 ♗e5) Black might have provoked White into weakening his position: 13.0-0 d6 14.f4 ♗xc3 15.♘xc3 ♕b6+ 16.♔h1 ♗f5∓.

12.♗g2

12.♘a4? ♘g4−+; 12.h3 a5!∓.

12...d6

12...♘g4!? would be too direct (patzerish), i.e. 13.0-0 ♕f6 (13...d6!? 14.h3 ♘e5):

A) 14.♕e1 d6 15.♗b2 ♗d7 (15...♕h6!? 16.h3 ♘e5 17.♕c1 ♕xc1 (17...♕g6 18.♘a4 ♘d3 19.♕d2 ♗d8 20.♘f4 ♘xf4 21.♕xf4 ♗d7 22.♘c3 ♗g5=) 18.♖axc1 ♘d3 19.♖c2 ♘xb2 20.♖xb2 ♗f5=) 16.♖a2 ♘a6∓;

B) 14.♗f4 g5 15.♘e4 ♕h6 16.h3 ♖xe4 and now:

B1) 17.♗xb8? ♘xf2−+;

B2) 17.♕c1 ♖xe2 18.♗xg5 (18.♕xc8+ ♔g7−+) 18...♕f8 19.hxg4 d6∓;

B3) 17.hxg4 ♖e8 (17...♖xe2? 18.♗xg5! ♕xg5 19.♕xe2+−) 18.♗d2 d6 19.♘c3 ♘d7 20.♘e4 ♖xe4 21.♗xe4 ♘e5 with Black's initiative.

Not too bad, on second thought!

13.0-0

On the immediate 13.♘a4 play may continue 13...♗g4 14.♖a2 ♘bd7 with active piece play for Black.

13...♘bd7

13...a6 14.♗f4 ♘h5 15.♗d2 ♗g4∓.

14.h3?!

14.♘a4 ♗c7 15.♘d4 ♘e5∓.

14...a6 15.♘f4

15.♗f4 ♘e5 16.♘d4 ♗d7∓.

15...♘e5 16.♖a2

The b6-bishop still plays its part, as you witness 16.♘h5 ♘xh5 17.♕xh5 ♗d4∓; and 16.♘d3 ♗d4 17.♗b2 ♘c4∓.

16...♗d7

16...♗f5 17.g4 ♖c8 18.♘a4 ♗b1 19.♖b2 ♗e4 20.♘xb6 ♕xb6∓.

17.♘h5

Other simplifications do not really help: 17.♘d3 ♖c8 18.♘xe5 dxe5 19.♗b2 ♗d4∓; 17.♘e4 ♘xe4 18.♗xe4 ♖c8∓.

17...h6!

17...♖c8 was also good, but it would take some creativity: 18.♗g5 ♖xc3 19.♗xf6 gxf6 20.♕d2 ♖e3! 21.fxe3 f5 22.h4 ♘g4 and Black attacks.

18.♔h2?!

18.♔h1 ♖c8 19.♗b2 ♘xh5 20.♕xh5 ♗d4 21.♘e4 ♗xb2 22.♖xb2 ♗b5∓.

If you think 18...♗xf6+ was better, you are right; after 18...♔xf6 19.♗f4 the onlookers would have had to wait a little longer for the KO, but due to his weaknesses White's situation remains critical.

18...♖c8 19.♗b2

Or 19.♘xf6+ ♕xf6 20.♘e4 ♕g6 21.♖c2 (21.♗f4 ♗b5−+) 21...♖xc2 22.♕xc2 ♖c8−+.

The matter is ripe for settlement.

19...♘fg4+! 20.♔h1

On 20.♔g1 Black also crashes through: 20...♘xf2 21.♖xf2 ♗xf2+ 22.♔xf2 ♕b6+ 23.♔f1 ♘c4 24.♗c1 ♘e3+ 25.♗xe3 ♕xe3 and everything falls apart.

20...♘xf2+ 21.♖xf2 ♗xf2 22.♘e4 ♗a7 23.♘xd6

23...♗a4(!)

The interpolation.

24.♕xa4 ♕xd6 25.♖a1 ♕g6 26.♕d1 ♘d3

White now decided he had had enough, and resigned.

Marc Santo Roman   2360
Andras Adorjan   2555

Cannes 1986 (8)

1.e4 c5 2.♘f3 e6 3.d4 cxd4 4.♘xd4 ♘f6 5.♘c3 d6 6.g4 h6 7.h4 ♘c6 8.♖g1 h5

9.gxh5

On 9.g5 ♘g4 10.♗e2 d5!∓ is a tough central counter-thrust – see the game Rodriguez-Adorjan above.

9...♘xh5 10.♗g5 ♘f6 11.♕d2 ♕b6 12.♘b3 a6 13.0-0-0 ♗d7 14.♖g3 ♖c8 15.♕e2

15.♔b1!? ♕c7 16.a4 ♘h5 17.♖f3 ♘e5 18.♖h3 is unclear.

15...♕c7 16.♗g2 ♗e7 17.♖e3?!

Anything but this! Let's say 17.♖h3 b5 18.a3 ♘e5 (18...b4!? 19.axb4 ♘xb4 20.♘d4 g6∓) 19.h5 a5, but anyway it's Black who is calling the shots here.

17...♘e5 18.f4 ♘c4 19.♖ed3?

19.♖h3.

19...♘h5!

Now the white position collapses.

20.♖h3

20.♗xe7 ♘xf4 21.♕e1 (21.♕f2 ♘xd3+ 22.cxd3 ♘xb2 23.♕xb2 ♕xc3+ 24.♕xc3 ♖xc3+ 25.♔b2 ♖xb3+ 26.axb3 ♔xe7−+) 21...♔xe7∓.

20...f6 21.f5

21.♗f3 g6∓/−+.

21...fxg5 22.hxg5 ♗xg5+ 23.♔b1

23...♔e7?!

The right idea, but the immediate 23...♘xb2! was more convincing, for example: 24.♔xb2 (24.♖xh5 ♘xd1 25.♘xd1 ♖xh5 26.♕xh5+ ♔f8−+) 24...♗f6 25.♔b1 ♗xc3 26.♖xh5 ♔e7−+.

24.♖xh5?

My previous move gave White the chance to play 24.fxe6 ♗xe6 25.♖xh5 ♖xh5 26.♕xh5. After 26...♘a3+ 27.♔a1 ♗f6 28.e5 the situation is totally unclear.

24...♖xh5?

Again, 24...♘xb2! was winning.

25.♕xh5 ♗f6

Here, 25...♘a3+ 26.bxa3 ♗f6 would have failed to an efficient hoovering operation by White: 27.e5! ♗xe5 28.f6+ ♗xf6 29.♘d5+ exd5 30.♖e1+ ♗e5 31.♕h4+ with equality.

26.♗h3?

The very end.

His last chance to bail out was 26.fxe6! ♗xe6 27.♗h3! (27.e5!?) 27...♗f7 28.♘d5+ ♗xd5 29.exd5 ♘a3+ 30.♔a1 ♘xc2+ 31.♔b1 ♘a3+ 32.♔a1 with a draw.

26...♘a3+

Also, 26...♗e8−+.

27.♔c1 ♗xc3 28.fxe6 ♗e8 29.♕e2 ♗e5 30.bxa3 ♕c3 31.♕d3 ♕b2+ 32.♔d2 ♗b5

Now White will be hoovered. He resigned.

Here is a crazy game between two romantic souls.

Istvan Bilek
Andras Adorjan
Hungary tt 1986

1.♘f3 c5 2.e4 e6 3.♘c3 a6 4.g3 b5 5.♗g2 ♗b7 6.d3 d6 7.0-0 ♗e7

Preventing the idea 8.♘g5 followed by the march of the f-pawn for the moment, though also after 7...♘f6 8.♘g5 ♗e7 9.f4 h6 10.♘h3 0-0 11.f5 b4 12.♘e2 exf5 13.♖xf5 ♘c6 Black is doing well.

8.♘d2

Bilek's funny patent.

8...♘c6

8...♘f6 9.e5 ♘d5 (9...♗xg2 10.exf6=) was also playable, e.g., 10.♘xd5 ♗xd5 11.♗xd5 exd5 12.♕g4 0-0 (12...dxe5 13.♕xg7 ♗f6 14.♕h6 ♕d6 15.♘f3 ♘d7 16.♗g5 0-0-0 17.♖fe1±) 13.♘f3 ♕d7 14.♕xd7 ♘xd7 15.♖e1 ♖fe8=.

9.f4 ♘f6 10.f5 0-0 11.fxe6

Trying to exploit the light squares.

11...fxe6 12.♗h3 ♘d4 13.♘f3 e5

13...♔h8!? 14.♘g5 e5=.

14.♗g5 ♕b6

The standard Sicilian liquidation with 14...♘xe4!? 15.♘xe4 ♗xe4 (15...♘xf3+

16.♖xf3 ♖xf3 17.♗xe7+−) 16.dxe4 ♗xg5 worked here, too.

After 17.c3 ♖xf3 18.♖xf3 ♘xf3+ 19.♕xf3 ♕e7 Black is a pawn up, but the position has been simplified and the bishops are of opposite colour.

15.♘h4

In case of 15.♕d2 b4 White can hold with the unattractive-looking 16.♘a4 (16.♘e2 leaves too many pieces hanging: 16...♘xe4 (16...♘xf3+ 17.♖xf3 ♘xe4 18.♖xf8+ ♖xf8 19.dxe4 ♗xg5 20.♕xg5 c4+−+) 17.dxe4 ♘xf3+ 18.♖xf3 ♖xf3 19.♗xe7 c4+ 20.♔h1 ♖f7−+) 16...♘xf3+ 17.♖xf3 ♕c6 18.♗e6+ ♔h8 19.♗xf6 ♗xf6 20.♗d5 ♕c7 21.♗xb7 ♕xb7 22.♖af1=.

15.♗xf6 ♖xf6 16.♘xd4 cxd4 17.♖xf6 invites another promising exchange sacrifice: 17...dxc3+ 18.♖f2 ♖f8 19.♕e2 cxb2 20.♖b1 d5 21.♔g2 dxe4 22.♖xf8+ ♗xf8 23.dxe4 ♕g6∓.

15...c4

Black has taken over already.

16.♗e3 d5 17.exd5

17...♗c5

17...♘xd5! was winning: 18.♘xd5 ♗xd5 19.♗g2 (19.c3 ♗xh4 20.cxd4 ♗g5 21.♗f2 ♖xf2 22.♖xf2 ♗e3−+) 19...♗xg2 20.♘xg2 ♖xf1+ 21.♔xf1 (21.♕xf1 ♗c5−+) 21...♗c5 and White is ripe for the slaughter.

18.dxc4

If 18.♗f2 ♘xd5 19.♘e4 (19.♘xd5 ♗xd5 20.♗g2 (20.c3 ♖xf2 21.♖xf2 ♘f3+ 22.♘xf3 ♗xf2+ 23.♔f1 ♖f8 24.♗g4 cxd3)

20...♕b7−+), now 19...♘b4 intends a strong piece sacrifice after 20.♘xc5 ♕xc5 21.c3 ♘xd3 22.cxd4 exd4 when the centre pawns and long diagonals will prove too much for White.

18...♘xc2 19.♕xc2 ♗xe3+ 20.♔h1 bxc4 21.♗g2 ♗d4 22.♘e4?

A more active defence was 22.♘f5! ♖ad8 (22...g6) 23.♘e4.

22...♘g4! 23.♘g5

Now 23.♘f5 would run into 23...♖xf5 24.♖xf5 ♘e3 25.♕f2 ♘xg2! when the long diagonal becomes fatal for White, for example: 26.♕xg2 ♕xb2 27.♕xb2 ♗xb2 28.♖d1 (28.♖b1 ♗xd5) 28...♗d4.

23...♕h6

23...g6!−+.

24.♘e6

In time-trouble he might have tried 24.♗e4 ♕g5 25.♗xh7+ ♔h8 26.♘g6+, but after the queen sacrifice 26...♕xg6 Black's bishops decide the issue: 27.♗xg6 ♗xd5+ 28.♗e4 ♖f2 29.♖xf2 ♗xe4+.

Also insufficient is 24.♕xc4 ♕xg5 25.d6+ ♔h8 26.♗xb7 ♕d2 27.♗g2 ♘f2+ 28.♖xf2 ♖xf2 29.d7 ♕xb2 30.♕c8+ ♖f8−+.

24...♖f2!

Normally this ought to decide the issue – just like:

A) 24...♘e3 25.♖xf8+ (25.♕a4 ♘xf1 26.♘xf8 ♖xf8 27.♖xf1 ♖xf1+ 28.♗xf1 ♗xd5+ 29.♘g2 ♕e6−+) 25...♖xf8 and again, Black's bishops will carry off the victory after the knight takes on g2:

26.♕e2 (26.♕a4 ♘xg2 27.♕d7
(27.♘xf8 ♘xh4 28.♕d7 ♕f6–+)
27...♘xh4 28.♕xb7 ♕f6–+)
26...♘xg2 27.♘xg2 ♖f2 28.♔f1 ♗xd5
29.♖xf2 ♗xf2 30.♕xf2 ♕xe6–+;

B) 24...♘f2+ 25.♔g1 ♕xe6 26.dxe6
♘d1+ 27.♔f2 (27.♔h1 ♖xf1#)
27...♖xf2 28.♕xf2 ♗xf2+ 29.♔f1
♗xg2+ 30.♘xg2 ♘xb2 31.♔xf2 ♖e8∓.

25.♖xf2
25.♕xc4 ♖xg2–+.

25...♘xf2+ 26.♔g1 ♘g4+ 27.♘xd4
27.♔h1 ♘e3 28.♕e2 (28.♕a4 ♘xg2
29.♕d7 ♘xh4 30.♕xb7 ♖f8 31.♘xd4
exd4 32.gxh4 ♕f4–+) 28...♘xg2
29.♕xg2 ♗xb2–+.

27...♕e3+
Continuing the attack. The endgame after
27...exd4 28.♕e4 ♕e3+ 29.♕xe3 ♘xe3
should win. Everything works for Black,
but unfortunately White refuses to break.

28.♔h1 ♘f2+
It was again time to consider the favourable endgame after 28...exd4 29.♘f5
♕d3∓.

29.♔g1 ♘d1+
Still wanting to keep the queens on the
board. Objectively better was either
29...♘d3+ 30.♔h1 ♕xd4 31.♘f5 ♕xb2
32.♕xb2 ♘xb2 33.♘d6 ♖b8 34.♖b1 c3
or 29...♘g4+ 30.♔h1 exd4 31.♘f5 ♕d3∓.

30.♔f1 exd4 31.♖xd1
Similar was 31.♕xd1 ♖f8+ 32.♗f3
(32.♘f3 ♗xd5 33.♕e2 ♗xf3∓) 32...g5
33.♕e2 ♕xe2+ 34.♔xe2 gxh4 35.♖d1
hxg3 36.hxg3 ♖e8+. The position is
equal – Black's c4- and d4-pawns can
easily be stopped.

31...♖f8+ 32.♘f5?
The wrong square.
After 32.♘f3 ♗xd5 33.♖e1 ♗xf3
34.♖xe3 ♗e4+ 35.♔e1 ♗xc2 Black still
has an edge, but in this endgame it's
better for White to have the knight to be
able to attack the pawns: 32.♗f3 ♗xd5
33.♖e1 ♗xf3 34.♖xe3 ♗e4+ 35.♕f2
dxe3 36.♕xf8+ ♔xf8 37.♔e2 is a draw.

32...d3!
White probably counted on 32...g6
33.♖e1 d3 34.♖xe3 dxc2 35.♖c3 ♖xf5+
36.♔e2 ♖e5+ 37.♔d2 ♗xd5 38.♗xd5+
♖xd5+ 39.♔xc2 ♖h5 40.h4 ♖a5 41.a3=.

33.♕f2

33...♕xf2+?
In time-trouble I missed the win with
33...♖xf5! 34.♕xf5 ♕e2+ 35.♔g1
♕xd1+ 36.♗f1 ♕e1 37.♕e6+ (37.♕d7
♕e3+ 38.♔g2 d2! and there is no
perpetual) 37...♕xe6 38.dxe6 ♗f3
39.♔f2 d2 40.♗xc4 ♔f8–+.

34.♔xf2 ♖xf5+ 35.♔e3 ♗xd5
Due to White's activated pieces the
endgame is quite dangerous for Black, for
example: 35...♖e5+ 36.♔d4 ♖e2 37.d6+–.

36.♗xd5+
He could have won the exchange by
36.g4 ♖g5 37.h4 ♖e5+ 38.♔d4 ♗xg2
39.♔xe5, with winning chances.

36...♖xd5 37.♖c1?
Underestimating Black's nasty reply.
37.b3! was still a draw: 37...♖e5+ (37...
cxb3=) 38.♔d4 ♖e2 39.bxc4 ♖xh2
40.♖xd3 ♖xa2 41.c5=.

37...♖e5+

38.♔d4?

This fails tactically. More tenacious was 38.♔f3, but White is in trouble in any case:

A) 38...♖d5 39.♔e3 ♔f7 40.♔d2 ♖b5 and now:

A1) 41.♖xc4 ♖xb2+ 42.♔xd3 ♖xh2 (42...♖xa2 43.♖h4 h6) 43.♖f4+ ♔g6 44.♖g4+ ♔h6 45.a3 g6 46.♔e3 ♖b2 47.♖a4 ♖b6 and Black can still try;

A2) 41.♔c3 should save the game with careful play:
41...♔g6 (41...♔f6 42.♖b1 ♖h5 43.h4 ♖c5∓) 42.a4 ♖b7 (42...♖b3+ 43.♔xc4 ♖xb2 44.♔xd3 ♖xh2∓) 43.♖b1 ♔f5 44.♔xc4 ♖d7 45.♔c3 ♔e4 46.♖e1+ ♔f3 47.♔d2 ♔g2 48.♖e3 ♖b7 49.♔xd3 ♖xb2 50.♖e7.

B) More logical is 38...♖e2 39.♖xc4 ♖xh2 40.♖a4 d2 41.♖d4 d1♕+ 42.♖xd1 ♖xb2 and White still has a tough job holding.

38...♖e2 39.b3

39.♔xc4?? ♖c2+−+; 39.♖xc4 d2−+.

39...cxb3 40.axb3 d2

Now it's game over.

41.♖d1 ♖xh2 42.♔c5 ♖g2 43.b4 ♖xg3 44.♖xd2 ♖g5+ 45.♔c4 ♖g6

White resigned.

In my youth, grandmaster Bilek was one of my teachers. I became a good pupil by listening to his words.

Anna Akhsharumova	2290
Andras Adorjan	2560

New York 1987

Akhsharumova was not at all a sitting duck, or a fragile female. She had played sensationally earlier on in the tournament.

1.d4 ♞f6 2.c4 e6 3.♞f3 b6 4.♞c3 ♝b7 5.a3 d5 6.cxd5 ♞xd5 7.♕c2 ♞xc3 8.bxc3 c5 9.e4 ♞d7 10.♝f4 ♝e7

10...cxd4 11.cxd4 ♕c8 12.♕b1.

11.♝d3

Here is a small bunch of alternatives:

A) 11.d5?! exd5 12.exd5 0-0 (12...♝xd5? 13.0-0-0!+−) 13.♖d1?! (13.c4 g5!?)

analysis diagram

13...g5! (fantastic!) 14.♝e3 (14.♝c1 g4 15.♞d2 ♝xd5 16.♞c4 ♝e6 17.♝d3 or 14.♝g3!? g4 15.♞d2 ♝g5 are unclear) 14...g4 and now:

A1) 15.♕f5 gxf3 16.♝d3 (16.♝h6 ♖e8−+) 16...♞f6−+;

A2) 15.♞g1 ♝g5 16.♕f5 ♝xe3 17.fxe3 ♕h4+ 18.g3 ♕e7 19.♝d3 f6 20.♕xg4+ ♔h8 with initiative;

A3) 15.♞d2 f5 16.h3 (16.g3 ♝xd5 17.♝c4 ♞e5 18.0-0 ♝xc4 19.♞xc4 ♞f3+∓; 16.f4 ♞f6∓) and now:

A31) 16...f4?! is too nice to be sound: 17.hxg4 ♝h4 18.♞f3 fxe3 19.♖xh4 exf2+ 20.♕xf2= (draw, 41) Lputian-Adorjan, Hastings 1986;

A32) 16...♝g5! 17.♝xg5 (17.hxg4 ♝xe3 18.fxe3 ♕g5) 17...♕xg5 18.c4

(18.hxg4 ♖ae8+ 19.♗e2 ♗a6 20.c4 ♕xg4 21.♕d3 ♕xg2) 18...♖ae8+ 19.♗e2 ♕h4! 20.g3 ♕h6!.

B) 11.♗b5 0-0 12.0-0 ♘f6 13.♖fe1 a6 14.♗d3 ♖c8 ½-½ Browne -Adorjan, New York 1987 – a sudden draw.

11...0-0 12.0-0 ♖c8 13.♕e2 ♘f6 14.♖fe1 cxd4 15.cxd4 ♖c3 16.a4

First 16.♗d2 ♖c8 and then 17.a4 was better, as we will see.

16...♕a8 17.♗d2

17...♖xd3! 18.♕xd3 ♗xe4

Destruction of White's centre, which gives Black abundant compensation for the exchange.

19.♕e2 h6

19...♖d8!?.

20.♖ac1 ♗xf3 21.♕xf3 ♕xf3 22.gxf3 ♘d5

Who needs a rook if you can have a knight on such a square?

23.♖c6 ♖d8 24.♗e3 ♖d7 25.♔g2 ♔h7

Also possible was 25...♗g5!? 26.♗xg5 hxg5 when only Black can play.

26.f4 ♔g6 27.♔f3 ♔f5 28.♖b1 ♗b4 29.♖b2 g6 30.♖b3 h5 31.♖b2 ♔f6

31...♖d6!? also favours Black; White has to play 32.♖b5.

32.♖b3 ♔e7 33.♗c1 ♗d6 34.♗a3?!

Cold, cold.

34.♗d2.

34...♗xa3 35.♖xa3 ♔f6 36.♔e4 ♘e7 37.♖c2 ♘f5 38.♖d3 ♖d5

39.♖dd2 ♖a5 40.♖a2 ♘e7 41.♖dc2 ♖f5 42.♖a3 ♘d5 43.♖f3 ♔g7 44.♖c4 ♘f6+

44...a5 45.h3; 44...a6 45.♖c6 h4.

45.♔d3 g5!?

A clever idea, but the execution is badly timed; 45...a6.

46.♖e3?

Running out of patience.

46.♖g3! would probably have held, for instance: 46...g4 (46...♖xf4? 47.♖xg5+ ♔h6 48.♖g2 ♘d5 49.♖c8=) 47.f3 ♖xf4 48.fxg4 (48.d5!?=) 48...hxg4 (48...♖xg4 49.♖c7 ♖xg3+ 50.hxg3 a5=) 49.h3 (49.d5!?=) 49...a6 50.hxg4 ♘d5 51.g5 b5 52.axb5 axb5 53.♖c5 b4 and after 54.♖c1 or 54.♖b5 it should be a draw.

46...♖xf4 47.d5 ♖xc4 48.♔xc4 ♘xd5

But it's all over now.

49.♖a3 g4 50.a5 ♔g6 51.♔b5 bxa5 52.♖xa5

Better was 52.♔c5!? ♘f4 53.♔d4 ♘h3 54.♔e3 f5 55.♖xa5 f4+ 56.♔e2 ♘g1+ 57.♔f1 ♘f3 58.♔g2 h4 59.h3 ♘e1+ 60.♔f1 gxh3 and now 61.♖a3 still puts up a fight, but the position smells anyway.

52...♘c3+ 53.♔c4 ♘e4 54.♖a2 ♘g5 55.♖a1 ♘f3 56.♖h1 h4

Now further resistance is futile.

57.♔d3 ♔g5 58.♔e2 h3 59.♖c1 ♘xh2 60.♖c7 f5 61.♖h7 e5 62.♖h8 ♘f3 63.♔f1 e4 64.♖h7 ♔f4 65.♖h8 e3 66.fxe3+ ♔g3 **0-1**

Not crystal-clear, but entertaining.

Matthias Steinbacher 2340
Andras Adorjan 2520

Germany Bundesliga 1988/89 (1)

I played in the Germany Bundesliga 1 for Kirchheim (Heidelberg). My debut was not very impressive and here my opponent felt he was close to drawing.

31.♘xa6??

31.♗xb5 axb5 32.♔f1 d3 33.♘xd3 ♘c4∓. However...

31...d3!

... destroyed his illusion. White resigned in view of 32.♘b4 d2.

Bela Perenyi
Andras Adorjan

Budapest ch-HUN rapid 1988

1.e4 c6

The underestimated, 'passive', wonderfully solid, flexible, dynamic counter-attack, the Caro Kann!

2.d4 d5 3.♘c3 dxe4 4.♘xe4 ♘d7 5.♗c4 ♘gf6 6.♘g5 e6 7.♕e2 ♘b6 8.♗d3 h6 9.♘5f3 c5 10.dxc5 ♗xc5 11.♘e5 0-0 12.♘gf3 ♘bd7 13.0-0 b6

14.b4?!

A 'greenhorn' decision.

14.♖d1 ♘xe5 15.♘xe5 ♕e7 16.♗f4 ♗b7 with mutual chances; or 14.b3.

14...♘xe5

14...♗d6 15.♗b2 ♘xe5 16.♘xe5 ♗b7 17.a3 was White's intention.

15.♘xe5 ♗d6

15...♗xb4 16.♘c6 ♕d6 17.♘xb4 ♕xb4 18.♕f3 ♗d7 19.♗a3 ♕a5 (19...♕a4) 20.♗xf8 ♖xf8 is supposed to be worse for Black, but it's not true!

16.♗b2 ♗b7 17.a3 ♕c7

17...♕e7! 18.♘g4 ♘xg4 19.♕xg4 ♕g5 20.♕xg5 hxg5∓ Schneider-Adorjan, Reykjavik 1982.

18.f4 ♖fe8

18...a5!? looks dangerous after 19.♘g4 ♘xg4 20.♕xg4, but Black defends with 20...f5 21.♕g6 ♕f7 22.♗xf5 ♕xg6 23.♗xg6 ♗xf4∓.

19.♔h1 ♖ad8 20.c4 a5! 21.♗c3?!

21.c5 bxc5 22.b5 a4 is also good for Black. It might have been best just to take on a5.

21...axb4 22.axb4

22.♗xb4 ♗c5∓.

22...♘d5!

23.♗d4?

After this the complications favour Black, who controls the d-file. Better was 23.cxd5 ♕xc3 24.♗b5 ♖e7 25.dxe6 ♖xe6 26.♖ad1 with chances to hold.

23...♘xb4 24.♗b1 ♗c5 25.♗b2 ♗d4

Now White's position hangs by a thread. Perenyi opts for the flight forward.

26.♖a3 f6 27.♗xd4 ♖xd4 28.♕h5 ♖e7 29.♕g6 f5 30.♘g4?

This loses – White does not get enough for the piece. But 30.♖h3 ♖d2 31.♖g3 ♕c5 or 30.♖g3 ♕d6 were also unattractive.

30...fxg4 31.♕h7+ ♔f8 32.♗g6 ♖f7 33.♕h8+ ♔e7 34.♕g8 ♔f6 35.f5

Black's turn!

35...♗xg2+! 36.♔xg2 ♖d2+ 37.♖f2 ♖xf2+ 38.♔xf2 ♕xh2+ 39.♔f1 ♕f4+ 40.♔g2 ♕e4+ 41.♔g1 ♖d7

White resigned.

Poor Bela Perenyi was my friend and partner, and he was a great attacker. He beat practically the full elite ranks of Hungary (including Portisch and Ribli). But he hardly ever managed even a draw against me. I could play in his style as well, only more strongly.

Corral
Andras Adorjan
Mazatlan Wch rapid 1988

1.d4 ♘f6 2.c4 e6 3.♘c3 ♗b4 4.e3 c5 5.♘e2 cxd4 6.exd4 d5 7.c5

7...e5!?

A rapid gamble. 7...0-0 8.a3 ♗a5 9.g3 ♘c6 is 'normal'.

8.dxe5?!

A customer!
8.a3!? ♗xc3+ 9.♘xc3 exd4 10.♕xd4 ♘c6 (10...0-0 11.♗b5) 11.♗b5=.

8...♘g4 9.♗f4?!

A) 9.e6!? 0-0 10.♘f4 d4 11.a3! ♗a5 12.♕xg4±;

B) 9.h3 ♘xe5 10.♗f4 ♕e7 with Black's initiative (10...♘bc6);

C) 9.♘f4?! d4 (9...0-0 10.♗e2 d4 11.a3 ♗a5 12.♗xg4 dxc3 13.0-0=) 10.e6 0-0 transposes to A.

9...♗xc5 10.♘d4 0-0

Or 10...♘c6 11.♗b5 0-0 12.♗xc6 ♕b6 with unpleasant pressure on b2 and f2.

11.♗e2?

He could just keep his position together with the more acute 11.h3 ♘xe5 12.♗xe5 ♖e8 13.♘f3 d4 14.♗b5 ♘c6 15.0-0 dxc3 16.♕xd8 ♖xd8 17.♗xc3 ♗e6 18.♖ac1=.

11...♘xf2!

Like in a fairy-tale!

12.♔xf2 ♘c6 13.♘b5

Retreating the bishop invites a few queen checks, e.g.: 13.♗e3 ♘xd4 14.♗xd4 (on 14.♘a4 ♘xe2 15.♗xc5 ♖e8 16.♕xe2 ♕h4+ wins back the piece) 14...♕h4+ 15.♔e3 ♕g5+ 16.♔f3 (16.♔f2 ♕f4+) and now 16...♗g4+ wins, as does 16...f6!, for example: 17.e6 ♕f5+ 18.♔e3 ♕e5+ or 18.♔g3 ♗d6+ 19.♔h4 g5+ 20.♔h5 g4+ 21.♘h4 ♕g5#.

13...a6 14.♖c1 ♕b6

15.♖xc5?

15.b4 ♗xd4+ 16.♘xd4 ♕xd4+ 17.♕xd4 ♘xd4, with a worse endgame, was best under the circumstances.

15...♕xc5 16.♗e3 axb5 17.♘e6?

Not tricky, but rather blind.

17.♘xb5 ♕e7 was hopeless as well.

17...♕e7??

Twin blindness. 17...fxe6+ was with check.

18.♘xf8 d4 19.♗f4

19.♗xd4 loses a pawn to 19...♔xf8!.

19...♕xf8 20.♗xb5 ♕b4

Or also 20...♖xa2 21.♗xc6 ♖xb2+ 22.♔g3 bxc6 23.♕xd4 ♖b3+ 24.♔f2 ♗e6 when the combination of bishop with c-pawn is strong.

21.♕b3 ♕xb3 22.axb3 ♖a2 23.♖d1 ♖xb2+ 24.♔f1 ♗g4 25.♖a1 h6 26.h3 ♗e6 27.♗xc6 bxc6 28.♖a8+ ♔h7 29.♖d8 ♗d5

30.e6 ♗xe6

Or 30...fxe6–+.

31.♖xd4 ♗xb3 32.♖d2 ♖b1+ 33.♔f2

White lost on time. 33...♗d5 should win.

Janez Barle 2425
Andras Adorjan 2540
Reykjavik 1988

The Panov Caro-Kann – razor-sharp!

1.e4 c6 2.d4 d5 3.exd5 cxd5 4.c4 ♘f6 5.♘c3 g6 6.cxd5 ♘xd5 7.♕b3 ♘b6 8.d5 ♗g7 9.♗e3 0-0 10.♖d1 ♘a6!

There follows a model example of a counterattack.

11.♘f3

11.♗xa6 bxa6 12.♘ge2 (12.♗d4 ♗xd4 13.♖xd4 e6 14.d6 e5 15.♖d1 ♖b8 16.♘ge2 ♗e6 17.♕c2 ♘c4 18.b3 ♘xd6 19.0-0 ♖c8∓) 12...a5 13.♕b5 a4 14.♗d4 ♕d6 15.♘e4 ♕d7 16.♕c6 ♗xd4 17.♖xd4 ♖d8 18.h4 ♕f5∓.

11...♕d6!

12.a3?

Not a strong novelty. On 12.♗e2 ♘c5 13.♕b5 Black has the fabulous 13...♘ca4!! 14.♘e4 (14.♘xa4 ♗d7) 14...♕d7 15.b3 ♘c3 16.♕xd7 ♗xd7 17.♘xc3 ♗xc3+ 18.♔f1 ♖fd8 19.a4 ♗f5 20.♗xb6 axb6 21.♗c4 ♖a5 22.♔e2 ♗e4∓.

12...♘c5 13.♕b5

13.♕a2 ♘ca4 14.♗d4 e5 15.dxe6 and now:

A) 15...♘xc3!? 16.exf7+ ♖xf7 17.bxc3 ♗e6 18.♕b2 ♖e8 19.♗e2 ♗c4 20.♗xg7

analysis diagram

20...♕xa3!! (how about it, folks?) 21.♕xa3 ♖xe2+ 22.♔f1 ♖a2+ 23.♔g1 ♖xa3 24.♗d4∓;

B) 15...♕xe6+ 16.♕xe6 ♗xe6 17.♘xa4 ♘xa4 18.♗xg7 ♔xg7 19.♖d4 ♖fe8 20.♗e2 ♘xb2 21.0-0 ♗f5∓.

Finally, after 13.♕b4 here it comes again:

13...♘ca4! 14.♕xd6 exd6 15.♘xa4 ♘xa4 16.b3 ♘c3 17.♖d2 ♘b1 18.♖a2 ♗f5 19.♗c4 b5!∓.

13...♘ca4!

13...♗xc3+ 14.bxc3 ♘e4 15.♕b3 ♗g4!= (15...♗d7 16.♖d4! is unclear).

14.♘e4

14.♘xa4 ♗d7−+.

14...♕d7 15.♕b3!?

A) 15.♕a5 ♘xb2! 16.♗xb6 axb6 17.♕xa8 ♘xd1 18.♔xd1 ♕xd5+ 19.♘ed2 ♗g4 20.♕a4 ♗xf3+ 21.gxf3 ♖d8 22.♕c2 ♗h6 is a nice, long, forced, and winning line;

B) 15.♕b4 ♕f5! (15...♘xb2 16.♖d4 ♗xd4 17.♗xd4 ♘2a4 18.d6 ♕c6 19.♗d3 ♗f5 (19...♖e8 20.0-0 ♗f5−+) 20.dxe7 ♗xe4 21.exf8♕+ ♖xf8−+) and now:

B1) 16.♘g3 ♕c2−+;

B2) 16.♗xb6 axb6 and now:

B21) 17.♕xe7 ♘xb2 18.♖d2

analysis diagram

18...♖xa3!! (18...♗d7 also wins, but we prefer the alternative) 19.♕xa3 ♕xe4+−+;

B22) 17.b3 ♘b2 18.♖d2 ♖xa3!! 19.♕xa3 ♕xe4+ 20.♗e2 ♕b1+ 21.♗d1 ♘d3+−+;

B3) 16.♘h4 ♕e5 17.♖d4 ♗f5∓.

C) 15.b3 ♕g4 16.♕b4 ♘c3 17.♘xc3 ♕xb4 18.axb4 ♗xc3+ 19.♗d2 ♘xd5∓.

15...♘xb2 16.♗b5 ♕g4 17.♘g3 ♘xd1 18.h3

Catch!

18.♕xd1? ♗c3+ 19.♔f1 ♗d7−+;

18.♔xd1? ♖d8 19.h3 ♕e6−+.

18...♘xe3!

Whoops!

Less strong, and less attractive, though still good, was 18...♕xg3 19.fxg3 ♘xe3 20.♕xe3 ♘xd5∓.

19.hxg4 ♘xg2+! 20.♔f1 ♘f4

White's position is a chaos. He tries to confuse the issue with a desperate attack:

21.♘g5 h6 22.d6

22...exd6!

22...hxg5!? was also possible, but after 23.dxe7 Black would have had to find 23...♖e8!! 24.♗xe8 ♗e6∓.

23.♘5e4 ♗xg4 24.♖h4 ♗e6

24...h5! would have finished more quickly, for instance: 25.f3 ♗e6 or 25.♘xd6 ♖ad8 26.♕e3 ♘bd5.

25.♕f3 ♘fd5 26.♘xd6 ♘c3!

27.♘ge4

27.♔g1 ♘xb5 28.♘xb5 ♗d5 and the bishops rule.

27...♖ad8

Second-best, though good enough. 27...♘xb5 would have won a piece: 28.♘xb5 (28.♘f6+ ♗xf6 29.♕xf6 ♘d7–+) 28...♗c4+ 29.♔g1 ♗xb5 30.♘f6+ ♗xf6 31.♕xf6 ♘d7 32.♕b2 ♗c6 33.♖xh6 f6 34.♖xg6+ (34.♕c2 ♖f7–+) 34...♔f7 35.♖g3 ♖ae8–+.

28.♘f6+ ♗xf6 29.♕xf6 ♖xd6 30.♕xc3

30.♖xh6?? ♗h3+.

30...♖c8 31.♕b2 h5 32.♗e2 ♖c5 33.a4?!

33.♖d4 ♖xd4 34.♕xd4 ♘d7 and Black's extra pawns will bring him the victory.

33...♗d7 34.♖d4

34.♕a3 ♖dd5∓.

34...♘xa4

In mutual time-trouble I'm making it harder for myself.

34...♖xd4 35.♕xd4 ♖c1+ (35...♖f5!? or 35...♖a5 may be stronger) 36.♔g2 ♗xa4 37.♗xh5! ♖c4 (37...gxh5 38.♕d8+ ♔h7 39.♕d3+=) 38.♕d8+ ♔g7 39.♗f3∓.

35.♕d2??

35.♖xa4! ♗xa4 36.♕a3 b6 37.♕xa4 a5 gave him some saving chances.

35...♖xd4 36.♕xd4 ♗c6 37.♕d8+ ♔h7 38.f3 ♖f5 39.♔f2 ♘c3 40.♗d3 ♖xf3+ 41.♔e1 a5 42.♗d2 ♘e4+ 0-1

Finita de la (tragi-)commedia.

There follows a clear strategic win with the help of several 'petite combinaisons'.

Bogi Palsson   2020
Andras Adorjan   2540
Reykjavik 1988

1.d4 ♘f6 2.c4 e6 3.♘c3 ♗b4 4.e3 c5 5.a3 ♗xc3+ 6.bxc3 b6 7.♗d3 ♗b7 8.f3

8.♘e2 is an error due to 8...♗xg2 9.♖g1 ♗e4 10.♗xe4 (10.♖xg7 ♗g6–+) 10...♘xe4 11.♖xg7 ♘xf2! 12.♕c2 ♕h4 13.♘g3

analysis diagram

and now 13...♘d3+!! (13...♔f8? 14.♕xf2 ♔xg7 15.♘f5++–) 14.♕xd3 ♔f8 and where have all the squares for the rook gone? Instead, 8.♘f3 0-0 9.0-0 ♗e4 10.♘g5 ♗xd3 11.♕xd3 ♘c6 12.e4 d6 keeps White's troubles limited.

8...♘c6 9.♘e2 0-0 10.0-0 ♗a6!
11.e4 ♘e8

White was threatening 12.♗g5.

12.♗e3

Better was 12.♕a4 ♘a5 13.dxc5 d6 (another gambit move is 13...♕c7!? 14.♗e3 d6 15.cxb6 axb6 and the pressure on c4 should be enough by way of compensation) 14.cxb6 ♕xb6+ (after 14...axb6 White can fill the hole on b5 by 15.♘d4 ♕c8 16.♘b5 and is slightly better after e.g. 16...♕c5+ 17.♔h1 ♘f6 18.♕b4 ♖fd8 19.♖b1) 15.♘d4 ♕c5 (straight for the c4-pawn) 16.♗e3 ♗xc4 17.♗xc4 ♘xc4 18.♗f2 ♕c7=.

12...♘d6!

The usual Nimzo pressure on c4 is increased from an unusual square.

13.dxc5

13.♕a4 is no use here since the ♗e3 is hanging: 13...♘a5 14.dxc5 ♘dxc4 15.♗xc4 ♘xc4 (also not bad is 15...♗xc4 16.♖fe1 ♕c7) 16.♕xa6 ♘xe3 17.♖f2 ♕c8 clearly favours Black.

13...♘xc4 14.♗xc4 ♗xc4 15.cxb6

15.♖b1 bxc5 (15...b5!? 16.♕c2 ♘e5 17.♖fd1 ♖b8∓) 16.♗xc5 d6∓ because taking on d6 would lose the knight. 15.♖e1 ♕c7 16.a4 ♘e5 and the knight is very active.

15...axb6

And BLACK is BETTER.

16.♖f2 ♕c7

16...d5 or 16...f5 were more aggressive.

17.♘d4 ♘e5 18.♖d2 ♗a6!

Or 18...♖fc8 19.a4 d5 20.exd5 ♗xd5 21.♗f4 f6∓.

19.♗f4 d6 20.♘b3

20.♘c2 ♖fd8∓.

20...♖fd8

White faces a difficult choice: with the knight on c4 he will have to defend miserably, but swapping the knight leaves him with the inferior minor piece.

21.♗xe5?! dxe5 22.♖xd8+ ♖xd8 23.♕c2 h6 24.h3 ♖d3 25.♖c1 ♕c4 26.♔h2 ♔h7 27.♕b2 ♖e3! 28.♖c2 28.♘a1 f5−+.

28...♗b5−+ 29.♘d2 ♕d3 30.♕b3

On 30.♕c1, 30...♖e2 finishes.

30...♖e2 31.a4 ♗e8 32.♕a2 ♖f2 33.♖b2 ♕e2 **0-1**

Although my opponent was not a chess genius, this game is a precious memory.

G. Kradolf
Andras Adorjan
Zurich simul 1988

In this simul I played Black on all boards.

1.c4 c5 2.♘f3 ♘f6 3.g3 b6 4.♗g2 ♗b7 5.0-0 g6 6.b3 ♗g7 7.♗b2 0-0 8.♘c3 d6 9.d4 cxd4 10.♘xd4 ♗xg2 11.♔xg2

11...d5=

I was not in a bloodthirsty mood – or I would have tried 11...♕c8!? 12.e4 ♘bd7 13.♕e2 ♕b7 14.♘d5 ♖fe8 with chances for both sides.

12.♕d3?!

12.cxd5 ♘xd5 13.♘db5=.

12...e5 13.♘db5?

A kamikaze act.

13.♘c2 d4 (13...e4 14.♕e3 dxc4 15.bxc4 ♕c8∓) 14.♘e4 ♘bd7∓.

13...a6 14.♘a3 d4 15.♘e4 ♘bd7

Black is clearly better here; it's just a matter of time before his centre pawns will start to roll.

16.♖ac1 ♕c7

16...♘xe4 17.♕xe4 ♘c5 18.♕c2 ♕c7∓.

17.♘xf6+ ♗xf6 18.b4 ♗g7

There was time, but the immediate 18...a5! was more forceful.

19.e3 ♖fd8 20.f3 ♕b7

20...♗h6! 21.f4 dxe3 22.♕xe3 exf4 23.♕d4 (23.gxf4 a5) 23...♕c6+ 24.♔g1 f6–+.

21.♖c2 a5 22.c5?

Running into a vicious reply. 22.exd4 exd4 23.bxa5 ♖xa5∓/–+.

22...e4! 23.fxe4

23.♕xe4 ♕xe4 24.fxe4 and now 24...d3 25.♖cf2 ♗xb2 26.♖xb2 axb4 27.♘c4 bxc5 rolls to a win.

23...♘e5 24.c6 ♘xc6 25.♕b3 a4 26.♕c4 ♘e5 27.♕c7 ♕xe4+   0-1

Tell me frankly: wasn't that a cute game?

Istvan Csom	2545
Andras Adorjan	2525

Hungary tt 1989

1.d4 ♘f6 2.g3 c5!? 3.d5

On 3.♘f3 my intention was 3...♕a5+!?. Playing Csom was often simply boring. He did not only play the Hedgehog. He was a Hedgehog man.

Now the options for White are:

A) 4.c3 cxd4 5.♘xd4 ♕d5 6.f3 e5 7.e4 ♕a5 8.♘b3 ♕d8=;

B) 4.♗d2 ♕b6 5.♘c3 ♘e4 6.dxc5 ♘xc3 7.cxb6 ♘xd1 8.♔xd1 axb6 9.♘c3 e6 10.♘b5 ♘a6 11.e4=;

C) 4.♕d2 ♕xd2+ 5.♘bxd2 cxd4 6.♘xd4 g6 7.♗g2 ♗g7 8.0-0 (8.♘b5 ♘a6 9.0-0 0-0);

D) 4.♘c3 cxd4 5.♘xd4 ♘e4 6.♗d2 ♘xd2 7.♕xd2 ♘c6 8.♗g2 g6=.

3...b5! 4.♗g2 d6 5.♘f3

5.a4 b4 6.c4 g6 (6...bxc3); 5.e4 g6 6.♘e2 ♗g7.

5...g6 6.c4 a6

6...bxc4!?.

A good Benko for Black without having sacrificed anything.

7.a4 b4

A positional blunder. 7...bxc4! gave Black the upper hand, for example: 8.♘fd2 a5 9.♘xc4 ♘a6 10.0-0 ♗g7 11.♘c3 0-0 12.♗g5 ♘b4 13.♕d2 ♖b8.

8.b3!

The only way of developing the bishop on c1.

8...♗g7 9.♗b2 0-0 10.♘bd2 ♖a7! 11.0-0 e5 12.dxe6

He might have preferred to keep the position closed by 12.e4 ♘g4 13.a5 ♘d7 14.♘e1 ♘h6 (14...f5) 15.♘d3, though 15...f5 will come.

12...♗xe6

12...fxe6!? could be better: 13.♕c2 (13.♘g5) 13...♖e7 14.♖ad1 ♗b7 15.♗xf6 ♗xf6 16.♕d3 ♕c7 17.♘e4 ♗g7 with good chances along the f-file and with well-timed central pawn pushes.

13.♖a2

Not 13.♕c2? ♗f5 when 14.e4 loses a pawn to 14...♘xe4 15.♘xe4 ♗xb2 16.♕xb2 ♗xe4 17.♖ad1 ♘c6 18.♖fe1 ♗xf3 19.♗xf3 ♘d4 20.♖xd4 cxd4 21.♕xd4 ♖e7 22.♖d1 ♖e5.

13...♖e8

14.♘g5

A good, provoked shot. White is taking his chances too.

14.♕a1 gives Black all the play in the centre after 14...d5 (less good is 14...♘c6 15.♘g5 ♘a5 16.♘xe6 ♖xe6 17.e3= or 14...♗f5!? 15.♖e1 ♘c6=) 15.cxd5 (15.♘g5 d4) 15...♗xd5 16.♖e1 (16.e3 ♘c6 17.♕b1 (17.♖c1 ♘a5 18.♖xc5 ♘xb3 19.♖xd5

♕xd5∓) 17...♘a5 18.♗a1 ♘e4∓) 16...♖d7 17.e4 ♗xe4 18.♘xe4 ♖xe4!.
Or 14.♗xf6 ♗xf6 15.♘e4 ♗e7! (15...♖d7 16.♘xf6+ ♕xf6 17.♖d2 ♗f5 18.♘e1 ♗e4 19.♘d3=) 16.♘e1 ♗f8 and Black is ready to expand.

14...♗f5 15.♘h3

15.♖e1 ♖ae7; 15.e4 ♗d7 16.f4 h6∓.

15...♗g4! 16.♖e1

16.f3 ♗xh3 17.♗xh3 ♘c6 18.♖e1 ♖ae7 19.♗g2 (19.e4 ♘d4∓) 19...d5∓; 16.♘f3 ♘e4 17.♗xg7 ♔xg7∓; 16.♘f4 g5.

16...♖ae7 17.♘f4

17...g5!

Now or never!

17...♘h5 18.♗xg7 ♘xf4 19.gxf4 ♔xg7 hands the initiative to White after 20.♘f1 ♕d7 21.♖d2 – the e2-pawn is easily defended, but its colleague on d6 is not.

18.♗xf6

18.♕a1 ♘bd7 19.♘d5 ♖xe2−+ or 18.♘d5 ♘xd5 19.♗xg7 ♔xg7 (19...♘e3!? 20.fxe3 ♔xg7) 20.♗xd5 ♖xe2 (20...♗xe2?! 21.♕a1+ ♔g8 22.♘e4 ♖xe4 23.♗xe4 ♖xe4 24.♖axe2 ♖xe2 25.♖xe2 ♘c6 26.♕e1 ♔f8=) 21.♖xe2 ♖xe2∓ both just lose the e-pawn.

More intricate is the attack on the bishop, but Black obtains a clear advantage by pushing through: 18.h3 gxf4 19.hxg4 fxg3 20.f3 d5 21.♘f1 dxc4 22.♕xd8 ♖xd8 23.bxc4 ♘c6 or 18.f3 gxf4 19.fxg4 fxg3 20.h3 d5 21.g5 ♘e4.

18...♗xf6 19.♘d5

19.♗h3? is bad due to 19...♗xh3 20.♘xh3 ♕d7 21.♔g2 ♘c6 – now just compare all of White's pieces with Black's!

19...♖xe2 20.♖xe2 ♗xe2

Certainly not 20...♖xe2?, walking into a pin:

A) 21.f3 ♗d4+ 22.♔h1 ♕e8; or

B) 21.h3 ♗d4 22.♔h2 (22.hxg4 ♖xf2 23.♔h1 ♕f8–+; 22.♘e4 ♖xf2 23.♕xd4 ♖xg2+ 24.♔xg2 ♗xh3+ 25.♔xh3 cxd4–+) 22...♘c6 23.♖c2 ♘e5 doesn't work for White;

C) But 21.♗f1 leaves Black nothing but 21...♖xd2 22.♕xd2 ♘c6 23.♗g2 ♘d4 24.♕d3 ♗f5 25.♗e4=.

21.♕e1

21.♘xf6+ ♕xf6 22.♘e4 ♖xe4 23.♖xe2 ♖d4 might have been a better chance for White to stay afloat.

21...♔g7

Even 21...♔f8 was possible. After 22.♕b1 ♗h5 23.♕xh7 ♔g6 24.♕h3 ♔g7 White has his pawn back, but his pieces are totally uncoordinated.

22.♘e4

22.♘xf6 ♕xf6 23.♘f1 (23.♘f3 ♕e7 24.♘xg5 f6 25.♘f3 ♘c6 26.♘e5 ♗f3 27.♗xf3 ♘d4∓) 23...♕e5 24.♘e3 ♗h5∓.

22...♗d3 23.♖d2 ♗xe4 24.♗xe4?

Already short of time, White commits the decisive error.

24.♖e2 ♘c6 25.♖xe4 ♖xe4 26.♗xe4 ♘d4 27.♕d1 ♕e8 would still have given Black some work to do.

24...♘c6 25.♖e2?

Doubles! 25.♕b1 ♘d4 26.f3 ♕d7∓.

25...♘d4 26.♖e3

26...♖xe4   **0-1**

A game of great complexity, with many ups and downs – and a wonderfully dramatic memory.

Nandor Schlusnik
Andras Adorjan
Budapest rapid 1990

1.e4 c5 2.♘f3 d6 3.d4 cxd4 4.♘xd4 ♘f6 5.♘c3 a6 6.f3 ♘c6 7.♘b3
7.♗e3.

7...g6 8.♗e3 ♗e6 9.♕d2 ♖c8 10.0-0-0 h5 11.♔b1 ♗g7 12.♘d4
12.♕f2!?.

12...♘xd4 13.♗xd4

13...h4

13...♕a5 or 13...♕c7 are normal, but I was not in my right mind that day.

A rapid game against a weaker player can drive anyone crazy.

14.♕f2 ♕a5 15.♗b6 ♕h5 16.♗e2 ♔f8
16...♕h6.

17.h3 ♘d7

17...♕g5!? would have gotten the queen back into the game.

18.♗d4

18.f4!±.

18...♕a5 19.♘d5 ♗xd5 20.♗xg7+ ♔xg7 21.♖xd5 ♕a4 22.♕d4+ ♕xd4 23.♖xd4

23...g5∓

Now it's chess again.

24.f4!? gxf4 25.♗g4 e6?!

Allowing White some activity. The transition to the rook ending was more favourable: 25...♖c7 26.♗xd7 ♖xd7 27.e5 ♖h5 28.♖e1 (28.exd6 e5 with a huge centre) 28...♖g5 29.exd6 ♖xd6 30.♖xf4 ♖xg2 31.♖xh4 e5 32.a3 f6 and Black wins.

26.♖xd6 ♘e5 27.♗e2 ♖hd8 28.♖hd1?

28.♖xd8 ♖xd8 29.♖f1 ♘g6 30.c3 ♔h6 31.♔c2 offered better drawing chances.

28...♖xd6 29.♖xd6 ♔f6 30.c3

Retreating wouldn't hold out much longer: 30.♖d1 ♖g8 31.♗f1 ♖g3 32.♔c1 f3−+. White's bishop is just awful.

30...♖g8 31.♗f1

31...f3! 32.gxf3

32.♖d2 ♔g5 and the king walks in.

32...♖g1 33.♖d1 ♘xf3 34.♔c1 ♘g5 35.c4 a5

35...♘xe4 – I swear I saw it!

36.♖e1 ♔e5　　　　　　　　　　**0-1**

Stark
Andras Adorjan
Germany Bundesliga 1989/90

Playing the Scheveningen well is just pure pleasure. Try it!

1.e4 c5 2.♘f3 e6 3.d4 cxd4 4.♘xd4 ♘f6 5.♘c3 d6 6.♗e2 ♗e7 7.0-0 0-0 8.♗e3 a6 9.f4 ♕c7 10.♔h1 b5 11.a3 ♗b7 12.♗f3 ♘bd7

Without White having done anything stupid, BLACK is already BETTER. Just wait and see!

13.♘b3

13.♕e1 ♖ac8 14.♖d1 ♘b6∓.

13...♖ac8 14.♕e2 e5 15.f5 ♖fe8 16.♖ad1 ♘b6 17.g4

17.♗c1 ♘a4 18.♖d3 ♕b8∓.

17...♘a4! 18.g5

The problem is that White cannot hold his centre together, e.g., 18.♘xa4 bxa4 19.♘d2 ♕xc2 20.g5 ♘xe4 21.f6 ♗f8 22.♔g1 d5∓.

18...♘xc3 19.bxc3 ♘xe4

The situation is already hopeless for White.

20.♕g2 d5 21.g6 fxg6 22.fxg6 ♘xc3 23.♕h3

23.gxh7+ ♔h8−+.

23...h6 24.♗xh6

A desperate try for an attack.

24...gxh6 25.♕e6+ ♔h8 26.g7+ ♔xg7 27.♗e4

Quite ingenious.

27...♗g5! 28.♕g6+ ♔h8 29.♖f7 ♕xf7 30.♕xf7 ♖e7 31.♕g6 dxe4 32.♘c5 ♘xd1 33.♘xb7 ♖xb7 34.♕xa6 ♖bc7 35.♕xb5 ♖g7   0-1

Indeed, this all happened in a FIDE-rated game.

Peter Meister	2420
Andras Adorjan	2520

Balassagyarmat 1990 (4)

This was a very strange GM tournament, with five Soviets (Tseshkovsky, Rashkovsky, Fominikh among others), six Germans and only me representing Hungary. And winning it too!

1.d4 ♘f6 2.c4 e6 3.♘f3 b6 4.g3 ♗a6 5.♕b3 ♘c6

If 5...c5 6.d5.

6.♘bd2 ♘a5 7.♕a4 ♗b7

8.♗h3?!

Hard to understand. True, this whole line is a joy to play for Black anyway.

There is no accounting for some people's taste.

8.♗g2 c5 9.dxc5 (9.0-0 ♗c6 10.♕c2 cxd4 11.♘xd4 ♗xg2 12.♔xg2 ♖c8 with counterplay) 9...bxc5 (9...♗xc5 10.b4 ♗c6 11.♕a3 ♗e7 12.♕c3 ♘b7 is unclear) 10.0-0 ♗e7 11.♖d1 0-0=.

8...♖c8!?

Logical and good. 8...♗e7 9.0-0 0-0 10.♗g2 c5 11.dxc5 bxc5 12.♕c2 ♕b6 13.b3 ♘c6 is comfortable; 8...g5!? can be played by people who are nearing their second childhood.

9.0-0 c5 10.dxc5 ♗xc5 11.b4 ♗c6 12.♕a3

12...♗xf3 13.exf3 ♗e7 14.c5

What could the poor fellow do? If 14.♗b2 ♘c6 15.c5 a5 his queenside crumbles — all thanks to that early queen sortie.

14...♘c6 15.♘b3 0-0 16.b5

16.♕a4?! ♘d5 17.♗d2 ♘e5 18.♗g2 (18.♔g2 d6 19.f4 ♘c4 20.♗e1 dxc5 21.bxc5 ♘b2 22.♕e4 bxc5 23.f5 e5∓) 18...♘c4∓.

16.♗d2 a5 and White is KO!

16...♘e5

16...♘a5 17.♘xa5 ♗xc5 18.♕d3 bxa5 was also strong.

17.♕xa7

In the event of 17.♗b2 ♘c4 18.♕a4 ♘xb2 19.♕d4 it seems as if Black has been fooled, but after 19...♘d5 20.♕xb2 ♗f6 the joke is on White.

17...bxc5 18.f4 ♘d3 19.♕a5 ♘d5 20.♕xd8 ♖fxd8

Winning in the ending is not a shame with black.

21.♗e3 ♗f6

Also, 21...c4 22.♘d4 ♗a3.

22.♖ad1 c4 23.♘d4 ♖b8 24.♖d2

Or 24.a4 ♘c3 with deadly forks.

24...♘xe3 25.fxe3 ♗xd4 26.exd4 ♖xb5

There is no more hope for White here.

27.f5 ♖c8 28.a4 ♖a5 29.♖b1 exf5

29...e5 or 29...♖xa4 were winning as well.

30.♖c2 ♖xa4

30...g6 31.♗f1 ♖c6–+.

31.♗xf5 ♖b4 32.♖d1 ♘b2 33.♖e1 ♔f8 34.♗xd7 ♖d8 35.♗c6 ♘d3 36.♖a1 ♖xd4 37.♖e2 g6 38.♖a8+ ♔g7 39.♖e7 ♖b1+ 40.♔g2 ♖b2+ 41.♔f3 c3 42.♖aa7 ♔h6   0-1

Do not play over the last 13 moves!

Gilles Andruet	2355
Andras Adorjan	2520

Paris 1990 (4)

1.d4 ♘f6 2.c4 e6 3.♘f3 b6 4.g3 ♗a6 5.b3 b5!?

Neither better nor worse than the 'theoretical' moves. Only different, original, risky. And – mine!

6.cxb5 ♗xb5 7.♗g2 ♗b4+ 8.♗d2 a5 9.0-0

9.♗xb4 axb4 10.♕d2 ♕e7 11.♕g5 seems to win a pawn, but... 11...d5 12.♕xg7 ♖g8 13.♕h6 c5 14.dxc5 ♕xc5 15.0-0 ♔e7 16.♖c1 ♕xf2+ 17.♔xf2 ♘g4+ 18.♔g1 ♘xh6 and Black has the pawn back, with an unclear position.

9...0-0 10.♖e1

10.a3 ♗xd2 (10...♗e7) 11.♘fxd2 d5 12.♘c3 c6=.

10.♘c3 ♗xc3 11.♗xc3 ♘d5 12.♗d2 a4 13.♖e1 ♘c6 14.e4 ♘de7 15.d5 exd5 16.exd5 ♘xd5 17.♗g5 ♘f6 18.♘d4 ♘xd4 19.♗xa8 ♘e2+ 20.♖xe2 ♗xe2 21.♕xe2 ♕xa8 22.♗xf6 gxf6 23.♕g4+ ♔h8 24.♕xd7 (24.bxa4 ♕d5 25.♖d1 ♕e6) 24...axb3 25.♕d4 bxa2 26.♕xf6+ ♔g8 27.♕g5+ ♔h8 28.♕f6+ ½-½ Barus-Adorjan, Novi Sad ol 1990.

10...♗c6

Typical. 10...♘c6?! would put Black's pieces on the wrong foot, for example: 11.a3! ♗e7? (still better is 11...♗xd2 12.♘bxd2=) 12.♘c3 (12.e4 d5 13.e5 ♘e4) 12...♗a6 13.e4 d5 14.exd5! ♘xd5 15.♘xd5 exd5 16.♕c2+–.

11.♘e5?

In his craving for a draw, White misunderstands the important elements in the position. The g2-bishop will be sorely missed.

11.♕c2 ♗e4 12.♕b2 ♘c6 13.a3 ♗e7
14.♘c3 ♗xf3 15.♗xf3 ♘xd4 16.♗xa8
♕xa8 with fine compensation, e.g.,
17.♗e3 ♘f5. 11.a3!?.

11...♗xg2 12.♔xg2 ♕c8! 13.♕c2
13.a3 ♕b7+ 14.e4 ♘xe4 15.♕f3 ♗xd2
16.♘xd2 ♘d6∓; 13.e4 d6 14.♘f3 ♘bd7
15.a3 ♗xd2 16.♘bxd2 ♕b7∓.

13...c5! 14.dxc5
After 14.♗xb4 ♕b7+! 15.e4 cxb4 White's
position is bleeding from many wounds.

14...♗xc5 15.♘f3 d5!
15...♗b4!? 16.♘c3 ♕b7 17.♘a4 ♖e8∓.

16.♘c3 ♗b4

17.♕b2?
This only helps the opponent.
17.♖ac1! was a more pointed defence,
offering better chances to hold.
For example: 17...♕b7 (17...♗a3??
18.♘xd5+−) 18.♘a4! (18.♕b2 ♘e4)
18...♘a6 19.♕c6! ♕xc6 (19...♕e7
20.♘b6 ♗xd2 21.♘xd2 ♘b4 22.♕c5

♕xc5 23.♖xc5 ♖a6 24.♘c8 ♘xa2
25.♖a1=) 20.♖xc6 ♘e4∓.

**17...♕b7 18.a3 ♗e7 19.♘a4 ♘e4
20.♗e3 ♘d7 21.♔g1**
Sad necessity. After 21.♗d4 f6 Black's
pawns will come as a steamroller.

21...e5!
And BLACK is winning.

22.♖ec1
22.♘xe5 ♘xe5 23.♕xe5 ♗f6 loses big
material.

22...♗f6 23.♖c2 d4 24.♗d2
24.♗c1 ♖fc8 25.♖xc8+ ♖xc8 26.♗d2
(26.b4 ♕b5) 26...♘xd2 27.♘xd2 e4−+.

24...♘xd2 25.♖xd2
25.♘xd2 e4 26.♕c1 e3 27.♘f3
d3 28.♖c7 ♕d5 and Black wins.
Picturesque, isn't it?

25...d3!
A nice thematic finish! Handshake.
If 26.♖c1 dxe2 27.♘e1 ♗g5−+; 26.e4
♕xe4 27.♘e1 ♕b7−+; and 26.exd3
♕xf3−+.

Chapter 8
Black Magic in the Tal Memorial 2013

Tal Memorial Tournament			BLACK	White	BLACK	White
Boris Gelfand	6/9	(+3 -0 =6)	(+2 -0 =2)	(+1 -0 =4)	3/4	3/5
Magnus Carlsen	5.5/9	(+3 -1 =5)	(+0 -0 =4)	(+3 -1 =1)	2/4	3.5/5
Shakhriyar Mamedyarov	5/9	(+1 -0 =8)	(+1 -0 =4)	(+0 -0 =4)	3/5	2/4
Fabiano Caruana	5/9	(+3 -2 =4)	(+3 -0 =2)	(+0 -2 =2)	4/5	1/4
Dmitry Andreikin	5/9	(+1 -0 =8)	(+1 -0 =3)	(+0 -0 =5)	2.5/4	2.5/5
Hikaru Nakamura	4.5/9	(+4 -4 =1)	(+3 -1 =0)	(+1 -3 =1)	3/4	1.5/5
Sergey Karjakin	4/9	(+0 -1 =8)	(+0 -1 =4)	(+0 -0 =4)	2/5	2/4
Viswanathan Anand	3.5/9	(+1 -3 =5)	(+0 -1 =3)	(+1 -2 =2)	1.5/4	2/5
Alexander Morozevich	3.5/9	(+1 -3 =5)	(+1 -2 =2)	(+0 -1 =3)	2/5	1.5/4
Vladimir Kramnik	3/9	(+0 -3 =6)	(+0 -1 =4)	(+0 -2 =2)	2/5	1/4

It happens about once in a hundred years in chess tournaments, that BLACK is not only OK but heavily superior. In the Memorial tournament for the 'Wizard of Riga' in Moscow, 2013, Black won almost twice as many (11) games as White (6). All the games won by Black can be found here in this chapter with my analyses. Naturally, this result was shocking for many. Even I, who firmly believe that Black has even chances in a chess game, could hardly believe what was happening. I'm not using these facts as evidence for my thesis. I prefer scientific proof. Anyway, people win and lose in practical games because they/we are feeble. True, White is ahead in the statistics, but this is just because people are trained to believe that he should be. A friend of mine (who is a mathematician – otherwise a harmless man) says: 'Even if the balance turned to Black's favour for 50 years this would still prove nothing.'

Here are just a few important arguments for the 'BLACK IS OK' thesis:
'To move in the initial position is not only a right but also a duty (zugzwang). It also means a responsibility which is not to everybody's liking', wrote Arpad Földeak, an excellent chess historian, in 1995. The following statistics were produced by him too.

Hastings 1895

	White	BLACK
Chigorin	7/10	9/11
Lasker	6/10	7.5/11
Steinitz	6.5/11	6.5/10
Teichmann	4.5/10	7/11
Schlechter	5/11	6/10
Blackburne	5/11	5.5/10
Bird	3.5/10	5.5/11

Before I forget: in this tournament, all the participants played 21 games. Hard to believe, but it's true: all of them scored better with black – even those who played more games with white!

Otherwise it's just a silly superstition which says that it's White, who moves, first takes the initiative, and decides the direction of the game and the structure of the position. It's incredible that such a twisted idea still stands today. One handy refutation is: if White begins with 1.e4, Black has no less than 9 plausible replies. Let's see once again: 1....g6, 1...♞f6, 1...e6, 1...e5, 1...d6, 1...d5, 1...c6, 1...c5, 1...♞c6. Who then is the one who determines the course of the game? Think it over, and sooner or later you will rid yourself of the 'White to play and...' superstition.

A few years ago, Endre Vegh composed a complete repertoire for White in the 1.e4 and 1.d4 openings, where for Black, however, the target is only on the Sveshnikov and the Slav. Fasten your seatbelts: in both cases the white side needed twice as much work! We refer you to Chapter 9 for this repertoire.

Tal Memorial 2013 | Final standings

1	Gelfand	2755	2900	*	½	½	½	1	1	½	1	½	½	6
2	Carlsen	2864	2846	½	*	½	½	0	1	½	½	1	1	5.5
3	Mamedyarov	2753	2819	½	½	*	½	½	1	½	½	½	½	5
4	Andreikin	2713	2823	½	½	½	*	½	½	½	½	½	1	5
5	Caruana	2774	2817	0	1	½	½	*	0	½	1	1	½	5
6	Nakamura	2784	2777	0	0	0	½	1	*	1	0	1	1	4.5
7	Karjakin	2782	2738	½	½	½	½	½	0	*	½	½	½	4
8	Morozevich	2760	2701	0	½	½	½	0	1	½	*	0	½	3.5
9	Anand	2786	2698	½	0	½	½	0	0	½	1	*	½	3.5
10	Kramnik	2803	2654	½	0	½	0	½	0	½	½	½	*	3

In the Tal Memorial in 2013, Vishy Anand, the reigning World Champion, suffered a loss on the very first day. Perhaps his thoughts were already on the coming title match with Magnus Carlsen in Chennai – in any case it wasn't to be the Indian's tournament.

- Analyses by AA and IM Endre VEGH -

Viswanathan Anand 2786
Fabiano Caruana 2774
Moscow 2013 (1)

1.e4 e5 2.♘f3 ♘c6 3.♗b5 a6 4.♗a4 ♘f6 5.0-0 ♗e7 6.♖e1 b5 7.♗b3 0-0 8.h3 ♗b7 9.d3

Trendy – White avoids the longish concrete lines.

9...d5 10.exd5 ♘xd5 11.♘bd2

11.♘xe5 was the testing move: 11...♘xe5 (11...♘d4!? looks promising too. For example: 12.♘d2 c5 13.♘df3 ♘xb3 14.axb3 ♖e8) 12.♖xe5 ♕d6 13.♖e1 ♖ae8 14.♘d2 ♘f6 15.♘f3 c5 16.♗g5 ♗d8 with the type of activity for the pawn which is typical for this line.

11...f6 12.c3

12.a3!?; 12.a4 ♕d7.

12...♔h8 13.♗c2

Passive. More appealing was 13.d4!? exd4 14.cxd4 ♖e8 (14...♗b4 with counter-chances) 15.♘e4 ♕d7 16.a3 ♖ad8

17.♕d3 ♘b6 (17...♕f5 18.♗c2; or 18.g4!? ♕d7 19.♗c2 g6) 18.♘g3 (18.♗f4 ♘c4!).

13...♕d7

13...b4!? came into consideration as well: 14.c4 (14.♘e4?! bxc3 15.bxc3 f5) 14...♘f4 15.♘b3 ♘e6 16.d4 ♘exd4 17.♘fxd4 ♘xd4 (17...exd4!? 18.♗e4 ♕d6 19.♘xd4 ♕xd4 20.♕xd4 ♘xd4 21.♗xb7 ♖ae8 22.♖b1 ♗d6 23.♗d2 a5) 18.♘xd4 exd4 19.♕h5 d3 20.♗xd3 ♕xd3 21.♖xe7 ♕d6 22.♕e2 ♖ad8=.

14.♘b3 a5 15.a4 bxa4 16.♖xa4

16...♘cb4

In New In Chess 2013/5, Caruana wrote that he was already 'committed to a pawn sacrifice' here: 'For the pawn I eliminated White's bishop, and I was happy my king would finally feel secure.'

17.♖xa5 ♘xc2 18.♕xc2 ♘b6

With hindsight, Caruana thought he should have played more energetically with 18...g5.

19.♖xa8 ♖xa8 20.♘bd2 g5! 21.♘h2

21.d4!? is an interesting possibility: 21...g4 22.hxg4 ♕xg4 23.♘e4 ♖g8 24.♘g3 h5 25.♘h2 (25.♘xe5!? fxe5 26.♖xe5 ♗g5 27.♗xg5 ♖xg5 28.♕d2 ♖xe5 29.dxe5 ♔g7 30.♕d8 ♘d5 with a likely draw) 25...♕g7 (25...♕g6 26.♕xg6 ♖xg6 27.dxe5 h4 28.exf6 ♗xf6 29.♘e4+−) 26.♘f3 ♕g4 27.♘xe5 (27.♘h2=) 27...fxe5 28.♖xe5±.

21.♘e4 was solid and good.

21...♖d8 22.d4 exd4

22...♘c6!? 23.♕e4 (23.♘df3 ♖xd4!) 23...♕xe4 24.♘xe4 exd4 is at least OK for BLACK, for example: 25.♘g4 dxc3 (25...♔g7? 26.♘xg5+−) 26.♘exf6 ♗xf6 27.♘xf6 ♔g7 28.♗xg5 ♔g6 29.♘xh7 ♖h8 30.♖e6+ ♔xh7 31.bxc3#.

23.cxd4 ♗b4 24.♖e2 ♕xd4 25.♘df1?

A little passive. After 25.♕xc7 ♖d7 26.♕c2 ♕d5 27.♘hf3 ♔g7 White would at least have a pawn for his troubles.

25...♕c5

25...♕d5!? 26.f4 (26.♘f3 ♗a6!−+; 26.♘e3 ♕d6∓) 26...♗a6 27.♖f2 ♗d3 is killing.

26.♕xc5 ♗xc5 27.♖c2 ♗d6 28.♘g4 ♔g7 29.♗d2 ♔g6 30.♘ge3 f5

It's unlikely that Anand had catered for a massage like this...

30...♖a8 was not bad either.

31.♘c4 ♗xc4 32.♖xc4 ♖a8 33.♖c1 f4 34.♗c3 h5 35.♘d2 ♗d5 36.f3 ♗c5+ 37.♔f1 ♗e3 38.♔e2?

38.♖e1 was somewhat tougher.

38...♗c4+ 39.♔e1 ♖e8−+ 40.♔d1 ♗xd2 41.♔xd2 ♖e2+ 42.♔d1 ♖xg2 43.♗d4 ♗e2+ 44.♔e1 ♗xf3 45.♖xc7 ♖e2+ 46.♔f1 ♖h2 47.♖g7+ ♔f5 48.♗e5 ♔xe5   0-1

The first black victory had been born in the Tal Memorial. Who would have believed that it would be followed by 10 (ten!) more?

The second white player who lost is familiar to us. However, Hikaru Nakamura would bounce back (and forth again...) in this, bizarre for him, tournament.

Hikaru Nakamura 2784
Shakhriyar Mamedyarov 2753

Moscow 2013 (1)

1.d4 ♘f6 2.c4 e6 3.♘f3 d5 4.♘c3 ♗b4 5.♕a4+

Rare, and not really good. The common move is 5.♗g5.

5...♘c6 6.e3 0-0 7.♗d2 dxc4 8.♗xc4 a6 9.0-0 ♗d6 10.♖ad1 e5 11.dxe5 ♘xe5

12.♗e2

12.♘xe5!? ♗xe5 13.f4 ♗d6 14.♕c2.

12...♕e7 13.♘g5

13.♕c2 ♘xf3+ 14.♗xf3 ♗g4 is very comfortable for Black too.

13...♗f5 14.e4 ♗d7 15.♕c2 h6 16.♘f3 ♖fe8 17.♖fe1 ♖ad8 18.g3?!

Strangely enough, White is already worse without having made any apparent errors.

18...♘eg4 19.h3?

This proves to be a decisive mistake. 19.♗d3 was the lesser evil: 19...♗c5 20.♖e2 ♘xf2!? 21.♖xf2 ♗c6 22.♔g2 (22.♗e1 ♘xe4 23.♘xe4 ♗xe4 24.♗xe4 ♗xf2+ 25.♔xf2 ♖xd1 26.♕xd1 ♕xe4∓) 22...♗xf2 23.♔xf2 ♕c5+ 24.♔g2 ♘xe4 25.♘xe4 ♕xc2 26.♗xc2 ♗xe4∓.

19...♘xf2! 20.♔xf2 ♗xh3

White could even resign here.

21.♔g1

21.♘d4 ♗c5 22.♗e3 ♕e5 is also over and out.

21...♗xg3 22.♗f1 ♗xe1 23.♖xe1 ♗g4 24.♗g2 ♗xf3 25.♗xf3 ♕d6 26.♖e2 ♕g3+ 27.♗g2 ♘g4 28.♘d1 ♖e6 29.♘e3

There is no salvation in either 29.♘f2 ♖c6 30.♕b3 ♕xb3 31.axb3 ♖c2 32.♘xg4 ♖dxd2–+ or 29.♗e1 ♕h2+ 30.♔f1 ♖xd1! 31.♕xd1 ♖f6+ 32.♗f2 ♖xf2+ 33.♖xf2 ♘e3+ 34.♔e2 ♘xd1 35.♔xd1 ♕g1+ 36.♔e2 ♕b1–+.

29...♖c6 30.♕b1 ♕h2+ 31.♔f1 ♕f4+ **0-1**

For some reason people cannot imagine that it's possible to be worse early in the game with white. Well, this is a good example!

Nakamura bounced back with victories against Kramnik, Karjakin, Caruana and Anand in the next four rounds. But then he completely collapsed and lost three games in a row, against Gelfand, Carlsen and Morozevich. In Huffington Post, Lubos Kavalek spoke of a 'rambunctious performance'.

Like Anand, the American had been playing a lot in the preceding months – perhaps too much.

Nakamura said two years later that he didn't remember that Black was scoring so well in this tournament.

Apparently, though everyone wants to draw a number that gives one more white game in the pairings, after a tournament it's no longer so important whether they have taken their points with white or black. 'But any time you see more black victories, people will have been trying too hard with white, especially when players are almost of the same level', was Nakamura's analysis.

Vladimir Kramnik	2803
Hikaru Nakamura	2784

Moscow 2013 (2)

1.c4 ♘f6 2.♘c3 g6 3.g3 ♗g7 4.♗g2 0-0 5.d4 d6 6.♘f3 ♘bd7 7.0-0 e5 8.b3 ♖e8 9.e4 c6 10.♗e3 exd4 11.♘xd4 ♘c5 12.f3 ♕e7 13.♖e1

13.♘de2!?.

13...a5 14.♕c2 ♗e6 15.♖ad1

15...a4?!

Playing to lose in a sharp tussle, but Kramnik proves to be better at hara-kiri. After 15...♗c8 16.♕d2 ♘fd7 17.f4 (17.♘de2 ♗f8 (17...f5!?) 18.f4 f5 is unclear) 17...♘f6 18.h3 White is slightly better.

16.b4 ♘cd7 17.♘xe6 ♕xe6

17...fxe6 18.♘xa4 d5 19.cxd5 exd5 20.♘c5 was out of the question for Black.

18.♘xa4 ♘e5 19.c5! ♕c4

Seeking complications. 19...dxc5 20.f4 ♘ed7 (20...♘eg4 21.♗xc5+−; 20...♘c4 21.♗c1+−) 21.e5 ♘d5 22.♗xd5 cxd5

23.bxc5 ♕c6 24.♘c3 would give Black no chance to survive.

20.♕b3! dxc5 21.♘b6

21.f4! was the clearest way to win.

21...♕xb3 22.axb3 ♖ad8 23.bxc5 ♘fd7 24.♘a4 ♘f8 25.♖d6

25.♔f1!? ♘e6 26.♔e2±.

25...♘e6 26.♖ed1 ♖a8 27.h3

27...♘c4

The only way to get counterplay. However, it is not the position on the board but the psychological state of the players which changes.

28.bxc4 ♖xa4 29.♖d7

29.♗f1!? ♗f8 30.♔f2 still allowed Black some compensation. But now White's game rapidly deteriorates. The proud c5-pawn becomes a weakness.

29...♖b4 30.f4 ♗f8 31.♔h2 ♗xc5 32.♗c1 ♖a8 33.f5 ♘f8 34.♖7d3 ♖xc4 35.♗h6 ♗e7!

Safeguarding his position first. 35...♖a2 would be an inaccuracy: 36.♖d8 f6 (36...♖cc2?! 37.♖xf8+! ♗xf8 38.♖d8 ♖xg2+ 39.♔h1 ♖h2+ 40.♔g1 ♖hg2+ 41.♔f1 ♖af2+ 42.♔e1 ♖e2+ 43.♔d1 ♖d2+ 44.♗xd2 ♔g7 45.f6+ ♔xf6 46.♖xf8 ♖xg3 47.h4 ♖g4 48.♗g5+ ♔g7 49.♖e8 h6 50.♗d8 g5 51.hxg5 hxg5 with a little edge – most probably a draw) 37.♖xf8+ ♗xf8 38.♖d8 ♔f7 39.♖xf8+ ♔e7 40.♔g1 ♖cc2 41.♗f1 ♖c3 42.e5 is unclear.

36.♖1d2 b5 37.♖f3 b4 38.e5 gxf5 39.♖xf5 ♘g6 40.♖df2 ♗f8 41.♗g5 b3

White is dead. He resigned 18 moves later.

There were people who noted that Black's success was achieved not quite without the opponent's help, like in this game. Very true. But in the games won by White, did Black not make any mistakes there? Or would that be natural?

Fabiano Caruana had his own streak in the tournament. He lost two games with white – both against the Najdorf. Shortly before the tournament he had lost two more Najdorfs with white. Boris Gelfand, who is famous for his smooth opening play – and also for his Najdorfs – quipped the following about their game in an interview in New In Chess: '...he obviously was better prepared. After the opening he had an extra hour, but my experience in the Najdorf proved to be a more important factor.' Two years later he recalled: 'Caruana was far ahead in preparation in this game. At some point I'd spent an hour more than him. In a certain position, he tried to remember rather than to think. Then he made a positional mistake, allowing me to play 26...d5-d4. After that, I was better.'

In other games since then it has turned out that this line favours White. In this game Caruana seems to have fallen victim to a well-known phenomenon: too much preparation, too little concentration.

Of course the balance between the two is what it is all about, and is one which Gelfand has been able to maintain on a high standard for almost three decades. 'You have to work day after day to improve yourself', he says, after working hard with his second Khuzman for more than 20 years.

'The motivation is to do something better than yesterday.'

Fabiano Caruana 2774
Boris Gelfand 2755
Moscow 2013 (2)
1.e4 c5!

It is hard to play for a win in the Petroff, Boris realized.

2.♘f3 d6 3.d4 cxd4 4.♘xd4 ♘f6 5.♘c3 a6 6.f3 e5 7.♘b3 ♗e6 8.♗e3 ♗e7 9.♕d2 0-0 10.0-0-0 ♘bd7 11.g4 b5 12.g5 b4 13.♘e2 ♘e8 14.f4 a5 15.f5 a4 16.fxe6 axb3

This is a key position in certain circles.

17.cxb3

17.exf7+ ♖xf7 18.cxb3 ♖xa2 19.♘g3 was stronger.

17...fxe6 18.♗h3

18.♔b1 ♖xa2! and now:

A) 19.♔xa2 ♕a8+ 20.♔b1 (20.♗a7 ♕xa7+ 21.♔b1 ♘c5 with excellent play for Black) 20...♕xe4+ 21.♕d3 ♕xh1 22.♗h3 ♕c6 23.♗xe6+ ♔h8∓;

B) 19.♗h3 ♕a5 20.♗xe6+ ♔h8 21.♗xd7 (21.♗c4 ♘c7 22.♘c1 (22.♘g3?! ♖c8!) 22...♖a1+ 23.♔c2 ♘b6 with a dangerous initiative) 21...♖a1+ 22.♔c2

♕c7+ 23.♘c3 ♖xd1 24.♕xd1 ♕xd7 25.♘d5 ♘c7 26.♘xe7 ♕xe7 27.♖f1 ♖b8 with an approximately even game.

18...♖xa2 19.♗xe6+ ♔h8 20.♘g3 ♘c7 21.♗c4 ♕a8∓ 22.♖hf1 ♖xf1 23.♖xf1 ♖a1+ 24.♔c2 ♖xf1 25.♗xf1 d5! 26.h4?!

Better was first 26.exd5 ♘xd5 and then 27.h4 with counterchances.

26...d4! 27.♗g1 ♘e6 28.♕e2?!

This is bad, but the alternatives were no better. For example: 28.♔b1 g6−+.

28...♘dc5 29.♕c4 ♘f4!?

29...h6!∓.

30.♕f7 ♕f8 31.♕c4

31.♕xf8+ ♗xf8 32.♗c4 ♘g2 33.♘f5 ♘e1+ 34.♔d1 ♘f3 35.♗f2 g6 was already losing for White.

31...g6

The following labyrinth of variations was indeed too hard to calculate in a practical game. Please buckle up!

31...♘g6!? 32.h5 (32.♘f5 ♘xe4 33.♘xe7 ♘xe7 34.♗g2 ♕f4−+) 32...♕f4 33.hxg6 ♕xg3 34.♕f7 d3+ 35.♔b1 hxg6 36.♗f2 (36.♕xe7 ♕xg1−+) 36...♕g4 37.♔a2 ♘xb3! 38.♕xg6 (38.♕xb3 d2−+; 38.♗e3 ♕d1−+) 38...♘c1+ 39.♔b1 d2 40.♗c4 ♗f8 41.♕f7 ♕xe4+ 42.♔a1 ♕xc4 43.♕xc4 d1♕ 44.♕h4+ ♔g8 45.♕c4+ ♔h7 46.♕h4+ (46.g6+ ♔h6 47.♗e3+ ♔h5 48.♗xc1 b3−+) 46...♔g6 47.♕e4+ ♔f7 48.♕f5+ ♔e8 49.♕xe5+ (49.♕c8+? is weaker due to 49...♕d8 50.♕e6+ (50.♕xc1 ♕a8+ 51.♔b1 b3−+) 50...♗e7 51.♕g8+ ♔d7 52.♕d5+ ♗d6 53.♔b1 b3 54.♕b7+ (54.♔xc1 ♕c8+−+) 54...♕c7 55.♕xc7+ ♗xc7 56.♔xc1 ♔e6 57.♔d2 ♗a5+ 58.♔d3 ♔d5−+) 49...♗e7 50.♕b8+ ♕d8 51.♕b5+ ♕d7 52.♕b8+ ♗d8 (52...♕d8 53.♕b5+ forced 53...♕d7 54.♕b8+ ♔f7 55.♕f4+ ♔g8 56.♕xc1 ♕d5∓) 53.♕e5+ ♔f8 54.♕f4+ ♔g8 55.♕xc1 ♕a4+ 56.♔b1 b3∓.

32.♗f2?

32.♕xb4!? was a better try, for example:

A) 32...♘xe4? 33.♗xd4! ♗xb4 (33...♕c8+? 34.♗c4!+−) 34.♗xe5+ ♘f6 (34...♔g8 35.♗c4+ ♕f7 36.♗xf4+−) 35.♗xf6+ ♕xf6 36.gxf6 ♘d5 37.♔d3 ♘xf6 38.♘e2 and White is slightly better;

B) But with 32...d3+ 33.♔b1 ♘h5! 34.♘xh5 ♕xf1+ 35.♔a2 ♕f8 36.♘f6 ♘d7 37.♕c3 ♘xf6 38.gxf6 ♗xf6 39.♕xd3 ♗xh4 Black keeps his advantage.

32...♘e2

Or 32...d3+ 33.♔b1 ♕d8−+.

33.♘h1 d3+ 34.♔d1 ♕f3 35.♗xc5 ♕xf1+ 36.♔d2 ♘f4 37.♘g3 ♕g2+ 38.♔c1 ♕xg3 39.♔b1 ♘e2 40.♕f7 ♕e1+ 41.♔a2 ♘c3+! 0-1

This was a real chess game. It's a shame that the Petroff was in fashion for such a long time at the 'club'. On the other hand, the Russian (which is what we call this defence) did a fine 'BLACK IS OK' job. Most games ended in a draw. And if White was not able to do much with his extra tempo in a symmetrical position, then what is the problem?

This was Gelfand's first black win in the tournament – out of two. He didn't recall that there were so many other black wins in this event. 'But my games with Caruana and Nakamura were certainly memorable. I played well in them, whereas they didn't.'

Carlsen's comment on his tournament was as follows: 'Especially my play with black was at best indifferent. I had four draws in those games and basically in all of them I was either suffering a little

26-28 Excellent moves Black!

32...Ne2 Knight sacrifice to gain Bishop + check! 33.Nh1 Didn't work!

bit or a lot and winning chances were zero.' (New In Chess)

♟ **Magnus Carlsen** 2864
○ **Fabiano Caruana** 2774
Moscow 2013 (3)

1.♘f3 ♘f6 2.g3 d5 3.♗g2 c6 4.0-0 ♗g4 5.c4

5.d4 ♘bd7 with mutual chances; 5.d3 ♘bd7 6.♘bd2 e5 7.e4 ♗d6.

5...e6 6.cxd5 ♗xf3 7.♗xf3 cxd5 8.♘c3 ♘c6 9.d4 ♗e7 10.e3

Carlsen does not rush things.

10...0-0 11.b3 ♕a5 12.♗b2 ♗a3 13.♕c1 ♗xb2 14.♕xb2 ♖fc8

Dead even.

15.♖ac1 ♘e7

15...♕d8!? was just as good, but the text provokes a dubious pawn sac.

16.♘a4 ♘d7 17.♘c5?! ♘xc5 18.dxc5 ♖xc5 19.b4 ♖b5!

It's hard to believe that a great player like Carlsen missed this move.

20.a3 ♕d8

White does not seem to have enough compensation.

21.e4 a5! 22.exd5 ♘xd5 23.♖c5 ♕b6 24.♖xb5 ♕xb5 25.♗xd5 exd5 26.♖c1 ♖e8 27.♕d4 axb4 28.axb4 h6 29.♔g2 b6! 30.♖d1 ♖e4 31.♕xd5 ♕xd5 32.♖xd5 ♖xb4∓

A typical rook ending.

33.h4 ♔f8 34.♖d7 ♖e4 35.♖b7 ♖e6 36.g4

36.h5!? ♖f6 37.f4 g6 38.hxg6 ♖xg6 might have been harder to win for Black.

36...g5 37.f4 gxf4 38.♔f3 ♖f6 39.g5 ♖c6 40.♔xf4

40...h5!

This pawn will win the game.

41.♔f5 ♔g7 42.♖b8 ♖c5+ 43.♔f4 ♖b5 44.♔e4 ♖b1 45.♔f5 ♖b2 46.♔f4 ♖b4+ 47.♔e5 ♔g6 48.♖g8+ ♔h7 49.♖f8??

49.♖b8 still gave drawing chances.

49...♖xh4 50.♖xf7+ ♔g6 51.♖f6+ ♔xg5 52.♖xb6 ♖a4–+ 53.♖b8 ♔g4 54.♖g8+ ♔f3 55.♖f8+ ♔g3 56.♖g8+ ♔h2 57.♔f5 h4 58.♖b8 h3 59.♔g5 ♖e4 60.♔f5 ♖e2 61.♖g8 ♖g2 62.♖d8 ♖f2+

White resigned.

Caruana had learned his lesson well. Carlsen's improvisation backfired this time. It seems he had left his sense of danger in the hotel...

Anish Giri tweeted with regard to this game: 'I am pretty sure Magnus is losing the rook endgames because he just sees too much. No sarcasm.'

Excellent

Fabiano Caruana 2774 ○
Hikaru Nakamura ● 2784
Moscow 2013 (4)

1.e4 c5 2.♘f3 d6 3.d4 cxd4 4.♘xd4 ♘f6 5.♘c3 a6 6.f3 e5 7.♘b3 ♗e6 8.♗e3 h5!?

This set-up has become standard, in order to slow down the attack with g2-g4.

9.♕d2 ♘bd7 10.♘d5

10.0-0-0 ♗e7 11.♔b1 ♕c7 leads to a different structure.

10...♘xd5 11.exd5 ♗f5 12.♗e2

12.♗d3 – see move 17.

12...♖c8 13.♖c1 ♕h4+ 14.g3

14.♗f2!?.

14...♕f6 15.0-0 ♗e7 16.♘a5 ♖c7
17.♗d3 0-0 18.c4 ♗xd3 19.♕xd3
♖e8 20.b4 ♗f8 21.♖ce1 g6 22.♕d2!?

22.h4 might have been better.

22...♕f5 23.a4 ♘f6 24.♗b6

24.c5!.

24...♖cc8 25.f4?

Wrong; 25.♗e3.

25...e4 26.♗d4 ♖c7 27.h3 ♗g7
28.♕g2

28...b5!

A key move.

29.axb5 axb5 30.♗xf6

30.cxb5 ♘xd5 31.♘c6 ♘f6–+.

30...♗xf6 31.g4 hxg4 32.hxg4
♗d4+ 33.♔h2 ♕f6 34.♘c6 ♗b6

35.g5 ♕f5 36.c5

If 36.♕h3 bxc4–+.

36...dxc5 37.♘e5 cxb4 38.d6 ♖c3
39.♖xe4 ♔g7   **0-1**

At the end darkness came down on White.

Two weeks earlier, Nakamura had already had Black against Anand in Norway, winning in the Arkhangelsk Variation of the Ruy Lopez. Still in a winning mood in Moscow, the American decided on a little experiment. What followed was an 'exciting game, and one where I understood the urgency and danger in the position a little bit better than the World Champion', he wrote in New In Chess.

Viswanathan Anand   2786
Hikaru Nakamura   2784
Moscow 2013 (6)

1.e4 e5 2.♘f3 ♘c6 3.♗b5 g6

Nakamura still plays rare variations too.

4.0-0 ♗g7 5.c3 a6 6.♗xc6

6.♗a4.

6...dxc6 7.d4 exd4 8.cxd4 ♘e7

8...♗g4!?.

9.h3

Giving Black already something of a target, as Nakamura argued: a 'hook'.

9...0-0 10.♘c3 h6 11.♕b3

11.♗f4!?.

11...g5 12.♖d1 b6 13.a4 a5 14.♗e3
♘g6 15.d5

173

A little impatient. 15.♘e2!? was solid, e.g. 15...g4?! 16.hxg4 ♗xg4 17.♕c2 ♗xf3 18.gxf3 ♕f6 19.f4 with the idea ...♕h4 20.f5 or 20.♕xc6±.

15...c5 16.♘b5 g4

16...♗a6!?.

17.hxg4 ♗xg4 18.♗d2

18.d6!.

18...♕d7 19.♖ac1?!

19.♖e1!? seems to be better. It is rational to move the rook out of the pin. Later, ♘h2 may be coming.

19...c6

With 19...♖ae8 Black could activate another piece, but the text is okay too.

20.dxc6 ♕xc6∓ 21.♗c3

21.♖e1.

21...♗xf3 22.gxf3 ♖ad8?!

22.♘f4! 23.♖d6 ♕c8∓.

23.♖xd8 ♖xd8 24.♖d1 ♖d7 25.♖xd7 ♕xd7

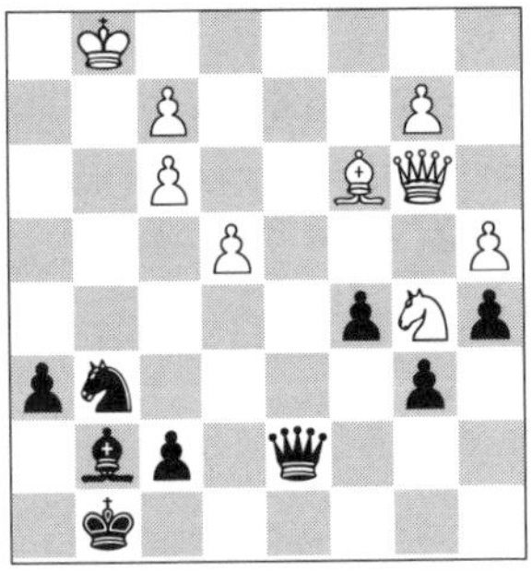

26.♕d5

This was not yet obligatory, but 26.♗xg7 ♔xg7 27.♕c3+ f6 28.♕e3 ♕h3 29.♘d6 ♘h4 30.♘f5+ ♘xf5 31.exf5 ♕xf5 32.♕e7+ ♔g6 33.♕e8+ ♔g5 should lead to Black's victory with practically two pawns up. However Nakamura himself wrote that he saw no way for Black to make progress after 34.♕e3+ ♕f4 35.♕b3!. Geza Maroczy, one of the greatest Hungarian chess players of all time, once said: 'If you win a game, always give your opponent some consolation by saying that at certain points he could have played better and

maybe held the game.' Nakamura's words are in the same gentlemanly spirit.

26...♕xd5 27.exd5 ♗xc3 28.bxc3 ♘e5?!

28...♔f8! with advantage to Black.

29.♘d6 ♔f8 30.♔h2??

After this mistake, resignation would be early, but it is hopeless to continue. 30.f4 was White's only chance. After 30.♔f1, Nakamura gave 30...b5!! as the only way to win.

30...♔e7 31.♘c8+ ♔d7 32.♘xb6+ ♔c7 33.f4 ♘f3+ 34.♔g2 ♘d2 35.♘a8+ ♔b7 36.d6 ♔c6 37.♘c7 ♔xd6 38.♘b5+ ♔d5 39.♔g3 ♔c4 40.♘d6+ ♔xc3 41.♘xf7 c4 42.f5 ♔d4 43.♘d6 ♔e5 44.♘b5 ♔xf5 45.f3 h5 0-1

Nakamura was doing fine with black for quite some time. I remember him playing my gambit in the Nimzo-Indian (4.♕c2 0-0 5.a3 ♗xc3+ 6.♕xc3 b5!?) in round 6 of the Wijk aan Zee tournament in 2011, against l'Ami.

In the next round, Nakamura, who had made his four points in a row by now, faced Gelfand. Here the chapter about these two opponents earlier in this book (Chapter 6) coincides with this chapter! At that point Nakamura was leading the event, and Gelfand was trailing him by half a point. 'To his credit, he played an open game', Gelfand reminisces. 'After about 20 moves, the computer said that White was better. Nakamura's second also claimed this after the game, and the live commentators agreed. But if you take a good look at the position, you will soon see that White is the one who has to be careful here.'

Hikaru Nakamura 2784
Boris Gelfand 2755
Moscow 2013 (7)

1.e4 c5 2.♘f3 ♘c6 3.d4 cxd4 4.♘xd4 ♘f6 5.♘c3 e5

(handwritten in left margin: Well balanced solid movement by Black.)

Gelfand is familiar with the Sveshnikov too. He threw in it a couple of times like against Leko (Polanica Zdroj 1998). That was a sharp game that ended in a draw.

6.♘db5 d6 7.♗g5 a6 8.♘a3 b5 9.♗xf6

Some play 9.♘d5 ♗e7 10.♗xf6 ♗xf6 11.c4, hoping for an opening advantage.

9...gxf6 10.♘d5 f5 11.c4

Very unusual here. 11.exf5 or 11.♗d3 are the main lines.

11...b4 !

11...♗g7!? with counterplay.

When he was confronted with 11.c4, Pavel Eljanov reacted in a different way, but also got a good game: 11...♕a5+ 12.♕d2 ♕xd2+ 13.♔xd2 ♗h6+ 14.♔d1 0-0 15.exf5 ♗xf5 16.cxb5 axb5 17.♗xb5 ♘d4 18.♘e7+ ♔g7 19.♘xf5+ ♘xf5 20.♗d3 ♘e7 21.♘b5 d5 22.♔e2 e4 23.♗c2 ♖ab8 24.a4 f5, and Black was fine, although in the end he lost, in Volokitin-Eljanov, Kiev 2012.

12.♘c2

12.♕a4 ♗b7 13.♘xb4 fxe4 14.♖d1±.

12...fxe4 13.g3

13.♘cxb4 ♘d4.

13...♗g7 14.♗g2 0-0 15.♗xe4 ♖b8 16.b3 f5 17.♗g2

17...e4

Gelfand wrote in New In Chess: 'Here I had to make a decision, and after a long thought I decided on the risky-looking pawn grab on a2, as I couldn't find anything to refute the idea. The point

is that once the a-pawn has been taken, Black will not have problems in almost any endgame as he has counterplay connected with ...a5-a4. Alternatively, 17...♔h8 18.0-0 ♗e6 19.♕e2 a5 20.♖ad1 ♕d7 21.♖d2 would lead to a normal game, typical for this opening.'

18.♖b1 ♕a5 19.0-0 ♕xa2 20.♘de3

20.f3!? was promising.

20...♕a5 21.♕xd6 ♖f6 22.♕f4 ♕e5 23.♕xe5 ♘xe5 24.♘d5 ♖f7 25.♘cxb4

25.f3!? exf3 26.♗xf3 ♘xf3+ 27.♖xf3 a5 28.♔g2 ♗d7 29.♔f2± (after 29.♖e1, a4 will always be hanging in the air).

25...a5 26.♘c2 ♖fb7

27.♘ce3?!

27.♖bd1!? was also indicated by Gelfand. But he had expected 27.♘d4, when he was hesitating between a simplifying line starting with 27...♘xc4, leading to a draw, or 27...a4 28.c5! a3 29.c6! ♖f7 30.♖a1. 'I had a feeling that Black should be fine here, but the lines are very complicated.'

27...♘c6 28.c5 ♖xb3 29.♘b6?

29.♖xb3 ♖xb3 30.♗h3 (30.g4! Gelfand).

29...♖xb1 30.♖xb1 ♗e6

Black is slightly better here. His a-pawn is a potential danger.

31.♗f1 ♗d4

31...♘d4!?.

32.♖b5 ♔f7 33.♘ec4 ♔g7 34.♘d6 ♔f6 35.♘a4?!

35.♔g2 ♗xc5 36.♖xc5 ♖xb6 37.♘e8+ ♔e7 38.♘g7∓.

27... Nc6 saves knight fork!

35...e3! 36.fxe3 **♗xe3+** 37.♔g2
♗d5+∓ 38.♔h3 **♖xb5** 39.♗xb5
♘e5 40.♘c3?

40.♘b6 ♗e6 41.♘e8+ ♔g5 42.♘c7∓
was bad enough too, but not easily
losing like the text move.

40...♗f3 41.♗e2 **♗xe2** 42.♘d5+
♔g5 43.♘xe3 ♘g4 44.♔g2

44.♘xg4? ♗f1#.

44...♘xe3+ 45.♔f2 ♘c4   0-1

Now the a-pawn decides.
Gelfand again took risk in order to get
dynamic counterplay, and got rewarded
for it. That's how a great artist plays in
the memory of Mikhail Tal!

Vladimir Kramnik   2803
Dmitry Andreikin   2713
Moscow 2013 (7)

1.d4 ♘f6 2.c4 e6 3.g3 ♗b4+ 4.♗d2
♗xd2+ 5.♕xd2 d5

An attempt to solve the problems of the
Catalan in a simple way.

6.♗g2 0-0 7.♘f3 c6 8.0-0 ♘bd7
9.♖c1 ♕e7 10.♕e3 dxc4 11.♖xc4
♘d5 12.♕a3

12.♕d2 ♘5b6 13.♖c1 e5=.

12...♖e8 13.♕xe7 ♖xe7 14.e4±

14.♖c2!? ♘5b6 15.a4 a5 16.♘bd2 e5
17.♘e4 also gave an edge.

14...♘5b6 15.♖c2 e5 16.♘bd2

Andreikin wrote in New In Chess:
'From this moment on many of my
opponent's ideas came as a surprise to
me.

For example, I was sure that the knight
would be better placed on c3.'

16...a5 17.a3

17.♘xe5!? ♘xe5 18.dxe5 ♖xe5 19.♘b3
with a slight advantage.

**17...g6 18.♖ac1 exd4 19.♘xd4
♘e5 20.f4 ♖d7! 21.♘e2?!**

21.♘4b3 ♘d3 22.♖d1 a4 23.♘c1 ♘xc1
24.♖dxc1 ♖d4 25.♘c4±; 21.♘4f3±.

21...♘g4

21...♘d3!? 22.♖d1 ♘a4 23.b3 ♘ac5±
was worth considering too.

**22.♘f1 ♖d8 23.h3 ♘f6 24.♖d2 ♗e6
25.♔f2**

25.♘d4!?±.

25...♘a4 26.♖cc2 ♘d7

27.♔e3??

A terrible blunder. Instead there were
several good options, such as 27.♘c1±,
27.♘d4±, or 27.♖d4±.

27...♗b3 28.♖c1 ♘db6!

That puts an end to this one.

29.♖d4 c5!

The rest was a formality. Kramnik
resigned on move 42.

Young Andreikin kept waiting
patiently, and took the first opportunity
to punish his great opponent for the
first error. This recalls Ulf Andersson's
true Grandmastery of positional play.
Alexander Morozevich also played quite
disastrously in his home town. It wasn't
until the ultimate round that he won
his first game – a quite shaky affair (see
below). The brilliant Russian lost three

[left margin handwritten:] White plays 44.Kg2 to fork both pieces After 44...Nxe3+! Nice but not enough 45.Kxe2

[right margin handwritten:] Back + forth Nothing exciting

games, two of them with black. As you can see in the table at the beginning of this chapter, the four lowest-placed participants were the only ones with negative scores with black. Morozevich's sole white loss went as follows:

Alexander Morozevich 2760
Fabiano Caruana 2774

Moscow 2013 (8)

1.e4 e5 2.♘f3 ♘c6 3.♘c3 ♘f6 4.d4 exd4 5.♘xd4 ♗b4 6.♘xc6 bxc6 7.♗d3

This variation has been a dead draw for decades.

7...d5 8.exd5 cxd5 9.0-0 0-0 10.h3 c6 11.♕f3

11...♖e8

11...♗d6! – here is a point for signing the peace treaty.

12.♗g5 h6 13.♗xf6 ♕xf6 14.♕xf6 gxf6 15.♘e2 ♗d6 16.♖ad1 ♗e6 17.♘g3 ♖ab8 18.♘h5 ♗e5 19.b3 ♔f8 20.f4 ♗b2 21.♖f3

It's not easy to find a sound plan for either side.

21...c5

21...♔e7.

22.♗h7 ♖b6 23.c3 ♗c8

23...d4!.

24.♖g3 d4 25.cxd4 ♗xd4+ 26.♔h2 ♗d7 27.♖g8+ ♔e7 28.♖e1+

Moro would have been better off with 28.♖xe8+ ♔xe8 29.♘g7+ ♔f8 30.♘f5 ♗xf5 31.♗xf5=.

28...♖e6 29.♖xe6+ fxe6 30.♖g7+ ♔d6 31.♖g6 ♖h8

Black is slightly better here.

32.♖xh6 ♗b5 33.g4 ♗d3 34.f5 ♗e5+ 35.♔g2 ♗e4+ 36.♔f2 ♗d4+ 37.♔e2 c4

38.g5??

Giving away the game as a present. 38.bxc4 ♖b8 39.fxe6 ♖b2+ 40.♔d1 was equal, and 38.♘xf6 ♗xf6 39.♖xf6 cxb3 40.axb3 ♖xh7 41.♖xe6+ ♔d5 42.♖a8 would also hold.

38...c3–+ 39.♘g3 c2 40.♘xe4+ ♔e5 **0-1**

This was the most spectacular suicide in the tournament.

But here is Moro's sole win of the event!

Hikaru Nakamura 2784
Alexander Morozevich 2760

Moscow 2013 (9)

1.d4 ♘f6 2.c4 e6 3.♘f3 d5 4.♗g5 ♗b4+ 5.♘bd2

Odd. 5.♘c3 is usual.

5...dxc4 6.e3 b5

6...c3 7.bxc3 ♗xc3 8.♖c1 ♗b4 9.♗d3 with compensation.

7.a4 c6

7...c5?! 8.axb5 cxd4 9.exd4 ♗b7 10.♗xc4 ♘bd7 11.0-0 0-0 with a clear pawn up for White.

8.♕c2 ♗b7 9.♗e2 ♘bd7 10.0-0 0-0 11.b3

11.♘e4!? was another promising option.

11...c3

11...cxb3, taking the a- and b-pawns, followed by 13...a5, could have given him an edge.

12.♘e4 h6 13.♗h4?! g5 14.♘xf6+ ♘xf6 15.♗g3 c5 16.♗xb5

16.axb5!? ♗e4 17.♕c1 c2 18.dxc5 ♗xc5 19.♖a4 ♕d5 and Black is clearly better.

16...♗e4 17.♕e2 ♖c8 18.♗a6 cxd4! 19.♘xd4 ♖c5 20.♖ad1 ♘d5

Better was 20...♕b6!?.

21.♘c2 ♕b6 22.♗c4

22.♗d3! was more appealing.

22...a5 23.♖d4

23.♘xb4! axb4 24.♖d4 ♗g6 25.e4 would have freed White's play and given him the upper hand.

23...♗g6 24.h4 ♖cc8

24...♖d8!?.

25.hxg5 hxg5 26.♖g4 ♗e7 27.e4 ♘f4 28.♗xf4 gxf4 29.e5

On 29.♖xf4, 29...♖fd8! was dangerous.

29...♔g7

30.♗d3?

Late by 8 moves. After 30.♘e1 ♖h8 31.♘d3 White would have been only slightly worse.

30...♖h8!

Black's attack is more than dangerous now.

31.g3 ♖h6 32.♗e4 ♖ch8 33.♕c4 fxg3 34.♖xg3

34...♖h4! 35.♕c6

White could have resigned here as well. If 35.♘e3 ♖d8!–+.

35...♕xc6 36.♗xc6 ♗c5

36...♖h3!?–+.

37.♖c1 ♖f4 38.♘e3 ♗d4 39.♗b5 ♔f8 40.♗c6 ♗xe5 41.♘d1 ♖b4 42.♖xg6 fxg6 43.♘xc3 ♔e7 44.♗g2 ♖xb3 45.♘e4 ♖d8 46.♖e1 ♖bd3 47.♔f1 ♖d1 48.♘c5 ♖xe1+ 49.♔xe1 ♖d4

Finally. White resigned.

So, Gelfand won two more games in this tournament. After the event Carlsen and Kramnik said that they, and the other participants, had made a lot of mistakes in this Tal Memorial, and that Gelfand had made the least mistakes. 'That's rather disrespectful', Gelfand thinks. 'This is always the case with big players. They won't say someone else has played very well, if they haven't played well themselves. There are very few top-level players who remain objective and respectful in such cases. Anand and Tal come to mind.'

NAKAMURA subtly outplayed!

Chapter 9
Who's the Boss?

The repertoire scheme given below was made by IM Endre Vegh, who is one of the world's leading analysts. His speciality is systematization. He has developed the *Chess Informant* code system further. There might be little holes here or there in this net. But my main argument here is that Black has many more deviations to which White has to have at least one serious weapon in the spirit of his 'superiority', while Black actually determines the direction in which events will develop.

Just one example. If Black wants to play the Sveshnikov he is supposed to study it deeply and to keep updating it. White's alternatives to avoid this crazy variation hardly promise him any advantage. See my earlier book on the Sicilian sub-variations from 2.f4 to the Closed Variation or 2.b3, 2.b4, or the Smith/Morra (*Your Black is OK Repertory*, VI/2 Sicilian subvariations, 1994). From this entire bunch, only 2.c3 is something that can be called serious. But not very.

All in all, there is sufficient evidence for the fact that against 1.e4 and 1.d4, which are the best first moves by far, Black can create a repertoire, as Evgeny Sveshnikov himself has admitted, with much less lexical work than White has to do. Or he can pick up two different variations to mix, depending on the opponent, the tournament situation, and his state of mind or mood. And it is possible to learn all this spending not more time and energy than it takes White to build up one serious weapon in every plausible line.

The material in this chapter provides 99% evidence about 'Who's the boss' (if anyone is...) in the opening. Not White. You can check it. White has to have something against every answer to 1.d4. If he plays 1.e4 he must be well prepared against nine plausible answers. Wake up, folks! I'm not talking rubbish! And if you say this is the third time in this book you read this, you have counted well. This is like the third call – it still gives you the chance not to be late to get closer to the chess truth, so that you could use it for your own benefit. Listen to me, and don't deny the facts!

White repertoire – 1.d4

1.d4

I. Various

1. 1...e5 (Englund)
2. 1...♘c6 2.c4 e5 (2...d5 – see Chigorin) 3.d5 ♘ce7 (3...♗b4+) 4.♘c3 ♘g6 (4...d6 5.g3; 4...♘f6 5.g3) 5.g3
3. 1...b5 2.e4 ♗b7 3.f3 a6 4.♗e3 e6 5.♘d2
4. 1...b6 2.c4 ♗b7 3.d5 e6 (3...e5) 4.a3 – see 1...e6 2.c4 b6 3.a3 ♗b7
5. 1...e6 2.c4 b6 3.a3 ♗b7 (3...g6; 3... f5) 4.♘c3 f5 (4...g6 5.e4; 4...♘f6 5.d5) 5.d5 ♘f6 6.g3
6. 1...g6 2.c4 ♗g7 3.e4 d6 4.♘c3:

179

a. 4...f5 (Bilek) 5.exf5 ♗xf5 6.♘f3;

b. 4...e5 5.♘f3 exd4 (5...♘c6 6.♗g5;
   5...♗g4 6.d5) 6.♘xd4 ♘c6 (6...♘e7
   7.♗g5) 7.♗e3 ♘ge7 8.h4;

c. 4...c6 5.♘f3;

d. 4...c5 5.d5;

e. 4...♘d7 5.♗g5;

f. 4...♘f6 – see King's Indian;

g. 4...♘c6 5.♗e3 e5 (5...♘f6) 6.d5 ♘ce7
   (6...♘d4 7.♘ge2) 7.g4 f5 (7...♘f6; 7...f6)
   8.gxf5 gxf5 9.♕h5+ ♚f8 (9...♘g6
   10.exf5 ♕h4 11.♕f3) 10.♗h3.

**7. 1...d6 2.c4 e5 3.d5 (Avrukh) 3...f5
   (3...♗e7 4.e4 ♗g5 5.♘d2) 4.e4 fxe4
   (4...♘f6) 5.♘c3 ♘f6 6.♘ge2**

**8. 1...c5 2.d5 e5 (Czech Benoni) 3.e4
   d6 (3...♘f6 4.♘c3 d6 5.f4) 4.♘c3 ♗e7
   (4...g6; 4...a6; 4...♘d7; 4...♘e7) 5.f4**

9. 1...f5 (Dutch) 2.♘f3 ♘f6 3.g3:

a. 3...e6 4.♗g2 d5 (Stonewall) (4...♗e7
   (Iljin-Zhenevsky) 5.0-0 0-0 6.c4 d6
   (6...d5 – see Stonewall) 7.♘c3 a5
   (7...♘e4 8.♕c2; 7...♕e8 8.♕c2) 8.b3
   ♕e8 9.♗b2) 5.0-0 ♗d6 (5...♗e7 6.c4

0-0 7.b3 c6 (7...♘e4; 7...b6; 7...♗d7
8.♗a3; 7...♘c6 8.♗a3) 8.♗a3) 6.c4 c6
7.b3 ♕e7 (7...0-0 8.♗a3) 8.♘e5 0-0
(8...♘bd7; 8...b6) 9.♘d2);

b. 3...g6 (Leningrad) 4.♗g2 ♗g7 5.0-0
   0-0 6.c4 d6 (6...c6) 7.♘c3:

b1. 7...e6;

b2. 7...a5;

b3. 7...c6 8.d5 e5 (8...♕a5; 8...♗d7;
    8...♕e8) 9.dxe6 ♗xe6 (9...♕e7
    10.♗f4) 10.b3;

b4. 7...♘c6 8.d5 ♘e5 (8...♘a5 9.♕a4 c5
    (9...b6 10.♕c2) 10.dxc6 bxc6 (10...♘xc6
    11.♖d1) 11.♘d4) 9.♘xe5 dxe5 10.♕b3;

b5. 7...♘a6 8.♖b1;

b6. 7...♕e8 8.♖e1 ♕f7 (8...c6; 8...♘c6;
    8...e5) 9.e4.

II. Queen's Gambit
   1...d5 2.c4

1. 2...c5

**2. 2...♗f5 (Keres) 3.cxd5 ♗xb1
   4.♕a4+ c6 (4...♕d7 5.♕xd7+ ♘xd7
   6.♖xb1 ♘gf6 7.♘f3) 5.♖xb1 ♕xd5
   6.♘f3 ♘d7 7.a3**

3. 2...♞c6 (Chigorin) 3.♘c3:

a. 3...e5 4.cxd5 ♘xd4 (4...exd4 5.dxc6 dxc3 6.♕xd8+ ♚xd8 7.cxb7 ♗xb7 8.bxc3) 5.e3 ♘f5 6.♘f3;

b. 3...♘f6 4.♘f3 ♗g4 (4...dxc4 5.e4 – see 4...dxc4) 5.cxd5 ♘xd5 6.e4 ♘xc3 7.bxc3 e5 8.d5;

c. 3...dxc4 4.♘f3 ♘f6 5.e4 ♗g4 6.♗e3.

4. 2...e5 (Albin's Counter Gambit) 3.dxe5 d4 4.♘f3 ♘c6 (4...c5) 5.g3 ♘ge7 (5...♗g4 6.♗g2 ♕d7 7.0-0 0-0-0 8.♕b3; 5...♗e6 6.♘bd2) 6.♗g2 ♘g6 7.♗g5;

5. 2...c6 Slav 3.♘f3 ♘f6 4.♘c3:

a. 4...♗g4 5.♘e5;

b. 4...♗f5 5.cxd5 cxd5 6.♕b3;

c. 4...♕b6 5.♕c2;

d. 4...g6 5.cxd5 cxd5 6.♗f4;

e. 4...a6 5.c5 ♘bd7 (5...♗g4; 5...♗f5; 5...g6) 6.♗f4 ♘h5 (6...g6) 7.♗d2 ♘hf6 (7...g6 8.e4) 8.♕c2;

f. 4...e6 5.♗g5:

f1. 5...♗e7 6.e3;

f2. 5...♘bd7 6.e3 ♕a5 (Cambridge Springs) 7.cxd5 ♘xd5 (7...cxd5; 7...exd5 8.♗d3 ♘e4 9.0-0; 7...♘e4) 8.♕d2 ♗b4 (8...♘7b6 9.♗d3) 9.♖c1;

f3. 5...dxc4 (Botvinnik) 6.e4 b5 7.e5 h6 8.♗h4 g5 9.♘xg5 hxg5 (9...♘d5 10.♘f3 ♕a5 11.♖c1) 10.♗xg5 ♘bd7 (10...♗e7 11.exf6 ♗xf6 12.♗xf6 ♕xf6 13.g3) 11.exf6 ♗b7 (11...♗h6; 11...♕a5) 12.g3 c5 13.d5 ♕b6 13...♕c7; 13...♘e5; 13...♘b6; 13...♘xf6 14.♗g2 ♗e7 (14...♗h6 15.♗xf6) 15.0-0 ♘xd5 16.♗xe7 ♚xe7 17.♘xb5 ♕b6 18.♘a3; 13...♗h6 14.♗xh6 ♖xh6 15.♕d2; 14.♗g2 0-0-0 15.0-0 b4 16.♘a4 ♕b5 (16...♕d6; 16...♕a6) 17.a3 exd5 18.axb4 cxb4 (18...d4) 19.♗e3;

f4. 5...h6 (Moscow) 6.♗h4 dxc4 7.e4 g5 (7...♗e7; 7...♗b4) 8.♗g3 b5 (8...♗b4) 9.♗e2 ♗b7:

f41. 9...b4;

f42. 9...♗b4;

f43. 9...a6;

f44. 9...♘bd7 10.d5 cxd5 (10...b4;
10...♗b7; 10...exd5) 11.exd5; 10.h4
g4 (10...b4) 11.♘e5 h5 12.0-0
♘bd7 (12...♗g7) 13.♕c2.

g. 4...dxc4 5.a4 ♗f5 (5...♘a6 6.e4;
5...e6 6.e4; 5...♗g4 6.♘e5 ♗h5
7.g3) 6.♘e5 ♘bd7 (6...e6 7.f3
♗b4 (7...c5 8.e4 cxd4 9.exf5 ♘c6
(9...♗b4 10.♗xc4) 10.♘xc6 bxc6
11.fxe6 fxe6 12.♗xc4) 8.e4 ♗xe4
(8...♗g6; 8...♘xe4) 9.fxe4 ♘xe4
10.♗d2 ♕xd4 11.♘xe4 ♕xe4+
12.♕e2 ♗xd2+ 13.♔xd2 ♕d5+
14.♔c2 ♘a6 15.♘xc4 0-0 (15...0-
0-0 16.♕e3) 16.♕f3) 7.♘xc4 ♕c7
(7...♘b6 8.♘e5 a5 (8...e6 9.f3) 9.g3)
8.g3 e5 9.dxe5 ♘xe5 10.♗f4 ♘fd7
(10...♖d8 11.♕c1 ♗d6 12.♘xd6+
♕xd6 13.♗g2) 11.♗g2 g5 12.♘e3.

6. 2...dxc4 (Queen's Gambit Accepted) 3.e4:

a. 3...b5 4.a4 c6 5.axb5 cxb5 6.♘c3;
b. 3...c5 4.d5 ♘f6 5.♘c3 e6 (5...b5
6.♗f4) 6.♗xc4 exd5 7.♘xd5 ♘xd5
8.♗xd5 ♗e7 (8...♗d6 9.♘f3) 9.♘f3;
c. 3...♘c6 4.♘f3 ♗g4 5.d5 ♘e5 6.♗f4
♘g6 7.♗e3 ♘f6 8.♘c3 e5 (8...e6)
9.♗xc4;
d. 3...♘f6 4.e5 ♘d5 5.♗xc4 ♘b6
(5...♘c6 6.♘c3 ♘b6 7.♗b5) 6.♗d3;
e. 3...e5 4.♘f3 exd4 (4...♗b4+ 5.♘c3 exd4
6.♘xd4) 5.♗xc4 ♗b4+ 6.♘bd2 ♘c6
7.0-0 ♘f6 (7...♘h6; 7...♕e7; 7...♗xd2;
7...♗e6; 7...♕f6) 8.e5 ♘d5·9.♘b3.

7. 2...e6 3.♘c3:

a. 3...f5 4.♘f3 ♘f6 5.♗g5;
b. 3...♗b4 4.a3 ♗xc3+ 5.bxc3 c5
(5...♘e7 6.e3) 6.e3;
c. 3...c6 4.e4 (Slav Gambit) 4...dxe4
(4...♗b4 5.cxd5 (5.exd5 Kasparov))
5.♘xe4 ♗b4+ (5...♘f6) 6.♗d2 ♕xd4
7.♗xb4 ♕xe4+ 8.♗e2 ♘a6 (8...♕xg2;
8...c5; 8...♘e7; 8...♘d7) 9.♗a5;
d. 3...c5 4.cxd5 exd5 (Tarrasch)
(4...cxd4 (Schara-Hennig) 5.♕a4+
♗d7 6.♕xd4 exd5 7.♕xd5 ♘c6
8.♘f3 ♘f6 9.♕d1 ♗c5 10.e3 ♕e7
11.♗e2) 5.♘f3 ♘c6 6.g3 ♘f6 (6...
c4) 7.♗g2 ♗e7 8.0-0 0-0 9.♗g5
cxd4 (9...♗e6; 9...c4) 10.♘xd4 h6
(10...♖e8 11.♖c1) 11.♗e3;
e. 3...♗e7 4.cxd5 exd5 5.♗f4 c6
(5...♘f6 6.e3) 6.♕c2;
f. 3...♘f6 4.cxd5 exd5 5.♗g5 ♗e7
(5...c6 6.e3 ♗f5 (6...♕b6 7.♕c2;
6...h6 7.♗h4) 7.♕f3 ♗g6 (7...♗e6
8.♗xf6 ♕xf6 9.♕xf6 gxf6 10.♗d3)
8.♗xf6 ♕xf6 (8...gxf6) 9.♕xf6 gxf6
10.♘f3) 6.e3 c6 (6...♘bd7 7.♗d3
♘f8 8.♘f3; 6...0-0 7.♗d3 ♘bd7
8.♘ge2) 7.♕c2 ♘bd7 8.♗d3:

f1. 8...h6 9.♗h4 0-0 (9...♘b6; 9...♘f8;
9...♘h5 10.♗xe7 ♕xe7 11.♘ge2)
10.♘ge2;

f2. 8...♘f8 9.♘ge2 ♘e6 (9...♘h5; 9...g6;
9...♘g6) 10.h4;

f3. 8...♘h5 9.♗xe7 ♕xe7 10.♘ge2;

f4. 8...0-0 9.♘ge2 ♖e8 10.0-0 ♘f8
(10...♘e4; 10...g6) 11.f3.

III. Indian Openings
1...♘f6 2.c4

1. **2...b6 3.♘c3**
2. **2...e5 (Budapest Gambit) 3.dxe5
♘g4 (3...♘e4 4.a3) 4.♗f4 ♘c6
(4...g5 5.♗g3) 5.♘f3 ♗b4+ 6.♘c3
♕e7 (6...♗xc3+ 7.bxc3 ♕e7 8.♕d5)
7.♕d5**
3. **2...d6 (Old Indian) 3.♘c3:**

a. 3...♗f5 4.f3;
b. 3...c6 4.e4 – see 3...♘bd7;
c. 3...e5 4.♘f3:

c1. 4...♘c6 5.d5;
c2. 4...exd4 5.♘xd4 g6 6.g3;

c3. 4...e4 5.♘g5 ♗f5 (5...♕e7 6.♕c2)
6.g4 ♗g4 (6...♘xg4 7.♘gxe4)
7.♗g2 ♗e7 (7...c6 8.♘gxe4; 7...♘c6
8.♘gxe4) 8.♘gxe4;

c4. 4...♘bd7 5.e4 – see 3...♘bd7 4.e4 e5
5.♘f3;

d. 3...♘bd7 4.e4 e5 5.♘f3 ♗e7 6.♗e2
0-0 7.0-0 c6 8.♗e3.

4. **2...c5 3.d5:**

a. 3...e5 (Old Benoni) 4.♘c3 d6 5.e4;
b. 3...b5 (Benko Gambit) 4.♘f3 g6:

b1. 4...a6 5.♕c2;
b2. 4...b4 5.a3;
b3. 4...bxc4 5.♘c3;
b4. 4...♗b7 5.♕c2;
b5. 4...d6 5.♕c2;
b6. 4...e6 (Blumenfeld Gambit) 5.♗g5
exd5 (5...h6 6.♗xf6 ♕xf6 7.♘c3;
5...♕a5+ 6.♕d2) 6.cxd5 d6 7.e4; 5.♕c2.

c. 3...e6 4.♘c3 exd5 5.cxd5 d6 (Modern
Benoni) (5...♗d6 (Snake Benoni)
6.♘f3 0-0 (6...♘c7 7.♗g5) 7.♗g5)
6.e4 g6 7.h3 ♗g7 8.♗d3 0-0 9.♘f3
b5 (9...a6 10.a4 ♘bd7 11.0-0 ♖e8

(11...♘h5 12.♗g5; 11...♕e7 12.♖e1;
11...♕c7 12.♖e1) 12.♖e1) 10.♘xb5
♖e8 (10...♘xe4 11.♗xe4 ♖e8
12.♘g5; 10...♗a6 11.a4; 10...♕a5+
11.♘c3) 11.0-0 ♘xe4 12.♖e1.

5. 2...c6 3.♘c3 – see Slav
6. 2...♘c6 (Black Knights Tango)
  3.♘f3 e6 4.a3
7. 2...a6 3.♘c3
8. 2...e6 3.♘c3 ♗b4 (Nimzo-Indian)
  (3...b6 4.e4; 3...c5 4.d5 – see
  Modern Benoni; 3...d5 4.cxd5 –
  see 1.d4 d5 2.c4 e6 3.♘c3 ♘f6
  4.cxd5) 4.♕c2:

a. 4...b6 5.e4:

a1. 5...c5 6.e5;
a2. 5...♗xc3+ 6.bxc3 ♗b7 (6...d6 7.f4)
    7.♗d3;
a3. 5...♗b7 6.♗d3.
b. 4...♘c6 5.♘f3 d6 6.♗d2 0-0 (6...e5;
    6...♕e7) 7.a3 ♗xc3 8.♗xc3;
c. 4...c5 5.dxc5 0-0 (5...♗xc5; 5...♘c6;
    5...♘a6; 5...♕c7) 6.a3 ♗xc5 7.♘f3 ♘c6
    (7...b6; 7...d5; 7...♕b6; 7...♕c7) 8.♗f4;

d. 4...d5 5.a3 ♗xc3+ (5...♗e7) 6.♕xc3
    ♘e4 (6...♘c6; 6...0-0; 6...c5 7.dxc5
    d4 8.♕g3; 6...dxc4 7.♕xc4 b6 8.♘f3)
    7.♕c2 c5 (7...0-0; 7...e5; 7...♘c6)
    8.dxc5 ♘c6 9.cxd5 exd5 10.♘f3
    ♗f5 (10...♕a5+; 10...♕f6) 11.b4;
e. 4...0-0 5.a3 ♗xc3+ 6.♕xc3 b6
    (6...♕e8; 6...♘e4; 6...b5; 6...d5)
    7.♗g5 ♗b7 (7...♗a6 8.♕f3; 7...c5
    8.dxc5 bxc5 9.e3) 8.e3 d6 9.♘e2

9. 2...g6 3.♘c3:

a. 3...d5 (Grünfeld Indian) 4.cxd5
    ♘xd5 5.e4 ♘xc3 (5...♘b6 6.h3)
    6.bxc3 ♗g7 (6...c5) 7.♗c4 0-0 (7...
    c5 8.♘e2 ♘c6 9.♗e3 cxd4 (9...0-0
    – see 7...0-0) 10.cxd4 ♕a5+ 11.♗d2
    ♕d8 (11...♕a3 12.0-0 0-0 13.♖b1;
    11...♘h5 12.d5 ♘e5 13.♗b5+)
    12.♗c3) 8.♘e2:

a1. 8...♘c6 9.0-0 b6 (9...e5 10.♗e3;
    9...♘a5 10.♗d3) 10.♗g5;
a2. 8...♕d7 9.0-0 b6 10.♗e3;
a3. 8...b6 9.h4;
a4. 8...c5 9.♗e3 ♘c6 10.0-0:

a41. 10...e6;

a42. 10...b6;

a43. 10...♘a5;

a44. 10...♗d7;

a45. 10...♕c7 11.♖c1 ♖d8 (11...♘a5;
11...b6) 12.♗f4 ♕d7 (12...e5;
12...♗e5) 13.d5 ♘a5 (13...♘e5)
14.♗d3;

a46. 10...♗g4 11.f3 ♘a5 12.♗d3 cxd4
13.cxd4 ♗e6 14.d5 ♗xa1 15.♕xa1
f6 16.♕d4;

b. 3...♗g7 4.e4 d6 (King's Indian):

5.♘f3 0-0 (5...b6; 5...a6; 5...c5; 5...♘bd7;
5...♘c6; 5...e5; 5...c6) 6.♗g5 c5 (6...h6;
6...♘bd7; 6...c6; 6...♘c6; 6...a6) 7.d5 e6
(7...h6; 7...♕a5) 8.♕d2 exd5 9.cxd5 a6
10.a4 h6 (10...♕a5; 10...♘bd7; 10...♖e8)
11.♗e3 ♖e8.

White repertoire 1.e4
1.e4

I. Various (Semi-Open Games)

1. **1...g5 (Basman)**

2. **1...a6 (Miles) 2.d4 b5 3.♗e3 ♗b7
    4.♘d2**

3. **1...b6 (Owen) 2.d4 ♗b7 3.♗d3**

4. **1...♘c6 (Nimzowitsch) 2.♘f3 d6
    (2...d5 3.exd5; 2...e5 3.♗b5) 3.d4
    ♘f6 (3...♗g4 4.♗b5) 4.♘c3**

5. **1...d5 (Scandinavian) 2.exd5 ♕xd5
    (2...♘f6 3.d4 ♘xd5 (3...♗g4 4.f3)
    4.♘f3) 3.♘c3:**

a. 3...♕d8 4.d4;

b. 3...♕a5 4.d4 ♘f6 (4...e5; 4...c6) 5.♘f3
    c6 (5...♘c6; 5...♗f5; 5...♗g4) 6.♗c4;

c. 3...♕d6 4.♘f3 a6 (4...c6) 5.g3.

6. **1...♘f6 (Alekhine) 2.e5 ♘d5 3.d4 d6
    4.♘f3 ♗g4 (4...♘b6 5.a4 a5 6.♗b5+;
    4...♘c6 5.c4 ♘b6 6.e6; 4...c6 5.c4;
    4...dxe5 5.♘xe5; 4...g6 5.♗c4) 5.♗e2**

7. **1...g6 (Modern) 2.d4 ♗g7 (2...c6)**
3.♘c3 d6 (3...c6 4.♘f3 d5 5.h3; 3...c5
4.dxc5) 4.♗e3 a6 (4...c6 5.♕d2) 5.♘f3

8. **1...d6 (Pirc/Ufimtsev) 2.d4 ♘f6**
3.♘c3 g6 (3...c6 4.f4; 3...e5 4.♘ge2)
4.♗e3 c6 (4...♗g7) 5.♘f3

9. **1...c6 (Caro Kann) 2.d4 d5 3.e5 ♗f5**
(3...♘a6 4.c3; 3...g6 4.c4; 3...c5
4.dxc5) 4.♘f3 e6 5.♗e2 c5 (5...h6;
5...♗g4; 5...♗g6; 5...♗e7; 5...♗b4+;
5...♘e7; 5...♘d7) 6.♗e3 cxd4 (6...♘e7;
6...♘d7; 6...♕b6) 7.♘xd4 ♘e7 8.c4

10. 1...c5 (Sicilian):

ALTERNATIVES WHITE
a. 2.♘c3;
b. 2.c3;

c. 2.♘f3:

The 'black hole' = Sicilian sub-variations
c1. 2...♕c7;
c2. 2...b6;
c3. 2...g6 3.d4 ♗g7 (3...cxd4 4.♕xd4)
4.c4;
c4. 2...a6 (O'Kelly) 3.c4;

c5. 2...♘f6 (Nimzowitsch) 3.e5;
c6. 2...♘c6 3.d4 cxd4 4.♘xd4:

c61. 4...d5 5.♗b5 dxe4 6.♘xc6 ♕xd1+
7.♔xd1 a6 8.♗a4 ♗d7 9.♘c3
♗xc6 10.♗xc6+ bxc6 11.♘xe4;

c62. 4...e5 5.♘b5 d6 (Kalashnikov) (5...
a6 6.♘d6+ ♗xd6 7.♕xd6) 6.♘1c3;

c63. 4...♕c7 5.♘b5 ♕b8 6.c4;

c64. 4...♕b6 5.♘b3 ♘f6 6.♘c3 e6
7.♕e2 ♗b4 8.♗d2;

c65. 4...g6 5.c4 (Maroczy):

c651. 5...♗h6;
c652. 5...♘f6 6.♘c3 d6 (6...♘xd4)
7.♗e2;
c653. 5...♗g7 6.♗e3 ♘f6 (6...♘h6)
7.♘c3 ♘g4 (7...0-0) 8.♕xg4
♘xd4 9.♕d1 ♘e6 (9...e5 10.♘b5)
10.♖c1.
c66. 4...♘f6 5.♘c3 e5 (Sveshnikov)
6.♘db5 d6 (6...h6) 7.♗g5 a6 8.♘a3
b5 (8...♗e6) 9.♘d5 ♗e7 (9...♕a5+
10.♗d2 ♕d8 11.c4) 10.♗xf6 ♗xf6
11.c4;

c7. 2...e6 3.d4 cxd4 4.♘xd4:

c71. 4...♗c5;
c72. 4...♛b6;
c73. 4...♘f6 5.♘c3:
c731. 5...♛b6 6.e5 ♗c5 7.♗e3 ♘d5
8.♘xd5 exd5 9.♗e2;
c732. 5...♗b4 6.e5 ♘d5 (6...♘e4
7.♛g4) 7.♛g4;
c733. 5...♘c6 6.♘db5 ♗b4 (6...d6
7.♗f4 e5 8.♗g5 – Sveshnikov)
7.a3;
c74. 4...♘c6 (Paulsen);

c75. 4...a6 (Kan) 5.♗d3:

c751. 5...g6;
c752. 5...♘e7;
c753. 5...♘c6 6.♘xc6 dxc6 (6...bxc6
7.0-0) 7.0-0;
c754. 5...♛c7;
c755. 5...b5;
c756. 5...♛b6 6.c3;
c757. 5...♗c5 6.♘b3 ♗e7 (6...♗a7
7.♛e2) 7.♛g4; 5.♘c3 ♛c7 (5...
a6) 6.♗e3 ♘f6 (6...a6 7.♛d2)
7.♛d2;
c8. 2...d6 3.d4 cxd4 4.♘xd4 ♘f6 5.♘c3:

c81. 5...♗d7 (Kupreichik) 6.♗g5;
c82. 5...♘c6 6.♗g5 (Richter-Rauzer) 6...
e6 (6...g6; 6...♛a5; 6...a6; 6...♛b6;
6...♗d7 7.♛d2) 7.♛d2 a6 (7...♗e7
8.0-0-0 0-0 (8...♘xd4) 9.f4)
8.0-0-0 ♗d7 (8...h6 9.♘xc6 bxc6
10.♗f4) 9.f4;
c83. 5...g6 (Dragon) 6.♗e3 ♗g7
(6...♘bd7) 7.f3 ♘c6 (7...a6) 8.♛d2
0-0 (8...♗d7) 9.♗c4 ♗d7 (9...♘a5;
9...a6; 9...♘a5; 9...♘xd4 10.♗xd4;
9...♘d7) 10.h4;
c84. 5...e6 6.g4 (Keres) 6...h6 (6...d5;
6...e5; 6...♗e7; 6...♘c6; 6...a6) 7.h4
♘c6 (7...♗e7 8.♖g1) 8.♖g1 h5
(8...d5 9.♗b5) 9.gxh5;
c85. 5...a6 (Najdorf) 6.♗e3 e5 (6...♘bd7;
6...♘g4; 6...e6 7.f3; 6...♘c6) 7.♘b3.

11. 1...e6 (French) 2.d4 d5 3.♘c3:

a. 3...f5;
b. 3...c5;
c. 3...♗e7;
d. 3...♘e7;
e. 3...♘c6;

f.   3...dxe4 (Rubinstein) 4.♘xe4:

f1. 4...♕d5;

f2. 4...♗d7;

f3. 4...♘f6 5.♘xf6+ ♕xf6 (5...gxf6);

f4. 4...♘d7 5.♘f3 ♘gf6 6.♘xf6+ ♘xf6 7.c3;

g.   3...♘f6 4.e5 (Steinitz) 4...♘fd7 (4...♘g8; 4...♘e4) 5.f4 c5 6.♘f3 ♘c6 (6...a6 7.♗e3) 7.♗e3 cxd4 (7... a6 8.♕d2) 8.♘xd4 ♗c5 (8...♘b6; 8...♕a5; 8...♗b4; 8...♗e7; 8...♘c5; 8... a6; 8...♘xd4 9.♗xd4; 8...♕b6) 9.♕d2;

h.   3...♗b4 4.e5:

h1. 4...f6;

h2. 4...♘e7 5.a3 ♗xc3+ 6.bxc3 c5 – see 4...c5 5.a3;

h3. 4...♕d7 5.a3;

h4. 4...b6 5.a3 ♗xc3+ (5...♗f8) 6.bxc3;

h5. 4...c5 5.a3:

h51. 5...cxd4 6.axb4;

h52. 5...♗a5 6.b4 cxb4 (6...cxd4 7.♕g4) 7.♘b5;

h53. 5...♗xc3+ 6.bxc3 ♘e7 (6...♕c7 7.♕g4; 6...♕a5 7.♗d2) 7.♕g4 ♕c7 (7...0-0 8.♗d3) 8.♕xg7.

II. Open Games
1... e5
1. 2.♘f3:

a.   2...♕e7;

b.   2...f5 (Latvian);

c.   2...d5 (Elephant);

d.   2...d6 (Philidor) 3.d4 ♘f6 (3...f5; 3... exd4; 3...♘d7) 4.♘c3;

e.   2...♘f6 (Petroff) 3.♘xe5 d6 (3...♕e7; 3...♘xe4) 4.♘f3 ♘xe4 5.d4 d5 6.♗d3 ♗e7 (6...♗d6);

f.   2...♘c6 3.♗b5 (Ruy Lopez):

f1. 3...♗b4 (Alapin);

f2. 3...♘a5;

f3. 3...♘ge7 (Cozio) 4.c3;

f4. 3...g6 4.c3;

f5. 3...♘d4 (Bird) 4.♘xd4 exd4 5.0-0;

f6. 3...d6 (Steinitz) 4.♗xc6+ bxc6 5.d4;

f7. 3...♗c5 (Cordel) 4.0-0 ♘f6 (4...♘d4 5.♘xd4 ♗xd4 6.c3 ♗b6 7.d4 c6 8.♗a4);

f8. 3...f5 (Jänisch) 4.♘c3:

f81. 4...♘d4;

f82. 4...fxe4 5.♘xe4 d5 (5...♘f6);

f83. 4...♘d6;

f9. 3...♘f6 (Berlin) 4.0-0 ♘xe4 (4...♗c5 — 3...♗c5 4.0-0 ♘f6; 4...d6) 5.d4 ♘d6 6.♗xc6 dxc6 (6...bxc6 7.dxe5) 7.dxe5 ♘f5 8.♕xd8+ ♚xd8 9.♘c3;

f10. 3...a6 4.♗a4:

f10-1. 4...♘ge7;
f10-2. 4...g6;
f10-3. 4...♗c5;
f10-4. 4...b5 5.♗b3 ♗b7 (5...♗c5; 5...♘a5);
f10-5. 4...f5;
f10-6. 4...d6;
f10-7. 4...♘f6 5.0-0:

f10-71. 5...♗c5 6.c3;
f10-72. 5...b5 (Arkhangelsk) 6.♗b3 ♗b7 7.d3;
f10-73. 5...d6 6.♗xc6+ bxc6 7.d4;
f10-74. 5...♘xe4 (Open) 6.d4 b5 (6...exd4 7.♖e1) 7.♗b3 d5 (7...♗e7 8.♘xe5; 7...exd4 8.♖e1) 8.dxe5 ♗e6 9.c3;
f10-75. 5...♗e7 6.♖e1 b5 (6...d6 7.c3 ♗g4 (7...0-0 8.d4) 8.d3) 7.♗b3 0-0 (7...♗b7 8.d4) 8.c3:
f10-751. 8...d5 (Marshall) 9.exd5 ♘xd5 (9...e4) 10.♘xe5 ♘xe5 11.♖xe5

c6 (11...♘f4; 11...♗b7; 11...♘b6; 11...♘f6) 12.d4 ♗d6 13.♖e1 ♕h4 14.g3 ♕h3 15.♖e2;

f10-752. 8...d6 9.h3:

f10-7521. 9...a5 10.d4 a4 11.♗c2 ♗d7 (11...exd4) 12.♘a3;
f10-7522. 9...♕d7 10.d4 ♖e8 11.♘bd2 ♗f8 12.d5;
f10-7523. 9...♗e6 10.d4 ♗xb3 11.♕xb3 d5 (11...♘d7; 11...♘a5; 11...h6; 11...♖b8; 11...exd4; 11...♕b8; 11...♕d7) 12.exd5 ♘a5 13.♕c2 exd4 14.cxd4 ♘xd5 15.♘c3 ♘xc3 (15...c6 16.♘e4) 16.♕xc3;
f10-7524. 9...♘d7 (Keres) 10.d4 ♗f6 (10...♘b6 11.♘bd2 exd4 (11...♗f6 12.♘f1) 12.cxd4 ♘b4 (12...d5 13.♗c2) 13.♘f1 c5 14.a3 ♘c6 15.♗e3) 11.a4 ♗b7 (11...♘a5 12.♗c2 ♘b6 (12...♗b7 13.d5) 13.b4) 12.♘a3 exd4 (12...♘b6 13.d5) 13.cxd4 ♖e8 (13...♘a5) 14.♗f4;
f10-7525. 9...♗b7 (Zaitsev) 10.d4 ♖e8 (10...♘a5 11.♗c2) 11.♘bd2 ♗f8 12.a4 h6 (12...♕d7; 12...g6; 12...exd4; 12...♘a5) 13.♗c2 exd4 (13...g6; 13...♖b8; 13...♘b8; 13...♕d7) 14.cxd4 ♘b4 15.♗b1 c5 (15...g6; 15...♕d7; 15...bxa4) 16.d5 ♘d7 (16...g6 17.♘f1) 17.♖a3;
f10-7526. 9...h6 (Smyslov) 10.d4 ♖e8 11.♘bd2 ♗f8 12.♘f1 ♗d7 (12...♗b7 13.♘g3 ♘a5 (13...

189

g6; 13...♛d7) 14.♗c2 ♘c4
15.b3) 13.♘g3 ♘a5 (13...g6)
14.♗c2 c5 (14...♘c4 15.b3
♘b6 16.♗b2) 15.b3 ♘c6
16.d5 ♘e7 17.♗e3;

f10-7527. 9...♘b8 (Breyer) 10.d4 ♘bd7
11.♘bd2 ♗b7 12.♗c2 ♖e8
(12...c5) 13.♘f1 ♗f8 14.♘g3
g6 15.a4 c5 (15...c6 16.♗g5;
15...♗g7 16.♗d3) 16.d5 c4
(16...♘b6 17.♛e2) 17.♗g5
h6 18.♗e3 ♘c5 (18...♚h7)
19.♛d2 h5 (19...♚h7)
20.♗g5.

f10-7528. 9...♘a5 (Chigorin) 10.♗c2
c5 11.d4 ♛c7 (11...♘c6 12.d5;
11...♗b7 12.♘bd2; 11...♘d7
12.♘bd2) 12.♘bd2 cxd4
(12...♖e8; 12...♖d8; 12...♗d7
13.♘f1 ♖fe8 14.♘e3; 12...♘c6
13.d5 ♘d8 (13...♘a5 14.b3.
14.a4 ♖b8 (14...♛b7) 15.axb5)
13.cxd4 ♘c6 (13...♗b7 14.d5;
13...♗d7 14.♘f1 ♖ac8 (14...♖fc8
15.♘e3) 15.♘e3) 14.♘b3 a5
15.♗e3 a4 16.♘bd2 ♗d7
(16...♗e6 17.a3; 16...♘b4 17.♗b1
♗d7 18.a3 ♘c6 19.♗d3. 17.♖c1.

Now we give an example of a more detailed repertoire for Black, based on the Slav (against 1.d4) and the Sicilian Sveshnikov (against 1.e4).

Black Repertoire
1.d4 d5

1. 2.c3
2. 2.e3
3. 2.e4
4. 2.♗f4
5. 2.g3
6. **2.♘c3 ♘f6:**
a. 3.♘f3;
b. 3.♗g5 ♘bd7 4.♘f3;
c. 3.♗g5 ♘bd7 4.♕d3 e6;
d. 3.♗g5 ♘bd7 4.f3 c5;
e. 3.♗g5 ♘bd7 4.♘f3 g6.

7. **2.♗g5 f6:**
a. 3.♗h4 ♘h6;
b. 3.♗f4 ♘c6.

8. **2.c4 c6:**

a. 3.♗f4 dxc4;

b. 3.e3 ♘f6 4.♗d3 e5;
c. 3.♘c3 ♘f6 4.♗g5 ♘e4;
d. 3.♘c3 ♘f6 4.cxd5 cxd5 5.♗f4 ♘c6 6.e3 a6;
e. 3.♘c3 ♘f6 4.e3 a6:
e1. 5.b3 ♗f5;
e2. 5.♗d3 ♗g4;
e3. 5.♕c2 g6.

9. **2.c4 c6 3.♘f3 ♘f6:**
a. 4.g3 dxc4;
b. 4.♘bd2 ♗f5;
c. 4.♕c2 (4.♕b3) dxc4 5.♕xc4 ♗f5;
d. 4.e3 a6:
d1. 5.♘bd2 ♗f5
d2. 5.♗d3 ♗g4
d3. 5.a4 ♗g4
d4. 5.♕c2 ♗g4.

10. **2.c4 c6 3.♘f3 ♘f6 4.♘c3 a6:**

a. 5.♗f4 dxc4;
b. 5.♕c2 dxc4;
c. 5.h3 e6;
d. 5.b3 ♗g4;
e. 5.cxd5 cxd5:
e1. 6.♗g5 ♘e4
e2. 6.♗f4 ♘c6:
e21. 7.e3 ♗g4;
e22. 7.♖c1 ♗f5...;
f. 5.♕b3 e6;
g. 5.g3 dxc4;
h. 5.♗g5 ♘e4:
h1. 6.h4;
h2. 6.♗h4;
h3. 6.♗f4.
i. 5.♘e5 ♘bd7 6.♗f4 dxc4...

191

j.   5.a4 e6:
j1. 6.g3;
j2. 6.♗g5...
k.   5.c5 ♘bd7 6.♗f4 ♘h5;
l.   5.e3 b5:
l1. 6.cxd5;
l2. 6.c5 g6;
l3. 6.b3 ♗g4:
l31. 7.h3 ♗xf3 8.♕xf3:
l311.8...e5;
l312.8...♘bd7;
l32. 7.♗e2 ♘bd7...

Black repertoire
1.e4 c5

1. 2.a3
2. 2.b4 d5:
a.   3.e5 ♘c6;
b.   3.exd5 cxb4 4.d4 ♘f6.

3. 2.b3 b6:
a.   3.c4;
b.   3.♗b2 ♗b7.

4. 2.c4 ♘c6
5. 2.♗c4 e6
6. 2.d3 ♘c6
7. 2.g3 d5:
a.   3.d3;
b.   3.♘c3 d4;
c.   3.exd5 ♕xd5:
c1. 4.♕f3 ♕d8;
c2. 4.♘f3 ♘c6:
c21. 5.♗g2 ♕e6+;
c22. 5.♘c3 ♕e6+.

8. 2.f4 ♘f6:
a.   3.d3;
b.   3.e5 ♘d5;
c.   3.♘c3 d5 4.e5 d4.

9. 2.d4 cxd4:
a.   3.♕xd4;
b.   3.c3 dxc3:
b1.4.♘f3 cxb2 5.♗xb2 e6;
b2.4.♘xc3 ♘c6.

10.2.c3 d5

a.   3.d3;
b.   3.exd5 ♕xd5 4.d4 ♘f6:
b1. 5.♗e3;
b2. 5.♘f3 e6:
b21. 6.♘bd2;
b22. 6.♘a3;
b23. 6.♗e3;
b24. 6.♗d3;
b25. 6.♗e2.

11.2.♘c3 ♘c6:

a.   3.♗b5;
b.   3.f4 g6 4.♘f3 ♗g7:

b1. 5.♗e2;
b2. 5.♗b5 ♘d4;
b3. 5.♗c4 e6;
c. 3.g3 g6 4.♗g2 ♗g7 5.d3 d6.
c1. 6.f4 e6 7.♘f3 ♘ge7.
c2. 6.♗e3.

12.2.♘f3 ♘c6:

a. 3.♗e2;
b. 3.♗c4;
c. 3.b4;
d. 3.b3;
e. 3.c4;
f. 3.g3;
g. 3.d3;
h. 3.c3.

i. 3.♘c3:
i1. 3...g6 – Dragon;
i2. 3...e5.

j. 3.♗b5 g6:

j1. 4.c3;
j2. 4.0-0 ♗g7:
j21. 5.♖e1;

j22. 4.0-0 ♗g7 5.c3 ♘f6:
j22-1. 6.d4;
j22-2. 6.♕e2;
j22-3. 6.e5;
j22-4. 6.♖e1;
j23. 4.♗xc6 dxc6.

k. 3.d4 cxd4 4.♘xd4 ♘f6 5.♘c3 e5:

k1. 6.♘xc6;
k2. 6.♘de2;
k3. 6.♘b3;
k4. 6.♘f5.

k5. 6.♘db5 d6:

k51. 7.♗e3 a6 8.♘a3 ♖b8;
k52. 7.a4;

k53. 7.♘d5 ♘xd5 8.exd5 ♘e7:
k53-1. 9.c3;
k53-2. 9.c4.

k54. 7.♗g5 a6 8.♘a3 b5:
k54-1. 9.♘ab1;

k54-2. .9.♘d5 ♗e7:

k54-21. 10.♘xe7 ♘xe7:
k54-211. 11.♕f3 ♗g4;
k54-212. 11.♗d3 ♗b7;
k54-213. 11.♗xf6 gxf6:
k54-2131. 12.♗d3;
k54-2132. 12.♕d2;
k54-2133. 12.c4;
k54-2134. 12.♕f3;
k54-22. 10.♗xf6 ♗xf6:
k54-221. 11.c4;
k54-222. 11.g3;
k54-223. 11.c3 0-0:
k54-2231. 12.♘c2 ♗g5 13.a4 bxa4
          14.♖xa4 a5:
k54-2231a. 15.b4;
k54-2231b. 15.♗b5;
k54-2231c. 15.♗c4.

k54-3. 9.♗xf6 gxf6 10.♘d5 f5:

k54-31. 11.♘e3;
k54-32. 11.♕d3 fxe4 12.♕xe4 ♗g7;
k54-33. 11.g3;
k54-34. 11.♘xb5 axb5 12.♗xb5 ♘d7;
k54-35. 11.♗xb5 axb5 12.♘xb5 ♖a4;
k54-36. 11.c3 ♗g7;

k54-37. 11.exf5 ♗xf5:
k54-371. 12.♕f3 ♘d4 13.♘c7+ ♕xc7
          14.♕xa8+ ♔e7;
k54-372. 12.♗d3 e4;
k54-373. 12.c3 ♗g7;
k54-3731. 13.♕f3;
k54-3732. 13.♘c2 0-0 14.♘ce3 ♗g6.

k54-38. 11.♗d3 ♗e6:

k54-381. 12.c4 ♕a5+:
k54-3811. 13.♕d2;
k54-3812. 13.♔f1 fxe4;
k54-382. 12.c3 ♗g7:
k54-3821. 13.0-0;
k54-3822. 13.♕f3;
k54-3823. 13.♘c2;
k54-3824. 13.♘xb5;
k54-3825. 13.♕h5 ♖g8;
k54-3826. 13.♕xh7;
k54-3827. 13.♖g1;
k54-3828. 13.0-0;
k54-3829. 13.c4;
k54-38210. 13.f4;
k54-38211. 13.0-0-0;
k54-38212. 13.c3;
k54-38213. 13.g3.

k54-383. 12.0-0 ♗xd5 13.exd5 ♘e7:
k54-3831. 14.♘xb5;
k54-3832. 14.c4;
k54-3833. 14.c3.

Chapter 10
Black is Brutal IV (1991 – 1999)

I was awarded the title of best Hungarian male chess player in 1991, among other things finishing second in the 1991 Super Championship behind Judit Polgar. In addition, I collected the Hungarian national title in 1992 and 1993 too. I was a member of the Hungarian A-team at the European Team Championship in Debrecen, 1992, and won a brilliancy prize for my game against Giorgadze. This game is one of the classics that can be found in this book – of the eight beauty prizes in my career, this was the only one that won me a real prize: 1000 US dollars.

From the early 1990s until 1999, Peter Leko was my pupil (in several 'waves', the last one being between 1996 and 1999). He was an ideal student: a genius who loved chess, and was industrious; a very good fighter and even a lovable boy. His age was very close to that of my own daughters.

I am inactive since 2000, but only as far as tournament chess is concerned. I'm still trying to exercise creative thinking, as opposite to a shockingly large and growing part of the human race.

Rogelio Barcenilla   2435
Andras Adorjan   2525
Bacolod 1991 (5)

1.e4 c5 2.♘f3 e6 3.d4 cxd4 4.♘xd4 ♘f6 5.♘c3 d6 6.g4
Bayonett auf! The Keres Attack.
6...h6 7.♖g1 ♘c6 8.h4 h5 9.gxh5
On 9.g5 ♘g4 10.♗e2 d5! turns the tables – Black got dangerous counterplay for the pawn and won in Sznapik-AA and Schmittdiel-AA, Dortmund 1984.
9...♘xh5 10.♗g5 ♘f6 11.♗e2 ♗e7 12.h5

12...e5
Black can also go for counterplay on the queenside by 12...a6!?, e.g. 13.♗e3 ♖h7

(13...♔f8!? 14.h6 g6) 14.f4 ♗d7 15.♕d2 b5 16.a3 b4 17.axb4 ♘xb4.
13.♘b3
13.♗xf6 gxf6 14.♘xc6 bxc6 15.♗c4 ♗f8 (less good is 15...f5 16.♕f3 and White attacks) 16.♕e2 ♗h6 leaves Black slightly better – his king is safer.
13...♗e6 14.♗e3
14.♗h4 invites the famous simplifying trick 14...♘xe4 15.♗xe7 (15.♘xe4 ♗xh4 16.♘xd6+ ♔f8∓) 15...♘xc3 16.♗xd8 ♘xd1 17.♖xd1 ♖xd8 18.♖xg7 a5∓.
14...♔f8 15.♕d2 a5
15...♘xh5 looks dangerous, but it works: 16.♖h1 g6 17.♘d5 ♗h4 18.0-0-0 ♔g7=.
16.♖d1
He could have stopped the march of the a-pawn with 16.a4 ♘b4 17.h6 g6 18.0-0-0 ♖c8 19.♗f3 b5 20.axb5 a4 21.♘a1 ♕a5 22.♔b1 a3 23.♘b3 ♕a8!? (23...♗xb3 24.cxb3 a2+ 25.♔a1±) 24.♗g5 ♕a7 and the situation is unclear. If 16.h6 g6.
16...a4 17.♘c1 a3∓ 18.b3 ♖c8 19.f4?
Groundless.
19.h6 g6 20.♗f3 ♘d4!; 19.♖g2 ♕a5 20.♘d3 ♘d4−+.
19...exf4 20.♗xf4 ♘xh5

195

21.♗xd6

21.♖h1 runs into 21...♗h4+ 22.♔f1 ♘xf4 23.♕xf4 ♘e5−+.

21...♘b4!?

21...♗xd6 22.♕xd6+ ♕xd6 23.♖xd6 ♘f6 was a more prosaic way.

22.♖h1

22.♗xe7+ ♕xe7 23.♖h1 ♕c7 24.♕d6+ ♕xd6 25.♖xd6 ♖xc3 26.♖d8+ ♔e7 27.♖xh8 ♖xc2 28.♔f2 ♘f4 29.♔e3 g5 also leaves Black clearly better.

22...♕xd6 23.♕xd6

23.♗xh5 ♕g3+−+; 23.♘d3 ♕g3+ 24.♔f1 ♗h3+−+.

23...♘xc2+!

Nice!

24.♔f2

24.♔d2 ♖xd6 25.♔xc2 ♗e5 26.♖d3 g6−+.

24...♗xd6 25.♖xd6 ♔e7 26.♖b6 ♖xc3 27.♖xb7+ ♔f6 28.♖xh5 ♖xh5 29.♗xh5 ♘d4−+

Or 29...♘a1−+.

30.♘e2 ♖c2 31.♔e3 ♘xe2 32.♗xe2 ♖xa2 33.♖b6 ♖a1 34.♖a6 g5 35.♔d4 a2 36.♔c3 ♔e5 37.♗d3

♖b1 38.♖xa2 ♖xb3+ 39.♔c2 ♖xd3 40.♖a5+ ♔xe4 41.♖xg5 ♖d5   0-1

Excellent

| Yrjö Rantanen | ⬤ | 2415 |
| Andras Adorjan | 10 | 2525 |

Jyväskylä 1991 (3)

1.e4 c5 2.♘f3 e6 3.d4 cxd4 4.♘xd4 ♘f6 5.♘c3 d6 6.♗e2 ♗e7 7.0-0 0-0 8.♗e3

Avoiding 8.f4 ♕b6!?, which brought me victory in a few games, see Yearbook No. 112. The idea is to continue by 9.♔h1 ♘c6 10.♘b3 ♕c7!, losing a winning tempo compared to the 'main line' ...♗d7/g4 and ...♗c8!.

8...a6 9.f4 ♕c7 10.♔h1

10.a4 is the sober move.

10...b5 11.♗f3?! ♗b7

12.e5?

Consistent but overoptimistic.

12...dxe5 13.fxe5 ♘fd7 14.♗f4

Now this is a loss of tempo. But White's position is already inferior: 14.♗xb7 ♕xb7 15.♕h5 ♘c6 16.♘xc6 (16.♘f3 g6) 16...♕xc6 and Black will have all the play after ...f7-f6!.

14...b4

14...♘c6!?.

15.♘b1?

This undevelopment of the knight is more than White's position can bear. After 15.♘e4 ♘xe5 16.♕e2 ♘bd7 Black is just a clear pawn up, but 15.♗xb7 ♕xb7 16.♘a4 (16.♘ce2∓) 16...♖c8 17.♕h5 ♘c6 gave better chances of salvation.

15...♞c6 16.♞xc6 ♝xc6 17.♞d2 ♜ad8 18.♝xc6

On 18.♜c1, 18...♝xf3 19.♞xf3 ♛a5 lays bare another weakness.

18...♛xc6 19.♜f3 f6 20.exf6 ♝xf6 21.♜b1

21...♞b6!

Slightly better than 21...e5!? 22.♝e3 e4; Black redeploys his pieces first.

22.♛e1 e5! 23.♝g3 ♛xc2 24.♞e4 ♞d5 25.♜f2 ♛c6

Or first 25...♛c4 26.b3 and then 26...♛c6.

26.♛e2 ♞f4! 27.♝xf4

The pawn grab 27.♞xf6+ ♜xf6 28.♛xe5 fails to 28...♞xg2! with a decisive attack: 29.♜xf6 (29.♜xg2 ♜d2) 29...gxf6 30.♛c7 ♛d5−+.

27...exf4 28.♜xf4

28.♞xf6+ ♜xf6 doesn't help much – the possibility of the ...f4-f3 push makes things worse for White.

28...♝xb2!! 29.♜xf8+ ♜xf8 30.♛d3 ♝c3 31.♞g5

No time for 31.♜c1 ♜e8 32.♞xc3 due to the back-rank problems – 32...bxc3.

31...♛g6 32.♛d5+

After the exchange of queens White's a-pawn would also soon fall as well.

32...♚h8 33.♜d1 h6 34.♞e6 ♜e8 35.♞c5 a5 36.♜f1 ♛f6! 37.♜d1 ♛e5

Or 37...♛f2 38.♞d3 ♛e2 39.♜g1 ♜f8 and White has no moves left.

38.h3 ♛g3

White resigned. An eventful game, not without errors. He could defend against the threat of 39...♝e5 by 40.♞e4, but after 40...♛f4 he is finished. The bishop on c3 has an uncanny control over White's pieces.

38...♛xd5 39.♜xd5 ♜e1+ 40.♚h2 ♝e5+ 41.g3 ♜e2+ 42.♚g1 ♝xg3 would have won a little further on in the endgame.

| Peter Lukacs | 2495 |
| Andras Adorjan | 2535 |

Hungary tt 1991

1.d4 ♞f6 2.c4 g6 3.♞c3 d5 4.cxd5 ♞xd5 5.e4 ♞xc3 6.bxc3 ♝g7 7.♝c4 c5 8.♞e2

The old main line, but still popular.

8...♞c6 9.♝e3 0-0 10.0-0 ♛c7 11.♜c1 ♜d8 12.♝f4 ♛d7

12...♝e5!??! is a very strange and hardly good option, though it was played twice by Grünfeld expert Peter Svidler.

13.d5

13...♞e5

[margin notes, handwritten:] 36...♞f6 sacrifice for mate Re1#

[margin notes, handwritten, vertical left:] 28... ♝xb2 is a beautiful move, leaves f4 rook hanging, also after all exchanges Kf1 mate!

[margin notes, handwritten, vertical right:] Good opening position by both!

[handwritten:] QGD ● 7

A 'novelty' I found over the board. The fact is that this had been played already, but I did not know about it. Later it was employed too. See my games in Yearbook No. 116.

14.♗xe5 ♗xe5 15.f4 ♗g7 16.♕b3 ♖b8 17.a4 ♕c7 18.♖b1 ♔h8 19.♘g3 ♗d7

19...a6!? creates a hole White can jump in: 20.e5 ♗d7 21.♕b6 ♕xb6 22.♖xb6 ♗xa4?! (22...g5 23.♘e4 gxf4 24.♖xf4 ♗e8 25.♘g5 ♗xe5 26.♖xf7; 22...f6) 23.♘e4 ♗c2 (23...f6 24.d6 fxe5 25.♘g5 ♗e8 26.fxe5 ♗xe5) 24.♘xc5=.

20.e5!?

After 20.♗b5!? Black can wriggle out with a few crisp moves: 20...♗xb5 (20...c4!?) 21.axb5 c4 22.♕b4 ♕d6! 23.♕xc4 ♖bc8 24.♕a2 ♕b6+ 25.♔h1 ♖xc3 26.e5!? ♖d3 27.d6 (27.♖fd1 ♕xb5!) 27...exd6 28.♘e4 d5 29.♘d6 ♔g8 30.♖fd1 ♕d4 31.♖xd3 ♕xd3 32.♘xb7 ♖b8 33.♘d6 ♗h6 34.g3 ♗f8∓ (Leko).

20...a6 21.♘e4?

In this case, 21.♕b6 ♕xb6 22.♖xb6 f6! would give Black sufficient counterplay. But now White gets lost in a tactical scramble.

21...b5 22.axb5 axb5 23.d6 exd6

24.♗xf7

24.exd6 ♕a7 25.♖a1 ♕b6−+; 24.♘xd6 bxc4 25.♘xf7+ ♔g8 26.♕xc4 ♗e6!−+.

24...c4−+ 25.♕b4 ♗f5 26.♘xd6 ♗xb1 27.♖xb1 ♗f8 28.♗d5

28...♖xd6!   **0-1**

After 29.exd6 ♗xd6 the white queen is caught!

Angelo Young   2245
Andras Adorjan   2525
Manila 1991

1.d4 ♘f6 2.♘f3 g6 3.c4 ♗g7 4.♘c3 d5 5.cxd5 ♘xd5 6.g3 ♘b6 7.♗g2 ♘c6 8.0-0!?

8...0-0

Black could take the pawn − White gets compensation but no advantage: 8...♘xd4 9.♘xd4 ♕xd4 and now:

A) 10.♘b5 ♕c4 11.♕b3 0-0 12.♕xc4 ♘xc4 13.♘xc7 ♖b8 14.♘d5 ♗g4 15.h3 ♗e6 16.♘xe7+ ♔h8 17.♘d5 (17.♖b1 ♖bd8 18.e4 ♘d2 19.♗xd2 ♖xd2 20.♖fd1 ♖c2=) 17...♘xb2 18.♖b1 ♘a4 19.♗f4 ♖bd8 20.e4 b6 and White has to centralize to equalize;

B) 10.♕xd4 ♗xd4 11.♘b5 ♗e5 12.♗f4 (12.f4 a6) 12...♗xf4 13.gxf4 0-0 (13...♔d8 14.♖fd1+ ♘d7 15.♖ac1 c6 16.♘d4 with a dangerous attack for the

(handwritten marginalia, left side): Too bad for the White Queen! It will fall by Black Bishop PIN, 28 Rxd6!

(handwritten, right side): QGD

pawn, even without queens) 14.♘xc7 ♖b8 15.♖fd1 ♗g4 16.♔f1 ♖fd8 17.♘b5 and the game is more or less balanced.

9.a4?!

Tricky but wrong. Black has good counterplay after either 9.d5 ♘a5 10.♗f4 c6 or 9.e3 e5 10.d5 ♘e7 (10...e4!?).

9...a5

This is a normal handling of such bluffs. 9...♘xd4? would now play into White's hands: 10.♘xd4 ♕xd4 11.♕xd4 ♗xd4 12.a5 (12.♘b5 ♗e5 13.f4 a6 14.fxe5 axb5 15.♗h6 bxa4 16.♗xf8 ♔xf8 with compensation) 12...♗xc3 13.axb6 ♗d4 14.bxc7 ♖b6 15.♗f4±.

10.♘b5

10.d5 ♘b4 11.e4 c6 12.♘h4 ♗d7 13.♕e2 (13.♖e1 ♖c8∓) 13...cxd5 14.exd5 ♖c8∓.

10...♘b4 11.♗f4 ♘6d5 12.♗d2 c6 13.♘c3 ♗g4 14.♘xd5 ♘xd5 15.♗c3?!

The lesser evil was 15.♘e5!? ♗e6 16.f4 ♘f6 17.e3 ♗d5∓.

15...♕b6 16.e3 ♖fd8 17.♕c1 ♕a7

17...c5!? was interesting, but only equal after 18.dxc5 ♘xc3 19.cxb6 ♘e2+ 20.♔h1 ♘xc1 21.♖axc1 ♖a6 22.h3 ♗xf3 23.♗xf3 ♖xb6 24.♖c5=.

18.h3

18.♘e5 ♗xe5 19.dxe5 ♘xc3 20.♕xc3 ♕b6 gives Black the edge due to his control of the d-file and the half-open b-file.

18...♗f5

18...♗xf3 19.♗xf3 ♖ac8 was just OK.

19.♘d2

19...e5!

Oh yes!

20.♘b3

On 20.♗xd5, 20...♖xd5! is even stronger than the capture with the pawn thanks to a nice point: 21.e4 exd4! 22.exd5 ♗xh3 23.♖e1 dxc3 and Black gets beautiful play with the two bishops. Quite bad was 20.dxe5 ♘xc3 21.♕xc3 ♖d3 and White's position is cracking.

20...♘xc3 21.bxc3 ♖ac8 22.♖d1 b6 23.♕b2 h5? 24.♔h2?

Setting a self-trap. 24.dxe5 ♗xe5 25.♘d4 ♗d7 was still not so clear.

24...♕c7 25.♖d2?

25.dxe5 ♗xe5 26.♘d4 ♗d7 was already advantageous for Black now due to his counterplay against g3.

White wants to crash through in the centre, but...

25...h4!

... is just in time.

26.♖ad1 ♖d7 27.e4 hxg3+ 28.fxg3 ♗e6 29.d5 cxd5 30.exd5 ♗f5 31.d6

31.g4 fails tactically now to 31...e4+ 32.♔g1 ♗xc3 33.♕a2 ♗xd2 34.♕xd2 (34.♖xd2 e3; 34.♘xd2 ♕c5+ 35.♔h1 ♕xd5!) 34...♗e6−+ and Black wins back the piece due to the pin on the d-file) 34...♗e6−+ with another pin.

31...♕d8 32.♗d5

32...♗h6

32...♕g5! was really Brutal.

33.g4?

Better was 33.♖f2. Now White's kingside is an open house.

33...♗xd2 34.♕xd2 ♗e6

34...♗xg4 was even prettier: 35.hxg4 ♕h4+ 36.♔g2 ♕xg4+ 37.♔f2 ♕xa4 38.♕g5 ♕f4+ 39.♕xf4 exf4 and Black wins as the d-pawn will also perish.

35.♗xe6 fxe6 36.♕h6 ♕f6–+ 37.♔g1 ♖f8

37...♖xc3 38.♖f1 ♕g7 also sufficed. The knight on b3 is having a bad day.

38.♘d2 ♖xd6 39.♖f1 ♕g7 40.♖xf8+ ♔xf8 41.♕e3 ♕f6 42.♕h6+ ♔g8 43.♔g2 ♖d3 44.h4 e4 45.h5 ♕g7 46.♕xg7+ ♔xg7 47.♘xe4 ♖e3 48.♘d6 gxh5 49.gxh5 ♖xc3 50.♔f2 ♔h6 51.♔e2 ♔xh5 52.♔d2 ♖c6 53.♘f7 ♖c4 54.♘d6 ♖xa4   0-1

Jacek Gdanski  2430
Andras Adorjan 2530

Polanica Zdroj 1991 (5)

1.e4 c5 2.♘f3 e6 3.d4 cxd4 4.♘xd4 ♘f6 5.♘c3 d6 6.♗c4 ♗e7 7.♗b3 ♘a6!

'A knight on the rim is dim'... not in this or, for that matter, similar cases! On a6 this one has more options than on d7.

8.♕f3 ♘c5 9.♗g5 a6

Also strong was 9...♕a5 10.♗xf6 (10.♗d2 ♘cxe4! 11.♘xe4 ♕e5 12.♗a4+ ♔f8 13.0-0-0 ♕xe4 is a healthy pawn) 10...♗xf6 with pressure on the centre.

10.0-0-0 ♗d7 11.h4 ♖c8 12.♔b1 b5 13.a3 ♕b6 14.♖he1 0-0!

But of course now!

15.♕g3 ♔h8

There was no rush, but 15...a5! was more attractive:

A) 16.♘f5 exf5 17.exf5 ♕d8 and now after 18.♖xe7 ♕xe7 19.♘d5 Black has the strong queen sacrifice 19...♘xd5! 20.♗xe7 ♘xe7 21.f6 (21.♕xd6 ♗xf5) 21...♘f5 and White has no compensation;

B) 16.♗h6 ♘h5 17.♕g4 b4 18.axb4 axb4 and Black comes first on the queenside: 19.♘ce2 ♕a5 20.♘c1 ♖a8 21.♗a2 b3 22.cxb3 ♘d3 23.♗d2 ♕a6–+.

16.f4 b4 17.axb4 ♕xb4 18.e5 dxe5 19.fxe5 ♘g8 20.♘f3?

Still better was 20.♘e4!? ♗a4 with unclear complications.

20...♕b7

20...♘xb3! 21.cxb3 ♖xc3! was a nicer finish: 22.♖xd7 ♖xb3 23.♖e2 ♖b8 24.♕f2 ♖a3! with annihilation along the a-file: 25.♕d4 ♕a5 26.♗xe7 ♘xe7 27.♖xe7 ♖a4–+.

21.♗xe7

With 21.♘d4 White could have put up a defence, for example 21...a5 22.♕f3.

21...♘xe7 22.♘g5?! ♗c6 23.♕f2

23.♗c4 h6 24.♘f3 ♖b8 25.b3 ♕b4 26.♘d2 ♘f5 and White cannot keep his act together.

23...♘xb3   24.cxb3   ♕xb3–+ 25.♘xf7+ ♔g8 26.♖f1 ♘d5 27.♖d3 ♘xc3+ 28.♖xc3

Vicious takes by both.

In the left margin, handwritten: *Excellent Black movement!* and *Error Game*

28...♗e4+

Or 28...♕b4–+.

29.♔a1 ♕a4+ 30.♖a3 ♕d7 31.♕e1 ♗xg2 32.♖g1 ♖xf7 33.♖xg2 ♖cf8 34.♖g1 ♕b5 35.♕c3 ♕d5 36.♖c1 ♖f3 37.♕c5 ♖f1 38.♕c3 ♕h1 39.♖xf1 ♖xf1+ 40.♔a2 ♖a1+ 41.♔b3 ♕d5+ **0-1**

The endgame is simply lost after 42.♕c4 (42.♔c2 ♕d1#; 42.♔b4 ♕b5#) 42...♖xa3+ 43.bxa3 h5–+.

Pavel David	2400
Andras Adorjan	2530

In the margin, handwritten: *Opening?*

Zalaegerszeg 1991 (3)

1.c4 g6 2.e4 e5 3.♘f3 ♗g7 4.d4 exd4 5.♘xd4 ♘f6!

The key move of the Adorjan System – see Yearbook 93, as well as the BLACK IS OK Zero Copy, page 43.

On 5...♘e7 6.♘c3 ♘bc6 7.♗e3 0-0 8.♗e2 f5, White keeps an edge with 9.♕d2. The mistake 9.exf5? ♗xd4! 10.♗xd4 ♘xf5 is notorious – the strong grandmaster Valery Chekhov fell for it in 1992 against Yuri Meshkov... and drew.

6.♘c3

6.e5 ♘e4 7.♕e2 d5 is the first point: 8.f4 (on 8.exd6 0-0! is the dynamic solution: 9.dxc7 ♕xd4 10.cxb8♕ ♖xb8 11.♕e3 ♖e8–+; 8.cxd5 ♕xd5) 8...0-0.

6...0-0 7.♗e2 ♖e8 8.f3 c6 9.♗g5 h6 10.♗h4

10...d5

That's the idea!

11.cxd5

11.exd5 cxd5 and now:

A) 12.0-0!? ♘c6 13.♗f2=;

B) 12.♗xf6 ♕xf6 (12...♗xf6 13.♘xd5 ♘c6 14.♘xc6 bxc6 15.♘xf6+ ♕xf6 16.0-0 ♕xb2∓) and now:

B1) It's no good to go for the win of the exchange with 13.♘xd5 ♕xd4 14.♕xd4 ♗xd4 15.♘c7 ♗d7 (even 15...♖e7!? 16.♘xa8 ♘c6 looks good) 16.♘xa8 ♖c8 17.0-0-0 ♘c6 18.♖d3 ♗e6 19.♖b3 b6 and White has to give the knight – then materially he is still alright, but Black's pieces rule the board;

B2) 13.♘db5 ♘a6 14.0-0 (14.cxd5 ♕b6! gives Black a dangerous attack) 14...dxc4 15.♗xc4 ♗e6∓.

11...cxd5 12.exd5 g5 13.♗f2 ♘xd5 14.♘db5 ♗e6 15.0-0 ♘c6 16.♘xd5 ♗xd5 17.♘c3 ♗e6 18.♗b5

18.♖e1 ♕a5 19.♗f1 ♖ad8 20.♕c2; 18.♗d3 ♗e5 19.♖e1 ♗d4; in both cases Black's predominance in the centre gives him an edge.

18...♖c8 19.♘e4?!

The queenless middlegame after 19.♕xd8 ♖exd8 20.♖fd1 ♘d4 21.♗f1 (21.♗xd4

♗xd4+–+) 21...a6 wasn't very attractive, but the game continuation is worse.

19...a6 20.♗d3 ♘b4 21.♘d6 ♘xd3

21...♗e5! was pretty and fast: 22.♘xc8 ♘xd3 (a nice turnaround!) 23.♘b6 ♗xb2 24.♘a4 ♗xa1 25.♕xa1 ♘xf2 26.♖xf2 ♕a5 27.♘c3 ♕e5 with crushing centralization.

22.♕xd3 ♗c4

23.♕d1 ♗xf1

The liquidation 23...♗e2 24.♖e1 ♗xd1 25.♖xe8+ ♕xe8 26.♘xe8 ♖xe8 27.♖xd1 ♗xb2 is similar.

24.♘xe8 ♕xd1

Also winning was 24...♕xe8 25.♕xf1 ♖c2 26.♖e1 ♕d7.

25.♖xd1 ♗e2 26.♘d6 ♗xd1

More accurate was 26...♖c2 27.♖b1 b5 28.b4 ♖xa2 and Black is winning.
27.♘xc8 ♗xb2 28.♗c5 b5 29.♘d6 ♗c2 30.♔f2 ♗e5 31.g3 f5 32.h3 ♔g7 33.g4 f4 34.♘b7 ♔f6 35.♔e2 h5 35...♗b1 36.a3 ♗a2 with the unpleasant threat of 37...♗c4+ and either 38...♗f1 or 38...♗d5 (or 37.♘d6 ♔e6).

36.♗b6 ♗b1 37.♘c5 *B♗ error*

37...♗xa2?

In mutual time-trouble Black makes things hard for himself. Stronger was 37...hxg4 38.hxg4 (38.♘d7+ ♔e6 39.♘xe5 gxh3 40.♘g4 ♗xa2 41.♗d8 ♗c4+–+) 38...♗d6–+.

38.♘xa6?

38.♘d7+ ♔e6 39.♘xe5 would have forced an opposite-coloured bishops ending which probably cannot be won: 39...♔xe5 40.♗d8 (40.gxh5 ♔f5) 40...hxg4 41.hxg4 ♗d5 42.♗xg5 b4 43.♗h6 a5 44.♗g7+ ♔e6 45.♗f8 ♗c6 46.♗h6 ♔e5 47.♗g7+ ♔d5 48.♔d3 (48.♗h6 a4 49.♗xf4 a3 50.♗c1 ♔c4 51.g5 ♔c3) 48...♗b5+ 49.♔c2 a4 50.♗f8 ♔c4 ♗d6 and White holds the draw.

38...hxg4 39.hxg4 ♗c4+ 40.♔d2 ♗b2 41.♘c5 ♔g6 42.♗d8 ♗d5

And Black won on move 56.

A clock simul against the Turkish juniors playing all 11 games with black takes courage.

Guner Bulent
Andras Adorjan
Istanbul clock sim 1991

1.d4 ♘f6 2.♘f3 e6 3.c4 b6 4.♘c3 ♗b7 5.♗g5 h6 6.♗h4 g5 7.♗g3 ♘h5 8.e3 ♘xg3 9.hxg3 ♗g7 10.♗d3 ♘c6 11.g4 ♕e7 12.a3 0-0-0 13.♕a4

13...h5

Typical. Alternatives were: 13...f5 14.gxf5 exf5 15.0-0-0 f4; or 13...♔b8 14.0-0-0 ♖hf8.

14.gxh5 g4 15.♘d2

On 15.♘g1, 15...g3 gives good chances (or also 15...f5 16.♘ge2 ♕g5).

15...f5 16.0-0-0 ♔b8

17.c5?

Too ambitious. After the better 17.♘e2 ♕g5 18.♘g3 (18.c5), 18...♘xd4! was interesting (18...♘e7): 19.exd4 ♗xd4.

17...f4?

Simply 17...bxc5 18.♗a6 (perhaps 18.♘b3!?) 18...♗xa6 19.♕xa6 cxd4 was winning. There is no attack – at least not for White. But now there is something that looks like it.

18.♗a6 fxe3

18...g3 19.♗xb7 ♔xb7 20.fxg3 fxe3 21.♘de4 d5 22.cxd6 ♖xd6 23.♘xd6+ ♕xd6 24.♘e2 ♗h6 does not give enough compensation.

19.fxe3   ♕g5   20.♖de1   ♖xh5 21.♖xh5 ♕xh5

22.♘c4?

Admirable aggression. 22.♗xb7 ♔xb7 23.♘de4 d5 24.cxd6 cxd6 25.♕b5 would have been equal.

22...♕h2∓ 23.♘b5? ♕xg2 24.♔b1 g3 25.♖c1

White has brought up all his forces against the black king, but it doesn't work. Or shouldn't.

25...♕e4+ 26.♔a2 ♕d3??

26...♗f8 should still be winning.

27.♖c3?   *CLEANS HOUSE!*

The bad placement of the black queen gave White a nice winning motif here: 27.♘xc7 ♔xc7 28.cxb6+ axb6 29.♗xb7 ♔xb7 30.♕b5+−.   *Attack starts*

27...♕f1   28.cxb6   axb6   29.♗xb7 ♔xb7

30.♘cd6+??

Of course he should have used the other knight: 30.♘bd6+ cxd6 31.♕b5. Then Black would have had to give the queen by 31...♕xc4+ 32.♕xc4, but it doesn't look good. *knight sacrifice*

Rook sacrifice 36. Rxc1+ After sacrificing pieces white had nothing left to play with!

Nice opening for Black!

30...cxd6 31.♘xd6+ ♔c7 32.♘b5+ ♔b7 33.♘d6+ ♔b8 34.♖b3

34...g2 35.♖xb6+ ♔c7 36.♖xc6+ dxc6 37.♕a7+ ♔xd6 38.♕c5+ ♔d7   0-1

Zoltan Varga
Andras Adorjan
Budapest rapid 1992
1.d4 ♘f6 2.c4 g6 3.d5 b5!?

The so-called Danube Gambit. The move suddenly entered my head in 1968, when I was analysing the game Meleghegyi-P.Szilagyi for *Magyar Sakkelet*, and mentioned it in the article. Zoltan Ribli, with whom I have worked together for 10 years, played it first, in 1974. The press editors of IBM 1978, where I played the move against Roman Dzindzichashvili, dubbed it the Danube Gambit for its similarity to the Volga Gambit (developed by another fellow-countryman, Pal Benko!).

The difference is that after 4.cxb5 a6 5.bxa6 Black plays 5...c6! with active piece play.

4.♘a3? bxc4 5.♘xc4 ♗b7 6.♘e3
The picturesque 6.e4 ♘xe4 7.♘a5 ♗c8 (7...♗a6) 8.♕d4 ♘f6 favours Black.

6...c6 7.d6
After 7.dxc6 ♘xc6 Black emerges from the opening with several tempi up. But now where is White's compensation for the d6-pawn?

7...exd6 8.♘f3 d5 9.a3 ♗g7 10.g3 0-0 11.♗g2 ♘a6 12.0-0 ♘c5 13.♕c2 ♘ce4 14.♖d1
14.b4 a5 15.♗b2 ♖e8−+.

14...♖e8 15.h3 ♕b6 16.g4 ♖e7 17.g5 ♘h5 18.♘g4 ♖ae8 19.♗e3

19...♕c7?!
An unforced error; 19...c5!−+.

20.♖xd5 ♘f4
20...c5 21.♖dd1 d5−+ would still win. Now it gets messy.

21.♗xf4 ♕xf4 22.e3 ♕c7
22...♕b8.

23.♖ad1 c5
23...d6!.

24.♘f6+ ♘xf6 25.♖xc5 ♕b6 26.gxf6 ♗xf6 27.♘d4 ♗xg2 28.♔xg2 ♕b7+ 29.♔g1 ♖e5
29...♗xd4 30.♖xd4 ♕f3 can be parried by 31.♕d1 ♕xh3 32.♕g4 ♕xg4+ 33.♖xg4 d6 and Black's advantage in this ending is not great.

30.♖xe5 ♖xe5

31.♔f1??

Time-trouble; he had to play 31.♔h2, of course.

31...♕h1+

31...♖h5 32.♕b3 ♕a8 was an alternative.

32.♔e2 ♕xh3 33.♘f3 ♕h5?

Stronger was 33...♖f5! 34.♕e4 ♗xb2 35.♖xd7 a5 and Black still holds all the trumps.

34.♖xd7 ♖f5 35.♕e4 ♗xb2
36.♖xa7 ♔g7 37.a4∓ 0-1 (time)

Giorgi Giorgadze	2525
Andras Adorjan	2535

Debrecen Ech tt 1992 (4)

1.d4 ♘f6 2.c4 g6 3.♘c3 d5 4.cxd5

Come on! This is not today's lesson! We were expecting something else: 4.♕b3.

4...♘xd5 5.e4 ♘xc3 6.bxc3 ♗g7
7.♗b5+?!

The revival of a line which had been considered harmless earlier. I faced it four more times in the following months (fashion will be fashion), with a positive score (BLACK IS OK!, as we all know).

7...c6 8.♗a4 b5 9.♗b3 b4 10.♗e3

10.♗b2 bxc3 11.♗xc3 ♗a6 12.♘e2 0-0 13.0-0 ♘d7 14.♖c1 and now:

A) Not the hasty counterblow 14...e5?, which surprisingly loses on the spot: 15.♗b4! (15.d5? ♘c5! 16.♗b4 ♘d3 17.♗xf8 ♘xc1 18.♕xc1 ♕xf8 19.♖e1=) 15...♖e8 16.♗xf7+!;

B) But rather the cool rook move 14...♖e8!, getting ready for active counterplay: 15.♕c2 (15.f4 e6 16.♗a4 ♖c8 17.♗a1 c5 18.dxc5 ♗xa1 19.♖xa1 ♖e7 and Black will collect the c-pawn in the end: 20.c6 ♘c5 21.♕xd8+ ♖xd8 22.♖fd1 ♖c8 23.♘c3 ♘xa4 24.♘xa4 ♖xc6; 15.e5 e6 is unclear) 15...e5 16.♖fd1 ♕h4. Now White's best option is to take on e5. Then he can win the pawn on c6, but this opens lines for Black's pieces.

10...bxc3 11.♖c1 ♘d7 12.♘e2

12.♖xc3 c5=.

12...♗a6 13.e5

A pandemonium would be the result of 13.♘xc3 c5 (13...♖b8 14.e5=) 14.dxc5 ♕a5 15.♗xf7+ (15.♗d4? is bad due to 15...♘e5) 15...♔f8 (15...♔xf7? 16.♕d5+) 16.♕xd7 ♗xc3+ 17.♖xc3 ♕xc3+ 18.♔d1 ♖b8 19.♗b3 ♗c4 20.c6 ♖b4!=.

Black's counterchances are also sufficient after 13.♖xc3 c5 14.♗c4 ♕a5 or 13.f4 ♖b8 14.♘xc3 0-0.

13...♕a5!

This is how you play in the Grünfeld spirit!

14.♕c2?!

The touchstone of the whole thing is, naturally, 14.e6, with crazy complications, where either party can get lost easily. Unfortunately, it was the most beautiful line that got refuted. It took White four years though. 'Little' Dao Thien Hai unleashed a great novelty, against no other than my 'accomplice' IM Endre Vegh. In Variation A2, the Vietnamese youngster prevented the 'miracle line' 17...♖d2!! by 17.♘xc3! ♗xf1 18.♕f3!! (line A22 below). Poor Endre got so confused that he allowed Dao to take his rook 'for free' after 18...♔d8 19.♕xc6 ♕c7 20.♕xc7+ ♕xc7 21.♘a4+. It is also true that any 'improvements' promised only torture. But, as the two sides make moves in turn, Black can throw in 15...♖d8! in his turn (AA-Leko, 1997). After this, there are no more fireworks, just the logical outcome of a chess game: 16.♔b3 ♖f8! 17.♕c3 ♕b5 18.♗c4 ♕xc4 19.♕xc4 ♗xc4 20.♖xc4 c5! 21.0-0 (21.dxc2? ♘e5) 21...cxd4 22.♗xd4 ♘b6 with a peaceful end. It looks like this:

A) 14.e6 fxe6 15.♗xe6 (15.♘f4 e5 16.♘e6 ♗f6∓) 15...♖b8 (better is 15...♖d8) and now:

A1) 16.♘xc3 ♘c5! (16...♖b2? 17.♕f3! (White has to act quickly and decisively: 17.♖c2? ♘c5!–+; 17.♗xd7+ ♔xd7 18.♖c2 ♖hb8∓) 17...♘f6 18.♕xc6+ ♔f8 19.♗b3+–;) 17.dxc5 ♗xc3+ 18.♗d2 ♗xd2+ 19.♕xd2 ♕a4∓;

A2) 16.0-0 ♖b2 and here it is:

A21) 17.♖e1 ♖d2!! (also good is 17...c2 18.♕d2 ♕xd2 19.♗xd2 ♗xe2 20.♖xe2 ♗xd4) 18.♕b3 ♖xe2 19.♖xe2 ♗xe2 20.♕b7 ♕d8 21.♕xc6 ♗d3 22.♖xc3 (22.g4 c2) 22...♗f5, keeping the extra piece while White's attack peters out;

A22) 17.♘xc3! ♗xf1 18.♕f3!! ♗d3 (18...♗b5 19.♕f7+ ♔d8 20.♕xg7 ♖e8

21.d5!±) 19.♕xc6 ♕d8 20.♘d5 ♔8 20.♕c3±.

B) 14.f4 ♘b6 (14...c5) 15.♘xc3 ♘c4 with an advantage due to White's unsafe king;

C) If 14.♘xc3 ♖d8 15.♕f3 0-0 16.♕xc6 ♗xe5 17.♕a4 ♗c7 and Black still has counterplay against the king.

14...c5

15.♕e4?

A little naive, don't you think so? Yes, you have to be very specific and sharp in the royal game, but those with a healthy way of thinking will be guided quite reliably by their so-called 'feeling for chess'.

So let's repeat the lesson: there are 2 (two) kings on the board. And one more important popular wisdom: you can never checkmate the enemy king without attacking pieces!

Never!

15.♗xf7+!?. A bolt from the blue! 15...♔xf7 16.e6+ and now:

A) 16...♔xe6? 17.♕e4+ ♔d6 18.♗f4+ e5 19.dxe5+ ♘xe5 (19...♔e6 20.♕c6++–) 20.♖d1+ ♔e6 21.♕d5+ ♔f5 22.♗xe5 ♗xe5 23.♘g3+ ♔f6 24.♕c6+ ♔g7 25.♖d7+ ♔h6 26.♘f5+ ♔g5 27.h4+ ♔xf5 28.♖f7++–;

B) 16...♔g8 17.exd7 cxd4 (17...♖d8 18.dxc5 ♖xd7 19.0-0 ♖b7 20.♕e4!±; 17...♗xe2 18.♕xe2 cxd4 19.♕c4+ ♔f8 20.♗xd4 c2+ 21.♔e2 ♖d8 22.♖xc2=) 18.♕b3+ (18.♘xd4!) 18...♔f8 19.♘xd4 c2+ 20.♗d2 ♕e5+ and now:

B1) 21.♕e3? ♕xd4! (21...♕xe3+ 22.♗xe3 ♔f7 23.♖xc2 ♖hd8=) 22.♕f3+ ♗f6 23.♕xa8+ ♔g7 24.♕f3 ♗d3 25.h4 (25.♕e3 ♖d8) 25...♕xd7 26.h5 ♕e6+ 27.♕e3 ♕xe3+ 28.♗xe3 ♗c3+ 29.♗d2 ♗b2 30.hxg6 ♔xg6 31.♖h6+ ♔f7 32.♖c6 ♗xc1 33.♗xc1 ♖d8 34.♖c7 ♗f5 35.♗d2 a6 with winning chances in the ending;

B2) Best for White is 21.♗e3! ♕a5+ with a perpetual.

C) However Black can still win by 16...♔f8! 17.exd7 ♖d8 18.dxc5 ♖xd7 19.♘xc3 ♔f7 20.♗d2 (20.c6 ♖d6–+) 20...♖hd8–+;

15...0-0 16.♗xf7+

16.e6 cxd4! 17.exf7+ (17.♘xd4 ♘c5 18.exf7+ ♔h8 19.♘c6 ♕a3–+) 17...♔h8 18.♗xd4 c2+ 19.♔f1 (19.♘c3 ♕xc3+!–+) 19...♕d2–+.

16...♔h8!?

The other road probably led to Rome as well. But by this road, we also have a band playing. Enjoy the music!

16...♔xf7 and now:

A) 17.e6+ ♔g8 18.exd7 ♗xe2 19.♔xe2 cxd4 20.♗xd4 ♕xa2+ 21.♔d3 ♖ad8! 22.♖c2 (22.♗xg7 ♕d2+ 23.♔c4 ♖f4–+) 22...♕a6+ 23.♔e3 ♗h6+ or 23.♔xc3 ♖xd7 24.♗xg7 ♕a3+, Black wins in either case;

B) 17.♕d5+ e6 18.♕xd7+ ♔g8 19.♕xe6+ ♔h8 20.f4 (20.♘xc3 cxd4 21.♗xd4 ♖fd8 22.♗e3 ♖ac8 23.♗d2 ♖xd2 24.♔xd2 ♗h6+ 25.♔d1 ♖d8+ 26.♔c2 ♗d3+ 27.♔b2 ♗xc1+ 28.♖xc1 ♖b8+ 29.♔a1 ♕xc3+–+) 20...♗e2 (20...♖ab8–+) 21.♔xe2 cxd4 22.♗xd4 ♖xf4 23.♗e3 ♕b5+ 24.♔e1 ♕d3 25.♗xf4 ♕e4+, and Black wins.

17.♘f4

So that's what it was all about! He's threatening 18.♘xg6+ and 19.♕h4 mate. You don't want to get too optimistic about it, as 17...g5 wouldn't have been sufficient to parry the danger, even though the variations are somewhat more complicated (see the next comment).

17.f4 ♖ab8 18.♗b3 (18.♗e6 ♖b2 19.♘xc3 cxd4 20.♕xd4 (20.♗xd4 ♘c5 and the king remains caught in the centre) 20...♘xe5!–+) 18...c4 19.♗c2 ♗b7 and White will have to give up a few pawns;

White also collapses after 17.♗d5 cxd4 18.♗xd4 ♖ac8.

17...♖xf7!

The time has come. White now pays dearly for forgetting the number of kings on the board (= 2).

17...g5? and now:

A) 18.♘e6 cxd4 19.♘xf8 ♖xf8–+;

B) 18.♘h3 cxd4 19.♘xg5 c2+! 20.♗d2 ♕xe5–+;

C) 18.♘g6+? hxg6 19.h4 (19.♕xg6 ♖xf7–+; 19.♗xg5 ♖xf7–+) 19...♖xf7 20.hxg5+ (20.e6 ♖ff8 21.hxg5+ ♔g8 22.♕xg6 ♘f6–+) 20...♔g8 21.♕xa8+ ♘f8 22.♕e4 cxd4 23.♕xd4 ♕xa2 24.♕d1 ♗xe5–+;

D) But 18.♗b3! wins for White! – 18...cxd4 19.♗c2 d3 20.♘xd3+–. Black would

(left margin, rotated) 16. ♗xf7 excellent! ♖xf7 gives white game ;

have to resort to 18...♖xf4! 19.♕xa8+ ♖f8 20.♕d5 to limit his disadvantage.

18.♕xa8+ ♖f8 19.♕d5

Three other queen moves also lose: 19.♕xa7 cxd4 20.♕xd7 c2+! 21.♗d2 ♕xe5+−+; 19.♕c6 cxd4 20.♗xd4 ♖xf4 21.♕xc3 ♕b5−+; 19.♕e4 cxd4 20.♕xd4 ♘xe5−+.

19...♕b5!

Much stronger than 19...♘b6?! 20.♕xc5 ♕xa2 21.♕xc3 and after 21...♖xf4 22.♕d2 I never found a win for Black.

20.♕b3

20.a4 ♕b2 21.♕xd7 ♖xf4−+.

20...cxd4 21.♕xb5 ♗xb5 22.♘e6

22.♗xd4 ♖xf4 23.♗xc3 ♘c5!−+.

22...dxe3 23.♘xf8 ♘xe5!!　　　0-1

A picturesque final position! This game was awarded the brilliancy prize in this European Team Championship.
The lines are:

A) 24.♖xc3 ♘f3+!;

B) 24.fxe3 ♘d3+ 25.♔d1 ♘xc1 26.♔xc1 ♗xf8−+;

C) 24.♘e6 ♘d3+ 25.♔d1 (25.♔e2 ♘xc1+ 26.♔xe3 ♘xa2−+) 25...♘xc1 26.fxe3 ♘xa2 27.♔c2 ♗a4+ 28.♔b1 ♗b3−+.

Jacek Gdanski　　　2500
Andras Adorjan　7　2550
Debrecen Ech tt 1992 (5)

1.e4 c5 2.♘f3 e6 3.d4 cxd4 4.♘xd4 ♘f6 5.♘c3 d6 6.g4 h6 7.♗g2 ♘c6 8.h3 a6 9.♗e3?!

In fact the most popular move. If 9.♘xc6 bxc6 10.e5 ♘d5 11.♘xd5 cxd5 12.c4 dxe5 13.cxd5 ♗b4+ 14.♗d2 ♗xd2+ 15.♕xd2 ♗b7 16.♖d1 0-0 17.0-0 exd5 18.♗xd5 ♗xd5 19.♕xd5 ♕f6 20.♖fe1 (20.♕d6 ♕g5∓) 20...♖ad8 21.♕e4 ♖d4! 22.♖xd4 exd4 23.♕d3 ♖d8 24.b4 h5 25.a4∓.

9...♘e5!

10.♕e2

10.f4 ♘c4 11.♗c1 e5!? (11...♕b6 12.b3 e5 13.bxc4 exd4 14.♘d5=) 12.♘de2 exf4 13.♘xf4 ♗e7 14.♕d4 ♘e5 15.♗e3 0-0 16.0-0-0 ♗e6 with counterchances.

10...g5! 11.0-0-0 ♕c7 12.f4 gxf4 13.♗xf4 b5

(½-½, Bologan-Sax, Manila ol 1992)

14.♘b1?

You cannot waste so much time in a sharp position like this. Normal was 14.♖hf1 ♘fd7, although Black's position is very solid.

14...♗b7 15.♘d2 ♖c8 16.♗g3 ♗e7

16...♗g7!? had its points too.

17.♔b1 ♘fd7 18.♖hf1 h5! 19.gxh5 ♘f6

* Italian game Mate!

The game is positionally over. White now tries to fish in troubled water. There are two kings on the board – a fact that is frequently overlooked by attacking players.

20.♘2f3

20.♗h4 runs into the little trick 20...♘xh5! 21.♗xe7 ♘g3.

20...♘c4!

One of the roads really leading to Rome. Wrong is 20...♘xe4? 21.♘xe5! ♘xg3 22.♕f2 ♗h4 23.♗xb7 ♕xb7 24.♕xf7+ ♕xf7 25.♘xf7±.

21.♘g5?

The central thrust does not convince either: 21.e5 ♘e4 (21...dxe5 22.♘xe5 ♗xg2 23.♕xg2 ♘xe5 is still good, but it gives White some chances with 24.♘xe6!) 22.♕e1 (22.exd6 ♘xg3 23.dxc7 ♘xe2 24.♘xe2 ♘e3–+) 22...d5 with a solid plus. Better is 21.♗h4.

21...♘xb2!

Whoops!

22.♔xb2

22.♘gxe6 fxe6 23.♘xe6 ♕c4–+.

22...♕c3+ 23.♔b1 ♕xg3 24.h4 ♖c4 25.♖d3 ♕xh4 26.♘df3 ♕xh5 27.e5

27.♖h1 ♕xh1+ 28.♗xh1 ♖xh1+ 29.♖d1 (29.♔b2 ♘xe4 30.♘xe4 ♗xe4 31.♖d1 ♗f6+–+) 29...♘xe4 with heavy consequences: 30.♘xe4 ♖xd1+ 31.♕xd1 ♗xe4 32.♘e1 ♖b4+–+.

27...♘d5 28.♖h1 ♕xh1+ 29.♗xh1 ♖xh1+ 30.♘e1

30.♔b2 ♖b4+ 31.♖b3 ♖b1+!–+.

30...♗xg5 31.c3 ♘f4 0-1

Black wins Bish + Rook for Queen!

This game was played 'the day after' the previous game Giorgadze-Adorjan, which got a brilliancy prize. Apparently our team captain thought I was OK with BLACK!

Piso
Andras Adorjan
Gabarone 1992 (8)

This rapid game was played in Gaborone, Botswana, in a tournament where I took the black pieces in all 11 games, still winning the tournament... with 10½ points. I got there as part of a GMA training mission for African talents.

22...♖xc3! 23.♗xf6 ♘xf6 24.g5

If 24.bxc3 dxe4, catching the bishop.

24...dxe4–+ 25.gxf6 exd3 26.fxg7+ ♗xg7 27.♖xd3 ♖xd3 28.cxd3 e4 29.f6 ♗h6 30.dxe4 ♗xe4 31.♘xe4 ♖xe4 32.♕g2 ♗e3+ 33.♖f2 ♗xf2+ 34.♔xf2 ♖e2+ 35.♔xe2 ♕xg2+ 0-1

The following game was played two weeks after the European Team Championship. It shows the way theory progresses today.

* **Attila Groszpeter** 2520
Andras Adorjan 2550 10
Budapest ch-HUN 1992

1.d4 ♘f6 2.c4 g6 3.♘c3 d5 4.cxd5 ♘xd5 5.e4 ♘xc3 6.bxc3 ♗g7 7.♗b5+?! c6 8.♗a4 b5 9.♗b3 b4 10.♕f3 0-0 11.♘e2 bxc3!N

9...b4 if white takes, Black gets Bxd4!

11...e5?! had been played in Kramnik-Adorjan, Debrecen Ech tt 1992. In that game Black spent more time developing his queenside, and lost.

12.0-0

Black cannot be tamed on the queenside anyway: 12.♕xc3 ♗b7 13.♕b4 (13.f3 ♘d7 14.♗a3 c5∓) 13...♕c7 (13...♘d7!? 14.♗e3 c5) 14.♖b1 (14.♗a3 ♘a6!?) 14...♗a6 15.♗c4 c5! 16.dxc5 ♘c6 17.♕a4 ♗xc4 18.♕xc4 ♘e5 19.♕c2 ♕xc5!∓ – nice, isn't it?
If 12.h4 h5!?.

12...♗a6 13.♖d1

13.e5 ♘d7 14.♖d1 c5 – typical Grünfeld counterplay against the centre! 15.♗e3 and now:

A) 15...♕a5? 16.♗xf7+! ♔h8 17.♘f4!+−;

B) 15...♕c7 16.♗xf7+! ♔h8 (16...♖xf7 17.♕xa8++−) 17.♘f4!+−;

C) But 15...cxd4! gives Black an edge: 16.♗xd4 c2 17.♗xc2 ♕c7∓, winning the e-pawn: 18.♗d3 ♗xd3 19.♕xd3 ♘xe5 20.♕e4 ♕c6.

13...c5!

The only move, but a good one.

14.dxc5

14.♗d5 c2! 15.♖d2 cxd4 16.♘xd4 (16.♗xa8 d3−+) 16...♗xd4 17.♗xa8 (17.♖xd4 e6 18.♗g5 ♕b6−+) 17...♗xa1! 18.♖xd8 ♖xd8 19.♗d5 e6 20.♗g5 exd5 and Black wins – he has too much material for the queen.

14...♕a5 15.e5

15...♘c6!

This is the key move!

16.♕xc6

Too many white pieces are hanging after 16.♕xc3?? ♗xe2 or 16.♘xc3? ♘xe5 17.♕e3 ♘g4.

16...♗xe2 17.♖e1

17...c2!

Again this irritating desperado!

18.♖xe2

Better chances of salvation were offered by 18.♗e3 and now:

A) 18...♗xe5 19.♗xf7+ ♔g7 (19...♔xf7 20.♕d5+ ♔f6 21.♗g5+ ♔xg5 22.♕xe5+ ♖f5 23.♕e3+ ♔f6 24.♕xe2 ♕xc5 25.♖ac1=) 20.♖ac1 ♖ad8=;

B) 18...♗d1 19.♖axd1 cxd1♕ 20.♖xd1 ♖ad8 (20...♗xe5? allows the drawing combination 21.♗xf7+ ♔xf7 22.♕d5+ ♔f6 23.♗g5+ ♔xg5 24.♕xe5+ ♔h6 25.♖d4 ♖f5 26.♖h4+ ♖h5 27.♕e3+ ♔g7 28.♖xh5 gxh5 29.♕xe7+=) 21.♖c1 ♗xe5 22.♕b7 e6 and Black consolidates, but the game is far from over.

If 18.♗xf7+ ♔h8 19.♗e3 (19.♗g5?
♖ad8 20.♗d5 ♗d1–+) 19...♖ad8
20.♗d5 ♗xe5 21.♖ac1 ♗d1 and Black
keeps the upper hand.

18...♕c3 19.f4

19.♗xc2 ♕xa1 20.♖e1 ♕c3 21.♖e2
♖ac8–+; 19.♗xf7+ ♔h8–+; 19.♖xc2??
♕e1#.

19...♖ad8!

And it's all over now (baby blue).
The rook enters the back rank, with a
decisive attack.

20.♔f2 ♕xa1 21.♖xc2 ♖d1 22.♗d2

22.♗e3 ♖f1+ 23.♔g3 ♗xe5!–+;
22.♗b2 ♖f1+ 23.♔e3 ♕e1+ 24.♖e2
♕b4 25.g3 g5! 26.fxg5 ♕g4 27.♔e4
♕xg5+ 28.♔d3 ♖d8+ 29.♔c4 (29.♔c2
♖c8) 29...e6! and there is no rest for the
white king.

22...♖d8–+ 23.♗c3 ♖f1+ 24.♔g3

24.♔e3 ♕d1 25.♕e4 ♗h6! 26.g3
♖d3+–+.

24...♖d3+ 25.♔h4 ♖xf4+ 26.g4

26...♖xg4+! 27.♔xg4 ♕d1+   0-1

OK? – 28.♔f4 ♗h6+ 29.♔e4 ♖e3#.

Tibor Tolnai	2495
Andras Adorjan	2550

Budapest ch-HUN 1992

1.♘f3

Surprise! Tolnai was a wild tactical GM
who worked together with IM Perenyi,
and he always played 1.e4. Did he want
a draw?

**1...♘f6 2.c4 b6 3.♘c3 ♗b7 4.d4 e6
5.♕c2 c5 6.dxc5 ♗xc5 7.♗g5 h6
8.♗h4 ♗e7 9.e3**

9.♖d1 ♘a6.

9...0-0 10.♗e2 ♘a6!?

Yes – on the rim. A good alternative
was 10...d5 11.0-0 ♘bd7 12.♖fd1
♖c8 13.♖ac1 dxc4, intending after
14.♘e5 to sacrifice the queen with
14...♘xe5 15.♖xd8 ♖fxd8 with ample
compensation.

11.0-0 ♘c5 12.♖fd1 ♘fe4 13.♗xe7

13.♗g3 loses the momentum: 13...♘xc3
14.♕xc3 ♘e4 and Black has the
initiative.

13...♕xe7 14.♘d2?!

Simple and good was 14.♘xe4 ♘xe4=.

14...♘xc3 15.♕xc3 d5 16.♗f3

He could have contested the c-file with
the more astute 16.b4 ♘d7 17.cxd5
♖fc8 18.♕b2 ♗xd5 19.♗a6 ♖c7 20.e4
♗c6 21.♖ac1=.

16...♖fd8 17.h3

Black is a little more active now. He
could have tried 17.b4!? ♘a6 18.a3
♖ac8 19.♕b3 (19.b5 ♘c5∓) 19...dxc4
20.♘xc4 ♗xf3 21.gxf3 ♘c7∓.

17...dxc4! 18.♗xb7

18.♕xc4 ♖ac8 also favours Black.

**18...♘xb7 19.♘xc4 ♖ac8 20.♕a3
♕xa3 21.♘xa3 ♘c5 22.♘b5 a6**

23.♘c3?!

Active play is vital in such positions!
White could have kept the balance with
23.♘d6 ♖c6 (23...♖c7 24.♘c4 ♖xd1+

25.♖xd1 ♘a4 26.b3 b5 27.♖d8+ ♔h7 28.♘e5 ♘c3 29.a3=) 24.♘c4 ♖dc8 (24...♘d3 25.♘e5 ♖cd6 26.♘c4=) 25.♘e5 ♘c7 26.♖d6 f6 27.♘f3 ♖c6=.

23...♘d3 24.♖d2 ♘e5! 25.♖xd8+
25.♖ad1 ♖xd2 26.♖xd2 ♔f8∓.

25...♖xd8 26.♖d1 ♖c8 27.♖d4 ♔f8 28.♔f1 ♔e7 29.♔e2 ♘c4 30.♘d1 b5 31.♖d3 b4 32.f4?
32.a3 ♘xb2! 33.♘xb2 ♖c2+ 34.♔f3 ♖xb2 35.axb4 ♖xb4 36.♖a3 ♖b6 37.♖a5∓/–+; 32.b3 ♘a3∓; 32.♖b3 ♖b8 33.♖d3 (33.♘c3? bxc3! 34.♖xb8 c2–+) 33...a5 34.a3∓.

32...a5 33.a3?
White got himself into a worse position and now loses patience.
33.♖b3 ♖b8 34.a3? bxa3! loses too, but 33.♖d4 was more tenacious.

33...♘xb2! 34.♘xb2 ♖c2+ 35.♔f3
35.♖d2 ♖xd2+ 36.♔xd2 bxa3 and the a-pawn decides.
35...♖xb2 36.axb4 ♖xb4
36...axb4.
37.♖c3 ♖b7 38.♖a3 ♖a7 39.♔e4 ♔d6 40.♔d4 a4 41.♖c4 f5
Fine was 41...♖a8 42.♔d4 (42.♔b5 ♔d5 43.♔b6 ♔c4–+) 42...e5+! 43.♔c4 (43.♔e4 exf4 44.exf4 ♔c5) 43...♔e6 44.g4 f5 45.♔c5 g5; or also the immediate 41...g5.
42.♔b5 ♖b7+ 43.♔c4 ♖a7 44.♔b5 ♖b7+ 45.♔c4 ♖b2 46.♖xa4
46.g4 ♖b3! 47.♖xb3 (47.♖xa4 ♖xe3–+) 47...axb3 48.♔xb3 ♔d5 49.♔c3 ♔e4 50.♔d2 fxg4 51.hxg4 ♔f3–+.

46...♖xg2 47.♖a7 g5 48.♖a6+ ♔e7 49.♖a7+ ♔f6 50.♖h7 ♔g6 51.♖e7 ♔f6 52.♖h7 gxf4! 53.♖xh6+
53.exf4 ♔g6 54.♖e7 ♖e2–+.
53...♔g7! 54.♖xe6

54...f3
A pretty finish: 55.♖a6 f2 or 55.♔d3 ♖g1–+.
White resigned.

The silent Argentinian GM Gerardo Barbero lived in Hungary for quite some time. He got married to Ribli's former wife and they had a son. But he fell fatally ill and died rather young. Rest in peace...

Gerardo Barbero		2485
Andras Adorjan	♟	2530

Hungary tt 1992
1.d4 ♘f6 2.c4 g6 3.♘f3 ♗g7 4.g3 c5 5.♗g2 cxd4 6.♘xd4 0-0 7.♘c3 ♘c6 8.♘c2 d6 9.0-0 ♗e6
9...♗d7!? is a good alternative: 10.b3 ♕a5 11.♗b2 ♖fc8 12.e3 a6 13.♘d4 ♖ab8 14.♘d5 ♘xd5 15.cxd5 ♘xd4 16.♗xd4 ♗xd4 17.♕xd4 ♕c3 18.♕h4 ♗b5 19.♖fe1 ♖c7 20.e4 ♕d2∓.

10.b3 ♕d7 11.♖e1?!
By omitting further development with 11.♗b2 ♗h3 12.♘e3 ♖ab8 13.♕d2 a6 14.♘cd5 White now loses the initiative.
11...♗h3 12.♗h1 ♘g4

BLACK WINS PAWN WITH KNIGHT SACRIFICE 35.Nxb2 – Rc2+

13.♗d2

Careful but passive. If 13.♗b2 ♕f5 14.f3?! (14.♗f3 ♖ad8=/∓)

analysis diagram

14...♕xc2!! is a fantastic turn: 15.♕xc2 ♗d4+ 16.e3 ♘xe3 17.♕f2 ♘c2 18.♕xd4 ♘6xd4 19.♖xe7 ♘xa1 20.♗xa1 ♘c2 21.♗b2 ♖fe8 22.♖xe8+ ♖xe8 23.♘e4 ♖e6 24.♗c3 h6 and Black wins.

13...♕f5! 14.f3 ♕c5+! 15.e3 ♘f6 16.♖c1 a6!

Black is more than OK here. The white kingside pawns are 'soft' and need constant attention.

17.a4?!

17.♘a4 ♕h5 18.♘d4 ♘e5 hardly changes the situation.

17...♖fd8

Or the more speculative 17...♘e5!?∓.

18.♘e2 ♖ac8 19.♘cd4

19.♘f4 ♗f5 20.g4 ♗d7 is still somewhat better for Black; White is now a little overextended on the kingside. 19...♘b4!

Avoid exchanges when you're pressing!

20.♘f4 ♗d7 21.♘c2 ♘xc2 22.♕xc2 b5! 23.axb5 axb5 24.♕d3 ♕b6 25.cxb5 ♗xb5 26.♕b1

In the endgame after 26.♕d4 ♕xd4 27.exd4 ♖xc1 28.♖xc1 e5 White's pieces are unfortunately placed.

26...e5! 27.♘d3 ♖xc1 28.♖xc1 ♗h6 29.♖e1

29...♖c8

29...♘d5! won as well, exploiting (as before) White's pawn weaknesses 'in front of' his king: 30.f4 (30.♔f2 ♖c8–+) 30...exf4! 31.♗xd5 fxe3 32.♗c1 ♕d4 33.♗c4 ♗c6 34.♖f1 ♕e4 35.♗xf7+ ♔h8 36.♗b2+ ♗g7 37.♗xg7+ ♔xg7 38.♕b2+ ♔h6–+.

30.♘f2 ♘d5 31.♘g4

Or 31.♕e4 ♘c3.

31...♗g7 32.♖c1 ♖xc1+ 33.♕xc1 ♗d7 34.♕c4 ♗e6 35.♕d3

35.♕a4 loses a pawn to 35...h5 36.f4 ♘xf4 (36...hxg4? 37.♕a8+) 37.♘f2 ♘h3+ 38.♘xh3 ♗xh3 39.♕e8+ ♗f8 40.♗d5 ♕a7, and Black consolidates.

35...♘b4! 36.♕b1

Or 36.♕c3 ♘d5 37.♕d3 f5 38.♘f2 ♗h6 39.♘d1 f4.

36...h5 37.♘f2 d5 38.♘d3?

A mistake in time-trouble.

38...♗f5! 39.♗xb4 ♕xe3+ 40.♔g2 e4! **0-1**

Romuald Mainka	2550
Andras Adorjan	2550

Polanica Zdroj 1992

Sometimes work does not pay off immediately. But it's never in vain!

1.e4 c5 2.♘f3 e6 3.d4 cxd4 4.♘xd4 ♘f6 5.♘c3 d6 6.♗e2 ♗e7 7.0-0 0-0 8.♗e3 a6 9.a4 ♘c6 10.f4 ♕c7 11.♔h1 ♖e8 12.♗g1 ♖b8 13.♕d3

13...e5!?N

Kasparov and I had been working this novelty out before the first K vs K match in 1984.

Instead, 13...♘xd4 14.♕xd4 e5 comes down to the sacrifice of an exchange: 15.♕a7 exf4 16.♗b6 ♖a8 17.♕xa6 ♖xa6 18.♗xc7 ♖c6 19.♗a5 ♖xc3 (or also 19...g5 20.♗b5 ♗d7 21.♗xc6

♗xc6 with compensation) 20.♗xc3 ♘xe4 21.♖xf4 ♘xc3 22.bxc3 ♗e6 may be tough for Black, but another interesting option is 13...b6!? 14.♘xc6 ♕xc6 15.♗f3 ♕c7 16.♖ad1 ♗b7, with an unclear position.

14.fxe5

The point of the pawn push is that Black gets the e5-square for his knight in all variations:

A) 14.♘f5 ♗xf5 15.exf5 exf4 16.♖xf4 d5;

B) 14.♘b3 exf4 (14...b6 15.♕c4 ♗d8 16.♘d5 ♕d7 is unclear) 15.♕c4 (15.♖xf4 d5 16.♖af1 dxe4 17.♘xe4 ♘e5∓; less good is 16...♘b4 17.♕f3 dxe4 18.♘xe4 ♘bd5 19.♘xf6+ ♘xf6 20.♗d3 – wrong squares for the knights) 15...♗e6 16.♘d5 ♖ec8! 17.♖xf4 ♕d8 18.♕d3 ♘e5 19.♕d2 ♘g6∓ YES! BLACK is BETTER in all variations.

14...dxe5 15.♘f5

15.♕g3!? ♘xd4 16.♗xd4 ♗d8! 17.♗e3 ♔h8 18.a5!? ♗e6 19.♗d3 (19.♗b6 ♕c6 20.♗xd8 ♖bxd8 is also slightly better for Black) 19...♖c8 20.♗b6 ♕d6 21.♗xd8 ♖exd8 22.♕h4 ♕e7 with good central pressure.

15...♗xf5 16.♖xf5

16...♘d4!?

Kasparov's move.

17.♗xd4

Or 17.♖ff1 ♖bd8 and Black takes over.

17...exd4 18.♕xd4

If 18.♘d5 ♘xd5 19.♖xd5 (19.exd5 ♗d6 20.♖af1 ♖e3 21.♕d2 ♖be8) 19...♗f6 and Black is better.

18...♗d6!?

18...♖bd8!? is not bad either, for example: 19.♕c4 ♗d6 20.♕xc7 ♗xc7 and White will have to shed his extra pawn eventually: 21.♗d3 ♗e5 22.♘d5 (22.♖af1 ♗xc3 23.bxc3 ♘xe4 24.♗xe4 ♖xe4 25.♖xf7 b6 26.h3 ♖xa4 27.♖b7 ♖f8 28.♖d1 ♖af4=) 22...♘xd5 23.exd5 g6 24.♖f3 ♗xb2 25.♖b1 ♖xd5 26.g4 ♗e5 27.♖xb7 ♖d4 28.a5 ♖xg4=.

19.♖af1?

A big mistake. Correct was 19.♘d5! ♘xd5 and now:

A) 20.♖xd5 ♗xh2 (20...♗e5 21.♕c4) 21.♖d7 ♕f4 and White is in grave danger – probably his best option is the exchange sacrifice 22.♖xf7 ♕h6 23.♖xg7+;

B) The best recapture is 20.♕xd5 and now:

B1) 20...♗xh2? 21.♖af1 ♖e7 22.♗c4 ♖f8 23.♖xf7 ♖fxf7 24.♖xf7 ♖xf7 25.♕xf7+ ♕xf7 26.♗xf7+ ♔xf7 27.♔xh2 ♔e6 28.♔g3 ♔e5 29.♔f3 b6 (29...h5 30.a5 g5 31.♔e3 h4 (31...g4 32.g3+−) 32.♔f3+−) 30.c3+−;

B2) 20...g6 21.♖xf7! (21.♖f3 ♖e5 22.♕d4 ♖e7 23.♕c4 ♗xh2∓) 21...♖xf7 22.♕xd6 ♖bd8 23.♕b4 ♕e7=;

B3) 20...♖bd8 21.♖af1 ♖d7 22.♗c4 ♖e5! 23.♕d3 ♖xf5 24.♖xf5 ♗xh2 25.♖d5 ♖xd5 26.♗xd5 ♗d6 27.♗xb7 ♕e7 28.g3 ♕xb7 29.♕xd6 ♕xe4+ 30.♔g1 ♕e1+ 31.♔g2 ♕e2+ 32.♔h3 ♕f1+=;

B4) Crucial is 20...♗e5 21.♕c4! and now:

B41) 21...♖c8 22.♖xe5 (22.♕xc7 ♖xc7 23.♖xe5 ♗xe5 24.c3=/±) 22...♗xe5 23.♕xc7 ♖xc7 24.♖d1 f5 or 24.c3 ♖d7, both with compensation;

B42) 21...♕e7 22.♖af1 ♖f8 23.♗d3 ♖xf5 24.exf5 ♕f6 25.♕d5=;

B43) 21...♕xc4 22.♗xc4 ♖xf5 23.exf5 ♔f8 24.♖d1 ♖d8 with a drawish ending.

19...♗e5 20.♕d3

There was the escape clause 20.♘d5 ♗xd4 21.♘xc7 ♖ec8 22.♘d5 ♖xc2 23.♘xf6+ gxf6, but White would also be in for a rough ride in that case.

20...♗xc3 21.bxc3 ♖e7! 22.♖5f4

This way White does not derive much pleasure from his 'plus pawn'. If 22.♗f3 ♖d8! 23.♕e3 ♕c4 24.♗g1; but his best chance was 22.♖xf6 gxf6 23.♗g4 with a much-needed change of scenery, and probably sufficient compensation.

22...♖be8 23.♕c4 ♕xc4 24.♗xc4

24...♖c8!?

A nice switch. Also good was the handy 24...♖xe4 25.g3 ♖8e7! (25...♖xf4 26.♖xf4 ♖e4 27.♖xe4 ♘xe4 28.♗d5 ♘c5 29.a5 is unclear; 25...♔f8 26.♔g2 ♖xf4 27.♖xf4 ♖c8 28.♔f3 ♔e7 29.♔e3 g5 30.♖d4 ♖c5∓) 26.♖xe4 ♘xe4 27.♖f3 g6, giving Black a big advantage.

25.♗b3 ♖xc3 26.♖d1 ♖c8

26...h6 27.♖d8+ ♔h7 28.♖f8 ♔g6 29.h3 ♖cc7∓.

27.♖d4 ♖ce8 28.♗d5 ♘xd5
29.♖xd5 *Even piece trades*

29...g6?!

Best was 29...h6! to put pressure on the e4-pawn with ...g7-g5. Now:

A) 30.g3? g5 31.♖f6 ♔g7 32.e5 (32.♖dd6 ♖xe4 33.♖xh6 ♖xa4–+) 32...♖xe5 33.♖xe5 ♖xe5 34.♖b6 ♖e7 with good winning chances;

B) 30.♔g1 ♖c8! 31.♖d2 (31.♖f2 ♖xe4 32.♖d7 ♖e1+ 33.♖f1 ♖xf1+ 34.♔xf1 ♖xc2 35.♖xb7 ♖c4–+) 31...♖c4 32.a5 g5 33.♖f6 ♔g7–+.

30.♔g1

Obviously, crucial was 30.♖d4!? and now:

A) 30...f5 31.♔g1 fxe4! 32.♔f2 b5 33.♔e3 ♖c7 34.axb5 axb5 35.♖fxe4 ♖xe4+ 36.♖xe4 ♖xc2 37.♖g4 ♔g7 38.♔d3 ♖c5∓;

B) 30...g5!? is still radical and good, for example: 31.♖g4 (31.♖f5 ♖xe4! 32.♖xg5+ ♔f8 33.♖xe4 ♖xe4 34.♔g1 ♖xa4 35.♖c5 and Black should be able to win) 31...f6 32.h4 h6 33.♖b4 ♖c8 34.hxg5 fxg5–+;

C) 30...♖c8 31.♖f2 (31.c4 ♖c5 intending 32...♖a5) 31...♖c3 32.♔g1 ♖ec7 (32...♖e3 33.♖f4 ♖c7∓) 33.♖fd2 ♖xc2 34.♖xc2 ♖xc2 35.♖b4 ♖c7 36.♔f2 ♔f8 37.♔e3 ♔e7 38.♔f4 ♔d6–+.

30...♖c8! 31.e5

31.♖d2 ♖c4–+.

31...♖xc2 32.h3

If 32.♔f1 ♖ec7 with the nasty threat of 33...♖a2–+.

Black takes PAWN / ead 31 Rxc2

32...♖e2 33.♖b4 ♖2xe5 34.♖xe5 ♖xe5 35.♖xb7 ♖e4 36.a5 ♖e5 37.g4 ♖xa5 38.♖c7 ♖a2   **0-1**

Fruit of the work done together with Garry – after 8 years!

Xu Jun   2540
Andras Adorjan   2550
Shenzhen 1992 (6)

What an awful tournament did I have right after the Manila Olympiad. But this game was a consolation for my suffering.

1.♘f3 c5 2.c4 ♘f6 3.♘c3 ♘c6 4.d4 cxd4 5.♘xd4 e6 6.a3 ♗e7 7.e4

The alternative is 7.♗f4 but White cannot really take advantage of the dark squares in this line:

A) 7...d5 8.cxd5 ♘xd5 9.♘xc6 bxc6 10.♗d2 ♗a6 (less good is 10...♗f6 11.♕c2 ♖b8 12.e3 0-0 13.♗d3 h6 14.0-0=/±) 11.♕a4 ♕b6 12.e4 ♗xf1 13.♔xf1 ♘xc3 14.♗xc3 0-0 15.♕d4 ♕b5+ 16.♔g1 ♗f6 17.e5 ♗e7 18.h4 ♖fd8 19.♕g4 ♖d3 20.♖h3 ♖xh3 21.♕xh3 ♖d8=;

B) 7...d6 8.♗g3 (8.♘db5?? e5 9.♗g5 a6–+) 8...♘h5 9.e3 ♘xg3 10.hxg3 ♕b6∓;

C) 7...0-0 8.e4?! d5 and now:

C1) After 9.e5 the e-pawn becomes weak: 9...♘d7 10.cxd5 exd5 11.♘xc6 bxc6 12.♗e2 ♖e8 13.0-0 and now Black can take the pawn and weather the storm by 13...♗f8 14.♗d3 ♘xe5 (or also 14...g6). White can win it back only by giving up the bishop pair: 15.♗xh7+ ♔xh7 16.♕h5+ ♔g8 17.♗xe5 ♕d7 18.♖fe1 ♕f5 19.♕xf5 ♗xf5 and Black is better;

C2) 9.cxd5 exd5 10.exd5 ♘xd5 11.♘xc6 bxc6 12.♘xd5 cxd5 13.♗e2 ♗f6 also favours Black due to his better development.

7...0-0

8.♘b3

A) 8.♗e2 d5=;

B) There is still 8.♗f4?!, but again 8...d5 is a dynamic reaction;

C) 8.♘db5 d6 9.♗e2 (9.♗f4? doesn't work here due to 9...e5 10.♗g5 (10.c5 dxc5−+) 10...a6−+) 9...a6 10.♘d4 ♕c7 11.0-0 ♘xd4 12.♕xd4 b6 with counterplay;

D) 8.♘f3 b6 9.♗f4 d6 10.♕d2 ♘a5 11.♖d1 ♗a6.

8...b6 9.♗e2 ♗a6!?

You might have expected 9...♗b7 10.♗f4 d6 11.0-0 ♖c8=.

10.♗e3

10.f4 ♖c8 11.♗e3 d6 12.0-0 ♘b8 13.♘d2 and here the central break 13...d5 is extremely strong: 14.cxd5 exd5 15.exd5 (15.e5 d4 16.♗xa6 ♘xa6 17.exf6 ♗xf6∓) 15...♖xc3! 16.bxc3 ♘xd5 17.♗d4 (17.♗xa6 ♘xe3 18.♕e2 ♘xa6−+) 17...♗c5!−+.

10...♖c8 11.f4 d6 12.♗d3?!

A loss of time. White is having constant trouble defending the c4- and e4-pawns. Also insufficient is 12.♖c1 ♘b8 13.♘d2 d5 14.cxd5 exd5 15.♗xa6 ♘xa6 16.♘xd5 ♘xd5 17.♖xc8 ♕xc8 18.exd5 ♗c5∓.

Best under the circumstances is to try to finish his development with 12.0-0 and now:

A) 12...♘a5 13.♘xa5 bxa5 14.♕d4 ♘d7 15.♖ad1=/± ♕b6 (15...♘b6 16.b3 a4 17.♘xa4 ♘xa4 18.bxa4 ♕c7 19.♕xa7 ♕xa7 20.♗xa7 ♗xc4 with compensation);

B) 12...♘b8 13.♘d2 d5 14.exd5 exd5 15.♘xd5 ♘xd5 16.cxd5 ♕xd5 17.♗xa6 ♘xa6 18.♘f3 ♕b5∓.

12...♘d7 13.♗e2

A sad retreat. He should have played 13.0-0 ♘c5 14.♗xc5 bxc5 with chances for both sides.

13...♘c5 14.♘d2

14.♘xc5 bxc5 15.0-0 ♘d4 16.♗xd4 cxd4 17.♕xd4 d5 18.b4 ♗xc4 19.♕xa7 ♖c7 20.♕b6 ♗xe2 21.♘xe2 dxe4 22.♖fd1 ♕c8∓.

14...♗h4+!

15.g3

15.♗f2 ♗xf2+ 16.♔xf2 f5! or 16...♘d4!? – in both cases Black has a clear advantage.

15...♗f6 16.♖c1 ♘d4 17.♗f1

17.0-0 was still the lesser evil. With the ♔ on e1 you cannot hope for mercy.

17...e5 18.b4

18.♘d5 exf4 19.♗xd4 (19.♗xf4 ♖e8−+) 19...♗xd4 20.b4 ♘e6 21.♘f3 ♗e5∓/−+.

18...♘ce6 19.f5

Trying to keep the position closed, but in the end this won't wash. The desperate 19.♕a4 ♗b7 20.♕xa7 also loses: 20...♗c6 21.♘d5 ♗xd5 22.exd5 ♖a8 23.♕b7 exf4 24.♗g1 ♘g5−+.

19...♗g5! 20.♘d5

Better was 20.♗xg5 ♕xg5 21.♔f2 (21.fxe6? ♕e3+ followed by 22...fxe6 when f2 and also c4 are under threat) 21...♗b7, but it still looks dangerous.

20...♘c7 21.♕g4 ♗xe3 22.♘xe3

217

22...♘e8!

22...b5 was also promising, but the text is more thematic.

23.♕d1 ♘f6

23...♕g5 24.♖c3 ♘f6 25.♗g2 ♗xc4 26.♘exc4 b5∓.

24.b5

24.♗d3 runs into the break 24...b5.

24...♗b7 25.♗g2 ♕c7 26.g4

26.♘c2 ♘xf5−+; 26.0-0 ♕c5 27.♖e1 ♖fd8; 26.a4 ♕c5, driving White crazy due to all the pins in the position.

26...♕c5

26...♘xb5 27.g5 ♘d7 28.f6 g6−+.

27.g5

27.♔f2 h6−+.

27...♘e6!−+

... and here we are!

Good, but less attractive, was 27...♕xa3 28.♔f2 ♘d7.

28.♘c2 ♘xg5 29.♕e2 h6 30.h4 ♘gh7 31.♖b1 d5 32.exd5 ♘xd5 33.♗xd5

33.♕f2 ♘f4!−+.

33...♗xd5 34.♘e3? ♗xh1　　　**0-1**

Andrei Purtov   2440
Andras Adorjan   2550
Zalakaros rapid 1992 (4)

Black can be better even after 10 moves!

1.♘f3 ♘f6 2.g3 c5 3.♗g2 g6 4.0-0 ♗g7 5.d3 0-0 6.e4 ♘c6 7.♘c3

7.♘bd2.

7...d5 8.exd5 ♘xd5 9.♘xd5

9.♗d2 e6.

9...♕xd5 10.♖e1?!

10.♘d2.

10...♕h5!

Very unpleasant.

11.♘d2??

An awful blunder. He could have kept his disadvantage within limits by 11.♕d2 ♗h3∓ or 11...♗g4∓; or 11.♘g5 ♕xd1 12.♖xd1 ♗g4∓.

11...♕xd1 12.♖xd1 ♘b4 13.c3 ♘xd3 14.♘b3 c4 15.♘a5 ♗g4! 16.f3

If 16.♖d2 ♘xc1 17.♖xc1 ♗h6 18.f4 e5.

16...♗e6 17.♘xb7 ♖ab8 18.f4 ♗g4 19.♖d2

19...e5!

Brutal.

20.♘d6

20.fxe5 ♗h6! 21.♖xd3 ♗xc1–+.

20...exf4 21.♘xc4 ♘xc1 22.♖xc1 f3–+ 23.♗f1

All the tactics work for Black: 23.♘e3 ♗h6 24.♘xg4 ♗xd2.

23...♗h6 24.♖cd1 ♗xd2 25.♖xd2 ♖fd8 26.♖xd8+ ♖xd8 27.♘e5 h5 28.h3 ♗e6 29.♘xf3 ♖d1 30.♔f2 ♗xa2   **0-1**

Imre Horvath	2360
Andras Adorjan	2530

Zalakaros rapid 1992 (7)

1.g3 c5 2.♗g2 g6 3.c4 ♗g7 4.♘c3 ♘c6 5.d3

5...b6

5...e6 6.♘f3 ♘ge7 is a very good system for Black.

6.e4

6.♘f3 ♗b7 7.0-0 ♘f6 8.e4 0-0 9.h3 d6.

6...♗b7 7.♘ge2 ♘f6 8.0-0

8.e5 ♘g4 9.f4 d6 10.h3 ♘h6 and BLACK IS OK.

8...0-0 9.h3

Here 9.e5?! already works against White as after 9...♘e8 10.f4 d6 his centre crumbles.

9...d6 10.♗e3 ♘d7 11.♕d2

11.d4 was the right way to play here: 11...e5 (11...cxd4 12.♘xd4 ♘c5 13.b3 a5) 12.dxe5 dxe5 13.♘d5 ♘d4 is unclear.

11...a6 12.f4?!

It was still better to fill the hole in the centre by 12.d4.

12...♘d4 13.♗f2 e5 14.♘xd4 cxd4 15.♘d5 ♗h6! 16.♕b4 ♘c5 17.fxe5 ♗xd5 18.exd5

18...dxe5!

18...♘xd3 19.♕xd6 ♘xf2 is not so clear after 20.♕xd8 (20.♔xf2 ♗e3+ 21.♔e2 ♕g5 with chances for both sides) 20...♘xh3+ 21.♗xh3 ♖axd8.

19.♖ad1 f5

19...♕d6 20.♕e1 b5∓.

20.♕e1 ♕d6 21.b4

Making things worse.

21...♘a4 22.♖b1 ♖ae8 23.♖b3 f4 24.gxf4 exf4 25.♗e4 ♕f6 26.♔h1 f3 27.♗g3 ♘c3 28.♖b2 ♕g5

Soft killing. 28...♖xe4 29.dxe4 d3–+ or 28...♘xe4 29.dxe4 ♗e3 might have been the hard way.

29.d6 ♘e2 30.♔h2

30...♖xe4! 31.dxe4 d3 32.e5 f2! 33.♗xf2 ♕xe5+ 34.♗g3 ♕xb2

35.♖xf8+ ♗xf8 36.d7 ♕d4 37.c5 bxc5   **0-1**

Istvan Csom	2475
Andras Adorjan	2545

Gyula HUN-ch 1993 (6)

26...♘c3!

Very unpleasant! Not that such a move is unusual in this line – just the contrary. Taking advantage of the weakness of c3 combined with other elements of the position is always 'hanging in the air'.

27.♘xc3?

Wrong! The surprise effect and the shortage of time paralysed Csom. 27.♗xb7? loses to 27...♘xe2+ 28.♔f1 ♕xb7.

The only way to offer serious resistance was 27.♗xc3 ♗xf3 and now:

A) 28.exf3 dxc3 29.♘xc3 ♖xc4! (29...♕xd3 30.♖c6! ♕xf3 31.♕d5 with compensation) 30.dxc4 (30.♕xc4 ♖c8−+) 30...♕d2! 31.♘a2 (31.♕c2 ♖e1+−+; 31.♖c2 ♖e1+ 32.♔g2 ♕d3−+) 31...♖e2−+;

B) 28.♗xd4 ♗d5 29.♗xg7 ♗xc4 30.♕b2 (30.♖xc4 ♔xg7 31.♘c3 ♕e6!∓) 30...♗xb5 (30...♕xb5 31.♖xc4 (31.♕a1 ♗e6 32.♖xc8 ♗xc8 33.♗h8 f6 34.♗xf6 ♕c6 35.♗h8 ♖e7−+) 31...♕xb2 32.♗xb2 ♖xc4 33.dxc4 ♖xe2=) 31.♖xc8 (31.♗xh6? ♖xc1+−+) 31...♖xc8 32.♗xh6 (32.♗h8 f6−+) 32...f5 33.♘c3 ♗c6 34.♗e3.

analysis diagram

A strange position. Black is surely better, but at least White has a pawn for the exchange. It's not so easy to mobilize the passed pawns while White has some – at the moment still slightly abstract – attacking dreams against the somewhat exposed black king's position.

27...♗xf3 28.♖xc8

28.exf3 dxc3.

28...♖xc8 29.♘e4 ♖xc1+

29...♗xe2!? would fall for a trick that wouldn't save White anyhow: 30.♖xc8+ (30.♗xh6 ♖xc1+ 31.♗xc1 ♕h3 32.♘d2∓) 30...♖xc8 31.♕xf7+ ♔xf7 32.♘d6+ ♔e6 33.♘xc8 ♗xd3 34.♘xa7 ♔d5−+.

30.♗xc1 ♗xe2

31.♗xh6?

A blunder, of course, but the game was over anyhow. This way the end comes a little faster.

31...♕h3   **0-1**

And you know what happened? Poor Csom lost no less than four more games after this, and dropped to the bottom of the table. Me? I won three out of the next four and defended my national Hungarian title. But let me tell you again: while there is no such thing as 'bad luck', things depend on nuances quite often.

The following game was played at the first ever Rainbow chess tournament on this globe. The initial position and the rules are 100% the same as in the traditional chess game.

Dao Thien Hai
Andras Adorjan
Budapest rapid 1994

This Rainbow chess game was played in the Bela Papp Memorial.

1.c4 g6 2.e4 e5 3.♘f3 ♗g7 4.d4 exd4 5.♘xd4 ♘f6 6.♘c3 0-0 7.♗e2 ♖e8 8.f3 c6

9.♘b3
9.♘c2 d5!; 9.♗g5 h6 10.♗h4 d5.
9...a5

9...d5 is also sound. Compared to the normal King's Indian my system gains a tempo by playing ...d7-d5 at once. 10.cxd5 cxd5 11.♘xd5 (11.exd5 ♕b6 12.♕d4 ♘bd7=) 11...♘xd5 12.♕xd5 and now:

A) 12...♕c7!?, with compensation for the pawn, was given by Stohl in Yearbook 93;

B) 12...♕xd5 13.exd5 ♘a6 14.♔f2 ♘b4 15.♖d1 ♖d8 16.♗c4 ♗f5 17.a3 ♖ac8 18.♗g5 (18.♘a5 ♘c2∓) 18...f6 19.axb4 ♖xc4∓;

C) 12...♕h4+ 13.g3 ♕f6 14.0-0 (14. f4 ♘c6 15.e5? (better is 15.♔f2∓) 15...♘xe5 16.fxe5 ♖xe5 17.♕c4 ♗e6 18.♕f4 ♕e7−+) 14...♘c6 15.♖b1 ♗e6 16.♕g5 a5 with compensation.

10.♗e3
Other ways were:

A) 10.c5. This attempt to fix Black's queenside pawns backfires: 10...a4 11.♘d4 b6 12.cxb6 (12.♘xa4 bxc5−+) 12...♕xb6 13.♘xa4 ♕b4+ 14.♘c3

analysis diagram

and now a nice queen sacrifice: 14...♘xe4! 15.a3 (15.fxe4 ♗xd4−+) 15...♕xc3+ 16.bxc3 ♘xc3 17.♕d3 ♗xd4 18.♕xd4 ♘xe2 (18...♖xe2+ 19.♔f1 ♗a6 is another attractive option) 19.♕d6 ♘xc1+ 20.♔d1 ♘e2 and Black has all the chances;

B) 10.♗f4 a4 11.♘xa4 ♖xa4 12.♗xb8 d5 and now:

B1) 13.♘d2 ♖a8 14.♗g3 (14.♗f4 ♘h5−+) 14...dxe4−+;

B2) 13.cxd5 loses right away to 13...♘xe4!;

C) 10.a4 stops ...a5-a4, but leaves a hole on b4 and thus facilitates ...d7-d5 again: 10...♘a6 (but not 10...d5 11.cxd5 cxd5 12.♗g5) 11.♗f4 d5 12.cxd5 cxd5 13.♘xd5 ♘xd5 14.♕xd5 ♕xd5 15.exd5 ♘b4 16.♖d1 ♗f5∓.

10...a4 11.♘c5 a3 12.0-0

If 12.b4 d5, making White suffer on the open long diagonal.

12...d5 13.bxa3

A) 13.cxd5 ♘xd5 is a well-known resource;

B) 13.b4 ♘g4 14.fxg4 (or 14.♗d4) 14...d4;

C) After 13.b3, 13...♘g4 14.♗d4 ♘e3 15.♗xe3 d4 is less good due to 16.♗f2.

13...♖xa3

Also nice was 13...♘xe4 14.fxe4 d4−+.

14.♗d4

Otherwise the knight on c3 is in a bad fix: 14.♕c1 ♖xc3 15.♕xc3 ♘xe4−+; or 14.♘5a4 ♘fd7 15.♗d4 (15.♕c1 ♖xc3 16.♘xc3 d4 17.♗g5 ♖a5) 15...♗xd4+ 16.♕xd4 dxc4−+.

14...dxe4 15.fxe4 ♘xe4!

Winning a pawn and the game.

16.♗xg7 ♘xc3 17.♗xc3 ♖xc3

First exchanging the queens was good too.

18.♕xd8 ♖xd8 19.♖fd1 ♖e8 20.♗d3 ♔f8 21.♗f1 ♖c2 22.♗d3

A little more tenacious was 22.♖ab1 ♖xa2 23.♘xb7 ♗g4; more convincing for Black was 21...♖a3 on the previous move. Now Black can slowly but surely convert his plus pawn.

22...♖b2 23.♘db1 ♖xb1+ 24.♖xb1 ♖e7 25.♗f1 ♔e8 26.♘b3 ♔d8 27.♔f2 ♔c7 28.♘c5 ♘d7 29.♘a4 ♖e5 30.♘c3 ♖h5 31.h3 ♖a5 32.♖e1 ♘e5 33.a4 ♗e6 34.♖e4 ♘d7 35.♖e1 ♘b6 36.g4 h5 37.gxh5 ♖xh5 38.♔g3 ♘xc4 39.♘e4 ♖e5 40.♔f2 ♘b2 0-1

Laszlo Börcsök   2185
Andras Adorjan   2530
Budapest rapid 1995

Even a rapid game can be splendid.

1.e4 c5 2.♘c3 e6 3.g3 d5 4.exd5 exd5 5.d4?!

This leads to an inferior position.

5.♗g2 gives White nothing either: 5...♘f6 6.♘ge2 d4 7.♘e4 ♘xe4 8.♗xe4 ♗d6 9.0-0 0-0 10.d3 ♘d7! 11.♗f4 ♘f6 12.♗xd6 ♕xd6 13.♗g2 ♗g4∓.

5...cxd4 6.♕xd4 ♘f6 7.♗g2 ♘c6 8.♕d1

8...♗g4

Also interesting was 8...d4!? 9.♘ce2 ♗c5∓; or 9.♘e4 ♗b4+ 10.♗d2 ♕e7 11.♕e2 ♘xe4 12.♕xe4 (12.♗xe4 ♗xd2+ 13.♔xd2 0-0 with the idea 14.♗xc6 ♕b4+) 12...♗xd2+ 13.♕xd2 ♗e6 with attack.

9.♗f3

On 9.♘ge2 Black can try 9...♗c5!? because taking the pawn is too dangerous for White: 10.♘xd5?! ♘d4 11.♘dc3 ♕a5!−+.

9...♗xf3

9...d4 10.♗xg4 dxc3∓.

10.♘xf3 d4 11.♕e2+ ♗e7 12.♘e4 0-0 13.0-0 ♖e8 14.♘xf6+ ♗xf6∓ 15.♕d3 ♘b4 16.♕b3

Heavy piece exchanges 13–18

16...♛d5! 17.♛xd5

17.♛xb4 ♛xf3 18.♗d2 ♛f5 is also very unpleasant for White.

17...♘xd5 18.♖d1?

With 18.♗d2 White should have prevented Black's next move.

18...♘b4 19.♗f4 ♘xc2

19...♖e2! was even stronger.

20.♖ac1 ♖e2?

And now, more accurate was 20...♖ac8! 21.♖d2 ♘b4 22.♖xc8 ♖xc8 23.♘xd4 ♖d8 24.♘b5 ♖xd2 25.♗xd2 ♘xa2 26.♘xa7 ♗xb2 and Black should win this ending.

21.♔f1 ♖ae8

22.♘g1??

22.♗e5 ♗xe5 23.♔xe2 ♗f4+ 24.♔d3 ♘b4+ 25.♔xd4 ♗xc1 26.♖xc1 ♘c6+ 27.♔d3 would have drawn.

22...d3!–+ 23.♖xd3 ♖e1+ 24.♖xe1 ♖xe1+ 25.♔g2 g5

Or 25...♖b1 26.♘f3 ♖xb2 27.a4 g5 28.♗d2 g4 29.♘e1 ♖xe1+ 30.♗xe1.

26.♗b8 ♖a1 27.♖b3 ♘e1+ 28.♔h3

28...h5 29.g4 ♖xa2 30.♖xb7 ♘d3 31.♗xa7 ♗xb2?

Silly. After 31...♘f4+! White would have had to give a piece to prevent mate: 32.♔g3 ♖a1 33.♘f3 h4+ 34.♘xh4 ♘e2+ 35.♔f3 ♘g1+ 36.♔e4 gxh4 37.b4 ♖e1+ 38.♔f5 ♗b2 and Black wins.

32.♗e3?

32.gxh5 would have equalized.

32...♗f6

32...♗e5 33.♘f3 ♘f4+ 34.♗xf4 ♗xf4 35.gxh5 ♖xf2 36.♔g4 f5+ 37.♔xf5 ♖xf3 38.♔g6 ♔f8 39.h6=.

33.gxh5 ♘xf2+

34.♔g2??

A losing mistake in time-trouble; 34.♗xf2 ♖xf2 35.♔g3 would have held the draw.

34...♘d1+ 35.♔f3 ♖a3 36.♔e4 ♖xe3+ 37.♔f5 ♖e6 38.♔g4 ♔g7 39.♘f3 ♖e4+ 40.♔g3 g4 41.h6+ ♔xh6 42.♘d2 ♖d4 43.♘b3 ♗e5+ 44.♔g2 ♖d3 45.♖b5 f6 46.♖b7 ♖h3 47.♖b5 ♖xh2+ 48.♔g1 g3 49.♖d5 ♘f2 50.♘d2 ♘h3+ 0-1

Books Best Game!

10

Zoltan Gyimesi 2500
Andras Adorjan 2530

Budapest ch-HUN 1995 (8)

1.d4 ♞f6 2.c4 e6 3.♞f3 b6 4.g3 ♝a6 5.b3 ♝b4+

5...b5!? (Dobosz/Adorjan) is original, and playable too.

6.♝d2 ♝e7 7.♝g2 d5 8.♝c3 ♞e4 9.♝b2 ♞d7 10.0-0 0-0 11.♞c3 ♞xc3 12.♝xc3 dxc4 13.♞d2

13...cxb3!?

Playing for a win by giving up the exchange. More or less equal was 13...♜c8 14.♞xc4 ♝f6 15.♛c2 c5 16.d5 exd5 17.♝xd5 ♝xc3 18.♛xc3 ♛e7 19.♝f3 ♜fe8 20.♜ad1 ♞e5 21.♛xe5 ♛xe5 22.♞xe5 ♜xe5 23.♜d2 ♚f8 24.♜fd1 c4.

14.axb3

14.♝xa8 b2 (14...♛xa8 15.axb3 ♝b5 also gives good compensation) 15.♝xb2 ♛xa8 16.♛a4 ♛c8=.

14...♝b5 15.♝xa8 ♛xa8 16.♜e1 ♜d8 17.♜a2

It may have been better to occupy the centre with 17.e4 and now:

A) 17...c5?! 18.d5±;

B) 17...♝f6 18.♛c2 ♛b7 (18...c5 19.dxc5 ♝xc3 20.♛xc3 ♞xc5 21.b4 ♞d3 22.♜e3±) 19.♞c4 a5±;

C) But after 17...♞f6! 18.♛f3 a5 Black's compensation is promising.

17...a5

Black is pursuing a flank strategy, keeping his options in the centre open.

If 17...♝f6 18.♛c2 a6 19.♝a1 c5 20.dxc5 ♝xa1 21.♜exa1 ♞xc5 22.b4 ♞d7±; 17...a6 18.e4 ♞f6 19.♛c2 c5!?=/±.

18.e4 ♞f6 19.f3?

19...h5?!

Ultra-modern. 19...c5! 20.dxc5 ♛c6 21.♛a1 (21.b4 ♝xc5+ 22.♚g2 axb4 23.♝xf6 gxf6∓; 21.♛c1 ♝xc5+ 22.♚g2 ♜d3) 21...♛xc5+ 22.♚g2 ♜d3∓ was 'normal'.

20.♚g2 h4 21.♞c4 ♛c6 22.♜c2

After 22.♝a1 ♝xc4 23.bxc4 ♝b4 24.♜h1 ♛xc4 25.♜c2 ♛b5 26.♜xc7 Black can keep the initiative with some hard work: 26...♛g5 27.♜c2 (27.♛c1 ♝d2! 28.♛c2 hxg3 29.hxg3 ♝f4) 27...hxg3 28.hxg3 ♞h5 29.g4 ♞f4+ 30.♚f1 ♛b5+ 31.♚f2 ♛g5 or 31...e5, with counterchances; in such positions the knight is not worth less than a rook.

22...♝xc4 23.bxc4 ♛xc4 24.♝xa5 ♛b5 25.♝c3 ♞h5?

A silly provocation. 25...c5, with compensation, was good enough.

26.f4

26.♛d2 ♛b3.

26...♞f6 27.♛e2 ♛a4?

27...♛xe2+ 28.♜exe2 c5 29.dxc5 ♝xc5 still gave good chances for the material. But now, without the knight, it becomes problematic.

28.d5! exd5 29.♝xf6 ♝xf6 30.e5± d4

What else? If 30...♝e7 31.♜xc7+−.

Excellent

31.exf6?
31.♖xc7 won easily.
**31...d3 32.♖a2 ♕c6+ 33.♕f3 h3+
34.♔f2 ♕c5+**

Now Black is winning!
35.♖e3
The h3-pawn is a nail in White's coffin:
35.♕e3 ♕d5 36.♕d2 ♕g2+ 37.♔e3
♖e8+ 38.♔xd3 ♖d8+−+; or 35.♔f1 d2
36.♖ea1 ♕c4+ 37.♕e2 d1♕+ 38.♖xd1
♖xd1+ 39.♔f2 ♕d5−+.
35...d2 36.♖a1 ♕c1 37.♖d3
A nice line is 37.♕d1 ♕xa1! 38.♖e8+
♖xe8 39.♕xa1 c5 (39...♖e1? 40.♕a8+
♔h7 41.♕f8+−; 39...♖d8−+) 40.♕d1
♖d8 41.fxg7 (41.♕g4 g6−+) 41...♔xg7
42.♔e2 ♔f8 and the black pawns can
start rolling.
37...♖e8 38.♕d1 ♕c5+ 39.♔f1
39.♔f3 ♕c6+ 40.♔g4 ♕e6+ 41.♔h4
♕xf6+ 42.♔xh3 ♕f5+ loses the rook.
**39...♖e1+   40.♕xe1   dxe1♕+
41.♖xe1 ♕c6 42.♖d8+ ♔h7 43.♖e5
♕h1+ 44.♔f2 ♕xh2+ 45.♔f3 ♕g2+
46.♔g4 h2 47.fxg7 ♔xg7   0-1**
As Tartakower predicted, the player committing the penultimate mistake won.

Alexander Sherzer   2490
Andras Adorjan   2525
Hungary tt 1995

Excellent — 10

**1.e4 c5 2.♘f3 e6 3.d4 cxd4 4.♘xd4
♘f6 5.♘c3 d6 6.♗e2 ♗e7 7.0-0
0-0 8.f4 a6 9.a4 ♘c6 10.♔h1 ♕c7
11.♗e3 ♖e8 12.♕e1**

12...e5!?
Also produced by Kasparov/Adorjan,
1984.
13.fxe5
A) White can never play 13.♘f5?
♗xf5 14.exf5 d5;
B) 13.♘b3 ♘b4!;
C) 13.♘f3 ♘b4!? (13...exf4 14.♗xf4
♗e6) 14.♗d3 ♘g4 with good counterplay;
D) 13.♘xc6 ♕xc6 14.♗d3 (14.♗f3
♗e6 15.a5 ♖ac8) 14...exf4 15.♖xf4
♗e6 16.♗d4 and the knight lands on
e5: 16...♘d7 17.♕g3 ♘e5 with double-
edged play.
13...dxe5 14.♕g3
No good was 14.♘f5? ♗xf5 15.exf5
(15.♖xf5? ♘d4) due to the Kasparovian
ploy 15...♘d4, with advantage to Black.
14...♘xd4 15.♗xd4 ♗d8! 16.♗e3 ♔h8
Maybe it's hard to believe, but BLACK
is already BETTER here. Not, however,
16...♗e6? 17.♗h6.
17.♖ad1 ♗e6 18.♗g5 ♗e7?!
Now White creates pressure against f6.
This could have been avoided by 18...♘g8!
19.♗e3   ♖c8   (19...♘f6=)   20.♗d3
(20.♗g4 ♘f6 21.♗f5 (21.♗xe6 fxe6=)
21...♗xf5   22.♖xf5   ♕c4)   20...♘f6
21.♗g5 ♘h5! with Black's advantage.

19.♕h4 ♖ad8

20.♖d3?!

A novelty at the time. Black is doing well after the other options:

A) 20.♗d3 ♘g4;

B) 20.♖xf6!? ♖xd1+ (20...♗xf6 21.♗xf6 ♖xd1+! 22.♗xd1 – see 20...♖xd1+!) 21.♗xd1 ♗xf6 22.♗xf6 gxf6 23.♕xf6+ ♔g8 24.♕g5+ ♔f8 25.♕h6+ ♔e7.

20...♘g8! 21.♖g3 ♗xg5

Good. But superior was 21...f6! 22.♗e3 f5 23.♕h3 (23.♗g5 f4 24.♖d3 ♗xg5 25.♕xg5 h6∓) 23...f4 24.♕xe6 fxg3.

22.♕xg5 f6 23.♕h4 ♖d4! 24.♗g4 ♗f7 25.♗h5

Black can also parry 25.♖h3 by 25...♗g6 26.♗f5 ♗xf5 27.♖xf5 ♘h6 28.♖xf6? ♕xc3!–+.

25...♖ed8 26.♖h3 ♘h6 27.♗e2 ♗c4

More subtle was the regrouping 27...♗g6! and ...♘f7.

28.♗xc4 ♕xc4 29.♖hf3 ♘f7 30.b3 ♕c6

30...♕e6!.

31.♕h5

31...♘d6??

An awful blunder in mutual time-trouble. 31...♕e6! was still good.

32.♖h3 h6 33.♖xf6! ♔g8

33...gxf6 34.♕xh6+ ♔g8 35.♕g6+ ♔f8 36.♕xf6++–.

34.♖g3 ♕e8 35.♖fg6

35.♖xg7+! ♔xg7 36.♕xh6+ ♔g8 37.♕g5+ was winning.

35...♖d7 36.♕xh6??

Sherzer returns the favour. The luft 36.h3 would still have won for White.

36...♘f5!! 37.♕c1 ♘xg3+ 38.♖xg3 ♕h5 39.♖f3 ♕g5!?

39...♖d2 was winning.

40.♕f1 ♖d2?

Another mistake on the last move before the time control. 40...♖d8 41.♖f5 ♕d2 42.♘d5 ♕d1∓.

41.♘d5??

41.♕c4+ would have drawn, cf. 41...♔h7 42.♖h3+ ♔g6 43.♕e6+ ♕f6 44.♖g3+ ♔h7 45.♖h3+=.

41...♖xc2 42.h3? ♖c1 43.♖f8+ ♔h7

White resigned.

A tragicomic fight!

Pal Petran   2470
Andras Adorjan   2530
Budapest ch-HUN 1995 (2)

This game was played with a Rainbow chessboard, about which we shall talk later. There are unpleasant opponents for everybody – IM Petran was one for me. But I did produce an original shot in this game!

1.♘f3 c5 2.c4 ♘f6 3.♘c3 e6 4.e3 g6!?/?!

Very 2016!

5.d4 ♗g7

6.♗d3?!

A) 6.dxc5 ♘a6 7.♕d6 ♕a5=;

B) 6.e4!? is more ambitious: 6...0-0!? (6...cxd4 7.♕xd4 ♘c6 8.♕d6 ♕e7 9.♗f4 ♘g4) and now:

B1) 7.d5 exd5 8.cxd5 ♖e8 9.♗d3 b5 10.♘xb5 c4 11.♗xc4 ♖xe4+ 12.♗e2 ♕a5+ 13.♔f1 (13.♘c3 ♘xd5) 13...♗a6 14.a4 ♗xb5 15.♗xb5 a6 16.♗d2 ♕b6 17.♗d3 ♖e8 with compensation;

B2) 7.e5 ♘g4 leads to an exchange sacrifice which is interesting because of White's lag in development: 8.♗g5 (8.h3 cxd4 9.♕xd4 ♘xe5 10.♘xe5 d6 11.♘xf7 ♖xf7 (11...♗xd4 12.♘xd8 ♗xf2+ 13.♔e2 ♗b6∓) 12.♕d2 ♘c6∓) 8...♕a5 9.♗e7 cxd4 10.♗xf8 ♔xf8 11.♕xd4 ♘xe5 12.♘xe5 ♗xe5 13.♕d2 ♘c6 with compensation (13...♗xc3 14.bxc3 ♘a6 is unclear).

C) 6.♗e2 would be the normal move: 6...0-0 7.0-0 d6 (7...cxd4 8.♘xd4 (8.exd4 d5 is OK for Black) 8...♘c6 9.b3 ♘xd4 (9...d5 10.♗a3 ♘xd4 11.exd4 ♖e8) 10.exd4 d5=) 8.e4 ♘c6 9.d5 ♘d4 10.dxe6 ♘xe6 11.h3 ♖e8 12.♗e3 b6 13.♕c2 ♗b7 14.♖ad1 ♘xe4 15.♘xe4 ♘d4 16.♘xd4 cxd4 17.♘f6+ ♕xf6

18.♗xd4 ♕g5 19.g3 ♗xd4 20.♖xd4 ♖e6 with a draw in 32 moves, Portisch-Suba, Luzern 1985;

D) 6.d5 exd5 7.cxd5 0-0 transposes to a Benoni with an extra tempo for Black.

6...0-0 7.0-0 cxd4

Stronger was 7...b6! with the idea 8.♕e2 (8.d5 is better) 8...♗b7 9.b3 ♘c6 10.♗b2 ♘b4! 11.♗b1 d5∓.

8.exd4

Or 8.♘xd4 ♘c6.

8...d5 9.♕e2?

Much better was 9.♗g5! dxc4 10.♗xc4 h6 (10...♘c6 11.♘e4) 11.♗xf6 (11.♗h4 ♘c6) 11...♗xf6 12.d5 exd5 13.♘xd5 ♘c6 (13...♗xb2 14.♕d2 ♗g7 15.♖ad1 ♘c6 16.♖fe1 ♗e6 17.♕f4) 14.♕e2. Now Black takes over.

9...♘c6 10.♖d1

10...♘b4! 11.b3 b6! 12.♗a3 a5

Black is already superior. There is no way for White to undertake something active.

13.♘b5?

13.♘e5 ♗a6 with pressure.

13...♗a6! 14.♖ac1?

He could have relieved the pressure somewhat by 14.♗xb4 axb4 15.a4 bxa3 16.♖xa3 dxc4 (16...♗b7 17.♖xa8 ♗xa8; 16...♗xb5 17.♖xa8 ♕xa8 18.cxb5 ♕a3) 17.bxc4 ♗xb5 18.♖xa8 ♕xa8 19.cxb5, but after 19...♘d5 Black still calls the shots.

14...♗h6!

Winning!

15.♗xb4

After 15.♖b1 dxc4! 16.bxc4 ♗xb5 17.cxb5 ♘fd5, the knight is a monster; even more dreadful than in the game.

15...axb4 16.♖c2 dxc4! 17.bxc4 ♗xb5 18.cxb5 ♘d5 19.♗e4

If 19.♕e1 ♘c3, for example 20.♖a1 ♗g7 and Black calmly collects the d-pawn.

19...♘c3 20.♖xc3 bxc3 21.♗xa8 ♕xa8 22.♕c2 ♕a3 23.♘e5

A cute line is 23.♖b1 ♖a8 24.♖b3 ♕xa2 25.♕xc3 ♕xb3!, highlighting yet another of White's problems.

23...♖a8 24.♕e4

24.♕d3 ♗f4 25.♖f1 ♗xe5 26.dxe5 ♖c8−+.

24...♕xa2 25.♕f3 c2

All White gets is a few checks.

26.♕xf7+ ♔h8 27.♕f6+ ♗g7   0-1

Torsten Behl
Andras Adorjan
Ubach rapid 1996

My opponent in this game is Torsten Behl, my clubmate in the Lohmar team.

1.e4 c5 2.♘f3 ♘c6 3.d4 cxd4 4.♘xd4 ♕c7 5.c4

5.♘b5!? ♕b8 6.♘1c3 is interesting.

5...♘f6 6.f3

On 6.♘c3, grabbing the e-pawn is possible but risky: 6...♘xe4?! (6... e6) 7.♘xe4 (7.♘db5 ♕a5) 7...♕e5 8.♘b5 ♕xe4+ 9.♗e2 ♕e5 10.g3 with compensation.

6...e6 7.♗e3

An interesting position where many sharp lines are possible.

7...a6

7...d5!? comes down to a dynamic pawn sacrifice after 8.♘b5 ♗b4+ 9.♘d2 ♕d8 10.a3 ♗e7 11.cxd5 exd5 12.♗f4 0-0 13.♘c7 ♘h5 14.♘xd5 ♘xf4 15.♘xf4 ♗d6 and soon Black's attack against the uncastled white king will start rolling (a recurrent theme in this book!);

On 7...♗c5, 8.♘b5 does not work (neither does 8.♘xe6 ♗b4+) in view of 8...♕a5+ 9.♕d2 ♗xe3 10.♕xa5 ♘xa5 11.♘c7+ ♔e7 12.♘xa8 ♗c1 13.♘d2 ♗xb2 14.♖d1 ♗e5 and the knight is lost.

8.♗e2 ♗d6 9.g3 b6 10.♘c3 ♗b7 11.♕d2 ♗c5 12.♖d1 0-0 13.♔f2

13.0-0 d5!? (13...♖ab8) 14.exd5 exd5 15.cxd5 ♘xd4 16.♗xd4 ♘xd5=.

13...♖ad8

This can only mean one thing...

14.♘c2 d6 15.a3 ♘e7 16.b4 ♗xe3+ 17.♕xe3 d5!

Again: BLACK is not OK but BETTER!

White should've traded Queens at 24. Qxa2!

18.cxd5

18.c5 bxc5 19.♕xc5 ♖c8 20.exd5 ♕b8! and Black wins, as 21.♕xe7 loses the queen to 21...♖fe8;

18.exd5!? exd5 19.♘a4 b5! and it looks as if White will have to sacrifice a knight to avoid worse.

18...exd5 19.e5 ♘f5–+ 20.♕f4 ♕xc3 21.♕xf5

21...♘e4+! 22.fxe4 ♕xc2 23.♖c1 ♕b2

No queen trades with an unsafe white king!

24.♖c7 ♗c8 25.♕f3

25.♕f4 f6.

25...♕xe5 26.♖hc1 ♗e6?!

26...dxe4!–+.

27.♗d3?

27.exd5 ♗xd5 28.♕e3 ♕f6+ 29.♔g1 b5.

27...g6

27...f5!–+.

28.♕e3

Now Black wins with a prosaic second pawn grab:

28...♕b2+ 29.♖1c2 ♕xa3 30.exd5 ♗xd5 31.b5 ♖fe8 32.♖2c3 ♕a2+

Heavy Piece exchanges

33.♖c2 ♖xe3 34.♖xa2 ♖xd3 35.bxa6 ♗xa2 0-1

White Blunders Bxa2

Kocur
Andras Adorjan
 9
Ubach rapid 1996

I played all of my games in this tournament with black as well.

1.e4 c5 2.c3 g6 3.d4 cxd4 4.cxd4 d5 5.e5 ♗g7 6.♗d3 ♘c6 7.♘e2 ♘h6

Also possible is the direct 7...f6!? 8.exf6 (less good is 8.f4 ♘h6∓) 8...♘xf6 9.0-0 0-0 10.♘bc3 e6=.

8.0-0 0-0 9.♘bc3 ♘f5 10.♗c2 ♗e6 11.f3 ♕b6

The attack on d4 was best prepared with the surprising 11...♖c8!, which leads to some fascinating tactics after 12.g4 ♘fxd4! 13.♘xd4 ♕b6 14.♗e3 ♗xe5 15.♘a4 (15.♘cb5 ♘xd4 16.♘xd4 ♖c4 17.♘f5 ♕xb2–+; 15.♘ce2 ♘xd4 16.♗xd4 ♗xd4+ 17.♘xd4 ♖c4–+) 15...♗xd4! 16.♘xb6 ♗xe3+ 17.♔g2 ♗xb6.

analysis diagram

A fantastic picture! BLACK is much more than OK!

12.♘a4

Kicking back the queen, but White could have removed the threats to d4 with 12.♗xf5! gxf5 (12...♗xf5 13.♘xd5 ♕a5 14.♘e3=/±) 13.♘a4 ♕d8 14.♗g5=.

UNCOMMON Sicilian Opening.

Excellent sequence played by Black. 13...Nfxe(4-16. (handwritten left margin)

12...♕c7 13.♖f2

13...♘fxd4!? 14.♘xd4 ♘xd4 15.♕xd4 ♗xe5 16.♕d2

16.♕c5!? was more careful, cf. 16...♗xh2+ (16...♕xc5 17.♘xc5 ♗d4 18.♘xe6 fxe6 19.♗d2 is unclear) 17.♔h1 ♖ac8 and the position is hard to assess, though Black certainly has practical chances. If 16.♕h4 b5.

16...♗xh2+ 17.♔f1 d4 18.b3

18.♕xd4 b5 19.♗h6 ♗e5 20.♕c5 bxa4 21.♕xc7 ♗xc7 22.♗xf8 ♔xf8 leads to an endgame of the type we often find in this book; Black's bishop pair plus pawn more than make up for the minus exchange.

18...b5 19.♘b2

19...d3?

Why the hell do I play such moves? 19...♖fd8∓.

20.♗xd3

The pins along the d-file are insufficient after 20.♘xd3 ♖fd8 21.♕e3 ♗f5 22.♗b2 ♖ac8 23.♖d1±.

20...♖fd8 21.f4 ♗g3 22.♖f3 ♗h4 23.f5 ♗xf5 24.♕h6??

White could still bail out to a slightly better endgame with 24.♕f4 ♕xf4 25.♗xf4 ♗f6 26.♗xf5 gxf5 27.♖b1 e6.

24...♕h2

Winning.

25.♗f4 ♕h1+ 26.♔e2 ♕xa1

26...♕xg2+ 27.♔e3 ♕xb2−+.

27.♗e5 ♗f6

Time-trouble; better was 27...♕e1#.

28.♖f1 ♗xd3+ 29.♘xd3 ♕xa2+ 30.♔e3 ♖xd3+ 31.♔xd3 ♕xb3+ 32.♔e2 ♗xe5 33.♖h1 0-1

Emil Anka
Andras Adorjan
Budapest rapid 1996 (9)

1.e4 c5 2.♘f3 d6 3.d4 cxd4 4.♘xd4 ♘f6 5.♘c3 a6 6.♗e3 ♘c6 7.f3

7...d5!?

Not bad! It prevents g2-g4.

8.exd5

Simpler is 8.♘xd5!? ♘xd5 9.exd5 (9.♘xc6 bxc6 10.exd5 ♕xd5 – or 10...cxd5 and BLACK is OK!) 9...♕xd5 10.♘xc6 ♕xc6 11.♗d3 e6 12.♕e2 ♗c5=.

8...♘b4!?

An interesting try to keep the game alive.

9.♕d2

9.♗c4 ♘fxd5 10.♘xd5 ♘xd5 11.♘b3 ♗e6 (11...♘xe3?? 12.♗xf7++−) 12.♗c5 b5 13.♗d3 ♕c7 14.0-0 ♘f4 15.♗e3 ♘xd3 16.cxd3 ♗d5 17.♖c1 ♕d8=/∓.

9...♘bxd5 10.♘xd5 ♘xd5 11.♗f2

Sharper was 11.0-0-0!? e6 (no time to take on e3) 12.♗f2 ♗e7 13.♔b1 0-0=.

11...e5 12.♘b3 ♗e7 13.♗c4 ♗e6 14.0-0

Now 14.0-0-0?? is off due to 14...♗g5.

14...♖c8 15.♗xd5 ♕xd5 16.♕xd5 ♗xd5 17.c3 f6 18.♖ad1 ♗e6

BLACK is BETTER, of course; the bishop pair makes the difference.

19.♗e3 ♔f7 20.f4 exf4 21.♗xf4 ♖hd8 22.♗e3 b5 23.♘c1 h5 24.a3 h4 25.h3 g5 26.♘d3

26.♖xd8 ♖xd8 27.♗xg5?? ♗c4 loses big material due to the back-rank threats.

26...♗b3 27.♖d2 ♔g6 28.♗d4 ♗c4 29.♖e1 ♖d7 30.♘f2 ♗c5 31.♗e3?

Objectively best was 31.♘g4 ♖cd8 32.♖e4 ♔f5 33.♖e3∓/∓, but it's no fun for White.

31...♖e7 32.♘d1 ♖ce8 33.♔f2 f5 34.♗xc5 ♖xe1 35.♘e3 ♖8xe3!

A nice finish.
White resigned.

BENKO

Tea Lanchava	2265
Andras Adorjan	**2530**

Groningen 1996 (10)

I managed to lose some 30 Elo points in this tournament. I played reasonably but committed horrible blunders. The following game was (more or less) an exception to this pattern.

1.d4 ♘f6 2.c4 c5 3.d5 b5 4.cxb5 a6 5.b6 d6 6.♘c3 ♘bd7 7.a4 a5 8.e4 g6 9.♗b5 ♗g7 10.f4?!

Often not very good in the opening phase of the Benko, as it weakens the dark squares in White's camp.
10.♘f3 is preferable.

**10...0-0 11.♘f3 ♘xb6 12.0-0 ♘e8!
13.♗c6 ♖b8 14.♘b5?!**

14.♖e1 ♗d7∓.

14...♘c7?

14...♗b7!?±.

15.♕e1 f5!

Now White's proud centre crumbles.

16.e5 ♘cxd5 17.♕xa5?

17.♗d2 ♘b4∓.

17...♘b4!−+ 18.♘a7 ♕c7 19.♗b5 ♖a8 20.♗c4+ d5

20...♔h8 won outright.

21.♗e3 ♖xa7 22.♕xc5 ♕xc5 23.♗xc5 dxc4 24.♗xb6 ♖a6 25.a5

♘d5 26.♗c5 ♗b7 27.♖fc1 ♖fa8
28.♖xc4 ♖xa5 29.♖ac1

29...♘xf4 30.♖xf4 ♗h6 31.♖fc4
♗xc1 32.♖xc1 ♗xf3 33.gxf3 ♖a1
34.♖xa1 ♖xa1+ 35.♔f2 ♔f7 36.f4
♖h1 37.♔g3 ♖b1 38.b4 ♖b2 39.h4
♖b3+ 40.♔f2 ♔e6 41.♔e2 ♔d7
42.♔d2 e6   0-1

| Ralf Kleeschaetzky | 2295 |
| Andras Adorjan | 2525 |

Balatonbereny 1996 (1)

Here is a true coffeehouse game.

**1.♘f3 c5 2.c4 g6 3.d4 cxd4 4.♘xd4
♗g7 5.e4 b6!?**

5...♘c6 is the common move.

**6.♘c3 ♗b7 7.♗e2 d6 8.♗e3 ♘f6
9.f3 0-0 10.0-0 ♘bd7 11.♖c1 ♖e8
12.♕d2 a6 13.♖fd1 ♖c8**

14.♘d5

14.b3!?.

14...e6 15.♘xf6+ ♘xf6 16.♘b3 d5

There we go. But in this case the manda-
tory push doesn't equalize right away.

17.c5 b5 18.♘a5 ♗a8 19.a4?!

Good was 19.e5 ♘d7 20.f4=; Black has
little air to breathe.

19...bxa4

Better seems to have been 19...dxe4!?
20.axb5 exf3 21.gxf3 ♕xd2 22.♗xd2
axb5 23.♗xb5 ♗xf3 24.♗xe8 ♘xe8∓
– the c5-pawn must fall.

20.♗xa6

Here, 20.c6!?± was very dangerous.

20...♖b8 21.e5 ♘h5 22.f4

Too many pieces are hanging for
22.g4 to be good: 22...♗xe5 23.gxh5
♖xb2-+.

22...d4

23.c6??

An 'unforced error' and a decisive one.
23.♗xd4 ♘xf4 24.c6 ♘d5 25.♘b7
♗xb7 26.♗xb7 ♕c7 27.♖e1 ♖xb7
28.cxb7 ♕xb7.
23.♕e1 ♖xb2 24.c6 (24.♗f1!? ♗xg2
25.♗xd4 ♖a2 26.♗xg2 ♘xf4 is
unclear) 24...♕b6 25.♗xd4 ♖xg2+
26.♔xg2 ♕xa6 27.♗e3 ♖c8. In both
cases Black has good compensation but
not much more.

**23...♕b6-+   24.♕xd4   ♕xa6
25.♕a7   ♕xa7   26.♗xa7   ♖bc8
27.g3**

The problem is that White cannot
maintain the centre: 27.♗e3 g5 28.g3
gxf4 29.gxf4 f6. He tries to make his
queenside majority count, but it's too
late.

**27...g5 28.♖d4 gxf4 29.gxf4 ♗h6
30.♖xa4 ♘xf4 31.♖cc4 ♘g6 32.b4**

Beautiful opening positions by both!

♘xe5 **33.b5** ♖ed8 **34.♗d4** ♘xc4
35.♖xc4 ♖xd4   **0-1**

Ivan Ivanisevic   2540
Andras Adorjan   2485
Szeged 1997

Benko

This game was played in the last round and brought me my first full point against the young Serbian champion.

**1.d4 ♘f6 2.c4 c5 3.d5 b5 4.cxb5
a6 5.♘c3 axb5 6.e4 b4 7.♘b5 d6
8.♗f4 ♘bd7 9.♘f3?!**

An unsound pawn sac, which was in fashion at that time.

9.♗d3 h6!? 10.h4 g6 11.♘f3 ♗g7∓.

9...♘xe4!? 10.♕e2

Less dangerous is 10.♗d3 f5 11.♗xe4 (11.0-0 g6 12.♖e1 ♗g7 13.♗xe4 fxe4 14.♖xe4 0-0∓ or 14.♗g5 ♘f6 15.♘d2 0-0∓) 11...fxe4 12.♘g5 ♘f6 13.0-0 g6 14.f3 ♗g7 (14...♕b6!? 15.a4 bxa3 16.♖xa3 ♖xa3 17.♘xa3 ♕b4∓) 15.fxe4 ♕b6 16.a4 bxa3 17.♖xa3 ♖xa3 18.♘xa3 0-0! 19.♘c4 ♕b4 20.♕c2

20...♘g4 (20...♘xd5! 21.exd5 ♖xf4 22.♖xf4 ♕e1+ 23.♖f1 ♗d4+–+) 21.g3 ♗d4+ 22.♔h1 ♗a6 23.b3 ♖b8 (23...♘e3!–+) 24.♕e2 h5 25.e5 dxe5 (25...♕xb3 26.♕e4 ♘f2+! 27.♖xf2 ♕b1+–+) 26.♕e4 ♖b6 ½-½, Jozsef Dobos-Adorjan, Balatonbereny 1996. As you see, I missed several easy wins in that game. After 27.♘xb6 ♕xb6 28.♘e6 ♔h7 29.♘g5+ ♔g7 30.♘e6+ ♔h7 the position is equal.

10...f5!

10...♘df6 loses to 11.♘g5 ♗f5 12.f3 ♘xd5 13.♘xe4 ♗xe4 14.♕xe4 e6 15.♗c4 ♘xf4 16.♕xf4 ♗e7 17.♖d1 0-0 18.♘xd6 ♗g5 19.♕g4 ♕f6 20.♘e4 ♕e5 21.♔xg5 1-0 T.Metz-Reimer, Bellheim 1994.

11.♘g5 ♘df6 12.f3 ♘xd5

Definitely not 12...♘xg5?? 13.♘xd6++–.

13.♘xe4!

13.fxe4? ♘xf4 14.♕f3 e5 15.exf5 ♖b8 16.♘e4 (16.♕c6+ ♕d7 17.♘c7+ ♔e7 18.♘d5+ ♘xd5 19.♕xd5 ♕xf5 20.♖d1 ♖b6 21.♘e4 ♕e6–+) 16...♗xf5∓.

13...♘xf4

13...fxe4 14.♕xe4 is not clear.

14.♘bxd6+?!

14.♘exd6+ is better but not good enough: 14...♔d7 15.♕e5 (15.♘f7 ♘xe2 16.♘xd8 ♘d4 17.♘f7 ♘c2+ 18.♔f2 ♘xa1 19.♗c4 e6 (19...♗a6∓) 20.♘xh8 ♘c2 21.♘f7 (21.♗xe6+ ♔c6) 21...♔e7∓) 15...exd6! and now:

A) 16.♕xf4 ♕e7+ 17.♔f2 ♕f6∓;

B) 16.0-0-0 and now:

B1) 16...♘g6? 17.♖xd6+!+−;

B2) 16...♕g5 17.♔b1 with a white initiative;

B3) 16...♕f6 17.♕xc5 (17.♕xf4? ♖xa2−+) 17...♘e6! (17...d5? 18.♕c7+ ♔e8 19.♖e1+! ♗e7 20.♘d6+ ♔f8 21.♕d8+!+−) 18.♖xd6+ ♗xd6 19.♕xd6+ ♔e8 20.♕c6+ ♔e7 21.♕xa8 ♕e5∓;

B4) 16...♔c6! Bravo! 17.♕xf4 ♖xa2 18.♔b1 ♖a5 19.♕c4 ♔b6−+.

14...exd6 15.♘xd6+ ♔d7 16.♕b5+ ♔e6

17.♗c4+?!

This doesn't work. The black king is ultra-exposed, but there are always pieces to help him out:

A) 17.♘xc8 ♖xc8 18.♕c4+ ♔e5! 19.♖d1 ♕c7 20.g3 ♘g6−+;

B) 17.♕c4+ ♘d5! (17...♔f6 18.♕f7+ ♔g5 19.h4+ ♔h6 20.g4! g6 21.g5+ ♔h5 22.♘e8!±) 18.♘xc8 ♖xc8 19.0-0-0 ♖c6 20.g4 ♖d6∓.

17...♔f6−+ 18.♘e8+ ♔g6 19.♖d1 ♕e7+ 20.♔f2 ♗e6 21.♗xe6 ♖xe8 22.♗xf5+ ♔xf5 23.♖he1 ♘e2 0-1

It was all home-made: I had prepared the variation together with Peter Leko, who was my pupil at the time.

Jozsef Boer
Andras Adorjan
Budapest rapid 1998

This game, also played in the Bela Papp Memorial, was not bad. But the analyses beginning with 9...♘d7 are really sparkling.

1.d4 ♘f6 2.c4 g6 3.♘c3 d5 4.♘f3 ♗g7 5.♕b3 dxc4 6.♕xc4 0-0 7.♗f4 ♘a6 8.e4 c5 9.d5?!

If 9.dxc5 ♘d7!? is an interesting idea.

analysis diagram

This move has never been played before or since!

A) 10.c6 bxc6 11.♕xc6? (11.♖d1 ♘ac5) 11...♘b4! 12.♕a4 (12.♕xa8 ♘c2+ 13.♔d1 ♘b6+ 14.♔xc2 ♘xa8∓) 12...♘d3+!! 13.♗xd3 ♘c5−+ 14.♗c7 ♘xd3+ 15.♔e2 ♘xb2;

B) 10.b4 is the test. Now:

B1) 10...♘dxc5! was my original intention: 11.♖d1 ♗e6 12.♘d5 ♘d7 (12...♘a4 13.♕c2 ♘b2 14.♖d2 (14.♘f6+ ♗xf6 15.♖xd8 ♖fxd8 16.♗xa6 bxa6 17.0-0 ♖ac8 18.♕b1 ♗c4 19.♗e5 ♗xf1 20.♕xb2 ♗e2 21.h3 ♖d1+ 22.♔h2 ♗xf3 23.♗xf6 exf6 24.gxf3 ♖c6∓) 14...♖c8 15.♕b1 ♗xd5 16.♖xd5 ♕b6 17.♗xa6 ♕xa6 18.e5 ♘a4∓) 13.♕b5 ♘b6 14.♘f6+

analysis diagram

14...exf6! This is the big finesse! 15.♖xd8 ♖fxd8 16.♕a5 ♘c4 (16...f5 17.♗xa6 bxa6

18.0-0 fxe4 19.♘d2=/∓) 17.♗xc4 ♗xc4 (keeping the white king in the centre and thus always retaining attacking chances) 18.♘d2 ♗d3 19.f3 f5 20.♔f2 ♗c3 21.♗g5 ♗xb4 22.♕xd8+ (a good counterchance for White, but the bishops remain strong) 22...♖xd8 23.♗xd8 ♘c5 24.♘b1 (24.♘b3 fxe4 25.♗e7 b6 26.♘xc5 bxc5 27.fxe4 ♗xe4 28.♖c1 ♗d5 29.♗xc5 ♗xc5+ 30.♖xc5 ♗xa2 31.♖a5=) 24...♘e6 25.♗f6 fxe4 26.fxe4 ♗xe4 27.♖d1 ♗c5+ 28.♔g3 ♔f8 with roughly equal chances;

B2) 10...♘b6!? was found later and is also playable:

B21) 11.cxb6 loses material after 11...♗e6, while Black keeps the initiative as well: 12.♘d5 ♗xa1 13.bxa7 ♖xd5 14.exd5 ♖c8 15.♕e4 (15.a8♕ ♖xc4 16.♕xd8 ♖e4+−+) 15...♘c3+ 16.♘d2 ♘xb4 17.♗c4 ♕a5;

B22) 11.♕b3 ♗e6 12.♕a3 ♘c4 13.♗xc4 ♗xc4 14.♗e5 (14.♘e5 ♗xe5 15.♗xe5 ♕d7 16.♖d1 ♕g4 17.♗g3 ♖fd8 18.f3 ♖xd1+ 19.♔xd1 ♕g5 20.♔c2 h5 with an attack for Black) 14...♗xe5 (14...♘h6 15.b5) 15.♘xe5 ♕d4 16.♘f3 ♕d7 17.b5 ♗xb5 18.♖d1 ♕e8 19.♕b3 ♗c6 and now 20.♕a3 or 20.♕c4 ♖c8 offers mutual chances: White is finally able to castle, but his c5-pawn is weak.

The other move for Black after 9.dxc5 is 9...♗e6 10.♕b5 ♗d7 11.♕xb7 ♘xc5 with compensation.

9...e6 10.♖d1

The question is whether White can maintain the pawn after 10.d6:

A) 10...♘h5 11.e5 and now:

A1) 11...♗b4!? 12.0-0-0 (12.♗g5 f6 13.exf6 ♘xf6 14.0-0-0 ♘bd5 unclear) 12...b5 13.♕e4 (13.♕xc5?! ♘xa2+ 14.♘xa2 ♘xf4 15.♘b4 ♗b7 16.♔b1 ♗e4+ 17.♗d3 ♖c8 18.♕e3 ♘xd3 19.♘xd3 ♗d5∓) 13...♗b7 14.♕xb7 ♘xf4 15.♗xb5 ♘fd5 (worse is 15...♕a5 16.a3±) 16.♘xd5 ♘xd5 17.♗c4 ♖b8 18.♕xa7 ♘b6 with attack;

A2) 11...♘xf4 12.♕xf4 ♘b4 13.0-0-0 f6 and Black will blast open the centre, with highly unclear consequences.

B) A little better seems to be the immediate 10...♘b4! 11.♕b3 (11.♘b5 e5!; 11.e5!? ♘c2+ 12.♔d2 ♘xa1 13.exf6 ♗xf6 14.♕xc5 ♗d7 15.♕c7 unclear) 11...♘h5 12.♗e3 ♕xd6 13.♖d1 ♕c7 14.a3 ♘c6 15.♗xc5 ♖d8 16.♖xd8+ ♘xd8 17.♗e3 ♗d7 18.♗e2 ♘f4 19.♗xf4 ♕xf4 20.0-0 ♖c8 21.g3 ♕c7 22.♖d1 a6 and with his bishop pair and pressure on the c-file Black holds the trumps.

10...exd5 11.exd5 ♖e8+ 12.♗e2 ♗d7?!

12...♗f5!? 13.d6 ♘e4 wins the d-pawn, but White has compensation after 14.d7 ♖e7 15.0-0 ♘xc3 16.bxc3 ♖xd7 17.♘e5 ♗xe5 18.♗xe5.

13.0-0?

Passing the initiative to Black because White's pieces are unfortunately placed. Necessary was 13.♗e5! ♕b6 14.0-0 ♖ad8 15.♖fe1=.

13...b5! 14.♕d3

14.♕b3 c4 15.♕c2 (15.♕a3 ♕b6−+) 15...b4 16.♘b1 ♖c8∓; 14.♘xb5 ♖e4 is the same trick that also decided the playoff in the 2015 Qatar Open between Yu Yangyi and Carlsen.

14...c4

Just winning.

15.♕b1

15.♕c2 b4 (15...♗f5!?) 16.♘b1 and now 16...♖c8 is best, since here 16...b3!? 17.♕xc4 ♖e4 fails to 18.♖d4 bxa2 19.♘c3.

15...b4−+ 16.♗xc4 ♗f5 17.♕c1

Or 17.♗d3 ♗xd3 18.♕xd3 ♘c5 19.♕b5 bxc3 20.♕xc5 ♘e4 – everything with tempo! Black wins.

17...bxc3 18.♗xa6 ♕b6 19.♗d3 cxb2 20.♕b1 ♘xd5 21.♗xf5 ♘c3 22.♕c2 gxf5 23.♘e5 ♘xd1 24.♕xf5 ♖xe5 25.♗xe5 b1♕   0-1

Sandor Sulyok 2305
Andras Adorjan 2490
Pecs 1998

The first FIDE-rated Rainbow chess game in Hungary!

1.d4 c5 2.e3

2.d5; uncommon and interesting would be 2.dxc5!? e6 3.♘c3 ♗xc5 4.♘e4.

2...cxd4 3.exd4 ♘f6 4.♘f3 d5 5.♘e5!?

After 5.c4 we could have gone 'back' to a famous line in the Panov Caro-Kann: 5...♘c6 6.♘c3 ♗g4 7.cxd5 ♘xd5 8.♕b3 ♗xf3 9.gxf3 e6 10.♕xb7 ♘xd4 11.♗b5+ ♘xb5 12.♕c6+ ♔e7 13.♕xb5 ♕d7 14.♘xd5+ ♕xd5 with chances for both sides.

5...g6 6.♘d2 ♗g7 7.♗b5+

7.♗d3 0-0 8.c3 ♘c6 9.♘df3 ♘xe5 10.♘xe5 ♘d7 11.♘xd7 ♗xd7 12.0-0= would be solid and not very exciting. But the simplification after the text favours Black.

7...♘bd7 8.♘xd7 ♗xd7 9.♕e2 0-0 10.0-0

10.♗d3 ♖e8 11.0-0 ♕c7∓; 10.♗xd7 ♘xd7 11.♘f3 ♖e8 12.0-0 e5!? 13.dxe5 ♘xe5 14.c3 ♘c4∓.

10...♗g4! 11.f3 ♗f5 12.♘b3 ♕b6 13.♗d3 ♗xd3 14.♕xd3

14...e5!

More forceful than 14...♖fe8 15.♗e3 ♘d7∓.

15.♗e3 e4 16.♕d2

After 16.fxe4 ♘xe4 17.♘c5 ♖fe8 Black has pressure.

16...♖fe8 17.♘c5 ♗e7 18.♖ae1?

18.b3 ♖ae8.

18...exf3 19.gxf3 ♕xb2 20.♖b1 ♕xa2 21.♖a1

21.♘xb7 ♖b8 22.♖a1 ♕c4 23.♘a5 ♕c8 is also very bad for White.

21...♕c4 22.♖fb1

22...♖xe3! *Brilliant Finish*

Finishing in style.

23.♕xe3 ♘g4 24.♕d3 ♗xd4+ 25.♔f1 ♘e3+   0-1

Robert Hübner *English* 2560
Andras Adorjan *Opening* 2490
Frankfurt rapid 1998

This game was played in a double-round 8-player rapid tournament held as a tribute to Hübner. All of his former opponents in Candidates matches got invited. Smyslov could not play, however, because of his fatal illness.

1.c4 c5 2.♘f3 g6 3.d4 ♗g7 4.d5

4.e4 ♕b6!? with counterchances.

4...b5 5.e4!?

5.cxb5 a6 6.e4 axb5 7.e5 ♗a6 looks like a very modern Benko Gambit. The white centre is not necessarily strong.

5...♘f6 6.e5 ♘g4 7.♕e2 d6 8.exd6

8.e6 fxe6 9.dxe6 ♗b7 10.♘g5 ♕a5+ 11.♘d2 ♘e5 and the pawn on e6 does not achieve much; 8.♗f4 0-0 9.h3

♘xe5 10.♘xe5 dxe5 11.♗xe5 ♗xe5
12.♕xe5 ♘d7∓.

8...♕xd6 9.♘c3

9.h3 ♘e5 10.♘a3 ♗xf3+ 11.♕xf3 a6
12.cxb5 ♗b7 13.♗c4 ♘d7 with free
play for the pawn.

9...bxc4 10.♗g5 ♘a6

An interesting option was 10...♗xc3+!?
11.bxc3 ♘d7 12.♖d1 f6∓.

11.♕xc4 0-0

11...♘e5 12.♘xe5 ♕xe5+ 13.♗e3 0-0=/∓.

A very original position has arisen.

12.♗e2 ♘b4 13.0-0 ♘e5?

The d5-pawn wasn't poisoned here,
so 13...♗xc3! 14.bxc3 (14.♕xc3
♘xd5 15.♕c4 ♗e6 16.♖ad1 ♖ad8∓)
14...♘xd5 looks good, when 15.♖fd1
♗e6 16.h3 ♘gf6 17.♕h4 ♕b6 18.♗d2
gives White some compensation.

14.♕h4 ♖e8 15.♖ad1 ♗a6?!

Better was 15...♗f5.

16.♘xe5 ♗xe5 17.♗xa6 ♕xa6?

17...♘xa6 18.♘e4±.

18.♗xe7 ♘d3 19.♘e4

Good enough. But cleverer was 19.d6
♘xb2 20.d7 ♗xc3 21.dxe8♕+ ♖xe8
22.♖c1±.

19...♘xb2 20.♖b1 ♘c4 21.♖b3

21.d6 ♘xd6 22.♘f6+ ♗xf6 23.♕xf6
♖xe7 24.♕xe7 ♘f5 25.♕xc5 ♕xa2
26.♖a1+−.

With little time on the clock (the time
limit was 25 minutes), now a parade of
errors starts.

21...♕xa2?

21...♖ac8 22.d6+−.

22.♖h3?

22.♘f6+ ♗xf6 23.♗xf6 h5 24.♕xc4+−.

22...h5 23.♕g5??

23.d6 ♘d2 24.♘f6+ ♗xf6 25.♕xf6
♕c2 26.♖e1±.

23...♕e2 24.♖h4

24...♘d2!!

Whoops! Black is very much OK!
24...♗d4 25.h3 ♘d2 26.♕xd2 ♕xd2
27.♘xd2 ♖xe7 28.♘b3 ♗e5 29.♘xc5
♖d8∓.

25.♘xd2

25.♕xd2 ♕xd2 26.♘xd2 ♖xe7∓.

25...♖xe7 26.♘f3 ♖ae8 27.♕c1

27.♖xh5 fails to 27...♘d4! (threatening
28...♕xf2+) 28.♕c1 (28.♘xd4?
♕xf1+−+) 28...♗b2 29.♕g5 ♖e5
30.♘xe5 ♖xe5 31.♕d8+ ♖e8 and the
♖h5 cannot be saved.

27...♗f6 28.♖c4?

28.♖a4∓.

28...♗b2 29.♕c2

29.♕f4 ♖e4 30.♖xe4 ♕xe4 31.♕d2
♖b8∓.

29...♕xc2 30.♖xc2

30...♗d4?

30...♗a3! was just winning.

31.♖d1??

The rook ending is a draw after 31.♘xd4 cxd4 32.♖d2 a5! 33.d6 (33.♖xd4? ♖e4 34.♖xe4 ♖xe4 35.♖d1 ♔f8 36.f3 ♖b4 37.d6 ♔e8 38.♖e1+ ♔d7 39.♖e7+ ♔xd6 40.♖xf7 ♔c5∓) 33...♖a7 34.♖xd4 a4 35.♖a1 a3 36.d7 ♖d8 37.h4=.

31...♖d8 32.♘xd4 ♖xd5–+ 33.♔f1 cxd4 34.♖cd2 ♖ed7 35.♔e2 a5 36.♖a1 d3+ 37.♔f3 ♖e7 38.♖a3 ♖f5+ 39.♔g3 ♖e2 40.♖xe2

Or 40.♖axd3 ♖fxf2.

40...dxe2 41.♖e3 a4 42.♖xe2 ♖a5

White plays on for too long from here on.

43.♔f4 a3 44.♖a2 ♔g7 45.♔e4 ♔f6 46.♔d4 ♔f5 47.♔c4 ♖a8 48.♔d4 ♔f4 49.♔d3 h4 50.h3 f5 51.♔c2 g5 52.♔b1 g4 53.♖c2 ♖b8+ 54.♔a1 ♖b2 55.♖c4+ ♔g5 56.f4+ ♔f6 57.♖c6+ ♔e7 58.hxg4 fxg4 59.♖h6 ♖xg2 60.♖xh4 ♔f6 61.♖h5 ♖f2 0-1

Lajos Portisch	2600
Andras Adorjan	2490

Frankfurt rapid 1998

'Your problem is not that you make mistakes', I said good-willingly to Lajos. 'It's that you are afraid of the time scramble from the very beginning!' 'Come on', he replied. 'And anyway there is still one more round today.' 'And who do you play?' 'You!', he said.

1.d4 ♘f6 2.c4 g6 3.♘c3 d5 4.♘f3 ♗g7 5.♗f4 0-0 6.e3 c5 7.dxc5 ♕a5 8.♖c1 ♖d8

Better is 8...dxc4 9.♗xc4 ♕xc5 10.♗b3 ♘c6 11.0-0 ♕a5=.

9.♕a4

The famous 'Anti-Timman' Grünfeld, with which several Dutch players made trouble for the Dutch GM for some time.

9...♕xa4

9...♕xc5 may be a good practical chance, starting wild complications. Here are some sample lines: 10.b4 ♕c6 11.b5 (11.♕a3 ♗f5 12.cxd5 ♘xd5 13.♘xd5 ♕xd5 14.♗c4 ♕d7 15.0-0± (15.b5±) 15...a6 16.♗c7) 11...♕c5 12.♕b3 a5 (12...♗g4 13.♘a4 ♕c8 14.♗e2=) 13.a3!±. With this move White keeps control and stands better. After 13.♘a4 ♕b4+ 14.♕xb4 axb4 15.♘b6 ♖xa2 16.♗xb8 b3, we get some sharp skirmishes leading to an equal ending after 17.♘d4 b2 18.♖b1 ♖a1 19.♗d3 dxc4 20.♘xc4 ♗e6 21.♘xe6 fxe6 22.♘xb2 ♖xb1+ 23.♗xb1 ♖xb8.

10.♘xa4 ♘c6

11.♘c3?

11.♘e5! was the only good move, for example:

A) 11...♗e6 12.♘xc6 bxc6 13.♗e5 dxc4 (13...♖d7 14.cxd5 ♘xd5 15.♗xg7 ♔xg7 16.a3±) 14.♗xc4 ♗xc4 15.♖xc4 ♖d5 16.♗xf6 ♗xf6 17.♔e2 ♖ad8 18.♖c2 and Black's compensation for the pawn is gone;

B) More tricky is 11...♘a5, but White stays on top after 12.b4 ♘xc4 (12...♘e4 13.cxd5 g5 14.♘xf7 ♔xf7 15.♗c7 ♖xd5 16.bxa5 ♗e6 17.a6) 13.♘xc4 dxc4 14.♗c7 (14.♗xc4 ♘d5 with compensation) 14...♖d7 15.♗a5=;

C) Quite solid is 11...♘xe5 12.♗xe5 ♗d7 13.♘c3 ♗c6 14.♗xf6 (less good is 14.cxd5 ♘xd5 15.♗xg7 ♔xg7 16.♘xd5 ♗xd5 17.a3 a5 with good counterplay along the d-file) 14...♗xf6 15.♘xd5 ♗xd5 16.cxd5 ♖xd5 17.♗c4 ♖g5 18.♖c2. White looks a bit better here, but Black can keep him busy, e.g.: 18...♖c8 19.b4 ♖xg2 20.♗d5 ♖g4 21.♗xb7 ♖c7 22.c6 ♖xb4 23.0-0 ♗e5;

D) 11...♗d7 12.♘xd7 ♖xd7 13.cxd5 ♘xd5 14.♗g3 ♖ad8 15.♖d1 and as soon as White develops his kingside, he will be slightly better;

E) 11...♘h5 is dubious as Black's pieces start to look awkward after 12.♘xc6 bxc6 13.♗c7 ♖d7 14.♗a5 d4 15.g4 ♘f6 16.g5 (16.♗g2!? ♘xg4 17.♗xc6 ♖b8 18.♔e2±) 16...♘g4 17.♗h3 ♖b7 18.exd4±.

11...♘e4 12.♗e2

12.♘b5 doesn't work. Black is fine after 12...♗e6 13.♘fd4 ♘xd4 14.♘xd4 ♘xc5∓. The exchanges after 12.cxd5 play into Black's hands: 12...♗xc3+ 13.bxc3 ♖xd5 14.c4 ♖xc5 15.♘d4 e5 16.♘xc6 exf4 17.♗d3 bxc6 18.♗xe4 fxe3 19.fxe3 ♗e6 and White has too many weak pawns. 12.♘xd5 ♗xb2 13.♖d1 ♗g4 is also fine for Black, who is better developed.

12...♗xc3+!

Oh YES! Now BLACK is BETTER!

13.bxc3 dxc4 14.♗xc4 ♘xc5

Black controls the open file and has a better structure.

15.0-0

15.♘d4 ♗d7∓; 15.♗c7 ♘d3+ 16.♗xd3 ♖xd3 17.♔e2 ♖d7 18.♗g3 b6 19.♖hd1 ♗a6+ 20.♔e1 ♖ad8∓.

15...♗e6 16.♗xe6 ♘xe6 17.♗g3 ♖ac8 18.♘d4 ♘c5

18...♘a5!?∓.

19.♖fd1 f6 20.f3 ♔f7 21.♗f2?

21.e4 was a better defence.

21...♘e5 22.♖b1 a6 23.e4 b5

I could have gone for the c3-pawn right away: 23...♘a4! 24.♘e2 (24.♖xb7 ♘xc3

25.♖d2 and now the back-rank trick 25...♘xe4!–+) 24...♖xd1+ 25.♖xd1 ♘xc3 26.♘xc3 ♖xc3∓/–+.

24.♘e2 ♘a4 25.♗d4 ♘c4–+

Game (practically) over.

26.h4 h5?!

Quite convincing was 26...e5 27.♗f2 (27.♗a7 ♘d2–+) 27...♘d2 28.♖a1 ♘b2–+.

27.♔f2 e5?!

27...♘ab2 28.♖g1 e5–+.

28.♗a7 ♘d2

28...♘ab2–+.

29.♖a1 ♘xc3?

In time-trouble I keep 'forgetting' the move 29...♘b2, when a knight finally gets to the d3-square after circling around it for the entire game.

30.♘xc3 ♖xc3

31.♗b6??

We both failed to see the backward king move with which White could exploit the pin on the ♘d2: 31.♗e3 ♖c2 32.♔e1! (or first 31.♔e1 ♖c2 32.♗e3) 32...♘c4 33.♖xd8 ♘xe3. Black should still be winning here, but it's a lot more difficult. For example: 34.g3 ♖g2 35.♖c1 ♖g1+ (35...♘c4 36.♖d7+ ♔e6 37.♖cd1 ♖xg3 38.♔f2 ♖h3 39.♖c7 ♖xh4 40.♔g3 ♖f4 41.♖c6+ ♔e7 42.♖c7+=) 36.♔d2 ♘c4+ 37.♔c2 ♖g2+ 38.♔c3 ♖xg3.

31...♖d7??

Losing material. Instead, 31...♖d6, after which the knight can retreat to c4, was winning.

32.♗a5 ♖c2 33.♔e1 ♘xf3+ 34.gxf3 ♖xd1+ 35.♔xd1

35.♖xd1 ♖xa2∓.

35...♖f2

Luckily the compensation is still good. Very good.

36.♗e1

36.♖c1=.

36...♖xf3 37.♖c1 ♖d3+

Better was 37...g5!.

38.♔e2 ♖a3 39.♖c7+ ♔e6 40.♖c6+ ♔f7 41.♖c2?

It's hard to play for White without much time. 41.♖c7+ ♔e8 42.♖c6 ♖xa2+ 43.♔d3 would have drawn.

41...g5!∓ 42.hxg5 fxg5 43.♗b4

43.♗d2 g4.

43...♖a4 44.♖c7+ ♔e6 45.♗d2 ♖xe4+ 46.♔f3 ♖a4 47.♗xg5 ♖xa2 48.♖h7 b4 49.♔e4 b3 50.♖h6+ ♔d7 51.♖b6 b2 52.♗f6 h4!

53.♗xe5

53.♗xh4 ♖a4+ 54.♔f5 (54.♔xe5 ♖a5+ 55.♔d4 ♖b5−+) 54...♖xh4 55.♖xb2 a5 56.♔xe5 ♔c6 wins because the white king is cut off.

53...h3 54.♗b8

54.♔f5 a5 55.♖d6+ ♔c8 56.♖b6 ♔d7 and it's a draw.

54...a5 55.♔d3??

He could have drawn with 55.♗e5 ♖a4+ 56.♔d3 or the more active 55.♔d5 ♔e7 56.♗e5 a4 (56...♔f7 57.♖f6+ ♔g8 58.♖b6) 57.♖b7+ ♔d8 58.♔e6 b1♕ 59.♖xb1 ♖c2=.

55...a4−+ 56.♗d6 ♖a1 57.♖xb2 ♔xd6 58.♔c4 ♖h1 59.♖d2+ ♔c6

White resigned.

One of my rare victories over Lajos Portisch.

Ferenc Portisch
Andras Adorjan
Hungary tt 1999

IM Ferenc Portisch (the junior brother of 'Lajos the Great') had a plus score against me ever since the 1966 Hungarian championship, and was never beaten by me. Until this very last game we played...

1.d4 ♘f6 2.c4 c5 3.d5 a6!? 4.♘c3

4.♘f3; 4.a4 e6 (4...d6) 5.♘c3 exd5 6.cxd5 d6 leads to a Benoni (or a Snake Benoni with 6...♗d6!?).

4...b5!? 5.cxb5 axb5 6.♘xb5 d6 7.f3

The simple 7.♘c3 is the most common move here.

7...♕a5+

7...e6!? 8.♘c3 exd5 9.♘xd5.

8.♘c3 ♗a6 9.e4 ♗xf1 10.♔xf1 g6 11.♘ge2 ♗g7 12.g3 0-0 13.♔g2 ♘bd7 14.♖b1 ♘e5 15.b3 ♘e8 16.♗d2

Or 16.♗g5 f5 17.♖f1 h6.

Objectively White is better. He has an extra pawn too. But there is compensation, in the form of activity for Black, which matters a lot in complicated positions like this.

16...♘c7 17.a4 ♕a6 18.b4?!
18.♘f4 ♖fb8 19.♕e2=.
18...cxb4 19.♖xb4 f5 20.♘f4 g5!?
Escape forward!
21.♘h5
21.♘b5? would lose to 21...♘xb5
22.axb5 ♕a2.
21...g4 22.f4
He should not have been afraid and
have played 22.fxg4! fxg4 23.♗f4,
closing the f-file. On ...♘f3 White then
has h2-h3.
22...♘f3 23.♘xg7 ♔xg7

24.♖f1?
A mistake.
24.♗e3 ♖fb8 gave Black good
compensation, but 24.♕c2!± gave an
edge while 24.h3 ♖ab8 25.♖xb8 ♖xb8
26.hxg4 fxg4 27.♘e2 ♕c4 28.♗c3+
♔g8 29.♕c2 ♖b4 30.e5 ♕e4 31.♕xe4
♖xe4 32.♔f2 ♘xd5 33.exd6 exd6
34.a5 ♖c4 35.♖c1 ♖a4 36.♖d1 was
even.

24...♖ab8 25.♘b5 ♘xb5 26.axb5
♖xb5 27.♗c3+ ♔g8 28.♕e2 ♖a5
29.♕xa6 ♖xa6 30.♖b7??
Zeitnot!
After 30.exf5 ♖a3∓ (not 30...♖xf5
31.h3 h5 32.♖b7=) Black still has the
upper hand; but White could have
forced an equal ending with 30.h3 ♖c8
31.hxg4 fxg4 32.♖b3 ♖a4 and now the
exchange sac 33.♖xf3.

30...♖c8–+ 31.♗b2
31.♗b4 fxe4 32.♖xe7 ♖c4 is also game
over.
31...♘d2
White resigned because of 32.♖c1 ♖xc1
33.♗xc1 ♘xe4 34.♗b2 ♔f7 and with
the weak d5-pawn there is no chance
of survival.
This first ever victory of mine over
Ferenc, an unusual Benko Gambit but
with many Benko Gambit features, did
not have so much beauty, but showed
two feeble people putting up a decent
fight.

Chapter 11
All Kinds of Reflections

In 1995 I published an essay titled **'BLACK IS OK** – or the Presumption of Innocence in the Game of Chess' in some chess magazines and on some websites. In it I said: 'In criminal law, the suspect is entitled to the presumption of innocence until it is proved beyond reasonable doubt that he is guilty. In chess I presume – in the spirit of the presumption of innocence – that the initial position is equal. It is White who has to prove that he can get an advantage. Naturally, starting the game should not be mistaken for taking the initiative!

But come on, you trouble-maker! It has been known for centuries that in the initial position, White, thanks to his right to make the first move, has an advantage. That is their answer. And if incidentally we really start a debate there is always their favourite bye-bye word: 'Statistics'. And sometimes they add 'the figures don't lie'. Now let's stop here. True, the overall statistics show a plus for White almost every time, in any kind of tournament. But you can find a few splendid exceptions in this book, produced by messrs Gelfand and Nakamura, and by the participants of the Tal Memorial tournament in 2013. Plus, somewhat earlier, Hastings 1895. And if you don't hate facts you can have a look at some of the official FIDE lists of the first 100 men and 50 women. Believe your own eyes: with the exception of six players, every one of them has a plus with black.

Ever since the birth of 'BLACK is OK – or the Presumption of the Innocence in the Game of Chess' I received many reflections, which I answered and published whenever I had the opportunity. Many of them can be found in my books *BLACK is still OK* (2004) and *BLACK is OK forever!* (2005), both with Batsford. Many pros and cons, prosaic and sometimes also stylistically brilliant, from all over the world. Some of these reflections are quite similar to each other, others are very different.

The two key questions asked were the following:
1. *What is the outcome of a perfect game?*
2. *Subjective feelings and experiences about playing with Black or White.*

Below are excerpts from the letters of every living soul who answered my questions. Of course there were many other views, for example reviews in New In Chess, and I have noticed that the phrase 'BLACK IS OK' became as common as any other evaluation in analyses, like $\pm$, $=$, $-+$ etc. Like 'Catch 22'. Now there is also proof that I could have become the Hungarian Salvador Dali – if I had been discovered in time. But unfortunately the drawing given on the previous page is the only one I'm able to make. It is a kind of ad. The Hungarian word 'Elötte' means 'Before', 'Utána' means 'After'. It's just a fun thing. I think I like to promise mistakes to my readers. This sketch can now be found in many places in the world: I used to give it together with my autograph.

The sketches are followed by a collection of the most interesting fragments from the many letters and comments I received and/or found about my thesis BLACK IS OK!. I'm sure you will find a lot of wisdom in them!

In my opinion, at least two-thirds of all 'tested' openings give White an apparent advantage. The root of the problem is that very few people know which are the openings where Black is really OK. Those who find these lines have nothing to fear, as **Black is indeed OK**, but only in these variations! – *Lajos PORTISCH (GM, 1994)*

I worked mostly on my repertoire with black, and allotted only the time I had left to my white games, although the elaboration of a good repertoire for White is more time-consuming, as one is forced to prepare for a wide range of openings, whereas for Black it is satisfactory to have one or two openings 'in stock'. In addition to that, when people play with white they always try to prove that White is better, and they often go beyond the limit of reasonable risk. Then Black can take over the initiative, and he is stronger because he is better prepared! And I still hold that, from a theoretical point of view, the tasks of White and Black in chess are different: White has to strive **for a win**, Black – **for a draw!** – *Evgeny SVESHNIKOV (GM, 1994)*

The prevalent style of play for Black today is to seek dynamic, unbalanced positions with active counterplay, rather than merely trying to equalize. – *Lucina GHINEA (2014)*

The fascinating thing is that although the greatest modern players have rejected the classical approach set out by such champions of the 19th and early 20th century as Steinitz and Capablanca, who asserted that Black should try to equalise rather than fight for an advantage, in master chess overall the modern counter-attacking defences give no better results for Black than the dour forward-defensive block favoured by the old school (...) The reason why some of us prefer to play with the black pieces is because we prefer counter-attack to attack. We don't want to charge at our opponents like a jousting knight, but instead feel more comfortable digging a hole, covering it, and then lying in wait for the enemy to fall in. – *Dominic LAWSON (2010)*

From the early days of the game, strong players overwhelmingly believed that the first player to move had some advantage, though it wasn't clear how big this advantage was. Most importantly, it was realized this advantage wasn't enough to ruin the game: Black won plenty of games even at the highest levels, a fact that remains true to this day. – *Edward SCIMIA (About.com Guide)*

Both chess composers and tournament players know the concept of *zugzwang*. This is a position where the side to play has no 'healthy' moves, and any possible move makes his position worse. There may be players who feel awkward if they have to play first because they find it difficult to choose from numerous possibilities, putting their cards on the table in a way. Perhaps they feel that they make life easier for Black, as the second player's choice is much more limited. When he has Black, the same person may await with malicious joy how White solves this unpleasant problem (or considered unpleasant by him at least!). – *Arpad FÖLDEÁK (chess historian, 1995, Hungarian chess monthly 'Sakkélet')*

It does certainly appear that White has a slight advantage over Black. The advantage is so small, however, that it could be easily attributed to psychology alone. Unless you are an expert player, the first-move advantage can generally be ignored. – *Mark BEL-JAARS (http://EzineArticles.com/2594764)*

Chess games are not linear and do not follow a uniform pace throughout the game. There are many tempos lost and gained by both sides in the course of a game. The pace ebbs and flows; the advantage swings back and forth. As the game changes its character, the importance of the first move may have long lost much of its relevance to the position. In fact, Black has as much right to determine the character of the game (...) Who moves (or strikes) first is not as important as much as whether the player moving second has adequate countermeasures, or even evasive techniques. That is what makes chess so intriguing and, most of all, a fair game. – *Baaim* SHABAZZ, *Ph.D.* (2008, *The Chess Drum's 65th Square*)

I've only recently begun devoting a lot of my time to chess and decided two weeks ago to almost completely study black openings and defensive games, since then I've won far more games than I have lost. I think the reason is that when your playing White, **Black is usually happy to accept a draw**. The other reason I can think of is that most players don't expect Black to go on the attack so they overlook attacking variations in favour of defensive ones, this has the effect of disconcerting them when they can't find an answer and they lose the initiative even when in a better position. – *Anne CAZ* (noir_lord@yahoo.com)

I suspect that a lot of the advantage White holds is psychological at various levels, as you suggest. Somehow the game is always viewed in terms of White's moves, rather than Black's. Typically, working through a game *one tends to sit looking at the board from White's side* (...) I'm suggesting that assuming White and Black both play well the result will be a draw. Consequently, the first person to make a mistake should lose (and, of course, they should be the last person to make a mistake as well!). In that instance it seems to me that White is always one step closer to making a mistake than Black is; the fact that Black can achieve the quickest mate seems fair testimony in this regard. – *Ian ASH* (ian@dchip.com)

I also worked with **Morozevich**, who had amazing results with black. For two reasons: he worked on his Black openings a lot more than on White. His opponents often over-pressed in the opening since they felt obliged to get an edge. – *Alex BABURIN* (ababurin@iol.ie)

I have formed the view that one reason why White has an advantage is due to the accepted printing standard for chess diagrams, which are ALWAYS published from White's side of the board. I think this causes many players to develop a much better 'FEEL' for White positions. – *David CHRISTIAN*

I am much better with black, and prefer it to White. With white I am under pressure not to let the advantage slip and constantly over-play (...) I have always been reluctant to throw the first punch, I am a counter-puncher, and I much prefer playing Black. It is in man's nature to defend his territory, not to conquer others! Or at least it should be. – *Eric SCHILLER* (US)

With regard to the latest debate raging within the magazine (CHESS) about players finding it easier to play with black rather than white, dare I suggest that in reality this has nothing to do with the 'Ol' Black Magic', as some would call it, but more to do with the fact that you tend to learn and therefore know your defences much better, and as Black you find it much, much easier reacting to your opponents advances? – John HENDERSON (2002)

In the case of correspondence players above Elo 2500 the success rate rises to 57:43 in favour of White. In my opinion this may be a sign for a practical white advantage, because relatively stronger players are more able to use this advantage than relative weaker ones. Psychology plays no or only a very small part (...) Of course it is totally indifferent whether you have Black or White in any position. Decisive is the position itself. In my opinion the positions are a little bit more difficult to master on the black side of the board. – Peter HERTEL (corr GM, Germany)

The presumption of equality is just that: a presumption. I.e., it is impossible to prove anything mathematically at present. So, the presumption that in the initial position 'White is better, or slightly better' is just what it is: a presumption. Now if 'the position is equal' or 'White is better' are both presumptions, which of them should we take? Clearly, the second! ... – Henrique HENRIQUES (Lisbon, Portugal)

I believe the specific openings chosen (and becoming proficient in complicated openings) have much more to do with having the advantage and winning, than whether playing with the white or black pieces. – Kenneth BACHMAN (Florida)

I still think White has a 'very slight' edge in practical chances. This may be simply a prejudice on my part. If you play well enough, it doesn't matter. – Kevin BONHAM (Hobart, Tasmania)

With equally good, i.e. correct play from both sides, a game ends (has to end) with a draw. However, I make the restriction that it is somewhat more difficult for Black than for White to stay within the drawing range. In certain opening variations, the extra tempo does count (...) the right to play first does NOT guarantee an automatic win, but it is indirectly responsible for Black's slightly higher loss ratio. – Friedrich WOLFENTER (Stuttgart)

As you must know very well yourself, we have played only a tiny portion of all possible chess games so far. It doesn't prove anything that White had the better score in the past 300-400 years. If Black had scored better, it wouldn't prove anything, either. – György NEGYESI (Budapest)

There are games played by two where one of the following three statements is true: a/the first player wins; b/draw; c/the second player wins. These are mathematically proven facts for certain games! Naturally, this only holds IF BOTH PARTIES PLAY PERFECTLY! For most games, however, this question cannot be decided. If a game has a simple drawing or winning strategy, it's a mathematical game, and it's not worth playing any more. If the strategy is very complicated, or the proof does not provide us with a strategy to be followed, the game can still be played, it is not influenced by the theoretical decision. As for chess, nobody has been able to say anything so far, so nobody has been able to say Black is NOT OK!!! – Zoltan BLAZSIK (mathematician)

I like your basic concept: I don't think it can be proved mathematically that Black is 'worse'. — Mikhail GOLUBEV (Odessa, Ukraine)

I hope that the start position is not a 'mutual zugzwang' (when White loses!) — so, if we are OK and still able to play chess, then we can be OK with black and with white too. — Gene VENABLE (Chess Watch)

Based on my long experience, I would say that White has a better score in junior tournaments and in rapid and blitz, or when people play fast in time trouble in classical games. In 'normal' chess, however, White has no advantage. Only in the players' heads. — Igor LYASHKEVYCH (Magdeburg)

White wins, I was always led to believe that this was so. — Tom COOPER (Ireland)

I normally enjoy the games more and some of my best wins have been with black. I like counter-attack and the 'reduced pressure' from team-mates expecting a win. — Martin COBHAM (Derby & Mickleover Chess Club)

I cannot agree that White's advantage is some form of collective hallucination. I do not think chess players 'presume' White is better. This is inferred from having the privilege of moving first and confirmed by the statistics from actual play. There are, of course, individuals who play better with black (...) A large part of Morozevich's being so dangerous with black can be explained simply by the fact that he has studied the Slav Defence so thoroughly that he knows far more about it than most, or all, of his contemporaries. — Allan JACKSON (Australia)

Such is the complexity of chess that after not many moves, we will find ourselves in a position we could not have predicted. It is players who play best in those unforeseen positions who triumph. As Tarrasch did not quite say, 'After the Opening the Gods have placed the Middlegame'. — David SANDHAM

I usually prefer Black, simply because I feel I'm more in control of the type of opening I wish to play. — Alain CUERRIER (alzy@dsuper.net)

After I read somewhere that Bobby Fischer said, 'My world changed when I realized Black could play to win not just draw!', I felt that's profound. This way it became possible for him to win against Taimanov and Larsen 6-0! — Damon WEST (Texas, U.S.A.)

I myself prefer Black, simply because I can decide where I will take the game, as opposed to White, where he simply dictates 1.e4 or 1.d4. When White moves first, he generates something to attack so it is not White having the initiative, or having gained an advantage; it is the opposite, White loses equality the moment he moves, when he does he immediately gives Black something to attack, something to form his own plans around, whereas with White, he is always on the defensive, defending what he has done or what pawn he has pushed. Therefore it is Black who should most naturally be expected to win instead of White. — Kevin SCHWARZER

When I started to play chess, I preferred the white pieces. This resulted in the fact that all the games I won I achieved with white and I usually lost (and drew sometimes) with black. So at one point I realized that I was doing it all wrong when I concentrated on White only and I began to focus on playing with black. Right now, I enjoy very much playing with black and, more importantly: I am not afraid to play with black. Right now, my wins, draws and losses are more equally balanced. Last season I even won more games with black than with white. – Peter VYVEY (pvyvey@ vub.ac.be)

I think the tournament situation influences the balance. In Black's favor! I mean, as Black people don't play for a win anyway while as White they usually do. In a tournament however, they might play for a draw as White when it is enough to reach the desired position in the tournament. This might bring down the number of white wins. – 'Johan' (fa367611@skynet.be)

I think that playing with white mainly means a psychological advantage, you have more ways to force your style in the game with white than with black. Players can find a lot of good systems and gambits with white, while Black must have in most of the variations some disadvantage in space or weakness in structure. There was always a great difference in my scores by colour. – Jozsef FORGACS (Debrecen)

Already decades ago it was proved that in the game of chess both players have a strategy which doesn't lose. (The evidence isn't constructive so this strategy isn't built up yet.) This is not the only case when a mathematically proved statement is ignored in practice. – Tamas BINDER (mathematician)

The logical outcome of a perfect game is a draw – think of the communicating vessels: the level of water isn't effected by where the liquid is poured in (the final score is a 'draw' = same level). – Laszlo LEOPOLD (Romania)

My score is better with white, I work more on my white repertoire and I have more self-confidence playing with this colour. As Black I am often satisfied with a draw, it's more important to avoid defeat than to win. There's more than 100 Elo points difference in my performance by colour. I don't understand it, after all in both cases I am the player who directs the pieces. – Viktor ERDÖS (GM)

People think 'White is better' not only because a) it's a prejudice wrongly believed by them; b) the theory is built up in a deformed way, but unfortunately because c) in his mind, his chess, this is the truth. That is why it is so difficult to prove that 'BLACK IS OK', the players who are 'taught that White is better' really play better with white and worse with black. The only way to fight this is to defeat them. (...) In tournament chess the expectation of white players is a very heavy burden. Too heavy. It often happens that White – who is programmed by everybody, including him-/herself, to win – dreams of winning in an equal position and, overdoing it, even loses. – Sandor LISZNYAI (psychologist)

In my opinion it's more difficult to play Black than White against either stronger or weaker opponents, but between similar opponents the colour isn't of great importance. I agree with GM Portisch: BLACK IS OK – if (s)he finds the right lines! – *Zoltan MEDVEGY (GM)*

You haven't convinced me of the fact that people generally like to play with white. I know this, but I have another attitude. My favourite openings are the Grünfeld and the Najdorf. It depends on the opponent which colour I prefer. If (s)he enters into the main Najdorf, I prefer Black, but against opponents playing 1.e4 c5 2.c3 or stable systems with g2-g3, I would rather be White. – *Petra PAPP (WGM, 2015)*

If the chess world were to take Andras Adorjan [AA]'s thesis seriously, we might witness the end of draw-death, or at the very minimum, experience more dynamic games and consequently see better results from the black side of the board. Even the practical measure of *making all diagrams in the book presented to the reader with black at 'the bottom' forms a consistent part of AA's agenda.* As if to say 'this perspective' rather than the universal presentation of viewing the board from the white side, which is a form of **conditioning!** – *Phil INNES (Chessville, 2005)*

The idea of Black trying to 'equalize' is questionable. I think it has limited application to a few openings, rather than being an opening prescription for Black in general. (...) Black's chances increase markedly by playing good openings, which tend to be those with flexibility and latent potential, 'rather than those that give White fixed targets or that try to take the initiative prematurely.' He also emphasizes that 'White has "the initiative", not "the advantage".' Success with black depends on seeing beyond the initiative and thinking of positions in terms of 'potential'. – *Jonathan ROWSON (GM, 2005)*

Because of the presumption of White being better, the juncture of the game at which Black frees his game or neutralizes White's plans has often been automatically assumed to give him equality, even though in dynamic openings, the exhaustion of White's initiative very often means that Black has seized it with advantage. – *John WATSON (IM, 1998)*

Several GMs score better with black. The common belief is that these players are temperamentally suited to defence, to a passive approach to the chess fight and to reactive replies. In his book *BLACK is OK!* Adorjan disproves this with games from his practice. The real explanation lies in the dynamic nature of his opening repertoire. (...) On the other hand, the term 'defence' is improperly associated with some openings, just to make the players on the black side feel threatened. (...) In terms of the mathematical games theory, chess is a game of complete information, and Black's information is always greater – by one move! – *Mihai SUBA (GM, 1991)*

Black can play for a win without moral responsibility and unobserved. The psychological situation is the following: Black is the attacked side, the one in an unfavourable situation, and the audience's sympathy is for him/her. There is always something heroic about Black's struggle, even if (s)he gets carried away and does something (s)he regrets later. So (s)he is the only one who can profit from this business. If (s)he happens to lose the game... so what? It can be predicted by all the odds. Any other result is unfavourable for the opponent. All Black has to do is make it a bit more conscious so that the opponent could not even realise that (s)he also intends to win. (S)he can prepare for the opponent's favourite 'winning' openings, and find something new in them. Actually White has not one but two opponents. Him/herself as well! – *Ervin NAGY (IM, psychiatrist)*

It's a very feeble excuse for failure to say that you played Black. I use it all the time. I suppose we're all prejudiced on this subject, and so Kevin Schwarzer's claim that 'when White moves he loses equality' and 'immediately gives Black something to attack' is quite refreshing. It would mean that a great player like Tigran Petrosian, by doing next to nothing, must have had a terrific score with white! I also like GM Suba's argument that 'Black's information is always greater – by one move'. These advantages might just outweigh White's tiny objective plus in the starting position. I do play for a win also with black, you know. I even believe that if Black manages to equalize after the opening, he has proved he has played better than his opponent, so in fact he is already better at that point. I guess White's advantage is objective while Black's advantage is subjective – psychological. They may roughly outweigh each other but they are different in nature. So perhaps we should say: in the starting position there are chances for both sides. Admittedly, this sounds less catchy than 'Black is OK!' – *Peter BOEL (the Netherlands, 2016)*

SwitChess – funny and useful

1.e2-e4 (or anything else)

SwitChess is very good for training and exhibition. It is played according to the rules of traditional chess. The only difference is that the two camps change places in the starting position. BLACK is to start, and his pieces are standing in the places of White's pieces, and White's replies are in the place of BLACK's.

This mutation creates odd and comical pictures, but it is not *art pour l'art*!

It is an *experiment*. They say it is better to play with white. If this is really so, it might be just because of White's right (and duty) to a make the first move. However almost all the associations connected with BLACK are negative. We have collected close to hundred of such combinations. For example: BLACKmail, BLACK sheep (the shame of the family), BLACK spot (a place of danger or difficulty), BLACK death (the plague). Even the word BLACK itself has dark associations already, for example: angry, threatening (a BLACK look); wicked, sinister, deadly (BLACK-hearted); gloomy, depressed, sullen (a BLACK mood).

In short: the aim of our test rapid tournament – the World Premier of which was on the 21st of August 2009 in Szombathely (Hungary) – was to learn whether moving first or playing White in the game gives an advantage?

Naturally, we cannot draw solid conclusions from just one tournament.

But I was sure that there would be interesting games and I was eager to see the statistics of this tournament...

Here are the figures: The first mover won 22, the second 17, and there were only 9 draws in a total of 48 games (6 rounds). Here is a game by the winner, GM Adam Horvath:

Andras Dankhazi
Adam Horvath

Szombathely SwitChess (1) 2009

1.e4 c5 2.♘c3 e6 3.d3 ♘c6 4.g3 a6 5.♗g2 b5

6.a3 ♗b7 7.♘ge2 ♘ge7 8.0-0 g6 9.♗e3 d6 10.d4 cxd4 11.♘xd4 ♗g7 12.♕d2 ♘e5 13.b3

13...♘g4 14.♖ad1 ♘xe3 15.♕xe3 0-0 16.f4 ♕b6 17.♘ce2 ♖ac8 18.♘f5 ♕xe3+ 19.♘xe3

♗b2 20.a4 bxa4 21.bxa4 ♗a3 22.♔h1 ♗c5 23.♘c4 d5 24.e5 ♗a8 25.♘d2 ♘f5 26.♖b1 ♘e3 27.♖fc1 ♘xg2 28.♔xg2 ♗e3 29.♘b3 d4+   0-1

This is a game you cannot convert and play over in ChessBase, but only by hand. As a demo program you can find it on http://home.hu.inter.net/~prochess/rainbow.htm.

There's a danger for you, readers – that my **Swan Song Nr.2's** subject will be 'Alternatives to Playing the Royal Game with Traditional Rules'.

Sveshnikov

Grünfeld

Chapter 12
Connections

A Tribute to...

There are people who pretend that all their achievements are theirs alone. They are the lonely heroes. For this book I got the idea to pay tribute to those of my partners whom I learned, worked with, or taught in my chess career, as a second, or maybe the opposite. For each of them I wanted to give a game which he won with black. The outcome was astonishing. I don't know how many partners I had expected to come up with, but 43 was surely more than surprising. I have to note that some of the people on this list I don't like very much by now (and vice versa), but all the same we once worked together and that cooperation was fruitful.

Karoly JOCHA (1944)

My elder brother 'Karcsi' was the person who taught me how to play chess when I was 8-9 years old. Needless to say I was suffering in most of our games. Until I studied my first chess book *Hogyan sakkozzunk?* ('How to play chess?') by Laszlo Alföldy on my own. Karoly barely managed to swallow the turning of the tables after that. He became my 'manager' (which meant not more than accompanying me to my tournaments, which were held mostly in the evenings far away from our home). As a consolation (not), later he became one of the best sports writers in Hungary!

Karoly Jocha
Andras Jocha
Budapest 1962

1.d4 d5 2.c4 e5 3.dxe5 d4 4.♘f3 ♘c6 5.♗f4

5.g3 and 5.a3 are the main moves here. In two more moves we are completely 'out of book'.

5...h6 6.h4 ♗e6 7.♘bd2 ♕d7 8.g3 a5 9.♗g2 0-0-0 10.♕c2 ♗c5 11.♘b3 ♗b6 12.0-0 ♗f5 13.♕d2 a4 14.♘c1

Here White could have obtained a winning attack by 14.c5! ♗a7 15.e6 fxe6 16.♘a5 with the idea ♘e5.

14...f6 15.exf6 ♘xf6 16.a3 ♖de8 17.♕d1 ♘g4

It was time to attack the bishop by 17...♘h5.

18.♖e1??

Completely unnecessary. 18.♕xa4 followed by ♕b5 gives White the initiative as well as two pawns.

18...g5! 19.hxg5 hxg5 20.♗xg5

Better was 20.♘xg5 to keep the bishop in place, but 20...♘ce5 gives Black compensation. 20...d3! may be even stronger.

20...♕h7?

Again, 20...d3!, when 21.e3 ♘ce5 22.♘xe5 ♘xe5 gives Black a strong, probably winning attack.

21.♕xa4 ♗a5?

Allowing the bishop to be locked up by 22.b4, which could have been avoided by 21...♗c2!.

22.♗h4? ♗c2 23.♕b5 ♘ge5

23...♗xe1.

24.♘d3 ♘xd3 25.exd3 ♗xe1 26.♘xe1 ♗xd3 27.♘xd3 ♕xd3 28.♗xc6 bxc6 29.♕xc6 ♕f5 30.♕a8+ ♔d7 31.♕a4+ ♔d6 32.♕a6+

After 32.♖d1 White's attack would have come first.

32...c6 33.♖c1

33...♖xh4! 34.c5+ ♔d7 35.♕b7+ ♔d8 36.♕a8+ ♔e7 37.♕b7+ ♔f6 **0-1**

Laszlo SIMONYI (1907-2001)

My career started as many others' careers: I went to the nearby park (Petofi Square) to watch the old uncles playing chess. On these occasions there are usually some spectators, who sometimes make comments as well. And so did I, after a few days of warming up. Yes, but I was only ten. It was a blasphemy and it shocked them, as if it were a cow talking. They invited me to play, saying 'show us if you can play so well'. There was no joy for them that afternoon. But then came (Simonyi) 'Laci Bacsi', who was a teacher (like my mother) and a second-category player. He beat me 1.5-0.5, and I was discovered. He took me to his club, and... I will never know whether his showing up was an incident (he lived nearby) or whether some of the losers had rushed out to get him, to save their honour. Anyway, I have a lot to thank him for, which I am doing here again.

Attila Simonyi
Laszlo Simonyi

Hajduszoboszlo 1995

This was the world's first colour chess game, between the 90-year-old Laci Bacsi and his grandson Attila (9).

1.e4 e5 2.♗c4 ♗b4 3.♕f3 ♘f6 4.c3 ♗c5 5.♘e2 0-0 6.d4 exd4 7.cxd4 ♗b4+ 8.♘bc3 ♘c6 9.♗e3 d6 10.h3 ♗e6 11.♗d3 a6 12.0-0-0 h6 13.♕g3 ♘h5 14.♕f3 ♘f6 15.e5?

This doesn't quite work.

15...dxe5 16.dxe5 ♘xe5 17.♗h7+ ♘xh7 18.♖xd8

Now, instead of playing the prosaic 18...♘xf3 Black decides to attack:

18...♖fxd8 19.♕xb7 ♘d3+ 20.♔c2

Bravely forward!

20...♗f5

White resigned.

21.♔b3 ♖ab8 would have been a fitting finish.

Bela PAPP (1920-1988)

I read somewhere that 18 people qualified for the Guinness Book of Records by squeezing themselves inside a Trabant (which is a small car made in East Germany). Stupidity, which is highly recognized, as it seems. 'Bela Bacsi' never received such honours, although he was a wizard and his life's work as a trainer was unique. We, his formal pupils, organized a very strong tournament as a tribute to him in 1986. Justice was done.

As long ago as 1962, playing in a lower class in Simonyi Laci Bacsi's team, I noticed that there was a team composed of youngsters, some of them still children. So my brother took me to their training session. I played with a lad called 'Robi' Papp (no relative to Bela Bacsi), and he barely beat me. Then, to my great surprise, Uncle Bela invited me to his other team, the ASI (*Angyalföldi Sport Iskola*). This club achieved something hardly ever equalled by anybody. By winning all the leagues from the lowest class, they stepped up each and every year. The big difference between similar performances in the present and the past was that this team of his was not systematically strengthened with new legionaries. The ASI was composed of the original members. We followed a primitive method by developing year by year according to the expectations, which became higher and higher. Between 1962-64 I was a member of this dream team, playing on last board. Until some idiots dissolved both of Bela Papp's teams – of which ASI qualified to the first league. The great man had to start all over again. Uncle Bela had an incredible gift for discovering talent, and for helping those who had enough love for chess and were industrious. His enthusiasm radiated from him. He passed away in 1988. He was awarded with the Master Trainer title only in 1986. May God bless him! His 300 pupils – among them two grandmasters and quite a few IMs – will never forget him.

Laszlo Pacsay
Bela Papp
Hungary tt 1970

1.d4 e6 2.♘f3 ♘f6 3.c4 ♗b4+ 4.♗d2 ♗xd2+ 5.♘bxd2 d6 6.e4 e5!? 7.dxe5 dxe5 8.♘xe5 ♕d4 9.♘d3 ♗e6

He could have regained the pawn by 9...♘c6 10.e5 ♘g4 11.♘f3 ♕xc4

(11...♕e4+ 12.♕e2 ♕xc4 13.h3 ♘h6 is unclear) 12.h3 ♘h6, which looks risky but is quite OK.

10.♗e2 ♘c6 11.0-0 0-0-0 12.♖c1 ♘xe4! 13.♘f3 ♕f6 14.a4 g5 15.♖fd1 g4 16.♘d2

16...♖xd3 17.♘xe4

17.♗xd3 ♕xf2+ 18.♔h1 ♘c5 is the crucial line. White can hold on with 19.♕a3 ♘xd3 20.♕xd3 ♖d8 21.♘e4 ♕xb2 22.♕e3 ♖xd1+ 23.♖xd1 ♕e5 24.♕h6 b6 but Black is doing fine here.

17...♖xd1+ 18.♖xd1 ♕xb2

Now Black is simply a healthy pawn up.

19.♗d3 ♕e5 20.♖b1 ♖d8 21.♕c2 ♘d4 22.♕b2

22...♘f3+ 23.gxf3 ♕xb2 24.♖xb2 ♖xd3 25.fxg4 ♗xg4 26.♖d2 ♖xd2 27.♘xd2 ♔d7 28.f3 ♗f5 29.♔f2 ♔d6 30.♔e3 ♔c5 31.♘b3+ ♔xc4 32.♘a5+ ♔b5 33.♘xb7 ♗c8

White's Knight is Trapped

34.♘d8 ♗e6 35.a3 c5 36.f4 ♗d5 37.f5 ♔b6 38.♔f4 ♔c7 39.♔e5 ♗b3

White resigned.

Istvan Podhola
Bela Papp

Budapest 1974

1.c4 d6 2.d4 ♘d7 3.♘c3 e5 4.d5 g6 5.e4 ♗g7 6.♗d3 a5 7.♗e3 ♘e7

A novelty at the time. Larsen had played 7...♗h6 against Westerinen in Helsinki 1969, 7...b6 had been played twice. We are now moving towards a chain struggle.

8.♘ge2 f5 9.f3 0-0 10.0-0 f4 11.♗f2 g5 12.g4 h5 13.h3

13.gxh5 is no use – Black starts his slow attack with 13...♖f6.

13...♘f6 14.♕b3

14.c5!? – time for some action on the other side.

14...hxg4 15.hxg4

15...♗xg4!? 16.fxg4 ♘xg4

16...♕c8 looks even better.

17.♖fc1 ♕e8 18.♔f1 ♕h5 19.♘g1 ♕h2

19...♘xf2 20.♔xf2 ♕h2+ followed by 21...f3 was winning.

20.♘d1 ♘e3+ 21.♔e1 ♘g2+ 22.♔d2 g4 23.♔c3

The flight forward didn't help: 23.♕xb7 g3 24.♗a7 ♖xa7 25.♕xa7 f3 (not immediately 25...♘c8?! 26.♘f3) and Black's attack is unstoppable.

23...g3 24.♘f3 ♕h5 25.♗e2

25...♘f5 26.exf5?!

He could hang in there with 26.♗g1!?.

26...e4+ 27.♔c2 a4 28.♕a3 gxf2 29.♘xf2 ♘e3+ 30.♔d2 exf3 31.♗d3 ♕h2 32.♖f1 ♘xf1+ 33.♖xf1 ♗d4

White resigned.

Mario Seifart
Bela Papp

Budapest 1984

1.e4 c5 2.♘f3 e6 3.♘c3 ♘c6 4.♗b5 ♘d4 5.a4 a6 6.♗c4 ♕a5 7.♖a2 ♘e7 8.♘xd4 cxd4 9.♘e2 ♘c6 10.c3 ♘e5 11.d3 dxc3 12.♘xc3

12...d5! 13.exd5 exd5 14.♗b5+

14.♗xd5 runs into 14...♗b4, but the computer still finds something for White: 15.0-0! ♗xc3 16.bxc3 ♕xd5 17.c4 ♕d6 18.♗a3! and Black will have to give back the piece: after 18...♕xd3 19.♕e1 f6 20.f4 ♗e6 21.fxe5 0-0-0 the game is equal.

14...axb5 15.axb5 ♕xa2 16.♘xa2 ♖xa2 17.♕e2

White wins back the piece, but Black gets the initiative for it.

17...♗b4+ 18.♔d1 f6 19.d4 ♗g4 20.f3 ♗e6 21.dxe5 0-0 22.♕d3?

22.♕e3!.

22...♖a1 23.♕b3 ♗a5 24.♔e2 ♖e8 25.♔f2 ♗b6+ 26.♔g3 ♗c7 27.f4 fxe5 28.♖d1 ♖f8 29.♔f2 ♗b6+ 30.♔g3 ♖f6 31.h3 e4 32.♕c2 ♖a8 33.♗d2 ♖c8 34.♕a4?! d4 35.♖c1 ♖d8 36.♔h2 e3 37.♗e1 d3

38.♗c3 d2 39.♖a1 e2 40.♗xd2 ♖xd2 41.♕b4 ♖d8 42.♖e1 ♖d1 43.♖xe2 ♗g1+ 44.♔g3 ♖d3+   0-1

GM Laszlo BARCZAY (1936-2016)

What a wonderful person 'Laci' was! He was one of those very rare players who carried the grandmaster title both in correspondence chess and in 'normal' chess. He even wrote poems, which are brilliantly strange. At the time we first met I was 14, and he became my mentor. If I remember well, we analysed mostly crazy gambits such as the Marshall, the Traxler and a bit of the King's Gambit. I was amused by his sparkling fantasy and was lucky to be a board boy when he played his game against Sapi during the Hungarian Championship in 1963. As the age difference became unimportant, we became friends. And that is what we remained. Thank God!

P.S.: On the 7th of April 2016 God called Laszlo to Him. I had the honour of exchanging the last e-mails with him only a few days before. The B-group of the traditional Zalakaros Open was dedicated to his memory.

Laszlo Sapi
Laszlo Barczay
Budapest ch-HUN 1963

1.d4 d5 2.c4 e6 3.♘f3 c6 4.♘c3 ♘f6 5.♗g5 dxc4 6.e3

6.e4 is the main variation.

6...b5 7.a4 ♗b4 8.♗e2 ♘bd7 9.0-0 ♕b6 10.♕c2 ♗b7 11.♖fd1 a6 12.♖ac1

Better is 12.b3.

12...c5! 13.♘e5 ♘xe5 14.dxe5 ♗xc3 15.bxc3

15.♗xf6 gxf6 16.♕xc3 was better.

15...♘e4 16.♗f4 b4 17.a5 ♕xa5 18.cxb4 cxb4 19.♗f3

19...♖c8 20.♗xe4 b3!

The point.

21.♕b1 ♗xe4 22.♕xe4 0-0 23.♖xc4 b2 24.♖xc8 ♖xc8 25.♕b1 ♕c3 26.e4 a5 27.♗e3 a4

27...♕b3 was easier, but in that case we would have missed the following finish.

28.♗d4

28...♛xd4! 29.♖xd4 ♖c1+ 30.♖d1 ♖xb1 31.♖xb1 a3

White resigned.

GM Gedeon BARCZA (1911-1986)

It was the autumn of 1965. And I was having a nice time with some of the best juniors, attending a lecture (which was rubbish, like always). We were standing in the foyer of the headquarters of the Chess Federation. And then Gedeon Barcza from the editorial board of *Magyar Sakkelet* (Hungarian Chess Life) came out.

He recognized me(!), came up and said: 'Bandi, we received your letter and your analyses. Very nice, and we will publish it. Write more!' (I had sent a reader's letter with a correction to a game by Marshall). And he took his leave. Surely this was one of the happiest moments in my life. And, encouraged by the grandmaster, I went on to write more. Much more!

This is my 14th book, folks! Besides countless articles and analyses. And this great man edited my works for years, tactfully and supportively. He was patient too, which was necessary in cases when I got the move numbers wrong... I was like his fifth child and I tried to prove myself worthy of this status. Just one more line. The Grandmaster's two daughters, Györgyi and Noémi, studied with Uncle Bela (Papp). High spirits met! I confess, a little late, that I was in love with Noémi Barcza, but she could only see the little boy in me... Still, even now I can see her pretty face with the same emotion. Don't tell anybody!

GM Laszlo Szabo was more successful in tournament chess, but there were quite a few occasions when G.B. beat him. Barcza was famous for his ability to convert small advantages into a win. When they were both playing in several of the Hungarian Championships,

Szabo would sigh: 'Barcza has nothing again — surely he'll win'.

**Laszlo Szabo
Gedeon Barcza**

Leningrad 1967

1.e4 c6 2.♘c3 d5 3.d4 dxe4 4.♘xe4 ♗f5 5.♘g3 ♗g6 6.h4 h6 7.♘f3 ♘d7 8.♗d3 ♗xd3 9.♛xd3 ♛c7 10.♗d2 ♘gf6 11.0-0-0 0-0-0 12.c4 e6 13.♗c3 ♗d6 14.♘e4 ♗f4+ 15.♔b1 ♘e5 16.♘xe5 ♗xe5 17.♛e3

17.♘c5!?, keeping the knights on, would have given White more play.

17...♘xe4 18.dxe5?!

18.♛xe4 ♗f6 19.♖h3 ♖he8 is unclear. White has more space, while Black has some pressure on the centre.

18...♖xd1+ 19.♖xd1 ♖d8

He could also try the immediate 19...♘xc3+ 20.♛xc3 ♖d8, with slightly more than 'nothing'. White's best option may be 20.bxc3!, however, when White can oppose on d4.

20.♖d4?!

Accurate was 20.♖xd8+ ♛xd8 21.♔c2 ♘xc3 22.♔xc3 ♛xh4 23.♛xa7 ♛e4 24.♛c5 ♛xg2 25.♛f8+ ♔c7 26.♛xf7+ with a draw.

20...♘xc3+

21.♛xc3?

Again, the anti-positional 21.bxc3 gave better counterchances: 21...♖xd4 22.♛xd4 (22.cxd4? ♛e7!) 22...c5 23.♛e3 ♛c6 24.♔b2 b6 25.♛g3! with a very interesting ending where White's chances do not look worse.

21...c5!

Now White has problems already.

22.♖xd8+

22.♖g4 g6.

22...♕xd8 23.g3 ♕d1+ 24.♕c1 ♕e2 25.♕f4 ♕d1+ 26.♕c1 ♕d3+! 27.♔a1 ♕e2 28.f4 ♕f2 29.g4 ♕xh4 30.♕g1 b6 31.a3 ♔c7 32.♕g2 ♕d8 33.♕e4 ♕d1+ 34.♔a2 ♕d4 35.♕c2 ♕xf4 36.♕a4 a5

White resigned.

GM Istvan BILEK (1932-2010)

We were playing in the same club for some 10 years. That's how we befriended, which was of course an honour for me. He was my second in the U-20 World Championship in Stockholm 1969. And he helped me coming second, in a field that had Karpov as the winner, playing Ulf Andersson, Torre and others as well. It was fine and, by the way, the best performance by any Hungarian until then. Bilek had a brilliant tactical mind, an amusing fantasy, and he was a lazy swine. This last remark comes from himself. I am only confirming it.

As Lajos Portisch once said: 'Talent is 99% diligence'. Bilek Pista took things easy and missed quite a few successes he could have achieved. I still learned a lot from him. For example, the 'delayed Benoni': 1.d4 ♘f6 2.c4 c5 3.d5 d6 4.♘c3 g6 5.e4 ♗g7 6.♘f3 0-0 7.♗e2 e6 8.0-0 ♖e8 9.dxe6 ♗xe6 10.♗f4 ♘c6 11.♗xd6 ♘d4, as the main line goes. I beat Uhlmann (IBM 1971) and Forintos (1973) with this weapon. Thanks!

Ludek Pachman
Istvan Bilek

Kecskemet zt 1964

1.d4 ♘f6 2.c4 d6 3.♘c3 g6 4.e4 ♗g7 5.f3 0-0 6.♗e3 b6 7.♗d3 ♗b7 8.♘ge2 c5 9.d5 e6 10.g4

This plan, in combination with the king's move to f2, turns out to be dubious, as is nicely demonstrated by Bilek.

10...exd5 11.cxd5 ♖e8 12.♕d2 ♘bd7 13.♔f2 ♘e5 14.♘g3

14...♗xd5!

Even stronger looks 14...♘fxg4+!? 15.fxg4 ♕f6+ 16.♔g2 ♕f3+ 17.♔g1 ♘xg4 18.♘f1 ♘xe3 19.♘xe3 ♗d4 20.♘d1 ♗xd5 21.♕f2 ♗xe4 22.♗xe4 ♕xe4, winning back the material with interest, and winning the game. However, after 16.♔e2! ♕f3+ 17.♔e1 ♗h6! 18.♘d1 ♗f4 19.♖g1 ♕xg4 (threatening 20...♘f3+), the computer gives 21.♗e2 or 21.♕e2 with approximate equality. So contrary to what was thought at the time, the text move is better.

15.♘xd5

After 15.g5 (15.♗b5 ♗c6) 15...♗c4! 16.♗xc4 ♘xc4 17.♕e2 ♘xe3 18.gxf6 ♗h6! Black is a good pawn up, and a second one on f6 is on the way.

15...♘xd5 16.exd5 ♕f6 17.♗e4 ♘xg4+ 18.♔g2 ♘xe3+ 19.♕xe3 ♕xb2+ 20.♕e2

Leading to a lost endgame, but 20.♔h3 f5 was hopeless.

20...♕xe2+ 21.♘xe2 ♗xa1 22.♖xa1 b5 23.♔f2 ♖e5−+ 24.♖d1 ♖ae8 25.♘c3 a6 26.♗d3 ♔g7 27.♗f1 ♖h5 28.h3 ♖h4 29.♘e4 ♖hxe4! 30.fxe4 ♖xe4 31.♖d3 b4 32.♔f3 ♖e1 33.♗e2 a5 34.♖e3 ♖a1 35.♖e7 ♔f6 36.♖d7 ♔e5! 37.♖xf7 ♖xa2 38.♖xh7 a4

**39.♗d3 ♖a3 40.♔e2 g5 41.♖g7 ♔d4
42.♗f5 ♖e3+ 43.♔d2   0-1**

IM Laszlo LIPTAY (1937)

'Lipi' has never been a profi, since he practiced as a doctor – of inner medicine and psychiatry. From him first I heard that the only difference between a psychiatrist and a patient is that the former has the keys. One day he could not find the keys, and escaped from psychiatry for good. He was my senior (just like the persons mentioned above), but he liked me for some reason (not everybody hates me – only a majority) and showed me a couple of opening ideas. He was the man who showed me the first appearance of the Grünfeld line 5.♕b3 dxc4 6.♕xc4 0-0 7.e4 a6 (Kozlov-Lukin, 1969). Later this became known as the Hungarian Variation of the Russian System (true, Alekhine already played it in his World Championship match against Euwe...).

Another thing he provided me with was a weapon against the English. When I was nineteen, I played reasonably well, and I had a repertoire, but I couldn't find anything solid against the English. He showed me something which served me for a lifetime. I can propose it also to you, dear reader. It goes: 1.c4 c5 2.g3 g6 3.♗g2 ♗g7 4.♘c3 ♘c6 5.♘f3 e6! followed by ...♘ge7. This handling of the line promises active counterplay, and is a pleasure to play. Among others, I beat Csom with it in the 1993 Hungarian championship. I'm grateful to the good Doc for all this.

**Vlastimil Jansa
Laszlo Liptay**

Budapest tt 1970 (8)

**1.g3 c5 2.♗g2 g6 3.c4 ♗g7 4.♘c3
♘c6**

5.a3

Wisely refraining from 5.♘f3 e6 6.0-0 (on 6.d4 cxd4 7.♘b5 there is the sharp 7...d5 8.cxd5 ♕a5+ 9.♘d2 ♕xb5 10.dxc6 ♘e7 with mutual chances) 6...♘ge7 7.d4 ♘xd4 (7...cxd4 8.♘b5 0-0 9.♘bxd4 d5 is also possible). Now 8.♘xd4 cxd4 9.♘b5 d5 10.cxd5 ♘xd5 11.♘xd4 0-0= runs along the above-mentioned lines, and after 8.♘e4 Black does best to return the pawn with 8...0-0 9.♘xc5 ♘xf3+ 10.♗xf3 d5 unclear, Ruck-Adorjan, Budapest ch-HUN 1995.

5...a5

5...a6!?.

After 5...e6 6.b4 is premature in view of 6...♘xb4! 7.axb4 cxb4 8.♘b5 (8.d4 bxc3 9.♘f3 ♘e7 does not offer any compensation) 8...♗xa1 9.♕a4 ♗g7 and Black is clearly better.

In reply to 5...b6 White can still go for 6.♖b1 (6.b4 ♗b7), for example: 6...♖b8 7.b4 cxb4 8.axb4 ♗b7 9.e4 (9.♘a2? ♘xb4! and Black was clearly better in Petrosian-Ftacnik, Sochi 1977) and now, interestingly, Black can aim at the weak point c4 by either 9...♘e5 or also 9...a5!? 10.bxa5 ♗xc3 11.dxc3 ♘xa5.

**6.♘f3 e6 7.0-0 ♘ge7 8.d3 0-0 9.♖b1
d5 10.cxd5**

An interesting, and as far as I know still untried, way to solve the problem of the long diagonal is 10.♘a4!? b6 11.b3.

**10...exd5 11.♗d2 b6 12.♘a4 ♗d7
13.♕b3 ♖a6 14.♗f4 h6 15.h4 ♗e6**

Black is strong in the centre. White now tries the flight forward.

16.e3 d4 17.♕b5 ♕c8 !

Catching the queen!

18.♗d6 ~~Sneaks in~~

18...♘a7 19.♘xb6

Limiting his loss to two minor pieces for a rook, but it won't do.

19...♘xb5 20.♘xc8 ♘xc8 21.♗xf8 ♗xf8 22.a4 ♘ba7 23.exd4 ♘c6!

Activity!

24.dxc5 ♗xc5 25.♖bc1 ♗a7 26.♖fe1 ♘8e7 27.♘e5 ♘xe5 28.♖xe5 ♘f5 29.♖c6 ♖xc6 30.♗xc6 ♘d4 31.♖xa5?

Desperate, but the plus pawns are no match for Black's minor trio. After 31.♗g2 ♗b6 Black would also in complete control.

31...♘xc6 32.♖a6 ♗d5 33.b4 ♗d4 34.b5 ♘b4 35.♖d6 ♔f8 36.b6 ♗c5 37.♖d8+ ♔e7 38.♖b8 ♘a6 39.♖h8 ♗xb6 40.♖xh6 ♗f3 41.♖h8 ♗d8 42.d4 ♘b4 43.♔f1 ♘d5 44.♔e1 ♘f6

Calmly collecting the a-pawn!

45.♔d2 ♗c6 46.♔e3   **0-1**

IM Laszlo NAVAROVSZKY (1933-1996)

'Navar' was on friendly terms with Liptay. He liked to read – mostly the 'Bible of the Devil' (playing cards). He wasn't such a great player, but he led the Hungarian gold medallist team in Buenos Aires 1978 as a captain. He played the Caro-Kann very well, and invented the 'Navary' – see the game below! With this line he won a couple of games, and so did I. Among them a victory over Karpov in 1969, which you have seen in Chapter 5, Black Is Brutal II.

**Bela Sandor
Laszlo Navarovszky**

Budapest ch-HUN 1954 (10)

1.♘f3 ♘f6 2.d4 g6 3.g3 ♗g7 4.♗g2 0-0 5.0-0 d6 6.c4 ♘bd7 7.♘c3 a6

This is the so-called 'Navary', which means (please use a Hungarian accent) Navarovszky variation.

8.h3

8.e4!? is the alternative.

8...c5 9.♗e3

On 9.d5!? Black can try 9...b5.

9...♖b8 10.dxc5 ♘xc5 11.♘d4 e5 12.♘c2 ♗e6 13.b3

A little sharper and maybe better is 13.b4!? ♘cd7 14.♕xd6 ♗xc4 15.♖fd1.

13...♕c7 14.♕d2 b5 15.cxb5 d5!

Not 15...axb5 16.♘b4 and Black loses the vital d5-square.

16.b6 ♕c8

On 16...♕xb6 17.b4 d4 there is the simplifying line 18.bxc5 ♕xc5 19.♘xd4 exd4 20.♗xd4 ♘e4! when Black has active play for the pawn in the endgame.

17.♘xd5?

The piece sacrifice 17.♖ac1! d4 18.♘xd4 exd4 19.♕xd4 was strong. After the text White's pieces will be awkwardly placed.

17...♗xd5 18.♗xd5 ♖d8 19.♘b4 ♘ce4 20.♕d3 ♕xh3 21.♖fd1 ♗f8 22.♕c4 ♖bc8 23.♘c6?

Stronger was 23.♗xf7+ ♔g7 24.♗e6 ♖xc4 25.♗xh3 ♖xd1+ 26.♖xd1 ♖xb4. White still looks worse here, but he can force a draw with 27.♖c1! ♘d5 28.♖c7+! ♔f6 29.♖c6+ or 28...♔h8 29.♖c8.

23...♖xd5! 24.♖xd5 ♖xc6 25.♗c5
25.♕xc6 ♘g4–+; 25.♕d3 ♖c3–+.
25...♖xc5 26.♖xc5 ♗xc5
White resigned.

IM Karoly HONFI (1930-1996)

received the grandmaster title post mortem, only barely missing it in his life.

A real gentleman in the jungle, that was Honfi. And although there was a time-gap of two decades between us, we were true friends (he mistakenly thought I was a noble soul as well...). He would dress in lilac all over, including his hat, making the impression of a young god even when he was not so young any more. He belonged to the old, classical generation. A little dogmatic too: he was somehow convinced that if he had occupied the centre (e4-d4), and had his bishops on c4 and f4, then the case was as good as closed...

He presented me with an idea in the Dragon which he never got on the board (as is usually the case). I employed it against Ribli (1968): 1.e4 c5 2.♘f3 ♘c6 3.d4 cxd4 4.♘xd4 g6 5.♘c3 ♗g7 6.♗e3 ♘f6 7.♗c4 d6 8.f3 ♕a5 9.♗b3 ♗d7 10.♕d2 0-0 11.0-0-0 ♖fc8 12.♔b1 ♘e5 13.♕e2 a6 14.f4 ♗g4 15.♘f3

15...♖xc3! and went on to win – made by 'Karcsi' Honfi.

**Bela Papp
Karoly Honfi**
Budapest 1984

Excellent
Book Best
10

1.e4 c5 2.d4 cxd4 3.c3 d3
No gambit pawns for Karcsi.
**4.♕xd3 ♘c6 5.f4 d6 6.♗e2 g6
7.♗e3 ♗g7 8.♘f3 ♘f6 9.♘bd2 0-0
10.h3 a6 11.g4 b5 12.♘d4 ♗b7
13.♗f3?** *Watch out Black!*

**13...♘e5! 14.fxe5 dxe5 15.♘2b3
exd4 16.cxd4 ♖c8 17.0-0 ♕c7
18.♘c5?**
Putting the cat among the pigeons. Safer was 18.e5 ♗xf3 19.♖xf3 ♘d5 20.♖af1.
**18...♕g3+ 19.♔g2 ♖xc5 20.dxc5
♗xe4 21.♕d2 ♘d5**
21...♗xg2 22.♗f4 ♕xh3 23.♕g2 ♕xg2+ 24.♔xg2 ♘xg4 was quite enough, but the text even wins a piece since White cannot protect both bishops.
22.♖f2
22.♗f4 ♘xf4 (22...♗d4+ 23.♔h1 ♕xh3+ 24.♗h2 ♕xg2+ 25.♕xg2 ♗xg2+ 26.♔xg2 ♘e3+–+) 23.♖xf4 ♗xg2–+.
**22...♘xe3 23.♖e1 ♗h6 24.♖ee2
♗xg2 25.♖xg2 ♘xg2 26.♖xg2
♗e3+** *Vicious ending!* **0-1**

IM Ervin NAGY (1945)

Needless to say, Ervin was a pupil of Bela Bacsi (Papp) too. We first met in 1962! He was surely talented, but he became a doctor – even worse, a psychiatrist... but he kept his love for chess. He made his necessary IM-norms

Gambit opening by white! Beautiful uncommon Rook sacrifice + discovered Attacks by Black! 18-26.

in tournaments during his holidays. He has written a book titled *Our psyche in chess/-ck* about chess-psychology, which I've been editing since 1993. With no publisher, and many other duties, it is still only a manuscript, although a few parts have appeared in Hungarian and English (*BLACK IS OK! Zero Copy*, 1992 and *BLACK is Still OK!*, 2004). Moreover, he was my psychiatrist between 1981 and 1993, on friendly terms but with sincere devotion. He is seventy now, and still working and playing. This speaks volumes about his moral too. Tribute to him.

Laszlo Barczay
Ervin Nagy
Budapest ch-HUN 1968
based on notes by Nagy

1.e4 g6 2.d4 d6 3.f4 ♗g7 4.c3
♘c3.

4...♘f6 5.♕c2

5.♗d3 is more natural.

5...0-0 6.♘f3 c5 7.dxc5 dxc5 8.♗e3

8...♕c7

Black could already have exploited White's loose development with 8...♘g4! 9.♗xc5? ♕c7 with a nice advantage.

9.♘a3 a6 10.0-0-0 ♘g4 11.♕e2 ♘xe3 12.♕xe3 b5

With his two bishops and free piece play Black is already better also here.

13.e5 ♗e6 14.♔b1 ♘d7

It wasn't too early for 14...b4!.

15.♘g5 ♗f5+

Better was 15...♗g4.

16.♗d3 ♗xd3+ 17.♖xd3 ♘b6 18.e6 f5 19.♕g3 ♖f6 20.♕h4?!

He should have covered the e-pawn with 20.♖e1. It's still Black who is attacking here.

20...h6 21.♘f7 ♖xe6 22.♘xh6+ ♔f8

23.♖hd1?

23.♘c2 was necessary. Now the pressure along the c-file becomes unbearable.

23...b4 24.cxb4

24.♘c2 bxc3.

24...cxb4 25.♘xf5

Despair. The black queenside attack remains.

25...gxf5 26.♕h7 ♖h6 27.♕xf5+ ♖f6 28.♕h7 bxa3 29.♖g3 e6 30.♖xa3 ♕c5 31.♖b3 ♖f5 32.a3 ♖c8 33.♔a2 ♕c4 34.♖d3 ♖b5 35.f5 ♖xb3 36.♖xb3 ♘d5 37.fxe6 ♖b8 38.♕f5+ ♗f6 39.e7+ ♔xe7

White resigned.

GM Zoltan RIBLI (1951)

We first met Ribli in 1964 during the Asztalos Honorary in Pecs. He lived there, and I was taken there as a present for winning the U-20 Hungarian Championship. I beat him 1.5-0.5. He wasn't very happy with that, but we started working together although we couldn't meet frequently (as happened later with me and Kasparov). Later on he also became an inhabitant of Budapest, and our co-operation became intensive. In 1975 Gyula Sax joined us, completing the 'Great Three'. Somewhat later, Laci Vadasz became the plus-1 person. Our work was very successful, even enjoyable. But alas! – the members of the National Team were also rivals for decades. I played two matches of six games with Ribli. The first encounter I won, so I could participate in the U-20 World Championship in Stockholm. Exactly 10 years later, in 1979, I qualified for the World Championship Candidates against Ribli, and he got mad. He took revenge outside the chessboard. As Vonnegut wrote: So it goes...

Gyula Sax
Zoltan Ribli

things go bad for white after Queen takes a7 knight!

Budapest ch-HUN 1972
based on notes by Ribli

1.e4 c5 2.♘f3 e6 3.d3 ♘c6 4.g3 d5 5.♘bd2

From the Sicilian to the King's Indian Attack.

5...♘f6 6.♗g2 ♗e7 7.0-0 0-0 8.♖e1 b5 9.e5 ♘d7 10.♘f1 b4!? 11.h4 ♗a6!?

11...a5 12.♗f4 would have transposed to the famous game Fischer-Myagmarsuren, Sousse izt 1967, which Fischer won in brilliant style.

12.♘1h2 ♗b5 13.♗f4

13.♗g5!? a5 14.♘g4 ♖c8 15.♕c1 c4 16.d4 c3 17.b3 a4 18.♗h3 unclear, A.Antunes-J.Sanchez, Havana 1992 (draw, 44 moves).

13...a5 14.♘g5

A standard attacking idea for White in this line is 14.♘g4!? with the idea ♗g5.

14...♕e8! 15.♘g4

15.♕h5 ♗xg5 16.♕xg5 (16.hxg5?! f5 works against White). Here Ribli gives 16...a4 17.♘g4 ♔h8 as unclear. Black might also try 16...c4!?.

15...♘d4 16.c3 ♘f5 17.c4!

Excellent Knight movement by both.

17...dxc4!!

Black could not allow the e5-pawn to be freed: 17...♗c6? 18.cxd5! ♗xd5 (18...exd5 19.e6±) 19.♗xd5 exd5 20.e6± (Ribli). With the exchange sacrifice Black manages to take over the initiative.

18.dxc4 ♗xc4 19.♗xa8 ♕xa8 20.♕xd7 ♖d8 21.♕a4!?

The alternative was 21.♕c7 ♖c8 22.♕d7 ♖d8 with a draw.

21...♘d4 22.♘h2! *saves Nf3 fork!*

22.♖e3!? h5! (first chasing the knight to a more passive square before winning the queen) 23.♘h2 ♗b5 24.♕d1 ♘e2+ 25.♕xe2 ♗xe2 26.♖xe2 ♖d3 is comparable to the game; White is OK materially but Black has the initiative.

22...♗b5 23.♕d1 ♘e2+ 24.♕xe2 ♗xe2 25.♖xe2 ♖d3 26.♘e4 ♕d5

26...c4 and 27...c3 might have been annoying.

27.♘f1 h6 28.b3 a4!

29.♘fd2

Ribli indicated 29.bxa4 c4 30.♘d6 c3 31.♘e3 as slightly better for White, but today's silicon monster comes up with 31...♕f3!, winning a piece with 32...g5 on the next move.

29...g5!

Also strong here, based on the pin created on move 32.

30.hxg5 hxg5 31.♘xg5?

He should have struggled on with 31.♗e3 ♕xe5 32.♖c1 ♕b2 33.♖ee1, but after 33...f5 it's no picnic either.

31...♗xg5! 32.♗xg5 ♕d4! 33.♖ae1 ♖xg3+ 34.♔f1 ♖xg5

Winning the piece back, and not even losing the exchange after it... an impressive piece of calculation!

35.♘f3 ♕d5!

The rook is taboo due to mate on h1.

36.♖e3 ♖f5 37.♔e2 axb3 38.axb3 c4   0-1

After 39.♖d1, 39...♖xf3! (Ribli) is the killer: 40.♖xf3 ♕xe5+ 41.♖e3 ♕h5+ followed by 42...c3.

GM Gyula SAX (1951-2014)

Gyula was the third musketeer of the Big Three. He joined Ribli and me in 1975 (in my memory, it was earlier). Then came an extra person, Laci Vadasz, and our work was fruitful. Just like Ribli, Sax became a great tournament player, a World Championship Candidate too. It's difficult to say how long we lasted. One thing is for sure: before and during the Buenos Aires Olympiad (1978) we were still co-operating. One surprising 'fait divers': although he was the more successful player, my personal score against him was 7-1. Like hell. It's hard to believe, even for me...

Aleksandar Matanovic	2505
Gyula Sax	2550

Buenos Aires ol 1978 (14)

This game was played in the final round of the event.

1.e4 c5 2.♘f3 e6 3.d4 cxd4 4.♘xd4 ♘f6 5.♘c3 ♘c6 6.♘db5 d6 7.♗f4 e5 8.♗g5 a6 9.♘a3 b5 10.♗xf6 gxf6 11.♘d5 f5 12.♗d3 ♗e6 13.♕h5 ♗g7 14.0-0 f4 15.c4 bxc4 16.♗xc4 0-0 17.♖ac1 ♘e7

17...♖b8!? became more popular later on.

18.♖fd1 ♖c8 19.♘xe7+ ♕xe7 20.♕e2

Better was 20.♖c3 ♔h8 21.b3 f5 22.♖h3±, Short-Sax, St John 1988.

20...♔h8 21.♗xa6

Gaining a massive advantage on the queenside, but unfortunately the centre is the place where the game will be decided.

21...♖xc1 22.♖xc1 f5 23.exf5 ♗xf5 24.♘b5

White should perhaps have tried to achieve a blockade on the light squares with 24.♗c4 e4 25.f3.

24...e4 25.♘c3?!

On 25.♕d1, 25...e3! is strong.

25...♕g5

The immediate 25...f3! was stronger, but things have become very difficult for White anyway.

26.f3 exf3 27.♕xf3 ♗g4 28.♕d5 ♗e5 29.♘e4 ♕g7 30.♗f1

30.♖c2 or 30.♘f2 would have prolonged White's agony.

30...f3 31.♖c2 fxg2 32.♗xg2 ♗f3 0-1

White forfeited on time in a totally lost position.

GM Laszlo VADASZ (1948-2005)

Laszlo Vadasz (Laci) was a very strong positional player. He was good-natured, so, for example, he was once Ribli's

29-34! Nice Queen Pin on f2 pawn, giving black Rook skewer! White answers with Knight fork! 35.Nf3!

second. When he was getting old and had lost much of his strength because of a heavy sickness, somebody asked me how on earth had he become a member of the Golden Team in 1978? At that time we were clubmates, and on friendly terms (as ever). So I asked him this. He quietly said: 'You know before the Olympiad I won eight GM tournaments in a row.' That was a good answer! For this and other achievements he deserves a tribute.

Mikhail Tal	2620
Laszlo Vadasz	2490

Tallinn 1977   *Modern Defence*

based on notes by Vadasz

1.e4 g6 2.d4 ♗g7 3.c3 d6 4.f4 ♘f6 5.e5 dxe5 6.fxe5 ♘d5 7.♘f3 0-0 8.♗c4 c5! 9.0-0 cxd4 10.cxd4 ♘c6 11.♘c3 ♗e6 12.♗b3

12.♘g5? is very bad for White due to 12...♘xc3 13.♘xe6 ♘xd1 14.♘xd8 ♖axd8 15.♖xd1 ♘xd4 and Black wins.

12...♘a5!? 13.♘g5 ♘xc3! 14.bxc3

Again, 14.♘xe6? is losing: 14...♘xd1 15.♘xd8 ♘xb3 16.axb3 ♖fxd8 17.♖xd1 ♗xe5–+.

14...♗d5 15.e6!?

Tal probably didn't fancy 15.♗xd5 ♕xd5 16.♕g4 h6 17.♘e4 ♘c4, but here 18.♕h4! would still have set Black some problems.

15...♘xb3 16.exf7+

16.axb3 f6 is fine for Black.

16...♖xf7! 17.♘xf7

17...♕a5! 18.♘h6+ ♔h8

18...♗xh6 19.♗xh6 ♘xa1 20.♕e1 ♕c7 21.♕f2 ♕c8 (or 21...♔h8!?) is also equal.

19.♖b1?

The only move was 19.c4 and now:

A) 19...♗xd4+?! 20.♔h1 ♗xa1 21.axb3 ♗g8! – the bishop should not go to c6, as was suggested at the time, but the resulting position is not appealing for Black;

B) 19...♘xc1 20.♕xc1 ♗xd4+ 21.♔h1 ♖c8 22.♘f7+ ♔g8 23.♘h6+ with a draw;

C) Even 19...♘xa1 seems to be possible, e.g. 20.cxd5 ♕xd5 and now White can either give a perpetual with 21.♘f7+ ♔g8 22.♘h6+ or try for more with 21.♕e2.

19...♘xc1 20.♘f7+

Not 20.♕xc1 ♕xa2! and Black wins in view of 21.♖b2 ♗xh6!.

20...♗xf7 21.♕xc1

On 21.♖xf7, 21...♕xa2 is again deadly.

21...♗c4

Black is winning, and Vadasz converted without problems:

22.♖f2 ♕c7 23.♕e3 b5 24.h4 ♕d6 25.♖d1 ♗f6 26.g3 ♖d8 27.♖dd2 a5 28.♔g2 ♗d5+ 29.♔g1 ♕e6 30.♕f4 ♕e4 31.♕xe4 ♗xe4 32.♔f1 ♖c8 33.♖fe2 ♗d5 34.♖e3 g5 35.h5 g4 36.♖f2 b4 37.♖c2 ♗xd4 38.♖xe7 ♖f8+ **0-1**

GM Lajos PORTISCH (1937)

We played three training matches, beginning in 1988. Surprisingly, I didn't win any of them. He was so childishly eager and I didn't want to spoil his joy. Also he had been one of the best players of the world for decades...

We played our first (serious) game in 1968 – an Evans Gambit ending in a draw. Our balance became somewhat shady for me. We became friends, which is nice and strange. You couldn't find two persons in the whole world being so different. Mutual respect did it all. He's a great man.

When he was 50 he suddenly started singing. He is a bass-baritone, and dead serious in everything he does. Indeed he reached a certain level, and he has a repertoire close to Placido Domingo's. He has given many concerts. Frankly speaking, it's easier to respect him than to love him, but I have friendly emotions toward him, and in a peculiar way he returns them. We are both idealists, that is the point.

Excellent

| Mikhail Tal | 2615 |
| Lajos Portisch | 2625 |

Varese 1976 *Najdorf*

based on notes by Forintos in Chess Informant

1.e4 c5 2.♘f3 d6 3.d4 cxd4 4.♘xd4 ♘f6 5.♘c3 a6 6.♗g5 e6 7.f4 ♕b6 8.♕d2 ♕xb2

The notorious Poisoned Pawn Variation, still played by some daredevils in the 21st century.

9.♘b3 ♕a3 10.♗xf6 gxf6 11.♗e2 ♘c6 12.0-0 ♗d7 13.f5

Nowadays 13.♔h1 and 13.♗h5 are more popular.

13...♘e5 14.fxe6 fxe6 15.♗h5+ ♔d8

On 15...♔e7? Forintos indicated 16.♖ad1!, intending ♘b1. In 2010 a game by two amateurs saw 16.♖xf6!, which ended in a draw after 16...♗g7(±); Black cannot take as then White gets a mating attack.

16.♖ab1

16.♖xf6 ♗e7 is unclear.

16...♖c8 17.♘e2 ♗e7 18.♘f4 ♔c7 19.♗e2 ♔b8 20.♘a5?

Better was 20.♘d4.

20...b5! *Black gains tempo!*

A very daring move, with the point 21.c4? ♗d8!.

21.♘b3 ♗d8! 22.♔h1 ♗b6

With great consolidation. Black has covered all the soft squares well. The pawn on f6 is sacrificed for beautiful piece play.

23.♘h5 ♖c7 24.♘xf6 ♗c8 25.♘g4 ♘c4 26.♗xc4 ♖xc4 27.♘f6

Forintos gave the following attractive lines: 27.♖f7 ♕xa2! 28.♖a1 ♕xc2 29.♕xd6+ ♗c7 30.♖xc7 ♖xc7 31.♖c1 ♖d8!–+; this is confirmed by today's computers. But in the line 27.♘e3 ♖xe4 28.♕c3 ♗d4! (28...♖g8? 29.♕c6!) 29.♕d3 Black should play 29...♗b7! instead of Forintos' 29...d5,

23.Nh5 White finds weak spot

analysis diagram

as it turns out that White has the stunning move 30.♘c4!! ♕a4 (forced) 31.♘d6 and Black is in trouble.

27...♕b4! 28.♕d1 ♕c3! 29.♖c1

29.♕xd6+ ♗c7 30.♕e7 (more tenacious is 30.♕d3 ♕e5 31.g3) 30...♕e5 31.g3

Excellent movement

♖xc2 with the idea 32...♖h2+, e.g. 32.♕g7 ♖d8 followed by 33...♖xa2.

29...h5! 30.♖f3 ♕e5–+

Centralization!

31.♕d2 ♔a8 32.♖d1 ♗c7 33.♘a5 d5! 34.g3 ♗xa5 35.♕xa5 ♖xc2 36.♕b6 ♕b2 37.♕g1 dxe4 38.♘xe4 ♗b7

Finally the bishop comes into action, and it is immediately decisive.

39.♖e3 ♖f8 40.a4 ♕e5   0-1

IM Bela PERENYI (1953-1988)

Poor Bela died very young in a car crash. He was on his way to Saloniki to see Ildiko Madl, his fiancée. Ildi was a heroine to finish the Olympiad, even beating Litinskaya and becoming Olympic Champion together with the Polgars.

Perenyi was a very sharp attacking player. With both colours! Beating practically the whole Hungarian elite – except me. We were not only on good terms, we also worked together on certain subjects. For example, the so-called Delayed Benoni (1.d4 ♘f6 2.c4 c5 3.d5 and here first ...g7-g6/♗g7/0-0/d7-d6 and only after that ...e7-e6). The guy was fantastic. The trouble was, when he put '=' behind a variation, it was sure to be better for White. He didn't really understand the position, only chasing his romantic dreams. This was common – I'm a lunatic too.

| **Anthony Miles** | 2610 |
| **Bela Perenyi** | |

Porz 1986

1.d4 ♘f6 2.c4 c5 3.d5 e6 4.♘c3 exd5 5.cxd5 d6 6.e4 g6 7.♗d3 ♗g7 8.♘ge2 0-0 9.0-0 ♘g4 10.♗f4

On 10.h3 ♘e5 11.♗c2 Black plays 11...♘a6! and now:

A) 12.a3!? c4 13.♗e3 b6!? 14.f4 ♘d3 15.♗xd3 (15.b4!) 15...cxd3 16.♕xd3 ♘c5 17.♗xc5 (17.♕c2 ♗a6!) 17...bxc5 18.♖fe1 ♖b8 with nice counterplay for the pawn, Zsinka-Perenyi, Hungary 1982;

B) 12.f4 ♘c4 13.b3 ♘b6 is unclear. It will take Black a while to bring his knights back to life, but White cannot undertake much in the meantime.

10...♘a6! 11.♕d2

11.♗g3 h5! with initiative, Zsu.Polgar-Perenyi, Fonyod 1983.

11...♘e5 12.♗c2 ♘c4 13.♕c1 ♘b4 14.♗b1 ♘e5 15.♕d1?!

Avoiding the draw with 15.♕d2 ♘c4 16.♕c1 ♘e5.

15...♕a5! 16.a3 c4 17.♕d2

Here White offered a draw.

17...♘bd3 18.b4!

18.♗xd3? cxd3 19.♘g3 ♘c4 and 20...♘xb2, but 19.♘d4! ♘c4 20.♕xd3 ♘xb2 21.♕d2 is still equal.

18...♕d8 19.♗xd3

19.♗g5 f6 20.♗e3 (20.♗h6 a5!) 20...f5! would give Black a nice initiative.

19...♘xd3 20.♗g5 ♕e8 21.♘c1?!

Here and on the previous move, 21.♗h6 was preferable.

21...f5! 22.♘xd3 cxd3 23.exf5

Another game with very bold Piece sacrifices to achieve mate!

What else would? Unsure conclusion?

On 23.♕xd3 f4! wins a piece.
23.f3 ♕e5 24.♖ac1 fxe4 25.♘xe4 ♗f5! also creates problems for White.

23...♗xf5 24.♖fe1 ♕c8 25.♖ac1 ♕c4! 26.♗e7 ♗e5! 27.♘e2!?

Both 27.♗xf8 ♗f4 and 27.♖xe5 dxe5 28.♗xf8 ♖xf8 also lose for White.

27...♕xd5 28.♗xf8 ♖xf8 29.♖c7!?

Here White offered a draw again. His idea is 30.♕h6. If 29.♘g3 ♗d7, again threatening 30...♗f4. But now Black starts a raging attack.

29...♗h3!! 30.f3

The only move – on 30.gxh3 comes the second bishop sac 30...♗xh2+ 31.♔xh2 ♖xf2+ with mate in a few moves.

30...♖xf3!   *Bold Sacrifice!*

With the point 31...♖f1+. Not 30...♗xg2? in view of 31.♕h6 and White wins.

31.gxf3

If 31.gxh3 ♗xh2+ as above; 31.♘g3 or 31.♘c3 loses to 31...♕d4+ 32.♔h1 ♖f2.

31...♗xf3 32.♕g5 ♗f6 33.♕g3 d2! 34.♖ec1

34.♖b1 obviously loses to 34...♕xe2 35.♕xh3 ♗d4+ 36.♔h1 ♕e4+−+.

The best defence was 34.♖cc1! ♕xg3+! (34...♕xe2? 35.♕b3+!+−; 34...dxc1♕ 35.♖xc1 ♕f5 36.♕f4! with chances of survival; 34...♕f5!) 35.hxg3 (35.♘xg3 ♗d4+ 36.♔h1 ♗d7! 37.♔g2 ♗b2!) 35...♗b2! 36.♖ed1! (36.a4? ♗xc1!−+; 36.♖cd1 dxe1♕+ 37.♖xe1 ♗xa3 and Black is clearly better) 36...dxc1♕ 37.♘xc1 ♗g4 38.♖e1 ♗f5! (38...♗xa3

39.♘d3! with the idea 40.♖a1) 39.a4 ♔f7 (not 39...♗c2 40.a5 ♗c3 41.♖c8+ ♔f7 42.♖c8) with some winning chances for Black.

34...♕xe2 35.♖c8+ ?

On 35.♕xh3? Black gives mate with queen, bishop, and pawns: 35...♗d4+ 36.♔h1 d1♕+! 37.♖xd1 ♕xd1+ 38.♔g2 ♕g1+ 39.♔f3 ♕e3+ 40.♔g4 h5+ 41.♔h4 ♗f6#!

35...♗xc8 36.♖xc8+ ♔g7 37.♖c7+

37...♔h6??

In time-trouble Black blunders terribly. Winning was 37...♗e7! 38.♖xe7+ (on 38.♕c3+ ♔h6! is correct: 39.♕h3+ ♕h5 40.♕e3+ ♕g5+−+) 38...♕xe7 39.♕c3+ ♕e5 40.♕xd2 d5.

38.♕f4+

Black had overlooked this check. He had considered only 38.♕h3+.

38...♗g5 39.♕f8+ ♔h5 40.♖xh7+ ♔g4 41.♕c8+??

Again, time-trouble. The players had to make 50 moves until the time control. 41.h3+! ♔g3 42.♕xd6+ would have won.

41...♔f4??

He should have played 41...♔f3! 42.♖h3+ ♔f4 43.♕f8+ ♔g4 44.♕c8+ with a draw.

42.♖f7+?

42.♕f8+ would have won the queen and the game after, e.g., 42...♔e4 43.♕e8+ ♔d3 44.♕b5+.

42...♗f6!?

42...♔e3 43.♕e8+ ♔d3 44.♕b5+ was a draw.

43.♖xf6+ ♔g5

44.♖xg6+!

It would have been even harder after 44.h4+!? ♔xh4! (44...♔xf6?? 45.♕f8++−) 45.♕h8+ ♔g5 46.♖xg6+ ♔xg6 and believe it or not, but this is a perpetual check!

Losing is 44.♕d8? ♕g4+ (44...d1♕+? 45.♖f1+) 45.♔h1 ♕e4+ 46.♔g1 (46.♖f3+ ♔g4−+) 46...♕d4+ 47.♖f2+ ♔h5!−+.

44.♖xd6 d1♕+ 45.♖xd1 ♕xd1+ is also drawish.

44...♔xg6 45.♕g8+ ♔f5 46.♕f7+ ♔e4 47.♕e6+??

Again, time-trouble! 47.♕e8+ ♔d3 (47...♔f3 48.♕h5+=) 48.♕b5+ is a draw.

47...♔d3 48.♕b3+ ♔d4 49.♕b2+ ♔e4 50.♕c2+ ♔e3

50...♔f4!.

51.♕b3+ ♔d4 52.♕b2+ ♔e4 53.♕c2+ ♔f4 ☞ **0-1**

With all its mistakes, an epic endgame.

IM Janos TOMPA (1947)

Can you believe we first met in 1962? Of course, it was with Bela Bacsi (Papp)'s junior team ASI. That's a lot of time. Janos became and stayed an IM, although his talent destined him for more. But he has an incredible record of activities as a trainer, captain, second, etc. It's not far-fetched to say that his missions were countless. And successful too!

He became one of my seconds in 1978, and in this capacity he expressively taught me how to play the Nimzo (4.e3 b6), which worked against Farago, and the Queen's Indian. He was with me at the Riga Interzonal, and did an excellent job. He was one of my seconds when I played against Hübner in 1980. That is a sad memory. Later on we met in several team events: in 1985 (the World Team Championship in Luzern), he was the second who analysed the position of my adjourned game against Seret in such a way that I won the game by following the lines he had found. From the beginning till the end. See also the fragment of my game against Mednis (1979) in Chapter 7 (Black Is Brutal III).

Igor Zaitsev
Janos Tompa 9
Moscow tt 1971   Ruy Lopez

1.e4 e5 2.♘f3 ♘c6 3.♗b5 a6 4.♗a4 ♘f6 5.0-0 ♗e7 6.♖e1 b5 7.♗b3 d6 8.c3 0-0 9.h3 ♘a5 10.♗c2 c5 11.d4 ♕c7 12.♘bd2 cxd4 13.cxd4 ♗b7 14.♘f1 ♖ac8 15.♖e2

15...d5!? 16.dxe5

On 16.♘xe5, 16...♘xe4 was the idea. But perhaps 16...dxe4 is also feasible, increasing the bishop's diagonal and gaining the d5-square for his pieces. If White tries to round up the e4-pawn, Black can do the same with the d4-pawn. *EP*

16...♘xe4 17.♘g3 f5 18.exf6 ♗xf6 19.♗xe4 dxe4 20.♘xe4

Beautiful opening. Heavy piece exchanges 16.-20.

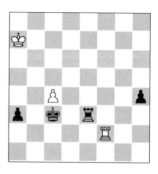

20...♕c6!

Black has a lot of space in compensation for the pawn, and already posts his queen on the long diagonal in case White takes on f6 with the knight. The point will become clear five moves later.

21.♕e1 ♘c4 22.a4? bxa4 23.♕b4 a3 24.♘xf6+ ♖xf6 25.b3

Better was 25.♖e7. Black can try 25...♖xf3, but then 26.♖xb7 equalizes. 25...♗a8! keeps all the possibilities on the board.

25...♖g6!! 26.♕xc4+ *wow*

26.♖e7 is no longer possible, as the long diagonal is already too vulnerable. Black wins with 26...♖xg2+! 27.♔xg2 ♕xf3+ 28.♔f1 ♕h1+ 29.♔e2 ♗f3+ 30.♔d3 ♕f1+ 31.♔c3 ♘b2+. So White is forced to enter a worse ending with opposite-coloured bishops.

26...♕xc4 27.bxc4 ♗xf3 28.♖e3 ♗xg2 29.♗xa3 ♗xh3+ 30.♔h2 ♗e6 31.♖c1

If 31.c5 ♖f8 and White has to give the f-pawn to avoid getting mated.

31...♗xc4 32.♖e7 h6

More efficient was 32...♖gc6 33.♗b2 ♗f7.

33.f4 ♖cc6 34.f5 ♖g4 35.♗b2 ♖d6

35...♖c5! won more easily as the f-pawn cannot move due to mate on h5.

36.♖xg7+?! ♖xg7 37.♗xg7 ♔xg7 38.♖xc4 a5! 39.♖c7+

On 39.♔g3 ♖a6 40.♖c7+ ♔f8 (or 40...♔f6? 41.♔f4, e.g. 41...a5 42.♖h7 with a draw) the draw is instructive: 41.♖c8+ ♔e7 45.♖c7+ ♔d8 46.♖c5!.

39...♔f6

40.♔g3

On 40.♖a7!? Black would have had to tread carefully:

A) 40...♖d2+? 41.♔g3 ♖a2 42.♖a6+ ♔xf5 43.♖xh6 is a theoretical draw. The Vancura Defence can come in handy here for White. Of course there are several possibilities for both players, but an exemplary line could be: 43...a4 44.♖b6 a3 45.♖b3 ♔e4 46.♔h3 (46.♖f3 is too early, because of 46...♖a1 47.Kg2 ♖g1+! (47...a2? 48.♖a3=)) ♖a1 47.♔h2 ♔d4 48.♖g3 and now we have reached a Vancura position. The way to draw here is as follows: White will stick with the pawn on a3 until Black's king goes to b4 (to protect the pawn intending to move the rook). When the king reaches that square, White gives checks from the rear. If Black is impatient and moves the pawn to a2 at once, White will put his rook behind the pawn by ♖a3. This time, if Black's king reaches b3 or b2 (again to defend the pawn with the idea to move the pawn), White will give checks from behind (for instance, from a8-b8). There is no way Black can make progress here;

B) 40...♖d5! 41.♖a6+ ♔xf5 (41...♔g5 42.f6 ♔g6 43.f7+ makes things worse) 42.♖xh6 ♔e4 43.♔g3. It seems as if a similar ending has been reached as in the line with 40...♖d2+, but there is a big difference here. Behind the pawn, the rook is better placed than in front of its pawn! In this case, Black can play 43...♖f5!, cutting off the white king. Still,

(handwritten margin notes, rotated left side)
White gets 1 pawn up 20.Nxe4! 26. Rg6 White's #3 Knight is pinned! Heavy piece exchanges! Black steals! 27. Bxf3, White can't return capture, 27-30 Discover check

the win is not elementary here, but we cannot always expect things to be easy! An exemplary line: 44.♖a6 ♔e3 45.♖a8 (45.♔g4 ♖f4+ and the a-pawn goes to a4 next) 45...♖g5+ 46.♔h4 ♔f4 47.♖a7 ♖f5 48.♖a8 ♔f3 49.♖a7 ♖f4+ and the a-pawn can be set in motion.

40...♔g5! 41.♔f3 ♖d5

Not 41...♖a6? when 42.♔e4 draws.

42.♔e4 ♖xf5   **0-1**

GM Jozsef PINTER (1953)

Pinter was one of my seconds in my Candidates' match against Hübner. It was my choice. A wrong one. At that time he was speaking of himself only as 'the two-time Hungarian Champion'. Indeed, that he was, having won the title twice in the absence of the four best players (Portisch, Ribli, Sax, Adorjan). He became a very strong grandmaster not much later, mainly thanks to his fantastic performances with white. On the other hand, when I had passed an invitation to Bajmok (Yugoslavia) to him in 1980, he lost all his seven black games in return for his eight white victories!! He has written close to twenty books.

Later, Lajos Portisch had three seconds too vs. Hübner, but he got so disgusted that for some time he appointed his late wife Kati as his only 'bodyguard'. She did not understand a thing about chess, but she was Lajos's faithful partner for 40 (forty) years.

Lajos Portisch	2625
Jozsef Pinter	2515

Budapest ch-HUN 1984

based on notes from Chess Informant no. 37

1.d4 ♘f6 2.c4 e6 3.♘f3 d5 4.♘c3 c5 5.cxd5 ♘xd5 6.e4 ♘xc3 7.bxc3 cxd4 8.cxd4 ♘c6 9.♗c4 b5 10.♗e2 ♗b4+ 11.♗d2 ♕a5 12.♗xb4

12.a4 ♗xd2+ 13.♕xd2 bxa4 14.♕xa5 ♘xa5 15.♖xa4 gives White a comfortable plus.

12...♕xb4+ 13.♕d2 ♗b7!

This dynamic move was new at the time. Farago had played 13...a6 in 1975 against Baumbach. After 13...♕xd2+ 14.♔xd2 a6 15.♖ac1 White is slightly better, as subsequent games have proved.

14.a3

Now 14.♕xb4 ♘xb4 15.♗xb5+ ♔e7 16.0-0 ♗xe4 is just equal.

14...♕xd2+ 15.♔xd2 a6 16.a4! b4 17.a5!?

17.♖ac1! would have kept some pressure. Now Black quickly creates counterplay in the centre and along the long diagonal.

17...♖d8 18.♔e3 f5! 19.exf5 exf5 20.♗c4! ♔e7! 21.d5 ♔f6!

A brilliant concept. After 21...♘b8 22.♔d4! White would gain the upper hand, so Pinter sacrifices a piece for a hunt on the exposed white king.

22.dxc6

Certainly not 22.♖he1? ♘e7.

22...♖he8+ 23.♔f4 ♖e4+

23...g5+ was thought to have been wrong, but may have been better than the text: 24.♔g3! (24.♘xg5? ♖d4+ 25.♔g3 ♖g4+ 26.♔h3 ♗xc6 favours Black, who wins his piece back) 24...f4+ 25.♔h3 (25.♔g4?? h5+–+) and now:

A) 25...♗xc6 26.♖he1 h5 27.♖xe8 ♖xe8 28.♘d2 ♗d7+ 29.g4 ♗xg4+ 30.♔g2 ♗e2 and Black can still fight;

B) But stronger is, like in the game, 25...♗c8+ 26.g4 h5 27.♔g2 hxg4

271

28.♘e1 ♗f5! (28...♖d2? 29.♘d3!) with the main point that after e.g. 29.♗xa6 the b-pawn marches very fast.

24.♔g3 ♗c8

24...♖g4+ 25.♔h3 ♗xc6 26.♗xa6 favours White, e.g. 26...♖g6 27.♖hc1! ♖h6+ 28.♘h4 ♗d5 29.♖cb1 b3 and now he has to give back the piece with 30.♗b7! ♗xb7 31.♖xb3, with an edge in the endgame as ...g7-g5 can be prevented by f2-f4.

25.♖ac1

The following try is also interesting: 25.♗xa6! ♗xa6 26.♖hd1 ♖xd1 27.♖xd1 ♖g4+ 28.♔h3 ♖c4 29.♖d6+ ♔e7 30.♖d7+ ♔f6 31.♖b7 g5! 32.♖b6 and now Black forces a fantastic draw with 32...g4+ 33.♔g3 ♗c8 34.♘e1 f4+ 35.♔h4 g3! 36.hxg3 f3+! 37.♔h5 ♖c5+ 38.♔h4 (38.♔h6?? ♗g4! loses!) 38...♖h4+ etc.

25...♖g4+ 26.♔h3 f4 27.♘e5?

It's a draw after 27.♗xa6 ♖g3+ (other moves fail) 28.♔h4 ♖g4+ (not 28...g5+? 29.♔h5 ♗g4+ 30.♔h6 ♖g8 31.hxg3 ♖g6+ 32.♔xh7 ♗f5 33.♖h6!+− or even 33.♔h8!!+−) 29.♔h3!.

The white king cannot move to h5 because of the ...♖d5 check. But there is a win if White keeps Black's second rook under control: 27.c7! ♖g3+ 28.♔h4 ♖g4+ 29.♔h5! ♖e8 (or 29...♖d6 30.♖hd1) and now 30.♗e6!! decides, e.g. 30...♗xe6 31.♖he1 with the deadly threat of 32.♖xe6+.

27...♔g5!!−+

Similarly here, after 27...♔xe5 28.♖he1+ ♔f6 29.♗e6! White has the advantage.

28.♘f7+

Or 28.♘f3+ and now:

A) After 28...♔h6 29.♖he1! Black has a mating trick that doesn't work: 29...♖g3+ 30.♔h4 g5+! (not 30...♖xf3 31.♗e6!=) 31.♘xg5 ♖g4+ 32.♔h3 ♔xg5! 33.♖e5+ ♔f6 34.♖e6+ ♗xe6 35.♗xe6 ♖g7! and after 35.c7 ♖xc7 36.♖xc7 ♔xe6 the rook ending seems to be a draw;

B) But much stronger is 28...♔h5! 29.♗f7+ g6 30.♖c5+ ♖g5+ 31.g4+ ♗xg4+ 32.♔g2 ♖xc5 and Black wins.

28...♔h5 29.♗e2 ♖d3+! 30.g3

30.♗f3 ♖xf3+ 31.gxf3 ♖g3#.

30...f3! 31.♖c5+

31.♗xf3 ♖xf3 32.♔g2 ♖xf7.

31...♖g5+ 32.g4+ ♗xg4+ 33.♔g3 fxe2+   **0-1**

An endgame with many fantastic points.

IM Tamas HORVATH (1951)

Horvath Tamas was a good buddy and he did well on all the occasions when he was my second. Also with the preparations. He helped me to become a World Championship Candidate against Ribli in our dramatic match (1979). He was with me during my tragic match with Hübner (1980). Halfway our 10-game match, Hübner was leading by 2 points, just like Ribli (1979) who had a 2½-½ lead in 6 games against me in 1979. But against him I won the next two games, and with a final draw I qualified thanks to my better Berger-Sonneborg in Riga. Miracles are usually not repeated, so against Hübner I won the 6th and was almost winning in the 7th, but finally, in Game 9 I made an awful blunder and stalemated him in a rook ending instead of taking another pawn, in which case he would have been ready to resign. Tamas also helped me in the Toluca Interzonal. He was the captain of the Hungarian (men's) team from time to time − a normal person on this responsible post.

We were 'believers' in the Sveshnikov. We wrote two books on the subject, and later on he published another, exclusively with his own games. We had some complicated analyses of the crazy kind. In the Riga Interzonal I made 2.5/3 with the Sveshnikov, including a fine win against Ljubojevic.

Tamas claims that he was the first who played the Sveshnikov. I personally saw the scoresheet. The trouble is there were quite a few others, and all of them pioneers. To my knowledge, Tal-Shamkovich was the very first game, in 1955.

Anyway, in the next game he plays originally, sacrificing his queen. Bravo!

Bela Perenyi	2310
Tamas Horvath	2410

Zamardi 1979

1.e4 c5 2.♘f3 ♘c6 3.d4 cxd4 4.♘xd4 ♘f6 5.♘c3 e6 6.♘db5 d6 7.♗f4 e5 8.♗g5 a6 9.♘a3 b5 10.♗xf6 gxf6 11.♘d5 f5 12.♗xb5 axb5 13.♘xb5 ♖a4

Black's best reply to the sacrifice, introduced in 1978 by Mark Tseitlin against the later Junior World Champion Mark Diesen, who then reproduced it in the same year against Honfi.

14.♘bc7+ ♔d7 15.0-0 ♖xe4 16.♕h5 ♘d4!

17.c3

The move that is preferred by most players nowadays. If 17.♕xf7+ ♔c6! 18.♘b4+ (18.b4 ♕d7 19.b5+ ♘xb5 20.♕xd7+

♗xd7 21.♘xb5 ♔xb5 22.a4+? ♔c6 23.♘f6 ♖c4 0-1 Velimirovic-T.Horvath, Stara Pazova 1983) 18...♔b7 19.♘b5+ ♕d7 20.♕d5+ ♔b6 21.a4 ♘e2+? (21...♘xb5!) 22.♔h1 ♖xb4 23.a5+ ♔a6 24.♕a8+ ♔xb5 25.♕d5+ ½-½ Szabo-T. Horvath, Oberwart 1979.

17...♘e2+ 18.♔h1 ♔c6! 19.g3

White cannot achieve anything by 19.b4 ♘f4 20.b5+ ♔b7 21.♕xf7 ♕d7 and the endgame after 22.♕xd7 ♗xd7 23.a4 ♖c4 24.♘xf4 exf4 25.♘d5 ♗g7 is winning for Black.

19...♖g8 20.♕f3

On 20.♖ae1 Black has the attractive move 20...♖gg4! 21.f3? (White can hang on by 21.♕xf7 ♖g7 22.♘e6!) 21...♘xg3+ 22.hxg3 ♖h4+ 23.gxh4 ♖xh4+ 24.♕xh4 ♕xh4+ 25.♔g2 f4–+.

20...♕xc7!!

A brilliant way to break the deadlock.

21.♘xc7 ♔xc7 22.♕h5

22.♕d3 f4 23.f3 leads to a kind of dynamic equality:

A) 23.♖ae1 ♗b7 24.f3 fxg3 25.♖xe2 ♖xe2 26.hxg3! (26.♕xe2? g2+ 27.♕xg2 ♖xg2 28.♔xg2 f5–+) 26...♖xb2 27.♕c4+ ♔b6 28.♕xf7 ♖xg3 29.♕xf8 ♖g6!? (29...♖h3+=) 30.♖d1 ♔a7 31.♕f7 ♖h6+ 32.♔g1 ♖g6+;

B) 23.f3 fxg3 24.♖g1 ♘xg1! 25.fxe4 (25.♕xe4 ♘xf3!) 25...♘h3 26.♕c4+ ♔d8 27.hxg3 ♖xg3 28.♕xf7 ♗e7 29.a4 and White can sacrifice his rook for the bishop on f3 and then build on his queenside pawns.

22...♖g6 23.♕xh7

23.♖ae1 ♗b7 with a deadly attack, for example 24.f3 ♘xg3+ 25.hxg3 ♖xe1 26.♖xe1 ♖h6−+.

23...♗e6 24.♖ad1 ♖eg4 25.♕h8 ♖g8 26.♕h3

White defends well for the moment, though 26.♕h7! may have been the most accurate move here. 26.♕h5 would lose to 26...f4 27.♖fe1 fxg3 28.♖xe2 gxf2 29.♖xf2 ♗d5+!.

26...f4 27.♖fe1

27.♕h7! was still the most tenacious, although Black has an ingenious way to catch the queen: 27...♖8g6 28.♔g2 f3+! 29.♔xf3 (29.♔h1 ♖h6 30.♕d3 ♖g8! with the lethal threat of 31...♖xh2+!) 29...♘xc3! 30.bxc3 e4+ 31.♔g2 ♖h6 with winning chances.

An uncanny similarity with the previous game!

27...♖xg3

Winning the queen due to the mate threat on g1 resp. d5. Even stronger would have been 27...fxg3 28.♖xe2 ♗d5+ 29.♖xd5 (29.♔g1 gxh2+ 30.♔xh2 ♖g2+ 31.♕xg2 ♖xg2+ 32.♔h3 ♗c6−+) 29...gxf2−+, but Horvath has no problems converting now.

28.♕xe6 fxe6 29.fxg3 f3 30.♖xe2 fxe2 31.♖e1 d5 32.♖xe2 ♔d6 33.♔g2 ♗h6 34.a4 d4 35.♔f3 d3 36.♖e1 ♔d5 37.c4+ ♔xc4 38.♔e4 d2 39.♖d1 ♔b3 40.♔d3 ♖d8+ 41.♔e2 ♔xb2 0-1

IM Jeno DÖRY (1951)

I can't recall our first meeting, but since we are of a similar age, it must have been ages ago. He was never determined – he was realistic about his chess future and switched to a civil profession in 1992. But still he remained the head of the Youth Committee of the Hungarian Chess Federation for many years, and did this job well (unpaid work). Sure he had some headaches, as children usually have parents... Jesus Christ on the cross! However we did some paperwork together: 1. *Winning with the Grünfeld* (1986), 2. *BLACK IS OK!* (1988), and 3.The Zero Copy of the *BLACK IS OK!* periodical (1992), both published by Batsford. I'd like to forget the Szirak 1987 Interzonal, in which I committed hara-kiri. Jeno and Endre Vegh were my seconds, but it was not their fault.
Jeno Döry was/is somebody who keeps his word. Nowadays that is not very common.

Rainer Gruenberg
Jeno Döry

Stockholm 1984

1.d4 ♘f6 2.c4 e6 3.♘c3 ♗b4 4.e3 c5 5.♘e2 cxd4 6.exd4 0-0 7.a3 ♗e7 8.d5 exd5 9.cxd5 ♖e8 10.d6 ♗f8 11.g3 b6 12.♗g2 ♘c6 13.♘b5 ♗a6 14.a4 ♖e6

Alternatives are 14...♖c8!? or 14...♘e4!?.

15.0-0

More principled was 15.♗f4! ♕e8 16.0-0! ♖xe2 (16...♗xb5? 17.axb5 ♖xe2 18.bxc6 dxc6 19.♗xc6 ♕xc6 20.♕xe2 ♗xd6 21.♖fc1±) 17.♘c7 ♕c8 18.b4! (18.♘xa8 ♖xb2 gives Black good counterchances) 18...♘xb4 19.♗xa8 ♖c2 20.♘xa6 ♕xa6 21.♗g2±, a line by Ron Henley.

15...♗xd6 16.♗h3

Weak would be 16.♘ed4? ♘xd4 17.♘xd4 ♖c8! 18.♘xe6 dxe6 19.♖e1 ♗b4 and Black has all the fun.

16...♗c5 17.♗xe6 fxe6 18.♗f4

Other ways to trade off the black king's bishop are 18.♗e3 ♘e5 19.♗xc5 bxc5 20.f4 ♘c4 21.♕c1 d5 22.b3 ♘a5 23.♕xc5 ♘xb3 24.♕c6 ♗xb5 25.axb5 ♘xa1 26.♕xe6+ ♔h8 27.♖xa1 ♕f8! and Black's chances are not worse; or 18.♘f4!? with the idea ♘f4-d3xc5.

18...♘d5 19.♕d2 ♕f6 20.♗d6 ♗xd6 21.♘xd6 ♕f3 22.♘b5?

Giving the b7-square to the black bishop proves immediately fatal. He should have played 22.♖fe1! ♘e5!? 23.♘d4 ♕h5 24.b4! to close off the bishop, with good play. Dangerous is 24.f4?! ♘d3 25.♖e4 (if 25.♖ed1 ♖f8, threatening 24...♘5xf4) 25...♘f6.

22...♘e5 23.♘ed4

On 23.♖a3?, 23...♕xa3! is already good, but much stronger is 23...♗b7!.

23...♗b7 24.♕d1

24.♖fd1 ♘e3! 25.♘xf3 ♘xf3+ 26.♔h1 ♘g5+ 27.f3 ♗xf3+ 28.♔g1 ♘h3#.

24...♕g2+! 25.♔xg2 ♘f4+ 26.♔g1 ♘h3#   **0-1**

LOVASS Laszlo (1964)

I may be subjective: Laci could have been one of the world's leading minds in computer chess if he had not remained a one-man band for too long. He has developed all by himself (and not being a strong player) his own program called Prochess, re-baptised SuperPro. This was before there was ChessBase, and it had extra services that were comparable. IM Dr Ervin Nagy simultaneously tested it, and occasionally I did too. But he couldn't find an honest distributor (are there any?), so he did the creation, the developing, the marketing, and the servicing. GMs Peter Leko and Zoltan Almasi praised his work publicly and so did I.

Later on, he decided to have a minimum of two meals a day and for that reason turned his talent to other fields. Successfully.

But he is the man who created my Rainbow Chess program. This is something by which you can play and analyse Rainbow, Colour, SwitChess and traditional chess, of course with the same rules. Also you can follow any tournaments, even online, if there are .pgn games. Leslie was my co-author in some parts of my books where his special knowledge was needed. He has a long-standing connection with the Benko family. First he was dating the pretty Palma, Pali's daughter, later he lectured and edited one of the brilliant GM Benko's books.

| **Gyula Letay** | 2265 |
| **Laszlo Lovass** | 2305 |

Hungary tt 1994/95 (8)

1.e4 e5 2.♘f3 d6 3.d4 exd4 4.♘xd4 g6 5.♘c3 ♗g7 6.♗e3 ♘f6 7.f3 0-0 8.♕d2 ♘c6 9.♗e2 ♖e8 10.0-0-0 ♘xd4 11.♗xd4 ♗e6 12.g4 c5!?

Often in such positions it's a good idea to sacrifice the d6-pawn for some action.

13.♗e3 ♕a5 14.♕xd6

14...♘xe4!?

More 'solid' was 14...♘d7 15.♕d2 b5! and Black has a strong attack almost out of nothing!

15.fxe4

Giving Black a beautiful initiative for nothing. Better was 15.♘xe4 ♕xa2 16.c3 ♗b3!? (instead of taking the immediate draw by 16...♖ad8 17.♕xd8 ♕a1+ 18.♔c2 ♕a4+=) and now:

A) 17.♕d3 ♕a1+ 18.♕b1 ♕xb1+ 19.♔xb1 ♗xd1 20.♖xd1 f5 leads to an equal endgame after 21.♗c4+ ♔h8 22.♗b5 ♖e5 23.gxf5 gxf5 24.♗f4 fxe4 25.♗xe5 ♗xe5 26.fxe4 ♗xh2 27.♖d7;

B) 17.♗d3 ♖ad8 18.♗b1 ♖xd6 19.♗xa2 ♖xd1+ 20.♖xd1 ♗xa2 21.♗xc5 b6 22.♗d4 ♗d5 23.♗xg7 ♗xe4 24.fxe4 ♔xg7 25.♖d4 ♔f6 leaves Black with a slight initiative in the endgame.

15...♗xc3 16.a3 ♖ac8 17.♕d3 ♗e5

Threatening 17...c4 with devastation.

18.♕b5 ♕c7 19.h4 a6 20.♕a4 b5 21.♕xa6 ♖a8

21...♖b8!? 22.♗xb5 ♖ec8 was also winning.

22.♕xb5 ♖ab8 23.♕xc5 ♗xb2+ 24.♔d2 ♖bd8+ 25.♗d3 ♕g3

This invasion should decide the issue. In the following Black has various other ways to continue the attack, but on move 35 he actually nearly blows it.

26.♖dg1 ♕f3 27.♕b6 ♖b8 28.♕a7 ♖bc8 29.♗d4 ♕f4+ 30.♗e3 ♕f3

31.♗d4 ♕f4+ 32.♗e3 ♗c3+ 33.♔c1 ♕d6 34.♔d1 ♗c4 35.♔e2

35...♗xd3+?

35...♖xe4 would have finally blown White's cover.

36.cxd3 ♖b8 37.♕a4?

Allowing the rook on b2 loses at once. After 37.♖b1 ♖bd8 Black is still attacking, but things have become highly unclear, e.g. 38.♖bd1 ♕e6 and now:

A) 39.♖hg1 ♕a2+ 40.♔f3 ♖d6 41.♖gf1 ♕h2 42.g5 f5 43.♖f2 ♕xh4 44.♔e2;

B) 39.♖hf1! ♕xg4+ 40.♖f3 ♖d7 41.♕c5 ♗e5 42.♕b5 f6 43.♖g1 ♕e6 44.♕c4.

37...♖b2+ 38.♔f3 ♕f6+ 39.♔g3 ♗e5+ **0-1**

IM Adam SZIEBERTH (1967)

'I don't have any good games', said Adam when I asked him for one. This is of course not quite true – see the one below. On the other hand, he doesn't play tournament chess but only team competition. He has the ambition to raise his three children by decent work. Which is tough. He is a professional translator (English-Hungarian). As for our co-operation and friendship, it has its roots in both of us being Bela Papp's pupils. Adam translated the whole BLACK IS OK! Zero Copy (1992). Later on the 'Presumption of Innocence in the Game of Chess' essay was born in 1995. It is the key line of BLACK IS OK!. Finally he was very helpful during the work on my later books *Black is still OK!* and *Black is OK forever!*.

Miklos Orso	2410
Adam Szieberth	2325

Hungary tt 1996/97

1.d4 ♘f6 2.c4 c5 3.d5 b5 4.a4

An odd move, frequently encountered on club level to avoid theory.

4...b4

4...bxc4 is OK, but Black wants to take away some squares from the queen's knight. A slightly more subtle way to do this is 4...♕a5+ 5.♗d2 b4.

5.♗g5 ♘e4 6.♗f4

6...e5!? 7.♗xe5

7.dxe6!? fxe6 8.e3 is also interesting.

7...d6 8.♗g3 ♕f6 9.♕c1 g6 10.♘d2 ♘xd2

Slightly better may be 10...♘xg3!? 11.hxg3 ♗g7. Black has the bishop pair, and there is no danger along the h-file.

11.♕xd2 ♗g7 12.♖b1?

A little more comfortable was 12.♕e3+!? ♔d8 13.♖a2.

12...♗f5 13.e4 ♗xe4 14.♕e2

Better was 14.♖d1, but Black has a great game after 14...0-0.

14...♔d7

Already winning big material. White decides to play on for a bit, but it gets worse.

15.♕xe4 ♖e8 16.♕xe8+ ♔xe8 17.♗d3 ♘d7 18.♘f3 ♗h6 19.♗h4 g5 20.♗g3 g4 21.♘h4 ♘e5 22.♗xh7 ♘xc4 23.0-0 ♗g5 24.♖fe1+ ♔d7 25.♗d3 ♘xb2 26.♖xb2 ♕xb2 27.♘f5 ♕d2 28.♗b5+ ♔c7 29.f3 gxf3 30.gxf3 b3 31.a5 ♕xa5 32.♗c4 b2 33.♗xd6+ ♔b6 34.♖b1 ♕c3 35.♗a2 ♗e3+ 36.♔h1 ♕c1+ 37.♔g2 ♕c2+ 38.♔h1 ♕xf5 39.♖xb2+ ♔a5 40.♔g2 ♖h8 41.♗c7+ ♔a4

White resigned.

IM Lajos GYÖRKÖS (1958)

I don't really remember when we worked together – it must have been in waves. He is a tall, strong man – and, true to this type: tame. We have completed quite a lot of lines but never finished our book about queen's pawn openings. A pity! It was supposed to be another part of the BLACK IS OK! repertoire, following the Grünfeld, Sveshnikov, Sicilian sub-variations, and Rare openings – finishing with 1.c4 and 1.♘f3. One sometimes sees booklets that promise a 'complete repertoire' for Black. I don't like such garbage.

These days Györkös has become the 'Big Arbiter', working almost continually in this capacity. I don't believe this was his dream. I think he deserves something better from life.

Jozsef Horvath
Lajos Györkös

Budapest 1982

1.e4 c5 2.♘f3 d6 3.d4 cxd4 4.♘xd4 ♘f6 5.♘c3 e6 6.♗e3 ♘c6 7.♗c4 a6 8.♗b3 ♗e7 9.♕e2 ♕c7 10.0-0-0 ♘a5 11.g4 ♘xb3+ 12.axb3 b5 13.g5 ♘d7

14.♞f5

A well-known sacrifice.

14...exf5 15.♞d5 ♛d8 16.exf5 ♝b7 17.f6 gxf6 18.gxf6?

18.♖he1 ♝xd5 19.♖xd5 ♖g8 20.gxf6 (20.♝f4!?) 20...♞xf6 21.♖f5 ♖g6 was first seen in Kupreichik-Beliavsky, USSR 1974. White can now play 22.♝b6 ♛d7 23.♛f3 ♖b8 24.♖xf6 ♖xb6 25.♛a8+ ♛d8 26.♖xe7+ ♚xe7 27.♖xf7+, with some advantage, as has happened in 8 games (3 white wins, 5 draws).

18...♝xd5 19.fxe7

After 19.♖xd5 ♞xf6 White won't see his piece back, but now also Black takes over and the whole thing is rounded off quickly.

19...♛a5! 20.♖hg1 ♛a1+ 21.♚d2 ♛xb2 22.♛d3 ♛e5 23.♖g5 ♝e4 24.♛d4 ♛xd4+ 25.♝xd4 f6   0-1

IM Zoltan NEMETH (1959)

Again I don't know the exact time when we analysed together. I guess it was twenty years ago. The subject was some lines of the English Opening. The fruits were OK. Zoli was (and is) a stubborn person. Once we got a 3/2 rook ending. I said 'It's a draw.' But he disagreed: 'I don't believe it, let's see it!' It became a matter of personal prestige...

Nowadays he is the publisher and editor of the only Hungarian chess magazine, called *Magyar Sakkvilag* ('Hungarian Chess World').

**Solymosi
Zoltan Nemeth**

Correspondence game 1986

1.e4 c5 2.c3

Not a big deal in my opinion, which I vented in a Survey in Yearbook 117. But Evgeny Sveshnikov, who I have known for 45 years, wrote a big book on it in 2010! I still think Black has no problems.

2...d5 3.exd5 ♛xd5 4.d4 e6 5.♞f3 ♞f6 6.♝d3 ♝e7 7.0-0 0-0 8.c4 ♛d7

He can also play 8...♛h5 or 8...♛d8.

9.♛e2?

Play becomes more direct if White takes the pawn: 9.dxc5 ♖d8 10.♞e5 ♛d4 (10...♛c7 11.♝f4 ♞c6 12.♖e1 ♞b4 13.♞c3 ♛xc5 14.♖e3 ♞xd3 15.♖xd3 ♖xd3 16.♛xd3 ♞h5 17.♛f3 ♞xf4 18.♛xf4 f6 and Black will consolidate his slightly better position) 11.♛e2 ♞bd7 12.♞xd7 ♝xd7 13.♝e3 ♛e5 14.♞d2? (after 14.♞c3, in Polasek-Mozny, Prague 1988, a draw was agreed. Also here Black should continue with 14...♝c6) 14...♝c6 15.♞b3 (15.♖ab1 loses even more quickly to 15...♖xd3 16.♛xd3 ♞g4 17.g3 ♛h5 18.♖fd1 ♖d8) and the following may not surprise you: 15...♖xd3! 16.♛xd3 ♞g4 17.♝f4 (17.g3 ♛h5 18.h4 ♞e5-+) 17...♞xf4 18.♛g3 ♛xg3 19.hxg3 a5-+ Rosentalis-Karpesov, USSR 1984.

9...cxd4 10.♞e5 ♛d8 11.♞d2 ♝d7 12.f4 a5

Also after 12...♞c6 13.b3 ♛c7 14.♝b2 ♖ad8 White won't get his pawn back.

13.g4 g6 14.♘df3 ♘c6 15.f5 exf5 16.gxf5 ♘h5 17.♕g2

Better was 17.♗h6 when 17...♗f6!? 18.fxg6 hxg6 19.♗xf8 ♗xe5 20.♗h6 ♘f4 gives two pawns and good play for the exchange.

17...♗f6 18.fxg6 ♗xe5 19.gxf7+ ♔h8 20.♘xe5 ♘xe5 21.♕e4

It's starting to look dangerous, but the attack can be easily warded off:

21...♖g8+!

Elegant – but at least as strong was 21...♘xf7 22.♖xf7 ♕g8+ 23.♔h1 ♗c6.

22.fxg8♗

It really says so in the game score.

22...♕xg8+ 23.♔f2

23.♕g2 ♗h3.

23...♘g4+ 24.♔g1 ♘e5+ 25.♔f2 ♖e8! 26.♕xd4 ♕g7 27.♕c3

On 27.♗e3 Black crashes through with 27...♘xd3+ 28.♕xd3 ♕xb2+ 29.♗d2 (29.♔d2 ♕f6+ 30.♔e2 ♗g4+) 29...♕f6+–+ 30.♕f3 ♕h4+. He could have played similarly after the text (27...♘xd3+ 28.♕xd3 ♕f6+), but now he starts to make things difficult for himself.

27...♕f6+ 28.♔e2 ♘f3+??

There was still only one win here: 28...♘xc4+ 29.♔d1 ♕xc3 30.bxc3 ♗a4+ 31.♗c2 ♖d8+ 32.♔e1 ♗xc2. The text fails to a miracle which is not recognized as such by both players.

29.♗e3 ♘f4+ 30.♔xf3 ♗c6+

31.♔f2??

The mate variation after 31.♔g3 is nice: 31...♖g8+ 32.♔f2 ♖g2+ 33.♔e1 ♕xc3+ 34.bxc3 ♘xd3+ 35.♔d1 ♗a4#.

But he could have cleared the third rank for his queen by 31.♗e4!!, for example 31...♗xe4+ 32.♔f2 and now on 32...♖e5 either 33.♗d4 or 33.♗xf4 wins because he can interpose the queen on g3. So 32...♘d3+ 33.♔e2 and Black has no follow-up.

31...♖e5 32.♔e1

The desperate 32.♕xe5 runs into a fork: 32...♘xd3+ 33.♔e2 ♕xe5 34.♔xd3 ♗e4+ 35.♔e2 ♕xb2+ 36.♗d2 ♕d4 and Black wins.

32...♖xe3+ 33.♔d2 ♖xd3+ 34.♕xd3 ♕xb2+ 35.♕c2 ♕d4+   0-1

IM SCHNEIDER Attila (1955-2003)
Schneider Attila became Hungarian Champion, as a result of which he got invited to the Hungarian Super Championship in 1984 (which was won by me). Attila achieved tournament successes, but his real field was chess-writing. He produced a lot of his own books but was in some cases my co-author. A very good one.
He died very early. Rest in peace!

Laszlo Barczay	2445
Attila Schneider	2365

Budapest 1982 (12)

1.d4 ♘f6 2.c4 e6 3.♘f3 b6 4.g3 ♗a6 5.b3 ♗b4+ 6.♗d2 ♗e7 7.♘c3 c6

8.e4 d5 9.♕c2 dxe4 10.♘xe4 ♗b7 11.♗d3

11.♘xf6+ might have saved him some agony, but after 11...♗xf6 12.♗d3 c5! 13.♗e4 ♘c6 Black is already better.

11...c5 12.♗c3 ♘c6 13.dxc5 bxc5 14.0-0 ♕c7 15.♖ad1 0-0-0 16.♕e2??

16.♘eg5 was necessary.

16...♖xd3 17.♖xd3 ♘xe4

And Barczay resigned right away. On 18.♕xe4 Black wins by 18...♘d4! 19.♕g4 ♘xf3+ 20.♖xf3 ♕c6 21.♔g2 f5 22.♕f4 ♗g5.

Attila MESZAROS (1965)

Attila was and is a real patzer. He knew and experienced this, but his true love for chess led him to play a large number of opens, not bothering about the result. He is a computer expert, and he already was one in 1992 when he edited the *Black is OK! Zero Copy* and the Hungarian version of *Black is OK!* (1988, Batsford). I'm grateful to him for the good job he did.

He was the General Secretary of the Hungarian Chess Federation for two years recently.

Zsofia Polgar	2415
Attila Meszaros	2350

Budapest rapid 1992 (5)

1.e4 c5 2.♘f3 ♘c6 3.d4 cxd4 4.♘xd4 ♘f6 5.♘c3 ♖b8!? 6.♗c4 ♕b6

This looks a little awkward.

7.♘b3 a6 8.0-0 e6 9.♗f4 e5 10.♗g5± ♗e7 11.a4

She wants to chase the queen to better squares. Strong was 11.♘d5! with the point 11...♘xd5 12.♕xd5 ♗xg5? 13.♕xf7+ ♔d8 14.♕xg7.

11...0-0 12.♗xf6 ♗xf6 13.♘d5 ♕d8 14.a5 ♗g5

Now Black is more or less OK.

15.♕d3 ♔h8 16.g3 d6 17.f4 exf4 18.gxf4 ♗h6 19.♔h1

19...f5 20.♖ae1 fxe4 21.♕xe4 ♗f5 22.♕g2 ♘xa5 23.♘xa5 ♕xa5 24.♖e7 ♖be8

White has no attack, for instance 25.♖fe1?? ♕xe1+.

25.b4 ♕d8 26.♖fe1 ♗d7 27.♖xe8 ♗xe8 28.♗d3 ♗c6 29.♗e4 ♕h4 30.♖g1 ♖e8 **0-1**

IM Endre VEGH (1957)

An extra-class player he could have become, but he didn't. Somehow he wasted his talent and time. But we have been working together for 33 years (with pauses). And he is an excellent theoretician. He has an ability that I've never seen elsewhere, to systematize things, and he has a deep understanding of the royal game. Once (I don't know exactly when) he became a member of Topalov's team. For a year or so. He was the co-author of my first ever BLACK IS OK! article, published in New In Chess in December 1985.

Excellent positioning by Black. 29.♗e4 key move for Black.

In many cases and forms he did help me in my writings and in the preparation for my games. For example, as my second in the Szirak 1987 Interzonal.
To tell the truth I have no idea how he manages to earn his living. It's not much fun to be an ageing chess player.

Gyula Sax 2513
Endre Vegh *10* 2252
Zalakaros 2011 (9)
(Notes by Endre Vegh)
We played this game in the last round, starting at half past eight in the morning. I think this already says quite a lot about the possible preparation and tuning up... This is mainly regretful against an opponent whose nearly 3000 games are known and easily accessible with a computer, who had splendid combinative skills, and had already written his name into the imaginary golden book of chess by means of his several nice victories for a long time.
1.e4 c5
Playing the Sicilian Defence against GM Sax is not a real life insurance, but I thought that in choosing the Najdorf Variation I could be in for an interesting game.
2.♘f3 d6 3.d4 cxd4 4.♘xd4 ♘f6 5.♘c3 a6 6.f4
One of the favourite continuations of my opponent. He had been playing this for a long time, with really good results. 6.♗e3 was also expectable.
6...e5 7.♘b3
This is much rarer than 7.♘f3, which is also met by 7...♘bd7.
7...♘bd7 8.♗e3
After spending nearly 40 minutes on this move. The rather sharp-looking 8.g4 also came into consideration. My first idea in reply to this was 8...d5!?.
8...♗e7 9.♗e2 0-0 10.0-0 b5
We should have made these moves without spending so much time,

keeping more time for the more problematic positions later.
11.a4
A natural reaction. 11...♗b7 also crossed my mind but I thought the text move could not be worse. So:
11...b4!? 12.♘d5 ♗b7
12...♘xe4?? is of course a blunder because of 13.♗f3! and White wins (13.♘xe7+? would be mistaken: 13...♕xe7 14.♕d5 ♘df6 15.♕xa8 ♗b7 16.♕a7 ♖a8 17.♕b6 ♘d5 with Black's advantage).
13.♘xb4
13.♘xe7+?! is clearly worse, because after 13...♕xe7 14.♗d2 a5 the balance tips in Black's favour.
13...♘xe4
13...♖e8!? is an interesting and fully correct move.
14.♘d5 ♘ef6
14...♘df6!?.
15.♘xe7+ ♕xe7 16.♘a5 ♗e4 17.c4
17.♕d2 ♖fe8 18.fxe5 ♘xe5 19.♗d4 ♗g6 unclear; 17.♘c4 d5 18.fxe5 (18.♘xe5 ♘xe5 19.fxe5 ♘d7!) 18...dxc4 19.exf6 ♘xf6 20.♗d4 ♖ad8 21.c3 ♕e6 unclear.
17...♖fe8 18.♖f2
I think this type of position is easier to play with black. His pieces are harmoniously developed and they properly control the centre. It is really difficult to find a good and effective plan for White.
18.♖e1 came into consideration too.
18...♖ab8

I think it is worthwhile to get thoroughly engrossed in this position. The longer one considers it, the more one realizes that White is already confronted with serious resistance here.

19.♗f3?!

19.♗f1 ♗a8; 19.♕d2 ♗a8.

19...♖ec8

19...exf4! 20.♗xf4 ♘e5! and Black would have had a better position.

20.♗a7 ♖a8 21.♗e3 ♖ab8

21...♗xf3!?.

22.♕d2

White avoids the repetition of moves in spite of his lack of time (approximately 2 minutes with a 30 seconds' increment after each move).

22...♗xf3 23.♖xf3 ♘e4 24.♕e1 ♘df6

This does not look bad, but today I would play differently because I have found a stronger move.

24...♖xb2 was not possible because of 25.♗c1, however after 24...exf4! 25.♖xf4 (25.♗xf4 ♖xb2) 25...g5! 26.♖f3 ♖xb2 Black is a pawn up with excellent play.

25.b4!

Gyula reacts strongly.

25...d5!

Nearly a must, because I could not expect anything good from passive play. The threat was 26.b5. I already saw here that I would have to sacrifice an exchange for a pawn.

26.fxe5 ♕xe5 27.♖d1

27.♗f4 ♕d4+ 28.♗e3 (28.♔h1 ♖xb4!) 28...♕e5.

27...dxc4 28.♗f4 ♕e6 29.♗xb8 ♖xb8 30.♔h1

This was not forced yet, but quite understandable in time pressure. 30.♖d4 was obviously better.

30...♘g4!

The threat is 31...♘ef2+.

31.♕g1 c3

31...h6! was also perfectly good. The explanation is simple: after Black

makes a luft the b4-pawn is already en prise.

32.h3

32...♘gf6

Taking into consideration the time pressure, 32...c2! would have created exciting complications, the outcome of which seems to be more favourable for Black in case both sides make the best moves. It may be worthwhile to use this position as a tactical exercise for youngsters:

A) 33.♖e1 ♖c8 34.hxg4 (34.♘b3 ♘ef2+ 35.♖xf2 ♘xf2+ 36.♕xf2 ♕xb3–+; 34.♖c1 ♕d6 35.♘b3 ♘gf2+ 36.♖xf2 ♘g3+ 37.♔h2 ♘e2+–+; 34.♖xe4 ♕xe4 35.♘b3 ♖d8 36.hxg4 ♖d1 37.♖f1 ♕e2–+) 34...♕h6+ 35.♖h3 ♕d2 36.♖c1 (36.♘b3 ♘f2+ 37.♔h2 ♕f4+ 38.g3 (38.♖g3 ♘xg4+ 39.♔h3 ♘f2+ 40.♔h2 f5 41.♖e3 ♖c6–+) 38...♕f3–+) 36...♘f2+ 37.♔h2 ♘xg4+ 38.♔h1 ♘f2+ 39.♔h2 ♘xh3–+;

B) 33.♖c1 ♖c8 and now:

B1) 34.hxg4 ♕h6+ 35.♖h3 ♘f2+! 36.♕xf2 (36.♔h2 ♘xh3 37.gxh3 ♕d2+ 38.♔h1 ♖c3–+) 36...♕xc1+ 37.♔h2 ♕b2–+;

B2) 34.♕d4 ♕e5! 35.♕xe5 ♘xe5 36.♖e3 ♘f2+ 37.♔g1 ♘fd3–+;

B3) 34.b5 ♘e5 (34...axb5!? 35.axb5 ♘e5∓) 35.♖b3 ♕h6 36.♖e3 (36.b6 ♘f2+–+) 36...♕f4 37.♕e1 ♘f2+ 38.♔g1 ♘fd3 39.♖xc2 (39.♖xd3 ♕xc1! (39...♘xd3 40.♖xc2!) 40.♕xc1 ♘xd3–+) 39...♖xc2 40.♖xd3 h6 41.♖e3 axb5 42.axb5 ♖c5∓.

33.♕d4 ♖c8?

The game stumbles from Black's point of view due to this careless move. After the event, quite a lot of things tend to come to light, of course... 33...♕e8 or 33...h6 was good.

34.b5! axb5 35.axb5 h6?

Now this is not the same as before... 35...♖b8.

36.♘c6

36.b6! was stronger, after which White's position can be considered to be winning!

36...♔h7 37.♕d3 ♔h8 38.♔g1 ♕b3 39.♖b1 ♕a2 40.♖c1

40.♖e1 ♕b2!?.

40...♕b2

We have reached the time control.

41.♖c2 ♕b3 42.♖e3 ♖e8 43.♖ce2 ♕e6 44.♕d4 ♕b3 45.♘b4 ♕b1+ 46.♖e1?

This gives away the advantage. The road to victory is as follows, according to my analyses:

46.♔h2 ♕f1 47.♘a2! (after 47.♖xe4 ♘xe4 48.♖xe4 ♖xe4 49.♕xe4 ♕xb5 it is not yet easy to convert this into a win for White) 47...c2 48.♕c4 ♕f4+ 49.g3 ♕b8 50.♖xc2+–.

46...c2! 47.♕c4

47.♘d3 ♕xb5 48.♖c1 (48.♖xe4 ♖xe4 49.♖xe4 ♕b1+!) 48...♖c8 49.♖xe4 ♘xe4 50.♕xe4 ♖d8 51.♘e1 (51.♘f2 ♖d2) 51...♕c5+ 52.♔h1 ♖d1 53.♖xc2 (53.♕f4? ♕e7–+) 53...♖xe1+ 54.♕xe1 ♕xc2 55.♕e8+ ♔h7 56.♕xf7=.

47...♘d6!

48.♖xe8+?

The losing move. Quite a lot of people would have played this automatically... 48.♕c3 ♖xe3 49.♕xe3 ♕xb4–+.

48.♕xc2 was the only line leading to a draw: 48...♕xb4 49.♖xe8+ ♘fxe8 50.♖b1 ♕d4+ 51.♔h1 ♘c4 52.♖b4 ♘ed6 53.b6 ♕e3=.

48...♘fxe8 49.♕c3 ♘e4! 50.♕e3 ♕xb4 51.b6 ♘8f6 52.♖c1 ♘d5 53.♕d3 ♕xb6+ 54.♔h2 ♕d6+ 55.g3

55.♔g1 ♘b4 56.♕xe4 ♕d1+ 57.♔h2 ♕xc1 58.♕e8+ (58.♕xb4 ♕f1–+) 58...♔h7 59.♕e4+ g6 60.♕c4 ♘d5–+.

55...♘b4!   **0-1**

IM Gyula FEHER (1959)

A friend and a good buddy for 13 years, Gyula is somebody without any sparkling talent. But he does understand chess, and he loves it. He published a magazine called MOST (an acronym meaning Hungarian Chess Informant in our language). It was a quality product, which served our chess players and teams. It had a circulation of only 600 copies but it was spread all over the country. He ran the magazine for ten years, until the uninterested Hungarian chess society considered the annual 20 Euros too much for 13 issues. I don't think he made any money with it anyway. He was my second four times, and was very helpful. We won two Hungarian Championships in 1992 and '93. I wish there were more people as devoted as he. Unfortunately, honesty and modesty don't pay as well as noisy dilettantism does. Tribute to him!

Endre Vegh	2330
Gyula Feher	2375

Budapest 1996

based on notes by Gyula Feher

1.d4 ♘f6 2.c4 g6 3.♘c3 d5 4.♘f3 ♗g7 5.♗f4 0-0 6.♖c1 dxc4 7.e4 b5!?

A novelty by Adorjan.

8.♘xb5

8.e5 ♘d5.

8...♘xe4 9.♗xc7!?

Taking the bait. The alternative is 9.♗xc4; on 9.♘xc7 Black has 9...e5!.

9...♕d7 10.♗xc4 a6 11.♘a3 ♘c6

Of course the ♗c7 is poisoned. Quick development is what Black wants!

12.0-0

12...♗b7!

12...♕xc7 was possible now; after 13.♗d5 ♗f5 14.♕e2 ♘c5!? things start to get interesting..

13.♗e5?!

13.♗b6 ♖ab8 (intending 14...♗a8) and now:

A) 14.♖e1 ♗a8 15.d5 (15.♖xe4 ♖xb6 leaves the white pawns vulnerable: 16.d5 ♘b4 17.♗b3 ♘xd5 18.♘c4 ♖bb8 with chances for Black; the text is an interesting simplification that opens up the black bishops, but White can hold) 15...♖xb6 16.dxc6 ♕xd1 17.♖cxd1 ♗xb2 18.♗xf7+ ♔xf7 19.♘c4 ♖xc6 20.♖xe4 ♖c5 and now White may keep the balance with 21.♘fe5+ ♔g7 22.♖e2;

B) 14.b3 is slow but White may just keep his position together with 14...♗h6 15.♖c2 (15.♘e5 ♘xe5 16.dxe5 ♘d2 17.♖e1 ♕f5 with the idea ♗g2) 15...♘b4 16.♘e5 ♕f5 17.♖b2, but Black has the freer play for the pawn.

13...♗h6 14.♖b1

14.♖c2 ♖ad8 (not 14...♘b4 15.♖e2 ♘d6 16.♗xd6 ♕xd6 17.♕b3! and suddenly White liberates himself) 15.♗b3 ♘g5 16.♘xg5 ♘xe5 17.♖c5 ♗xg5 18.dxe5 ♕f5 and with his two strong bishops Black has a good initiative.

14...♖ad8 15.♕e2?

15.♖e1 ♘xe5 16.dxe5 ♕c6 17.♕e2 ♘d2 18.♖bd1 leads to the game; but 15.♕b3 ♘a5 16.♕b4 was a better way to keep Black busy: 16...♘xc4 17.♘xc4 e6 18.♘b6 ♕c6 (threatening 19...♘d2) 19.♘c4 ♕b5!? (19...♕d7=) 20.♕xb5 axb5 21.♘e3 (or 21.♘b6 f6 22.♗c7 ♖de8 23.♖fe1 ♗e7) 21...f6 22.♗c7 ♖d7 23.♖fc1 ♘d6 with compensation.

15...♘xe5 16.dxe5 ♕c6!

Now many threats are hovering over White's head.

17.♔h1

After 17.♖bd1 ♘d2 18.♖fe1 Black continues with the lovely strike 18...♖d4! (18...♘xf3+ 19.♕xf3 ♕xf3 20.gxf3 ♗xf3 21.♖xd8 ♖xd8 22.♗xa6 ♖d4 also looks promising, but White has an elegant saving clause in 23.♗e2! ♖g4+ 24.♔f1 ♗g2+ 25.♔g1 ♗f3+=) 19.b3 ♖e4! 20.♕d3 ♖g4 with a decisive attack.

17...♘d2 18.♖bc1 ♕b6

Not 18...♘xf3 due to 19.♗xf7+ ♖xf7 20.♖xc6 ♗xc6 21.e6 ♖f6 22.♕xa6 when things are totally unclear.

19.♘xd2 ♖xd2 20.♕e1 ♕d4!?

Black wants to crash through with 21...♗g4, but the prosaic 20...♕xb2! was stronger, e.g. 21.♖b1 (21.♘b1 ♖d4 22.♖c3 ♗d2!-+) 21...♗xg2+ 22.♔xg2 ♕xa3 23.e6 f5 with good winning chances.

21.f3

Again, if 21.e6 f5.

21...♖d8 22.♗b3 ♖xb2

Black could have obtained a winning attack with the pretty sacrifice 22...♖xg2! 23.♔xg2 (on 23.♖c7 ♕d2! wins) 23...♗xc1 24.♕xc1 ♕g4+ 25.♔f2 (25.♔h1 ♗xf3+ 26.♖xf3 ♕xf3+ 27.♔g1 ♖d4-+) 25...♕xf3+ 26.♔e1 ♕e4+

27.♔f2 ♖d3 28.♗d1 (28.♗xf7+ ♔g7!–+) 28...♖h3 and there is no defence.

23.♖c7 ♗d5 24.♘c4

There was no time to catch the black rook by 24.♘c2 in view of 24...♕b6! 25.♕c3 ♗xb3 26.♕xb2 ♕xc7 27.axb3 ♖d2–+.

24...♗xc4 25.♖xc4 ♕d2 26.♕g3?!

It's quite understandable that White would not enjoy the endgame after 26.♕xd2 ♖dxd2 27.♖g4 ♗e3 28.h4 (28.♖c1 e6 29.♖e4 ♗a7 30.♖ec4 ♖xg2 31.♖4c2 ♖bxc2 32.♗xc2 ♖f2–+; 28.f4 e6 29.♖g3 ♗xf4 30.♖gf3 ♖xg2!–+; 28.♖d1) 28...h5! 29.♖xg6+ ♔f8 30.♖g3 ♗f4 31.♖h3 ♖xg2; or 26.♖g4 (the better move) 26...♕xe1 27.♖xe1 ♖dd2 28.h3 ♗g7 29.f4 e6, because even here Black keeps pressure. But after the text White gets severe back-rank problems.

26...♕e2 27.♖e1

On 27.♖g1 Black can force a winning queen ending with 27...♗e3 28.♖e4 ♖xb3 29.axb3 ♖d1 30.♖xe3 ♖xg1+ 31.♔xg1 ♕xe3+ 32.♕f2 ♕xb3.

27...♖xb3!

The back rank! On 27...♗d2 28.♖xe2 ♖b1+ White would have had the problematic rescue 29.♕e1! (29.♖e1? ♗xe1–+) 29...♗xe1 30.g4 when his troubles appear to be over.

28.axb3

There is nothing better: 28.♖e4 ♕xe4! 29.♖xe4 ♖d1+ 30.♖e1 ♖bb1; and if 28.♖xe2 ♖b1+ 29.♕e1 ♖dd1 30.♖ce4

there is the nice finish 30...♗d2!, or, similarly, 29.♖e1 ♖dd1 30.♖e4 ♗d2 31.h4 ♗xe1.

28...♖d1 29.♖e4 ♕f1+!　　　**0-1**

GM Peter LEKO (1979)

I was Peti's trainer for about three years. It was the time when he reached the world elite. I've never seen another talent like him, except for Kasparov. The little guy was loving chess industriously and had a very good fighting spirit. At that time he did not played this short-moving chess that he does now. I do not know what happened to him to make him such a constant draw-king. In those years he achieved his most precious victories with black over Topalov, Kramnik, Van Wely (twice) and quite a few others. He produced several opuses using my novelties. He gave me credit for them, and I never took away the honour from him – after all it was he who actually played and won those games. There was a strong emotional connection between us too, partly because he is as 'old' as my own daughters. Later he became a person who was easy to respect but harder to love.

| Ludger Kürholz | 2295 |
| Peter Leko | 2465 |

Budapest 1993

1.d4 ♘f6 2.c4 c5 3.d5 b5 4.cxb5 a6 5.♘c3

An alternative to 5.bxa6 that can lead to sharp play.

5...axb5 6.e4 b4 7.♘b5 d6 8.♗f4 g5!

Benko's own recommendation.

9.♗xg5 ♘xe4 10.♗f4 ♗g7!

10...♕a5 11.♗c4 ♗g7 was the old continuation; in *Attack with Black* (2012) Aveskulov recommends 10...♘f6 as the 'most precise move – anticipating White's ♕e2 idea, the knight drops back to a secure square and puts pressure on White's isolated d5-pawn'.

An excellent Alteration of Benko Opening!

11.♕e2 ♘f6 12.♘xd6+

12.♗xd6 ♘xd5 13.♖d1 0-0! hands over the attack to Black, as White's kingside is still 'in its infancy'.

12...♔f8 13.♘xc8 ♕xc8 14.d6

Trying to keep the momentum, but the kingside problem remains.

14...exd6 15.♗xd6+ ♔g8 16.♕f3?

And therefore he should have played 16.♘f3.

16...♘c6! 17.♘e2

17.♗xc5 would be suicidal due to 17...♘e5 18.♕e3 ♘d5 19.♕c1 ♕e6 20.♗e3 ♘g4.

17...♕e8! 18.♗xc5 ♘e4 19.♗e3 b3! 20.♘c1?

Not 20.a3 ♘b4!–+. The only move was 20.♘g3 ♘xg3 21.♕xg3 ♘b4 22.♗c4 ♘c2+ 23.♔e2 ♕c6 24.♗xb3 ♕b5+ 25.♔f3 ♕b7+ 26.♔e2 – why do such positions always end in draws?

20...♘d4!

20...♘b4?! would run into 21.♗d3!.

21.♗xd4 ♗xd4 22.♗e2

The losing move. An ingenious defence was 22.♗c4! with the idea 22...♗xb2 (as in the game) 23.0-0 ♗xa1 24.♘xb3 with very good compensation. The best reply may be 22...♖a4! 23.♗xb3 ♗xf2+ 24.♔d1 ♖d4+ 25.♘d3 with a crazy position – Black still has an attack, but the ♗/♕xf7+ resource is always in the air.

22...♗xb2 23.♕g4+ ♔f8 24.♘xb3 ♗c3+ 25.♔f1 ♗xa1 26.♘xa1 ♖xa2 27.♘b3 ♖b2 28.♗d3

28...♖xf2+?!

A nice direct win was 28...♘xf2!! 29.♕d4 ♘xd3 30.♕xh8+ ♔e7 and White has no checks – he will lose the rook or the knight.

29.♔g1 ♖b2

Not everything wins here – after 29...♖g8 30.♕xe4 ♖gxg2+ 31.♕xg2 ♕e1+ 32.♗f1 ♖xg2+ 33.♔xg2 ♕e4+ 34.♔g1 ♕e3+ 35.♔g2 ♕xb3 36.♗e2 the computer does give a win for Black, but try it in a practical game!

30.♕xe4 ♖xb3 31.♔f2?!

The problem is that after 31.♕xe8+ ♔xe8 32.♗f1! ♖b2! 33.h3 ♖g8! the white rook remains boxed in: 34.♔h2 f5! 35.♖g1 f4 36.♗c4 ♖g5 and Black wins.

31...♖b2+ 32.♔f3

This 'refreshing' walk won't do the white king any good.

32...♕d8! 33.♖e1 ♖g8 34.♗f1 ♕f6+ 35.♔e3 ♕c3+   0-1

This game was played in the final round of the First Saturday Tournament – it meant the first GM norm for Peti Leko!

13ᵗʰ World Champion Garry KASPAROV (1963)

We met in Banja Luka 1979, where he made his international debut by winning a strong GM tournament. With a two-point margin! We somehow befriended there, and our co-operation lasted until 1986. We had difficulties in communication, but still we found a way to do it. I wrote in English and he answered in Russian.

I was his second with four matches (Karpov 1984, Andersson 1985, Timman 1985 and Miles 1986). When I was preparing for my Candidates match with Ribli I got a telegram from him: 'I hope you didn't beat Larsen and Miles to lose against Ribli'. When the tragicomedy was over I got another telegram, which said: 'Always believed you'd win. Garry'. I didn't. The 6-game match started with a 2½-½ score for Ribli...

I always considered Garry to be as great a champion as Fischer. He was a maximalist in every way. It's a pity he turned for the worse and accused one of his seconds, Evgeny Vladimirov, who was a nice loyal guy, of betraying him in 1986. It was rude and completely groundless. Then I wrote a book on him called in Hungarian *Kaszparov feketén-fehéren* ('Kasparov black and white'). It was almost 400 pages. It contained practically all the games he had played until then. Later on it was published under the title *Quo Vadis Garry?* in German and Norwegian. I still adored him as a player but sharply criticized him as a man. Garry was raging, but he never called me a traitor. At least, not in public... We made up in 1997 in Linares. And when Peter Leko played my Sveshnikov novelty against him (1.e4 c5 2.♘f3 e6 3.♘c3 ♘c6 4.d4 cxd4 5.♘xd4 ♘f6 6.♘xc6 bxc6 7.e5 ♘d5 8.♘e4 ♗b7N) he took half an hour to meet it. When in the post-mortem the position after 8.♘e4 ♗b7 was reached, he looked up and asked: 'Adorjan?'.

Robert Hübner   2620
Garry Kasparov   2740

Brussels 1986

1.d4 ♘f6 2.c4 g6 3.♘c3 d5 4.♘f3 ♗g7 5.♕a4+?!

Still this move was later adopted by guys like Ivan Sokolov, Etienne Bacrot, Wang Hao and Peter Svidler.

5...♗d7 6.♕b3 dxc4 7.♕xc4 0-0 8.e4

The major alternative is 8.♗f4 ♘a6 (8...♗c6) 9.e4 c5 10.dxc5 (10.e5 ♘h5) 10...♗e6 11.♕b5 ♗d7 12.♕xb7 ♘xc5 13.♕b4 ♘e6 with good centralized play, better development and open lines for the pawn.

8...b5!

8...a6 9.e5 favours White; after 9...♘e8, 10.h4 looks dangerous.

9.♕b3

The point is that after 9.♘xb5 ♘xe4 10.♘xc7 ♘c6 11.♘xa8 ♕a5+ 12.♗d2 ♘xd2 13.♘xd2 ♘xd4 14.♘c7 ♖c8 15.♖c1 ♕e5+ 16.♔d1 ♗h6 Black has a very dangerous attack – who would want to sit behind the white pieces here? A funny losing line, by the way, is 16...♗b5? 17.♖c5! ♗e2+ 18.♔e1.

9...c5 10.e5

A novelty at the time. 10.dxc5 ♘a6.

10...♘g4 11.♗xb5

The complications favour Black after 11.♕d5 cxd4! (11...♘c6!? 12.♕xc5 ♖c8! is unclear) 12.♘xd4 (12.♕xa8 dxc3 followed by ...♕b6, and Black is clearly better) 12...♕b6 13.♗xb5 ♗xe5.

11...cxd4 12.♘xd4 ♗xb5

12...♗xe5!? 13.♕d5 ♕b6! with a nice initiative (13...♗xb5 14.♘dxb5 ♘d7∓).

13.♘dxb5 a6 14.♘a3 ♕d4! 15.♕c2

Or 15.0-0 ♕xe5 16.g3 ♕h5 with a promising attack for no material.

15...♘c6 16.♕e2 ♕xe5! 17.♕xe5

The endgame after 17.♘c4 ♕xe2+ 18.♘xe2 ♘b4 19.0-0 ♖ac8 is unappealing for White.

17...♘gxe5 18.0-0 ♘d3

Gazza's dreaded octopus...

19.♖b1 ♖ab8 20.♖d1 ♖fd8 21.♔f1 f5! 22.♔e2 ♘ce5!

23.♘a4

Hübner is putting up stubborn resistance. There was not much hope for White in the following lines: 23.♗g5? h6! 24.♗xe7 ♖d7 25.♗h4 g5; 23.f4? ♘xc1+ 24.♖dxc1 ♘d3; 23.g3 ♘xc1+ 24.♖dxc1 ♘d3 25.♖d1 ♘xb2; or 23.♗e3 f4 24.♗c1 g5.

23...♖d6

23...♖b4? would allow the save 24.♘c5!. 23...♖bc8 probably posed White a less difficult choice than the text; after 24.♘b6 (24.f4? ♖xc1 25.♖bxc1 ♘xc1+ 26.♖xc1 ♘d3–+) 24...♖c6 25.♘bc4 ♘xc4 26.♘xc4 ♖xc4 27.♖xd3 ♖c2+ 28.♗d2 ♖b8! Black has a clear advantage in the endgame, but White is still alive.

24.♗e3?!

Hübner prefers to go down in flames. Lines like 24.f4 ♖d4 25.fxe5 ♘xc1+ 26.♖bxc1 ♖xa4 27.♘c4 ♗xe5!–+ or 24.♘c4 ♘xc4 25.♖xd3 ♖xd3 26.♔xd3 ♘a3 27.♖a1 e5! 28.f3 e4+! look pretty dramatic, but perhaps White could sit tight with 24.b3!? or even 24.g3!?.

24...f4 25.♗c5 f3+ 26.gxf3 ♘f4+ 27.♔e3

Or 27.♔f1 ♖xd1+ 28.♖xd1 ♘xf3 29.♗xe7 ♘xh2+ 30.♔g1 ♘f3+ 31.♔f1 and now the unstoppable 31...h5! 32.♖d8+ ♖xd8 33.♗xd8 h4 34.♗c7 ♘d2+! 35.♔g1 ♘d3 36.b3 ♗d4 37.♗b6 ♗xb6 38.♘xb6 h3.

27...♖f6 28.♗xe7?

Time-trouble; more tenacious was 28.♗d4! ♖f5! 29.♗xe5 ♗xe5 30.♘c4.

28...♘g2+ 29.♔e2 ♖xf3 30.♗d6

30.♖d8+ ♖xd8 31.♗xd8 would be quicker than the game: 31...♘f4+ 32.♔f1 ♘g4 33.♗b6 ♘xf2 34.♗xf2 ♗d4 and Black wins.

30...♘f4+ 31.♔f1 ♘g4! 32.♖d2

After 32.♗xb8 ♖xf2+ 33.♔g1 ♖g2 mate follows.

32...♖e8 33.♘c4

33.♗xf4 ♖xf4 34.♘c5 ♖e5 35.♖d8+ ♗f8 36.♘d7 ♘xh2+ 37.♔g2 ♖g5+! also leads to mate: 38.♔h1 ♖h4 39.♖xf8+ ♔g7–+.

33...♘xh2+ 34.♔g1 ♘g4 35.♖f1

35...♗d4!

Weaving the final mating net.

36.♗c5

36.♘c5 ♗xf2+ 37.♖dxf2 ♖g3+ 38.♔h1 ♘xf2+ 39.♖xf2 ♖e1+–+.

36...♖g3+ 37.♔h1 ♖h3+ 38.♔g1 ♘h2!   **0-1**

Jozsef 'Szenya' SZENTGYÖRGYI (1949-??)

A multi-faceted genius with whom I made a burlesque and wrote songs. He played one game in my blindfold simul in 1970. I beat the poor fellow, who had to play Black. Below is the only game by him I could find, as he quit tournament play early. He has a candidate of master strength. I will make a cuckoo of it: one game that White won in this book. He was interested in many other (board) games: he published the first book in Hungarian about Dama, for instance. As usually happens, we had many quarrels while giving birth to the Kasparov book (which is inevitable with a work of this size and importance) and split at the end. From time to time I heard about him. Naturally good people like to blah-blah about whether he had died or was still alive. For a long time I have thought that it was a present of God, him appearing in my life. And this feeling will not change.

Andras Adorjan
Jozsef Szentgyörgyi
Budapest blindfold simul 1970

1.c4 e5 2.♘c3 c5 3.g3 ♘c6 4.♗g2 d6 5.e3 ♗e7 6.♘ge2 ♗f5 7.d4 ♘f6 8.d5 ♘b8 9.0-0 ♕c8 10.f4 exf4 11.♘xf4 ♘bd7 12.♘h5 ♘xh5 13.♖xf5 g6

14.♖xh5! gxh5 15.b3 ♗f6 16.♗b2 ♗e5 17.♘h3 ♕d8 18.♕xh5 ♕f6 19.♖f1 ♕e7 20.♗xd7+ ♕xd7

21.♘e4! ♗xb2 22.♖xf7 0-0-0 23.♖xd7 ♖xd7 24.♕f5 ♔c7 25.♘g5 ♖e7 26.♘e6+ ♔b6 27.♕f2 ♗e5 28.a3 a5 29.♔g2 ♖a8 30.e4 ♔a6 31.b4 axb4 32.axb4 b6 33.bxc5 bxc5 34.♕a2+ ♔b7 35.♕b3+ ♔c8 36.♕b5 ♖a2+ 37.♔h3 h5 38.♕c6+ ♔b8 39.♕b6+ ♖b7 40.♕d8+ ♔a7 41.♘c7 ♖b8 42.♘b5+ ♔a8 43.♕c7 h4 44.♕c6+ ♖b7 45.♘xd6

BLACK resigned.

Peter BOEL (1963)
The Internet and other high-tech facilities are both a blessing and a damnation of our age. Many people fall victim to becoming dependent on them; instead of building up human connections, friendships etc., escaping to a virtual world. Which threatened to prevent them from leading normal lives. I don't have many friends, but those I have are by my side since as early as the sixties, seventies. The trouble is we are all ageing and don't see each other as much as we used to. I have lost two of my best friends within a year: Antal Papp and GM Laszlo Bárczay.

But there is also a very positive side to cosmic speed telecommunication. I've met and became friends with quite a few wonderful people all over the world by means of electronic letters. One of them was a Hungarian-born poet who is a classical translator too, Imre Gyöngyös (New Zealand), who translated some of my poems, one of which you can read in the Foreword to this book ('The Blackout Fright', page 9). I don't remember the exact time and occasion we met, and the same goes for quite a few other Hungarian-born partners in foreign countries. They could all be called presents of Providence. Like Peter Boel, my co-author.

For years he was the one who, as the Managing Editor of the Yearbook with New In Chess, edited my articles. As the years passed by we discussed many things, from actual events to general questions as well, besides the professional work. He is an intelligent and highly cultured man, and on top of everything truly modest. For me to have him as a friend means an oasis in the sands of the noisy and aggressive crowds. Thanks, Peter! He is a club-player (ASV, Arnhem) and a many-time winner of Dutch chess journalists' events. Let's see a game by him, annotated by the winner himself.

Otto Wilgenhof
Peter Boel

Arnhem rapid 2015

1.d4 ♘f6 2.♘f3 g6 3.c4 c5 4.d5 b5 5.cxb5 a6 6.b6 d6 7.♘c3 ♗g7 8.e4 ♘bd7 9.♗e2 0-0 10.0-0 ♖b8 11.♘d2 ♘xb6 12.f4?

Funny, but here the pawn is just in the way of White's pieces, and moreover the diagonal towards White's king is dangerously opened.

12...e6 13.dxe6 fxe6

This pawn formation is a joy for both Benko and King's Indian players.

14.♘c4?

Allowing a trick. 14.♘f3 was more or less equal.

14...♘xe4 15.♘xe4 ♘xc4 16.♗xc4 d5 17.♗d3

17.♘xc5 dxc4! is quite lethal already due to the threatened check on d4 (less convincing is 17...♕b6?! 18.♗e3).

17...dxe4 18.♗xe4 ♗xb2

Also good was 18...♕d4+ 19.♕xd4 ♗xd4+ 20.♔h1 ♗b7 and Black dominates completely – largely thanks to White's 12th move!

19.♖b1? ♕d4+?!

It's nice when all the tricks in a position seem to be going my way, but objectively better was 19...♕xd1 20.♖xd1 ♗d4+ 21.♔h1 ♖xb1 22.♗xb1 ♗b7 – see the comment to move 18.

20.♔h1 ♕xe4 21.♗xb2?

Thanks to Black's inaccuracy on move 19 White had a more staunch defence here with 21.♖xb2 ♖xb2 22.♗xb2 ♗b7 when 23.♕d2 might hold – now both sides have an extremely strong long diagonal.

21...♗b7 22.♕d2?

Better was 22.♖f2 or 22.♖g1, but in both cases 22...♖xf4 should suffice.

22...♖bd8 23.♕f2 ♖xf4 24.♖g1 ♖d2 25.♖xf4 ♕xf4 26.♗c1

I like playing against my teammate Wilgenhof. Our games are always wild and full of tricks. Here I have been winning for a long time, and still he manages to come up with something. All Black's pieces are hanging, but still he has various wins thanks to some beautiful geometrical motifs.

26...♖xg2

In fact, 26...♗xg2+ 27.♕xg2 ♖d1+ would have won even more quickly.

27.♗xf4 ♖b2+

Nice!

28.♕g2

And now everyone was expecting 28...♖xb1+ with mate, but I managed to find a worse win:

28...♗xg2+

And of course Otto gave up anyway.

(margin, rotated) Excellent ending!

GM Kevin SPRAGGETT (1954)

I baptised Kevin 'the Canadian Bastard' in St. John in 1987. By which I understood that he got very little help (if any) from the Canadian Chess Federation when preparing for and playing his Candidates match against Andrei Sokolov, who was the favourite. I offered him my services for free. Kevin was a very strong player, but the openings he prepared with black were just wrong. So I intervened and we switched to the Caro-Kann. The reason I proposed it was that my last four games with Gyula Sax had been comfortable for me. Also you can see attacking players getting upset when they don't get a chance to set up a direct attack. Kevin played the Caro in all his black games and was doing fine, even though he lost the very first one. He qualified for the Candidates match against Jussupow. We split. All the same, the naughty boy used one of my novelties, with success. Anyway I'm still glad that I was able help a true fighter like him, in the most important match of his life.

| Jan Timman | 2640 |
| Kevin Spraggett | 2550 |

Montpellier ct 1985

based on notes from Chess Informant

1.d4 e6 2.c4 ♗b4+ 3.♗d2 ♕e7 4.e4 d5!?

A novelty at the time. 4...♘f6.

5.e5 ♘c6 6.♘f3 ♗xd2+ 7.♕xd2

7.♘bxd2.

7...dxc4!

8.♗xc4 allows 8...♕b4, but also 8...♘h6!?.

8.♘c3 ♘h6 9.d5?!

Allowing an interesting piece sacrifice. After 9.♗xc4 0-0 10.0-0 ♖d8 White has a solid plus.

9...♘xe5

The only move; if 9...exd5? 10.♘xd5 ♕d8 11.0-0-0 0-0 12.♕f4±.

10.♘xe5 exd5 11.♕e2!?

He could return the piece by 11.♕xd5 f6 12.0-0-0 fxe5 13.♗xc4 for an initiative, but 13...c6! keeps the balance. After 14.♕d6 ♕xd6 15.♖xd6 ♗d7 White gets the e-pawn back, but Black finishes his development.

11...♗e6 12.0-0-0 c6

Not 12...0-0-0 13.♘b5!± with a big blockade on d4.

13.♘f3! 0-0 14.♘d4 ♖ae8 15.g3 b5?!

15...♕c7 16.♘xe6 fxe6 17.f4 e5! and Black is slightly better; 15...♕f6 16.♘xe6 ♖xe6 17.♕d2 ♘g4 is unclear.

16.♘xe6! fxe6 17.f4

17...e5!

Disrupting a very nice image, but he had to do something. If (ugly!) 17...b4? 18.♘a4!±.

18.fxe5

If 18.♕xe5 ♕xe5 19.fxe5 ♘g4! White has problems.

18...♘f7

18...b4.

19.e6 ♕xe6 20.♕xe6 ♖xe6 21.♘e2?

With time-trouble already approaching, White misses a tactic that would maintain an edge: 21.♗g2 with the point 21...b4?! (better is 21...g5 with the idea ...♔g7) 22.♘xd5! cxd5 23.♗xd5.

21...♖e3! 22.♔b1 ♘e5 23.♘f4?

23.♘d4! ♖f2 24.♗h3 g6 25.♖df1 ♖d2 26.♖d1 – you know.

23...g5 24.♘e6 ♖f5 25.♘d4

Now 25.♗h3 g4 26.♖hf1 fails to 26...♘f3!, threatening 27...♘d2+. Meaning that White gets squeezed to death now.

25...♖f2 26.g4 ♖e4 27.h3 b4 28.♘c2 a5 29.a3? b3 30.♘d4 ♖d2!   0-1

GM Suat ATALIK (1964)

Suat Atalik – whom I called the Turkish Capa – was an astonishing surprise when we met in Istanbul during my training mission in 1991. Turkey at that time was a desert from the viewpoint of quality in chess. There were some enthusiastic young players, but most of them were just 2300+. Suat was about 200 Elo points above them. And not once did I see him sitting at his board and staying there until the game ended. Another exceptional virtue of his is his memory. Once I was thinking about the whereabouts of a certain Uhlmann-Gligoric game. The guy said: 'It was Sarajevo 1983. And you played in that tournament.' He picked up *Chess Informant* and showed it to me with a wicked smile.

Suat Atalik is a brave man too. Not only did he marry a chess player, but he dared to attack her in the last-round game of an open with black – and won too. But I try not to think of what happened at home after the game...

Ekaterina Atalik	2444
Suat Atalik	2607

Kavala 2010 (8)

notes by Suat Atalik

It is always difficult to play your spouse, but especially so in a critical round in a tournament. Katya was a candidate for the first woman's prize in the tournament at the time and I had already drifted away from any man's prize. Apart from the many Kafkasians who were surprised about the course and the result of the game, the encounter attracted a lot of attention, despite its quality.

1.d4 ♘f6 2.c4 e6 3.♘c3 ♗b4

I was never a good Nimzo-Indian player, and I should either learn more about it or cut it out.

4.e3 0-0 5.♗d3 d5 6.♘f3 b6 7.cxd5 exd5

8.♘e5!?

Very sharp, but a little premature since ...♗b7 has not been played yet.

8.0-0 ♗b7 9.♘e5 (9.a3 ♗d6 10.b4 a6 11.♕b3= is universally accepted as the best line for White) 9...♗d6 10.f4 c5 11.♕f3 ♘c6 12.♕h3 g6 13.♔h1 ♖e8 14.♗d2 ♗f8 15.♗b5 ♕c8 is unclear; White has the attack but Black is not worse.

8...c5

8...♘bd7!? was a move I considered due to the strange move order: 9.0-0! (9.♘c6? ♗xc3+ 10.bxc3 ♕e8 11.♗a3 ♘c5 12.♘e5 ♘xd3+ 13.♕xd3 c5 14.0-0

♕a4 with attack) 9...♗b7 (9...♗xc3?! 10.bxc3 ♕e7 (10...♘xe5? 11.dxe5 ♘e4 12.c4 ♗b7 13.♕c2±) 11.f4 ♘e4 12.c4 ♗b7 13.♕c2±) 10.f4 c5 is another scheme similar to the above-mentioned line, this time with ...♘bd7 instead of ...♘c6: 11.♗d2 ♘e4 12.♘xe4 dxe4 13.♗c4 ♗xd4 14.♕xd2 ♘xe5 15.fxe5 ♗d5 16.b3 and Black should keep the balance.

9.0-0 ♗b7

9...♗a6?! 10.♗xa6 (10.♘b5 c4; 10.♘c6 ♘xc6 11.♗xa6 cxd4 12.exd4 ♗xc3 13.bxc3 ♘a5 unclear) 10...♘xa6 11.♘e2=.

10.♘e2!

Now with my bishop stuck there I had to push ...c5-c4.

10...c4 11.♗c2 ♘c6 12.f4 b5 13.♘g3 ♘e7 14.f5!?

Again too ambitious. 14.♗d2 ♗d6 (14...♕a5 15.♗xb4 ♕xb4 16.♕e2±) 15.♕f3 ♕c7, unclear, was an option.

14...♔h8?

... and too cautious!

14...♗d6 15.♘g4 ♘xg4 16.♕xg4 f6 17.♘h5 ♖f7 unclear.

15.♘h5 ♘eg8 16.♘f4 ♗d6 17.♗d2 ♕e7

I chose this move from among many other options: 17...♘h6!?; 17...a5 18.♗e1; 17...b4 18.♖f3 (18.♕f3 ♕c7; 18.♕e1 a5 19.♕h4 ♘h6 unclear) 18...♘h6 19.♖h3 with attack.

18.♖f3 ♗xe5?

I wanted to be consequent and grab the pawn since the alternatives are scary as well:

A) 18...a5 19.♖h3 ♗xe5 (better is 19...♘h6 like in the previous alternative) 20.dxe5 ♕xe5 21.♗c3 ♕d6 22.g4 with an attack;

B) 18...♘e4 19.♗xe4 dxe4 20.♖h3 ♗xe5 21.dxe5 ♕xe5 22.♗c3 ♕xf5 23.♖h5 ♕c8 24.♕d4+−;

C) 18...♘h6 19.♖h3 b4 20.♘h5 (20.♗e1!?) 20...♘xh5 (20...♖fe8

21.♘xf6 ♕xf6 22.♘d7 ♕e7 23.f6 ♕xd7 24.fxg7+ ♔xg7 25.♕h5 ♖e6 26.♕g5++−) 21.♖xh5 ♗xe5 22.dxe5 ♕xe5 23.♖f1 (23.♗xb4? ♕xb2) 23...c3 24.bxc3 bxc3 25.f6 ♕xh5 26.fxg7+ ♔xg7 27.♗xc3+ f6 28.♖xh5+−.

19.dxe5 ♕xe5 20.♗c3 d4

21.♗xd4!!

This came as a terrible surprise for me. 21.exd4? ♕d6 and Black is clearly better.

21...♗xf3 22.♕xf3+−

It is not easy to understand at first sight why Black is lost. However, two bishops combined with the g-pawn's march and the g6-square makes the position impossible to defend for Black. My mistake was that I had failed to assess this many moves ago, while Katya had!

22...♕e7

22...♕d6 23.g4 does not change much (23.♖d1!?).

23.g4 ♘d7

23...♖ad8 24.g5 ♘e8 25.f6 ♘gxf6 26.gxf6 ♘xf6 27.♘h5 ♖xd4 28.exd4 ♘xh5 29.♕xh5 f5 should also be lost.

24.♕g3?!

24.f6!? was more direct: 24...♘gxf6 25.g5 ♘e5 26.♕h3 h6 27.gxf6 ♕xf6 28.♕g3 ♖fe8 29.h4! (avoiding the queen exchange on g5) 29...♕xh4 30.♕xh4 ♘f3+ 31.♔f2 ♘xh4 32.♖h1 ♘g6 33.♘xg6+ fxg6 34.♖xh6+ ♔g8 35.♖xg6 ♖e7+−.

24...♘gf6?

I rejected 24...f6 with a passive defence after 25.♘e6 ♖fc8 – White is slightly better.

25.g5 ♖g8

25...♘e4? 26.♗xg7+ ♔xg7 27.f6++−.

**26.♕h4   ♘e5   27.gxf6   gxf6+
28.♔f2**

This is the natural square for White's monarch, but even 28.♔h1 was adequate: 28...♖ad8 (28...♕b7+ 29.e4) 29.♗e4+−.

28...♖g4

28...♖ad8   29.h3+−   (29.♖e1   ♖g4 30.♕h6+−); 28...♘g4+ 29.♔f3 ♘e5+ 30.♔e2 ♖g4 31.♕h6 ♖ag8 32.♖f1+−.

29.♕h3 ♖ag8

30.♖d1!

The last important move by White, and Black is on the ropes.

30.♗xe5?!   ♕xe5   31.♘g6+   fxg6 32.♕xg4 ♕xb2 33.♕d1 ♕e5 probably leads to a perpetual.

30...♖8g5

30...♖4g5 might have turned out to be better.

31.♗e4! ♕d6 32.♗f3

32.♔e2!? ♖g1 33.♖xg1 ♖xg1 34.♕h6 ♘g4 35.♕h4 ♘e5 36.♘d5 ♔g7 37.♗c5!+−.

32...♖xf4

A) 32...♘xf3 33.♕xf3 ♖h4 34.h3 ♖xf5 35.♗c3+−;

B) 32...♘d3+ 33.♖xd3 ♖xf4 34.exf4 cxd3 35.♗xf6+ (35.♔e3) 35...♕xf6 36.fxg5 ♕xg5 37.♕g4+−.

33.♗xe5??

All of a sudden Katya, under the spell of time-trouble, erred unexpectedly.

She overestimated Black's drawing chances in the line 33.exf4 ♘d3+ 34.♖xd3 cxd3 35.♔e3 (35.♗xf6+ ♕xf6 36.fxg5 ♕xb2+ (36...♕xg5 37.♕h5 ♕d2+ 38.♔g3 ♔g7 39.♕g4++−) 37.♔e3 d2 38.♕g4+−) 35...♖g1 36.♕h6 ♔g8 37.♕xf6 ♕xf6 38.♗xf6+−.

33...♖xf3+ 34.♕xf3 ♕xe5   0-1

By this win I still did not get anything in the tournament, while Katya had to share third place in the women's competition.

FM Zsolt FÜSTHY (1963)

A highly intelligent character, talented in plenty of ways, and an idealist spirit, all hidden in one body. Bela Bacsi (Uncle Bela Papp)'s eyes could not miss the small boy's chess skills in a simul. Zsolt became a leading figure in the next wave of exceptional promises. We have 13 years between us (to my disadvantage...) and became personal friends, and club-mates as well. Otherwise he's an odd 'boy'. I could have sworn he would stay a bachelor for ever, but fortunately I was wrong. (Unlike other people I am wrong sometimes and, being a feeble man, I am not ashamed to confess it). He married when he was well over 40 and became a father of two twin daughters at fifty! How about that? He is a successful yet honest lawyer who won my case against the Hungarian Chess

Federation's gangsterism (they illegally took away from me the right to play in the zonal in 1995, which I had gained by winning the Hungarian Championship in 1993; and also kept me away from both the Open and the round-robin Championship in 1995 which brought 1.3 million HUF to the B.Papp Foundation in 2003. We were the founding members. He worked for free, and I used the bastards' money for organizing tournaments and helping handicapped chess players.

Being one of my pupils in the Statisztika Club, Zsolt threw in my Jocha Gambit against the Middle Gambit 21 years after its birth. And he did not regret it.

Janos Havasi
Zsolt Füsthy
Hungary tt 1986

1.e4 e5 2.d4 exd4 3.♕xd4 ♘c6 4.♕e3 f5!?

Always nice to see what can happen if you play something in the opening you just cannot play.

5.exf5+ ♗e7 6.♗d3 ♘f6 7.♘e2 0-0 8.0-0 ♘b4

Going after the bishop and, consequently, the f5-pawn. Another option was 8...d5 9.♘f4 ♕d6 10.♖e1 ♘g4 11.♕f3 ♘ce5 12.♕xd5+ ♕xd5 13.♘xd5 ♗c5 14.♗e3 – see Antal-Adorjan, Hungary tt 1965. Even stronger was 13...♗h4! and now 14.♗e3 ♘xd3 15.cxd3 ♖xf5 16.♘xc7 ♘xe3! or 14.♖e2 ♘xd3 15.cxd3 ♗xf5. What's the use of White taking a pawn on f5 when his own pawn becomes so weak? Moreover, according to Nimzowitsch, the whole complex surrounding a weakness is weak.

9.♘d2
9.♘f4!?.

9...d5 10.♘g3 ♘g4 11.♕d4 ♘xd3 12.♕xg4

Or 12.♕xd3 ♘h6 when White can still try to create some kind of initiative with 13.c4.

12...♘xc1 13.♖axc1 g6 14.♘f3 ♗xf5 15.♘xf5 ♖xf5 16.♖cd1 ♗d6 17.♖d3 ♕f6 18.c3 ♖e8

Seizing the open file. Also promising was 18...♖f8 when White will have trouble maintaining the equilibrium.

19.♘d4??

19.♕a4! would have made it harder for Black to coordinate his forces.

19...♖xf2! 20.♖f3
20.♖xf2 ♖e1+.

20...♖xf1+ 21.♖xf1

After 21.♔xf1 ♕e7 the attack along the e-file decides, e.g. 22.g3 c5 or 22.♔g1 ♕e1+ 23.♖f1 ♗xh2+–+.

21...♗xh2+   **0-1**

GM Andras 'Kisbandi' FLUMBORT (1984)

When I left Peter Leko in 1999 I felt light as a balloon. I could have stayed with him forever. He got his first invitation to Linares, Western sponsors joined in. My fee surely would have been multiplied. No way. I was not a poor devil anyhow, and it was not Kasparov throwing me out and shouting traitor like he did with Vladimirov. No! After seven years of not asking or accepting money for my services, my stomach told me I must leave. Thank God I could always afford to remain myself and not become part of any machine. Other people have to deal with their guilt after deliberate wrongdoings. I don't like to hate myself, and my criticism does not only target others.

I've been asked what pupil I would like to have after geniuses like these. My answer was: an orphan! And that was what happened. When 'Kisbandi' (little Andy) showed up in my harbour, he had already lost his mother. He was only 18. (My father died when I was 17 – also of cancer.) We had a 'human interview' – after all it's not the same sitting 6-8 hours a day opposite a sympathetic, talented guy, or opposite some spoiled brat, who hates the whole procedure and makes you feel like a prostitute. Without fear of starvation!? The boy was thrilling. Well educated in many ways, intelligent with a sparkling humour, especially after the encouraging first half hour. So we lived and worked together for three weeks in our home. In return for my efforts I did not get a penny – they sent 400 eFt (a thousand HUF) to the B. Papp Foundation. He got full board and lodging. No girls, but he was in love with one already. The whole thing sounds like a fairy-tale, although certainly we had problems too. Who cares?

Then the sponsorship stopped and anyhow he lived in the country, in Nagykanizsa. It was more of a (grand-) master course than a continuous training. But he definitely got the message that BLACK IS OK!, and at least partly because of that became a reasonably strong GM. But parallel to that, he studied brilliantly at the University, and although he was helping Richard Rapport for some time, he became another lawyer friend. To tell the truth, we broke up 14 years ago, for I found he was a jolly good fellow with just anybody, be he a nice guy or a sinner. And I have a weak stomach. I would be dead in five minutes if I played everybody's darling.

Jump! In 2015 he invited me to an event in the quality of organizer. Fortunately I was not able to be present as a has-been puppet, but I sent a letter in a friendly tone, offering to make up in conditions that were not exactly mine, but were correct. He gladly said yes. Months passed before we met again, because not much later I collapsed and spent months in hospitals due to kidney problems. Poor Bobby! He passed away because of chronic kidney problems.

Very recently I again met with this 32 years' old tall (he had grown 10cm but lost as much of the hair on his head) lawyer, who will surely get the nickname 'Naughty' in his profession. I like humour and decency. Believe it or not, only on that evening we drank pertu. I'm still 34 years older than him, which means he can even call me Bandi, but preferably Bandi Bacsi. No matter what the future will bring, this nice mutual gesture has washed away the bad memories.

Thanh Hoang	2426
Andras Flumbort	2414

Budapest 2002 (7)

based on analyses by Lubomir Ftacnik

1.d4 ♞f6 2.c4 g6 3.♞c3 d5 4.♞f3 ♝g7 5.♛b3 dxc4 6.♛xc4 0-0 7.e4 ♞a6 8.♝e2 c5 9.d5 e6 10.0-0 exd5 11.exd5 ♝f5 12.♝f4 ♞d7

A natural move in such positions, first played by Tukmakov. Nowadays the straightforward 12...♜e8 is more popular.

13.♜ad1 ♞b6 14.♛b3

White wants to keep an eye on his passed pawn on d5. 14.♛b5 ♜c8 15.d6 ♜e8 16.♝g5 ♛d7 17.a4 c4 18.♞d4 ♜c5 19.♛xd7 ♝xd7 20.♝e7 ♜a5 21.♝f3 ♞c5 22.♞d5 ♞bxa4 ½-½ was Avrukh-Van Wely, Amsterdam 2001.

14...♞b4 15.♜d2

15...♘d3?!

Starting wild complications. Winning the pawn with 15...♗xc3? 16.bxc3 ♘4xd5 appears to be unwise in view of 17.♗h6 ♖e8 18.c4 ♖xe2 19.♖xe2+–; but 15...♖e8!? looked like a worthy alternative.

16.♗g5 ♕d7 17.♘h4?

If White does not succeed in exchanging the bishop on f5, this antipositional move will backfire on him. The best move was 17.d6! c4 (17...♕xd6? 18.♗xd3 ♗xd3 19.♘e4 c4 20.♘xd6 cxb3 21.♖xd3 bxa2 22.♖a1+–) 18.♕a3 f6?! 19.♗e3 ♖fd8 20.♘d4 ♘c8 (20...♕xd6 21.♕xd6 ♖xd6 22.♘xf5 gxf5 23.b3±; 20...♗f8!±) 21.♘xf5 ♕xf5 22.♗xd3 cxd3 23.♕b3+
♔h8 24.♖fd1 ♘xd6 25.♖xd3 (Ftacnik) wins for White, but on move 18 Black has better: 18...♖fc8! with the idea ...♖c6 and if necessary ...♗f8 looks good.

17...c4 18.♕c2

Trading queens doesn't help after 18.♕b5 ♕xb5 19.♘xb5 ♗e4 20.♗e7 ♖fe8 21.d6 ♘xb2 22.♘c7 c3 23.♘xe8 cxd2, but 18.♕a3! would have limited the damage.

18...♘b4 19.♕d1 ♗d3! 20.♘f3

Wholly unattractive was 20.a3 ♗xc3 21.bxc3 ♗xe2 22.♕xe2 ♘4xd5 23.♕f3∓.

20...♖fe8 21.♖e1

21.d6, to set up a pin on the d-file, does not work in view of 21...♕xd6 22.a3 ♗xc3 23.bxc3 ♘6d5! 24.cxb4

and now 24...♖xe2 25.♖xe2 ♘c3, winning.

21...♘6xd5 22.♘xd5 ♕xd5 23.♕a4

23.a3 ♗xe2 24.♖exe2 ♘d3.

23...c3!

Flumbort dominates the board, so he can afford to look for an immediate punishment of his opponent. The text is more forceful than 23...a5 24.♖ed1 ♕f5, which should also win.

24.bxc3

There are no tricks if White keeps the black pawn on c3 alive: 24.♖dd1 c2 25.♖d2 ♕b5 26.♕xb5 ♗xb5 27.a3 ♖ac8–+; 24.♕xb4 cxd2 25.♕xd2 ♗e4–+.

24...♗xc3 25.♖ed1 ♗xd2 26.♗xd3

26.♖xd2 ♖xe2.

26...♘xd3 27.♖xd2

27.♗xd2 ♘b2.

27...♕xg5! 28.♖xd3

28.♘xg5 ♖e1#.

28...♕f6 29.h4 ♖ad8 30.♖xd8 ♖xd8 31.♕xa7 ♖d1+ 32.♔h2 ♕f4+   0-1

Hoang Thanh Trang has never been a pupil of mine. But she was the strongest ever sole winner of the Bela Papp Memorial. This was when the tournament was composed not only of U-20 players but also of older IMs. She started with 7/7 and drew two games. She grew up in Hungary, speaks the language on a literary level, and is a charming person in all. A Hungarian citizen, with the male GM title, who has played for Hungarian teams, except last time, when she became a mother as well – of a baby girl that you can see on Facebook.

Olaf MÜLLER (1966)

A young and talented player was our next hero. A member of the SG Kirchheim team, composed entirely of players of his generation. They just qualified for the first Bundesliga when we found each other, so I became the leading player there, and a trainer as well. What happened was hard to believe: the inexperienced lads reached 7th place in 1988/89 (among 14) – me having an unbeaten plus-4 score, sharing the best player award in a tie with Hübner, Spassky and Christiansen. But Olaf! To say that he was causing us constant headaches is very mild. We felt a nervous breakdown hanging above our heads like the sword of Damocles when we watched his games. He always ended up in time-trouble (just like otherwise excellent players like Smejkal and Groszpeter). This Olaf won the game I give below both on time and in a winning position. In 26 moves. His opponent, Herbert Bastian, had a tremendous score with the Closed Sicilian, which he kept playing religiously. But I, who have always considered this variation dubious at best, simply made monkey of the whole set-up, not by being a wizard, but just by finding healthy, active moves during preparation. Bastian behaved like a gentleman, and complimented us afterwards. Later on I wrote an article for the *Europa Rochade* magazine titled 'Black Magic in the Bundesliga'. But the whole idea was so crystal-clear with no tricks at all, that any reader could understand. You too!

Herbert Bastian   2315
Olaf Müller   2355

Germany Bundesliga 1988/89

based on notes by Adorjan and Vegh in Chess Informant

1.e4 c5 2.♘c3 ♘c6 3.g3 g6 4.♗g2 ♗g7 5.d3 d6 6.f4 e6 7.♘f3 ♘ge7 8.0-0 0-0 9.♗e3 ♘d4 10.e5 ♕b6!

A novelty at the time, invented by Jo. Horvath. Alternatives are 10...♗d7!? 11.♘xd4 cxd4 12.♗xd4 ♗c6! with compensation (Adorjan) or 10...♘ef5.

11.♖b1?!

Too complacent! Crucial is 11.♘e4, e.g. 11...dxe5 12.fxe5 ♘ef5 13.♗f4 and if 13...♘xf3+ 14.♕xf3 ♕xb2 15.c3, White gets a strong attack for the pawn.

11...♘ef5 12.♗f2 ♘xf3+ 13.♕xf3 dxe5 14.♘a4 ♕c7 15.fxe5

15.♗xc5 loses too much time. Black takes the initiative with the Kasparovian exchange sacrifice 15...♗d7! 16.♗xf8 ♖xf8 17.♘c3 ♗c6, for example: 18.♘e4 exf4 19.♕xf4 ♕b6+ 20.♖f2 (20.♔h1 ♘e3 21.♖f2 f5–+) 20...♗d4 21.c3 ♗e3 22.♕f3 ♖d8 23.d4 ♗xe4 24.♕xe4 ♗xf2+ 25.♔xf2 ♘xd4! 26.cxd4 ♖xd4–+.

15.♘xc5 looks pretty sad too: 15...♘d4 16.♗xd4 exd4 17.♘b3 ♖b8 intending ...b7-b6 and ...♗b7 (17...♕xc2?? 18.♖fc1).

15...♗xe5 16.♗xc5

16.♘xc5 loses heavy material after 16...♘d4! 17.♕e4 ♕xc5 18.c3 ♖d8–+.

16...♗d7!

The same sharp trick, taking over the attack. Probably 16...♖d8!? was fine too, for example: 17.b4 ♗d7 18.b5 b6 19.♗f2 ♕xc2 20.♕e4 ♗g7 and Black is clearly better.

17.♗xf8 ♖xf8 18.♘c3 ♗d4+

Even stronger was 18...♕b6+!, when after 19.♔h1 (19.♖f2 ♗xc3−+) the long diagonal becomes White's undoing: 19...♘e3 20.♖fe1 ♘xg2 21.♖xe5 ♗c6 22.♖e4 (22.♘e4 ♘e3−+) 22...♘e3 23.♘a4 ♕a5 24.♕xe3 ♕xa4 and Black obtains a winning endgame.

19.♔h1

19.♖f2 ♗c6 20.♘e4 ♖d8 with a strong hold on White's position. The liberating try 21.c3 weakens the d3-pawn too much: 21...♗xf2+ 22.♔xf2 ♕b6+ 23.♔e2 (23.d4 ♘xd4 24.cxd4 ♗xe4 25.♕xe4 ♖xd4−+ is something we have seen before) 23...♕a6 24.a3 ♖xd3!−+.

19...♘e3

20.♕e4?

In time-trouble White puts his queen on a fatal square. It was already very difficult for him:

A) 20.♕xb7 ♕xb7 21.♗xb7 ♘xf1 22.♖xf1 ♖b8−+;

B) 20.♖f2 ♘xg2 21.♖xg2 ♗c6 22.♕e2 ♗xc3 23.bxc3 ♗xg2+ 24.♔xg2 (24.♕xg2 ♕xc3 25.♖xb7 ♕a1+−+) 24...♕xc3 should be winning for Black, as 25.♖xb7? ♕c6+ 26.♕f3 ♕xc2+ is hopeless;

C) The staunchest defence was 20.♕f4 ♕b6! 21.♘e2 e5 22.♕f6 ♘xf1 23.♕xb6 ♘xg3+ 24.♘xg3 ♗xb6 25.♗xb7 f5 with an endgame clearly favouring Black.

20...♕b6 21.♖f4 e5

Even stronger than winning material by 21...♗xc3 as White's major pieces in the centre are sitting ducks.

22.♘e2　♗c6　23.♘xd4　♗xe4 24.♖xe4 exd4 25.♗f3 ♖c8 26.♖e7 ♕f6　　　　　　　　　　　　　0-1

Torsten BEHL (1965)

The team of Lohmar played in a lower class and, not having a sponsor like Mercedes Benz, it stayed there – I believe also today. You know we Hungarians can be found in every spot of the world. Only we don't want to rule it, we just want to build and help. I was approached by Sandor ROZSA (no, not the legendary 'betyar' (= outlaw), the 19th century Hungarian Robin Hood) during a desperate period of my life. OK, there were quite a few such periods before and after that, but this one took the cake. Rozsa, who had lived in Germany for 26 years, and was a successful but honest businessman, lifted me up. I was separated from my wife after 18 years, with two daughters (we divorced soon after), and, as is well-known, the two main reasons for committing suicide are divorce and the death of some beloved person. Sandor played chess and even had some revolutionary reform ideas, but apart from this nightmare he was more than OK. He helped me (and Lohmar) financially and in a clear charity spirit. That saved me from going astray. God bless him!

Torsten, a big-bodied man, was often full of anxiety. He knew a lot, yet during the game he couldn't manage to express his real self, remaining a hidden treasure. Except I got an idea from him which I then used against one of the greatest attackers in the world, who seemingly got scared now. I wrote a theoretical article about the Grünfeld Indian with him and Uwe Fleischer for New In Chess, which they published. They even paid for it too. Not in a rush...

Gyula Sax — 2570
Andras Adorjan — 2485
Szeged 1997 (2) *Sicilian*

1.e4 c5 2.♘f3 d6 3.d4 cxd4 4.♘xd4 ♘f6 5.♘c3 a6 6.♗g5 e6 7.f4 ♘c6 8.e5 h6 9.♗h4

9...♘xd4!?

An innovation by Torsten. Two known alternatives are:

A) 9...g5 10.fxg5 ♘d5 11.♘xd5 exd5 12.exd6 ♗xd6 13.♕e2+ ♔f8 14.0-0-0 hxg5 15.♗f2 ♕f6 16.♔b1 ♗e5 17.♕f3 (½-½, 107) Baramidze-Dominguez Perez, Khanty-Mansiysk 2007;

B) 9...dxe5 10.♘xc6 ♕xd1+ 11.♖xd1 bxc6 12.fxe5 ♘d5 (12...♘d7 13.♘e4±) 13.♘e4 ♖b8 (13...♗e7 14.♗g3) 14.b3 (14.c4 ♖xb2 15.cxd5 ♗b4+ 16.♘d2 exd5µ) 14...♗e7 15.♗g3!N (½-½, 32) Adams-Anand, Linares 1997.

10.♕xd4

The magnificent point after 10.exf6? is 10...♘f5!!

analysis diagram

A) 11.fxg7 ♕xh4+ 12.g3 ♘xg3 13.gxh8♕ (13.gxf8♕+ ♖xf8 14.hxg3 ♕xh1 15.♕xd6 ♗d7 is the more prosaic win) 13...♘e4+ 14.♔e2 ♕f2+ 15.♔d3 ♘c5+ 16.♔c4 b5+ and White gets mated in all lines, e.g., 17.♔b4 a5+;

B) After the prosaic 11.♗f2 Black is better too: 11...♕xf6 12.♕d2 b5 13.0-0-0 ♗b7 14.♖g1 h5 15.♗d3. White has little space to manoeuvre around in.

10...dxe5 11.♕xd8+

After 11.♕xe5 ♗e7 (also interesting is 11...♗d6!? 12.♕d4 ♗e7 as the queenless middlegame is quite comfortable for Black) 12.♗d3 (12.♗e2 0-0 13.0-0 ♗d7 14.♖ad1 ♖e8 15.♗f2 ♕b8= or 15.♔h1 ♕b6 16.b3 ♖ac8∓) the simplification by 12...♘d7 13.♗xe7 ♘xe5 14.♗xd8 ♘xd3+ 15.cxd3 ♔xd8 favours Black with his better pawn structure, also in the event of 16.d4! b5! (16...♗d7 17.d5=).

11...♔xd8 12.fxe5 g5 13.♗xg5

A) 13.♗g3 ♘d7 14.0-0-0 (14.♗e2 ♗g7 15.0-0 ♔e7 16.♗h5 ♖f8 17.♖ae1 b5 18.♗f3 ♖b8=/∓) 14...♗g7 15.♗e2 ♔e7 allows Black to press on the weak outpost at e5, although taking it immediately is dubious: 16.♗h5!? and now:

A1) 16...♘xe5?! 17.♖he1±;

A2) 16...b5 17.♖he1 (17.♖hf1!?) 17...♗b7 18.♖e2 (0-1, 57) Paramos Dominguez-Dominguez Perez, Santa Clara 1999;

A3) 16...b6 17.♖he1 ♗b7=.

B) More promising for White is 13.exf6 like in the game: 13...gxh4 14.0-0-0+ ♗d7, when his slightly better structure and open rook files compensate for Black's bishop pair, for example:

B1) 15.♖d4 ♔c7 16.♖xh4 ♗c6 17.♘e4 ♖g8 18.g3 ♖g6 19.♗g2 ♗xe4 20.♖xe4 ♖xf6 21.♖c4+ ♔b6 22.♖c3 (22.♖d1 ♖f2!=) 22...♖b8=;

B2) 15.♘a4 ♔c7 16.♖xd7+ ♔xd7 17.♘b6+ ♔c6 18.♘xa8 ♗d6=;

B3) 15.♗e2 ♔c7 16.♗f3 ♖d8 17.♖d4 h3! (the vulnerable h-pawn does have its use!), and now:

B31) 18.gxh3 ♗d6 19.♖e1 ♗xh2 20.♗h5 ♗e8 21.♖g4 ♖f8 22.♖g7 ♗f4+ 23.♔b1 ♗g5 24.♖xe6 (24.♘e4 ♗h4 25.♖eg1 ♖d5∓) 24...♔b8 25.♖e1 ♗xf6 26.♖h7 ♗g5=/∓;

B32) 18.g3 ♗c5! 19.♖c4 ♔b6 20.♖e1 ♗b5! 21.♘xb5 axb5 22.♖h4 (22.♖ce4 ♖d4 23.c3 ♖xe4 24.♖xe4 ♗g1 25.♖h4 (not 25.♖e2? h5 26.♔c2 ♖h6 27.a3 h4 28.gxh4 ♖xh4 with a quite clear advantage) 25...♗xh2 26.♖xh3 ♗g1 27.♗h5=) 22...♗d4 23.♔b1 ♖d6 24.♖d1 e5 25.c3 ♖xf6 26.cxd4 ♖xf3 27.dxe5 ♖e3 28.♖xh3 ♖xe5=.

13...hxg5 14.exf6

14...♗d7!

A) Less good is 14...♔c7 as the king is exposed here: 15.♘e4 ♖g8 16.♗e2 (also interesting is 16.h4!? gxh4 17.♖xh4 e5 18.♖h5=) 16...g4 17.h4! gxh3 18.♖xh3±.

B) 14...♗d6! is a good alternative with accurate play:

B1) 15.0-0-0 ♔c7. Now it is harder for White's rooks to get at the black king: 16.♘e4 ♗f4+ 17.♔b1 ♗d7 18.♗d3 (18.g3?! ♗c6 19.♗g2 ♗e5) 18...♗c6 19.h3 (19.g3 ♗e5=) 19...♖ag8 with compensation;

B2) 15.♘e4 ♗e5 16.0-0-0 (16.♘xg5 ♔e8 17.♘e4 ♗xb2 18.♖d1 ♗e5 19.g3 ♗d7 20.♗g2 ♖c8! is slightly better for White, but Black has counterplay against the various weak pawns) 16...♔c7 17.g3 (17.♔b1 ♗d7 18.♘xg5 ♗xf6 19.♘xf7 ♖h4) 17...♗d7 18.♘xg5 and now:

B21) 18...♗c6? 19.♘xf7±;

B22) With 18...♗xf6 Black keeps pressure for the pawn: 19.♘f3 (19.♘xf7? ♖hf8! (19...♖h7? 20.♘d6 ♗c6 21.♗d3!±) 20.♘d6 ♗g5+ 21.♔b1 ♗c6−+) 19...♗c6 20.♗e2 ♖ad8;

B23) But best may be 18...♗xg3!? 19.♔b1 ♖xh2 20.♖xh2 ♗xh2 21.♘xf7 ♗f4 22.♗d3 ♖f8 23.♗g6 ♗c6 (23...♗e8 24.♘d8!) 24.♖e1 and White is so tangled up that he cannot be better here.

15.♘e4 g4

16.♖d1!?

A) Less to the point is 16.♘f2?! g3! 17.hxg3 ♖xh1 18.♘xh1 ♗c6 or 18...♗d6, both with tremendous compensation;

B) 16.♘g5 ♔e8 17.♖d1 ♗c6 18.♖d4 g3 19.h4 ♖h6 is also fine for Black;

C) 16.g3! ♗c6 17.♗g2 consolidates, but it doesn't give White any real winning chances since Black is simply too active, for example: 17...♕c7 and now:

C1) 18.♖d1 ♗c5!? (18...♗xe4 19.♗xe4 ♗c5 20.♖d3 ♖ac8!) 19.♖d2 ♗a7 with compensation;

C2) 18.0-0 ♖d8 19.♖ad1 ♖xd1 20.♖xd1 ♗xe4 21.♗xe4 ♖h6 22.♖f1 ♗d6=.

D) 16.h4! is a way to 'wash' White's Achilles' heel: 16...gxh3 17.♖xh3 ♖xh3 18.gxh3 ♔c7 and here White can still try for more, e.g.:

D1) 19.♖d1 ♗c6 20.♘g5 ♗d6 21.♘xf7 ♗g3+ 22.♔e2 ♖f8 23.♘g5 ♖xf6 24.♔d3 e5 25.♗e2 (25.♔c3 ♗h4!-+) 25...♗h4 26.♘e4 ♖f4 27.♘c3 ♖d4+ 28.♔e3 ♗g5+ 29.♔f2 ♖b4 30.b3 ♖f4+ 31.♔g1 ♖f6 32.♘d5+ ♗xd5 33.♖xd5 ♗e3+ 34.♔h1 e4 35.♖e5 ♖f2 36.♗g4 ♖xc2 37.♖xe4 ♗g5=/±;

D2) 19.♔f2 ♗c6 20.♖e1 ♗b4 21.c3 ♗d6!? 22.♘xd6 ♔xd6 23.h4 ♖h8 24.♔g3 ♖h6 25.♗d3 ♖xf6 26.♗e4 ♗xe4 27.♖xe4=.

16...♔c7 17.h4

Draw agreed. There could follow:

A) 17...gxh3 18.♖xh3 ♖xh3 19.gxh3:

A1) 19...♗c6 20.♘g5 ♗h6 (20...♗d6!?) 21.♘xf7 ♗f4 22.♗d3 (22.h4 ♗g3+ 23.♔e2 ♗xh4 24.♘e5=) 22...♖f8 23.♗g6 ♖g8 (23...♗e8 24.♘d8 ♗g3+ 25.♔e2 ♗b5+ 26.♔f3 ♖xf6+ 27.♔xg3 ♖xg6+ 28.♔f4=) 24.♗h5 ♖g2 with drawing chances, because Black is very active;

A2) 19...♗h6 and now:

A21) For 20.♘d6 ♗c6 21.♘xf7 see line A1;

A22) 20.♗d3 ♖g8 21.♔f2 ♗c6 22.♖f1 ♖g6 23.♔e2 ♖g2+ 24.♔f3=;

A23) 20.♗g2 ♗c6 21.♔f2 ♖g8 22.♗f3 ♗f4 (22...♖g6 23.♖e1 (less good is 23.♖d3 ♗xe4 (23...♗f4!?∓) 24.♗xe4 ♖xf6+∓) 23...♗xe4 24.♖xe4 ♖xf6 25.h4=).

B) 17...♖h6, allowing White to keep his passed h-pawn, is slightly risky, but also here his active pieces should be able to save him:

B1) 18.♗d3 ♗c6 19.♔e2 ♗xe4 20.♗xe4 ♖xf6 21.♖d3 ♖f4 22.♖c3+ ♔b8 23.♖c4 f5 24.♗d5 ♖xc4 25.♗xc4 ♔c7=;

B2) 18.h5 ♗c6 19.♘f2 ♖xf6 20.♘xg4 ♖f4 21.♘f2 ♗h6 22.♖h3 ♖g8 23.g3 ♖f3 24.♖d3 ♖xd3 25.♘xd3 ♗d6;

B3) 18.♖d3 ♗c6 19.♘f2 ♖xf6 20.♘xg4 ♖f4 21.♘e3 ♗h6 22.h5 ♖g8 with sufficient counterchances.

Correspondence IM Sandor 'Sanyi' DOBSA (1934-2005)

He was a piano-virtuoso, and the head of the Hungarian Radio's Studio 11 orchestra. For 40 years! A chess-lover too – an internationally known correspondence player who was proud to have 8 (eight) annotated games in Informant. He was very serious if needed, but cheerful and humorous if possible. His personality simply radiated sunshine and positivism. As an artist he got many deserved acknowledgements. From me he never expected any serious help in his correspondence games. On the other hand, he arranged my little piano pieces and pop-rock songs.

Once, in 1986, I initiated a movement called 'Moving Aid' (similar to 'Live

Aid') by chess players from Hungary and the rest of the world. On TV I made a live statement in Hungarian (and recorded in English). I composed a title song as well, which Sanyi arranged and recorded. He played several tunes with instruments in the studio and I sang my lyrics in English and Hungarian. There were charity simuls all over Hungary and it was supported by Bessel Kok (from the GMA) with 500 US dollars. Garry promised to make the symbolic first move but he didn't. At the time he was simultaneously lobbying for the ridiculous Lucena to overthrow Campomanes by trying to get African votes during the Dubai Olympiad. 'Moving Aid' never became an organization, all I have ever been able to rely on is spontaneous humanitarians.

Ours was a noble, naive and rather symbolic gesture. The money went to UNICEF. I still keep the recording and the notes. It was published in 1992 in the *BLACK is OK! Zero issue* (11,000 complimentary copies). I won't say everybody got a copy. But anybody who played in the 1992 Manila Olympiad got one of the 2000 that were distributed there. Also 1500 at the European Team Championship in Debrecen at the end of the same year. It was meant to be a periodical, but I did not have any back-up sponsors and I was not a multi-millionaire. I was never any good selling myself or anything else.

The Hungarian Radio is very near to the place where I live, so Sandor (Sanyi) visited me many times on his way home. 'Here I am, Andrishka' – my mother also called me that – and then a happy hour would start. He never brought sorrow, only joy, knowing my melancholy. 'Do you know that today Bahrein is a super power of correspondence chess? They have the

best computers. But for me the wonder of chess remains untouched. I'm trying to do my best, in the interest of my own ability. For me to play decently is not heroic but natural.' So said my great friend Sandor Dobsa, an unforgettable man whom I remember with gratitude and love. Such a personality, who found me worthy of his friendship.

Gergely Radnoti	2500
Sandor Dobsa	2500

Correspondence game 1996
based on notes by Dobsa in Chess Informant
1.e4 c5 2.♘f3 ♘c6 3.d4 cxd4 4.♘xd4 ♘f6 5.♘c3 e5 6.♘db5 d6 7.♗g5 a6 8.♘a3 b5 9.♗xf6 gxf6 10.♘d5 f5 11.♗d3 ♗e6 12.♕h5 ♖g8

13.g3
The main line. The second one is 13.c3.
13...♖g4 14.♘e3
After the violent attempt to break open the centre with 14.f4 things become exciting: 14...exf4 15.0-0-0 (15.♘xf4 ♕a5+ 16.c3 ♖xf4 17.gxf4 b4 18.♘c2 bxc3 19.b3±):

A) 15...fxg3 16.exf5 and now:

A1) 16...♖h4 runs into 17.♘c7+! ♔d7 18.fxe6+ ♔xc7 (18...fxe6? 19.♕f7+ ♗e7 20.♘xa8) 19.♕xf7+ ♗e7 20.hxg3, favouring White;

A2) 16...♗xd5 17.♖he1+ (17.♕xg4 ♗xh1 18.♖xh1 gxh2 19.♖xh2 ♘e5 is unclear) 17...♘e5 18.♕xg4 gxh2 (18...♗xa2) 19.♕h3 (19.♗xb5+ axb5 20.♖xd5 h1♕ 21.♖xe5+ dxe5 22.♖xh1

♗xa3 23.bxa3 ♕d6 24.♕g8+ and White may hold this endgame) and Black has good compensation;

B) 15...fxe4!? 16.♗xe4 fxg3 (16...♖c8 17.♘xf4±) 17.♘f6+ ♕xf6 18.♗xc6+ and now Black has to watch his step:

B1) 18...♔d8? is very dangerous: 19.♗xa8 ♖b4 20.c3 ♗h6+ 21.♔b1 ♕xc3 22.♖xd6+ ♔e7 (22...♔c7? 23.♖c6+) 23.♖xe6+ fxe6 and now the miracle save 24.♘c4!! almost turns the tables: 24...♗g7! (24...bxc4 25.♕c5++−) 25.♕g5+ ♗f6 26.♕c5+ ♔f7 27.♘d6+ ♔g7 28.♕xc3 ♗xc3 29.b3 still gives White an edge in the endgame;

B2) But a good winning chance is 18...♔e7! 19.♗xa8 ♗h6+ 20.♔b1 ♖b4 21.c3 ♕xc3 22.♕e2 (22.♕h4+ f6 23.♕xb4 ♕xb4 24.hxg3 ♗f5+ 25.♔a1 ♗g5−+) 22...♗g7 23.♖d2 ♕xa3 24.♗d5 ♗xb2 25.♗xe6 ♗e5+ 26.♗b3 ♖xb3+ 27.axb3 ♕a1+ 28.♔c2 ♕b2+! 29.♔d3 ♕c3+ 30.♔e4 ♕c6+ 31.♔e3 ♕xh1 and White's king is more clumsily placed than after the immediate 28...♕xh1.

14...fxe4

15.♗xb5

15.♘xg4!? had been played already in 1992, e.g. 15...exd3 16.cxd3 ♘d4 17.0-0 ♗f5 18.♖ad1 ♗g7 19.f3 (19. f4 or 19.♘e3 also give White an edge) 19...♗g6 20.♕h3 ♕g5 21.♕g2 and White has consolidated.

15...axb5 16.♘xg4 ♘d4 17.c3
If 17.0-0 b4.

17...♘f3+ 18.♔f1!

18...♖xa3!!
On any other king move this would have been immediately winning.

19.bxa3 ♕c8!
Black has a very dangerous attack along the light squares.

20.h3
20.♘f6+ ♔e7 21.♘g8+ ♔d8 and now:

A) 22.♔g2? loses to 22...♗g4 23.♕xh7 (23.♕xf7? ♗h3#) 23...♘g5 24.♕h4 ♗h3+ 25.♔g1 f6−+;

B) 22.h4! f5!? (22...♗h3+ 23.♖xh3 ♕xh3+ 24.♔e2 ♕e6! leads to a perpetual) wins a piece back, with an ongoing initiative due to the strong knight on f3: 23.♘f6 (23.♘h6 ♕c4+ 24.♔g2 ♕e2 25.♘f7+ ♔e7∓) 23...♔e7;

C) 22.h3 ♕c4+! 23.♔g2 ♕e2 24.♘f6 ♗g7 25.♘g4 e3! 26.♕xh7 ♖xg4 27.♖hf1 ♗d7 with a winning advantage.

20...♗f5 21.♘f6+
21.♘e3? loses material to 21...♗g6 22.♕g4 f5.

21...♔e7 22.♘d5+ ♔e6 23.♖d1 ♗g6

24.♘f4+ exf4 25.♕xb5 ♕xc3 26.♕d5+ ♔f6 27.gxf4 ♕xa3 28.h4

28.♔g2 ♘h4+ 29.♔g1 ♗f5−+.

The most tenacious was 28.♕b3!? ♕xb3 (28...♕a6+) 29.axb3 ♔e6, but the ending is no picnic for White.

28...♕a6+ 29.♔g2 ♕c8 30.h5

30.♔g3 doesn't help due to 30...h5 31.f5 ♗xf5−+.

30...♕g4+ 31.♔f1 ♗f5 32.a4 ♕xf4 33.a5 ♗g4

And White resigned. On, say, 34.a6, 34...e3! is the killer move: 35.a7 (35.fxe3 ♘d2+ 36.♔g2 ♗f3+ 37.♔f2 ♘e4+!) 35...♘h2+ 36.♖xh2 e2+ 37.♔g1 ♗f3 38.♕xf3 ♕xf3 39.♖a1 ♕d5!.

Sandor MESZAROS (1955)

Are you talented in any way? Or is your child? Of course, yes. Unless you are suffering from a fatal illness, you can dream of anything. Some even say that everybody is a genius, or, if not, may become one. It only needs a wizard. That is, a trainer – today we have millions of them – will get the best out of him. Effortlessly, with the help of analysing programs, etc. Fairy-tales like this however end in catastrophe if the pupil doesn't reach anything above mediocre level. A misguided, poor child, distressed, with suicidal ideas.

Sanyi Meszaros was surely talented. He loved chess and had promising results in his youth. But looking around, he realized that there were better players than him. Maybe not many, but still. He never abandoned chess; he follows the events and plays occasionally, but he has become 'only' a dentist. A renowned and trusted one. I let him take care of my teeth as well. Free of charge for him... Checkers (chess players) know his prices, but he charges them only half the money, out of loyalty. He is one of many friends of mine to whom I have to be grateful, with chess as our common passion though they have never been professionals. We have been friends since 1964, without a pause, from early childhood. And we will be till the very end, I'm sure. The game below he played against one of many Horvaths we have: a younger brother of IM Tamas Horvath.

Sandor Horvath
Sandor Meszaros
Hungary tt 1976

1.e4 c5 2.♘f3 e6 3.d4 cxd4 4.♘xd4 a6 5.♗d3 ♘f6 6.♘c3 ♕c7 7.f4 d6 8.♘b3 b5 9.a3 ♗b7 10.♗e3 ♘bd7 11.g4

11...d5 12.exd5 ♘xd5 13.♘xd5 ♗xd5 14.♖f1?

Now the king remains in the centre. Less bad was 14.0-0 ♗b7∓.

14...♗e7 15.♕d2 ♘f6 16.♘d4 ♘c5 17.g5 ♗e7 18.f5 ♘xd3+

18...e5? fails to 19.♗xb5+! (Houdini) 19...axb5 20.♘xb5 ♕b7 21.♕xd5! and White wins; 18...0-0-0 is better.

19.cxd3 e5 20.♖c1 ♕b7 21.♘e2 g6 22.♕c3 ♗d6 23.♗c5 ♖c8 24.b4

24...♔d7 25.fxg6

25.d4! would make for some more excitement.

25...hxg6 26.♖f6 ♗e6 27.d4 ♕d5

He could have taken on h2, but Black is better anyway.

28.♖d1 e4 29.♕e3 ♖h3 30.♘g3? ♗xg3+ 31.hxg3 ♖h1+ 32.♖f1 ♖ch8 33.♖d2 ♕c4 34.♕e2 ♕xe2+   0-1

Antal PAPP (1948-2015)

There is never a convenient time for something that is very sad. It's a heavy blow. Toni too was discovered by Bela Bacsi (Bela Papp) and we first met at the club in 1962. The chess club, of course. A brilliant mind he had (which wasn't difficult – he inherited it from his professor parents) that sparkled in many directions. He never stopped playing tournament chess – the last time for a small team just one month before his death. Could he even have become a grandmaster? These are irresponsible speculations, and he himself never toyed with the idea. He was befriended with me, and later with Ribli and Sax, and what's more, very warmly with Lajos Portisch. A catholic background. He admired us and, having become a fantastic lawyer, so to say served us in our legal cases – for free since we all humbly served Caissa, our common love. I shall never forget a report by him from a case he won for his client. He looked sad. 'But Bandi Bacsi! The other guy was right.' Thank God I was able to say goodbye to him, holding his hand, sitting by his deathbed. Rest in Peace, Toni!

Sometime in 1970 I played a blindfold simul against six candidate masters with a 3-3 result. Guess who of them was rude to me?

Andras Adorjan
Antal Papp
Budapest 1970
1.g3 ♘f6 2.♗g2 g6 3.d4 ♗g7 4.♘f3 d6 5.0-0

5.c4 ♘bd7 6.♘c3 c5 7.d5 h6 8.e4.

5...0-0 6.c4 ♘bd7 7.♘c3 c5 8.d5 h6 9.e4

9.♕c2 a6 10.a4 ♘g4 11.h3 ♘ge5 12.♘d2 f5 13.f4 ♘f7 14.♘f3±.

9...♘g4 10.♘d2 ♘de5

Since now the d3-square is available.

11.h3 ♘f6 12.f4 ♘d3 13.♘f3 ♘xc1 14.♖xc1 ♘e8

A time-consuming knight dance, but Black is perfectly OK here as he can deal with any thrust in the centre.

15.g4 a6 16.♕e1 b5 17.e5 bxc4 18.♕h4

Premature.

18...♖b8 19.♖c2 ♕c7

20.e6? fxe6 21.g5 h5 22.♖e2 ♖xb2

Other moves also win here, as White has deliberately ruined his position. The text is of course the most attractive way.

23.♖xb2 ♗xc3 24.♖c2 ♗h8 25.♘d2 c3 26.♘c4 ♘g7

He could also have set the pawns rolling with 26...exd5 27.♗xd5+ e6.

27.♘e3 ♘f5 28.♘xf5 ♖xf5 29.♗e4

29...exd5!

The bishop pair and pawn mass are killing.

30.♗xf5 ♗xf5 31.♖e2 d4 32.♕e1 ♔f7   **0-1**

Frederic FRIEDEL (1945)

Today everybody knows who he is. However, when I first met him during the Hamburg Open in 1980 he was not yet the (God-)Father of ChessBase but a member of a ZDF-BBC TV team making an experimental film about how chess players think. He approached me and I together with GM Helmut Pfleger I became an experimental partner. One of these tests was most memorable. It went as follows: They show a normal position to the person for 5 (10?) seconds. Then they covered it with something and the subject had to reproduce the position on an empty board piece by piece. I don't know about Helmut, but I managed to reproduce a complex position with 32 pieces with one slight mistake, putting my a1-rook on d1 instead of c1. Then came the shocking surprise: they showed me a board with the same number of pieces, but completely mixed up. My first reaction was: 'But this is hopeless!' I didn't even bother so much, and in the end there were some 3-4 pieces in their right places. That proved the presumption that chess players may have a photographic memory but in the game the interaction of the pieces heavily effects interception and remembrance.

We became friends in a way that he invited me to his home sometimes, when we discussed professional and personal matters. To tell you the truth, in friendship or in love there is no equality. What I mean by this is that one always gives more even if the other isn't trying to take advantage of the co-operation. He did me many more friendly services than I could ever fully return, except I helped him to get in touch with Garry Kasparov in 1985. There was a time when we tried to support Garry and keep suspicious persons like Andrew Page and the like away from him. Characters who always show up in a company of very successful people, and especially young and inexperienced ones. Our hero was blind, and the others' stomach was stronger than ours. Anyway! Fred and I kept contact, and from 1986 onwards he deservedly became a VIP, and a popular person not only because of his ChessBase empire, which he started to build with a fellow called Mathias Wüllenweber. Also his intelligence, humour and tactfulness gained him the sympathy of quite a few leading players. The last time I saw him was in Frankfurt-Dortmund 1998, where he tried to mend the old friendship between Garry and me, which half succeeded.

Frederic Friedel is somebody I haven't seen since 1998. This is unfortunate but not rare. It's not necessarily a broken-up friendship, but simply geographical distance. We get married, have children, and think we still have time for everything.

I cherish the pleasant and precious moments, and I have broken my back to find a game he won with black, but it seems that for him Fritz does all the playing...

Jimmy ADAMS (1947)

According to New In Chess 2013/3, Jimmy ranks among the 'strongest ever amateur chess players'. We met during the Evening Standard GM

Tournament in London 1975 where he was the bulletin editor (players: Timman, Sax, Adorjan, Nunn – whom I beat in a brilliancy prize game – etc.). Jimmy started to play at the age of 11 but relatively early withdrew from tournament chess although he had been enjoying tournament successes at home and abroad. With a 2300 Elo he was a FIDE Master.

But he is best known as an author, translator, and compiler of books on openings as well historical tournaments. His books *Mikhail Chigorin: The Creative Chess Genius* (1987) and *Johannes Zukertort: Artist of the Chessboard* (1989) are famous. He also made a collection of games and writings of the little-known Hungarian chess revolutionary and forerunner of the Hypermodern movement Gyula Breyer, who once proclaimed: 'After 1.e4 White's game is in its last throes!'

He also worked as an editor and served as an adviser for Batsford. He has helped publish well over a hundred chess titles, including games collections of Fischer, Lasker, and Petrosian. He became the editor of my two books *BLACK is still OK!* and *BLACK is OK forever!* (2004-5 Anova-Batsford). Did a fine job too. As the editor of CHESS magazine he published my essay 'The Presumption of Innocence in the Royal Game of Chess' and collected the readers' opinions for the book(s).

All in all, he provided a very high recognition of the BLACK IS OK! mission. Thanks, Jimmy!

A. Torn
James Adams
Islington 1968 (6)
1.e4 c5 2.♘f3 d6 3.d4 cxd4 4.♘xd4 ♘f6 5.♘c3 a6 6.f4 ♕c7 7.♗e2 g6

An early Dragadorf. But because of White's last move, what is considered the natural follow-up today, ...b7-b5, has to wait (♗f3).
8.0-0 ♗g7 9.♗f3 ♘bd7 10.♖e1

10...e5!
Possession of this point is essential, and as so often in this book we will see Black exchanging on f4 and planting a knight on e5, not worrying about the weakness on d6.
11.♘de2 0-0 12.♘g3 exf4 13.♗xf4 ♘e5 14.♔h1 h5!? 15.♘f1 ♘fg4 16.♖e2
Now White's pieces are stumbling over each other. He had to try something like 16.♗xg4 ♗xg4 17.♘d5 ♕c5 18.♕c1.
16...♗e6 17.h3 ♘xf3

18.♗xd6
Desperation. 18.gxf3 ♗xc3 19.♗xd6 (19.bxc3 ♕xc3! and White's kingside is in tatters) 19...♘f2+ 20.♖xf2 ♕b6 21.♔g2 ♖fd8 may have been better but was also quite attractive for Black.

18...♛b6 19.gxf3 ♞f2+ 20.♜xf2
♛xf2 21.♝xf8 ♝xh3

Of course. It's over.

22.♞e3   ♝xc3   23.bxc3   ♛xe3
24.♛d4   0-1

Phil INNES (1953) – Publisher of Vermont Views Magazine, USA

Shortly after BLACK is still OK! had been released in 2004, I received a very respectful message from someone who actually asked if I would mind if he wrote a 1500-character review of the book for Chessville. Needless to say, I said I would be glad if he did. After all no author writes for himself, and anyway he didn't need anyone's permission to express his opinion. And so he did. In a very extraordinary way. Very few of those who publish reviews actually bother to read their subject matter at all. Some take a quick look at it, but most of them ignore even the publisher's blurb on the back of the book. I don't suffer from persecution mania, so I don't think it only happens with my books – it's a quite common phenomenon. Such an attitude can cause damage. After all, many people buy books online without getting a chance to look into them. Do not misunderstand me, please. Nobody is supposed to agree with me on anything I say – especially when I claim that an 'axiom' that has been there for hundreds of years is an empty dogma and a form of mass psychosis. Let's have a debate! Everybody has a say, but let's not deny any facts. Phil, who also writes poetry, seems to agree.

He did read the book thoroughly, and analysed it in detail. Most of all, he understood that BLACK IS OK! is not just my hobby-horse but a scientific approach which has practical use too. Another person/good spirit whom I never met (although we intended to) and perhaps never will meet. Yet, we have kept in touch ever since and I enjoy his support: he draws my attention to events and writings concerning BLACK IS OK!. He is a friend. His *Vermont Views Magazine* publishes a different local picture every single day!

Epilogue

... and then Peter and me started writing the book. We selected and supervised the awfully extensive rough material, built on three decades of experience. Our deadline was February 16, 2016. This looked comfortable, but as it turned out so many times, sometimes it's easier to start from zero than to select from such a shocking lot of stuff you are strongly emotionally attached to. And of course we had other obligations as well. But we made reasonable progress and everything looked OK – like BLACK.

On the 28th of December 2015, I collapsed and was hospitalized, spending several months in clinics, asylums, call it what you like (I did not like). In the first place where I was taken, I didn't get so much as a diagnosis – not even a false one. At the second station they discovered I had been poisoned by an overdose of lithium. No, not a suicidal attempt, nor had I taken in too much of it at once, but my organism had stored it in various spots instead of regularly clearing it out. Let's not get hysterical, but realistic – my life was in danger. I got three dialyses (kidney) and survived the ordeal.

I write these lines on 7th June 2016. I have learned to walk again and my rehabilitation is on the way. It'll take at least half a year, but more probably a full year until I'll be my old self again. The trouble is that when I reach 67 this will mean I will be as I was when I was 65. And I assure you that was not pure enjoyment of life. By the way, I have PMD (psychomaniac depression, bipolar) since 1979, taking therapies and pills, like the damned lithium. Would you like a bite?

Here is a poem (composed by AA, translated by Imre Gyöngyös – New Zealand).

The Blackout Fright

Here stirs again the Blackout Fright,
descending on my mind: arrived;
like dog snarls on my breast so tight:
the mind arresting Blackout Fright.

This is my destined Blackout Fright;
with it I come and go alike;
and by that all my shirts are lined;
that wakes me up from mercy-hours!

From where to when, how long, what for?
Against heaven my fist I shall not lift!
But oh my God why was not yet enough?
My human self how long shall be adrift?

Lord, if it at all be possible,
rid my soul from this ghastly cramp!
I must not be just dust and sand!
Lord help, as help is only in your hand!

Does such horror come from your Will and Might?
How many times got me the Blackout Fright?
To serve my people is my only Will,
though swallowed hemlock could not make me ill.

Lord, who could peek into your greater Plan?
Your hand holds all the cards that 's really worth!
It does make all the happiness a sham,
while your subject writhes and devours the earth!

Lift me up, Father or trample me down:
already it seems all the same to me!
I had enough of my foul, thorny crown;
any less vital I will never be!

Let Thy Will be done -- as we ever quote!
It shall be so! - Adored and hated Lord!
My broken soul shall also be restored,
if you just say it with one sacred word!

Winston Churchill had a lifelong depression. When he was down he visualized a big black dog sitting on his chest while he was lying on the floor.

Bibliography

Adorjan, Andras: *Black is OK!*, Batsford, 1988.
Adorjan, Andras: *Black is OK!* quarterly (zero issue), 1992.
Adorjan, Andras: *Black is still OK!*, Batsford, 2004.
Adorjan, Andras: *Black is OK forever!*, Batsford, 2005.
Aveskulov, Valery, *Attack with Black*, Gambit 2012
Gelfand, Boris: *Positional Decision Making in Chess*, Quality Chess, 2015.

New In Chess Magazine
New In Chess Yearbooks

ChessBase MegaBase
Houdini 1.5a x64

Biography

Andras Adorjan (born Andras Jocha on March 31, 1950 in Budapest) is a Hungarian chess grandmaster and a former Candidate for the World Championship. Flourishing in the chess-minded capital of Hungary, he developed into one of the world's best junior players at the end of the 1960s. In 1969/70 he became European Junior Champion, and in 1969 he came second at the World Junior Championship in Stockholm, behind the later World Champion Anatoly Karpov. Adorjan became an International Master in that same year, and won the Grandmaster title in 1973. He won many tournaments in the 1970s and 1980s, including Varna 1972, Osijek 1978, Budapest 1982, Gjövik 1983, Esbjerg 1985 and the New York Open 1987. In 1978, he was a member of the Hungarian team that broke the Soviet hegemony to win the Olympiad in Buenos Aires. He was also on the team in 1984, 1986 and 1988, and never did Hungary end up lower than fifth place in those events. Adorjan was Hungarian champion three times, in 1984, 1992, and 1993.

In 1979 Adorjan finished joined third in the Riga Interzonal, qualifying for the Candidates matches. He beat his compatriot Zoltan Ribli in the tiebreaks after a dramatic match, and lost the quarter-final match to Robert Hübner after allowing the German GM to draw from a totally lost position.

Adorjan has a reputation of a world-class opening theoretician. He has worked with Peter Leko, the youngest grandmaster in the world and a world top player in his day, as well as with World Champion Garry Kasparov during several of the latter's crucial matches. In the 1990s Adorjan's activity as a player ceased, but he continued to write about chess, having published since the age of 15. He completed various books that circled around the thesis that 'Black is OK!' in chess. His first book on the subject of BLACK is OK! (1988) became a bestseller and a cult classic. He has also written many theoretical articles in magazines all over the world, including the New In Chess Yearbooks.

Some look upon Adorjan and his 'Black is OK!' mission as a Don Quixote, an epithet that the subject himself wears with pride. But his works have also received approval of many colleague grandmasters.

Index of Games

Chapter 6

Chapter 7

Chapter 8

Chapter 10

Chapter 11

Chapter 12

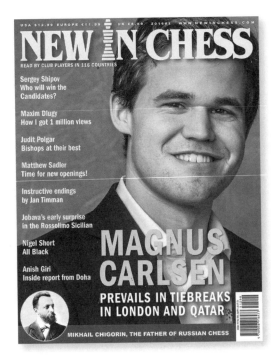
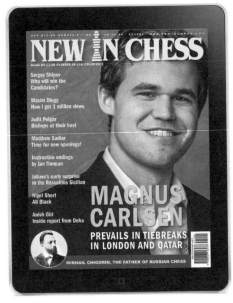